The Social Construction
of Race and Ethnicity
in the United States

SECOND EDITION

The Social Construction of Race and Ethnicity in the United States

Joan Ferrante
Prince Brown, Jr.

Northern Kentucky University

Prentice Hall

Upper Saddle River, New Jersey 07458

Library of Congress Cataloging-in-Publication Data

The social construction of race and ethnicity in the United States/[edited by] Joan
   Ferrante, Prince Brown, Jr.—2nd ed.
      p. cm.
   Includes bibliographical references and index.
   ISBN 0-13-028323-1
      1. United States—Race relations. 2. United States—Ethnic relations. 3.
   Race—Classification. 4. Ethnicity—United States—Classification. 5. United States—Race
   relations—Government policy. 6. United States—Ethnic relations—Government policy. I.
   Ferrante-Wallace, Joan, 1955 II. Brown, Prince.

   E184.A1 S667 2001
   305.8'00973—dc21   00-036322

Editorial Director: *Laura Pearson*
AVP, Publisher: *Nancy Roberts*
Managing Editor (editorial): *Sharon Chambliss*
Managing Editor (production): *Ann Marie McCarthy*
Production Liaison: *Fran Russello*
Project Manager: *Marianne Hutchinson (Pine Tree Composition)*
Prepress and Manufacturing Buyer: *Mary Ann Gloriande*
Cover Director: *Jayne Conte*
Cover Designer: *Kiwi Design*
Cover Image: *Jose Ortega/Stock Illustration Source, Inc.*

For permission to use copyrighted material, grateful acknowledgment is made to the copyright holders on pages 511–516, which are hereby made part of this copyright page.

The book was set in 11/13 Garamond light by Pine Tree Composition
and was printed and bound by Hamilton Printing Company.
The cover was printed by Phoenix Color Corp.

© 2001, 1998 by Prentice-Hall, Inc.
A Division of Pearson Education
Upper Saddle River, New Jersey 07458

Printed in the United States of America

10 9 8 7 6 5 4 3 2 1

ISBN 0-13-028323-1

Prentice-Hall International (UK) Limited, *London*
Prentice-Hall of Australia Pty. Limited, *Sydney*
Prentice-Hall Canada Inc., *Toronto*
Prentice-Hall Hispanoamericana, S. A., *Mexico*
Prentice-Hall of India Private Limited, *New Delhi*
Prentice-Hall of Japan, Inc., *Tokyo*
Pearson Education Asia Pte. Ltd., *Singapore*
Editora Prentice-Hall do Brasil, Ltda., *Rio de Janeiro*

To
James E. Blackwell
Horatio C Wood IV, M.D.

CONTENTS

◇◆◈◆◇

PART 4
The Persistence, Functions, and Consequences of Social Classification   289

PART 5
Toward a New Paradigm: Transcending Categories   359

Appendix A

Appendix B

Appendix C

PREFACE

◇•◈•◇

The Social Construction of Race and Ethnicity in the United States is a five-part book that gives special attention to the social construction of race and ethnicity in the United States. It offers an in-depth and eye-opening analysis of (a) the power of the U.S. system of racial classification to shape our understanding of race and race relations, (b) the way in which this system came into being and has been preserved/perpetuated, and (c) the real consequences this system has on life chances.

The Social Construction of Race and Ethnicity in the United States is not just a book of readings. Each of the five parts leads off with an in-depth essay or overview that grounds the set of readings in sociological theory. Readings were selected for their potential to stimulate critical thinking and self-examination. In addition, each reading begins with one or more study questions to help readers clarify/identify key concepts and issues.

The idea for this book grew out of our frustration with the misleading way in which the idea of "race" is treated in most textbooks that address this concept. Many authors, for example, accurately point out that race is not a meaningful biological concept, but then they proceed to define race in a way that highlights biological traits and to show photographs suggesting that race is a definitive, clear-cut attribute.

This book also developed out of a shared commitment to improve the quality of our teaching and to gain a fuller understanding of the impact that the idea of race has on a society that is consumed by it. The logic, organization, articles, and ideas evolved out of conversations with other teachers and from students responses to class material. As one example of how student input helped to shape this book, we asked students to respond in writing to the idea that "race" is a myth and is based on the false assumption that people can be divided into distinct racial categories. While there are always a few students not surprised by this idea, the majority cannot see how this is possible—as these sample comments show:

- *I don't understand how this is possible but I am open-minded about it.*
- *If there is no such thing as race, why can I look around at the people in the class and know their race?*
- *If race is a myth, why is race such a big deal in this country?*

Such responses motivated us to ask and answer several difficult questions that are central to this book: (1) How is it that racial categories are treated as mutually exclusive when we can identify many cases in which people have complex biological histories? (2) If classification schemes in fact are based on a false assumption, why do they seem so clear-cut? (3) Why have government officials spent so much physical and mental energy devising rules for classifying people according to race? (4) "Why do we so easily recognize races when walking down the street if race is a myth?" (Haney López 1994:19). (5) If race is a myth, should we dismantle classification schemes?

In writing and selecting the readings, we struggled with how to refer to "race." Should we always put the word *race* in quotation marks? Should we always qualify references to a person's race with the words *people classified as* black, white, and so on? In the end, we concluded that the idea of race is real if only because its consequences are real. However, we believe that people must shift their understanding of the meaning of race away from a term referring to clear biological divisions of humanity, to a term referring to "a way in which one group designates itself as 'insider' and other groups as 'outsiders' to reinforce or enforce its wishes and/or ideas in social, economic, and political realms" (Rorhl 1996:96). *The Social Construction of Race and Ethnicity in the United States* was created with the goal of helping readers make this conceptual transition.

Changes to the Edition

This new edition reorganizes the material of the first edition to fit with a major and historical change in the way the United States determines race. On October 30, 1997 the U.S. Office of Management and Budget [OMB] declared that for the first time in history of the United States, people could identify themselves on the census and other official forms as belonging to more than one racial category. The OMB has yet to decide how it will count people who identify with more than one race. One thing is clear: It will not use the term multiracial. The number of racial categories could change from the official categories of the 1990 census to as many as 63, depending on how people respond to the race question. This change in policy leads us to ask several questions, including the following: Why did this change occur? And how did the U.S. government account for people who identified with more than one race before October 30, 1997?

We have included approximately 20 new readings in the second edition. We have selected readings that speak to the constructed nature of race and the real consequences this social construction has had on people's life chances and on race relations in the United States. The longstanding belief that people fit neatly into clear-cut racial categories has supported a corresponding belief that the American experience is a series of separate and parallel stories of racial and ethnic groups. The new readings open our eyes to the idea that the American experience is a story of interracial intimacies, shared histories, and interconnected experiences. The system of racial classification, and the ways this system has been formally and informally enforced, has forced disconnections and separations among the "races" and has otherwise worked to keep these intersecting histories a "secret."

In addition to adding readings that show the consequences of racial classification, we have also selected readings that strengthen the discussion surrounding ethnic classification. The reading "What's in a Name?" offers insights into the origins of the term "Hispanic." "Theories of Ethnicity" adds a theoretical dimension. "Are Italian Americans Just White Folk?" uses the case of Italian-Americans to explore the ethnic experience and the many factors that affect that experience. The reading "Americans United by Myths" addresses two important questions: What's the common identity Americans share and how did this identity emerge?

We also added readings that specifically speak to the meaning of "whiteness. They are "Litigating Whiteness," "The Rules of Passing," "White Privilege Shapes the U.S.", and "More Thoughts on Why the System of White Privilege is Wrong."

Acknowledgments

The ideas in this book are not new. For example, *Race: A Study in Modern Superstition* by Jacques Barzun was published in 1937 and reissued in 1965. In the preface to the 1965 edition, Barzun states "This book is coming back into print because the idea of race it treats of, although repeatedly killed, is nevertheless undying" (pp. ix).

Recall also that W. E. B. Du Bois was preoccupied with the "strange meaning of being black here in the dawning of the Twentieth Century." His preoccupation was no doubt affected by the fact that his father, born in

Haiti, was of French and African descent and his mother, born in the United States, was of Dutch and African descent. In *The Philadelphia Negro: A Social Study,* Du Bois (1899) wrote about popular ideas of race and compared them to reality. Du Bois documented that blacks and whites married and paired off despite laws prohibiting marriage and that they did have children (who, by definition, cannot fit into one racial category).

We mention Du Bois and Barzun as a way of acknowledging those who came before but whose ideas were not received in the same way as those who now write about race as a social construction today. The dates on which many of the readings included in *The Social Construction of Race and Ethnicity in the United States* were originally published also point to the many contributors and to the long process behind the development of new paradigms.

To our knowledge, this is the first reader written and compiled with the exclusive goal of explaining race as a social construction. For this opportunity, we thank Alan McClare who signed the book in November 1995. We also thank Nancy Roberts and Sharon Chambliss for deciding to issue a second edition. Of course a revision plan depends on thoughtful and constructive reviewer critiques. In this regard, we express our deepest appreciation to the professors who served as reviewers:

Karen A. Callaghan, *Barry University*
Walter F. Carroll, *Bridgewater State College*
Abby L. Ferber, *University of Colorado-Colorado Springs*
Marguerite Marin, *Gonzaga University*
Valerie Ann Moore, *University of Vermont*
Sarah Willie, *Swarthmore College*

We are also grateful to those professors who reviewed the first edition:

Richard E. Bradfield, *Western New Mexico University*
Michael Collins, *University of Wisconsin*
Lillian Daughaday, *Murray State University*
Jan Fiola, *Moorhead State University*
Cecilia Garza, *Texas A&M International University*
Donald Hayes, *Sam Houston University*
Beverly M. John, *Hampton University*
Joane Nagel, *University of Kansas*
Ron Stewart, *State University of New York College at Buffalo*

We would like to thank our research assistants at Northern Kentucky University, Leigh Cherni (class of 2000) and Michael Vaughn, (class of 2001) who entered changes, and helped us track down books, articles, internet documents, and other materials we needed to revise this edition. Working with students as gifted as Leigh and Michael is one of the most rewarding experiences we have as college professors. We would also like to thank three Northern Kentucky University students from the class of 2000—Sara Fair, who wrote the box *"Juntos Como Hermanos: A Study of a Spanish-Language Catholic Church";* Ray Elfers, who took photographs of the families and other people who defy the "logic" of racial classification; and Anna Castellini who took photos for the essay "I Can't Imagine Being Any Other Race Than White." Many other Northern Kentucky University students (whose names remain anonymous) contributed case studies and quotes used in this book.

Special thanks to Annalee Taylor Ferrante, for handling the correspondence connected with securing permissions for the readings we reprinted. She also checked all references and quotes for accuracy, and maintained the files. We know of no person who could do this detailed work with the same level of care and accuracy as Annalee.

We dedicate this book to our mentors, Drs. James E. Blackwell and Horatio C Wood IV, M.D., whose guidance and support contributed to our academic and personal development and ultimately to the creation of this work.

Joan Ferrante
Prince Brown, Jr.

Introduction

◇◆◇◆◇

On October 30, 1997, the U.S. Office of Management and Budget (OMB) declared that for the first time in the history of the United States, people could identify themselves on the 2000 census and other federal forms as belonging to more than one racial category. While the number and names of the accepted racial categories have varied over time, the insistence that everyone belong to one category has until now remained constant. For the 1990 census, the U.S. government attempted to classify everyone within its jurisdiction as belonging to one of the four broad racial categories: (1) white; (2) black; (3) American Indian, Eskimo, Aleut; and (4) Asian or Pacific Islander.

We routinely ask students in our classes if they know of someone who might find it difficult to fit into one of these four categories—that is, did they know of someone who could identify with more than one of the four racial categories? (See Figure 1.1.) Almost everyone knows of someone who does not fit clearly into one racial category.[1] Here are some examples:

- *I am of mixed ancestry, but because I have to choose one category, I usually fill in the white category. I am Japanese-American, and I know many other Japanese-Americans. Many of us never know what circle to fill in. Just the other day, I took my brother to the doctor's office, and he asked me which one he should circle, and I told him white. Then he asked me which do I usually fill in and circle, because he was confused too. I told him I usually circle white.*
- *Carolyn, a tall white lady in her thirties, lives with her black husband in a small, predominantly white county. They have one daughter who is five years old and looks a great deal like her father. She is beautiful with long curly black hair, brown skin, and bright brown eyes. They are also awaiting the birth of a second child. Carolyn is already anticipating what the baby will look like.*
- *One of my friends has a dark complexion and long hair. Recently he was pulled over by a police officer and cited for speeding. The officer marked his race as Native American/Eskimo on the citation. Actually, my friend considers himself white with some Indian ancestry.*
- *I am Filipino, but my birth certificate says I am white. Also I was born in Virginia. My parents are both Filipino, however. Not too many people can figure out, without asking, that I am Filipino; they assume I am Asian.*

- *A friend of my mother is Vietnamese and her dad is white. She looks Vietnamese, and most people see her as just that. People who don't know have asked if she can speak English. She just looks at them, almost annoyed at the question because she speaks it plain as day. She was born in the United States and has lived here all her life.*
- *Kristen was born to a Native-American mother and an African-American father in 1974. Kristen's grandmother forced her daughter, who was only 16 years old, to give Kristen up for adoption. A white couple eventually adopted her. Kristen makes it a point to inform herself about Native American peoples. She belongs to the local chapter of the NAACP and is the black affairs editor of a college campus newspaper.*
- *I decided to write about myself: I came to the United States from Brazil two years ago. The most intriguing thing about the United States is its ideas about race. It is appalling how Americans insist on placing me in a racial category. Someone in this class asked me what race do I declare myself in situations in which I must list my race? I said "black," but one of my "white" friends said in complete disbelief, "You are not black!" While a "black" friend said, "I am very glad, I consider you a sister."*

These student-generated examples prompt us to ask several questions:

- Before the 2000 census, how did the U.S. government account for people who identified themselves as belonging to more than one race?
- If multiracial people existed before the year 2000, why did they *have to identify* with one race only?
- Why does the U.S. government classify people by race?
- After 210 years of insisting that people fit into one racial category, why did government officials change the classification rules for the 2000 census, allowing people to circle more than one racial category? (See Figure 1.2.) (See Box: "Potential Single and Multiple Race Categories for 2000 Census".)

This potentially revolutionary change in the way we ask the race question raises an even more important question: How is it that racial categories were treated as mutually exclusive for more than 200 years, when we can identify many cases in which people have complex biological histories? Maybe race is not a natural biological division of human beings into categories. Perhaps *race* refers to that which is produced through racial classification (Webster 1993). In other words, the fact that everyone seemed (and still seems) to fit into a single racial category is really the result of the *system* of racial classification used in the United States.

Figure 1.1 Race Question for 1990 Census

```
4. Race                              ○ White
   Fill ONE circle for the race that the    ○ Black or Negro
   person considers himself/herself to be.  ○ Indian (Amer.) (Print the name of the
                                               enrolled or principal tribe.)
   If Indian (Amer.), print the name of
   the enrolled or principal tribe.→    [                              ]

                                        ○ Eskimo
                                        ○ Aleut
                                            Asian or Pacific Islander (API)
                                        ○ Chinese        ○ Japanese
                                        ○ Filipino       ○ Asian Indian
                                        ○ Hawaiian       ○ Samoan
   If Other Asian or Pacific Islander   ○ Korean         ○ Guamanian
   (API), print one group, for example: ○ Vietnamese     ○ Other API↓
   Hmong, Fijian, Laotian, Thai,
   Tongan, Pakistani, Cambodian,        [                              ]
   and so on. →
   If Other race, print race.→          ○ Other race (Print race.)↑
```

Instructions for Question 4

Fill ONE circle for the race each person considers himself/herself to be.

If you fill the "Indian (Amer.)" circle, print the name of the tribe or tribes in which the person is enrolled. If the person is not enrolled in a tribe, print the name of the principal tribe(s).

If you fill the "Other API" circle [under Asian or Pacific Islander (API)], only print the name of the group to which the person belongs. For example, the "Other API" category includes persons who identify as Burmese, Fijian Hmong, Indonesian, Laotian, Bangladeshi, Pakistani, Tongan, Thai, Cambodian, Sri Lankan, and so on.

If you fill the "Other race" circle, be sure to print the name of the race.

If the person considers himself/herself to be "White," "Black or Negro," "Eskimo," or "Aleut," fill one circle only. Do not print the race in the box.

The "Black or Negro" category also includes persons who identify as African-American, Afro-American, Haitian, Jamaican, West Indian, Nigerian, and so on.

All persons, regardless of citizenship status, should answer this question.

Source: del Pinal and Lapham (1993: 448–49).

Figure 1.2   Race Question for the 2000 Census

Although 14 categories are listed, the Census Bureau ultimately collapses them into 5 official race categories, those categories are (1) American Indian or Alaska Native, (2) Asian, (3) Black, (4) White, (5) Native Hawaiian or Other Pacific Islander.

⑨ **What is your race? Mark one or more races to indicate what you consider yourself to be.**

❑ White
❑ Black or African American
❑ American Indian or Alaska Native—*Print name of enrolled or principal tribe*

_____

❑ Asian Indian	❑ Native Hawaiian
❑ Chinese	❑ Guamanian or Chamorro
❑ Filipino	❑ Samoan
❑ Japanese	❑ Other Pacific Islander—*Print race*
❑ Korean	_____
❑ Vietnamese	
❑ Other Asian—*Print race*	

_____

Perhaps the best example of how the U.S. system of racial classification has maintained an illusion that people fit into clear-cut racial categories can be found in the various criteria it has used to classify "mixed-race persons." As late as 1980, any person of mixed parentage was "classified according to the race of the nonwhite parent, and mixtures of nonwhite races are classified according to the race of the father, with the special exceptions noted above" (U.S. Bureau of the Census 1993:21). An example of a special exception applies to persons of mixed Negro and Indian descent. In such cases no matter what the father's race, the person is classified as Negro "unless the Indian ancestry very definitely predominates or unless the individual is regarded as an Indian in the community" (p. 21).

Consider the diagram taken from the U.S. Bureau of the Census (1994) interviewing manual (see Figure. 1.3). The diagram is a flowchart of decisions interviewers must make about *problem cases,* respondents who say they are more than one race or who name as a response a race not listed. Notice how the flowchart directs interviewers to classify the so-called problem respondent as belonging to one race.

The flaws of the racial classification scheme used in the United States are especially evident when we come across people who do not fit into a single racial category, who are forced into a single category, or who must choose between categories. Such cases tell us that race is not an easily

◆◇◆

Potential Single and Multiple Race Categories for the 2000 Census

For the 2000 census there are 63 potential single and multiple race categories, including six categories for those who marked exactly one race and 57 categories for those who marked two or more races. These 57 categories of two or more races include the 15 possible combinations of two races (for example, Asian and white), the 20 possible combinations of three races, the 15 possible combinations of four races, the six possible combinations of five races, and the one possible combination of all six races.

The 63 mutually exclusive and exhaustive categories of race may be collapsed down to seven mutually exclusive and exhaustive categories by combining the 57 categories of two or more races. These seven categories are white alone, black or African American alone, American Indian and Alaska Native alone, Asian alone, Native Hawaiian and Other Pacific Islander alone, Some other race alone, and Two or more races.

U.S. Bureau of the Census (1999)

◆◇◆

definable characteristic, immediately evident on the basis of physical clues, but that it is a category defined and maintained by people through a complex array of formal and informal social mechanisms.

The official system of racial classification used in the United States for more than 200 years is not unlike a classification scheme devised by a third-grade class in Riceville, Iowa. In 1970, teacher Jane Elliot conducted a classic experiment in which she divided her students into two groups according to a physical attribute—eye color—and rewarded them accordingly. She did this to show her class how easy it is for people (1) to assign social worth, (2) to explain behavior in terms of a physical characteristic such as eye color, and (3) to build a reward system around this seemingly insignificant attribute. The following excerpt from the transcript of the TV program "A Class Divided" (*Frontline* 1985) shows how Elliot established the ground rules for the classroom experiment.

> ELLIOT: *It might be interesting to judge people today by the color of their eyes . . . would you like to try this?*
> CHILDREN: *Yeah!*
> ELLIOT: *Sounds like fun doesn't it? Since I'm the teacher and I have blue eyes, I think maybe the blue-eyed people should be on top the first day. . . . I mean the blue-eyed people are the better people in this room. . . . Oh yes they are the—blue-eyed people are smarter than brown-eyed people. . . .*

Figure 1.3   Diagram of Procedures for Recording Problem Race Cases

The flow chart below offers several if-then scenarios to guide Census Bureau interviewers when they encounter "problem cases." Note that if respondents report more than one race or a race not listed on the census bureau form or card, they are asked a series of questions to "help" them select a single race category.

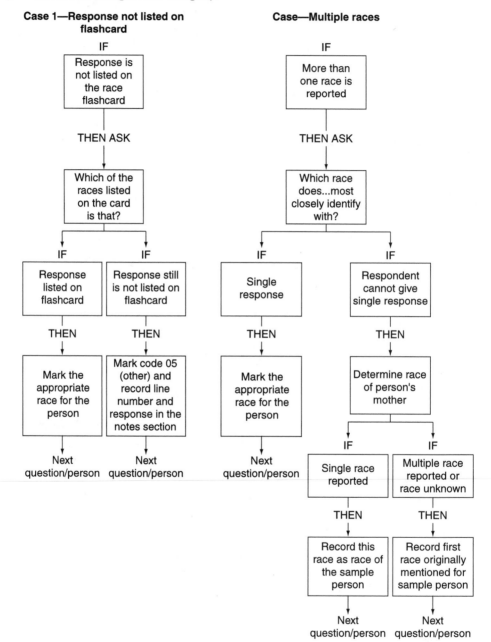

Source: U.S. Bureau of the Census (1994:C3–17).

BRIAN: *My dad isn't that stupid.*
ELLIOT: *Is your dad brown-eyed?*
BRIAN: *Yeah.*
ELLIOT: *One day you came to school and you told us that he kicked you.*
BRIAN: *He did.*
ELLIOT: *Do you think a blue-eyed father would kick his son? My dad's blue-eyed, he's never kicked me. Ray's dad is blue-eyed, he's never kicked him. Rex's dad is blue-eyed, he's never kicked him. This is a fact. Blue-eyed people are better than brown-eyed people. Are you brown-eyed or blue-eyed?*
BRIAN: *Blue.*
ELLIOT: *Why are you shaking your head?*
BRIAN: *I don't know.*
ELLIOT: *Are you sure that you're right? Why? What makes you sure that you're right?*
BRIAN: *I don't know.*
ELLIOT: *The blue-eyed people get five extra minutes of recess, while the brown-eyed people have to stay in.... The brown-eyed people do not get to use the drinking fountain. You'll have to use the paper cups. You brown-eyed people are not to play with the blue-eyed people on the playground, because you are not as good as blue-eyed people. The brown-eyed people in this room today are going to wear collars. So that we can tell from a distance what color your eyes are. [Now], on page 127—one hundred twenty-seven. Is everyone ready? Everyone but Laurie. Ready, Laurie?*
CHILD: *She's a brown-eye.*
ELLIOT: *She's a brown-eye. You'll begin to notice today that we spend a great deal of time waiting for brown-eyed people* (Frontline *transcript* 1985:3–5).

As soon as Elliot set the rules, the blue-eyed children accepted and enforced them eagerly. During recess, the children took to calling each other by their eye colors. Some brown-eyed children got into fights with blue-eyed children who called them "brown-eye." The teacher observed that these "marvelous, cooperative, wonderful, thoughtful children" turned into "nasty, vicious, discriminating little third-graders in a space of fifteen minutes" (p. 7).

On the first reading, you might dismiss this demonstration as interesting but as something that could never happen in real life. Eye color as a means of classifying and ranking people—how absurd! In addition to the obvious fact that eye color is an attribute over which people have no control, even the most simple-minded person could readily identify the flaw in this scheme: eye colors fall into more than two categories. Thus a two-category classification scheme could not accommodate people with green, hazel, gray, or mixed-color eyes (one blue eye and one brown eye, for instance). We might even laugh at the fact that the teacher and the children agreed to use collars as a way to clearly distinguish the brown-eyed people from the blue-eyed people. All of us can see that dividing people in this manner makes no sense.

Such a strategy is similar to racial classification in the United States in that people are classified according to criteria over which they have no control. Ernest Evans Kilker (1993) points out that state definitions of who is black have ranged from Georgia's "any known ancestry" to Ohio's "preponderance of blood." Other methods of determining race include "'exhibiting' a child of questionable race to a jury (e.g., Nebraska, California, North Carolina, Kentucky); showing photographs or even crayon portraits (notice the kinky hair) of family members of the individual in question; general reputation; and 'classification by association'—assigning 'color' based on the color of those the individual has normally associated with" (p. 252).

As in Elliot's third-grade experiment, a major shortcoming of the U.S. system of racial classification is that not all people fit neatly into the categories the U.S. government designates as important. Even so, as we will learn in this book, people have used, and still use, many conscious and unconscious strategies to make others fit into categories. Likewise, many people employ a number of strategies to make sure they themselves fit into some racial category.

In "Interpreting Census Classifications of Race," sociologist Sharon M. Lee (1993) points out that although the racial classification scheme in the United States has changed in significant ways over time, four dominant themes have prevailed: (1) a preoccupation with skin color as the defining indicator of race, (2) a belief in racial purity or in the idea that people can be classified as belonging to one race, (3) a pattern of transforming many ethnic groups into one panethnic racial group, and (4) general tendency to admit no sharp distinction between race, ethnicity, and national origin. Depending on how people answer the race question on the 2000 census, theme 1 and theme 2 may or may not still prevail. Themes 3 and 4, however, will still apply to the 2000 census.

The preoccupation with skin color (theme 1) suggests that the biological facts do not matter. As one of my students wrote:

> I can't be anything but what my skin color tells people I am. I am black because I look black. It does not matter that my family has a complicated biological heritage. One of my great-great-grandmothers looked white but she was of French and African-American descent. Another great-great-

grandmother looked Indian but she was three-fourths Cherokee and one-quarter black. My great-grandfather looked white but his sister was so black she looked purple. My coloring is a middle shade of brown, but I have picked up a lot of red tones in my hair from my Indian heritage. My family is a good example of how classifying people according to skin color is ridiculous.

The features of General Colin Powell are a more famous example of why skin color cannot be regarded as a reliable indicator of biological ancestry. Powell is referred to as a retired black/African-American general, but in reality he is the son of Jamaican immigrants with "African, English, Irish, Scottish, Jewish, and probable Arawak Indian ancestry" (Gates 1995:65). Similarly, Eldrick "Tiger" Woods, who classifies himself as "also Asian," is known as a "black" golf prodigy. "His mother, from Thailand, is half Thai, a quarter Chinese, and a quarter white. His father is half black, a quarter Chinese, and a quarter American Indian" (Page 1996:285).

Notice in both the 1990 and 2000 census race questions that each racial category encompasses a range of national origin and ethnic groups (themes 3 and 4). The category includes ethnic or national origin groups such as Chinese, Asian, Indian, Japanese, Korean, and Vietnamese (see Figure 1.2). Note in the instructions to the 1990 race question (see Figure 1.1), the "black" or "Negro" category includes persons who identify as "African-Americans, Afro-American, Haitian, Jamaican, West Indian, Nigerian, and so on." Keep in mind that people who identify as Haitian, Jamaican, West Indian, or Nigerian may be of *any* race, just as people who identify as American can be of any race. The point is that in the process of transforming many groups into one, the U.S. government makes no sharp distinction among race, ethnicity, and nationality.

In this book, we begin by considering the various ways in which racial classification schemes affect people's lives. Part 1, "The Personal Experience of Classification Schemes" includes a number of personal accounts. Each account points out that classification schemes are important to people's lives whether individuals fit clearly into a racial category or resist classification. Each personal account represents one or more of the following situations:

1. People who cannot be easily classified, and the discomfort and crisis of meaning others feel when they cannot easily place those people into an alleged racial category.
2. People classified as belonging to one racial category but raised by parents of another category.

3. People who do not fit others' conceptions of the racial category to which they claim to belong.
4. People for whom the racial categories to which they belong change from moderately important to extremely important.
5. People whose field of work (e.g., sports, literature, music, art) is classified as representing a particular racial category.
6. People who find that the racial categories to which they have been assigned dominate interpretations of what is taking place and the course of interactions.

Once we understand the tremendous significance of racial categories, we can identify the shortcomings of racial classification schemes. In Part 2, "Classifying People by Race," we present evidence showing that such schemes are based on at least two false assumptions: (1) that people can be divided into clear-cut categories so that everyone fits into one category only, and (2) that each category tells us something meaningful about the persons assigned to it and that differentiates them from people assigned to the other categories. If the assumptions supporting classification are problematic, then by extension, so are any generalizations we make about the people in each category. For example, the ongoing and seemingly endless debate as to whether attributes, such as intelligence (as measured by IQ tests), or behaviors, such as criminal activity (as measured by arrest rates), can be traced to racial or ethnic differences can be laid to rest. If it is clear that race is not a biologically meaningful category, then claiming that race explains differences in behavior proves simply to be a waste of time (Fish 1995).

In Part 3, "Ethnic Classification," we critique the U.S. system of ethnic classification. We do this for several reasons. First, as mentioned earlier, the U.S. government has followed a pattern of transforming many ethnic groups into one panethnic racial group. In addition, the U.S. government makes no distinction between race, ethnicity, and national origin. Second, according to official policy, the only ethnic categories which federal agencies must use when they collect and present data about the U.S. population are (1) Hispanic/Spanish origin and (2) not Hispanic/Spanish origin. Although federal agencies may use other categories, all categories must ultimately fall under these two official categories. Finally, we critique ethnic classification because many people believe that classifying people according to ethnicity is a more meaningful criterion than race.

Our goal in critiquing classification schemes is *not* to create "better" categories with clearer dividing lines, but to show the futility of trying to classify people in this manner at all. In other words, the goal is to explore how people come to define racial categories. And how do they come to see them as the clear-cut mechanisms they employ to maintain the illusion of pure categories. This goal is not to be confused with a desire to show that since there is no such thing as race, then "race" no longer matters. The important point is that people construct classification schemes that carry real consequences. Classification schemes are problematic because they are used to assign social significance and status value to categories over which the people most effected by being categorized have little or no control. When that occurs, persons who possess one variety of a characteristic (white skin versus brown, blond hair versus dark hair) are regarded as more valuable and more worthy of reward than persons who possess other varieties of characteristics. In other words, categories affect *life chances,* a critical set of potential social advantages including "everything from the chance to stay alive during the first year after birth to the chance to view fine art, the chance to remain healthy and grow tall, and if sick to get well again quickly, the chance to avoid becoming a juvenile delinquent—and very crucially, the chance to complete an intermediary or higher educational grade" (Gerth and Mills 1954:313).

In Part 4, "The Persistence, Functions, and Consequences of Social Classification," we ask if classification schemes in fact are so problematic, then why do they seem so clear-cut? The answer to this question is not simple. We identify at least eight factors that make classification schemes seem to be clear-cut and appear to be a natural way to divide people: ignorance of history, legal mechanisms, informal mechanisms, adhering to unexamined norms, ideology, social vulnerability, selective inattention, and the scientific method.

Finally, in Part 5, "Toward a New Paradigm: Transcending Categories," we examine the complex issue of challenging and modifying classification schemes. We consider the real consequences of current schemes and the advantages and disadvantages of modifying them. We recognize that classification, however arbitrary, is connected to discrimination. Although the first impulse may be to call for the elimination of all classification schemes, we must recognize that on some level we need these schemes to monitor discrimination and to appraise efforts to combat discrimination. Given this dilemma—classification as a mechanism supporting discrimination versus classification as a means of monitoring inequality and discrimination—we need a new paradigm to help us consider what categories mean, a new vocabulary to help us think about our position in relation to others, and a new framework to help us to discuss differences among people and across constructed categories. The readings in Part 5 are a first step in this direction.

Since racial categories are social constructions, we struggled with the question of how to refer to "race." Should we always put the word *race* in quotation marks? Should we always qualify references to a person's race with the words people *classified as* or *who identify as* black, white, and so on? In the end, we concluded that the idea of race is real if only because its consequences are real. We believe, however, that people must shift their understanding of the meaning of race away from a term referring to clear biological divisions of humanity, to a term referring to "a way in which one group designates itself as 'insider' and other groups as 'outsiders' to reinforce or enforce its wishes and/or ideas in social, economic, and political realms" (Rorhl 1996:96). Therefore, we continue to see race as an important concept for thinking about the structure of social relationships but we ask that readers work to make this important conceptual shift.

Notes

[1] Some additional examples from students in these two classes make this point even more clear:

- *I worked with a man with one set of grandparents who were mixed (one white, one black). His parents were also mixed. He looks black. This man is now married to a "white" woman, and their kids* look *black.*

    I don't know how we even came to talk of this one day. I always just thought he was black when he's very mixed up. We kind of just made jokes with him about it because he always said how when filling out applications he just checked "other."
- *I went to high school with a boy who grew up in America Somoa. His mother is from the United States and has Cherokee and Irish blood. His father is considered black but has African and Asian blood. My classmates and I never really talked about it, but we all knew he was different from the rest of us.*
- *An alum of my sorority is Cherokee Indian and white. Now she has married a Puerto Rican Hispanic, and they have a daughter who is classified as Hispanic on her birth certificate because her dad is.*
- *My sister's friend could not fit into any of the categories. Her mother is white and her father is black. I never asked her what she considered herself. I do remember when I was in high school and she was in junior high, a couple of the senior guys nicknamed her "mix." I know it hurt her feelings, but I don't know how she replied to the comment.*
- *I have a white friend from Nigeria who has a black boyfriend. They have a little girl who is light-skinned. The U.S. Census Bureau would probably have a hard time figuring out which racial group to put her in.*
- *When I was in high school I played football with a multiracial person. His mother was white and his father was black. He associated with both white and black students inside and outside of school. He lived in the black part of a segregated neighborhood. I think that if he* had *to choose a category he would circle the black category.*

PART 1

❖•❖•❖

The Personal Experience
of Classification Schemes

In this section, we explore the personal experience of racial and ethnic classification schemes. Obviously, personal experience is best understood on the level of *social interaction*, everyday events in which at least two or more people communicate and respond through language and other symbolic gestures in order to affect one another's behavior and thinking. When we encounter another, we make many assumptions about what that person ought to be. Judging from an array of clues, we anticipate his or her identity (or category) and the qualities that we believe to be ordinary and normal for a member of that category. We say "here is someone with a characteristic that places him or her in a certain category. Let me see how he or she fits my conception of what I believe a person in that category should be like." We do not say "here is a person, let me find out what he or she is like without making reference to that category" (Montagu 1964).

We will also consider several interaction situations: situations in which people claiming membership in a particular category do not fit others' conceptions of what someone in the category is like, situations in which people possess physical characteristics which others use to assign them to a particular category, and situations in which people possess ambiguous characteristics that do not allow others to easily place them into a category. We begin with the case of the Mashpee Indians, a group that does not fit others' conceptions of what Indians are supposed to be like.

The Mashpee Indians

Imagine that you have been selected as a jury member for a case in which you and fellow jurors are asked to decide whether a group of people who call themselves the Mashpee constitutes a tribe and whether the Mashpee people have managed to keep alive a core Indian identity over the past 350 years. This question is important for the Mashpee Wampanoag Council because the tribe is suing, in Federal District Court, a large land development company and other property owners to regain 16,000 acres of community land that they had lost in the mid-nineteenth century. Before the Mashpee can bring the suit to court, however, they must prove that they are the biological and cultural descendants of the Mashpee who inhabited the area when it was settled by colonists, and who subsequently lost their land in 1850. If the jury decides in favor of the Mashpee on the question of identity, they will not immediately win their claim to the disputed land. A favorable decision only gives the Mashpee the right to a second trial, which will address the land question. In theory, the identity trial is separate from the land trial.

The lawyers representing the Mashpee argue that in spite of enormous odds, the Mashpee have managed to keep alive a core Indian identity since 1850. The defense, on the other hand, argues that a Mashpee tribe never existed because the federal government never recognized them as a sovereign people. In fact, the town of Mashpee possesses no characteristics to distinguish it from any other small rural community in the United States (Brodeur 1978). At best, says the defense, the Mashpee can be described as a small, mixed community fighting for equality and citizenship, while abandoning most of its heritage by choice and coercion (Clifford 1988).

For 41 days, you listen to testimony from both sides, which centers around whether the Mashpee have lost their culture or distinct way of life. You listen to testimony from Mashpee who speak with New England accents; few of them look "Indian." In fact, some could pass as black; others, as white.

You learn that the Mashpee language has not been spoken commonly since 1800. One witness, in her seventies, recalls that some of her older relatives knew the language but that English was always spoken at home. She heard the old tongue spoken once when her grandfather's mother was sick and her grandfather held a long conversation with his mother. After that, the witness recalled her own mother saying "Dad, why didn't you tell me you could speak Indian?" When he did not answer, the witness followed up by asking "Grandpa, why didn't you tell us you could speak Indian? Why didn't you teach us?" He replied, "I just want my children to learn the English language and learn it as well as they can" (Clifford 1988:285–86).

During the testimony you learn that over the past three years, Mashpee Indians have intermarried with members of other Indian groups, with whites, with slaves, with Cape Verde Islanders,[1] with Hessian mercenaries employed to fight for England during the American Revolution (who later deserted from the British Army), and with black servicemen stationed nearby at Camp Edwards during World War II (Brodeur 1978).[2] Outsiders sometimes identify the Mashpee as "colored." The physical appearances of the Mashpee witnesses reflect this mixed racial and ethnic heritage. One teenage witness, the daughter of a Portuguese father and a Mashpee mother states that she considers herself Mashpee. When asked under cross-examination "How do you know you're an Indian?" she answers, "My mother told me" (Clifford 1988:301).

You learn from witnesses, who identify themselves as Mashpee, that Mashpee routinely move into and out of the community to go to college, to serve in the military, to look for work. Sometimes the moves are temporary; at other times, permanent. For example, one witness lived away from Mashpee for 18 years while he was stationed in Korea and Japan. After leaving the military, he held jobs in Philadelphia and Boston.

Finally, you hear the following kinds of exchanges between lawyers and Mashpee witnesses:

Q: *You don't eat much Indian food, do you?*
A: *Only sometimes.*
Q: *You use regular doctors, don't you?*
A: *Yes, and herbs, as well.*
Q: *How do you know your ancestry?*
A: *My mother, grandparents, word of mouth.*
Q: *What about being a devout Baptist and Indian?*
A: *Grandmother moon and the earth and all those things. . . . They are very dear to me, and I respect them. But I also respect God through my Christian belief. And to me God and the Great Spirit are the same.*

(Clifford 1988:287)

Q: *I notice you have a headband and some regalia?*
A: *Yes.*
Q: *How long have you been wearing such clothing?*
A: *Oh, I have been wearing a headband as long as needed, when my hair was long enough.*
Q: *How long has that been?*
JUDGE: *That which you have on there, is that an Indian headband?*
A: *It is a headband.*
JUDGE: *It has some resemblance to an ordinary red bandanna?*
A: *Right, that's what the material is, yes.*
JUDGE: *A bandanna you buy in the store and fold up in that manner?*
A: *Yes.*

(Clifford 1988:346)

After all the testimony, you are expected to decide whether the contemporary Mashpee are biological and cultural descendants of the 1850

Mashpee. What is your verdict? The jury in this case decides no. Anthropologist James Clifford (1988), who covered the case, argues that the Mashpee never really had a chance of winning the case in the first place because of the narrow way in which most people think about race and ethnicity. For most people these entities have clear boundaries, and when someone steps outside them he or she becomes contaminated, causing that person's claims to membership to become suspect. Because the Mashpee have intermarried with other Indian groups, with whites, with blacks, with Cape Verde Islanders (who can be of any race), and others, the jury cannot see the Mashpee as a separate people.

Likewise, the idea of a Mashpee culture carries associations of a distinct way of life, "of roots, of a stable, territorialized existence" (p. 338). Many people believe that a culture dies if historical continuity is broken. Few regard cultures as phenomena in flux, which adapt to or are transformed by changing circumstances. Because the Mashpee Indians could not point to a physical or cultural characteristic that set them apart or that had remained unchanged, the jury could not see how the Mashpee people could manage to keep alive a core Indian identity over the past 350 years. In addition, the members of the jury brought with them preconceived conceptions about what it means to be Indian that they may have "gleaned from old John Wayne movies and TV reruns of *The Lone Ranger*" (Riley 1992:136). For example, in this case a Mashpee could only be "Mashpee Indian" if they started fires with pieces of flint rather than using matches, if they hunted with bow and arrow rather than rifles, or if they wore deerskin rather than cotton clothing. The reading "Adventures of an Indian Princess" by Patricia Riley (1992) alerts us to some of the ways people pick up such preconceptions about Native Americans.

From the jury's viewpoint, no Mashpee who took the witness stand was an authentic Indian; all had become contaminated (voluntarily or involuntarily) by outside events. The Mashpee could not be authentic because, according to the impossible standards of authenticity, they would have had to remain "pristine" or untouched by the events going on around them over the past 350 years. It seems that the standards of authenticity become less rigid when the dominant groups in society benefit from more flexible standards.

Authenticity

Sociologist Richard Handler argues that the idea of authenticity is a "cultural construct of the modern Western world" (1986:2). He argues that "[o]ur search for authentic cultural experience—for the unspoiled, pristine, genuine, untouched and traditional—says more about us than about others" (p. 2). Handler hypothesizes that questions about authenticity become most relevant when ethnic or racial groups find themselves in a struggle for recognition, whether that recognition be for national sovereignty, for a separate category in the responses to the race question on the census, for the right to speak a language different from the dominant group, or for civil rights (i.e., the right to vote, free speech, and equal opportunity). Although the Mashpee land claim was, in theory, not part of the identity trial, one might speculate that the jury could not free themselves of this fact and considered only the question of identity in reaching a verdict.

The case of the Mashpee reminds us that ideas of authenticity are deeply embedded in judgments about whether people are members of the categories to which they claim to belong (Handler 1986). Thus every person, but especially those in categories outside the dominant group, are subjected to conscious or unconscious authenticity tests by those within and outside of the category to which they claim to belong. In the reading "Black Man with a Nose Job" by Lawrence Otis Graham (1995), we learn how Graham struggled with issues of authenticity when he decided to undergo rhinoplasty. He describes friends' and acquaintances' reactions to his changed bridge, nostrils, and profile—to his "longer, thinner nostrils." While white friends and classmates who had undergone the surgical procedure could justify their rhinoplasty with "I just want to look better," Graham cannot escape the question of whether he had launched an assault on his history, identity, culture, and people.

In a similar vein, writers who are not considered members of the dominant group are subjected to authenticity tests. In "Culture Wars in Asian America" by Garrett Hongo (1995), we learn that many reviewers and critics see it as their job to classify nonwhite authors as authentic or inauthentic and to question the ability of white authors to write about nonwhite experiences. Many people assume that writers classified as Asian-Americans write (or should write) "Asian-American literature." Classifying writers according to their race or ethnicity sets up a false distinction between so-called mainstream American literature and multicultural literature with all its subspecialities—African, Asian, Native American. Such a false distinction flattens differences, denies variation, represses independence among writers, and denies them "the legitimacy of their own interpretation of events" (Hongo 1995:27). Assuming an automatic correspondence between an author's race or ethnicity and his or her topic and writing style reveals an inability to see Asian-Americans and other groups as highly heterogeneous with regard to experience, national origin, and length of residence in the United States (Hongo 1994). The reading "Born and Raised in Hawaii but not Hawaiian" offers one example from a "Korean" perspective of the Asian-American experience. Note that the author Andrea Kim is a third generation Korean-American who at various points in her career identifies with Korean, Japanese, Hawaiian, and American cultures. At times Kim even rejects some elements of her "Korean" identity. Authenticity issues are central in the essay, "Don't Want to Be Black Anymore," by Yolanda Adams. Adams possesses the physical characteristics that would make her appear to be an "authentic black person" yet she lives in a white neighborhood. As an editor of a black newspaper, Yolanda is asked, "How can you represent and write about the black community if you don't live in a black community?"

Pressures to be authentic can make the challenged person feel as if he or she is under a microscope or is on stage performing before an audience (see **Conversations About "Authenticity"**). Here the dramaturgic model of social interaction offers some insights. Erving Goffman (1959), the sociologist associated with this model, views social interaction as though it were a theater and people as though they were actors giving performances to audiences. People in social interaction resemble actors in that they must be convincing to others and must demonstrate who they are and what they are about through verbal and nonverbal clues. In social interaction, as on a stage, people manage the setting, their dress, their appearance, their words, and their gestures to correspond to the impressions they are trying to make or to the image they are trying to project to their audience. This process is called *impression management.*

On the surface, the process of impression management may strike us as manipulative and deceitful. Most of the time, however, people are not even aware that they are engaged in impression management because they are simply behaving in ways they regard as natural. But when people are aware that an audience is skeptical about who they are, impression management can become a self-conscious, even deliberate, process. When this occurs, impression management presents people with a dilemma. If they do not conceal thoughts and behavior deemed inappropriate for or not expected of someone in their category, they risk offending or losing their audience. Yet, if they conceal their "true" feelings, wishes, or reactions, they may feel they are being deceitful, insincere, or dishonest, or that they are selling out. According to Goffman, the people involved weigh the costs of losing their audiences against the costs of losing their integrity. If keeping the audience is important, concealment is necessary; if showing our true reactions is important, we may risk losing the audience.

The point of the dramaturgical model and the "Conversations About Authenticity" is that they help us better understand the self-presentation and impression management issues members of dominant and subordinate

Conversations About "Authenticity"

- When I was about ten years old, I remember playing basketball with my 12-year-old cousin at a family event. This cousin was a role model in every aspect of my life. Among other things she taught me how to dress, how to put on makeup, and what music was "cool." That day I was wearing overalls, and I had left one of the buttons undone, so that one side of the bib was left hanging. When my cousin saw this she said, "Are you a wannabe?" I asked her what that word meant. She told me that a "wannabe" is someone who wants to be black. Then she buttoned my overalls into place. This experience made a great impression on my life even though I was a very young child. Why did leaving one button undone mean I wanted to join another race ?

- Problems began at my high school when a number of white males began to act "black." They began wearing their pants low on their hips, listening to R&B and rap music, and using what was considered "black" slang. These "wannabes" became the most hated group in my high school and their style caused heated debates as well as some fistfights. The "wannabes" were eventually banished from social circles and forced to change their style in order to fit in.

- I have a black female friend whose parents sent her to the best schools. She speaks "proper" English and is fluent in French. With the exception of maybe two black men, she has dated white men. She is considered white by all of our friends because she didn't fit into the mold of what a black woman should be. Many refer to her as a "wigger" because she went to "white" schools. In college she joined a white sorority instead of a black one. When I asked her how she feels about the things that people say about her, she replies "I am what I am, and I am not going to change because someone doesn't think that I act black!"

- In middle school, I remember hearing people say that if you were black and made good grades then you were trying to "act white." But if you were black and made average grades then you were considered to be acting your color.

- I have always been called "white." People call me this because I speak proper English and because I am not interested in the latest clothing trends or rap videos. I listen to alternative music, and I know nothing of the ghetto. When my peers aren't calling me "white," they call me "stuck-up" because they sense that I am uncomfortable around them. My parents chose to live in white neighborhoods to shelter me from the stereotype of what some call "niggers." When I was younger being called "white" really bothered me, but now I realize that I am better equipped to handle the business world (one cannot go into a place of business speaking slang), while my "ghetto" counterparts struggle to make it in the business world.

- I grew up in an all-white neighborhood and went to an all-white elementary school. The middle school I went to was predominantly black. In middle school I was seen as an "oreo" (black on the outside, white on the inside). Another kid at this school was also called the same thing. This kid's situation was a little bit different from mine, though. He was from Africa; his father was a doctor and his family was very well off. After a couple of months of middle school I was able to change the way I talked so that I was not made fun of every time I spoke. But it wasn't that simple for the African kid. No matter what he did, the other black students did not accept him. In fact, both the white and black students teased him by saying "You act whiter than a white person." By the time I graduated from middle school, I was very popular with all students at school. The African guy could only make it with some of the white kids; he never "broke in" to the social circles of the black students.

- There was only one black student in my high school graduating class. He acted white. He listened to country music, not rap. He drove a pickup truck and dressed country western with cowboy boots and flannel shirts. He spoke with a country drawl and did not use slang words. Once a white student asked him if he ever ate "chitlins and greens" and he said that he never even heard of chitlins. His entire peer group was made up of white students.

Continued

Conversations About "Authenticity" *(Continued)*

• I see dressing nicely as appearing professional and neat. Others see it as trying to be white. People also label language as black or white. I am not sure how I would describe my voice and speech but my friends, and even strangers, say I talk white. Older people think this is cute and respectful, but my peers see it as sounding like a white girl or they mistake my tone for being stuck-up. This has been a major obstacle for me in the past when it came to finding friends. I even tried to change the way I talked, so I wouldn't sound so white. That didn't work very well. It only served to make things worse. When I got to high school, it seemed that most people had grown out of this mind set. Outside of the occasional student who refused to get to know me as a person and classified me as a "black girl trying to be white," high school was a better experience. I thought that in college this would not even be an issue. But in college even those who got to know me well admitted that they didn't think I talked like a black girl; others came right out and called me white. I run into this when I answer the phone. Some-

one will ask for my roommate and also ask me if I'm white or black. I'll say that I'm black and the person on the other end, usually a guy, will act as if he doesn't believe me. What do they expect me to say? "Oh, I'm sorry. You're right, I'm wrong. I *am* white."

• I am biracial (mom's white, dad's black) and all my life I have been "accused" of acting too much like one race or the other. My black friends tell me I am acting "too white." My white friends say I am acting "too ghetto." To me, I am just acting like me, nothing more, nothing less.

• When I was in the sixth grade I remember being in a locker room after gym with three black students. One of the girls was looking at a picture of another girl's parents in which the father was black and mother was white. After examining the photograph for a few seconds one girl said "Oh great, we lost another one," meaning we lost another black man to the white world.

---

racial categories face. Nonwhites are taught, and also learn intuitively from their socializing experiences (the theater of life), that they must manage the impressions they make on on both dominant and subordinate group members. In the case of black and white youths, blacks learn that they had better not act "too black" when their audiences are primarily white adults and that they better not act "too white" when their audiences are black. Whites, on the other hand, learn that "acting black" in front of white audiences conveys the message that they are rebels or that they are dissatisfied in some way with the system. In any case, whites have the option of abandoning their rebellious self-presentations. Blacks, on the other, unless they can pass into the white race, daily confront the demands of two audiences. The different impression management issues speak to the varying and uneven effects of racial classification. In addition the impression management dilemma blacks face illustrates a double consciousness that W.E.B. DuBois descibes as "this sense of always looking at one's self through the eye's of others, of measuring one's soul by the tape of a world that looks on in amused contempt and piety." The double consciousness includes a sense of twoness: "an American, a Negro, two souls, two thoughts, two unreconciled strivings; two warring ideals in one dark body, whose dogged strength alone keeps it from being torn asunder."

To this point we have discussed situations in which people's racial and ethnic authenticity is questioned—that is they do not display the distinctive, popularly held, and imposed characteristic which places them solidly in the category of a Mashpee Indian, a black man, a black woman, an Asian writer, or a Korean man. But what happens when people display that distinctive characteristic which places them solidly in a social category? Here we can turn to Erving Goffman's theory of stigma for some insights.

Stigma

A *stigma* is an attribute that is deeply *discrediting*. That is, when someone possesses a stigma, he or she is reduced in the eyes of others from a multi-faceted person to a person with one tainted status. In addition, the attribute dominates the course of interaction and also the way others think about the person with the discrediting attribute. To illustrate these points, Goffman opens *Stigma: Notes on the Management of Spoiled Identity* (1963) with a letter written by a 16-year-old girl born without a nose. Although she is a good student, has a good figure, and is a good dancer, no one she meets can get past the fact she has no nose.

Consider the situation of Mitzi Uehara-Carter (1996) as she describes it in "On Being Blackanese." Uehara-Carter is both Japanese and Black, and people can't see her as mixed or even as Japanese. Her black heritage dominates the view others have of her to the point that they can only see her as black. As another example of how a stigma reduces a person in the eyes of others from a multifaceted person to a one dimensional being, consider the situation of noted historian John Hope Franklin (1990), where the element of race affects the ways in which people describe and evaluate his accomplishments:

> It's often assumed that I'm a scholar of Afro-American history, but the fact is that I haven't taught a course in Afro-American history in 30…years. They say I'm the author of 12 books on black history, when several of those books focus mainly on whites. I'm called a leading black historian, never minding the fact that I've served as president of the American Historical Association, the Organization of American Historians, the Southern Historical Association, Phi Beta Kappa, and on and on. The tragedy…is that black scholars so often have their specialties forced on them. My specialty is the history of the South, and that means I teach the history of blacks and whites. (1990:13)

Goffman was particularly interested in social encounters known as *mixed contacts* or interactions between stigmatized persons and normals. Goffman did not use the term *normal* in the literal sense of the "well-adjusted" or "healthy." Instead, he used it to refer to those people who are in the majority or who possess no discrediting attributes in the context of a particular setting. Goffman's choice of the word *normal* is unfortunate, because some readers forget how Goffman intended it to be used in the context of his thesis.

In keeping with this focus, Goffman wrote that *mixed contacts* are "the moments when stigmatized and normals are in the same 'social situation,' that is, in one another's immediate physical presence, whether in a conversation-like encounter or in the mere co-presence of an unfocused gathering" (Goffman 1963:12). According to Goffman, when normals and stigmatized interact, the stigma comes to dominate the course of interaction. In the reading "Six Case Studies," six students from Northern Kentucky University describe how one characteristic—skin color—can come to dominate the course of social interaction: specifically, how the parties involved define, interpret, and attach meaning to encounters.

A stigma comes to dominate the course of interaction in many ways. First, the very anticipation of contact can cause normals and stigmatized individuals to avoid one another. One reason the stigmatized and the normals choose to avoid each other is to escape the other's scrutiny. Persons of the same race and ethnicity may prefer to interact with each other so as to avoid the discomfort, rejections, and suspicions they encounter from people of another racial or ethnic group. Goffman (1963) suggests that the stigmatized individual has good reason to feel anxious about mixed social interaction and that "we normals will find these situations shaky too" (p. 18). Normals feel "that the stigmatized individual is either too aggressive or too shamefaced, and in either case too ready to read unintended meanings into our actions" (p.18). Normals may feel that if they show direct sympathetic concern toward the stigmatized, they are calling attention to differences when they should be "color-blind." Each potential source of discomfort for the stigmatized "can become something we sense he is aware of, aware that we are aware of, and even aware of our state of awareness about his awareness" (Goffman 1963:18).

A second way in which a stigma comes to dominate the course of mixed-contact interaction is that normals often define accomplishments by the stigmatized, even minor accomplishments "as signs of remarkable and noteworthy capacities" (Goffman 1963:14) or as evidence that they have met someone from that category who is an exception to the rule (i.e., he or she is just "like us").

As well as defining the accomplishments of the stigmatized as something unusual, normals also tend to behave according to a third pattern: interpreting the failings of the stigmatized, major and even minor, as related to the stigma. When normals observe a failing in a stigmatized person, they attribute the cause of the failure to the stigma and ignore other contributing factors that would cause anyone difficulty. The dynamic by which people attribute cause is similar to the process by which people attribute cause to a fall, when the person falling is a one-legged girl on a roller skate: "Whenever I fell, out swarmed the women in droves, clucking, and fretting like a bunch of bereft mother hens...they assumed that no routine hazard to skating—no stick or stone—upset my flying wheels. It was a foregone conclusion that I fell because I was a poor, helpless cripple" (Goffman 1963:16).

A fourth way in which a stigma comes to dominate mixed-contact interaction is that the stigmatized are likely to experience invasion of privacy, whether the invasion is experienced through stares, intrusive questions, or added scrutiny. If the stigmatized show their displeasure at such treatment, normals often treat such complaints as exaggerated, unreasonable, or much to do about nothing. Their argument is that everyone suffers discrimination in some way and that the stigmatized do not have a monopoly on oppression. Normals announce that they are tired of the complaining and that perhaps the stigmatized are not doing enough to help themselves. This is how one woman from Nigeria reacted to the situation of American blacks. In an excerpt from "What Will My Mother Say," Dympna Ugwu-Oju (1995) recounts the level of ignorance Americans have about Africa and the insensitive and downright humiliating questions they ask. In spite of these experiences, Ugwu-Oju, who did not see herself as a black person, dismissed American blacks' reactions to discrimination as "groundless whining" until she learned that, in the United States, she *was* black and that her skin color was the most prominent characteristic by which she was judged.

This discussion should not lead you to believe that the stigmatized are passive victims who are at the mercy of those in the dominant categories. Goffman describes at least five ways in which the stigmatized respond to people who fail to accord them respect or who treat them as members of a category. One way is to attempt to correct that which is defined as the failing, as when people change the visible characteristics that they believe represent barriers to status and belonging. The stigmatized may undergo cosmetic surgery, straighten their hair, bleach their skin, enroll in a school to change an accent, change friends, or dress in a different manner.

The stigmatized may respond in a second way. Instead of taking direct action and changing the visible attributes that normals define as failings, they may attempt an indirect response. That is, they may devote a great deal of effort to trying to overcome the stereotypes or to appear as if they are in full control of everything around them. They may try to be perfect—to always be in a good mood, to outperform everyone else, or to master an activity ordinarily thought to be beyond the reach of or closed to people in their category. The stigmatized may press harder to prove their own uniqueness and their difference from others assigned to their category.

In "Apologizing for Being a Black Male," Paul Andrew Dawkins feels constrained to modify routine behaviors, which most white males undertake without a second thought, so as not to frighten white women, a group that has been socialized to be "suspicious" of most black men, especially when they find themselves alone with a black man in a building, an elevator, or a parking lot. The simple act of using a public phone adjacent to one a white woman is using becomes for Paul Dawkins an occasion of profound reflection, hesitation, and self-doubt. While Dawkins does bring himself to use the phone, the woman's behavior (turning her back and drawing her purse in front of her) confirms that he still needs to be concerned that his most innocent act, misinterpreted, could be perceived as threatening and even lead to unwarranted police intervention (see **Conversations About the "Fear of Black Men"**).

❖◆❖

Conversations About the "Fear of Black Men"[1]

- Some of my co-workers at the fast food restaurant where I work are afraid when a black man comes to the drive-through window to pick up his order. They tell me they are always fearful he will pull out a gun, shoot them, and rob the place. Some go as far as asking me to wait on the black men. I laugh at them because I believe if they are not willing to wait on everyone, then they do not need to work there. When our store was eventually robbed my co-workers were shocked that it was two white men who held one of the night managers at gun point forcing her back into the store to open the safe. In defense of white people, my co-workers argued that the two white guys who robbed the store did so because they hang out with black people

- At night if I'm in a black neighborhood or a bad part of town, I am usually jumpy. Even though nothing has ever happened to me, I still get scared when I am approached by blacks at night.

Continued

[1]When asked to comment on the "fear of young black men," a few students made the following point: "We all walk fast past people at night, lock our car doors while driving through the projects, and have people walk us to our destinations at night rather than walk alone. Why? Not because the people we are walking past and driving by are black. We lock our doors because it is a bad part of town, regardless of what race or races of people are standing on the street corner. Being cautious is smart, not racist. I do all of the above when I am in a bad part of town, regardless of the racial makeup of people living there."

Conversations About the "Fear of Black Men" *(Continued)*

- My mom and my aunt left work pretty late one night from downtown Cincinnati. They were driving through a rough looking part of the city when they realized they had a flat tire. Neither my aunt nor my mom knew how to change a flat tire. Both were terrified, and they did not know what to do. Two black men walking down the street noticed the predicament they were in and approached my mom's car. With great hesitation my mom and aunt got out of the car. The two black men asked them if they wanted them to change the tire. Of course, my mom said yes. When the two men had completed the task my mom tried to give them money for their time and trouble. My mom said the two men were utterly insulted by her gesture and would not accept the money. They told my mom and aunt to have a safe trip home, and then proceeded to walk down the street.

- I find myself trying to just pass black people on the streets and not look at them or attempt to talk to them. I usually only react this way with young black men, but I can't explain why. One of my best friends is a 23-year-old black male, Stephen. I feel very comfortable when I am with him, and I do not have a problem.

- I don't feel like I am afraid of every young black man. Sometimes I feel like every black man hates me. No one has ever told me that, I think it is part of our society. You always hear about racial problems on the news, in the movies, or in the music. The media makes it sound like it is "us against them."

The talk shows have guests on their programs who are preparing for the "Great Race War"—the whites versus the blacks. It can be very frightening to see this and I find myself believing it. I do not want a racial war. I have no problem with black and white integration, but obviously some parts of our society do.

- Two of my friends and I were parked by the Newport flood wall on a Saturday night. We had the radio turned up playing "Too Short," by a popular rap artist. My friend, Eddie, saw three black men in the car next to us and immediately turned the radio down. I don't know what he was afraid of. The black men next to us did not even seem to notice that we were parked next to them. This didn't matter to Eddie, he was still afraid of something.

- I remember one time I went downtown in the middle of the day with my Grandma. We were stopped at a red light and there was a young black man standing on the corner waiting to cross the street. As soon as my Grandma saw him she reached over and locked the door. I asked her why she did that and she said she was just keeping us safe. At the time I didn't really think much about it, but now, as I look back, I feel that was a very prejudiced action. I often wonder what she would have done if a white man been standing there instead of a black man. I don't think she is racist, but I do know that she was raised to believe black people are inferior to white people. I wonder if her upbringing made her feel this way.

Another way for the stigmatized to show their uniqueness is to take special actions to distance themselves from others in their category, as in the following situation described by a student. It involved her participation in an introduction to sociology class and her Chinese roommate, Elizabeth:

Elizabeth's parents, who met each other more than 25 years ago while attending college in the U.S., speak Chinese at home and follow traditional Chinese practices. This is often a point of embarrassment to Elizabeth who often refers to them as being "straight off the boat." Elizabeth dates only blond-haired, blue-eyed U.S.-born boys. Recently Elizabeth's parents came to town for her graduation. Elizabeth acted embarrassed to be seen with them. When she introduced them she would say, "Aren't they the cutest little Chinese couple?" Her parents never said a word, but one time her mother looked at me and rolled her eyes. The entire day Elizabeth talked to her parents as if they were dumb. At one point, her father ordered filet mignon and Elizabeth said, "No, he will have the New York strip, medium well." Her mother interrupted her and said, "Your father knows what he wants for dinner; he doesn't need your help deciding." Elizabeth thinks that because her parents have thick accents they need help being understood. Actually no one had trouble understanding them.

Sometimes the stigmatized respond in a third way: They use their subordinate status for secondary gains, including personal profit, or "as an excuse for ill success that has come [their] way for other reasons" (Goffman 1963:10). If a nonwhite person, for example, levels a charge of racism and threatens to file a lawsuit in a situation in which he or she is justly sanctioned for poor work, academic, or other performance, then that person is using his or her status for secondary gains.

A fourth response is to view discrimination as a blessing in disguise, especially for its ability to build character or for what it teaches a person about life and humanity. Finally, the stigmatized can condemn all of the normals and view them negatively.

To this point, we have examined two kinds of situations: (1) situations in which people claiming membership in a particular category do not fit others' conceptions of what someone in the category is like and (2) situations in which people possess or react to characteristics that are treated as discrediting. Now we turn to a third kind of situation—in which people possess ambiguous characteristics which do *not* allow others to easily place them into a category.

The writing of sociologist Robert E. Park (1967) on the *marginal man* provides some insights about people in this kind of situation. The *marginal man* is a person facing a social dilemma. He or she belongs to two groups that society treats as separate entities which have no overlap. Given this larger social context, the marginal man is a cultural hybrid, a person living and sharing intimately in the lives of two seemingly distinct peoples. Yet, at the same time, the marginal man lives on the margins of two groups. Thus the marginal man is simultaneously an insider and outsider. As an outsider, the marginal man takes on the perspective of a stranger: He or she "is not radically committed to the unique ingredients and peculiar tendencies" of either group and "therefore approaches them with the specific attitude of 'objectivity.' But objectivity does not simply involve passivity and detachment; it is a particular structure composed of distance and nearness, indifference and involvement" (Simmel 1950:404). As a result of this position in relationship to each group, the stranger tends to survey "conditions with less prejudice; his [her] criteria for them are more general and more objective ideals" (Simmel 1950:405).

We look at five cases in which people are simultaneously insiders and outsiders. In the reading "Choosing Up Sides," author Judy Scales-Trent (1995) must come to terms with the dilemma of her self-identification as a "black" person and her physical features, which sometimes lead others to describe her as "white," in a society which does not handle anomalies very well. Although she is living proof that categories that are treated as clear-cut do not exist, most of the people she encounters struggle to find a way to place her in a single category: "I am perceived by some as white, by some as black, by yet others as a black person but 'really white.'" Scales-Trent finds that in order to survive as a person, she must question the very existence of categories and the absurdity of a classification system which asks people to "choose up sides" (p. 63).

In the reading "Identity Matters: The Immigrant Children," an excerpt from Marilyn Halter's *Between Race and Ethnicity* (1993), an interesting parallel to Scales-Trent's situation is represented. We are introduced to two Cape Verdean Americans, Joaquim A. "Jack" Custodio and Lucille Ramos. Both faced the dilemma of being identified by the larger society as black while self-identifying as white.

Sarah Van't Hul, in "How It Was for Me" (1995), describes the subtle prejudice she experiences from white people and the overt hostility she encounters from black people when they learn that she is a black person who has been adopted by a white family. Like Custodio and Ramos, Van't Hul comes to terms with her marginal status by questioning the constructed nature and meaning of racial categories.

In "Mojado Like Me" (1995) we encounter the case of Joseph Tovares, a free lance documentary film producer who poses as a Latino farm worker with two colleagues as part of an undercover story for ABC's "PrimeTime Live." Although it had been 25 years since Tovares had worked in the fields, he thought "there had developed a great distance between who I had been and who I had become." He learns that only a change of clothes and a 1979 Ford truck allowed him to pass easily as a "Mexican farm worker" and lose his status as a professional.

Finally we consider the marginal status of Yuri Korhiyama, a young Japanese woman, who was one of the estimated 120,000 people of Japanese descent (80 percent of whom were U.S. citizens) living on the West coast of the United States sent to internment camps during World War II. Japanese-Americans were forced from their homes and taken to desert prisons surrounded by barbed wire and guarded by machine guns. There was no evidence of anti-American activity on the part of those interned. Yet the wartime hysteria, combined with long-standing prejudices, led to the shipping of some men, women, and children to concentration camps. In "Then Came the War," Yuri Kochiyama (1992) recalls that before the war she was "red, white, and blue" and felt "very, very American." She worked in a local department store and remembered the town as wonderful and the people as very friendly. Yet when the war came everyone was yelling to get the "Japs" out of California. In this reading Kochiyama describes the strange meaning of being Japanese in the United States during this time.

The final reading, "I Cannot Imagine Being Any Race Other Than White" is a photoessay. The images and symbols in these photos represent one specific way of experiencing "whiteness" in the United States. The people featured in this essay believe that race is a clear-cut category and that they belong to the white race. In these photos, Anna Castellini documents the various ways "whiteness" is conveyed, and even celebrated through slogans on t-shirts, white power gestures, and cross lightings.

Notes

[1] The Cape Verde Islands make up a Portuguese territory located in the Atlantic Ocean off the coast of Africa, west of Senegal.

[2] There was a U.S.O. center for "colored" servicemen in Mashpee. To ease racial tensions between white and black servicemen, military authorities persuaded Mashpee residents to house a center for black servicemen. The town proved to be a friendly place, and after the war many black servicemen took up residence in Mashpee (Brodeur 1978).

Adventures of an Indian Princess

PATRICIA RILEY

◇◆◈◆◇

Study Question
What preconceptions about Indian culture do tourists pick up when they visit "Cherokee Country"? Connect this story with the outcome of the Mashpee Indian trial described in "Part I: The Personal Experience of Classification Schemes."

The dingy blue station wagon lumbered off the road and into the parking lot as soon as its driver spotted the garish wooden sign with the words INDIAN TRADING POST written in three-foot-high red, white, and blue letters. Beneath the towering letters was the greeting WELCOME TO CHEROKEE COUNTRY, accompanied by a faded and rather tacky reproduction of someone's idea of a Cherokee chief, complete with a Sioux war bonnet. A smaller sign stood next to the large one and attested to the authenticity of the "genuine" Indian goods that the store had to offer.

The driver, Jackson Rapier, foster parent extraordinaire, assisted by his wife and two teenage daughters, had decided, at first seeing the aforementioned sign from a distance, that coming upon this place must indeed have been an act of Providence. Only yesterday they had received their newest addition in a long chain of foster children, a young Cherokee girl, eleven or twelve years old, called Arletta. The social worker had told them that it was important for the girl to maintain some kind of contact with her native culture. When they saw the sign, they were all agreed that this trading post was just the ticket. It would be good for Arletta and they would all have a good time.

Mrs. Rapier twisted around in the front seat and looked at the dark girl wedged between her pale and freckled daughters, the youngest of whom was absorbed in the task of peeling away what remained of a large bubble of chewing gum from around her nostrils. Mrs. Rapier sighed, then tried to smile encouragingly at Arletta as she pushed bobby pins into her wispy red hair. "You're gonna love this place, honey. I just know you will."

"Yeah, Arletta," the eldest daughter said, making faces at her sister over Arletta's head. "You ought to feel right at home in a place like this. This looks like just your style."

"Just your style," the sister echoed and resumed picking the gum off her face.

Arletta looked around her, assessed the situation, and decided she was outnumbered. She knew they wouldn't hear her even if she voiced her objections. They never listened when she talked. When she had arrived at their home, they had seemed to be full of curiosity about what it was like to be Indian. But all the questions they fired at her, they eventually answered themselves, armed as they were with a sophisticated knowledge of Indian people gleaned from old John Wayne movies and TV reruns of *The Lone Ranger*.

Arletta imagined she could survive this experience. She had survived a great many things these last two years. Her father's death. Her mother's illness. An endless series of foster homes. She was getting tired of being shuffled around like a worn-out deck of cards. All she wanted right now was to be able to stay in one place long enough for her mother to track her down and take her home. She knew her mother must be well by now and probably getting the runaround from the welfare office as to her daughter's whereabouts. For the time being, staying with the Rapiers was the only game in town, and she felt compelled to play along. She arranged what she hoped would pass for a smile on her face and said nothing. Behind the silent mask, she ground her teeth together.

The midsummer sun blazed off the shiny chrome hubcaps someone had nailed above the trading post door and reflected sharply into their eyes, making the transition from air-conditioned car to parking lot momentarily unbearable. Mr. Rapier was the first to brave the thick, heated air. He wiped a yellowed handkerchief across his balding head, which had begun to sweat almost immediately upon leaving the car. He adjusted the strap that held his camera around his neck and waited while his wife and daughters quickly climbed out of the car and made their way with swift steps to a battered red Coke machine that stood beside the trading post's open door.

Arletta hung back, squinting her eyes against the brightness. She had no interest in the trading post and was determined to stay outside. Off to the left of the Coke machine, she saw a tall, dark man suddenly walk around the side of the building leading a fleabitten pinto pony with a blanket draped awkwardly across its back. Arletta had to laugh at the way he looked because a Cherokee, or any other kind of respectable Indian, wouldn't dress like that on

his worst day. Before her mother's illness, Arletta had traveled with her throughout the United States, dancing at one powwow or another all summer long. She knew how the people dressed, and she learned to recognize other tribes by the things they wore as well. This man had his tribes all mixed up. He wore a fringed buckskin outfit, with Plains-style geometric beaded designs, a Maidu abalone shell choker, and moccasins with Chippewa floral designs beaded on the toes. On his head was a huge, drooping feather headdress, almost identical to the one pictured in the sign beside the road. Arletta noticed that there was something else not quite right about the way he looked. His skin looked funny, all dark and light, almost striped in places. As he came closer, she could see that the dark color of his skin had been painted on with makeup and that the stripes had been made by the sweat running down his skin and spoiling the paint job. Arletta had never in all her life known an Indian who looked the way this man did.

After buying everything they wanted, the Rapier family came spilling out of the trading post just in time to be impressed by the cut-and-paste "Indian."

"Oh, Arletta," Mrs. Rapier said. "Look what you found. A real live Indian! Go on over there like a good girl, and I'll have Jackson take a nice picture of the two of you together. It's so seldom you ever see one of your own people."

Arletta froze. She couldn't believe Mrs. Rapier was serious, but then she knew she was. Mrs. Rapier and her entire family actually believed that the man they saw before them was a bonafide Cherokee chief. What is wrong with these people? she thought. Can't they see this guy's a fake?

Mr. Rapier walked behind Arletta and put his sweaty hands on both her shoulders. For a moment, she thought he was going to give her a reprieve, to tell her that she didn't have to do this, that it was all just a joke. Instead, he pushed her forward, propelling her toward the man with the rapidly melting face. She knew then that they were giving her no choice.

Mr. Rapier arranged the girl and the costumed man in what he thought was a suitable pose and stepped back for a look through his camera. Dissatisfied with what he saw, he turned and walked back into the trading post to return minutes later with an enormous rubber tomahawk, a bedraggled turkey feather war bonnet, a smaller version of the one worn by the costumed man, and a shabbily worked beaded medallion necklace with a purple and yellow thunderbird design. He thrust the tomahawk into Arletta's hand, plunked the headdress on her head sideways, and arranged the necklace around her neck with the quickness of a ferret. Surveying his creation, he smiled and returned to his previous position to adjust his camera lens.

"Smile real big for me, honey," he said. "And say the magic word. Say Cherokee!"

Mr. Rapier grinned, his pale beady eyes twinkled at his clever remark. Arletta felt her mouth go sour and a strange contortion of pain began to move around in the bottom of her belly.

The costumed man took her hand and squeezed it. "Come on now, honey. Smile fer the pitcher," he said. His breath was stale rye whiskey and chewing tobacco. Standing next to him, Arletta could smell the pungent sweat that rolled off of him in waves, making his paint job look even worse than it had when she first saw him. Her stomach felt as if she'd swallowed an electric mixer, and she bit her lips to keep the burning in the back of her eyes from sliding down her face. Through her humiliation, Arletta glared defiantly at the man be-

hind the camera and stubbornly refused to utter Mr. Rapier's magic word, no matter how much he coaxed and cajoled. Finally the camera whirred once like a demented bumblebee and it was done.

Mrs. Rapier dabbed at the perspiration that puddled in her cleavage with a crumpled tissue and praised her husband's photographic genius. "That was perfect, Jackson," she said. "You got her real good. Why, she looks just like an Indian princess."

Appeased by his wife's esteem, Mr. Rapier bought everyone a round of cold drinks and then shepherded Arletta and his rapidly wilting family back into the dilapidated station wagon for the long ride home. The superheated air inside the closed-up car was stifling. Arletta suddenly felt as if she were being walled up alive in some kind of tomb. The syrupy soda that had been so cold when she drank it boiled now as it pitched and rolled inside her stomach. She took off the hideous turkey feather headdress and dropped it, along with the phony rubber tomahawk, onto the floor of the car. Slowly, deliberately, Arletta removed the cheap beaded medallion with its crude rendering of a thunderbird from around her neck. Her fingers trembled as she ran them across the tops of the large, ugly, and uneven beads. Turning the medallion over, she read the tiny words printed faintly on the shiny vinyl backing, while the painful turbulence inside her stomach increased.

"Mr. Rapier, could you stop the car?" she said. "Mr. Rapier, I don't feel so good."

Mr. Rapier adjusted the knob on the air conditioner's control panel to high and drove on without acknowledging that Arletta had ever spoken. He was already envisioning how her picture would look in the photo album where he and his wife kept the captured images of all the foster children they had cared for over the years. He hoped she hadn't spoiled the shot with that stubborn expression of hers. He wanted to put it next to the one of the little black girl they had last year. She sure had looked cute all dressed up in those African clothes standing next to that papier-mâché lion at Jungle World.

Mrs. Rapier pulled down the sun visor and began to pull at her perspiration-soaked hair with jerky, irritated movements. She looked at Arletta in the visor's mirror and frowned.

"Arletta," she said, "you need to hush. You've just worn yourself out from the heat and playing Indian. You'll be just fine as soon as the car cools off."

For an instant, Arletta pleaded with her eyes. Then she threw up all over the "genuine" Indian goods: "Made in Japan."

"Arletta!" Mrs. Rapier screamed. "Look what you've done! You've ruined all those lovely things we bought. Aren't you ashamed of yourself?"

Arletta flashed a genuine smile for the first time that day. "No, ma'am," she said. "No, ma'am, I'm not."

Black Man with a Nose Job

Lawrence Otis Graham

◇◆◈◆◇

Study Questions

1. How will Lawrence Otis Graham know if his operation is a success?
2. Where does Graham get his images of "ideal" noses to show the plastic surgeon?
3. What are the "racial" issues bound up with Graham's decision to have rhinoplasty?
4. Do you think Graham can ever know if his decision to undergo rhinoplasty represents a wish to simply "look better" or a wish to look "less black"?
5. In a book published in 1999, Graham acknowledged that he had his nose surgically altered "so that I could further buy into the aesthetic biases that many among the black elite hold so dear" (Graham 1999:380). What do you think he means by this?

"**D**ad, slow down some."

The relentless spring breeze finally calmed as my father let up from the accelerator and swerved us into a right-hand lane.

This man, who was normally quite solicitous of his youngest son and who almost never drove above fifty miles per hour, was suddenly sighing indignantly over my interference with his driving speed.

"What's wrong?" I asked.

He stared straight ahead, occasionally glancing at the stream of cars that were now passing us by. "Nothing," he answered.

As we reached the Henry Hudson tollbooths that would take us out of Manhattan, three young black faces peered into the side window.

"What the hell happened to *you?*"

"Somebody fucked his shit up—look at that shit!"

Three black guys in their early twenties looked down from their Jeep into my open window and shook their heads with perverse amusement.

Determined to get a response, the driver finally asked, "You get shot?"

Dad moved us up another car length as I put the ice pack beneath my eyes and moved into a reclining position.

"Extra token and a receipt."

"My goodness—is everything all right in there?" the blue-jacketed toll woman asked as she stared into the backseat at my head: an oversized bowling ball of white gauze, plaster, and hospital tape. Unbeknownst to me, melting ice was quietly transforming the gauze-covered bloodstains, making them a more prominent red color and giving them a surreal, almost tie-dye-like quality underneath the white material.

I think I nodded faintly.

"Just a nose job," my father answered while retrieving his change.

"Really?" She seemed surprised by my father's air of nonchalance.

Or was it an air of contempt?

As I lay reclined, with my head practically in the backseat of the little maroon BMW, I wondered what my father thought of me now. A man of a different generation—born and raised in the segregated South—educated and trained in an almost exclusively black world, where the concept of an oxymoron readily included such things as a black man with a nose job.

For my entire life, until yesterday, I had displayed his same nostrils, bridge, and profile. Tomorrow I wouldn't. Tomorrow I'd look like someone else. Staring up at the back of my father's head, I realized that the success of my operation would be measured in direct proportion to how much differently my nose looked from his. It was a shameful contrast to make with someone I loved so much, but when looking at my sketches, it was an accurate one nevertheless.

"This is the one I want," I had said while handing the opened magazine to Dr. Wilson.

"Which?" he asked.

I scanned the well-lit Upper East Side office, then crossed my legs with an air of affected nonchalance. "I actually don't care. Any of those would do."

This black plastic surgeon—one who had been practicing on the Upper East Side for longer than my time on this earth—had no doubt met my kind before: that overly anxious patient who displays reckless confidence in the miracles of modern medicine. Walking the streets with desperation in our eyes and portfolios under our arms, we young, well-to-do seekers of cosmetic enhancement bear a strange resemblance to professional models, except that inside *our*

portfolios is a lifetime supply of dog-eared photos and print ads depicting *other people's* faces, features, and body parts that we wish *we* had been born with and that we hope can still be affixed—Mr. Potatohead-like—onto the various appendages and extremities of our bodies.

Having torn more than fifty or sixty shots of sharp-nosed, square-jawed, model-handsome, near-black-looking or practically black-looking men from some of the best store catalogs and hippest fashion magazines in New York, I felt I'd done more than my share of the legwork. I was now ready to pay whatever it cost and submit myself to whatever tests, X rays, computer imaging, or painful surgical procedures were necessary.

Dr. Wilson flipped ahead with a ruffled brow. "What magazine are these pictures from?"

I leaned over his desk and looked at the pages. "That's the Brooks Brothers catalog. But I've got lots of other noses and faces mixed in from other catalogs and magazines."

The good doctor—I'd been told one of the best in New York—had no idea of how long I'd agonized over this project. I'd been saving noses and profiles for the prior three years, tearing out pages from magazines, catalogs—even stealing a poster from a Boston red-line subway car one Sunday afternoon—all in the search for the right features. I stuck all this into a bulging April 1987 issue of *Ebony*.

"Mr. Graham," the sensitive doctor began as he reached for my chin and turned my head to either side. "There is only a certain amount of alteration that is possible, or even desirable, for any one nose."

"I know what you're going to say," I interrupted. "That you can't make me look like those guys because they have white noses. But if you notice, those are all *black* men on these pages I've given you. They're all *black*."

"Hmm."

The least black-looking collection of black men either one of us had ever seen compiled.

"Even if I *could* do this—and it would be unlikely—such a long thin prominent nose wouldn't work on your face."

"Okay, then what about this one?" I showed him a page from a nine-month-old *Sports Illustrated*.

The good doctor shook his head.

"But he's black too." Yeah, black and something else.

"Umm."

"What about this one?" I showed him several shots of a brown-skinned model in a *GQ* layout. Probably a black Cuban.

He waved me on.

I pulled out a recent issue of *Essence* and turned to the first of the paper-clipped pages, which featured models who were suddenly displaying darker skin and wider, flatter noses. "How about that?" I pointed to the *Essence* man who stood holding an elegant glass of whiskey.

"Why don't I sketch out what I think we can consider."

But I wasn't giving up yet. "Wait—let me just show you this last one. I got this tourism ad out of *Ebony*. You must at least be able to do *that*."

He looked down at the brownest of all my men. "Mr. Graham, that nose would never be in harmony with your lips and chin. They would never work together."

"My lips and chin?" I asked. I had to pause a few seconds and consider the significance of his remark. "Then change them," I finally howled. "Change them. I'll pay whatever it costs. Change them. Just change them!"

Sometimes it takes very little to send some of us down the slippery slope toward black self-hatred.

Eventually I entered a hospital on Manhattan's Upper West Side to undergo that common surgical procedure we all call rhinoplasty. While this procedure is performed nearly a hundred thousand times each year, I had the feeling that my case was different. It was shortly after being wheeled into the large, brightly lit recovery room that I became certain that I had just launched an assault on my identity and my people. But now it was too late to go back. I was, forever, a black man who had gotten a nose job.

Although I'd grown up in a white neighborhood where male and female adolescents got their noses narrowed, chins and cheeks enhanced, and skin chemically peeled as a coming-of-age ritual during junior high and high school vacations, I had never seriously considered plastic surgery for myself. Yes, I wanted to be thought of as more handsome, but no one in my family had ever undergone cosmetic surgery. For these white friends and classmates who had undergone surgical changes, their explanations focused simply on cosmetics: They wanted to look "better." Not surprisingly, no one ever seemed to impute any other motive or to psychoanalyze the real meaning of "better." For me and my family, physical appearance and its alteration were issues of ethnicity and heritage. Black people had wide nostrils, thick lips, protruding mouths, and dark skin—and any desire to change those features was, by definition, a negative commentary on our people and our own racial identity.

For the most part, I never even compared my looks to those of the white kids or white adults around me. During my adolescence, I did, however, draw contrasts with the young blacks in my own world of black professionals and their families who socialized in our black social clubs and vacation places. There were numerous occasions as a child, and later as an adult, hosting summer cookouts in Sag Harbor, Long Island, or Oak Bluffs, Martha's Vineyard; attending our Jack & Jill family gatherings; or partying at the Sisters of Ethos all-black dances at Wellesley College, when I'd run into dozens of well-to-do, light-skinned, straight-haired, thin-featured black childhood friends. After returning to the security of my own bedroom mirror, I would critique my features against those other blacks in my life who had "sharper," "nicer," "finer" (all words that meant more attractive and less Negroid) physical characteristics.

I would flatten my thick lips against my teeth, protrude my chin, and try but fail to attach a wooden clothespin on the wide fleshy tip of my nose. The pain of this primitive procedure was outweighed by the satisfaction I got from capturing a glimpse of longer, thinner nostrils.

Except for those occasions when I flipped through men's magazines or passed by some daytime or nighttime TV soap opera, it was rare that I ever compared my features to whites around me. Unlike young girls, I was fortunate that, as little boys, my brother and I weren't saddled with trying to find our image and, hence, our self-worth, in the similarities we shared with the face and features of a white Barbie or Ken doll. In spite of the ambivalence that I once had about my looks, I've always felt that black boys are far luckier than the black girls who get ambushed by white girls in school and summer camp who tell them, "You'd be really pretty if it wasn't for that black nappy hair of yours."

My color ambivalence manifested itself in many different ways during my adolescence.

I'm reminded of the Hasbro G.I. Joe army and astronaut set I used to play with. One afternoon I put brown shoe polish all over my 1967 G.I. Joe astronaut's pink body and later melted his tiny nose away with the heat from my Mattel "Creepy Crawlers" cooking iron. I don't know if I can ascribe my actions to black pride or a desire to punish Joe, but I never took him out in public after that.

Finally, after considering hundreds of magazine and catalog layouts and doctor's sketches, after writing a check for $4,000 to a black surgeon, and after having the operation, I still sometimes feel like I've upset the standard of blackness that I'd been raised to accept and appreciate.

When I told a former black classmate about my operation, she accused me of trying to pass out of the black race. It was hardly the sympathetic response I had expected from an intelligent woman who had been one of my first friends in law school. In fact, her contempt was so great and questions so numerous, I really began to wonder if she was right about my motives.

Did I have this operation in order to become less black—to have features that were more white? Had I bought into the white definition of beauty—the sharp nose, the thin lips, the straight hair? Did I think that my less Negroid-looking black friends were more attractive than me?

My wife says my decision is personal and that I shouldn't feel compelled to defend it or explain it to anyone else. I'd like to think she is right. Maybe she's right about not needing to justify my acts to white coworkers or white neighbors. But what about my black relatives, my black friends, my black co-workers, my black secretary? Don't I owe them an explanation? Don't I have to let them know I wasn't saying that I wanted to be white when I pared down my wider, rounder Negroid nose?

Of course, I could take the easy way out and tell onlookers that one's racial identity is not embodied in one's nose. It certainly should be obvious in my case. After all, my dark brown skin and curly black hair are still intact. A different nose won't make me look white. But that's really not the point I need to address, is it?

For two years prior to my operation, I agonized over the ethnic ramifications of cosmetic surgery. According to the American Society of Plastic and Reconstructive Surgeons, 640,000 cosmetic procedures were performed in the United States in 1994. Since the preponderance of those patients were white, I am fairly certain that many of them felt no obligation to justify their surgery to members of their ethnic group.

All of this leads me to conclude that my defenses are a wasted effort. While my white friends have guiltlessly selected profiles and implants with their surgeons, I was making a futile attempt to validate my ethnic loyalty by developing arguments to prove that a nose job would not make me less black.

I shouldn't have to defend my surgery any more than those 640,000 patients who pass under the scalpel each year—or for any person who makes any type of cosmetic change in his or her natural appearance. After all, an Italian person rarely feels guilty for turning his brown hair blond. Few Jewish people apologize for having their noses shaved down. Not many Asian people have to justify putting waves into their straight hair. Many people, in fact, are surprised to learn that in both Japan and Korea, as well as in the United States, it is quite common for male and female Japanese and Korean people of all ages to have their eyes done (for less than $1,500, a surgeon creates a more westernized eye by creating a fold in the eyelid that makes it

appear rounder) and their noses enhanced (for about $2,500, a surgeon creates a more Caucasian nose by raising the bridge and tip by inserting a plastic or cartilage implant). With so many other groups undergoing the same procedures, it is ludicrous for black cosmetic surgery to be taken as a form of heresy against the race.

I am discovering that many whites as well as blacks perceive a black person's cosmetic surgery as a sign of self-hatred or the desire to be less black—an accusation often aimed at singer Michael Jackson, who in spite of his claims about rare skin diseases and naturally changing bone structure, pinched his nose, bleached his skin, tattooed his eyes, enhanced his chin, and straightened his hair. Even black talk show host Montel Williams felt compelled to explain his nose job to his viewers. His claim: He'd done it because he'd had difficulty breathing. Whether we believe his explanation or not, none of us have the right to challenge such a decision.

An equally presumptuous attitude prevailed a while back with regard to colored contact lenses. No one objected when white actors, models, and consumers wore the cosmetic lenses, but when black talk-show host Oprah Winfrey wore them on TV, there was an immediate avalanche of attacks from both whites and blacks who could not understand why a black person would wear green contacts. White people seemed to be threatened by the notion that black people could actually avail themselves of cosmetic advances and appropriate the beauty characteristics that white people had theretofore defined as exclusively their own. Black audiences, too, looked at rich, powerful, and famous Oprah and feared that she was somehow about to "buy" herself out of the black race and leave us bereft of one more black heroine and role model. In the end, when the host held her ground on her black identity, black and white viewers wised up and realized that the ever dedicated and down-to-earth Winfrey wasn't going anywhere she didn't belong. Colored contacts weren't going to change her.

Black plastic surgery patients or contact lens wearers should not have to address the issue of ethnicity any more than white people who go to a tanning salon or get a collagen shot to thicken their lips—as so many white actors, models, and fashion-conscious citizens are doing today. Black people who get their hair straightened each month should be able to do so just because they want to sample a noncurly style.

Because I've narrowed my nose, some of my black friends say I have sought to deny my ethnicity, and oddly enough, some of my white friends—even those who have had nose jobs themselves—say I'm representative of the young black professional who wants to assimilate into the white cul-ture. Perhaps it is true that the media images and the white kids who surrounded me as a child sometimes caused me to judge my own attractiveness on some other group's standard of beauty, but I dismiss the suggestion that any black who seeks to alter his natural physical characteristics has turned on his people and attempted to "pass" as a member of some other race.

Once the bandages were finally taken off (a few years ago), friends discovered that I am no less black than I was before the operation. I still had the same black friendships, still supported the same black causes, and still maintained the same black consciousness. As my father, the stoic black southerner, was able to do, my friends continue to allow me to take pleasure in my new appearance. For them to view this as anything more than a cosmetic procedure would be to suggest that the culture, feelings, and the history of black people are awfully superficial.

Culture Wars in Asian America

Garrett Hongo

Study Questions
1. Describe the criticism Cynthia Kadohata received because of her novel *The Floating World.*
2. What issue did Robert Butler have to confront about his work?
3. What does Hongo's account of his exchange with a *Newsday* reporter tell us about how the media covers issues related to "race"?

During the summer of 1989, on a book tour after the publication of her novel *The Floating World,* writer Cynthia Kadohata, a Japanese American, was making a routine appearance at Cody's Books in Berkeley. The crowd was unusually large for a first-time novelist, packed with interested Asian American students and some UC faculty too. Her book had been receiving good notices in the mainstream press, and a chapter of it had run in *The New Yorker* prior to publication. She read quietly but clearly, with a fine delicacy of voice and a minimum of physical movement. The audience seemed charmed. But in the question and answer session that followed, she was chastised for not writing about the concentration camp experience. Her novel, partially set during the time of World War II, tells the story of an itinerant family of Japanese Americans wandering through the West and South in search of work, doing without community except for each other. It never once mentions the federally ordered evacuation of citizens of Japanese ancestry from the West Coast. But there was a powerful faction among Japanese American intellectuals who felt it was illegitimate of Kadohata to have refrained from any overt references to the internment camp experience.

"You mean to tell me that you have this family of Japanese Americans running around through Arizona, Colorado, and Utah, and you *never* say anything about the camps!" a scholar shouted from the audience. "You should be ashamed of yourself for falsifying our history!" he yelled.

More shouting ensued as a few other Asian Americans joined this public castigation. Kadohata responded by saying that she didn't *intend* to write about the camps, that her novel wasn't *about* the camps, that she was writing about a family of loners and misfits, writing from *her* experience, and that was that. She was then criticized for abdicating her responsibilities as a Japanese American writer, denounced for not fulfilling expectation, for not writing from the public truth of the time.

She told me later that the whole incident puzzled and upset her. It hurt that people, especially other Asian Americans, felt compelled to attack her for what she *didn't* write even more than for what she *did* write. Kadohata was wondering why there was so much vehemence, so much anger, and so much "attitude" among Asian Americans *against* Asian American writers. She hadn't defended herself then, but the episode made a deep and lasting impression. She told me that the next time she was out there, she'd be ready. She wasn't going to get beaten up again without a fight.

I once remarked that Asian America is so immature as a culture and so unused to seeing cultural representations of itself that, whenever representation does occur, many respond with anger because of the pain released. It is as if they recognize *their* story in the outlines of the story one of the writers is telling, but feel even more alienated rather than absolved because that story isn't theirs *exactly,* or doesn't present the precise tone and tenor of their inner feeling regarding an experience they feel the writer, as an Asian American, should understand. It's like a bunch of family members at a holiday dinner sitting around, trying to tell a story about a maiden aunt, a matriarch, or a black sheep. One starts it up, and, before you know it, six others chime in, saying the first didn't get it right, that their version is the one that is true and has all the facts. It has to do with issues of primacy, proprietorship, a claim of proper descent and legitimacy, and a claim to specialized knowledge. It is complex. And charged with passion. Whenever someone singles out a certain storyline, an interpretive angle, there are always those who would dispute its legitimacy, even to the point of trying to erode the confidence of the storyteller. . . .

A couple of years ago, I got a phone call at my home in Oregon from a reporter at *Newsday,* the daily paper for Long Island. Just the day before, Robert Olen Butler had been awarded the Pulitzer Prize in Fiction for his collection of short stories called *A Good Scent from a Strange Mountain.* The narrator of each story is Vietnamese, each a different survivor of the war in Vietnam, most of them living in this country. The reporter wanted to know what I, as an Asian American writer, thought about the prize being awarded to a white male who wrote stories in the personae of male and female Vietnamese refugees.

I told him I was personally delighted that Butler had won the Pulitzer, that I was glad that the prize had finally gone to someone who was known as a dedicated laborer in the fields of creative writing, who wrote for long years in obscurity, who wrote well and without recognition except from his peers in the business, who taught a heavy teaching load at a regional branch of a state university, who was a single parent who gave to his community and to the community of Vietnamese immigrants. I stalled, wanting a little time to think.

"Yes," the reporter said, "but what is your opinion about his being white and writing in the voices of Asians? Of him *adopting* the identity of Vietnamese individuals in order to write his fiction?"

I had suspected there was something hot behind his questioning. On matters of race, American culture has the chronic habit of organizing itself in terms of opposition first, even with regard to a book that, to me, was a sincere attempt to create commonality.

On the one hand, there was the history of stereotyping and ventriloquizing Asians in this country. There was certainly a history of abuse there. And it was a history that was vague in the minds of most Americans who were not Asians—an "invisible" history, one that did not penetrate daily consciousness unless one were oneself Asian American. Butler's collection of stories, in the act of taking on the voices of Vietnamese people, could be interpreted by some as perpetuating that tradition.

On the other hand, there was my own feeling that Butler's book was kind of a breakthrough for American books on the Vietnam experience. Until Butler published his stories, most every piece of writing from Americans had to do with the tragedy of the American experience in Vietnam. Tim O'Brien and Larry Heinemann had written powerful fiction from the point of view of American soldiers. Michael Herr had published nonfiction from a similar perspective, while Yusef Komunyakaa had written a stunning book of poems—it, too, based on his GI experience. Very little had been published from the Vietnamese point of view, and almost nothing about the Vietnamese experience in America. Butler's book had created characters and described an ethos much unknown to mainstream America— that of the Viet Kieu, Vietnamese survivors of the war who had emigrated to the United States and were struggling over their losses, their identity, and the difficulties of acculturation. Sympathetic without being sentimental, Butler's treatment gave the outlines of their lives great human dimension and humor without ignoring the multiple tragedies of their having lost homelands, loved ones, and a certain continuity of cultural identity. *A Good Scent from a Strange Mountain,* though written by someone who was white and not Vietnamese, could not easily be seen as yet another piece of "minstrelsy" by the white culture ventriloquizing the ethnic experience and colonizing the mind of the Other for the purpose of reinforcing cultural dominance. It is a work which seemed to me at once more complex than that, and yet I could not say so within the simplistic framework in which the reporter was asking his question.

I told the reporter that I couldn't give him a short answer and gave him the long one instead. I begged off making any kind of *ultimate* political judgment. Since I am not from the Vietnamese American community, I couldn't presume to speak to the issue of whether or not his characterizations and tales infringed upon some "right" of theirs to define themselves in our culture. I felt uncomfortable being asked to speak "as an Asian American," knowing that we are an extremely diverse group in terms of generations, cultures of origin, and economics. I urged him to ask a Vietnamese American. I told him that, by asking me for my opinion, I knew he was operating as if Asians in America were one vast, homogenous category, and making the false assumption that any one of us, no matter that our ethnicities were different, could speak "on behalf" of the entire race.

He tried to press me, but gave up after a few more exchanges. He couldn't pin me down because I didn't want to be. Frustrated, the reporter thanked me and hung up. It was obvious I hadn't helped his story angle. He wanted a fight between Butler and Asians, and he wanted me either to defend Butler or to attack him. He wanted my answers to be *simple* and unqualified. On one side or the other, I guess, on that issue, I was sitting on a fence. The reporter's coming to me was itself another act of racism, and I worried about participating in that.

But I continued to feel uncomfortable about the incident. Why couldn't I have given the reporter something more definitive? Why hadn't I been more ready to give a strong opinion on the matter? What was it that made me speak on both sides of the issue? Was I, in fact, in being so equivocal, acting as an apologist for white colonization of ethnic cultural space? Was I—of *all* things—acting like a goddamn Uncle Tom? What are the issues here and how could I rethink myself through them? I questioned myself but hesitated to bring it up among my friends, whether Asian or not. I feared policing and I feared judgment. I wanted some space to think. I decided to look for other writers who could help me to do this kind of thinking.

There was indeed a political dimension to this issue, but it is not one regarding a given writer's "right" to represent a culture. There is a profound difference between the idea that any group has an exclusive right to engage in authorized acts of cultural representation and the idea that cultural representations are not open to criticism, whether by a group or an individual critic. Although our system of prestige can itself be seen as a kind of rule of unwritten laws, I myself believe that we cannot, finally, create legislation regarding cultural properties in the verbal arts—i.e., provide cultural laws empowering and licensing only certain individuals to do what we will prohibit others from doing with regard to language and the arts.

At the same time, I do not think that anyone can be above being criticized for what they choose to do with this kind of liberty. I think we can applaud [David] Mura for raising a political objection to a work of art, but we can also critique—though not silence—Butler on political grounds for the work of art he has produced. I think we can critique Mura as well, and we can praise Butler too—for his humanistic politics as well as for his powerful artistry. The confusions, then, have less to do with the practices of the individual artists and much more to do with the way general thought in our culture (as enacted by media and the ephemeral communal mind) tends to oversimplify complex social and artistic issues, with the habitual comminglings and false oppositions of matters of art with matters of social justice. The problem, ultimately, has to do with confusing and, finally, conflating the two realms.

Born and Raised in Hawaii, But Not Hawaiian

Andrea Kim

◇◆◆◇

Study Questions
1. In what ways is Andrea Kim "Korean?"
2. What behaviors or thoughts make her "not Korean?"
3. How do most outsiders view Andrea?
4. What does the title "Born and Raised in Hawaii, But Not Hawaiian" mean?

My Asian background is Korean, and even in Hawaii, Koreans are a minority. The group that dominated my sense of culture the most are Japanese Americans. It pervades everything. In high school, my friends would talk about going to the YBA—the Young Buddhists Association. It's the counterpart to the YMCA. A lot of them went to the Buddhist temple—but it was nothing special. It was just as normal to hear someone say that, as for someone to say, "I'm going to the YMCA or the Catholic church."

You eat sushi, you pick up Japanese words, there are Bon dances in the summer. Ever since I was little I had Korean clothes but I would be just as familiar with a kimono. It's just as natural as if you were living in New York, and you were familiar with pretzels, roasted chestnuts, and Central Park.

There are certain stereotypes—such as Chinese are very prudent with their money, and that Koreans gamble a lot—but I found the Asian stereotypes to be stronger here on the mainland than in Hawaii. There wasn't a Japanese stereotype, because they were the norm.

If you were white you really stood out. I know in high school people would hang out in groups. It was like senior corner, Hawaiian corner, and for the whites, we called theirs haole (means foreigner, and usually applies to white people) corner. We didn't regard the whites as a minority. They sort of had an exotic appeal. I thought white people were very attractive. In fact I used to wish I had blue eyes and blond hair. In my high school, it was a fashionable thing for people to use Scoth tape, and make their eyes look more like whites. You can do it so that you make your lids have another fold. A lot of my friends in the summers would go to Japan because their families were there. They would have an operation to make their eyelids double. It was not an unusual thing. More people would dye their hair lighter—instead of black, they would make it brown. Actually, a fairly popular hairdresser in Hilo dyed her hair blond. Looking back at that it's really pathetic. But Hawaii is really an odd little world. If I hadn't gone away to college, there is so much I would never have realized.

I would never call myself a Hawaiian because there is an ethnic group that is racially Hawaiian. I say I am from Hawaii or I grew up there. You have an identity with the Hawaiian culture. That's the exciting thing about growing up in Hawaii—you're exposed to not only the Asian influence, but the Hawaiian influence as well. There are obvious signs of Hawaiian culture, such as hula dancing or luaus.

As for the locals—the Hawaiians—you have to feel sorry for them, because they weren't doing well at all. There are special programs and housing for them, but in general, native Hawaiians do not do well academically and that affect their whole lives. If they don't do well in school, it becomes very difficult to succeed. It is not a perception that the Hawaiians are an underclass—it is a truth. For instance, it is also true to say that, in general, blacks in this country make up the underclass. I mean we all know blacks who are educated, have gone to Ivy League schools, and are doing terrifically well. But in general, if I had to choose, I would never choose to be born black in the United States. I don't care what my advantages are economically, there is just so much discrimination. It is such a burden to handle, that I wouldn't willingly choose to be a black person. Similarly, in Hawaii, I wouldn't choose to be a Hawaiian person. You can overcome all of that. But if you come from an environment where education is not a priority, it makes it difficult for you for the rest of your life.

I didn't really socialize with people who are Hawaiian. One of my friends who is Japanese, married someone who is Hawaiian. That must have been a big shock to her family. It's a class thing. It's as if you're marrying someone who is a janitor, or something. I feel it's kind of marrying down when you marry Hawaiian. I mean to me, it's inconceivable. Why would I marry someone who is Hawaiian? They don't have my interests—they're not in my class. They're not in the top classes. I was the salutatorian in my high school class of seven hundred thirty students. I was in the top of all my classes in school. There weren't any Hawaiians in any of my classes. Maybe there were in gym class but that wasn't based on ability. So the only Hawaiians I saw in high school were hanging around in their corners. In May Day programs you would elect a court—a king and a queen—and they were usually Hawaiians. A lot of the Hawaiians are very good looking.

I shouldn't give you the wrong impression. There is a great deal of ethnic pride in Hawaii. People are proud of being Japanese, Korean, or whatever. But the whole ideology is that this is a melting pot, and people get along fine. The overriding identification was being American.

Family: My father was born in Korea, and my mother's mother was born in Korea. My father and grandmother were very active in the Korean Christian Church. The services are in Korean, and they are basically for those who are recently arrived to Hawaii. I played the piano, so for about two hours on Sunday I would be in this totally Korean environment. In the service, I knew the Korean word for psalm so that when I heard that word, I knew it was time for me to play the piano. And other than that I would sit there and daydream. My father was the lay leader. So for two or three years, I would hear Korean, but not really understand any of it.

It would have been nice if we had spoken Korean at home, but there was no way that could have happened. Because on my mother's side, the feeling was you were in America, so it was important to speak English. My grandmother came to Hawaii as a picture bride, and so on my mother's side we are third generation Korean American, which is quite old. My mother's parents weren't well educated at all. They had a farm in a very small town. It is even even smaller than Hilo. They supported themselves by raising chickens. My grandmother also had a kimchee business which my uncle is still running.

The lifestyle she grew up with was a marked difference from the lifestyle she and my father were able to give us. My mother was a schoolteacher—she's retired—and we went to the school where she taught. It was great to have your mom work at the school, because the other kids wouldn't mess with you. After school, we would study in the classroom and the library. All the teachers were Asian—predominately Japanese American. In our family, where my mother is one of eight kids, we are seen as very successful. I went to Bryn Mawr. My sister went to Swarthmore and has her PhD from Johns Hopkins. Her husband also has a PhD from Hopkins. My brother went to Berkeley. He's now in Hawaii and working for a top engineering firm. The fourth sister did miserably in school. This is the sister that is very good looking. Academics is not something you questioned. It was important to do well in school. It's like accepting the fact that the sun comes up in the morning in the East. It was just important to do well in school. But there was no conscious effort on my parents' part to make us study. They made it very easy for us to do well. One thing I will say is that they devoted a lot of time to us. In the summers we had school at home. My mother assigned us compositions. We had workbooks and my father taught us math. We were at least one or two years ahead of our grades in math.

I felt we were growing up in an all-American way. The whole family used to watch Lawrence Welk every Saturday. I thought we had a very typical upbringing, because the television is a major homogenizing influence. You see the same commercials as

some kid in California sees. I decided I was as American as anyone else. We recited the Pledge of Allegiance every day before class. We sang "America the Beautiful" before class began, from first to sixth grade.

We ate very American things—spaghetti, hot dogs. But whenever we had a family get together, we would have Korean food. My mother would make Korean marinaded beef, and it would be charbroiled. I learned how to make that by going to the family gatherings. We always had my grandmother's broiled beef, and of course, kimchee. So now when I entertain, the greatest compliment I can show my guests is to serve Korean food. It is food that is very nourishing to me. I was very close to my grandmother, and she taught me how to make it.

On the Mainland: It was great growing up with Asians all around me, but I didn't appreciate it until I left Hawaii. When I was seventeen, I graduated Hilo High School, and went to Bryn Mawr. It's a good school, but I remember the first day on campus, I thought I was in a time warp because the school had gothic architecture, and I had never seen so many whites in one place at one time.

But it wasn't until I started my professional career, as a journalist—my first job was in a small town in Massachusetts, a very white community—that I became really conscious of being Asian. If I went to a major department store, I would be the only Asian person on that floor. I worked at the paper for five years. Toward the end of that time, there were Southeast Asians that were moving into the area. Catholic charities were very active in settling Vietnamese refugees or the Hmong refugees into the area. But in terms of educated, professional Asians, there were very few.

We covered everything—fires, town meetings, school boards. As I was leaving city hall one day, one of the workers—a very nice elderly woman—said to me, "My you speak English so well, where did you learn it?" Her assumption was that I was not an American. That kind of attitude was something that really made me quite angry at first, because I am very proud of being American, and to me, that people would assume I wasn't, really was very upsetting.

The first apartment I got was in the poor section of town. I didn't know it at the time. It was just that the rent was cheap. The landlord was in my apartment fixing something one day. He wasn't very educated. He ran an auto body shop and the rental units were a side business. He asked "What do people like you do?" I felt like I was an animal in a zoo. But I guess he was actually well intentioned. He just meant that in his daily work, he didn't see any Asians, and he wondered how we spent our time because he never saw us. I responded by being very polite. I said, "People like me do usual things. It's just that there aren't many Asians in this town, so you probably won't see them." I mean if he had gone to some classical concerts, he would have seen some Asians there because there were some professionals in the area.

Usually if men ask you to go out with them, it's because they have some interest in Asians—they have taken karate, or something like that. But your standard white-bred male wouldn't think of asking me out at all. I'm not something that would appeal to them. I mean if they had gone to school with some Asians, or attended karate class, or if their teachers were Asian, they might be curious and ask me out, out of pure novelty. Other than that, most had not grown up with someone who's Asian, and this really hit home to me when I was working in a small town.

Dating and Marriage: Since I am a journalist and move around a lot, the social life isn't that good. But let me tell you about my sisters. They would never go out with an Asian man. I have two sisters younger than I. One is married. Her husband is very handsome. He has dark hair and blue eyes. His ethnic background is Swedish and French. They met in graduate school. He's from California. She's never gone out with someone who is Asian. My other sister is truly beautiful. She would never go out with an Asian either. I think it relates back to my father. He is truly one of the most brilliant people I know. And in many ways I think I take after him because he has amazing qualities of resourcefulness and perseverance. If he is playing table tennis, and is behind, he can turn that game around and win. I've seen him do it many times. Similarly, he taught himself to fix anything. He has a degree in chemical engineering. He is a chemist. But he can fix washing machines, televisions, and cars. He just went to the library and borrowed books.

However, he does not speak English well at all. He has a very strong Korean accent. Ever since I was a little girl, I have seen how people treated him because of that. They treat him as if he is an idiot. They would raise their voices, thinking that would help him understand them better. They treated him this way just because he sounds like an immigrant. So that was always very painful to me. I resolved that I did not want to sound like my father. So that's why it was important to me not to go to school in Hawaii. When we visited my cousins in California, I heard how differently they sounded, and I wanted to sound like them. I didn't want to sound like an Asian or like my father. So that is why I wanted to go to Harvard or Bryn Mawr. But that also had ramifications. Because my father was seen as the other, or the outsider—my mother is definitely American—there would be clashes between my father and mother on very basic things such as education. Usually my father would prevail, because my mother is a very gentle person. But it's like all of us were American except my father. He was really Korean. And he's very strict. And even today, he tries to tell me how to run my life, and he is five thousand miles away. So I think that had a very strong influence on why my sisters would never consider someone who is Asian as attractive. My father would embody a lot of unattractive things about Asians to them, he had this accent, he had strange ideas, and he just wasn't American. And why would you want to tie yourself to someone who is different and an outsider? You want to be accepted and like other kids. So I think that would explain why neither one of my sisters would go out with someone who is Asian.

Since I'm thirty-two and not married, and I would like to have kids and stuff, I would just like to find someone who is not boring and someone who would be accepting of the lifestyle I have as a journalist. I belong to a professional association for Asian journalists, and through them I feel I have developed pride as an Asian. I have found that the older I get, more and more of my friends tend to be Asians. In college that wasn't the case. Most of my friends were white. If I had my choice, I would love to marry a Korean American. I would love to have kids who are pure Korean. On my father's side we are descended from royalty. Koreans have a very high rate of marrying other groups, and frankly, if you are Korean and twenty-five, that's kind of old not to be married. It's changing a little now. But traditionally, when I meet old Korean people, and I tell them I am not married, I can tell they feel sorry for me. There are not that many eligible men around my age. Again, I can't marry someone who is fresh off the boat. That wouldn't work. I am very American and don't have enough knowledge of Korean to communicate. And being able to

communicate is very important to me. So if someone is Chinese or Japanese, that is okay, too. It's perfectly fine for a Chinese to marry a Japanese. But it's nice to marry someone from your own ethnic group, because the kids will have a very strong sense of their ethnic identity. I have cousins who are half Chinese, and it really depends on the mother, as far as how they identify themselves. I'm sure my children will have a very strong identity of being Korean, and it would be nice if they were pure Korean.

What I find really interesting is that if I had never left Hawaii, I would probably have married a white person because I remember very clearly in high school, that even if a guy was just average, but he was white, I thought he was really handsome. Because there were so few white people, they really stood out. All the subliminal messages to you from television commercials, movies, and magazines are that white is beautiful. All the models were white. You develop an image of what is beautiful. Now, I'm really into looking as Asian as I can. My hair is straight. Now I want to see how long I can get my hair to grow. I also want bangs. I would not dye my hair brown. If anything, I would dye it black because I'm getting grey hair.

Some of my closest and best friends are Japanese. But to be very honest, it would be difficult if I did marry someone who is Japanese, because Japan colonized Korea. My mother once said that in our family, no one married a Japanese. That is true because they married whites, Koreans or Chinese. In one case, one aunt married someone who is Hispanic. They are no longer married. But even that is more acceptable than marrying someone who is Japanese. I would say the likeliest prospect if I were to marry an Asian would be Chinese American, because they have been in this country longer, and I think they treat their wives quite well. They're used to having independent women. Probably I would marry a Chinese American, or someone who's Jewish. I think people who are Jewish have a lot in commone with Asians. They have similar values.

I have friends who are black. I like them. But I would never marry anyone who is black, because I think it would be a terrible handicap to have children who are half black and half Asian. I very much want to have a family, so it's not an option that I would marry someone for love and not have kids. So I would never marry someone who is black. My parents would be horrified also. They would never understand it. And I think when you marry someone, it is very important that they fit into your family. My parents had no problem with my sister marrying a white. My dad just wants us married. I talk to them every weekend. And recently my dad said, "Well, I hope this is the year you meet someone and get married." In this case I don't see it as pressure I don't need. I feel the same way, so it's okay. He's thinking about my welfare. He really thinks I would be better off married.

Physical Appearance: When I was little, My mother used to always make me curl my hair. I don't do that anymore. I think it's nice to have really straight hair. Another problem is my hairstylist. She thinks it is a sin to curl Asian hair. She's blond herself, and she thinks Asian hair is beautiful. She would not curl my hair anyway. But in Hawaii most people had perms because you wanted to look as Western as possible. So I have never considered my black hair anything special. Why should I? Everybody looked like me. Everybody had brown eyes and black hair. It wasn't until college that people would say to me, "You have such beautiful hair." They'd say, "When I was little, I wished I had black hair." It was a new idea to me that while I didn't have curly red

hair with blue eyes, they also didn't have straight black hair.

If they're Asian, people usually think I'm Chinese, because there are more Chinese and Japanese here in New York. Rarely do people think I'm Korean. Even when I go to Korean green grocers, they never think I am Korean. They usually think I'm Japanese. I'm never taken to be Korean. I think it's because they assume that if I were really Korean, I would speak to them in Korean. This is even when I speak my very limited Korean to them. Maybe it's because my hair is straight, and a lot of Korean women have perms. Generally Japanese women I notice don't have perms. I also wear my makeup to make myself look more Western. It doesn't matter to me either way, because I'm proud to be Asian. It's okay.

Work: My Asianness is left at the door when I go to work, because in many ways, I am a replaceable cog. I know if I quit my job, they can find someone tomorrow. But I would like to think that in some small way I make a difference. Little things I can do. When I see something offensive, or egregiously wrong, or stereotyping Asians, I try to edit it before the story goes around the world.

But some things you can't do anything about, and it's not worth going on the line for. This is a typical example: It is typical that we have stories out of Korea about how people eat dog meat. I hate this story. There is nothing I can do about it. A correspondent in Korea writes a story about dog meat, which is terribly insensitive. There is a huge, long history about why people eat dog meat or snake. In this country, dogs are revered pets, it's just distasteful. The mere idea that another human being could eat a dog, makes Koreans look very barbaric, whereas it's just a matter of culture. I mean, I would never eat dog meat, I would be ill. But I can understand that it's okay. It can be seen as very healthy. But still we have this story that perpetuates this idea. And this story didn't even mention any other Asian groups. It's just Koreans, and how with the Olympics coming up, the government wanted to shut down all these restaurants that served dog meat. So I just edited this story, made sure it was well organized, and passed it along. If I were more militant, or probably dumber, I would make a big issue about it. I can't change it. I'm going to save the fight for something that is really important. But I hate those stories. I would like to own my own newspaper. I would love to be in a position to hire my friends and really make some special product with a special statement. Sometimes people don't have the option or the liberty to express that special voice.

I think I'm very fortunate to be Asian American. Not only do we have a whole realm of Western culture, but we also have this whole world of Asian culture that is part of us. It's a feeling, that genetically, I'm one hundred percent Korean, and my ancestors come from that country. That's why I want my childrent to be able to say that also. But realistically, unless I compromise a lot about what is important to me, and marry someone just to have Korean kids—and I probably won't do that—my kids probably won't be Korean, they'll be half. And I will be really sorry about that because it's important to me to know that I am pure Korean.

Don't Want to Be Black Anymore

Yolanda Adams

Study Questions
1. Why is Adams more comfortable socializing with whites than with blacks?
2. What historical factors do you think are responsible for the black community's preoccupation with skin color?
3. Is the question, "How can you represent and write about the black community if you don't live in a black community?" a legitimate question to ask Adams?

If you're White, you're all right. If you're Brown, stick around. If you're Black, get back. If you're Black, get back. We used to chant this rhyme while jumping rope or playing hopscotch when I was a youngster. Though the games were innocent, the rhymes served as a primer on the importance of skin color in America.

My dark skin and kinky hair are not favored attributes in the Black community. "Your skin is too black," "Your nose is too wide," "Your hair is so nappy"—these were my badges of dishonor.

As a result, I am one of many who find it easier to work and live outside my community. Without regret, I am more comfortable socializing with Whites than with Blacks. To even say this is tantamount to treason. Black leaders consider me—and others like me—a threat to Black consciousness. They say we've turned our backs on our community and ignored sacrifices made for our advancement; we're unjustly labeled as sellouts for expressing this preference.

I grew up in a Black community and felt a degree of comfort being Black. Naive then, less so now, I have learned that color offers no comfort. Rather, it is used to pigeonhole or unfairly define me.

As a community, our Blackness, or lack thereof, is often noted in the descriptions we've coined to specify our color. One is either too black, too light, red, damn-near-white, jet-black, light-brown, paper-bag tan, high yella, graham-cracker brown, redbone, blue-veined, dark-brown, blue-black or "light-skinded."

I wonder if White folks categorize the different hues of whiteness with the same mindless dedication. Are they Liquid Paper white, soft tan, sunburned, milky-white, jaundice-yellow, pasty-beige, George Hamilton brown, frosty, too white, damn-near-black and "white-skinded"? I don't think so.

This fascination with color seems odd, considering that every label can be either an insult or a compliment. Though my skin color veers toward the dark end of the spectrum, I have never been Black enough to satisfy some. My mannerisms have been my Achilles' heel since youth. I was often taunted for being "proper" or "acting White" because of how I dressed and spoke. My mother can be blamed, or applauded, for making me the anomaly I am. She wouldn't allow split infinitives or Ebonies. She also forbade me to think less of myself because of class (we lived in a shotgun house) or color—and where I grew up, color affected class. In fact, she encouraged me to do just the opposite.

When I first moved to Dallas to helm a Black newspaper, a well-known community leader wanted to know where I lived. When I told her, she asked, "How can you represent and write about the Black community if you don't live in a Black community?" I didn't have an answer then, but I do now.

Our communities have become havens for drug abuse and lawlessness; they are economic wastelands. I think of Ethiopians who perished in the middle of the desert, and I wonder why they didn't just move near water. This is how I see our community. So I moved to a place where I can thrive, where I can take a walk without fearing I might get cut down by an errant bullet, where I feel comfortable going to sleep at night.

Living is not about being Black, and being Black is not all there is to living. I have never taken an oath of allegiance to the Black community. And I never will. I want the Technicolor version of the American Dream, not the Black-and-White parody I believe most of our leaders are striving to create. I reject their phony melting-pot fable.

For the record, I am not denying that I'm a Black female who hates and suffers from racism. And I'm not saying I want to be White. I simply want to be neither.

When people see me, they invariably look past the person and see my color. This is as true of Whites as it is of Blacks. At 21, as the only Black editor at an Atlanta publishing company, I was viewed as a smartass by both sides simply because I was young and Black. Nobody acknowledged the work and skill that got me the position.

I can't deny I have dark skin, but I refuse to carry all the baggage that comes with my color. For better or worse, I have decided I don't want to be Black anymore.

On Being Blackanese

MITZI UEHARA-CARTER

◇◆◇◆◇

Study Questions

1. What societal forces "push" Mitzi Uehara-Carter into the category "black"?
2. In spite of these societal pressures, how does she come to maintain a sense of "Japaneseness"?
3. What identity does she prefer?

"Umm...excuse me. Where are you from?"

"I'm from Houston, Texas."

"Oh...but your parents, where are they from?"

(Hmm. Should I continue to play stupid or just tell them.) "My dad is from Houston, and my mom is from Okinawa, Japan."

"And your dad is black then?"

"Yup."

"So do you speak Japanese?"

"Some."

"Wow. Say something."

This is not a rare conversation. I cannot count the number of times I've pulled this script out to rehearse with random people who have accosted me in the past. "That's so exotic, so cool that you're mixed." It's not that these questions or comments bother me or that I am offended by their bluntness. I think it's more of the attitudes of bewilderment and the exoticism of my being and even the slight bossiness to do something "exotic" that annoy me. I think I am also annoyed because I am still exploring what it means to be both Japanese and Black and still have difficulty trying to express what that means to others.

In many ways and for many years I have grappled with the idea of being a product of two cultures brought together by an unwanted colonization of American military bases on my mother's homeland of Okinawa. Author of "In the Realm of a Dying Emperor," Norma Field expressed these sentiments more clearly than I ever could: "Many years into my growing up, I thought I had understood the awkward piquancy of biracial children with the formulation, they are nothing if not the embodiment of sex itself; now, I modify it to, the biracial offspring of war are at once more offensive and intriguing because they bear the imprint of sex as domination." Of course this is not how I feel about myself all the time, but rather it is the invisible bug that itches under my skin every now and then. It itches when I read about Okinawan girls being raped by U.S. Servicemen, when I see mail order bride ads, when I notice the high divorce or separation rate among Asian women and GI's who were married a few years after WW II, when I see the half-way hidden looks of disgust at my mother by other Japanese women when I walk by her side as a daughter. Our bodies, our presence, our reality is a nuisance to some because we defy a definite and demarcated set of boundaries. We confuse those who are trying to organize ethnic groups by highlighting these boundaries because they don't know how to include us or exclude us. We are blackanese, hapas, eurasians, multiracial....

My mother has been the center of jokes and derogatory comments since my older sister was born. She was the one who took my sister by the hand and led her through the streets of Bangkok and Okinawa as eyes stared and people gathered to talk about the sambo baby. She was the one who took all my siblings to the grocery stores, the malls, the park, school, Burger King, hospitals, church. In each of these public arenas we were stared at either in fascination because we were a new "sight" or stared at with a look of disgust or both. Nigga-chink, Black-Jap, Black-Japanese mutt. The neighborhood kids, friends, and adults labeled my siblings and me with these terms, especially after they recognized that my mother was completely intent on making us learn about Okinawan culture. On New Year's Day, we had black-eyed peas and mochi. We cleaned the house to start the year fresh and clean. "Don't laugh with your mouth too wide and show yo teeth too much," my mom would always tell us. "Be like a woman." I had not realized that I covered my mouth each time I laughed until someone pointed it out in my freshman year in college. When we disobeyed my mother's rule or screamed, we were being too "American." If I ever left the house with rollers in my hair, my mom would say I shouldn't do American things. "Agijibiyo... Where you learn this from? You are Okinawan too. Dame desuyo. Don't talk so much like Americans; listen first." There were several other cultural traits and values that I had inevitably inherited (and cherish) being raised by a Japanese mother.

Growing up in an all Black neighborhood and attending predominantly Black and Latino schools until college influenced my identity also. I was definitely not accepted in the Japanese circles as Japanese for several reasons, but that introduces another subject on acceptance into Japanese communities. Now this is not to say that the Black community I associated with embraced me as Blackanese, even though I think it is more accepting of multiracial people than probably any other group (because of the one-drop rule, etc.). There is still an exclusion for those who wish to encompass all parts of their heritage with equal weight, and there is also a subtle push to identify more with one's Black heritage than the other part because "society won't see you as mixed or Japanese but BLACK." I can't count the number of times I have heard this argument. What I do know is that no society can tell me that I am more of one culture than another because of the way someone else defines me. I am Blackanese—a mixture of the two in ways that cannot be divided. My body and mentality is not split down the middle where half is Black and the other half is Japanese. I have taken the aspects of both worlds to create my own worldview and identity. Like Anna Vale said in Itabari Njeri's article "Sushi and Grits," my mother raised me the best way she knew how, "to be a good Japanese daughter."

My father on the other hand never constantly sat down to "teach" us about being Black. We were surrounded by Blackness and lived it. He was always tired when he came home from work. He'd sit back in his sofa and blast his jazz. My mom would be in the kitchen with her little tape player listening to her Japanese and Okinawan tapes my aunt sent every other month from California. My siblings and I would stay at my grandmother's house once in a while (she cooked the best collard greens), and when my mom came to pick us up she'd teach her how to cook a southern meal for my father. Our meals were somewhat of an indicator of how much my mom held onto her traditions. My father would make his requests for chicken, steak, or okra and my mom had learned to cook these things, but we always had Japanese rice on the side with nori and tofu and fishcake with these really noisome beans that are supposed to be good for you, according to my mom. (I swear she knows what every Japanese magazine has to say about food and health.) It was my mother who told us that we would be discriminated against because of our color, and it was my Japanese mother to whom we ran when we were called niggers at the public swimming pool in Houston. To

say to this woman, "Mom, we are just Black" would be a disrespectful slap in the face. The woman who raised us and cried for years from her family's coldness and rejection because of her decision to marry interracially, cried when my father's sister wouldn't let her be a part of the family picture because she was a "Jap." This woman who happens to be my mother will never hear "Mom, I'm just Black" from my mouth because I'm not and no person—society or government—will force me to do that and deny my reality and my being, no matter how offensive I am to their country or how much of a nuisance I am to their cause. I am Blackanese.

Six Case Studies

JOAN FERRANTE AND PRINCE BROWN

Study Question

Identify interactions or scenes in each case study that relate to Goffman's theory of stigma. Be sure to clearly identify those elements of Goffman's theory (i.e. mixed contacts, reactions of normals, reactions of stigmatized, etc) that apply.

We routinely ask students in our classes to write essays describing their personal experiences with race. We have read hundreds of essays over the years and have selected six to reprint in this reader.

Case Study 1

The intramural basketball league at school started two weeks ago and six friends and I entered as a team. Dan, another friend, wanted to play on my team but no one had asked him to join. One day in math class, two guys were talking about the basketball league and mentioned that they were organizing a team but were still short a few players. Dan asked if he could join their team. They said he could play with them and at that point everything seemed fine. But Dan didn't know one thing—he would be the only white guy on the team.

Dan lives around the corner from me and associating with black people isn't anything new to us so when Dan learned that all his teammates were black he didn't seem to have any problem with it. On the first night of intramural basketball, a few of my teammates and I arrived at the gym a little early so we could watch Dan play. When we walked in Dan was sitting on the sidelines so we went over and talked with him. Dan

had not broken a sweat even though it was almost half time. "How may points do you have?" I asked. He said, "Only two." Dan didn't sound too happy, so I just assumed that he was having a bad game. The second half started, and he was still sitting on the sidelines while his teammates subbed in and out for one another every few minutes. I went over to Dan and told him to "get his ass in there" and he said that his teammates wouldn't pass him the ball, so it was pointless to play. Finally Dan got up, walked onto the court, and yelled, "Who needs one?" His teammates looked around at each other. After a second, one guy said "I do." Dan took his place and play resumed. The teams ran up and down the court several times and still Dan didn't touch the ball. Then one teammate, someone with whom Dan had grown up, grabbed a rebound and passed the ball to Dan. Dan took the ball to the basket and scored. At that point all my teammates clapped for him. The fans in the stands who were all black looked at us like we were stupid. I thought to myself that Dan was probably better than half of the other players on his team but no one was giving him a chance to prove it.

Then later in the game something happened that made me kind of mad. I noticed that everyone on Dan's team was making mistakes during the course of the game, and it really wasn't a big deal to the fans. However when Dan lost control of the ball and it went out of bounds to the other team, everyone in the stands started laughing and making fun of him. When one of Dan's black teammates had made a similar mistake the audience did not utter a negative word and even offered encouragement. This really made me mad because it was just unfair. I knew Dan was a good player, he knew he was a good player, and the teammate who had passed him the ball knew he was a good player. The others just didn't give him a chance.

After the game we talked to Dan and he didn't have much to say about what had happened. I told him to shoot the ball every time he got it so he could prove that he was a good player. Once his teammates realized this they would accept him as part of the team. I think it is rather stupid that people judge others by their physical features but I guess this practice has been going on for so long that it will take some time before people change their thinking.

Case Study 2

I grew up in a very small town with a population of about 200 people. My family is Christian, Southern Baptist to be exact, and some rules in my home are quite strict. Some of those "rules" are no drinking, no premarital sex, no cursing, no lying, and no displays of jealousy. There was one other behavior that was strictly forbidden in my house, but it was not something that I was *fully* aware of until after the fact.

It was my first date with Mike and I was so nervous. I had met him at the county fair. We went out on our first date, then a second, and so on, and had a wonderful time. One thing that I noticed about Mike was

that he always wore a ball cap (not that there was anything wrong with that). On about our fourth date he didn't wear a ball cap; he actually fixed his hair. It was long I thought, as I got into the car, but it wasn't straight. It was "black," not just the color black, but the texture of a black man's hair.

I didn't understand; obviously I had led a very sheltered life. How could Mike have a black man's hair? I was confused. I sat in silence most of the night; I honestly did not understand. He must have thought me to be quite dumb. Eventually Mike asked me why I had been so quiet. I told him that I wasn't feeling well and I asked him to take me home. He was a gentleman and he took me home.

When he got home, he called me right away to see if I was feeling better. I told him yes. He asked me what was wrong. I knew that I had to ask about his race because it bothered me to the point I couldn't go out with him again. You see, I had met his mother, and supposedly met his father. So for me, I just didn't understand how someone could have two white parents and not be white? We sat up and talked on the phone for hours. He told me that the man I met was his stepfather. His father was in prison in California. He also told me that his biological father was black.

I sat in silence for awhile. I didn't know what to do or what to say. I had never had any problems with race. Some of the kids at my school were black and my best friend was dating a black guy, so why was this bothering me so? I figured it out. It was because I was falling for him. Most of the time falling in love is not a problem, but this time it was. It was because my parents are against interracial couples. I didn't consider us an interracial couple. He was mixed. Who was he supposed to date, only mixed-race girls?

His ancestry did not embarrass me; it did scare me. I told him when we were out together it would be best for him to wear a ball cap for safety sake. He understood and he liked me well enough that he didn't mind doing this small thing for me. We dated for a couple of months and no one in my family and none of my parents' friends caught on until one night when we were out at a local Festival. Mike had had a couple of drinks and was acting a little obnoxious. We were walking around with some friends and someone that Mike didn't like grabbed a hold of me and jerked me away from him. Mike heard me scream and turned around. He took off his jacket and his ball cap and handed them to someone. Mike was known for trouble, but he was also known to protect whoever he was with and that was all that he was doing. The fighting began and everything was chaotic. I had never been involved in a fight and never had I been the cause of one. It was over in a matter of minutes. However, what happened while the fight was going on was more traumatic than the fight. My aunt happened to be walking by at that time and noticed what I had noticed about Mike's hair a few months before. She did not approach me, nor did she say anything for a while to my parents. When she noticed that I was getting more attached to him, she called me.

The words that she said put me into shock, "I know that Mike is not white, and so do you. You can't let this go on, your parents would be devastated. You have to tell them, or I will." I didn't know what to do. I called Mike as soon as I got off the phone with her. He told me to tell my parents, that they wouldn't do anything. Well, I couldn't bring myself to tell them because I didn't want them to make us break up. Later, some other problems involving Mike arose, and it made my parents very upset. They told me that I was never

allowed to see him again. I didn't know what to do so I paged him. Mike came over to my house riding on a new motorcycle. He took his helmet off. As I was telling him the news my mom walked out on the porch to tell him to leave. That was when she saw his hair. She was pissed. She told him to leave immediately and to never see me again.

As soon as he left, I broke into tears and I tried to go to my room. My mom grabbed my arm and told me that there was a reason that we had to split up, but even if that reason didn't exist, it was better anyway, because her daughter could not date a "black boy."

Case Study 3

During the summer following my freshman year in high school, I worked briefly at a national bank. I had gotten a job there through an acquaintance. My little brother's friend's mother worked in the human resources department at the bank and asked if I wanted to work there because they had summer jobs for high school students. I said something along the lines of, "Yeah whatever, I guess I'll fill out an application."

On my first visit to the bank I was blown away by the size of the building. Coming in from the main entrance, the first room I entered was this gigantic four-story high lobby crowded with little cubicles where customers, I guess, came to speak with the bank tellers about their financial business. Everyone seemed like a genuine business man or woman.

The office where I worked was up on the tenth floor facing the river—I didn't have a view of it though. I sat at a little abandoned cubical with a computer that didn't work, or maybe I needed a code to log-in. Anyway—
Here's the problem:
There REALLY wasn't anything for me to do. My main, and only assigned duty it

seemed, was to answer the phones. Easy enough, right? Wrong!! Apparently there was this high school graduate sitting a couple of cubicles away from me doing the exact same thing. She was white, dressed like a typical business woman, knew everyone in the office well enough, always smiled and it seemed that whenever she answered the phone the caller knew who she was.

I was at a complete loss. It seemed like this girl had it made up in her mind that she was going to be the dominant summer temporary worker. There really wasn't enough phone calls for the both of us, so I gave up. I pretended to read some novel I saw laying around and buried my head in it the whole time I was there, all eight miserable, teary hours.

There were a number of other problems:

- The female secretary who was supposed to be my boss was nothing more than a scared, overworked, African-American peon who seemed to think that I knew nothing about computers and was either incapable, or too unreliable, to edit any documentation. She had no respect for me.
- The other white people constantly laughed and giggled at jokes which apparently I did not either understand or think funny. As a result, I just stared at them thinking that this world of theirs is bizarre—I did not feel comfortable at all.
- When I answered the phones, I did not know whom the callers were asking for, nor did I know how to answer their questions.

As time went on, nothing got better. I felt like a lost, useless, stupid little black boy surrounded by people who were most likely talking about me behind my back. At times I felt like crying and sometimes did. Sitting there for eight hours doing nothing made me feel like s_ _t. I thought to myself, working in a fast-food restaurant seems a lot more exciting than being around these white assholes.

And then it happened one day. I was asked to visit the Human Resources department to talk with the person who hired me. She said that the people in my office thought that I should leave. It shattered my feelings, but at the same time it was really what I wanted. I hated them—I really and truly hated everyone in that department.

I remember the last face I saw as I returned to the office to get my stuff. Someone called and one of the head guys of the office picked up the phone, he said, "Yeah, he's leaving right now." He was looking right at me when he said that. It was like I was a problem that needed to be solved. No one came to me and asked if I was having any trouble adjusting to the place. No one warned me or even hinted that they wanted me to leave. It just happened one day.

I stayed there for two of the longest weeks of my life.

Looking back now, comparing how I felt then to how I feel about successful white people today, my feelings haven't changed really. The office life seems full of fake laughter, stupid jokes, gossiping, fake personalities, bitches and sons-of-bitches. That type of setting was horrible and torturing for me back then. I was totally unprepared for that kind of experience. I had never interacted with so many white adults before. I was the only black kid there. I was only 16. There were times when I thought that I would rather work in a low-paying job for the rest of my life than to be around people like them.

If I knew then that I would be living today with three white roommates in college; working with white people on a college magazine; nominated by white people to work for the dean of the university; and having a white teacher (who I thought was a racist) anticipate the release of my publications, I would probably think that the James of the future (I, today) was a completely different person. Hhmm...

I guess giving in to the white people's way of doing things is the only way to escape poverty and ridicule. I don't know. Sometimes I get the feeling that it's all my fault for not being social enough; it's my fault for not being able to disguise my feelings. I have never felt oppressed or suppressed by white people. I just feel either angry or apathetic whenever I'm around them for the most part. There's too many of them.

Case Study 4

Thinking back, I know that I went out of my way to be overly friendly to two of my new roommates—Tanisha and Naomi. I believe I actually tried harder to be nice because they were black and I did not want to be considered racist. My overly nice behavior may have been enough to put them on edge (I wish I knew). I do know one thing, I do not think that my third roommate Tracy (who was white) and I had a chance of getting along with these girls.

For one thing, they had moved in a few days earlier than we did so they had already set up their stuff throughout the apartment. We did not communicate well from the very beginning. They made it clear through their monosyllabic responses to our questions, and feeble attempts at conversation, that they were not happy we were their roommates. I believe that they were disappointed that Tracy and I were white. It became two against two. Tracy and I moved into our

bedroom, and we never felt comfortable using the rest of the apartment.

Tanisha and Naomi had an answering machine which they kept locked in their bedroom. Therefore, Tracy and I never received messages. Also, they always had friends over, and their friends would spend the night in the living room. Sometimes their friends would be camped out at the apartment even when they were gone. I never felt comfortable walking into the apartment because there were often strange men sitting on the couch. They would be very inconsiderate and would leave their music on extremely loud late into the night. Maybe they were just lousy roommates who just happened to be black. That is a definite possibility, yet, it does not explain the way they treated Tracy and I. When talking to their friends, they referred to us as "the white girls" and would loudly make fun of us even when we were within earshot. We were a joke to them.

I have never in my life been treated so poorly as when I lived with these roommates. I believe that Tanisha and Naomi had classified us before allowing any real social interaction to occur. They judged us on our appearance alone, never taking an opportunity to get to know us for who we really were. I suppose the question I now ask myself is whether I did the same.

I have always taken an interest in people of different backgrounds. That is one of my reasons I declared a minor in Anthropology. Cultures and lifestyles that differ from my own intrigue me. In my household and among my friends I am known as a debater. I love to argue for minority rights, and often preach about the importance of teaching cultural diversity and foreign languages. I have always considered myself very open-minded and have casually dated international students. I wonder if I have been overzealous in my attempt to avoid being ethnocentric. I wonder if instead of appearing friendly, I appear patronizing as just one more white person pretending to care.

Perhaps Tanisha and Naomi treated us as they thought we would treat them. I still do not believe they were good roommates, and there was definitely a level of racism directed at us from them. I do not really have an answer to the questions that I have raised. All I can do is try to be more aware of how I communicate with others, and try to avoid categorizing them. I did not enjoy being placed in a category without my own say. It would not be fair for me to then characterize others based on their appearances.

Case Study 5

I grew up with a Catholic background, having gone to a Catholic school for twelve years. My mom worked in downtown Cincinnati and my father worked close to our home in northern Kentucky. My sister and I were hardly ever allowed to go downtown to visit my mother at work because around her workplace many people lived in poverty and the neighborhood was considered bad. But my mother had many close friends who were black, so we became accustomed to having multiracial friends growing up. In my house it was never a black and white thing, it was a people thing. My parents taught us no matter what shape, form, or color people come in, we should not treat them any differently, just treat them the way that we would want to be treated. So in my situation it never occurred to me that skin color would make me feel so uncomfortable and unsafe.

It was a Friday night, a couple weeks before Halloween, when my friends and I de-

cided to go to a haunted house. We all met at someone's house and piled into a van. As we reached our destination, we headed toward the line of anxious people. When we approached the booth to purchase tickets, I stood at the front of the group and began counting. As I reached the ninth person named Sean, it crossed my mind that there were eight white people and one black person in our group. I have known this person for a while, but had never really thought of him as "black" because he does not "act" black (his mom is white and his dad is black). His race really did not have that much effect on me until we went to a bar later that night.

After the haunted house, we decided to go to a bar owned by Sean's grandpa. As we pulled into the parking lot and got out of the van, I looked around and felt unsafe. We were downtown about 12:30 A.M. on a Friday night in a bad part of town. We all looked around and noticed that we were the only white people in sight. That is when it hit me, I was in a situation that was very unfamiliar. Heading towards the entrance to the bar, I thought of this race class and the word "mixed contacts" came to mind. We all followed our friend very closely into the bar and headed straight for the corner of the bar. As I looked around I realized that everyone was staring at us.

Everyone's eyes were fixed on us, and we heard some remarks that made us feel uncomfortable. The bartender started to talk to our friend and asked what we wanted to drink. As we waited for our drinks our friend introduced us to some people. I can remember overhearing one lady commenting that "we had nerve." That is when we decided to leave; we did not want any trouble. As we started to leave a woman began laughing. We asked what was so funny and she replied, "it's good to see some new faces in here!" So we all settled back in our seats as she began making conversation with all of us. While we were talking to her, others came over, some joined in, and some asked us to dance. Sitting back in my chair, I thought of a time in class when you said that it was hard for a black person to come into class late; he or she sticks out and many classmates attribute lateness to the person's race. That is when I thought about my friend and wondered how often he felt the same as we did that night. Did he feel awkward going to a party being the only "black," or actually "mixed," person there.

As I sat there I looked around and noticed that everyone was dancing or socializing and no one saw us as the only white people in the bar, but as people. Of course, there were a few that could not get over the fact that we were in a "black" bar but no one said a word to us after that.

I look back on that situation and see for the first time in my life that I was not in the majority, that I was the "stigmatized" person. When all of the people in the bar looked at me and I looked at them, all we could see was the color of our skin. At first we could not get past skin color but once we did, we began to see each other for who we are on the inside, people.

Case Study 6

My family has never considered race to be much of an issue. We live in a predominantly white neighborhood and attended predominantly white schools. I can remember having experiences at a young age with race, and a few of those experiences stick out in my mind. For most of my youth my dad was a social worker at the Community Center in Newport, Kentucky. His clients were mostly lower class "black" families. As daddy's little girl I went to many center-sponsored activities. I vividly remember one event. I was probably a fifth-grader or younger at the time. It was February and Black History Month. My dad was with some of his co-workers setting things up, and I sat by myself in the audience watching the program. I do not remember much of the show except for the dancers and the music. A group of "African" dancers came out dressed in authentic garments and danced like I had never seen. The men playing the music were beating on drums and playing strange-looking instruments. I can remember feeling each beat of the drum in the pit of my stomach. This was a whole new experience for me. I remember when the lights came on after the show. I looked around at the rest of the audience. I realized that I was one of very, very few white people there, most of whom were workers, like my dad. I didn't realize it then but this was probably the first of a very few times in my life that I was the minority. I remember being confused. Why were there no other white people there? Couldn't white people celebrate Black History Month too?

I remember another time I went to a Center activity with my Dad. It was Martin Luther King Jr. Day, and they were having a candlelight vigil and march in his honor. I remember again being one of very few white people. I was still pretty young, but seeing the looks on these peoples' faces and the feelings they were showing, I realized the strength of Martin Luther King. Some of the people were crying, some were singing and some like me were just thinking and walking. I was thinking that I would never ever have to go through what these people went through. I began to think how much this man accomplished. I remember I wanted to cry. I also remember that I could not cry. I couldn't cry because I felt that I was not allowed because I was white. I felt that since I was not black, I could not fully participate in this day. I felt that Dr. King would never mean to me what he means to "black" people. This caused even further confusion in my experiences with race.

My family has a big interest in all types of cars. My dad collects them and we all know about them. We have been to car shows and seen all kinds of cars. I remember one time I was driving with my dad through downtown Cincinnati. We saw a really nice car, I think it was a Jaguar. We pulled up next to it. He was looking at my dad's car and I was looking at his. He was a "black" man. After we drove away I said to my dad: "I bet he plays for the Bengals." My dad responded: "Why would you think that, be-cause he is black and has a nice car?" I shrugged my shoulders and realized the foolishness of my statement. I had con-cluded that because this man was "black" and driving a nice car that he was a profes-sional athlete. It never even crossed my mind that this man might have been a suc-cessful, smart businessman who had worked hard for his luxuries.

As you can see, I am still very confused by many aspects of race. I was confused when I was younger, and I doubt race will ever become crystal clear to anyone. It is such a complicated issue. However, through my own social interactions, I have learned and gained more information, thoughts, and views on race. These aspects will be ever-changing because race is ever-changing.

What Will My Mother Say

Dympna Ugwu-Oju

Study Questions

1. Describe how American ideas of Nigeria affected the questions they asked Ugwu-Oju.
2. Describe Ugwu-Oju's knowledge of black history and why her knowledge was so limited.
3. Why did she have difficulty at first seeing racism in the United States?
4. What was the turning point for Ugwu-Oju with regard to understanding her racial classification in the U.S.?

John and Delia provided me the basic necessities for survival in America. But as my first weeks extended into months, they realized that New York City was *too* much America for me to survive on my own and that a less intimidating setting would provide an easier transition to the life I was determined to live. I applied to colleges in Westchester County in New York State, all of them women's colleges. America or not, I sought an environment that was at least familiar, a life I understood—I settled for an imitation convent.

Briarcliff promised to meet all my needs. It was extremely small (about four hundred students), and students received so much attention it would almost be like living with Mama. Every dorm had a "mother"—an elderly spinster who used her unspent maternal love on the students. These dorm mothers provided the girls everything, from extra blankets when they were cold to a hug or a sympathetic ear.

True enough, when I got to Briarcliff in the fall of 1975, my whole experience of America changed. I lived in the dorm with girls my age, who, though they had differ-

ent orientations and concerns, drew me out of my lonely funk. Before I knew it, I was so immersed in college life—classes, perfecting my English, and Friday night mixers with cadets from West Point, undergraduates from Yale, and other neighboring coeds—that I hardly remembered to miss home. My friendship with my suite-mates was as immediate as it was at the convent school at Nsukka. The relationships that I formed at Briarcliff went beyond the bounds of college; my friends were quite generous and invited me to their homes during the holidays, and we've stayed close to this day.

On the down side, my classmates at Briarcliff exhibited an unusual level of ignorance where Africa was concerned, and many of their questions were not only insensitive but downright humiliating.

"Don't you people go around naked in Africa? You must be really uncomfortable in your clothes."

"How does it feel to be in real clothes?"

"How did you all manage to sleep on tree tops without falling?"

Even some of the professors were no better. One actually commented after he ascertained I was from Nigeria, "Aren't you lucky to be here, with that ugly communist takeover of your emperor's power!"

"Emperor?" I wondered. What in the world is he referring to?

Others merely told me, "It's so sad to see all those starving kids in your country on television." What starving kids? Well, maybe during the Nigerian-Biafran war, which had ended several years before.

I quickly discovered that even the most intelligent Americans did not know the first thing about Africa. Their most common mistake was viewing Africa as a country or even a city instead of a continent, and erroneously believing that everyone knew everyone else there. With time, I was able to laugh at their gross inaccuracies and even give them a dose of their own medicine. Idi-Amin's reign of terror, for example, took place in Uganda, a country in East Africa more than a thousand miles away from Nigeria. But my American inquisitors thought it was the next town over.

"What a terror, that bully Idi-Amin, what he's doing to your people," I was told more times than I can recall. I accepted the concept of "my people," for I accepted all Africans as my brothers and sisters. But if only they had stopped there.

"Do you know him? I hope you're not related to him," others sympathized.

After explaining several times the geographical relation between Uganda and Nigeria, I decided to join them at their own game. With the help of one of my professors, I came up with responses to the most common questions about Africa. To Idi-Amin, I responded, "Yes, he's my uncle, from the bad side of the family, of course. Too bad, your own uncle, Anastasia Somoza, isn't doing much better!"

"What are you talking about?" My poor American acquaintances became so confused.

To questions about sleeping on tree tops, I answered, "But of course, if that's what you're raised with, you get used to it."

"But what about the children; how do they get up there?" my inquisitors would seek further clarification.

"Oh, they used elevators," I responded with a straight face.

"Ah, of course," they responded, probably thinking that anything was possible in Africa.

Unfortunately, I can't say that the situation has gotten any better, and although more than twenty years have passed since my first arrival to the United States, I find the questions no more enlightened than before.

My education was by no means limited to what I learned in undergraduate or graduate school. Delia continued to undo what Mama had spent a lifetime putting into place.

My sister-in-law became for me the symbol of American womanhood: fearless, determined, and aggressive. She taught me independence in my thinking and actions: that I, and I alone, should dictate what I wanted to do with my life. Delia invalidated almost everything Mama taught me about womanhood; to her, it was about speaking up for oneself, looking everyone straight in the eye, and following one's heart. I'm quite sure that without Delia's guidance, my American experience would not have been as rich and encompassing as it was. She became my primary educator, pushing me way beyond the bounds of academia.

Delia introduced me to writings of radical African Americans, especially the women's perspective, areas that my extensive education in predominantly white colleges had not touched. I studied Maya Angelou, Angela Davis, and others; Delia selected the books I read with as much care as she would her young daughters.' We moved from slavery to the Civil War to the Reconstruction, from the civil rights movement to the women's movement. From there, I was guided to biographies of most American presidents as well as of other influential leaders, both national and international. I felt so deficient in knowledge, so unprepared for the world I was thrown into, that I read as fast as Delia could push the books my way. I had to write a summary of each book I read and present it to Delia before I could go on to another one.

Delia also opened my eyes to a part of life I never knew existed. She introduced me to Black America. On the day of my placement test as an incoming freshman at Malcolm-King College extension, as Delia drove me to the campus at 125th Street, we passed hordes of black people—men, women and children of all sizes and shades. In spite of my extensive study of America, I was surprised by the large number of blacks we saw.

"There are many, many Africans here in New York," I observed in a matter-of-fact way.

"They're not Africans, they're Americans," Delia replied, sounding indignant.

"But they look like Africans; where did they all come from?"

Delia looked at me as if I were an alien creature. "How can you not be aware of America's blacks?" she uttered in what I took to be disgust for my ignorance. How could any African not be aware of the existence of American blacks? The truth is that, my education about America notwithstanding, I believed (and I'm sure no one saw fit to contradict my erroneous assumptions) that all blacks, all descendants of American eighteenth-century slaves, were resettled in Liberia, Newfoundland, and the Caribbean countries. I was not aware that there were

any blacks left in America; there was nothing in the textbooks—no pictures, no clues—that could have led me to that understanding.

Everything I thought I knew of America contradicted what I was seeing on the streets of New York. The history and geography texts had treated slavery as a historical issue; blacks were not mentioned or pictured in the books I had read in Nigeria. In addition, we were caught in our own civil war during America's civil rights movement, and much to my shame, I had never heard the name of Martin Luther King, Jr., or of other leaders of the black community until I came to America. I was not aware of the millions of Americans who have a common ancestry with me; I was completely oblivious to terms like racism. My ignorance stared me in the face, and there in the car with my sister-in-law, I had nowhere to hide.

Without Delia, the black experience would have remained remote and abstract. She brought it home for me. Before she embarked on her law career, she'd been a teacher of African-American history, a subject she knew inside and out. She herself had marched in Washington, D.C., on the day of Martin Luther King's "I Have a Dream" speech, and she already possessed most of the resources I needed to understand what it means to be black in America.

It took a while before it would all come together for me, and it was several years before I could begin to identify myself as a black person. It's strange but true. I must have felt some affinity with the blacks I saw on my first outing and subsequently, but there was nothing about their speech, their walk, the whining about "the system," the drunks who swaggered even in the mornings as I walked to school, with which I could identify. I saw American blacks from a distance, and with or without my sister-in-law's lessons, I was at a loss to find what I could really embrace. I thought racism was a figment of their collective imagination, and I never hesitated to point out to the few black girls at Briarcliff with me that "racism only exists in people's minds." I just didn't believe it.

I was probably one of ten blacks attending Briarcliff. I felt that I was treated as well as anyone else. I mixed well with the other students. In fact, I chose to live with white students and we became fast friends. I saw no difference in our lives. I got as many A's as my white friends. I simply did not see how my black skin had anything to do with my life.

On the other hand, I noticed that the other black students flocked together, as if separating from each other, even for one minute, would diminish their identity. They breathed, talked, walked their blackness and would not allow anyone who was different to come close to them. They dismissed me as not being one of them. "She acts white," they explained to those who asked why I was excluded from their group. If any of them received an undesirable grade, it was easily explained. "The professor hates blacks."

I argued with Yolanda, the leader of the black group, about why she missed more than half of the class meetings of an international relations course she took with me. "What difference would it make? The professor would still find a way to fail me," she said resignedly.

"How come he doesn't fail me?" I challenged her.

"Because you're African; you talk different. You don't rub them the wrong way."

"But I'm just as black," I threw back at her.

"You just don't understand," she said and walked away. As hard as I tried, I simply couldn't understand that mind-set. How could they be so defeatist? How could they

give up before trying? There was no room for self-pity where I was raised. No circumstance was deemed too hard to overcome, even when all doors were slamming in one's face. Even during the war, when our huts were razed to the ground and we had no more than the rags on our backs, we continued our struggle to survive; we had no time to point fingers at our persecutors. Hadn't I personally gone through worse adversities than any of them could possibly imagine? Hadn't I passed through a war and survived hunger, danger, and deprivation? Hadn't my own mother gone through worse, traded like an animal and passed from hand to hand until no one wanted her? Hadn't she also picked up the pieces when her husband died and left her with seven children? What could they have suffered that could be worse than I had? But as Yolanda told me, I simply didn't understand, and she was right. I couldn't then. It took many more years of living in America before I could see the debilitating effects of racism.

I discovered my blackness at Syracuse, well into my fifth year in America. Suddenly, in something of a blinding revelation, I saw myself as a black person for the very first time. Of course, I'd known I wasn't white, but I did not see myself as black either. It was as though I believed I belonged in a no-color zone. I don't know how that could have happened, except to attribute it to growing up in Nigeria, where black people were in the majority. I probably could not make the transition to being a member of a minority.

At Syracuse, there were many more black students and professors than at Briarcliff, but the only other black woman in the journalism masters program was forced to drop out because she could not maintain the required B average. So I alone was left to answer sometimes irritating or embarrassing questions about blacks. My colleagues, at times, boxed me into a stereotype that even after five years in the country was hard for me to comprehend.

The turning point took place at a lunch meeting. I arranged to do a special feature article on students from countries with political instabilities. My partner in the assignment (Janelle, a white woman), two black Ethiopian students we were interviewing, and I were seated around a table at the College Center cafeteria, when another student in our program stopped by. "Janelle, you're outnumbered. There's only one of you to three blacks," he chuckled, before moving on.

My first reaction was that he had it wrong. "What in the world does he mean?" There were *two* black girls at the table, plus Janelle and me. "Who's the third black girl?"

Then it hit me. It felt like someone dropped a ton of bricks on my chest and knocked the wind out of me. For a few seconds, I was out of breath, was suffocating to death. "It's *me* he's talking about. I am the third black girl. I'm black, I'm black," I said over and over to myself, repeating what should have been obvious to me years ago. I don't remember much else of that meeting other than my sudden awareness of the color of my skin. And from that moment on, I began to see myself in a different light: as a black person in America. For the first time, I was aware of what others saw when they looked at me.

Armed with my new awareness, I no longer dismissed blacks' complaints of racism as groundless whining. I reinvestigated the plight of blacks, using Syracuse as my new laboratory. I truly began to understand how crippled they'd become as a result of institutionalized and internalized racism. I reviewed everything I came across for its black-white implications. I stared in every face I saw, looking for signs that they looked at me differently. I scrutinized every gesture, action, conversation, every nuance of friends, professors, and even strangers on the streets, for racial undertones. If I wrote a check at a store and was asked for an ID, even though my rational self understood the need for the ID, my first reaction was, "Did he do this because I'm black? Would he ask a white person for an ID?"

My black awareness was also the driving force behind my decision after I completed my master's program not to aggressively pursue a job with mainstream media organizations, but instead to accept a position as the editor of the *Syracuse Gazette,* the only weekly black newspaper in the central New York area. The job paid poorly but allowed me the independence to make the newspaper whatever I desired. It was also an excellent opportunity to explore the dimensions of being black in America. Each week, I built the newspaper around a major issue that I felt concerned blacks: issues of teenage parenting, feminism, poverty, more. I spent hour after hour interviewing disenfranchised blacks: black matrons in rundown public tenements, young black men in county holding cells awaiting arraignment, black teenage mothers battling welfare and child protective agency officers, black women in no-win relationships with their men. I was completely immersed, up to my elbows in it. By the time I left the paper, I thought I knew everything I needed to know.

Strangely, my new black solidarity did not cross over to my social life. I never once felt that I could relate to American blacks as anything other than colleagues or friends. I never dated a black American man, although I contemplated doing so from time to time. They were as strange to me as were Hausas and Yorubas. I felt their world too far removed from mine. They simply would not know my worth and would treat me as they treated their own women. When I considered serious relationships, especially marriage, it was always with an Ibo man. That never changed.

Apologizing for Being a Black Male

PAUL ANDREW DAWKINS

◇•◆•◇

Study Questions
1. Why was Paul Dawkins reluctant to get out of his car and use a pay phone next to one being used by a white woman?
2. After this incident how did Paul resolve to act in the future? Do you agree with his decision?

At times I've actually gone so far as to adopt what I consider a less threatening posture whenever I encounter a White woman, especially an older one, in places where we are alone together. While searching for a public pay phone recently in Durham, North Carolina, I found myself re-experiencing a situation I had encountered several times before in the 15 years I have lived in this my adopted country.

I had spied an available and, I hoped, functioning pay phone in a convenience store's parking lot and decided to pull in. There were two phones side by side. One was being used by a well-dressed, slightly older White woman.

As I pulled in and parked my car, I discovered, much to my dismay and chagrin, that I was a bit reluctant to get out of my car and use the phone while this woman was still there. In questioning my hesitation, I came to the puzzling conclusion that I did not want to make her "uncomfortable."

I was surprised, and yet not surprised, by my reaction. Surprised because I hadn't quite realized to what extent I had allowed others' perceptions of who I was to seep so pronouncedly into my psyche.

Thinking back, while I remained seated in my car, I realized that as an almost-40-year-old Jamaican-born man (who was aware of race relations in the United States before arriving here), I've found myself not wanting to make Whites, particularly White women, uncomfortable.

I've even found myself apologizing, at least internally, for being a Black male. At times I've gone so far as to adopt what I consider a less threatening posture whenever I encounter a White woman, especially an older one, in places where we are alone together. Sometimes I catch myself slowing down as I walk to my car in a parking lot if there's a White woman heading to a nearby car—I don't do this with White males or with men or women of other races, for that matter. I either reach loudly and obviously for my keys, or hold back until she is safely in her car, for fear that she thinks I'm a potential rapist, purse snatcher, or carjacker. I hold back because I don't want to relive the dignity-bruising experience of seeing her hasten her steps to her car, and/or hear the power locks being quickly, and loudly, activated, which happened once several years ago while I was attending graduate school in Chapel Hill, North Carolina.

Now as I walked up to the pay phone, I realized that this hesitation had, in fact, been coloring my actions over the years almost imperceptibly. I was also angry at myself. Had I been so influenced by the newspaper accounts, studies, and opinion polls I had read, which indicated that Whites, particularly White women, were fearful of Blacks, particularly Black males, that I felt the need to make constant apologies on behalf of all men of my race? It was an angry burden to carry, and it was getting way too heavy.

I neared the available phone. The woman had her back to me, and although she might have sensed that someone was approaching to use the other telephone, she did not turn around just then.

As I picked up the receiver to dial, she turned, as anyone probably would have, to see her new "neighbor." When she saw me, she turned back around. Almost subconsciously, I continued to observe her as she proceeded to pull the handbag that had been hanging by her side in front of her.

I decided that, this time, I would not continue to go out of my way to be accommodating. Previously I would have done something like taking my large business planner with me to the phone to make her aware that I was not a thug. After all, thugs don't usually carry business planners, I reasoned. Previously I would have spoken a little louder than necessary on the phone so she could hear not only my accent and diction but also the content of my conversation. Then she would realize I had a legitimate reason for being there—that I was a dignified, purposeful fellow human being!

This time, however, I decided I had had enough. I had to let it go. It had become too draining, too taxing, to apologize for being what I could not change, and for trying to apologize for every man with my pigmentation who might have done harm to someone like her at some time in the past.

I decided that from that point on I would not edit my actions. I forgot about my neighbor and completed my call in the same way I would have if a White male, Black female, or Hispanic male had been using a nearby phone. I determined that life was too short and that my self-respect was too valuable.

Choosing Up Sides

JUDY SCALES-TRENT

◇◆◆◇

Study Question
What does Judy Scales-Trent mean when she says, "We renounce the reality of our real families, and we embrace the unreal reality as a social construct"?

"**W**hatever he does, he had better not bring home a white girlfriend!" she exclaimed. We laughed. There were three of us, black women friends who had gotten together after a long absence, talking about our lives, our work, our men, and, of course, our children. Her son was not yet a teenager and would not be bringing anyone home for quite a while, but she was already clear about his choices.

I laughed too, but I sensed a vague discomfort at her words. It took me awhile to understand that feeling. But I finally understood that I was uneasy because she had rejected part of me, the white part, with her statement. And I was uncomfortable—fearful that my disguise might not hold, fearful that she might suddenly "see" that I was a white black woman. Michelle Cliff says it well: "She who was part-them felt on trembling ground." I also finally recognized that my laughter was dishonest: why laugh at my own rejection? But I did laugh, I laughed because, at that moment, my hunger to belong to that group of friends was stronger than my ability to be true to myself.

I thought about this for days. And what kept returning to my mind during that period were thoughts of Grandpa Tate, my father's maternal grandfather and the only white blood relative I ever heard of. I know

little enough about him. I know that he was born sometime in the 1860s, and that he was a barber. I know that he married my great-grandmother Mary in 1886. I think he loved and respected her: I have a silver-plated dish inscribed "1886–1911" that he gave her on the occasion of their twenty-fifth anniversary. I know he made enough money investing in real estate to raise ten children in comfort and send them off to college. I have a picture of Grandpa Tate with his wife and children, taken around 1905. They all look healthy and well dressed and well groomed. It is clear that Grandpa Tate took good care of them. I know he was white, of Scottish origins. I also know that his wife, and therefore all of his children, were black. I think of the contribution Grandpa Tate made to my family, to me, and I am not willing to reject him. I respect and honor his memory and claim him as a cherished relative.

Racism is so deeply embedded in our consciousness that we don't often realize that society asks us, on a regular basis, to reject part of our family when we are required to take sides in this tragic war game of race and color.

"Which side are you on, black or white?
There is a war going on.

Allegiance must be clear.
Choose!"

But choosing up sides means buying into the craziness of American-style racism. For there are many black Americans with white ancestors, and there are plenty of white Americans with black family members.

This is the way the American system works: if you have one parent or ancestor with African origins, you are black. You are not a member of the white family that might also claim you. That family must renounce you, and you must renounce it. You are in the black family, as will be all of your children and your grandchildren and your great-grandchildren. It is by thus redefining "family" to exclude their black family members that white Americans keep themselves and their "family" white. The notion of "family" in white America has very controlled borders: "family" stops where "black" begins.

The result is, then, that white people are all "white," and that black people are a wide range of colors—white, rosy, olive, tan, brown, reddish, black. We are forced to choose up sides, but the American rules dictate that choice. Real facts, like who your parents and grandparents were, don't matter: only social facts count.

Several years ago, a strange and sad incident took place at the law school. It involved a moot-court program sponsored by a national association of black law students. A young woman at the school who wanted to participate decided to join the local chapter of the association. But it was not as easy to join as she had expected, for although her father was black and she had African features, her mother was Puerto Rican. There was furious debate by the students in that chapter as to whether she could—or should—participate in a program for black students. Finally, they arrived at a solution.

If she would renounce her Puerto Rican mother, she could join the association.

I hope this sounds as sick to you as it does to me. Renounce her mother? Were they all mad? And yet is this not what we all require of ourselves, of our children? We do it all the time. We renounce the reality of our real families, and we embrace the unreal reality of a social construct.

Think about it for a minute: whom have you renounced today? and why?

Are we all mad?

There are two little girls whom I love. They are two years old. The world is theirs to explore, and they go at it full tilt. Anyone old enough to read these words would be hard-pressed to keep up with either of them for an afternoon. These little girls are sisters in the deepest sense of the word, for they are twins and have been together from their earliest watery memories. They speak their own language and giggle at their own secrets. But they are twins who do not look alike. One is brown, like her father; the other is fair, like her mother.

I once talked about the problems color would present them with their father, a nephew. And I wondered, would they too be forced to choose up sides? How would they choose? Whom would they renounce? How could they? And why should they be forced into such a cruel dilemma? Their father's family is from Africa and Scotland and other lands; their mother's family is from Scotland and other European lands. It is just as misleading to say that they are African American as it is to say that they are Scottish American, for their heritage is complicated and rich. And I wonder sadly if there is any chance that these little girls will ever be able to just be Americans.

Think about it, for it does not involve my family alone. It involves yours too. And we really should do better by our children.

Let me be clear. I am not claiming that I always see these complications. I often think and speak as if the categories "black" and "white" are real. I am just as hungry for a place to belong as anyone else. I am just as willing as others to choose up sides. But living on the margin forces me to live with, and therefore to see, the complications. And it is very complicated indeed. For the truth is that all Americans with some African ancestry are indeed "black," because that is how we are defined, and that is how white people treat us, and that is how we are raised. But the truth also is that "black" people are not *only* "black," since we also have ancestors who came from Europe and Asia and South America and the South Pacific; we have ancestors who were Cherokee, Choctaw, Lumbee.

I am torn by my understanding of both truths, which exist side by side at the same time, for it means that we both can and cannot choose up sides. It is holding both these truths in my hand at the same time that is so difficult—and so important—to do.

Identity Matters:
The Immigrant Children

MARILYN HALTER

◇❖◇

Study Questions
1. How do the cases of Jack Custodio and Lucille Ramos support the argument that race is not a biological fact but a social construction?
2. What strategies did Jack Custodio employ to influence how others identified him? How does Custodio identify himself today?
3. Why did he "give-in" to the U.S. conception of race?
4. List the various racial identities Lucille Ramos and her family members took on. Which identity is the most accurate? Explain.

Vivid in the recollections of many of the men interviewed for this study was the jolt to their self-concept that was experienced during military service in World War II. For most Cape Verdean American male immigrants, joining the United States armed forces meant a first step out of the protective shelter of their enclave. This critical juncture in their lives brought them face to face with the existence of segregated troops and a wider society that did not know or care about the ethnic identity of a Cape Verdean. Most were sent to black regiments, where they were forced to deal directly with the issue of race, both in terms of the racist treatment they received in the military and in having to confront the question of their own racial identification. As one Cape Verdean veteran said: "I grew up thinking of myself as brown-skinned Portuguese, not black at all. I remember telling this sergeant, a black guy, that I was Cape Verdean. He said, 'You ain't Portuguese nothing. You're a nigger.' It sounds incredibly naive, but I'd never thought of myself as black or white. I

was both, and neither. I was Cape Verdean. America wants you to choose sides."[1]

Some were assigned to white units where they were not accepted either. Those Cape Verdean recruits who were sent with white regiments into the southern states found it especially painful to try to come to terms with the ambiguity of their own ethnic and racial background and the rigid racial barriers of their surroundings. The immigrants and their children had largely been raised to think of themselves as Portuguese, thus white, but once outside the ethnic community, they faced an indifferent, often hostile world that labeled them black. Interaction beyond the New England region became more problematic. Belmira Nunes Lopes sometimes handled it in this way:

> My trips south have been very interesting, but I must admit that every time I went south I always acted as if I wasn't too well acquainted with the English language because I didn't want to be discriminated against on the buses and the trains. I

always put on a fake accent and I always managed to get away with it. I didn't want anybody to think I was an American black because I am darker than most so-called white persons. My mother had never been mistaken for a black woman. She had been taken sometimes for an Indian, but she could never speak English well. I decided that I was going to act as if I couldn't speak English well.[2]

The social and political events of the postwar era also penetrated the cocoon of the Cape Verdean enclave. Beginning with the civil rights movement, the 1960s were watershed years for Cape Verdean Americans, as the rise of black nationalism and its attendant emphasis on pride in one's African heritage had a transformative effect on many. The domestic social changes coincided with the struggles for liberation from Portuguese colonialism on the continent of Africa as well. At the time, the Cape Verde islands in collaboration with Guinea-Bissau were engaged in a protracted armed conflict to procure their independence. They did find some support for their cause among Cape Verdean, Americans, but there was also much resistance to the idea of Cape Verde breaking its long-standing ties with Portugal and switching to an African-identified political and cultural ideology. The process of rethinking racial identifications touched most Cape Verdean families in this period, often creating intergenerational rifts between the parents and grandparents who were staunchly Portuguese and their children who were beginning to ally themselves with the African American struggle not only in political thought but also in cultural expression. Some, who could, would let their hair grow out into Afros; others may have dressed in colorful dashikis, much to the dismay of their Portuguese-identified parents. Writing about the 1960s, Belmira

Lopes Nunes explained:

At that time, our idea of Portuguese culture was Cape Verdean culture, and that was the thing that we really wanted to stress. To us, to be Portuguese was synonymous with being Cape Verdean....The Cape Verdeans have been saying they were Portuguese all along. I was brought up to believe that I was Portuguese. My parents said they were Portuguese. Whenever anybody asked us what we were because we spoke a foreign language or because we looked different from any other group, we always said that we were Portuguese. All of a sudden to be told that you are an African, I think, is a shock to most people, certainly to my generation and to many of those of this generation also, the children of Cape Verdean parents who have made their children feel that they had some reason to be proud of the Cape Verdean heritage.[3]

Perhaps the most graphic example I can give to illustrate Cape Verdean ambivalence concerning African origins is the anecdote reported to me about a woman, now middle-aged, whose Cape Verdean father, from the time she was a baby, would continually stroke her nose from the inner edges outward in a pointing motion in order to try to control its shape and development. The girl's mother was African American, and the father feared his daughter would grow up to have a nose of broad and flat contours.

Following are excerpts from the oral histories of two Cape Verdean Americans that cogently illustrate the multifarious and shifting nature of racial meanings. Both Joaquim A. "Jack" Custodio and Lucille Ramos were born in the United States, children of Cape Verdean immigrants and lifelong residents in the New Bedford area. Each has a biography that has been punctuated by issues resulting from the ambiguity inherent in belonging to a nonwhite immigrant group.

Both demonstrate how they and their families have been subjected to the arbitrary design of racial classification in the United States. In both accounts, the decade of the 1960s looms large. While each individual has a unique story to tell, I have selected these two life histories particularly for inclusion here because their experiences within the arena of racial-ethnic definitions have a universality among the Cape Verdean American population as I have understood it.

When I asked Jack Custodio in July of 1988, "What would you call yourself today in terms of identity?" he replied with his characteristic mixture of dead seriousness and ironic humor, "I'm black—I'm not beautiful, but I'm black. Positively black." How he arrived at this self-designation follows:

The salient facts of my life are I was born September 6, 1914, in a cold water flat, at home—as usual, all the births were in New Bedford. I was born to a Cape Verdean mother and a Cape Verdean father, but it has to be noted that my mother was so fair that she could go any place, whereas my father would have to get in the back of the bus. He's what we call in my own lingo, *besh roulade cavasa sec,* which means "thick lips and nappy hair," and that is still used by Cape Verdeans.

The South End was the Cape Verdean ghetto, but it has to be noted that in New Bedford you had the West End, which was another ghetto, these were Afro-Americans, for the most part, slaves who had migrated north from the south, after the Civil War and there was *no* intermingling, there was no mixture, there was nothing. If you were in the West End that was it, if you were in the South End, you were in the South End. I grew up and my mother taught me to say, "Those damn niggers in the West End." I said it like any other little white boy.

This is where my identification dilemma was spawned. Because my mother always told me I was white. I went to a Cape Verdean school at which we were all treated as white officially but unofficially we got the worst teachers in regard to competence. The equipment, the material—all obsolete, the hand-me-downs from the other schools.

Now I can see it so clearly. There is a distinction. I have to bring in the white Portuguese here. The white Portuguese have been labeled *nhambobs* by Cape Verdeans. We never referred to ourselves as Portuguese in the context of the *nhambobs*. They were kept separate, not for definitions of race, but that's because they were different, they were *nhambobs*. But it was a concession, I can see that so clearly now, to the fact that we, as Cape Verdeans were not white like the *nhambobs* were. Now that I look back on it, we professed to be white. If you asked me my race, I would tell you white, if you pin me down, I would tell you Cape Verdean or Portuguese. But I wouldn't do that until you pinned me down, and then, of course, I wouldn't be able to do that when I went to New Britain, Connecticut. I couldn't get away with saying Portuguese or Cape Verdean there because they didn't know either one.

But it raises the point now of identification which was, of course, cultivated by my own background and environment—I was not black. And when I went to New Britain, Connecticut, I got into fights with these Polish and Italian kids and whipped every one of them. When I left New Bedford and those kids in New Britain called me "nigger," I was outraged. How dare they call me "nigger." I know where the "niggers" are. The "niggers" are in the West End of New Bedford. And I plopped them one. That was it. And, of course, one of the advantages of growing up in the ghetto, you learned how to use your hands real quick. It's a question of survival more than anything else.

I was in the eighth grade. I must have been around 12 or 13 because I always kept pace with the norms. My mother had married again and my stepfather got a good job in Connecticut and he sent for us. I spent a year or two there and when things opened up here again in this area, we moved back because by that time my white aunt owned a house in Fairhaven [across the river from New Bedford] and she allowed us to move into the top floor of her house. I loved Fairhaven. At that time, Fairhaven was particularly tolerant of Cape Verdeans in the context of Portuguese.

Both my mother and father were born in São Vincent. My stepfather was from São Nicolau. But my stepfather could go anywhere. He and my mother made an ideal combination. They could go anywhere. My stepfather was the leader of the Cape Verdean band and they always thought that it was a *nhambob* leading the Cape Verdean band. He was a white man—every definition of the white race—the texture of his hair, the features, the coloring, and he was white. I don't know anything about genetics but visibly there are a lot of Cape Verdeans that have been accepted by society as whites and once that happens then they don't want any black relatives. Both my mother and stepfather were firmly convinced in their own minds that they were white. This was not a question of passing. There was no need for them to masquerade.

There was no problem with the older people. The problem is with us who were born here. The dilemma—especially of looking black and being white. And, of course, if you looked white it was all right, but if you didn't look white, then forget about it.

So I grew up in New Bedford, and when I went to New Bedford high school, I immediately found out that the cards were stacked against me. Number one, my ambition was to be an attorney. But I ended up in a commercial course. Now had my mother or my stepfather been aware of all these things, they could have advised me. Guidance counselor? I still don't know what a guidance counselor is—at my age. That was unheard of. So I ended up in a commercial course. I ended up typing, shorthand, bookkeeping, I was very good at it. I even took up French as an elective. And, you know, I did very well in French. I went through four years of high school, and I didn't flunk a single subject. And I worked. If I hadn't been able to work at the Boys Club, I would never have been able to stay in high school.

Then I got out of high school—and lo and behold—talk about finding a job. That's when I began to have this dilemma of "What am I?" Because I'd call up, and I'd make an appointment. I'd show up, but I would never be hired. And inferior people were hired in regards to studies. And, of course, college was out of the question. I applied for a salesman job. These magazines, you know, and they'd send me back a letter. This oil company wanted a salesman in this area. And I'll never forget the letter they sent me back. "Please send a photograph," and when I'd send a photograph, they'd send back a letter, "at this time we cannot consider hiring. We don't think your qualifications..."

I can't believe that. This is in the early 1930s. And it was a little more subtle but you couldn't get a job at the *Standard Times,* [the New Bedford daily newspaper]—all white. The banks—all white. I couldn't even get a job driving a cab. Do you know they didn't hire black cab drivers in those days? I tried to get a taxi driver's job in the fifties. Was already married with children. They wouldn't hire me. Union Street Railway. Safety Cab. Wouldn't hire me. And the theory behind this—white women aren't safe with black taxi drivers. Still prevails.

After I got out of high school, it was the usual series of cranberry picking, strawberries, for minimum, for nonexistent wages—

and dishwashing. All the chefs in this area were Cape Verdeans. That was a good job for us in that sense. We were allowed those jobs. Mills had gone out. Goodyear. Revere Copper and Brass. Even Chamberlain discriminated very blatantly against Cape Verdeans. After I left high school, I ran into all these problems. And, of course, what am I? The confusion was so disconcerting. Tell everybody I'm Cape Verdean and they'd put me in the back of the bus.

In the merchant marine in the early 30s, I was a mess boy. When I went on a ship, I found out that down south, if I were waiting for a trolley, there are two places. Colored and white. Well, I would speak Spanish, well my Portuguese, pidgeon Portuguese and Spanish, I would be with my *cumpads,* male *cumpads,* the firemen who was white, but the motor man would look at me and allow me to sit in front because I was still a Cape Verdean, and I was not going to mix with quote "dem niggers." I wasn't going to do it that's all there was to it. They would view me with a suspicious eye, but they wouldn't throw me off the trolley. Then I'd get off the trolley car and I'd go uptown to a show in Newport News or Baltimore, mind you, this was in the early '30s. And they would not sell me an orchestra seat. You know, that's where I found out that that's where "Nigger Heaven" originated.

I've got to tell you this anecdote. In '38 and '39, I worked on this shrub as a relief fireman. And I had the car. And boy, it was a great thing to own a car in '38. All the other crewmen were dependent upon me for rides. From Bristol, Rhode Island, to New Bedford, we'd come home every other weekend. This was the lighthouse service, before it was taken over by the Coast Guard. Well, this guy, God bless his soul, Mach—Seraphim Olivera, Brava, typical Brava who would not identify. Strictly white. We made an agreement. We went to the show in Providence, and the agreement was, use my car, my gas but he'd pay

for the ticket. And he always prided himself on the fact that he was white. He used to tell me, "I won't go to the show with you—you're too black." He used to tell me this. Mind you, we were supposed to be friends. Of course, he resented the fact that—we had boxing gloves out there and every time we put on the gloves, I would kick the living daylights out of him. And I would do it deliberately, you see, because of his Brava feeling of being superior. We went to this show in Providence. Providence longshoremen told me this afterwards, but this show was notorious for not admitting blacks or Cape Verdeans downstairs. They still had the "Nigger Heaven" bit. So Mach went up—Mach was his nickname. *Mach* means male. Mach went up to the box and the woman didn't see me. And he asked for two orchestras. "Oh, no, no, no, no, there was vaudeville on. They're all sold out." So we went upstairs. Unknowing and innocent of the custom of the theater management. We get upstairs and lo and behold, downstairs is vacant. I told Mach, they won't let colored people sit downstairs. He says (all of this in *Crioulo*), "You are colored; I'm not colored." I says, "Well, you bought the tickets." He says, "Animal, the lady must have seen you. And refused to sell me the tickets." Now, I was out of the vision of the lady. I got hysterical. And all this was in his dialect. There he is, he bought the tickets but he's blaming me. He was so embarrassed and humiliated because they refused to accept him as white, which he was. That is a typical Cape Verdean story.

The feeling of animosity between the West End and the South End led to fights. The white Portuguese never, never accepted us in any way, shape, or form except they'd do it on a superficial basis. We had our own separate little areas. Cape Verdean Band Club, St. Vincent's Sporting Club. And if you weren't Cape Verdean. God forbid, if you married *American d'cor* [pejorative term for African American]. If my mother were alive right now knowing that both of my surviving daughters have married Afro-Americans, my mother would turn over in her grave.

You know, I had an inferiority complex when I was a kid. Of the three sisters' children, me and George were the ugly ones. It had nothing to do with shade. In fact some of my cousins were darker than me. We were nappy headed. It had nothing to do with color. My hair was considered *pret corvasa sec*. They had good hair and even though they may have been darker, their features were better. I was considered ugly and so was George—based on appearance and the texture of the hair.

So eventually, I lived in New Bedford. Public housing came into existence and I applied for it and was accepted. And Bay Village from Walnut Street right down to Canon Street was all Cape Verdean except for two Afro-American families. From Canon Street all the way down to Grinnell Street was all white. So then I found out, among other things that they violated the pact, which meant this was Cape Verdean. Why did they have those two Afro-American families in there? Now, this was in the forties. Which goes to show you the feeling I still retained—this Cape Verdeanism—even then. In the 1940s, I had to be in my thirties. I still resented Afro-Americans being brought into my neighborhood. I still had that in-bred inferiority.

By the time of the "searing" sixties, I had started to change. By that time I had bumped into Duncan Dottin, a sociologist from Cambridge, an Afro-American who lived in the West End. He was fascinated. Here he is talking to me and I'm calling him a "nigger," and here I am telling him I'm white. One thing I've got to give Duncan credit for, Duncan has never, never held this against me. He knew my background. But God bless the man. He knew my potential. He was able to develop it. If I've got to the stage now where I'm fairly

articulate and fairly knowledgeable, it's due to the fact that Duncan was the springboard.

I'll never forget the time when he said something about Langston Hughes and I said to him, "Who's Langston Hughes?" He wanted to hit me. I began to recognize one thing, while I was not a "nigger" and I was Cape Verdean, they didn't accept Cape Verdeans. And the more and more I looked around—you know the minute you hit School Street [the Cape Verdean neighborhood in New Bedford] you know where you are. I don't give a damn what they say, I don't give a damn if they speak a foreign tongue. You know they're not white. And if you're not white, man, in this country you've got to be black and when I say black—it is in the context of the oppression, the subjugation. So, who am I kidding?[4]

Lucille Ramos, mother of four and foster-mother of twenty-five children, has an intergenerational outlook on the Cape Verdean dilemma of social identity:

Being a Cape Verdean is special to me and to my children even more so—because we're a potpourri really, we're a mixture of people. I think we have both European and African influence. When I was younger our country was still ruled by the Portuguese government, we, we've gone through changes, you know. When we were young we were Portuguese because that was our mother country, and then we went through the Black part of our lives in the sixties. And now I think we finally know who and what we are, which is Cape Verdean, and it is something special. And we are different, we're different from the American Blacks and we're different from the Whites. We've taken from both cultures, and that makes us unique.

With the kids, I remember the first time I knew they were proud of being Cape Verdean was when they had clubs, in high school, like International Food, and they would ask everyone for ethnic foods, and right away the kids wanted to bring in Cape Verdean dishes. When they were young it wasn't so important, but they began to have more pride as they grew older. When we were young, we didn't really know that much about Cape Verdeanism. People just classified us as Portuguese because we were a Portuguese colony. Now since 1975 when Cape Verde gained its independence, I think it's become much more important to us, and in particular to our children.

Here in New Bedford, you know, we just kind of accepted the fact that we were Cape Verdean and that everybody knew what that meant. But when Cape Verdeans began to go away from the community, they began to have problems.

For instance, one of my sons was in the R.O.T.C., and they travel a lot. Everywhere he went he would say, "My name is Ramos," and everybody thought he was Spanish. And he would say, "No, I'm Cape Verdean." "What's a Cape Verdean?" they would all ask, so it became a thing to be able to tell them where the islands were, that we had our own language and dialect, had our own foods, music, and culture.

The older people may still say "We're Portuguese." That is how they were raised. But I think the New Bedford Portuguese always objected to us saying we were Portuguese, because they felt we really weren't....

In the sixties we had lots of problems here locally with the labels "Black" and "White." You see, up till then the kids identified themselves as Cape Verdean. But at that point they had to take a stand, especially in high school. You were either Black or you were White, there was no in-between. So you had to decide then, "Am I a Black or am I a White?" And nobody wanted to hear whether you were a Cape Verdean or not. It was just Black or White. The kids had a difficult time then because they had to make that decision.

People may not understand this, but it was very difficult because Cape Verdeans come in shades from pure white to ebony black. For instance, when my kids were going to the Greene school [a New Bedford public school in the South End], the teacher would identify the child's race by looking at him. I had three sons all in the school at the same time. I was a carpet joke, because I have three sons three shades; and one teacher identified one boy as Black, one teacher identified one as White, and one was identified as Mulatto. So I have three children identified as three different races.

But this kind of confusion was not unusual for me. I'm the fourth child in my family. I have three brothers older, and four of us were delivered by one doctor, and four of us delivered by another. In those days it was not the parent who determined the race—and you know how race goes on your birth certificate? Well, when my brothers went into the service their race was listed as Caucasian. So when I went for my marriage license, I remember the woman there said, "What is your race?" and I said "Caucasian," because I had just assumed I was listed Caucasian too. I remember this very distinctly because the place was crowded at the time, and she went and took out my birth certificate and said, in a very haughty voice "You're not Caucasian, you're colored!" And I said, "Whatever, my brothers were Caucasian." She said, "They must have had different fathers." I said, "No, we all have the same mother and father." She said, "That's impossible." But it was very true, and as far as I know, it is still true that the doctor who delivers the child names the child's race. And the amazing thing was the white doctor listed the children as Caucasian, and the Cape Verdean doctor listed the children as Colored.

But my mother and father had no idea what we were listed as until we had to go and get our papers. My husband, who's half and half, was listed as Caucasian in the service. We married when he got out of the service. We went to Dartmouth for his papers, and they said, "What is your race?" and he said, "Caucasian," and they went and said, "You're a Mulatto, you're a mixed breed, your father is a Cape Verdean and your mother is White." So you know you run into these kinds of things.

I remember when my children were born that was a big thing for me. I told the doctor right at the beginning. "I will identify their race, not you." He said, "Fine, you do the whole thing," and it was funny because, with all the trouble my husband and I went through, we could now choose—and these were the choices—it was either Black, White, or Mulatto. We chose Mulatto. It became a crisis for them in the sixties, though, when they had to make a choice. Especially so when you had several kids in the family and one was light and one was dark, because—to us it meant nothing, but to the White person it meant something, or to the person who identified as Black it meant something.

I think the majority of the kids now are coming around to saying they are Cape Verdean. But if it is a choice of identifying White or Black, I think they would choose Black. I think it was more difficult for the older ones, the parents and the grandparents, to accept that their children identified as Black. Some of the kids were even dropping the Cape Verdean altogether and it was just Black. There was lots of peer pressure and they felt you couldn't be in-between, you had to be one or the other, and if the color of your skin wasn't pure white, that didn't give you much choice to begin with anyway.

But it was very difficult for the parents and grandparents to accept this. Take my father-in-law for instance. He is an extremely dark man, and looking at him there would be no doubt in your mind that this is a Black man. But he does not consider himself a Black man. He was born on the Cape Verdean islands. He is now in his eighties, and he considers himself Portuguese—he does not identify as Cape Verdean. He is Portuguese and Portuguese is White. Do you know the ridicule that a Black man faces when he says, "I'm White, I'm Portuguese."

But you see the kids were not going to be ridiculed that way. They knew what they were, and the thing is, they have been able to accept the pride in it, which is the important thing. Whereas for the older people being White meant being—special. They didn't want to be in the minority. But our kids don't feel that way, they're Black and they're proud. That came about in the sixties. And I think they realize that "Well, I may be Black but I am Cape Verdean and I have my own culture within the Black, and I can be as proud of that as being Black."[5]

So they've gone through a lot of changes, which we have as well, as parents. So racially I think we've had our difficulties, and I think our children still have difficulties, although not so many now.

Notes

[1] Charles Andrade, Jr., quoted in Colin Nickerson, "Black, White or Cape Verdean?" *Boston Globe,* 29 Sept. 1983, p. 16.

[2] Maria Luisa Nunes, *A Portuguese Colonial in America: Belmira Nunes Lopes, the Autobiography of A Cape Verdean-American* (Pittsburgh: Latin American Literary Review Press, 1982), p. 193.

[3] Nunes, *A Portuguese Colonial in America,* pp. 144, 201.

[4] Interview with Joaquim A. Custodio, 28 July 1988.

[5] Lucille Ramos in *Spinner,* I, pp. 34–37.

How It Was for Me

SARAH VAN'T HUL

Study Questions
1. Van't Hul states "the racist attitude of whites was more inconspicuous than the overt anger from blacks, but both were equally powerful and disturbing." Give examples that support her generalization.
2. How did Van't Hul deal with her marginal status?

Nineteen seventy-two, the year abortion became legal, was the year of my birth. It was also the year that the Black Social Workers Association decided that white people should not be allowed to adopt black children. They said that it is more damaging for black children to be adopted by white parents than to be placed in foster care, because the adopted children would be stripped of their identity and culture. As a result of the BSWA's position, many black children have been left with no family and very likely a poor sense of identity.

When I was two months old I was adopted by a white family and brought from Toledo, Ohio, to Ann Arbor, Michigan, right around the time that the BSWA made its recommendation. There were few other black or biracial kids in the white middle-class community in which I was raised. Unsurprisingly, my first reaction toward white people was positive. I loved my parents, my sister, and my brothers. The friends I had were white, and if I didn't like somebody, I never associated my dislike of them with their appearance.

I distinctly remember when the difference in my appearance became an issue for me. On my first day of kindergarten all the other girls except me had on dresses and had long straight hair. I had on jeans and

had a very short Afro. It was instant alienation and embarrassment. The girls didn't want to play with me; they told me I had fat lips and a big nose, and that my skin looked like "pooh." The only friend I had at first was a boy who was black like me, and he was just *as shy as I was*. We played with each other during recess because nobody else would play with us.

My first lasting friendship was with a girl named Laurie. I think part of what attracted us to one another was simply that we were the same color, and she had been adopted by a white family also. We were both different, and if one of us was teased by anyone for our color, we no longer had to bear it alone; they would have to deal with both of us.

It was in these early years that I heard one of my mother's friends say, "Oh, what a beautiful girl!" If she had only known know much I cringed when she said that! I thought she was crazy, or just trying to be polite. Someone black can't be pretty. I thought; she should *know* that.

It wasn't long before I did have a lot of girlfriends, maybe just because I was friendly. But racism became a definite reality for me in the later years of grade school. I had a group of very close girlfriends and always seemed to get along with boys very well. Boys liked to play with me, because I was good at sports and didn't act "girlish." Wearing dresses was never my thing, and I was never afraid to fight. But when my girl-friends were beginning to date and have boys who had crushes on them, I found myself left out. The few boys that had the courage to date me soon let me know they didn't want to "go out with me," because I was black.

It took me a long time to feel comfort-able about dating any boys, and I became the "feminist" amongst my friends. Girls began to see me as a source of strength, for I appeared confident and self-sufficient. What my friends never understood was that my so-called feminist strength was much less a choice on my part than a method of coping with prejudice.

Family outings, too, were often much more pain for me than pleasure. What I be-lieved was my quirky family drawing so much attention in restaurants, I later real-ized was really subtle racism. Going out to dinner and on vacations was much like pulling teeth for me. In diners on the road (my father's favorite eating establishments) and in restaurants outside of Ann Arbor, I had to deal with seemingly endless silence, when my family of four white people and two black kids (one of my brothers is also black) entered a restaurant. Everything seemed to stop, except the music. The stares and the screaming silence filled me with shame and left a permanent scar.

When I was twelve years old, I lived in Switzerland for a year with my family. My self-consciousness hit its peak. Everybody stared at me. At least in Ann Arbor there were havens where I did not feel alienated. In Europe, it seemed like I was the only black person on the whole continent. I could not blend in. The school kids petted my skin and hair, as though I were an ex-otic creature. It was one of the most fright-ening experiences I have ever had.

The prejudice from white people was subtle, however, compared to the overt hos-tility that came from other blacks. My first exposure to groups of black people was in junior high, and, to my surprise, they com-pletely rejected me. I quickly found that if the black kids have a problem with you, they will get in your face and tell you ex-actly what's wrong. They immediately let me know that my problem was that I thought I was white. Before I even opened my mouth, the black kids told me who I was: a "white wannabe." (This was kind of ironic, because *they* had bone-straight hair, and I had a natural.) I talked funny, I dressed funny, I thought I was better than anyone else, and why didn't I straighten that nappy do? Black girls frequently wanted to fight me for simply being me. They wanted me to be ashamed for being different and to hold my head down instead of up. My retal-iation was verbal. I would try to show them that they were acting much worse than I was, and it was stupid for them to want to fight me when I had done nothing to them.

L'Tonya was a big black girl who tor-mented me throughout junior high and until the eleventh grade in high school. Every time I walked down the hall, she loudly made fun of me—about everything, from my hair and clothes to the way I stood. Be-cause I would never respond, teasing be-came unsatisfactory for her. One time when she and five of her friends caught me and one of my friends in the gym, she threw a basketball at my head, and then a chair. She called me all kinds of names and more than anything wanted to fight me. I told her I wouldn't fight her, and I didn't understand why she hated me so much. I don't re-member everything I said, but I remember I left her speechless for the first time. She continued to harass me, but I began to recognize my strengths and her weaknesses, and I began not to cringe or care as much.

In the eleventh grade, I had to take the California Achievement Test; I was put in a room with the other black kids. I wasn't on my own turf, and I was awaiting the teasing and snickering. Instead, one black boy had the courage to approach and talk to me in front of the rest of the kids. L'Tonya was in the room, and she didn't look too happy, but after the boy walked away, she came up to me and, to my amazement, apologized for all the times she had made fun of me. I felt triumphant: for once I was appreciated just for being me. But I didn't say, "That's O.K."; I didn't say anything at all. For three years she had made me feel completely disowned and ugly, when I had given her nothing but respect. Now she wanted my respect, and I didn't have any for her.

Through all of this, I learned not to take my true friends for granted, for I knew they had to like me for me, and they often had to deal with name-calling from others just because they were friends with me.

Before I could even put into words what I felt, I knew I was different from other people who looked like me, and I struggled a lot with how to bridge the gap between me and them. I wondered what I had missed out on and what made me so different. I learned to accept the only position available to me when around other blacks—the observer. In that position I gained another kind of insight into black culture, one that has helped me become more understanding as to why I posed a threat to them and they to me.

It was the hostility of black kids that first made me conscious that being black means a lot more than having darker skin; it carries a whole history and anger. I resented those kids for punishing me for being black and

confident, but I was also attracted to them for having more knowledge about black culture than I did.

In recent years, I have become very curious and interested in black awareness and identity. I have mainly taken the responsibility of educating myself both through reading and listening to others speaking about black issues.

Black history, past and present (in particular, the history of black women), has been one of my primary interests ever since I have been out of high school. I am starting to learn many of the answers to the "whys" I had growing up. It has been both a relief and empowering to learn about black culture. It is the whole other half of history I was never taught in school.

The racist attitude of whites was more inconspicuous than the overt anger from blacks, but they both were equally powerful and disturbing. Yet, since the rejection from blacks was obvious, I initially attached my immediate feeling of oppression to other blacks. As time has gone on, I have become more understanding (though not accepting) of the black kids' resentment and more aware and less tolerant of prejudice from whites.

Dancing saved my sanity. It has been my coping device. Often when I felt there was no one I could talk to or who would completely understand, dancing was the closest I could get to peace. I didn't start taking classes on a regular basis until late high school, but I would always dance in one of the free rooms of my house. My mother tells me that I started doing this as young as two years old.

As an aspiring dancer, I was not exposed to the latest moves in the black community, and although I would take classes in modern and ballet technique to strengthen myself, I never found a form of dance that I felt was completely my style. Instead, I made up my own style and created movements that felt right for my body.

Now as a dance major at the University of Michigan, I don't just dance for pleasure, but with purpose. I find that through my choreography, I can finally speak and be heard. I have connected with black and white people (both in the audience and fellow dancers) at a level I could never reach verbally. Through my dance I found mutual respect.

One of the most significant questions I am frequently asked when people see me dance is where did I learn those moves, and if I could teach them. I tell them that I made them up. Although their interest is flattering, I have begun to realize that the real question they want to know the answer to, once again, is how to classify me. I believe I have started to define my own class, in dance and in the rest of my life, which grows out of both black culture and white culture.

Although I sometimes wish that I had been raised in a black community, I am still very grateful for having been raised as I was. Having a family at all, and especially one that loves and supports me, is far more important to me than being raised in a specific community.

I experienced some of the best and worst of both cultures, which has given me a wealth of insight that I only recently have begun to appreciate and hope that I can pass on to others. When I was growing up, I often felt like I had no place. Now I have come to realize that by not having a comfortable place, I had to create my own, which at times seems to serve as a bridge. In this world, full of so much hate, I believe we need all the bridges we can get.

Mojado Like Me

JOSEPH TOVARES

◇•◆•◇

Study Questions
1. How did Joseph Tovares and his colleagues "pass" as Mexican laborers? How did Tovares know he had "passed"?
2. Describe the life of a "Mexican laborer" as experienced by Tovares.
3. How does Tovares' marginal status help us understand race in the United States?

Early last November, I caught a radio news story about Latino support for California's Proposition 187, the bill that sought to deny educational, medical, and other benefits to undocumented immigrants. The report suggested that there was support for the measure among established Mexican Americans. Like a lot of people, I was stunned by what I heard. The "send them back to where they came from" attitude of some of my fellow Chicanos left me shaking my head in disbelief. It seems as though, in the span of one or two generations, many of us have become blind to the strife of our ancestors. How short can our collective memories be?

I am not pointing fingers. Although I find the very idea of Proposition 187 to be rooted in racism and find it abhorrent, I too have moments when I forget how I got here in the first place. I hadn't realized the extent of my memory lapses until I accepted an assignment that vividly reminded me of where I had once been.

The Mambo Kings. That's what we jokingly called ourselves as we drove across California shooting an undercover story for ABC's "PrimeTime Live." We were three college-educated, U.S.–born Latinos, but for this story we dressed as farm workers,

spoke Spanish and broken English, and tried hard to look poor. There was Steve Blanco, a half Cuban American, half Puerto Rican from Miami and an ace freelance sound recordist; Gerardo Rueda, a first-generation Mexican American as well as a first-rate shooter and sound recordist; and me, a documentary producer, a Tejano/-Chicano with roots in Texas stretching back to pre-Alamo days who just happens to be Jewish. As we traveled across the state in our beat-up Ford pickup, drawing nervous stares from shop owners and accusatory glances from policemen, I learned something about who I am and remembered much about who I used to be.

Back home in San Antonio and Miami, we led the good life. We worked for the networks, made good money, dressed well, and drove nice cars. We were living out our parents' dreams—the dreams of immigrants who longed for a better future for their children. Our folks had nothing to complain about—we were making good money and working for a prestigious show. "Nachas," the Jews call it. It's how old folks describe the pride and joy their children bring to them. For years we had brought our parents much "nachas."

But over the years, like most television veterans, I had picked up some bad habits. There is an "us and them" attitude that permeates our business. We're on the inside and everyone else is on the outside. Objectivity often forces journalists to put up walls, and Latino journalists are no different. A wall had developed between myself and almost everyone else, including other Chicanos. I somehow saw myself as different. After all, I was a freelance professional and I worked steadily. No one guaranteed me work; I worked because I was good and because I had paid my dues.

After much hard work, I had achieved a measure of success that I felt I had earned. I had been through what most professionals of color go through in this country. As a student I had put up with all the nonsense from white teachers, from first grade through graduate school. I had put up with all the snide remarks from co-workers who had never worked with a "Mexican." All that was behind me now. I didn't have to put up with anybody. In my mind I was a success. I had accomplished much more than I was supposed to. But with that success came the wall that divided me from my people and from my past.

I got the call from "Prime Time Live" on a Sunday, and a few days later the job was set. Gerardo and I set out from San Antonio and Steve Blanco flew in from Miami a few days later. Susan Barnett, the producer, and Claudia Swift, the associate producer, had done their homework. Our job was to infiltrate work groups made up of Mexican workers, then determine their legal status and whether or not they were being exploited. Unconfirmed sources indicated that the workers were being illegally charged for transportation and tools. It was the old "company store" routine. In the end, the workers owed the boss money. If that wasn't bad enough, many workers were often forced to live in subhuman conditions deep inside our national forests. We suspected all of this was occurring under the watchful eye of the U.S. Forest Service, which awarded the contracts for reforestation. The scenario had the two most essential elements for a good story: clearly identifiable victims and bad guys.

We began our new, albeit temporary, life in old faded work pants, well-worn flannel shirts, and dusty work boots. Susan and Claudia provided us with the proper vehicle—a 1979 Ford truck that had been in so many accidents it was now composed mostly of Bondo.

At first the job reminded me of *Black Like Me,* a sixties book by John Howard Griffin in which a white man foolishly thinks he can understand what it's like to be a black man in America by temporarily changing his skin color. A friend would later kid me about my adventure, referring to it as "Mojado Like Me." Mojado is a pejorative term, the Spanish equivalent of "wetback." But I didn't need to change my skin color; nor was I venturing into completely new territory.

We entered the town of Lindsay, California, anxiously looking for work. We walked the streets, chatting with everyone we could. On street corners, in restaurants, and in bars, we searched out employment in the *sierra*, the mountains. We only spoke Spanish—not the Spanish we learned in school but the language of the campesinos. By the end of the first day we knew we were "passing." We knew by the help we received from real farm workers and others we approached for information on jobs. Waitresses, barkeeps, and people on the streets would all refer us to contractors. But we also knew we were "passing" by the stares we received. Cops, shopkeepers, businesspeople would look at us with suspicion and speak to us in condescending tones. I had forgotten what that felt like, and it took me back to Michigan, to 1969 and to endless rows of Christmas trees.

It had been almost 25 years since that summer in Michigan. That was the last time I worked the fields. My mom and dad, my older brother Raul, and I worked long days trimming Christmas trees while my younger brothers played in the adjoining woods. Using machetes, we "formed" the trees, making sure they looked like Christmas trees should. All day long we would swing those machetes. Another crew followed closely behind, "painting" the mature trees with a green dye. After that summer, Christmas never seemed the same. Years later when my wife, Munya, and I were planning to marry, she asked if I would be willing to keep a Jewish home. I don't think she knows how easy it was for me to give up the Christmas tree.

A lot had changed in 25 years. I had gone from campesino child to East Coast–educated, hip (or so I thought) Latino. But like a lot of Latino professionals, there had developed a great distance between who I had once been and who I had become. I never forgot where I came from, but the memory had become fuzzier with time.

I had forgotten how much baggage poverty carries. Being without money is only part of the story. There is a side to poverty, exacerbated by race, that is much more difficult to understand. It is subtle yet oppressive. It is communicated by stares, gestures, and tone. Unless you've been there, you can't possibly understand. I had tried very hard to leave those feelings of inferiority far behind. I had graduated from high school, won a scholarship to college, and obtained a fellowship at graduate school. I thought I had come a long way.

Yet, as I walked the streets looking for menial work, I realized that after all these years I had been only one change of clothes away from my past. A past I had tried to bury long ago.

The competition for jobs was stiff. There was a surplus of labor around, and it was hard to pin down the contratistas as to when they would get their contracts. We dogged one guy for days, hanging around his storefront office until he finally agreed to add us to his work crew. The entire time we were wired for video and sound, wondering if our mannerisms and movements would give us away and wondering what would happen if we were found out. After all, these were not Boy Scouts we were approaching for work. These were men who were accused of absconding with their workers' wages and abandoning them in the mountains without food or transportation. They would not take kindly to having their unethical behavior surreptitiously videotaped. Landing the job was a cause for some celebration—not only did we get work, we got it on tape. But the scope of the accomplishment was diminished by the severe reality of the work we were going to have to perform.

The work in the California mountains was more than hard—it was brutal. We left camp at six in the morning and returned around seven at night. The official term for the job is "manual release" but the other workers, all of whom were from Mexico and undocumented, simply called it "limpieza," or "cleaning." In "manual release," workers move along in a line, and with hoes, shears, and brute force, clear thick brush from around recently planted pine trees. Those little seedlings had value; in many ways they were much more valuable than we were. Lots of money went into planting those little trees, and we were there to protect them. The thick brush we were taking out had been robbing the pine trees of valuable nutrients and had to be removed. But it was no easy matter. Some bushes were bigger than we were and virtually impossible to completely take out. I hadn't worked that hard in a long time. There I was, my hands cut and scratched, my body completely covered in dirt, trying to chip away at thicket after thicket. We had no idea how much we would wind up being paid or when; no idea when we would eat lunch, no idea if we would get a break. Under the watchful eye of our patron, a fellow Chicano, we worked. At his request, several men sang old Mexican songs. The National Forest had been transformed into a hacienda.

The plan was for us to complete fourteen acres that first day of work, but we only finished six. Midway through the afternoon the boss gave us a pep talk. "The quicker we finish, the more money you make," he said. But the work was too much. The Mambo Kings were the first to quit. We got the pictures we needed and left.

Over the course of several days, we wandered among various work camps, taking more pictures and gathering information. Living in tents and working twelve hours a day proved too much of a strain for many of the laborers. Fresh workers were brought in to replace those who left. We were told that during a period of seven weeks more than 100 men had come and gone from the crew. Only two of the original fifteen men, a father and son, remained.

Their names were Gregorio and Pedro. Gregorio, the father, had been in the United States for a long time. Pedro, his son, had only just arrived. The boy claimed to be eighteen, but he had the face of a child. I was amazed as I watched Pedro work. His tools were not nearly as good as ours and

the effort required to cut through the heavy bush and ground cover was taxing even for the grown men. But Pedro, who worked without gloves, never complained.

All day we would crawl to reach the trunks of the large and thorny bushes—constantly on the lookout for dangerous snakes. We were allowed fifteen minutes for lunch and given a ten-minute break in the late afternoon. As we worked side by side, Pedro told me of his solitary trek across Mexico and into the United States He had come to search for his father, hoping to land a job and assist him in supporting the family back in Oaxaca. The father and son expected to make about $6,000 between them, but after seven weeks of grueling work, all they received was $300 each. The last time I saw them was on television, several months after their job ended. They were still hoping to get paid.

Our job with ABC News lasted three weeks, but the memory will be with me forever. I can still remember the pain of the distrustful stares, the agony of watching men being treated like animals, and the anger of seeing Chicano contractors exploit Mexican workers. The lessons from those three weeks were startling. It didn't matter how different I thought I was from these men who hail from places like Oaxaca and Michoacan. To virtually all the people I met, I was one of them. The walls that I had built turned out to be made of paper, and they quickly crumbled.

Barely a month after the odyssey began, I was back home attending my twentieth high school reunion. There were doctors, lawyers, accountants, and businessmen—a dozen Hispanic success stories. Drinking and dancing at the San Antonio country club, we represented the new Chicano middle class. Part of me felt very much at home there, and the feeling troubled me. As I tried to make sense of my conflict, I glanced down and touched a small scar on my left hand. The scar had been left there by a careless boy trying to work as a man 25 years ago in Michigan. Day dreaming and machetes don't mix. Effortlessly the band segued from a rock tune to a Mexican polka, and the Chicanos shifted into barrio gear and slid across the dance floor with ease. As my wife and I danced, I realized that it is impossible to leave one life behind and simply begin another. Our lives are built on a series of experiences and, like it or not, even the difficult ones count.

So what started out as a good job with lots of overtime potential turned into a cathartic event that changed my life. I had tried for years to bury unpleasant memories, to deny they even existed. My career had made it easy to do. But during those three weeks in California I was forced into a deep reexamination of myself. The experience made me confront ugly realities about how this society treats a hidden underclass. Most important, it made me realize how easy it is for many of us who have escaped to simply forget.

Then Came the War

YURI KOCHIYAMA

◇◆◈◆◇

Study Question

Describe the marginal status of Japanese-Americans during WWII. In particular list examples of how interned Japanese were still "Americans" even as they were isolated from the rest of the U.S. population.

I was red, white, and blue when I was growing up. I taught Sunday school, and was very, very American. But I was also very provincial. We were just kids rooting for our high school.

My father owned a fish market. Terminal Island was nearby, and that was where many Japanese families lived. It was a fishing town. My family lived in the city proper. San Pedro was very mixed, predominantly white, but there were blacks also.

I was nineteen at the time of the evacuation. I had just finished junior college. I was looking for a job, and didn't realize how different the school world was from the work world. In the school world, I never felt racism. But when you got into the work world, it was very difficult. This was 1941, just before the war. I finally did get a job at a department store. But for us back then, it was a big thing, because I don't think they had ever hired an Asian in a department store before. I tried, because I saw a Mexican friend who got a job there. Even then they didn't hire me on a regular basis, just on Saturdays, summer vacation, Easter vacation, and Christmas vacation. Other than that, I was working like the others—at a vegetable stand, or doing part-time domestic work. Back then, I only knew of two Japanese American girl friends who got jobs

as secretaries—but these were in Japanese companies. But generally you almost never saw a Japanese American working in a white place. It was hard for Asians. Even for Japanese, the best jobs they felt they could get were in Chinatowns, such as in Los Angeles. Most Japanese were either in some aspect of fishing, such as in the canneries, or went right from school to work on the farms. That was what it was like in the town of San Pedro. I loved working in the department store, because it was a small town, and you got to know and see everyone. The town itself was wonderful. People were very friendly. I didn't see my job as work—it was like a community job.

Everything changed for me on the day Pearl Harbor was bombed. On that very day—December 7—the FBI came and they took my father. He had just come home from the hospital the day before. For several days we didn't know where they had taken him. Then we found out that he was taken to the federal prison at Terminal Island. Overnight, things changed for us. They took all men who lived near the Pacific waters, and had nothing to do with fishing. A month later, they took every fisherman from Terminal Island, sixteen and over, to places—not the regular concentration camps—but to detention centers in places like South

Dakota, Montana, and New Mexico. They said that all Japanese who had given money to any kind of Japanese organization would have to be taken away. At that time, many people were giving to the Japanese Red Cross. The first group was thirteen hundred Isseis—my parent's generation. They took those who were leaders of the community, or Japanese school teachers, or were teaching martial arts, or who were Buddhist priests. Those categories which would make them very "Japanesey," were picked up. This really made a tremendous impact on our lives. My twin brother was going to the University at Berkeley. He came rushing back. All of our classmates were joining up, so he volunteered to go into the service. And it seemed strange that here they had my father in prison, and there the draft board okayed my brother. He went right into the army. My other brother, who was two years older, was trying to run my father's fish market. But business was already going down, so he had to close it. He had finished college at the University of California a couple of years before.

They took my father on December 7th. The day before, he had just come home from the hospital. He had surgery for an ulcer. We only saw him once, on December 13. On December 20th they said he could come home. By the time they brought him back, he couldn't talk. He made guttural sounds, and we didn't know if he could hear. He was home for twelve hours. He was dying. The next morning, when we got up, they told us that he was gone. He was very sick. And I think the interrogation was very rough. My mother kept begging the authorities to let him go to the hospital until he was well, then put him back in the prison. They did finally put him there, a week or so later. But they put him in a hospital where they were bringing back all these American Merchant Marines who were hit on Wake Island. So he was the only Japanese in that hospital, so they hung a sheet around him that said Prisoner of War. The feeling where he was was very bad.

You could see the hysteria of war. There was a sense that war could actually come to American shores. Everybody was yelling to get the "Japs" out of California. In Congress, people were speaking out. Organizations such as the Sons and Daughters of the Golden West were screaming "Get the 'Japs' out." So were the real estate people, who wanted to get the land from the Japanese farmers. The war had whipped up such a hysteria that if there was anyone for the Japanese, you didn't hear about it. I'm sure they were afraid to speak out, because they would be considered not only just "Jap" lovers, but unpatriotic.

Just the fact that my father was taken made us suspect to people. But on the whole, the neighbors were quite nice, especially the ones adjacent to us. There was already a 6 A.M. to 6 P.M. curfew and a five mile limit on where we could go from our homes. So they offered to do our shopping for us, if we needed.

Most Japanese Americans had to give up their jobs, whatever they did, and were told they had to leave. Executive Order No. 9066—President Roosevelt's edict[1] for evacuation—was in February 1942. We were moved to a detention center that April. By then the Japanese on Terminal Island were just helter-skelter, looking for anywhere they could go. They opened up the Japanese school and Buddhist churches, and families just crowded in. Even farmers brought along their chickens and chicken coops. They just opened up the places for people to stay until they could figure out what to do. Some people left for Colorado and Utah. Those who had relatives could do so.

The idea was to evacuate all the Japanese from the coast. But all the money was frozen, so even if you knew where you wanted to go, it wasn't that simple. By then, people knew they would be going into camps, so they were selling what they could, even though they got next to nothing for it.

We were fortunate, in that our neighbors, who were white, were kind enough to look after our house, and they said they would find people to rent it, and look after it till we got back. But these neighbors were very, very unusual.

We were sent to an assembly center in Arcadia, California, in April. It was the largest assembly center on the West Coast, having nearly twenty thousand people. There were some smaller centers with about six hundred people. All along the West Coast—Washington, Oregon, California— there were many, many assembly centers, but ours was the largest. Most of the assembly centers were either fairgrounds, or race tracks. So many of us lived in stables, and they said you could take what you could carry. We were there until October.

Even though we stayed in a horse stable, everything was well organized. Every unit would hold four to six people. So in some cases, families had to split up, or join others. We slept on army cots, and for mattresses they gave us muslin bags, and told us to fill them with straw. And for chairs, everybody scrounged around for carton boxes, because they could serve as chairs. You could put two together and it could be a little table. So it was just makeshift. But I was amazed how, in a few months, some of those units really looked nice. Japanese women fixed them up. Some people had the foresight to bring material and needles and thread. But they didn't let us bring anything that could be used as weapons. They

let us have spoons, but no knives. For those who had small children or babies, it was rough. They said you could take what you could carry. Well, they could only take their babies in their arms, and maybe the little children could carry something, but it was pretty limited.

I was so red, white, and blue, I couldn't believe this was happening to us. America would never do a thing like this to us. This is the greatest country in the world. So I thought this is only going to be for a short while, maybe a few weeks or something, and they will let us go back. At the beginning no one realized how long this would go on. I didn't feel the anger that much because I thought maybe this was the way we could show our love for our country. And we should not make too much fuss or noise; we should abide by what they asked of us. I'm a totally different person now than I was back then. I was naïve about so many things. The more I think about it, the more I realize how little you learn about American history. It's just what they want you to know.

At the beginning, we didn't have any idea how temporary or permanent the situation was. We thought we would be able to leave shortly. But after several months they told us this was just temporary quarters, and they were building more permanent quarters elsewhere in the United States. All this was so unbelievable. A year before we would never have thought anything like this could have happened to us—not in this country. As time went by, the sense of frustration grew. Many families were already divided. The fathers, the heads of the households, were taken to other camps. In the beginning, there was no way for the sons to get in touch with their families. Before our group left for the detention camp, we were saying goodbye almost every day to other groups who were going to places like Arizona and Utah. Here we finally had made so many new friends—people who we met, lived with, shared the time, and got to know. So it was even sad on that note and the goodbyes were difficult. Here we had gotten close to these people, and now we had to separate again. I don't think we even thought about where they were going to take us, or how long we would have to stay there. When we got on the trains to leave for the camps, we didn't know where we were going. None of the groups knew. It was later on that we learned so and so ended up in Arizona, or Colorado, or some other place. We were all at these assembly centers for about seven months. Once they started pushing people out, it was done very quickly. By October, our group headed out for Jerome, Arkansas, which is on the Texarkana corner.

We were on the train for five days. The blinds were down, so we couldn't look out, and other people couldn't look in to see who was in the train. We stopped in Nebraska, and everybody pulled the blinds to see what Nebraska looked like. The interesting thing was, there was a troop train stopped at the station too. These American soldiers looked out, and saw all these Asians, and they wondered what we were doing on the train. So the Japanese raised the windows, and so did the soldiers. It wasn't a bad feeling at all. There was none of that "you Japs" kind of thing. The women were about the same age as the soldiers—eighteen to twenty-five, and we had the same thing on our minds. In camps, there wasn't much to do, so the fun thing was to receive letters, so on our train, all the girls who were my age, were yelling to the guys, "Hey, give us your address where you're going, we'll write you." And they said, "Are

you sure you're going to write?" We exchanged addresses and for a long time I wrote to some of those soldiers. On the other side of the train, I'll never forget there was this old guy, about sixty, who came to our window and said, "We have some Japanese living here. This is Omaha, Nebraska." This guy was very nice, and didn't seem to have any ill feelings for Japanese. He had calling cards, and he said "Will any of you people write to me?" We said, "Sure," so he threw in a bunch of calling cards, and I got one, and I wrote to him for years. I wrote to him about what camp was like, because he said, "Let me know what it's like wherever you end up." And he wrote back, and told me what was happening in Omaha, Nebraska. There were many, many interesting experiences too. Our mail was generally not censored, but all the mail from the soldiers was. Letters meant everything.

When we got to Jerome, Arkansas, we were shocked because we had never seen an area like it. There was forest all around us. And they told us to wait till the rains hit. This would not only turn into mud, but Arkansas swamp lands. That's where they put us—in swamp lands, surrounded by forests. It was nothing like California.

I'm speaking as a person of twenty who had good health. Up until then, I had lived a fairly comfortable life. But there were many others who didn't see the whole experience the same way. Especially those who were older and in poor health and had experienced racism. One more thing like this could break them. I was at an age where transitions were not hard—the point where anything new could even be considered exciting. But for people in poor health, it was hell.

There were army-type barracks, with two hundred to two hundred and five people to each block and every block had its own mess hall, facility for washing clothes, showering. It was all surrounded by barbed wire, and armed soldiers. I think they said only seven people were killed in total, though thirty were shot, because they went too close to the fence. Where we were, nobody thought of escaping because you'd be more scared of the swamps—the poisonous snakes, the bayous. Climatic conditions were very harsh. Although Arkansas is in the South, the winters were very, very cold. We had a potbellied stove in every room and we burned wood. Everything was very organized. We got there in October, and were warned to prepare ourselves. So on our block, for instance, males eighteen and over could go out in the forest to chop down trees for wood for the winter. The men would bring back the trees, and the women sawed the trees. Everybody worked. The children would pile up the wood for each unit.

They told us when it rained, it would be very wet, so we would have to build our own drainage system. One of the barracks was to hold meetings, so block heads would call meetings. There was a block council to represent the people from different areas.

When we first arrived, there were some things that weren't completely fixed. For instance, the roofers would come by, and everyone would hunger for information from the outside world. We wanted to know what was happening with the war. We weren't allowed to bring radios; that was contraband. And there were no televisions then. So we would ask the workers to bring us back some papers, and they would give us papers from Texas or Arkansas, so for the first time we would find out about news from the outside.

Just before we went into the camps, we saw that being a Japanese wasn't such a good thing, because everybody was turning against the Japanese, thinking we were saboteurs, or linking us with Pearl Harbor. But when I saw the kind of work they did at camp, I felt so proud of the Japanese, and proud to be Japanese, and wondered why I was so white, white when I was outside, because I was always with white folks. Many people had brothers or sons who were in the military and Japanese American servicemen would come into the camp to visit the families, and we felt so proud of them when they came in their uniforms. We knew that it would only be a matter of time before they would be shipped overseas. Also what made us feel proud was the forming of the 442nd unit.[2]

I was one of these real American patriots then. I've changed now. But back then, I was all American. Growing up, my mother would say we're Japanese. But I'd say, "No, I'm American." I think a lot of Japanese grew up that way. People would say to them, "You're Japanese," and they would say, "No, we're Americans." I don't even think they used the hyphenated term "Japanese-American" back then. At the time, I was ashamed of being Japanese. I think many Japanese-Americans felt the same way. Pearl Harbor was a shameful act, and being Japanese-Americans, even though we had nothing to do with it, we still somehow felt we were blamed for it. I hated Japan at that point. So I saw myself at that part of my history as an American, and not as a Japanese or Japanese-American. That sort of changed while I was in the camp.

I hated the war, because it wasn't just between the governments. It went down to the people, and it nurtured hate. What was happening during the war were many things I didn't like. I hoped that one day when the war was over there could be a way that people could come together in their relationships.

Now I can relate to Japan in a more mature way, where I see its faults and its very, very negative history. But I also see its potential. Scientifically and technologically it has really gone far. But I'm disappointed that when it comes to human rights, she hasn't grown. The Japan of today—I feel there are still things lacking. For instance, I don't think the students have the opportunity to have more leeway in developing their lives.

We always called the camps "relocation centers" while we were there. Now we feel it is apropos to call them concentration camps. It is not the same as the concentration camps of Europe; those we feel were death camps. Concentration camps were a concentration of people placed in an area, and disempowered and disenfranchised. So it is apropos to call what I was in a concentration camp. After two years in the camp, I was released.

Going home wasn't much of a problem for us because our neighbors had looked after our place. But for most of our Japanese friends, starting over again was very difficult after the war.

I returned in October of 1945. It was very hard to find work, at least for me. I wasn't expecting to find anything good, just something to tide me over until my boyfriend came back from New York. The only thing I was looking for was to work in a restaurant as a waitress. But I couldn't find anything. I would walk from one end of the town to the other, and down every main avenue. But as soon as they found out I was Japanese, they would say no. Or they would ask me if I was in the union, and of course I couldn't be in the union because I had just gotten there. Anyway, no Japanese could be in the union, so if the answer was no I'm not in the union, they would say no. So finally what I did was go into the rough area of San Pedro—there's a strip near the wharf—and I went down there. I was determined to keep the jobs as long as I could. But for a while, I could last maybe two hours, and somebody would say "Is that a 'Jap'?" And as soon as someone would ask that, the boss would say, "Sorry, you gotta go. We don't want trouble here." The strip wasn't that big, so after I'd go the whole length of it, I'd have to keep coming back to the same restaurants, and say, "Gee, will you give me another chance." I figure, all these servicemen were coming back and the restaurants didn't have enough waitresses to come in and take these jobs. And so, they'd say "Okay. But soon as somebody asks who you are, or if you're a 'Jap,' or any problem about being a 'Jap,' you go." So I said, "Okay, sure. How about keeping me until that happens?" So sometimes I'd last a night, sometimes a couple of nights that no one would say anything. Sometimes people threw cups at me or hot coffee. At first they didn't know what I was. They thought I was Chinese. Then someone would say, "I bet she's a 'Jap'." And I wasn't going to say I wasn't. So as soon as I said "Yeah," then it was like an uproar. Rather than have them say, "Get out," I just walked out. I mean, there was no point in fighting it. If you just walked out, there was less chance of getting hurt. But one place I lasted two weeks. These owners didn't want to have to let me go. But they didn't want to have problems with the people.

And so I did this until I left for New York, which was about three months later. I would work the dinner shift, from six at night to three in the morning. When you are young you tend not to take things as strongly. Everything is like an adventure. Looking back, I felt the people who were the kindest to me were those who went out and fought, those who just got back from

Japan or the Far East. I think the worst ones were the ones who stayed here and worked in defense plants, who felt they had to be so patriotic. On the West Coast, there wasn't hysteria anymore, but there were hostile feelings towards the Japanese, because they were coming back. It took a while, but my mother said that things were getting back to normal, and that the Japanese were slowly being accepted again. At the time, I didn't go through the bitterness that many others went through, because it's not just what they went through, but it is also what they experienced before that. I mean, I happened to have a much more comfortable life before, so you sort of see things in a different light. You see that there are all kinds of Americans, and that they're not all people who hate "Japs." You know too that it was hysteria that had a lot to do with it.

All Japanese, before they left camp, were told not to congregate among Japanese, and not to speak Japanese. They were told by the authorities. There was even a piece of paper that gave you instructions. But then people went on to places like Chicago where there were churches, so they did congregate in churches. But they did ask people not to. I think psychologically the Japanese, having gone through a period where they were so hated by everyone, didn't even want to admit they were Japanese, or accept the fact that they were Japanese. Of course, they would say they were Japanese-Americans. But I think the psychological damage of the wartime period, and of racism itself, has left its mark. There is a stigma to being Japanese. I think that is why such a large number of Japanese, in particular Japanese-American women, have married out of the race. On the West Coast I've heard people say that sixty to seventy percent of the Japanese women have married, I guess, mostly whites. Japanese men are

doing it too, but not to that degree. I guess Japanese-Americans just didn't want to have that Japanese identity, or that Japanese part. There is definitely some self-hate, and part of that has to do with the racism that's so deeply a part of this society.

Historically, Americans have always been putting people behind walls. First there were the American Indians who were put on reservations; Africans in slavery, their lives on the plantations; Chicanos doing migratory work, and the kinds of camps they lived in; and even, too, the Chinese when they worked on the railroad camps where they were almost isolated, dispossessed people—disempowered. And I feel those are the things we should fight against so they won't happen again. It wasn't so long ago—in 1979—that the feeling against the Iranians was so strong because of the takeover of the U.S. embassy in Iran, where they wanted to deport Iranian students. And that is when a group called Concerned Japanese-Americans organized, and that was the first issue we took up, and then we connected it with what the Japanese had gone through. This whole period of what the Japanese went through is important. If we can see the connections of how often this happens in history, we can stem the tide of these things happening again by speaking out against them.

Most Japanese-Americans who worked years and years for redress never thought it would happen the way it did. The papers have been signed, we will be given reparation, and there was an apology from the government. I think the redress movement itself was very good because it was a learning experience for the Japanese people; we could get out into our communities and speak about what happened to us and link it with experiences of other people. In that sense, though, it wasn't done as much as it should have been. Some Japanese-Americans didn't even learn that part. They just started the movement as a reaction to the bad experience they had. They don't even see other ethnic groups who have gone through it. It showed us, too, how vulnerable everybody is. It showed us that even though there is a Constitution, that constitutional rights could be taken away very easily.

Notes

[1] Executive Order No. 9066 does not mention detention of Japanese specifically, but was used exclusively against the Japanese. Over 120,000 Japanese were evacuated from the West Coast.

[2] American soldiers of Japanese ancestry were assembled in two units: the 442nd Regimental Combat Team and the 100th Infantry Battalion. The two groups were sent to battle in Europe. The 100th Battalion had over 900 casualties and was known as the Purple Heart Battalion. Combined, the units received 9,486 purple hearts and 18,143 individual decorations.

"I Can't Imagine Being Any Race Other Than White"*

PHOTOS BY ANNA CASTELLINI

Many white persons in the United States hold ideas about "whiteness" and the stereotypes expressed and implied about non-whites in the photoessay. One of the clearest indications that this is true are the hundreds of thousands of votes received by known Klan leaders and sympathizers in political elections throughout the country. You might begin to analyze the essay by answering the study questions below.

1. The images and comments in the photoessay point to a strong concern about "white identity." Traditionally, the emphasis has been placed on the social identity of non-whites in race and ethnic relations. Why has the issue of white identity become of so much concern in the US in recent years?
2. How would you explain why some whites who have been privileged relative to non-whites historically by law, and today in custom and tradition, believe that they are discriminated against? Do you agree or disagree with their position?
3. What insights can you extract from the photos about the way white people of all ages are socialized to Klan beliefs since prejudices are not innate but learned?
4. What conclusions can you draw about the "ideal of whiteness" as a collective social consciousness?
5. Do you identify as white or non-white? What is the significance for you of the way you identify? How would you express how you feel?

*The quotes are the words of those who belong to various members of the Ku Klux Klan (KKK) organization and they are not necessarily the words of the specific people pictured.

Photos on pages 99–102, and 104 (bottom): Courtesy of Anna Castellini.
Photos on pages 103–104 (top):Courtesy of Don Romaine, Imperial Wizard of the N. Georgia White Knights.

"Today, many people have experienced integration firsthand and have seen the marked differences between the races. White people are no longer buying the 'equality' myth, (even though many pretend that they do) and have begun to doubt some of the anti-Klan hysteria that they have been fed in school, on television, and from movies. Once people understand that the Knights of the Ku Klux Klan won its first struggle for our people in the post-Civil War period, they naturally turn to it as an answer to today's crisis."

"No misrepresentations by prejudiced historians or by the aliens who control America's mass media can dim the luster of its [the Klan's] deeds, or rob it from its rightful place in history as the savior of the White south, and thereby, the preserver of the purity of the White race for all America."

"The future is on our side, it's only a matter of time. We want to take America back. We know a Yugslav nation can't hold up for too long."

"Whites won't have any choice but to take military action. It's our children whose interests we have to defend…it's only a matter of time."

"We light the Cross with fire to signify to the world that Jesus Christ is the light of the world. Where the Holy Light shall shine, there will be dispelled evil, darkness, gloom, and despair. The Light of Truth dispels ignorance and superstition as fire purifies gold and silver, but destroys wood and stubble. Therefore, by the fire of the cross of the Cavalry, we cleanse and purify our virtues by burning out our vices with the fire of His Word. By this Holy Light of the Cross, we shall persevere."

"The Klan robe and hood are not used by Klansmen for wrongdoing. In many old Christian rituals, as illustrated by the carrying of the Pastas in Spain, the hood was worn as a symbol of humility, of anonymity in doing good works. This was the conception of the hood when the Klan was ably led by General Forrest, and this is its true meaning for Klan members: Selflessness, dedication to our God, our nation, our race, our Klan brothers and sisters and our entire Klan movement."

"Those who hate our race and faith are all over the world, and we are there to face them."

"The 'racist' double standard: how Whites are made to feel guilty and 'hateful' for loving their own people and culture."

"My God is a racist and Hitler
is my hero."

"We must secure the existence if our people and a future for White children."—The 14 Words

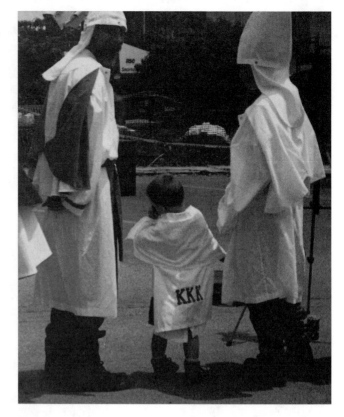

"I cannot imagine being any race other than white."

Can Family Members Really Belong to Different Races?

PHOTOS BY RAY ELFERS

◇◆◈◆◇

The idea that clear-cut racial categories exist is a fallacy if only because males and females from any alleged race can produce offspring. Millions of people in the world have mixed ancestries and/or possess physical traits that make it impossible to assign them to a single racial category. To illustrate this idea study the physical features of the children on pages 106–107. To what race does each belong? Study the physical features of each mother on pages 108–109. Can you match each child with his or her mother? Now look at the family photographs on pages 110–111 to see how many of your mother-child matches are correct.

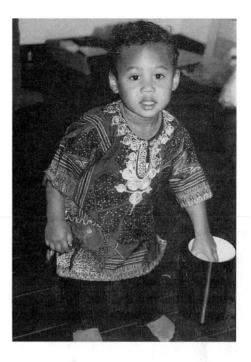

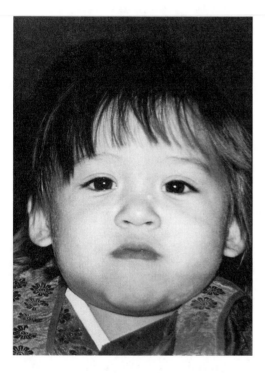

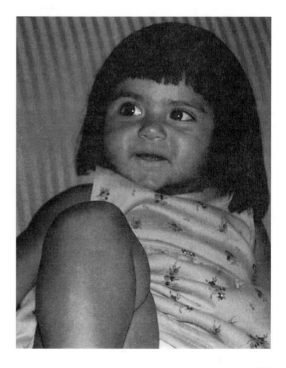

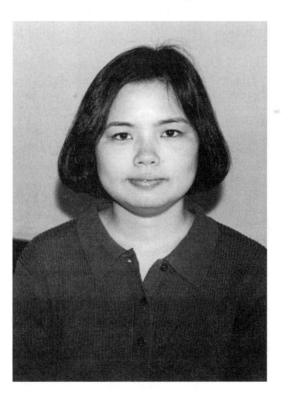

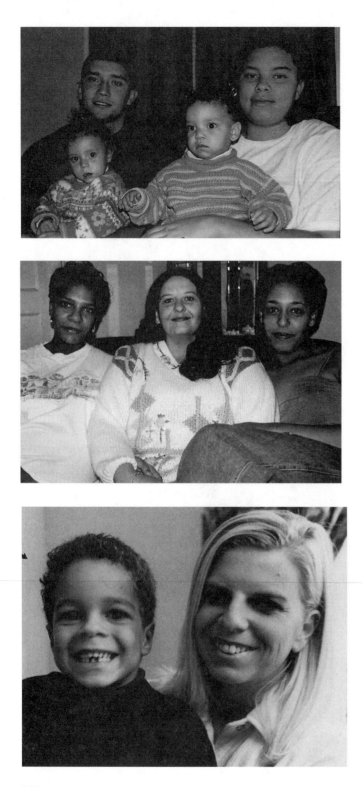

PART 2

◇•◆•◇

Classifying People by Race

In Part 1, we examined the personal experiences of racial classification in the United States. While every person had a unique story, the stories cannot be separated from the prevailing system of racial classification and the conception of race that supports it. Whether people fit into a racial category or not, the categories remain central to how people think about their own identity and the racial identity of others. In this section, we describe and critique the system of racial classification that has been used since 1790 in the United States, and we consider the system to be used beginning with the 2000 census.

Most people in the United States equate race with physical features. In their minds racial categories are assumed to represent "natural, physical divisions among humans that are hereditary, reflected in morphology, and roughly but correctly captured by terms like black, white, and Asian (or Negroid, Caucasian, and Mongoloid)" (Haney López 1994:6). This three-category classification scheme, and other category schemes for that matter, have many shortcomings, which immediately become evident when we imagine using them to classify the more than 6 billion people in the world.

Adding more categories, however, does not ease the task of classifying the billions of people in the world because racial classification rests on the fallacy that clear-cut racial categories exist. Why is this a fallacy? First, many people do not fit clearly into a racial category because no sharp dividing line distinguishes characteristics such as black skin from white skin or curly hair from wavy. This lack of a clear line, however, has not discouraged people from trying to devise ways to make the line seem clear-cut. For example, a hundred years ago in the United States there were churches that "had a pinewood slab on the outside door…and a fine tooth comb hanging on a string…" (Angelou 1987:2). People could go into the church if they were no darker than the pinewood and if they could run the comb through their hair without it snagging. At one time in South Africa, the state board that oversaw racial classification used a pencil test to classify individuals as white or black. If a pencil placed in the person's hair fell out, the person was classified as white (Finnegan 1986).

A second problem with the idea of clear-cut racial categories is that boundaries between races can never be fixed and definite, if only because males and females of any alleged race can produce offspring. Millions of people in the world have mixed ancestry and possess physical traits that make it impossible to assign them to any one of the five narrow racial categories currently used by the U.S. government. The media often presents mixed ancestry as a recent phenomenon connected to the dismantling of laws forbidding interracial marriages in 1967 and a subsequent societal openness to interracial marriage (which produce mixed race children). Since colonial days in the United States, however, "there has been intermixture between White and Indian, between White and Negro, and between Negro and Indian. While the offspring of such unions could not be biologically classified (and by their very existence defy the popular meaning of race), many of them did undoubtedly become accepted and identified with one of the three recognized stocks" (Pollitzer 1972:720). Evidence of this intermixing before 1967 is reflected in 1929 and 1949 studies of the racial ancestry of college students attending historically black universities. In the 1929 study, 78 percent of Howard University students were of mixed "racial" ancestry. In the 1949 study, 84 percent of the college students studied were of mixed ancestry (Meier 1949). The widespread existence of intermixing, however, seemed to have little effect on dismantling beliefs that distinct racial categories exist. It is important to note that in spite of their known mixed ancestry, the college students self-identified and were classified as "black."

A third shortcoming in systems of racial classification is that racial categories and guidelines for placing people in them are often vague, contradictory, unevenly applied, and subject to change. As examples of the arbitrary nature of classification rules, consider that for the 1990 census coders were instructed to classify as white those who classified themselves as "white-black" and to classify as "black" those who classified themselves as "black-white" (U.S. Bureau of the Census 1994). Likewise the National Center for Health Statistics (1993) has changed the guidelines for recording race on birth and death certificates. Before 1989, a child born in the United States was designated as white if both parents were white; if only one parent was white, the child was classified according to the race of the nonwhite parent; if the parents were of different nonwhite races, the child was assigned to the race of the father.[1] If the race of one parent was unknown, the infant was assigned the race of the parent whose race was known. After 1989, the rules for classifying newborns changed so that the race of the infant is the same as that of the mother (Lock 1993), as if identifying the mother's race would present no challenges.

Finally, in trying to classify people by race, we would find a tremendous amount of variation among people designated as belonging to a particular race. For example, people classified as Asian include, among other groups, Chinese, Japanese, Malayans, Mongolians, and Siberians. Likewise, there is considerable heterogeneity within the population labeled as "black" in the United States. Green (1978) identified at least nine distinct "cultural-ecological areas" for the native-born black population, including areas of Native American influence (Oklahoma and parts of Arkansas and Kansas) and French tradition (Louisiana, eastern Coastal Texas, and southwestern Mississippi). In addition,

> the black population includes immigrants from the Caribbean area and the African mainland. Almost half a million persons in the 1990 census indicated that they were of sub-Saharan African ancestry. The black population from the Caribbean basin countries is diverse and includes Spanish-speaking persons from Cuba, the Dominican Republic, and Panama; French-speaking persons from Haiti and other French-speaking Caribbean areas; Dutch-speaking persons from the Netherlands Antilles; and English-speaking persons from the former British colonies. (Williams, Lavizzo-Mourey, and Warren 1994:33)

Perhaps the strongest evidence that race is not a biological fact but a social creation is the different rules for classifying people into racial categories across societies and the shifting rules for classifying people within a single society. In the United States, not only have the rules governing classification changed but so have the categories. For example, in the United States a question about race has appeared on every census since 1790, although it was not until 1850 that the government included a question that clearly attempted to distinguish the black population from the white. Prior to 1850, except for the category free whites, the other categories could include people of any race. Over the past 200 years, the U.S. Bureau of the Census has used as few as three racial categories and as many as 14. (See Table 2.1). Although the rationale for determining the number and names of categories is the subject of a separate book, we can be sure that the various racial classification schemes reflect the prevailing ideologies of their times, and that to understand the various schemes and the changes in those schemes, one must place them in a larger social context.

Table 2.1　Categories Used by the U.S. Bureau of the Census to Designate Race, 1790–2000

1790, 1800, 1810

Free Whites	Slaves
All other Free Persons, except	
Indians not taxed	

1820, 1830, 1840

Free Whites	Free Colored
Foreigners, not	Slaves
naturalized	

1850, 1860

White	Mulatto
Black	Black slaves
Mulatto slaves	

1870, 1880, 1890, 1900, 1910, 1920

White	Chinese
Black	Indian4
Mulatto	Quadroon*
Octoroon*	Japanese

1930

White	All other
Negro	Indian
Chinese	Japanese
Filipino	Hindu
Korean	

1940

White	Japanese
Negro	Filipino
Indian	Hindu
Chinese	Korean

1950

White	Japanese
Negro	Chinese
American Indian	Filipino

1960

White	Hawaiian
Negro	Part Hawaiian
American Indian	Aleut
Japanese	Eskimo
Chinese	

1970

White	Chinese
Negro/Black	Filipino

(continued)

Table 2.1   (Continued)

1970

Indian	Hawaiian
Japanese	Korean

1980

White	Indian (American)
Black or Negro	Asian Indian
Japanese	Hawaiian
Chinese	Guamanian
Filipino	Samoan
Korean	Eskimo
Vietnamese	Aleut

1990

White	Samoan
Black or Negro	Guamanian
Indian (American)	Other API
Eskimo	Asian or Pacific Islander
Aleut	Chinese
Vietnamese	Hawaiian
Japanese	Korean
Asian Indian	

2000

White	Native Hawaiian
Black or African American	Guamanian or Chamorro
American Indian	Samoan
or Alaska Native	Other Pacific Islander
Asian Indian	Vietnamese
Chinese	
Filipino	
Japanese	
Korean	
Other Asian	

*Category applied to 1890 census only.
Source: U.S. BUREAU OF THE CENSUS (1999).

Based on the information presented in Table 2.1, one can readily identify at least two themes: (1) There has only been one category reserved for the population classified as white. In other words, there has been no attempt to further subdivide this white population even though the majority of people in the United States are classified as such. (2) At various times in history, the federal government has been preoccupied with identifying subdivisions within one broad racial category. In 1890, for example, there was an unusual emphasis placed on categorizing people according to degree of blackness. Notice that half the categories listed are devoted to this task. In 1930, five subcategories of "all other" were designated for people of Asian heritage, which at that time constituted only less than one-quarter of 1 percent (.002 percent) of the population (Lee 1993).

Sharon Lee (1993) points out that although the classification schemes in the United States have changed in significant ways over time, four dominant themes prevailed:

1. *A pattern of separating the population into two groups: white and nonwhite.*

The federal government's attempt to categorize people into two broad racial groups is the most enduring theme in the history of the United States. As mentioned above, there has been "a chronic concern with populations defined as non-White" (p. 82)[2]. As many as 13 categories have been used to classify the numerically smaller population designated as nonwhite with no corresponding effort to do the same with the majority population classified as white. Although definitions of who belongs to white and nonwhite categories have shifted over time,[3] up until 1980, rules for the Bureau of the Census in classifying persons of mixed biological heritage had never specified the white category as an option. In other words, according to the Bureau of the Census "any mixture of white and nonwhite should be reported according to the nonwhite parent."

2. *A belief in racial purity.*

The belief in the idea of racial purity is reflected in the absence of a multiracial category. Up until the year 2000 in the United States, categories were treated as mutually exclusive—that is, it is not possible for someone to belong to more than one category. The 1990 census asked respondents to "fill in ONE circle" for the race they consider themselves (and persons living within the same household) to be. If the person does not follow directions, census enumerators make every effort to assign people to one racial category even in instances where people give other kinds of responses.

Table 2.1 shows that there have been only a few attempts to identify multiracial populations. In 1890, the U.S. Bureau of the Census included the categories "Mulatto," "Quadroon," and "Octoroon"[4] in an attempt to identify the "partly Black" population and also gave special emphasis for identifying segments of the Native American population.[5] In the subsequent census, the categories "Quadroon" and "Octoroon" were dropped, never to appear again. The 1920 census was the last time the term "Mulatto" appeared. Since 1920, with the exception of an attempt in 1950 to count "special communities"[6] and an attempt in 1960 to identify those who are "part

Hawaiian," the U.S. government has not attempted to identify "partly white" or "mixed-race" populations. Such changes and omissions reflect the general acceptance of the "one-drop rule" in defining who is black or, for that matter, who is not white in the United States. These changes and omissions also reflect a belief in the idea of racial purity—that people can be, or rather are, assigned to one racial category no matter what the facts are with regard to ancestry. In the reading "Historical Origins of the Prohibition of Multiracial Legal Identity in the States and the Nation," Paul Knepper (1995) shows how this belief was incorporated into state and federal laws.

In making the decision to assign children of mixed parentage to the race of one parent, the government asks people to accept the idea that one parent contributes a disproportionate amount of genetic material to the child—so large a genetic contribution that it negates the genetic contribution of the other parent. The long-standing belief in racial purity suggests that other ideas about race were never considered or were dismissed as possibilities. Other ideas include creating new racial categories to accommodate mixed ancestry, dropping the idea of race as a valid way to categorize people (Scales-Trent 1995), and adopting the French and Spanish models.

> During the time Louisiana was a French or a Spanish colony—a time when liaisons between white men and black women were widespread and in some cases nearly formalized—the offspring was treated according to a Latin view of race that left room for a spectrum of colors between black and white. The French had eight terms to calibrate the spectrum—from "mulatre," for the product of a union between a black and a white, to words like "marabout" and "metis," to describe more complicated combinations. The Spanish managed to come with sixty-four terms. Then, in 1803, Louisiana was taken over by the Americans, who imposed what Edmonson refers to as a Germanic view of descent, common to Northern Europe and England: "When it comes to mixing between in-group and out-group, the offspring is flawed, and becomes a member of the out-group" (Trillin 1986:66–67)

3. A pattern of transforming many ethnic groups into one racial group.
"Federal Statistical Directive No. 15," an Office of Management and Budget document issued in 1977, and still in use today with some amendments (see "OMB's Decision: Revisions to Federal Statistical Directive No. 15"), outlines the standards for record-keeping, collection, and presentation of data on race and ethnicity. The amended directive names five official racial categories (up from four in the 1990 census) and two official ethnic categories. The five races are umbrella terms. That is, each is a

supercategory under which aggregates of people who vary according to nationality, ethnicity, language, generation, social class, and time of arrival in the United States are forced into one category (Gimenez 1989). For the 2000 census those supercategories are listed below:

American Indian or *Alaska Native* (any person having origins in any of the original peoples of North America, which by some estimates includes more than 2,000 distinct groups);

Asian (any person having origins in any of the original peoples of the Far East, Southeast Asia, the Indian subcontinent, including, for example, Cambodia, China, India, Japan, Korea, Malaysia, Pakistan, the Philippine Islands, Thailand, and Vietnam;

Black (any person having origins in any of the black racial groups of Africa);

White (any person having origins in any of the original peoples of Europe, North Africa, or the Middle East); and

Native Hawaiian or *Other Pacific Islander* (a person having origins in any of the original peoples of Hawaii, Guam, Samoa, or other Pacific Islands.

It is significant that the definition of the black category, unlike the definitions for the other four categories omits the words "original peoples" and substitutes "black racial groups of Africa."[7] If "original peoples" were included in the definition of black, every person in the United States would have to check this category. In the view of evolutionary biologists all people evolved from a common African ancestor. Moreover, how many people know enough about the original peoples of a geographic area to know whether they are descendants?

Judy Scales-Trent (1995) maintains that we are asking the wrong questions. The questions should not be where did your people originate? "but rather 'What countries did your people travel through on their way here from Africa?' Or maybe 'What was the most recent stop your people made on their trek to this place from Africa? Was it Denmark? Turkey? Bolivia? Vietnam?'" (p. 140).

4. *No sharp distinction between race, ethnicity, and national origin.*

Sociologist Martha E. Gimenez (1989) points out that the race question is poorly constructed in that it offers respondents racial, ethnic, and national origin categories as possible responses. As one example, under the Asian category, the Bureau of the Census lists ten national origin groups as examples. The ten national origin groups include Chinese, Filipino, Korean, Vietnamese, Japanese, and Asian Indian. These examples give the impression that race, country of birth, and/or national origin are one and the same. Consider the confusion these categories might pose for someone of Chinese ancestry who was born outside of China[8] (in Peru or Saudi Arabia, for example), and who then immigrated to the United States. The point of these examples is to show that when a person checks "Chinese," we don't know if it is because he or she is of Chinese ancestry or because he or she was *born in* China (not everyone born in China is of Chinese ancestry). Does the word "Chinese" trigger in respondents associations of biological heritage or associations related to their country of birth or their ancestors' country of birth before their arrival to the United States? It is not clear whether respondents should think about race as something related to their ethnicity, physical appearance, biology, country of birth, or national origin.

This critique of the U.S. system of racial classification tells us that there is no such thing as race. Yet, the belief that physical appearance denotes one's race seems so obvious that it is difficult for us to accept this conclusion. "The central intellectual challenge confronting those who recognize that races are not physical fact [is]: Why do we easily recognize races when walking down the street if there is no morphological basis to race? Why does race seem obvious if it is only a fiction?" (Haney López 1994:19). Not knowing the details of other people's lives, we search a person's physical features looking for the telltale "Negroid," "Caucasian," or "Mongoloid" features and proceed to assign them to racial categories on the basis of their most superficial traits—skin color, hair texture, hair color, cheekbone structure, eye color, eyelids, and so on (Piper 1992). Given the importance of the idea of race as a fixed, objective phenomenon, it is appropriate that we review the evidence discrediting the idea that race is a biological fact. In the reading "Biology and the Social Construction of the 'Race' Concept," by Prince Brown, Jr. we learn why most biologists and social scientists have come to agree that race cannot be a biological fact. Until the 2000 census those assigned the task of racial classification in the United States refused to consider genetic reality.

Ian F. Haney López cautions that even if race has no biological basis, we cannot call it a hallucination. *Biological race* is the illusion; *social race* is not. Haney López (1994) defines race in social terms as "a vast group of people loosely bound together by historically contingent, socially significant elements of their morphology and/or ancestry" (p. 7). In evaluating this definition, we must keep in mind that a race is not created simply because a subset of people share just any characteristic (height, hand size, eye color, or ancestry). It is the social significance ascribed to certain physical features and to certain ancestors, such as Africans, Europeans, or Asians, which define races. As Adrian Piper (1992) states, "What joins me to other blacks, then, and other blacks to another, is not a set of shared physical characteristics, for there is none that all blacks share. Rather, it is the shared experience of being visually or cognitively *identified* as black by a white racist[9] society, and the punitive and damaging effects of that identification" (pp. 30–31). If those physical features we associate with a specific race are *absent* in a person who claims to be of that race, or if those physical features are present in a person who claims *not* to be of that race, we accuse him or her of being "underhanded or manipulative, trying to hide something, pretending to be something [they are not]" (Piper 1992:23).

Even the U.S. Office of Management and Budget (OMB), which sets racial and ethnic classification policy and standard in the United States, acknowledged the social significance of race in Federal Statistical Policy Directive No. 15. The directive states that a person's mixed race or ethnic background was to be reported in a standard category that most closely reflects how others in the community recognize that person (Hunt 1993).

In the reading "The Mean Streets of Social Race," Ian F. Haney López (1994) expands on the social significance of race through the case of Piri Thomas, a Puerto Rican of mixed Indian, African, and European descent, who finds himself transformed into a black person upon moving to the United States with his family. López argues that race is *not* a fixed, inherited attribute, free of human intervention—something parents pass on to their offspring through their genes. Rather, race is a product of at least three overlapping and inseparable factors: chance (physical features and ancestry), context (historical, cultural, and social setting), and choice (everyday decisions).

We consider several other articles that emphasize the role of context in determining someone's race. The first is "'Indian' and 'Black' as Radically Different Types of Categories," by Jack D. Forbes. Forbes explains how the rules of racial classification change depending on whether a person is of African or Native American ancestry. In particular Forbes argues that "'blacks' are always 'blacks' even when mixed with white or American Indian. 'Indians,' however...must remain unchanged in order to be considered 'Indian.'"

Another factor (of many) that determines whether someone is Indian in the United States is federal recognition. The article, "Getting Recognized" is another example of the extreme effects of socially constructed racial classification schemes. As the authors note, no other ethnic group except Native Americans have been forced to "prove" that they are "authentic". Most significantly, Native Americans are not the one's who will make the judgement about their authenticity. Rather, a United States Congress dominated by elected officials classified as White will decide. The information in the article undermines all attempts to see this recognition process as a valid way of making up for past discrimination against Native Americans. If anything this process pits Native American groups against one another and encourages us to suspect the motives of those seeking recognition. First, some states recognize as Native Americans groups not recognized as such by the federal government. Second, some people who have lived as whites conclude that the economic value of being recognized as Native Americans outweighs the social ostracism that they know will follow. Third, the fact that it is relatively easy for many people to self-identify as Native American on one occasion and as White on other occasions makes clear the extensive degree of "race-mixing" that has occurred historically and in the present. Race-mixing, of course, compromises authenticity. Fourth, some people who now seek official recognition because of economic considerations were able to live as Whites without having that status challenged. Fifth, and finally, the article firmly establishes the "White" category as the ideal. To be white is the economically (relatively) secure, psychologically safe, and politically powerful status. All other statuses stigmatize those upon whom they are imposed, carrying a myriad of negative social consequences. These negative connotations are imposed even upon those who qualify for assistance because of past and present discriminations against their category. To fully appreciate the dilemma faced by Native American peoples in their efforts to achieve federal recognition see the Box: "Mandatory Criteria for Federal Acknowledgement That An American Indian Group Exists As An Indian Tribe." The externally imposed conditions cited in the box help to clarify the unique position of Native Americans as an internally colonized minority (see Section 4).

"The Memoirs of Madison Hemings" is significant on several counts in the debates about what constitutes race, how racial status is assigned, what privileges result from the assignment, and what behaviors are possible or not possible after an assignment or an assumption about race is made. Hemings' words take on greater credibility since recent DNA tests have shown that Madison Hemings is Thomas Jefferson's biological son with Sally Hemings (one of Jefferson's slaves and the half sister of Jefferson's wife). Several things about Madison Hemings' memoirs are worth noting. First, he offers a view of "race relations" from the viewpoint of an educated, formerly enslaved person who could recount firsthand his perception and experiences. Second, Hemings calls attention to the unprotected highly vulnerable status of black women who were frequently subjected to sexual alliances with their white owners (wanted or not). Third, the memoirs point to the frequency of interracial sexual liaisons between masters and slave women and the subsequent mating of their offspring with persons of all the different racial categories. Finally, we see the role of chance in determining racial classification as the Hemings' children could easily, pass for white, as several did.

◆•◆

Mandatory Criteria for Federal Acknowledgement
That An American Indian Group Exists As An Indian Tribe

The mandatory criteria are:

(a) The petitioner has been identified as an American Indian entity on a substantially continuous basis since 1900. Evidence that the group's character as an Indian entity has from time to time been denied shall not be considered to be conclusive evidence that this criterion has not been met. Evidence to be relied upon in determining a group's Indian identity may include one or a combination of the following, as well as other evidence of identification by other than the petitioner itself or its members.

  (1) Identification as an Indian entity by Federal authorities.

  (2) Relationships with State governments based on identification of the group as Indian.

  (3) Dealings with a county, parish, or other local government in a relationship based on the group's Indian identity.

  (4) Identification as an Indian entity by anthropologists, historians, and/or other scholars.

  (5) Identification as an Indian entity in newspapers and books.

  (6) Identification as an Indian entity in relationships with Indian tribes or with national, regional, or state Indian organizations.

(b) A predominant portion of the petitioning group comprises a distinct community and has existed as a community from historical times until the present.

  (1) This criterion may be demonstrated by some combination of the following evidence and/or other evidence that the petitioner meets the definition of community set forth in § 83.1:

    (i) Significant rates of marriage within the group, and/or, as may be cultur-

ally required, patterned out-marriages with other Indian populations.

    (ii) Significant social relationships connecting individual members.

    (iii) Significant rates of informal social interaction which exist broadly among the members of a group.

    (iv) A significant degree of shared or cooperative labor or other economic activity among the membership.

    (v) Evidence of strong patterns of discrimination or other social distinctions by nonmembers.

    (vi) Shared sacred or secular ritual activity encompassing most of the group.

    (vii) Cultural patterns shared among a significant portion of the group that are different from those of the non-Indian populations with whom it interacts. These patterns must function as more than a symbolic identification of the group as Indian. They may include, but are not limited to, language, kinship organization, or religious beliefs and practices.

    (viii) The persistence of a named, collective Indian identity continuously over a period of more than 50 years, notwithstanding changes in name.

    (ix) A demonstration of historical political influence under the criterion in § 83.7(c) shall be evidence for demonstrating historical community.

Continued

Mandatory Criteria for Federal Acknowledgement
That An American Indian Group Exists As An Indian Tribe *(Continued)*

(2) A petitioner shall be considered to have provided sufficient evidence of community at a given point in time if evidence is provided to demonstrate any one of the following:

(i) More than 50 percent of the members reside in a geographical area exclusively or almost exclusively composed of members of the group, and the balance of the group maintains consistent interaction with some members of the community;

(ii) At least 50 percent of the marriages in the group are between members of the group;

(iii) At least 50 percent of the group members maintain distinct cultural patterns such as, but not limited to, language, kinship organization, or religious beliefs and practices;

(iv) There are distinct community social institutions encompassing most of the members, such as kinship organizations, formal or informal economic cooperation, or religious organizations; or

(v) The group has met the criterion in § 83.7(c) using evidence described in § 83.7(c)(2).

(c) The petitioner has maintained political influence or authority over its members as an autonomous entity from historical times until the present.

(1) This criterion may be demonstrated by some combination of the evidence listed below and/or by other evidence that the petitioner meets the definition of political influence or authority in § 83.1.

(i) The group is able to mobilize significant numbers of members and significant resources from its members for group purposes.

(ii) Most of the membership considers issues acted upon or actions taken by group leaders or governing bodies to be of importance.

(iii) There is widespread knowledge, communication and involvement in political processes by most of the group's members.

(iv) The group meets the criterion in § 83;.7(b) at more than a minimal level.

(v) There are internal conflicts which show controversy over valued group goals, properties, policies, processes and/or decisions.

(2) A petitioning group shall be considered to have provided sufficient evidence to demonstrate the exercise of political influence or authority at a given point in time by demonstrating that group leaders and/or other mechanisms exist or existed which:

(i) Allocate group resources such as land, residence rights and the like on a consistent basis.

(ii) Settle disputes between members or subgroups by mediation or other means on a regular basis;

(iii) Exert strong influence on the behavior of individual members, such as the establishment or maintenance of norms and the enforcement of sanctions to direct or control behavior;

(iv) Organize or influence economic subsistence activities among the members, including shared or cooperative labor.

(3) A group that has met the requirements in paragraph 83.7(b)(2) at a given point in time shall be considered to have provided sufficient evidence to meet this criterion at that point in time.

(d) A copy of the group's present governing document including its membership criteria. In the absence of a

Continued

Mandatory Criteria for Federal Acknowledgement
That An American Indian Group Exists As An Indian Tribe *(Continued)*

written document, the petitioner must provide a statement describing in full its membership criteria and current governing procedures.

(e) The petitioner's membership consists of individuals who descend from a historical Indian tribe or from historical Indian tribes which combined and functioned as a single autonomous political entity.

(1) Evidence acceptable to the Secretary which can be used for this purpose includes but is not limited to:

(i) Rolls prepared by the Secretary on a descendancy basis for purposes of distributing claims money, providing allotments, or other purposes;

(ii State, Federal, or other official records or evidence identifying present members or ancestors of present members as being descendants of a historical tribe or tribes that combined and functioned as a single autonomous political entity.

(iii) Church, school, and other similar enrollment records identifying present members or ancestors of present members as being descendants of a historical tribe or tribes that combined and functioned as a single autonomous political entity.

(iv) Affadavits of recognition by tribal elders, leaders, or the tribal governing body identifying present members or ancestors of present members as being descendants of a historical tribe or tribes that combined and functioned as a single autonomous political entity.

(v) Other records or evidence identifying present members or ancestors of

Source: U.S. Department of Interior, Bureau of Indian Affairs (1999)

present members as being descendants of a historical tribe or tribes that combined and functioned as a single autonomous political entity.

(2) The petitioner must provide an official membership list, separately certified by the group's governing body, of all known current members of the group. This list must include each member's full name (including maiden name), date of birth, and current residential address. The petitioner must also provide a copy of each available former list of members based on the group's own defined criteria, as well as a statement describing the circumstances surrounding the preparation of the current list and, insofar as possible, the circumstances surrounding the preparation of former lists.

(f) The membership of the petitioning group is composed principally of persons who are not members of any acknowledged North American Indian tribe. However, under certain conditions a petitioning group may be acknowledged even if its membership is composed principally of persons whose names have appeared on rolls of, or who have been otherwise associated with, an acknowledged Indian tribe. The conditions are that the group must establish that it has functioned throughout history until the present as a separate and autonomous Indian tribal entity, that its members do not maintain a bilateral political relationship with the acknowledged tribe, and that its members have provided written confirmation of their membership in the petitioning group.

(g) Neither the petitioner nor its members are the subject of congressional legislation that has expressly terminated or forbidden the Federal relationship.

In "Litigating Whiteness" Ariela Gross uses the trial of Abby Guy (*Guy v. Daniel*) to outline "five ways of talking about race at trial": (1) race as a physical marker, (2) race as documented ancestry, (3) race as reputation, (4) race as association, and (5) race as reception in society. These five ways of talking again point to the fact that race is not a fixed inherited attribute, free of human intervention but a product of three overlapping factors: chance, context, and choice.

In the reading "Invoking Ancestors," Laura L. Lovett (1998) reminds us that while people may be assigned a racial category by the larger society, they have some choice over how they self-identify. Lovett argues that citizens classified as "colored" in the late nineteenth and early twentieth century claimed Indian ancestry (real and/or imagined) as a way to challenge the "very definition of the racial category assigned to them."

We close with two readings highlighting how the system of racial classification, with its emphasis on black-white categories, has shaped the "Asian" experience in the United States. In "Race Relations in Black and White" by Angelo N. Ancheta we learn that those classified as Asian have been at various times also classified as "near-black" and "near-white." In fact, in reaction to the U.S. legal model that limits one's options to black or white, Asian-Americans have sought, at various times, to be classified as white under the law. Ancheta argues that the special preoccupation with the black-white categories has left us with a model of race relations that ignores and marginalizes Asian-American experiences. One such experience that many people classified as Asian face is that, no matter what their ethnic category (Japanese, Chinese, Korean, Vietnamese), they are viewed as one-and-the-same.

A short "fact" sheet that appeared in *TIME* magazine a few weeks after the Japanese attacked Pearl Harbor illustrates this point. The "fact" sheet entitled, "How to Tell Your Friends From the Japs," is a vivid example. The "fact" sheet's focus on physical features alludes to the belief that "races" are set apart by physical/biological characteristics. While the "fact" sheet admits that it is difficult to tell young and middle-aged Chinese and Japanese men apart, the sheet asserts that, nonetheless, it is sometimes possible to do so. The writer claims that facial expression, posture, and body movements are all indicative of one's "race." Notice that, according to the "fact" sheet, Japanese facial expressions reflect arrogance, the Chinese are placid and kindly, and that aristocratic features are considered characteristic of Caucasian/whites.

Notes

[1] There was one exception to this rule: If either parent was Hawaiian, the child was assigned to the Hawaiian category (National Center for Health Statistics 1993).

[2] The experiences of Minty Nelson who is of black, white, and Native American ancestry represents one example of the Census Bureau's persistent efforts to classify respondents into one racial category. In a 1996 interview with a *Seattle Times* staff reporter, Nelson said she checked three racial categories on the census forms. Within a few weeks a Census Bureau representative knocked on her door to ask which racial category was correct.

"All three," Nelson replied.

Can't be all three, the middle-aged woman told her, just one.

Back and forth they went, their patience ebbing. The woman rolled her eyes, sighing in gusts; Nelson spoke in monotones. Twenty minutes later, drained from the experience, Nelson stopped. She told the woman to pick a box, any box, herself. (Strickland 1996)

[3] Before 1980, Asian Indians were considered white. Mexicans were considered a separate race in 1930 but in the 1940 census were classified as white.

[4] A *mulatto* is a person with one white and one Negro parent or any person with mixed Caucasian and Negroid ancestry. A *quadroon* is a person with one-quarter Negro ancestry. An *octoroon* is a person with one white parent and one parent who is one-eighth Negro.

[5] The 1880 and 1890 censuses gave the following instructions for coding responses related to Native American identity.

If this person is of full-blood of this tribe, enter "/." For mixture with another tribe, enter name of latter. For mixture with white, enter "W"; with black, "B"; with mulatto, "Mu."

If this is a white person adopted into the tribe, enter "W A"; if a negro or mulatto, enter "B A."

If this person has been for any time habitually on the reservation, state the time in years or fractions.

If this person wears citizen's dress, state the time in years or fractions since he or she has habitually so worn it.

If other than native language is spoken by this person, enter for English, "E"; Spanish, "S"; French, "F"; &c.

[6] The 1950 census instructed enumerators to "report persons of mixed white, Negro, and Indian ancestry living in certain communities in the Eastern United States in terms of the name by which they are locally known. The communities in question are of long standing and are locally recognized by special names, such as 'Croatan,' 'Jackson White,' 'We-sort,' etc. Persons of mixed Indian and Negro ancestry and mulattos not living in such communities should be returned as 'Negro'" (p. 99).

[7] This scheme also ignores the "original" black indigenous inhabitants of Tasmania, Australia, the Philippines, and the Melanesian Islanders of the Pacific.

[8] An estimated 32.3 million "Chinese" live outside of China in places like Peru (500,000), Saudi Arabia (769,000), and the various states of the former USSR (274,000) (Poston, Mao, and Yu 1994).

[9] By "a white racist society," Piper means the established and customary ways of doing things in society—the unchallenged rules, policies, and day-to-day practices that result in the oppression of people classified as nonwhites. Clearly the system of racial classification is an example of unchallenged rules, policies, and practices.

Historical Origins of the Prohibition of Multiracial Legal Identity in the States and the Nation

PAUL KNEPPER

◇◆◇◆◇

Study Question

Explain the following statement: "The system of racial classification in place today results not from the desire of multiracial persons to identify with [a] particular racial [group], but from statutory and case law developed during more than 200 years of legal history."

The United States recognizes no legal concept of multiraciality. Multiracial offspring are assigned to the race of the mother or father, depending on the state, or to the parent with the lower ascribed social status according to the rule of hypodescent. While some states, such as Hawaii, do not strictly enforce hypodescent, no state permits an adult to change an incorrect racial status recorded at birth.[1]

The federal government prohibits multiracial identity as well. The law requires that all federal agencies (as well as state agencies which must comply with federal record-keeping requirements) place persons in one of four racial categories: "American Indian/Alaskan Native," "Asian/Pacific Islander," "Black," or "White." Reporting agencies must assign "persons who are of mixed racial and/or ethnic origins" to a single category; multiracial persons may neither choose their racial group nor retain their mixed status.[2]

The legal prohibition of multiracial identity is curious, especially since, biologically or ethnologically, no pure races of humankind exist.[3] In fact, many Americans could claim to be of mixed ancestry. The majority of American Indians, virtually all Latinos, and significant portions of African and European Americans are descended from documentable multiracial genealogies.[4]

Why do the state and national governments prohibit persons of multiracial parentage from reporting their true racial identity? Federal reporting guidelines imply that official categories merely reflect prevailing social definitions, namely, that multiracial persons choose to identify with one racial community or the other. This explanation, however, ignores the role of government in imposing the ideology of discrete races. When Hawaii became the fiftieth state, the United States Census Bureau imposed mutually exclusive racial categories on a population that had until then used categories consistent with the islands' multiracial reality. When ten million Americans marked "Other" on the 1990 census schedule rather than check one of the four races supplied, the Census Bureau reclassified them as Hispanic.[5]

Racial categorization is more political than the government's explanation suggests.

Throughout American legal history, the states and the federal government have tended to impose a broad definition of "black" and a correspondingly narrow definition of "white." Both have countered pressures toward blurring racial distinctions with a greater delineation of racial lines.

The ideology of distinct races and legal efforts to support it began during the colonial period. Early lawmakers imposed mutually exclusive categories of race to sustain the distinction between master and slave. The Maryland Colonial Assembly, for example, enacted legislation in 1664 to clarify the position of persons identified as "Negro." The Act Concerning Negroes and Other Slaves stipulated that "all Negroes or other slaves already within the province, and all Negroes or other slaves to be hereafter imported into the province, shall serve *durante vita.*" While Africans in North America had formerly shared with other servants opportunities for eventual freedom, the Maryland law marked them unilaterally for lives of slavery.[6]

Maintenance of the institution of slavery required legal prohibitions of miscegenation and, not surprisingly, of attempts to determine the status of mixed offspring. Virginia enacted the first statute prohibiting all forms of miscegenation in 1661, providing that any white man or woman who married a "negro, mulatto, or Indian...bond or free" was liable to permanent banishment from the colony. The other colonies borrowed language from Virginia and, by the mid-eighteenth century, six of the thirteen colonies had enacted anti-miscegenation statutes.[7]

Colonial statutes classified multiracial persons or "mulattoes" with their black progenitors. In a departure from the normal doctrine of English law that the status of a child was determined by the status of the child's father, Virginia's 1662 law provided that "children got by an Englishman upon a Negro woman shall be bond or free according to the condition of the mother." Had Virginia followed English precedent, thousands of half whites would have been free. A 1664 Maryland law held that any English woman who married a slave would be a slave herself during the life of her husband. The law had the consequence of encouraging exactly the unions that it sought to prevent. It was rewritten in 1681 to provide that, when instigated by the master, "the woman and her issue shall be free."[8]

The policy of classifying mulattoes as black was enforced unevenly by state courts. Prior to the Civil War, several states accorded light-skinned mulattoes who possessed requisite wealth and education "white" legal standing. The Supreme Court of Ohio in 1831 extended to a "quadroon" woman the "privileges of whites" partly because the judges were "unwilling to extend the disabilities of the statute further than its letter requires" and "partly from the difficulty of ... ascertaining the degree of duskiness which renders a person liable to such disabilities." South Carolina's Court of Appeals adopted a similar position in 1846. The court recognized a third class of "negroes, mulattoes, and mestizos" in addition to "freemen" and "slaves." It noted "the constant tendency of this class to assimilate into the white" and found that the "question of the reception of colored persons into the class of citizens must partake more of a political than a legal character and, in the great degree, be decided by public opinion, expressed in the verdict of a jury."[9]

Other state courts insisted on a narrow and exclusive definition of white. In *People v. Hall* (1854), the California Supreme Court defined the words "Black, Mulatto, Indian and White person." The appellant, George W. Hall, a white man, was convicted of murder upon the testimony of Chinese witnesses. He challenged his conviction on the basis of a state statute providing that "[n]o Indian or Negro shall be allowed to testify as a witness in any action in which a white person is a party." The court cited the ethnological thinking of the day to indicate that "Indian" was a generic term for an Asiatic stock of humankind that included Chinese. "We are not disposed to leave this question in any doubt," the court concluded. "The word 'white' has a distinct signification, which *ex vi termini,* excludes black, yellow, and all other colors...The term 'black person' is to be construed as including everyone who is not of white blood."[10]

It was during the Jim Crow era, when white supremacists enacted a bewildering variety of laws requiring separations in public life, that racial categories acquired their modern rigidity. The United States Supreme Court's decision in *Plessy* v. *Ferguson* (1896) provided the legal rationale for discrimination based on race. It also determined the definition of race to be used.[11]

The *Plessy* case arose after a group of multiracial persons in New Orleans organized the Citizen's Committee to Test the Constitutionality of the Separate Car Law. The statute, Louisiana's Railway Accommodations Act (1890), required railway companies to provide "equal but separate accommodations for the white and colored races" and made it a misdemeanor for the conductor to seat members of different races in the same compartment. Homer Plessy, who appeared to be white, agreed to initiate the test. He then attempted to halt his trial with a writ of prohibition and argued that he was "of mixed descent, in the proportion of seven-eighths Caucasian and one-eight African blood," that "the mixture of colored blood was not discernable in him," and that he was entitled to the legal status of white citizens.[12]

Justice Henry Billings Brown, writing for the majority, acknowledged "a difference of opinion" among the states regarding the proportion of colored blood needed to create a colored person. The Court decided that legal definitions of race properly belonged to state governments and sustained the Louisiana law by finding that "the power to assign to a particular coach obviously implies the power to determine to which race the passenger belongs." The Court sympathized with railway employees who were compelled to sort out racial groups based solely on their appearance. "We are not prepared to say," Justice Brown wrote, "that the conductor, in assigning passengers to the coaches according to their race, does not act at his peril."[13]

Confusion over racial identity and the legal challenges that it presented continued throughout the Jim Crow period.[14] Whites, having been mistaken for blacks, brought considerable litigation against railway carriers required to seat them in separate cars. An Arkansas court ruled that a white woman forced to ride fifteen minutes in the "colored" section of a train coach was entitled to recover damages. In fixing the amount of the award, the court noted the absence of noise or misbehavior in the coach; the fact that other whites were riding with the sole black passenger; and the woman's age, degree of refinement, and her fear, nervous shock, and humiliation. In a 1912 Kentucky case, a woman won a $3,750 award for her shock and anguish because a conductor pushed her into a "colored" car and insulted her. White plaintiffs brought suit on similar grounds in Texas and Virginia.[15]

State legislatures responded with more stringent definitions of "whiteness." In constitutions, separate school laws, anti-miscegenation statutes, and other discriminatory legislation, state lawmakers institutionalized the "one-drop rule." Tennessee's segregation statutes defined "person of color" as "[a]ll negroes, mulattoes, mestizos, and their descendants, having any blood of the African race in their veins." Arkansas' prohibition of cohabitation of persons of "the Caucasian and of the negro race" defined "person of negro race" as "any person who has in his or her veins any negro blood whatever." Virginia's anti-miscegenation law limited "white person...only to such person as has no trace whatever of any blood other than Caucasian." Alabama unilaterally declared "negro" to include "mulatto" and mulatto to mean "a person of mixed blood descended on the part of the father or mother from negro ancestors, without reference to or limit of time or number of generations removed."[16]

State courts approved these definitions. The Supreme Court of Mississippi in 1917 decided that "colored," as used in the state constitution to provide for separate schools, included "not only Negroes but persons of mixed blood having any appreciable amount of Negro blood." Louisiana's court of last resort invoked a similar definition in reference to segregated railway cars. In *Lee* v. *New Orleans Great Northern R. Co.* (1910), the court held that the plaintiff, who argued that his children had been unlawfully assigned to the coach for "colored persons," had the burden of proof to establish that his children were "of the white race." The court acknowledged that "persons of color" may have descended from Indian parents, from a white parent, or from mulatto parents, but ruled that under the statute "colored persons" meant "all persons with any appreciable mixture of negro blood."[17]

The United States Supreme Court also approved. In *Rice* v. *Gong Lum* (1927), the Supreme Court of Mississippi prohibited a child of Chinese descent from attending the white school in her district. The court defined "white and colored races" as the "pure white or Caucasian race, on the one hand, and the brown, yellow and black races, on the other." The Supreme Court affirmed the *Rice* case the same year. Quoting the findings of the state supreme court, the Court declared that "the legislature is not compelled to provide separate schools for each of the colored races." Accordingly, the state had the authority to use "colored" in a broad rather than a restrictive sense in its social policy in order to preserve the purity of the white race.[18]

The federal judiciary supported the states' elastic definition of race in its interpretation of federal statutes, particularly immigration law. During the early decades of the twentieth century, Congress enacted immigration laws designed to restrict immigration of "inferior races." The Immigration Act of 1917 excluded immigration from Asia and the Pacific Islands. Immigration laws enacted during the 1920s further restricted immigration from Asia and established quota systems to reduce immigration from Southern and Eastern Europe.[19]

When challenged, federal courts supplied a narrow and exclusive definition of white. "White person" has been construed to exclude Afghans, Arabs, American Indians, Chinese, Filipinos, Hawaiians, Asian Indians, Japanese, and Koreans.[20]

Justice George Sutherland made explicit the federal judiciary's race definition policy in 1922. In *Ozawa* v. *United States,* the Court included persons of Japanese descent in the category of persons defined as "aliens ineligible for citizenship." Takao Ozawa, who had been born in Japan but had lived in California for 20 years, was not a "free white person" within the meaning of naturalization law. Ozawa argued that state courts had defined white as not black and, therefore, that "free white person" did not exclude Japanese. Justice Sutherland rejected Ozawa's contention and argued that state and federal courts had historically limited "white person" to "what is popularly known as the Caucasian race." Sutherland explained Congress's rationale: "The intention was to confer the privilege of citizenship upon that class of persons whom the fathers [framers] knew as white and to deny it to all who could not be so classified... The provision is not that Negroes and Indians shall be *excluded* but it is, in effect, that only free white persons shall be *included*." Although Justice Sutherland admitted that racial distinctions possess "no sharp line of demarcation," he held that Ozawa was "clearly of a race which is not Caucasian."[21]

The Court further narrowed its definition of white in *United States* v. *Bhagat Singh Thind*. In this case, Justice Sutherland found that, although Thind, "of high caste Hindu stock, born in Punjab," had been classified by "scientific authorities" as a member of the "Caucasian or Aryan race," he was not a "white person" entitled to naturalization under the law. The Court subjected Thind to a "racial test" not based on "scientific terminology" but upon "understanding of the common man." "It may be true that the blond Scandinavian and the brown Hindu have a common ancestor in the dim reaches of antiquity," Justice Sutherland wrote, "but the average man knows perfectly well that there are unmistakable and profound differences between them today."[22]

The system of racial classification in place today results not from the desire of multiracial persons to identify with particular racial groups, but from statutory and case law developed over more than two hundred years of legal history. No legal concept of multiraciality emerged in the United States owing to the legacy of slavery. Colonial legislatures attempted to fix discrete categories of black and white. Both the federal and state courts secured these distinctions during the era of "separate but equal." The judiciary has refused to recognize the multiple and overlapping ancestry of the American people, but it has consistently upheld efforts to separate black from white.

It would seem that to acknowledge the reality of multiraciality would expose official racial categories as fluid and elastic, not discrete, mutually exclusive divisions of humankind determined by biology or social interaction. The legal prohibition of multiracial identity developed because no system of oppression based on ancestry can operate in a social environment in which people recognize their multiple heritages.

Notes

[1] Kathy Russell, Midge Wilson, and Ronald Hall, *The Color Complex* (New York: Anchor Books, 1992), pp. 78–79.

[2] U.S. Department of Commerce, Office of Federal Statistical Policy, "Directive No. 15: Race and Ethnic Standards for Federal Statistics and Administrative Reporting," *Statistical Policy Handbook* (Washington, DC: Government Printing Office, 1978). "Hispanic" is represented as an ethnic category; it was created by Congress in 1976 (P.L. 94–311, 90 Stat. 688). Essentially, "Hispanic" subdivides the "white race" into ethnic groups of "Hispanic Origin" and "White, Not of Hispanic Origin."

[3] See, for example, UNESCO's "Statement on the Nature of Race and Race Differences," *The Race Concept* (Westport, CT: Greenwood Press, 1951).

[4] Maria P. P. Root, "Within, Between and Beyond Race," in Maria P. P. Root, ed., *Racially Mixed People in America* (Newbury Park, CA: Sage, 1992), p. 9.

[5] Felicity Barringer, "Ethnic Pride Confounds the Census," *New York Times,* May 9, 1993, p. E3.

[6] Assembly Proceedings (Maryland), 28–29 Liber WH & L (1664).

[7] 2 Laws of Va. 114–15 Hening (1823). *See also* George M. Fredrickson, *White Supremacy* (New York: Oxford University Press, 1981), p. 94.

[8] 2 Laws of Va. 170 Hening (1823). *See also* A. Leon Higginbotham, Jr., *In the Matter of Color* (New York: Oxford University Press, 1978), pp. 43–44; Fredrickson, *White Supremacy,* p. 101.

[9] *Gray* v. *Ohio,* 4 Ohio 353 (1831); *White* v. *Tax Collector of Kershaw District,* 3 S.C. 136 (1846). *See also Jeffries* v. *Ankeny,* 11 Ohio 372 (1842). Biracial persons were socially accepted as white in certain parts of the South as well. Virginia R. Dominquez, *White by Social Definition* (New Brunswick, NJ: Rutgers University Press, 1986).

[10] *People* v. *Hall,* 4 Cal. 399, 404 (1854). The early "one-drop rule,"—any known African ancestry and one is classified as black—is discussed in F. James Davis, *Who is Black?* (University Park: Pennsylvania State University Press, 1991), pp. 35, 49.

[11] The classic account of the Jim Crow period is C. Vann Woodward, *The Strange Career of Jim Crow* (New York: Oxford University Press, 1972).

[12] *Plessy* v. *Ferguson,* 163 U.S. 537, 538 (1896).

[13] *Id.* at 548–549.

[14] Derrick Bell, *Race, Racism and American Law* (Boston: Little, Brown, 1980), p. 84, n.3. Bell notes this confusion, and he cites the cases which follow.

[15] *Chicago R.I.&P.* v. *Allison,* 120 Ark. 54, 178 S.W. 401 (1915); *Louisville and N.R.R. Co.* v. *Richtel,* 148 Ky. 701, 147 S.W. 411 (1912); *Missouri K.&T. Ry* v. *Ball,* 25 Tex. Civ. App. 500, 61 S.W. 327 (1901); *Norfolk and W. Ry.* v. *Stone,* 111 Va. 730, 69 S.E. 927 (1911).

[16] 8396 Tennessee Code 417a1 (1942); Acts [Arkansas] No. 320, s. 3 (1911); Virginia Code 5099A (1924); Code of Alabama, Title 1, s. 2 (1927). Portions of these are reprinted in Pauli Murray, *States' Laws on Race and Color* (Cincinnati, OH: Women's Division of Christian Service, 1951).

[17] *Moreau* v. *Grandich,* 114 Miss. 560, 75 So. 434 (1917); *Lee* v. *New Orleans Great Northern R. Co.,* 125 La. 236, 51 So. 182 (1910). See also *State* v. *Treadway,* 126 La. 300, 52 So. 500 (1910).

[18] *Rice* v. *Gong Lum,* 139 Miss. 760, 104 So. 105 (1927); *Gong Lum* v. *Rice,* 275 U.S. 73 (1927).

[19] Immigration Act of 1917, 39 Stat. 874, 8 U.S.C. 173; Immigration Act of 1924, 43 Stat. 153, 8 U.S.C. 201.

[20] 613 C.J.S. s. 94 White (1989).

[21] *Ozawa* v. *United States,* 260 U.S. 178 (1922).

[22] *United States* v. *Bhagat Singh Thind,* 261 U.S. 404 (1922).

Federal Statistical Directive No. 15: Race and Ethnic Standards for Federal Statistics and Administrative Reporting

(as adopted on May 12, 1977)

THE U.S. OFFICE OF MANAGEMENT AND BUDGET

Study Questions

1. What is the minimum number of acceptable (a) race categories, (b) ethnic categories, (c) combined race and ethnic categories specified in Directive No. 15?
2. Does the Directive No.15 limit the collection of race and ethnic data to the categories identified in that document?
3. What kinds of reporting tasks require that Directive No. 15 be followed?

This Directive provides standard classifications for recordkeeping, collection, and presentation of data on race and ethnicity in Federal program administrative reporting and statistical activities. These classifications should not be interpreted as being scientific or anthropological in nature, nor should they be viewed as determinants of eligibility for participation in any Federal program. They have been developed in response to needs expressed by both the executive branch and the Congress to provide for the collection and use of compatible, nonduplicated, exchangeable racial and ethnic data by Federal agencies.

1. Definitions

The basic racial and ethnic categories for Federal statistics and program administrative reporting are defined as follows:

a. American Indian or Alaskan Native. A person having origins in any of the original peoples of North America, and who maintains cultural identification through tribal affiliations or community recognition.

b. Asian or Pacific Islander. A person having origins in any of the original peoples of the Far East, Southeast Asia, the Indian subcontinent, or the Pacific Islands. This area includes, for example, China, India, Japan, Korea, the Philippine Islands, and Samoa.

c Black. A person having origins in any of the black racial groups of Africa.

d. Hispanic. A person of Mexican, Puerto Rican, Cuban, Central or South American, or other Spanish culture or origin, regardless of race.

e. White. A person having origins in any of the original peoples of Europe, North Africa, or the Middle East.

2. Utilization for Recordkeeping and Reporting

To provide flexibility, it is preferable to collect data on race and ethnicity separately. If separate race and ethnic categories are used, the minimum designations are:

a. Race:
   American Indian or Alaskan Native
   Asian or Pacific Islander
   Black
   White
b. Ethnicity:
   Hispanic origin
   Not of Hispanic origin

When race and ethnicity are collected separately, the number of White and Black persons who are Hispanic must be identifiable, and capable of being reported in that category.

If a combined format is used to collect racial and ethnic data, the minimum acceptable categories are:
   American Indian or Alaskan Native
   Asian or Pacific Islander
   Black, not of Hispanic origin
   Hispanic
   White, not of Hispanic origin

The category which most closely reflects the individual's recognition in his community should be used for purposes of reporting on persons who are of mixed racial and/or ethnic origins.

In no case should the provisions of this Directive be construed to limit the collection of data to the categories described above. However, any reporting required which uses more detail shall be organized in such a way that the additional categories can be aggregated into these basic racial/ethnic categories. The minimum standard collection categories shall be utilized for reporting as follows:

a. Civil rights compliance reporting. The categories specified above will be used by all agencies in either the separate or combined format for civil rights compliance reporting and equal employment reporting for both the public and private sectors and for all levels of government. Any variation requiring less detailed data or data which cannot be aggregated into the basic categories will have to be specifically approved by the Office of Management and Budget (OMB) for ex-

ecutive agencies. More detailed reporting which can be aggregated to the basic categories may be used at the agencies' discretion.

b. General program administrative and grant reporting. Whenever an agency subject to this Directive issues new or revised administrative reporting or recordkeeping requirements which include racial or ethnic data, the agency will use the race/ethnic categories described above. A variance can be specifically requested from OMB, but such a variance will be granted only if the agency can demonstrate that it is not reasonable for the primary reporter to determine the racial or ethnic background in terms of the specified categories, and that such determination is not critical to the administration of the program in question, or if the specific program is directed to only one or a limited number of race/ethnic groups, e.g., Indian tribal activities.

c. Statistical reporting. The categories described in this Directive will be used at a minimum for federally sponsored statistical data collection where race and/or ethnicity is required, except when the collection involves a sample of such size that the data on the smaller categories would be unreliable, or when the collection effort focuses on a specific racial or ethnic group. A repetitive survey shall be deemed to have an adequate sample size if the racial and ethnic data can be reliably aggregated on a biennial basis. Any other variation will have to be specifically authorized by OMB through the reports clearance process. In those cases where the data collection is not subject to the reports clearance process, a direct request for a variance should be made to OMB.

3. **Effective Date**
   The provisions of this Directive are effective immediately for all new and revised recordkeeping or reporting requirements containing racial and/or ethnic informa-

tion. All existing recordkeeping or reporting requirements shall be made consistent with this Directive at the time they are submitted for extension, or not later than January 1, 1980.

4. **Presentation of Race/Ethnic Data**

Displays of racial and ethnic compliance and statistical data will use the category designations listed above. The designation *"non-white"* is not acceptable for use in the presentation of Federal Government data. It is not to be used in any publication of compliance or statistical data or in the text of any compliance or statistical report.

In cases where the above designations are considered inappropriate for presentation of statistical data on particular programs or for particular regional areas, the sponsoring agency may use:

(1) The designations "Black and Other Races" or "All Other Races," as collective descriptions of minority races when the most summary distinction between the majority and minority races is appropriate;

(2) The designations "White," "Black," and "All Other Races" when the distinction among the majority race, the principal minority race, and other races is appropriate; or

(3) The designation of a particular minority race or races, and the inclusion of "Whites" with "All Other Races," if such a collective description is appropriate.

In displaying detailed information which represents a combination of race and ethnicity, the description of the data being displayed must clearly indicate that both bases of classification are being used.

When the primary focus of a statistical report is on two or more specific identifiable groups in the population, one or more of which is racial or ethnic, it is acceptable to display data for each of the particular groups separately and to describe data relating to the remainder of the population by an appropriate collective description.

OMB's Decisions: Revisions to Federal Statistical Directive No. 15

THE U.S. OFFICE OF MANAGEMENT AND BUDGET

◇◆◈◆◇

This section of the Notice provides information on the decisions taken by OMB on the recommendations that were proposed by the Interagency Committee. The Committee's recommendations addressed options for reporting by respondents, formats of questions, and several aspects of specific categories, including possible additions, revised terminology, and changes in definitions. In reviewing OMB's decisions on the recommendations for collecting data on race and ethnicity, it is useful to remember that these decisions:

- retain the concept that the standards provide a minimum set of categories for data on race and ethnicity;
- permit the collection of more detailed information on population groups provided that any additional categories can be aggregated into the minimum standard set of categories;
- underscore that self-identification is the preferred means of obtaining information about an individual's race and ethnicity, except in instances where observer identification is more practical (e.g., completing a death certificate);
- do not identify or designate certain population groups as "minority groups";
- continue the policy that the categories are not to be used for determining the eligibility of population groups for participation in any Federal programs;
- do not establish criteria or qualifications (such as blood quantum levels)

that are to be used in determining a particular individual's racial or ethnic classification; and
- do not tell an individual who he or she is, or specify how an individual should classify himself or herself.

In arriving at its decisions, OMB took into account not only the public comment on the recommendations published in the **Federal Register** on July 9, 1997, but also the considerable amount of information provided during the four years of this review process, including public comments gathered from hearings and responses to two earlier OMB Notices (on June 9, 1994, and August 28, 1995). The OMB decisions benefited greatly from the participation of the public that served as a constant reminder that there are real people represented by the data on race and ethnicity and that this is for many a deeply personal issue. In addition, the OMB decisions benefited from the results of the research and testing on how individuals identify themselves that was undertaken as part of this review process. This research, including several national tests of alternative approaches to collecting data on race and ethnicity, was developed and conducted by the professional statisticians and analysts at several Federal agencies. They are to be commended for their perseverance, dedication, and professional commitment to this challenging project.

OMB also considered in reaching its decisions the extent to which the recommendations were consistent with the set of principles (see Section B of the Supplementary Information) developed by the Interagency Committee to guide the review of this sensitive and substantively complex issue. OMB believes that the Interagency Committee's recommendations took into account the principles and achieved a reasonable balance with respect to statistical issues, data needs, social concerns, and the personal dimensions of racial and ethnic identification. OMB also finds that the Committee's recommendations are consistent with the principal objective of the review, which is to enhance the accuracy of the demographic information collected by the Federal Government by having categories for data on race and ethnicity that will enable the capture of information about the increasing diversity of our Nation's population while at the same time respecting each individual's dignity.

As indicated in detail below, OMB accepts the Interagency Committee's recommendations concerning reporting more than one race, including the recommendation that there be no category called "multiracial," the formats and sequencing of the questions on race and Hispanic origin, and most of the changes to terminology.

OMB does not accept the Interagency Committee's recommendations concerning the classification of data on the Native Hawaiian population and the terminology for Hispanics, and it has instead decided to make the changes that follow.

Native Hawaiian classification.—OMB does not accept the recommendation concerning the continued classification of Hawaiians in the Asian or Pacific Islander category. **Instead, OMB has decided to break apart the Asian or Pacific Islander category into two categories—one called "Asian" and the other called "Native Hawaiian or Other Pacific Islander."** As a result, there will be five categories in the minimum set for data on race.

The "Native Hawaiian or Other Pacific Islander" category will be defined as "A person having origins in any of the original peoples of Hawaii, Guam, Samoa, or other Pacific Islands." (The term "Native Hawaiian" does not include individuals who are native to the State of Hawaii by virtue of being born there.) In addition to Native Hawaiians, Guamanians, and Samoans, this category would include the following Pacific Islander groups reported in the 1990 census: Carolinian, Fijian, Kosraean, Melanesian, Micronesian, Northern Mariana Islander, Palauan, Papua New Guinean, Ponapean (Pohnpelan), Polynesian, Solomon Islander, Tahitian, Tarawa Islander, Tokelauan, Tongan, Trukese (Chuukese), and Yapese.

The "Asian" category will be defined as "A person having origins in any of the original peoples of the Far East, Southeast Asia, or the Indian subcontinent including, for example, Cambodia, China, India, Japan, Korea, Malaysia, Pakistan, the Philippine Islands, Thailand, and Vietnam."

The Native Hawaiians presented compelling arguments that the standards must facilitate the production of data to describe their social and economic situation and to monitor discrimination against Native Hawaiians in housing, education, employment, and other areas. Under the current standards for data on race and ethnicity, Native Hawaiians comprise about 3 percent of the Asian and Pacific Islander population. By creating separate categories, the data on the Native Hawaiians and other Pacific Islander groups will no longer be overwhelmed by the aggregate data of the much larger Asian groups. Native Hawaiians will comprise about 60 percent of the new category.

The Asian, Native Hawaiian, and Pacific Islander population groups are well defined; moreover, there has been experience with reporting in separate categories for the Native Hawaiian and Pacific Islander population groups. The 1990 census included "Hawaiian," "Samoan," and "Guamanian" as response categories to the race question. In addition, two of the major tests conducted as part of the current review (the NCS and the RAETT) used "Hawaiian" and/or "Native Hawaiian," "Samoan," "Guamanian," and "Guamanian or Chamorro" as response options to the race question. These factors facilitate breaking apart the current category.

Terminology for Hispanics.—OMB does not accept the recommendation to retain the single term "Hispanic." **Instead, OMB has decided that the term should be "Hispanic or Latino."** Because regional usage of the terms differs—Hispanic is commonly used in the eastern portion of the United States, whereas Latino is commonly used in the western portion—this change may contribute to improved response rates. The OMB decisions on the Interagency Committee's specific recommendations are presented below:

(1) OMB accepts the following recommendations concerning reporting more than one race: When self-identification is used, a method for reporting more than one race should be adopted. The method for respondents to report more than one race should take the form of multiple responses to a single question and not a "multiracial" category. When a list of races is provided to respondents, the list should not contain a "multiracial" category. Based on research conducted so far, two recommended forms for the instruction accompanying the multiple response question are "Mark one or more..." and "Select one or more...." If the criteria for data quality and confidentiality are met, provision should be made to report, at a minimum, the number of individuals identifying with more than one race. Data producers are encouraged to provide greater detail about the distribution of multiple responses.

The new standards will be used in the decennial census, and other data producers should conform as soon as possible, but not later than January 1, 2003.

(2) OMB accepts the following recommendations concerning a combined race and Hispanic ethnicity question: When self-identification is used, the two question format should be used, with the race question allowing the reporting of more than one race. When self-identification is not feasible or appropriate, a combined question can be used and should include a separate Hispanic category co-equal with the other categories. When the combined question is used, an attempt should be made, when appropriate, to record ethnicity and race or multiple races, but the option to indicate only one category is acceptable.

(3) OMB accepts the following recommendations concerning the retention of both reporting formats: The two question format should be used in all cases involving self-identification. The current combined question format should be changed and replaced with a new format which includes a co-equal Hispanic category for use, if necessary, in observer identification.

(4) OMB accepts the following recommendation concerning the ordering of the Hispanic origin and race questions: When the two question format is used, the Hispanic origin question should precede the race question.

(5) OMB accepts the following recommendation concerning adding Cape Verdean as an ethnic category: A Cape Verdean ethnic category should not be added to the minimum data collection standards.

(6) OMB accepts the following recommendation concerning the addition of an Arab or Middle Eastern ethnic category: An Arab or Middle Eastern ethnic category should not be added to the minimum data standards.

(7) OMB interprets the recommendation not to add any other categories to mean the expansion of the minimum set to include new population groups. The OMB decision to break apart the "Asian or Pacific Islander" category does not create a category for a new population group.

(8) OMB accepts the following recommendation concerning changing the term "American Indian" to "Native American": The term American Indian should not be changed to Native American.

(9) OMB accepts the following recommendation concerning changing the term "Hawaiian" to "Native Hawaiian": The term "Hawaiian" should be changed to "Native Hawaiian."

(10) OMB does not accept the recommendation concerning the continued classification of Native Hawaiians in the Asian or Pacific Islander category. OMB has decided to break apart the Asian or Pacific Islander category into two categories— one called "Asian" and the other called "Native Hawaiian or Other Pacific Islander." As a result, there are five categories in the minimum set for data on race. The "Native Hawaiian or Other Pacific Islander" category is defined as "A person having origins in any of the original peoples of Hawaii, Guam, Samoa, or other Pacific Islands." The "Asian" cate-

gory is defined as "A person having origins in any of the original peoples of the Far East, Southeast Asia, or the Indian subcontinent including, for example, Cambodia, China, India, Japan, Korea, Malaysia, Pakistan, the Philippine Islands, Thailand, and Vietnam."

(11) OMB accepts the following recommendations concerning the use of "Alaska Native" instead of "Eskimo" and "Aleut": "Alaska Native" should replace the term "Alaskan Native." Alaska Native should be used instead of Eskimo and Aleut. The Alaska Native response option should be accompanied by a request for tribal affiliation when possible.

(12) OMB accepts the following recommendations concerning the classification of Central and South American Indians:

Central and South American Indians should be classified as American Indian. The definition of the "American Indian or Alaska Native" category should be modified to include the original peoples from Central and South America. In addition, OMB has decided to make the definition for the American Indian or Alaska Native category more consistent with the definitions of the other categories.

(13) OMB accepts the following recommendations concerning the term or terms to be used for the name of the Black category:

The name of the Black category should be changed to "Black or African American." The category definition should remain unchanged.

Additional terms, such as Haitian or Negro, can be used if desired.

(14) OMB decided to modify the recommendations concerning the term or

terms to be used for Hispanic: The term used should be "Hispanic or Latino." The definition of the category should remain unchanged. In addition, the term "Spanish Origin," can be used if desired.

Accordingly, the Office of Management and Budget adopts and issues the revised minimum standards for Federal data on race and ethnicity for major population groups in the United States which are set forth at the end of this Notice.

Topics for further research

There are two areas where OMB accepts the Interagency Committee's recommendations but believes that further research is needed: (1) multiple responses to the Hispanic origin question and (2) an ethnic category for Arabs/Middle Easterners.

Multiple Responses to the Hispanic Origin Question.—The Interagency Committee recommended that respondents to Federal data collections should be permitted to report more than one race. During the most recent public comment process, a few comments suggested that the concept of "marking more than one box" should be extended to the Hispanic origin question. Respondents are now asked to indicate if they are "of Hispanic origin" or "not of Hispanic origin." Allowing individuals to select more than one response to the ethnicity question would provide the opportunity to indicate ethnic heritage that is both Hispanic and non-Hispanic.

The term "Hispanic" refers to persons who trace their origin or descent to Mexico, Puerto Rico, Cuba, Central and South America, and other Spanish cultures. While there has been considerable public concern about the need to review Directive No. 15 with respect to classifying individuals of mixed racial heritage, there has been little comment on reporting both an Hispanic and a non-Hispanic origin. On many Federal forms, Hispanics can also express a racial identity on a separate race question. In the decennial census, individuals who consider themselves part Hispanic can also indicate additional heritages in the ancestry question.

On one hand, it can be argued that allowing individuals to mark both categories in the Hispanic origin question would parallel the instruction "to mark (or select) one or more" racial categories. Individuals would not have to choose between their parents' ethnic heritages, and movement toward an increasingly diverse society would be recognized.

On the other hand, because the matter of multiple responses to the Hispanic ethnicity question was not raised in the early phases of the public comment process, no explicit provisions were made for testing this approach in the research conducted to inform the review of Directive No. 15. While a considerable amount of research was focused on how to improve the response rate to the Hispanic origin question, it is unclear whether and to what extent explicitly permitting multiple responses to the Hispanic origin question would affect nonresponse to the race question or hamper obtaining more detailed data on Hispanic population groups.

Information on the possible impact of any changes on the quality of the data has been an essential element of the review. While the effects of changes in the Hispanic origin question are unknown, they could conceivably be substantial. Thus, OMB has decided not to include a provision in the standards that would explicitly permit respondents to select both "Hispanic origin" and "Not of Hispanic Origin" options. OMB believes that this is an item for future research. In the meantime, the ancestry question on the decennial census long form does provide respondents who consider themselves part Hispanic to write in additional heritages.

Research on an Arab/Middle Easterner category.—During the public comment process, OMB received a number of requests to add an ethnic category for Arabs/Middle Easterners so that data could be obtained that could be useful in monitoring discrimination. The public comment process indicated, however, that there was no agreement on a definition for this category. The combined race, Hispanic origin, and ancestry question in the RAETT, which was designed to address requests that were received from groups for establishing separate categories, did not provide a solution. While OMB accepted the Interagency's Committee recommendation not to create a new category for this population group, OMB believes that further research should be done to determine the best way to improve data on this population group. Meanwhile, the write-ins to the ancestry question on the decennial census long form will continue to provide information on the number of individuals who identify their heritage as Arab or Middle Easterner.

Biology and the Social Construction of the "Race" Concept

PRINCE BROWN, JR.

Study Questions
1. From a biological point of view, why is it impossible to classify people by race?
2. What are the shortcomings associated with using skin color, inherited diseases, or blood type as criterion for categorizing people into clear-cut racial categories?

Most people assume, with little or no thought, that when observing various human physical traits they are seeing different types of human beings, fundamentally different in their genetic makeup. They further assume that it is possible to take each human being and put that person in one of the several allegedly distinct categories that have been presented to them as different "races." In the United States, it has long been maintained that everyone could be classified using only three categories. A brief review of the history of the biological effort to explain variation in human characteristics will help us to understand why it is not possible to classify people by "race" (Diamond 1994; DOA 1986:238; Gould 1994; Livingstone 1962:279).

Current scientific investigations using genetic research and fossilized remains indicate that all modern humans evolved in Africa and migrated from there to the rest of the world (Stringer & Andrews 1988). Modern humans (*Homo sapiens*) include all of the people in the world today. All humans, regardless of their physical features readily exchange genes when they produce off-spring. The variations in human traits (phenotype), evident when we look at each other, are anatomical and physiological adaptations which help humans to increase their chances of survival and extend longevity in a particular environment.

Genetic elasticity is the tendency of human beings to exhibit a wide range of physical traits which they readily exchange with each other when they mate and produce children. No particular set of traits is limited to any one group or "race." And all groups are able to produce children with members of any other group. For example, while grey eyes are associated with a light complexion, they do occur among dark-complexioned people—as do brown eyes and black eyes. In the same vein, curly hair is associated with dark skin, but we all know light-complexioned people who also have curly hair. These common-sense illustrations help us to understand that no particular set of traits cluster together to form one group or "race."

Some people share similar traits (homogeneity) because they live in social isolation, which limits the availability of potential mates. Another reason why some people share similar traits is because the social rules (customs, laws) of their society (ideas about beauty, laws against interracial marriage[1]) prohibit them from mating with people whose features are different (Bell 1992:71–74). Of course we know that many people ignore the rules. When they do, we label their children "mixed-race" (Root 1992; Zack 1995).

Other words we use to label such children are Mulatto (one black and one white parent), Quadroon (one black grandparent and three white grandparents), and Octoroon (one black great-grandparent and seven white great-grandparents). The features of children born from these relationships will not mirror those of any one parent, grandparent, or great-grandparent but will appear as a blend of all of them (genetic elasticity). In biology we call the results of this blending and merging *heterogeneity*. It results from population contact and the preference[2] of people to mate with each other regardless of what rules are in place in society.

If human beings could be grouped into absolute "racial" categories, the differences should be evident at the most basic biological level—that of chromosomes or genes. What would we see if humans could be grouped into absolute "racial" categories? We would have groups of people unable to have children with any other groups. Each member of any one of the groups would be an exact duplicate of all of the other members of that same group. That is, there would not be any differences between people in the same group. Instead, what we find is that 75 percent of genes are identical (monomorphic) in all individuals regardless of the population to which they are socially assigned. The remaining 25 percent are genes which appear in more than one form

(polymorphic) (Lewontin et al. 1984). A single gene, for example, produces blood. But this gene can take more than one form, as is evident in the four (A, B, O, AB) different types of blood.

It has been shown that "…there is no gene known that is 100 percent of one form in one race and 100 percent of a different form in some other race" (Lewontin et al. 1984:122). That is, there is no gene for "race." Differences between people assigned to the same social group/"race" may be greater (eye color among whites) than those between individuals in two different groups (Nei & Roychoudhury 1972). In other words, if the genetic traits (blood type, inherited diseases) of a person are determined from a blood analysis, a geneticist would still not be able to say what that person's actual physical features (phenotype) will be. Likewise, when observing physical features, it is not always possible to predict genetic composition. For example, being able to see the physical features of a person does not allow one to say specifically what a genetic analysis of his blood will tell us. There is no known direct relationship between genetic makeup and physical features. This explains how two humans can produce a child with traits not visible in either of the parents.

Three sets of traits have been used to try to separate humans into absolute categories: (1) internal physiological features (metabolic rate, genetic diseases); (2) blood type; and (3) anatomical features (skin color, hair texture) (Marger 1991:20). None of these, however, can be shown to clearly distinguish any one group of people from any other.

Inherited diseases result from mutations[3] and may occur with a higher frequency in some groups than in others—but is not exclusive to those groups. This can be demonstrated by looking at two such mutations: lactase deficiency (inability to break down lactose) and sickle-cell trait and anemia (anti-malaria). Lactase deficiency may be present in up to 100 percent of South American Indians and West Africans, in 32 percent of people from England, and in 90 and 86 percent of Japanese and Greeks, respectively. The sickle-cell trait[4] is present in up to 16 percent of South American Indians, in up to 34 percent of West Africans, and in up to 32 percent of Greeks, but it is absent in the English and Japanese (Stein & Rowe 1989:186). If this criterion were used to assign "racial" status, some Greeks, some West Africans, and a smaller proportion of South American Indians would be placed in the same category. The refrain, again, is that inherited diseases do not enable the prediction of assigned "racial" status except within limits. Nor does assigned "racial" status enable us to predict the presence of inherited diseases.[5]

Lewontin et al. (1984) have reviewed the research literature relative to the feasibility of categorizing humans into absolute groups by blood type. If we know a person's blood type (A, B, O, or AB), we could not predict what "racial" group that person was assigned. Conversely, we could not predict blood type from observed physical features. While the proportion of a particular blood type differs for various groups…"no population was [is] exclusive of one blood type" (Lewontin et al. 1984:120). And of course, blood transfusions between alleged different "races" occur in hospitals all over the world every day.

The third set of traits, anatomical features, likewise, cannot be used to assign individuals to an alleged "racial" category. A range of colors, for example, can be found in all three socially constructed "racial" categories. East Indians (light tan to very dark),

Europeans (very pale to amber), and aboriginal Australians (tan to very dark) are all assigned to the "Caucasian/white" category. Straight hair is a characteristic of all three groups, as are grey, black, and brown eyes. Of course, possessing any of these traits does not prevent having children with people who do not possess them. Therefore, the term "race mixing" makes no sense—since distinct biological categories do not exist to begin with. Before we go further, it might help us to understand the wide range of human traits by reviewing some information about why some specific traits evolved.

Anatomical traits such as skin color, height, and lung capacity are all features which help individuals and groups to master their environment. Physical diversity (skin color, height) insures the success of humans by making it possible for us to exist in all known environmental zones (high and low elevation, cold and hot zones, etc.). Large lungs at higher elevations enable greater oxygen intake and more sustained physical activity. One of the features most often regarded as indicative of "race," skin color, has a complex evolutionary history (Wills 1994) and serves several different functions. Dark skin protects people from cancer by screening out the ultraviolet rays of the sun. It is logical, therefore, that people living along the Equator would be so complexioned.

What might appear to be distinctive "racial" traits are, in most cases, explainable by science. However, to fully appreciate the complexity of human morphology, it should be noted that this rule does not explain the case of South American Natives living on the Equator who are light complexioned. Geneticists point out that multiple genetic, as well as, environmental and cultural factors affect skin color (Stein & Rowe 1989:168).

This brief review of the biological bases for classification schemes indicates that "The popular division of the human population into three major racial groupings—Caucasoid, Mongoloid, and Negroid—is thus imprecise and largely arbitrary" (Marger 1991:21). "Racial" classification schemes cause people to be overly impressed with what can be seen (physical features) and to simplify that which is invisible (genes) and not well understood. Scientifically and socially, the slightest hint of a specific physical trait (e.g., colored equals Black/Negroid (Trillin 1986) is used to assign a "racial" label. If we construct a table of "races" using the three "arbitrary" categories traditionally employed by anthropologists, Caucasoid, Mongoloid, and Negroid, it can be shown that in reality "the biological category of 'race' is virtually meaningless" (Wali 1992:7).

Each cell in Table 1 represents a hypothetical person that almost everyone knows. The people *not* on the left-to-right diagonal are called "mixed race" or "interracial" (amalgamation). This simple table is much more representative of reality than the classification schemes people are socialized to carry around in their heads. It is at the same time deceptive. It would appear on first glance that there are nine different combinations of persons represented. A second look reveals six distinct combinations; NM and MN, MC and CM, and CN and NC are really the same combinations. MM, CC, and NN would appear to represent "pure races." What the table shows, however, is that each can produce offspring with all of the other persons as well each other. Thus what are assumed to be "pure races" do not function genetically as mutually exclusive categories. As the review of anatomical, blood composition, and inherited diseases data indicated, individuals are more alike than they are different. If every "race" can reproduce any other "race"—then, what is "race"?

Now imagine what possibilities would exist when offspring of those in Table 1 pair off with the partners shown in Table 2 and produce offspring. Table 2 illustrates what the results would look like. What appears to make perfect biological sense is that every human being is potentially the source of any trait that characterizes any other human being.

If the 81 persons from Table 2 are used to make yet another table, the number of "races" could expand exponentially. We normally do not think in terms of multiple biological ancestries. But this is more so the rule than the exception. In the United States alone there are millions of people who share European, African, and Native American ancestries (Forbes 1993; Trillin 1986).

The method for determining "race" has changed constantly (Norwood & Klein 1989) and, of course, no objective resolution is possible (Wright 1994). Both "race"

Table 1 Genetic Elasticity/Biological Amalgamation

		FEMALE RACE CLASSIFICATION		
		M	C	N
MALE RACE CLASSIFICATION	M	MM	MC	MN
	C	CM	CC	CN
	N	NM	NC	NN

M=Mongoloid, C=Caucasoid, N=Negroid.

Table 2   Genetic Elasticity/Biological Amalgamation

		PARTNERS								
		MM	MC	MN	CM	CC	CN	NM	NC	NN
OFFSPRING FROM TABLE 1	MM	MMMM	MMMC	MMMN	MMCM	MMCC	MMCN	MMNM	MMNC	MMNN
	MC	MCMM	MCMC	MCMN	MCCM	MCCC	MCCN	MCNM	MCNC	MCNN
	MN	MNMM	MNMC	MNMN	MNCM	MNCC	MCCN	MNNM	MNNC	MNNN
	CM	CMMM	CMMC	CMMN	CMCM	CMCC	CMCN	CMNM	CMNC	CMNN
	CC	CCMM	CCMC	CCMN	CCCM	CCCC	CCCN	CCNM	CCNC	CCNN
	CN	CNMM	CNMC	CNMN	CNCM	CNCC	CNCN	CNNM	CNNC	CNNN
	NM	NMMM	NMMC	NMMN	NMCM	NMCC	NMCN	CMCM	CMNC	CMNN
	NC	NCMM	NCMC	NCMN	NCCM	NCCC	NCCN	NCNM	NCNC	NCNN
	NN	NNMM	NNMC	NNMN	NNCM	NNCC	NNCN	NNNM	NNNC	NNNN

and color have been used as criterion to type the American population. Table 2 makes clear why the U.S. Bureau of the Census has avoided trying to define so-called "multiracial" people[6] (Wright 1994). And, why, in Brazil more than 64 "racial" categories are employed (Marger 1991). This is the sense in which "race" is a social/legal construction. It is a function of language, rather than a use of language to describe an objective reality.

First, given the facts cited in this essay, definitions of "race," such as that offered by Joseph Healy: "Biologically, a race is an isolated, inbreeding population with a distinctive genetic heritage" (1995:22), are simply another failed attempt at biological classification. Few populations in the world, any more, are truly isolated. Second, in the United States, individuals who are socially assigned to one alleged "racial" group intermingle, mate with, and have children with persons who are assigned to another group every day.

Finally, the critical point here biologically is that there is not a single known case of an isolated group not being able produce children with other people when they did come into contact. And, in fact, in every known case this is exactly what has happened. All human beings share a single gene pool with no known breeding restrictions under normal circumstances (Healy 1995, Montagu 1972). In fact, in Mexico and Brazil, where interbreeding has occurred for more than five centuries, the governments make little or no effort to classify people by race.

The development of the "race" doctrine is a social and political process (Hannaford 1994) that tells more about the history of relations between people who thought/think of—and define—themselves as different than it tells about what can be known using and practicing science. The majority of physical scientists (Wheeler 1995) are acknowledging this fact and are abandoning the term "race."

References

Bell, Derrick. 1992. *Race, Racism and American Law*. Boston: Little, Brown.

Diamond, Jared. 1994. "Race Without Color." *Discover:* 82–89.

DOA (Dictionary of Anthropology). 1986. Boston: G. K. Hall.

Forbes, Jack D. 1993. *Africans and Native Americans*. Chicago: University of Illinois Press.

Gould, Stephen Jay 1994. "The Geometer of Race." *Discover* (November): 64–69.

Hannaford, Ivan. 1994. "The Idiocy of Race." *The Wilson Quarterly* (Spring): 8–35.

Healy, Joseph F. 1995. *Race, Ethnicity, Gender, and Class*. Thousand Oaks, CA: Pine Forge Press.

Lewontin, R. C., S. P. Rose, and L. J. Kamin. 1984. *Not in Our Genes*. New York: Pantheon.

Livingstone, Frank B. 1962. "On the Non-Existence of Human Races." *Current Anthropology* 3(3): 279.

Marger, Martin. 1991. *Race and Ethnic Relations: American and Global Perspectives*. Belmont, CA: Wadsworth.

Montagu, Ashley. 1972. *Statement On Race*. London: Oxford University Press.

Nei, Masatoshi and Arun K. Roychoudhury. 1972. "Gene Differences Between Caucasian, Negro, and Japanese Populations." *Science* 177: 434–35.

Norwood, Janet L. and Deborah P. Klein. 1989. "Developing Statistics to Meet Society's Needs." *Monthly Labor Review* (October): 14–19.

Root, Maria P. P., editor. 1992. *Racially Mixed People in America*. London: Sage.

Stein, Phillip L. and Bruce M. Rowe. 1989. *Physical Anthropology*. New York: McGraw-Hill.

Stringer, C. B. and P. Andrews. 1988. "Genetic and Fossil Evidence for the Origin of Modern Humans." *Science* 239: 1263–68.

Trillin, Calvin. 1986. "American Chronicles: Black or White." *The New Yorker* (April): 62–78.

Wali, Alaka. 1992. "Multiculturalism: An Anthropological Perspective." *Report from the Institute for Philosophy & Public Policy* 12(1): 6–8.

Wills, Christopher. 1994. "the skin we'in." *Discover*: 76–81.

Wright, Lawrence. 1994. "One Drop of Blood." *The New Yorker* (July 25): 46–55.

Wheeler, David L. 1995. "A Growing Number of Scientists Reject the Concept of Race." *The Chronicle of Higher Education* (February 17): A8–A9, A15.

Zack, Naomi. 1995. *American Mixed Race*. Lanham, MD: Rowman & Littlefield.

Notes

[1] Interracial marriages were illegal in some states in the United States until 1967. In 1967, in *Loving* v. *Virginia* (388 U.S.1), the Supreme Court finally declared such states' laws unconstitutional.

[2] Social preferences (in this context) are learned, and oftentimes legally enforced, conventions societies use when choosing intimate partners and making mate selections.

[3] *Webster's New World Dictionary* (1989) defines *mutation* as "a sudden variation in some inheritable characteristic in a germ cell of an individual animal or plant, as distinguished from a variation resulting from generations of gradual change."

[4] A disorder in individuals in which red blood cells will develop into a sickle shape which, in turn, will clog capillaries, resulting in anemia, heart failure, etc.

[5] Scientists know that some traits are determined by the environment. They do not always fully know the exact mechanism that is at work to produce the changes, however. *See* Stein & Rowe (1989:50–53).

[6] On the few occasions when such an attempt was made, it proved highly unsatisfactory and the rules for assigning "race" were constantly changed. Increasingly, however, persons who self-identify as "multiracial" are demanding that a category be created for them.

The Mean Streets of Social Race

IAN F. HANEY LÓPEZ

Study Questions

1. Haney López identifies three factors which determine a person's race: chance (morphology and ancestry), context (social setting), and choice (everyday, ordinary decisions). Expand on the meaning of each factor.
2. Give examples from Piri Thomas's life to illustrate the role of each factor in determining race.

The literature of minority writers provides some of the most telling insights into, and some of the most confused explorations of, race in the United States.[150] Piri Thomas's quest for identity, recorded in *Down These Mean Streets,*[151] fits squarely within this tradition of insight and confusion. Thomas describes his racial transformation, which is both willed and yet not willed, from a Puerto Rican into someone Black.[152] Dissecting his harrowing experiences, piercing perceptions, and profound misapprehensions offers a way to disaggregate the daily technology of race. To facilitate this discussion, I employ the terms of chance, context, and choice: chance refers to morphology and ancestry, context to the contemporary social setting, and choice to the quotidian decisions of life. In the play of race, chance, context, and choice overlap and are inseverable. Nevertheless, I distinguish among these neologisms to focus on key aspects of how race is created, maintained, and experienced. Drawing upon these terms and using the ordeals Thomas recorded in *Down These Mean Streets* as a foil, I return to the definition proffered at the beginning of this essay, that a race is best thought of as a group of people loosely bound together by historically contingent, socially significant elements of their morphology and/or ancestry.

Chance

The first terms of importance in the definition of race I advance are "morphology" and "ancestry." These fall within the province of chance, by which I mean coincidence, something not subject to human will or effort, insofar as we have no control over what we look like or to whom we are born. Chance, because of the importance of morphology and ancestry, may seem to occupy almost the entire geography of race. Certainly for those who subscribe to notions of biological race, chance seems to account for almost everything: one is born some race and not another, fated to a particular racial identity, with no human intervention possible. For those who believe in biological race, race is destiny. However, recognizing the social construction of race reduces the province of chance. The role of chance in determining racial identity is significantly smaller than one might initially expect.

The random accidents of morphology and ancestry set the scene for Piri Thomas's racial odyssey. Seeking better prospects during the depression, Thomas's parents moved from Puerto Rico to Spanish Harlem, where Piri and his three siblings were born. Once in the United States, however, the family faced the peculiar American necessity of defining itself as White or Black. To be White would afford security and a promising future; to be Black would portend exclusion and unemployment. The Thomas family—hailing from Puerto Rico of mixed Indian, African, and European antecedents—considered themselves White and pursued the American dream, eventually moving out to the suburbs in search of higher salaries and better schools for the children. Yet in their bid for Whiteness, the family gambled and lost, because even while the three other children and Piri's mother were fair, Piri and his father were dark skinned. Babylon, Long Island proved less forgiving of Piri's dark skin than Spanish Harlem. In the new school, the pale children scoffed at Piri's claim to be Puerto Rican rather than Black, taunting Piri for "passing for Puerto Rican because he can't make it for white,"[153] and proclaiming, "[t]here's no difference...[h]e's still black."[154] Piri's morphology shattered not only the family's White dream, but eventually the family itself.

While the family insisted on their own Whiteness as the crucial charm to a fulfilling life in the United States, Thomas, coming of age amid the racial struggles of the 1950s and himself the victim of White violence, fought the moral hypocrisy he saw in their claim to Whiteness.[155] Piri unyieldingly attacked the family's delusion, for example challenging with bitterness and frustration the Whiteness of his younger brother José:

> José's face got whiter and his voice angrier at my attempt to take away his white status. He screamed out strong: "I ain't no nigger! You can be if you want to be....

But—I—am—*white!* And you can go to hell!"

But Piri persisted in attacking the family, one at a time:

> "And James is *blanco,* too?" I asked quietly.
>   "You're damn right."
>   "And Poppa?"
>   ..."Poppa's the same as you," he said, avoiding my eyes, "Indian."
>   "What kinda Indian," I said bitterly. "Caribe? Or maybe Borinquen? Say, José, didn't you know the Negro made the scene in Puerto Rico way back? And when the Spanish spics ran outta Indian coolies, they brought them big blacks from you know where. Poppa's got *moyeto* [Black] blood. I got it. Sis got it. James got it. And, mah deah brudder, you-all got it....It's a played-out lie about me—us—being white."[156]

The structure of this painful exchange casts a bright light on the power that morphology and ancestry wield in defining races. In the racially charged United States, skin color or parentage often makes one's publicly constructed race inescapable.

Piri's dark features and José's light looks are chance in the sense that neither Piri nor José could choose their faces, or indeed their ancestry. Yet, two important qualifications about chance should be made. The most important of these, that morphology and ancestry gain their importance on the social and not the physical plane, is the subject of the next part. The second caveat bears mention here. Upon reflection, what we look like is *not* entirely accident; to some extent looks can be altered in racially significant ways. In this respect, consider the unfortunate popularity of hair straightening,[157] blue contact lenses, and even facial surgery.[158] Or consider that in 1990 alone approximately $44 million was spent on chemical treatments to literally lighten and whiten skin through the painful and dangerous application of bleach.[159] It seems we minorities do not leave our looks to chance, but constantly seek to remake them, in tragic obeisance to the power of racial aesthetics in the United States.[160] Though morphology and ancestry remain firmly in the province of chance, that province daily suffers incursions of the will.

Context

Given Piri's status as a Puerto Rican with ancestral ties to three continents, there is a certain absurdity to his insistence that he is Black. This absurdity highlights the importance of context to the creation of races. Context is the social setting in which races are recognized, constructed, and contested; it is the "circumstances directly encountered, given and transmitted from the past."[161] At the meta level, context includes both ideological and material components, such as entrenched cultural and customary prejudices, and also maldistributed resources, marketplace inequalities, and skewed social services. These inherited structures are altered and altered again by everything from individual actors and community movements to broad-based changes in the economic, demographic, and political landscape. At the same time, context also refers to highly localized settings. The systems of meaning regarding morphology and ancestry are inconstant and unstable. These systems shift in time and space, and even across class and educational levels, in ways that give to any individual different racial identities depending upon [his or] her shifting location.[162] I refer to context in order to explain the phrases "historically contingent" and "socially significant" in the proffered definition of race.

The changes in racial identity produced by the shifting significance of morphology and ancestry are often profoundly disconcerting, as Piri Thomas discovered. In Puerto Rico, prevailing attitudes toward racial identity situated the Thomases, as a family not light enough to be Spanish but not so dark as to be Black, comfortably in the mainstream of society.[163] They encountered no social or economic disadvantages as a result of their skin color, and were not subjected to the prejudice that usually accompanies rigid racial constructs. However, the social ideology of race in the United States—more specifically, in New York in the late 1950s—was firmly rooted in the proposition that exactly two biological races existed. Such an ideology forced the Thomas family to define themselves as either White or Black. In the context confronting Piri, "[i]t would seem indeed that… white and black represent the two poles of a world, two poles in perpetual conflict: a genuinely Manichean concept of the world…."[164] Once in the United States, Thomas came to believe that he and his family were Black as a biological fact, irrespective of their own dreams, desires, or decisions. Yet, Thomas was not Black because of his face or parents, but because of the social systems of meaning surrounding these elements of his identity.

Consider how Thomas came to believe in his own Blackness. In a chapter entitled "How to be a Negro Without Really Trying," Thomas recalls how he and his fair-skinned Puerto Rican friend Louie applied for a sales job. Though the company told Thomas they would call him back, they hired Louie to start Monday morning. Thomas's reflections bear repeating:

> I didn't feel so much angry as I did sick, like throwing-up sick. Later, when I told this story to my buddy, a colored cat, he

said, "Hell, Piri...a Negro faces that all the time."

"I know that," I said, "but I wasn't a Negro then. I was still only a Puerto Rican."[165]

Episodes of discrimination drove Piri towards a confused belief that he was Black.[166] Aching to end the confusion, Piri traveled to the South, where he hoped to find out for sure whether his hair, his skin, and his face somehow inextricably tied him, a Puerto Rican, to Black America. Working in the merchant marine between Mobile, New Orleans, and Galveston, Piri experienced firsthand the nether world of White supremacy, and the experience confirmed his race; bullied by his White bosses, insulted by White strangers, confronted at every turn by a White racial etiquette of violence, Thomas accepted his own Blackness. "It was like Brew said," he reflected after his time in the South, "any language you talk, if you're black, you're black."[167] Suffering under the lash of White racism, Thomas decided he was Black. Thomas's Blackness did not flow from his morphology but from traveling the mean streets of racial segregation. His dislocations suggest a spatial component to racial identities, an implication confirmed in Thomas's travel from Spanish Harlem, where he was Puerto Rican, to Long Island, where he was accused of trying to pass [for white], to the South, where he was Black.[168]

Piri and his family were far from the first to face the Manichean choice between White or Black. The Chinese, whose population in the United States rose fifteenfold to 105,465 in the twenty years after 1850, were also initially defined in terms of Black and White. Thus in Los Angeles circa 1860 the Chinese area downtown was called "Nigger Alley."[169] During their first years in the

United States, as Ronald Takaki observes, "[r]acial qualities that had been assigned to blacks became Chinese characteristics."[170] Not only were the supposed degenerate moral traits of Blacks transferred wholesale to the Chinese, but in a fascinating display of racist imagination, Whites also saw a close link between Black and Chinese morphology. Takaki cites a commentator who argued that Chinese physiognomy indicated "but a slight removal from the African race,"[171] and he reprints a startling cartoon contrasting Anglo Uncle Sam with a Chinese vampire replete with slanted eyes, but also with very dark skin, woolly hair, a flat nose, and thick lips.[172]

In California, where the racial imagination included Mexicans and Indians as well as Blacks, the racial categorization of the Chinese involved their construction not only in terms of Blackness but also in terms of every non-White race, every rejected and denigrated Other. This point furnishes yet more evidence for the theory that racial identity is defined by its social context. Consider the 1879 play *The Chinese Must Go* by Henry Grimm of San Francisco. Notice the language Grimm ascribes to the Chinese characters, discussing, predictably, their nefarious Anti-American plot to destroy White labor through hard work:

> AH CHOY: By and by white man catchee no money; Chinaman catchee heap money; Chinaman workee cheap, plenty work; white man workee dear, no work—sabee?
>
> SAM GIN: Me heep sabee.[173]

The Chinese in this Grimm play speak in the language that Whites associated with Indians and Mexicans, making Sam Gin sound remarkably like Tonto playing out *The Lone Ranger*'s racial delusions. Thus, the Chinese were assigned not only their own peculiar stereotypes, like a fiendish desire to work for low wages, but also the degenerate characteristics of all the minorities loathed by Whites. Not coincidentally, three years after Grimm's play, the United States passed its first immigration law: The 1882 Chinese Exclusion Act.[174] In a telling example of law reifying racist hysteria, the Supreme Court upheld the Chinese Exclusion Act in part by citing the threat posed by the Chinese to White labor.[175] The first Chinese, like the Thomas family nearly a century later, entered a society fixated on the idea of race and intent on forcing new immigrants into procrustean racial hierarchies.

The racial fate of Piri and the Chinese turned to a large extent on the context into which they immigrated. Context provides the social meanings attached to our faces and forbears, and for this reason I write that races are groups of people bound together by *historically contingent, socially significant* elements of their morphology and/or ancestry. A race is not created because people share just any characteristic, such as height or hand size, or just any ancestry, for example Yoruba or Yugoslav. Instead, it is the social significance attached to certain features, like our faces,[176] and to certain forebears, like Africans, which defines races. Context superimposed on chance largely shapes races in the United States.

Choice in Context

Piri's belief that he is Black, and his brother José's belief in his own Whiteness, can in some sense be attributed to the chance of their respective morphology and the context of their upbringing. Yet, to attribute Thomas's racial identity only to chance and context grossly oversimplifies his Blackness. Thomas's father shared not only his social context, but his dark looks as well, making context and chance equal between them.

Nevertheless, his father insisted on his Whiteness, and explained this decision to Piri as follows:

> I ain't got one colored friend...at least one American Negro friend. Only dark ones I got are Puerto Ricans or Cubans. I'm not a stupid man. I saw the look of white people on me when I was a young man, when I walked into a place where a dark skin isn't supposed to be. I noticed how a cold rejection turned into an indifferent acceptance when they heard my exaggerated accent. I can remember the time when I made my accent heavier, to make me more of a Puerto Rican than the most Puerto Rican there ever was. I wanted a value on me, son.[177]

Thomas's father consciously exaggerated his Puerto Rican accent to put distance between himself and Black Americans. Thomas himself also made conscious and purposeful decisions, choices that in the end made him Black. As Henry Louis Gates argues, "one must *learn* to be 'black' in this society, precisely because 'blackness' is a socially produced category."[178]

Choice composes a crucial ingredient in the construction of racial identities and the fabrication of races. Racial choices occur on mundane and epic levels, for example in terms of what to wear or when to fight; they are made by individuals and groups, such as people deciding to pass or movements deciding to protest; and the effects are often minor though sometimes profound, for instance, slightly altering a person's affiliation or radically remaking a community's identity. Nevertheless, in every circumstance choices are exercised not by free agents or autonomous actors, but by people who are compromised and constrained by the social context. Choice, explains Angela Harris, is not uncoerced choice, "freely given, but a 'contradictory consciousness' mixing approbation and apathy, resistance and resignation."[179] Nevertheless, in racial matters we constantly exercise choice, sometimes in full awareness of our compromised position, though often not.[180]

Perhaps the most graphic illustration of choice in the construction of racial identities comes in the context of passing. Passing— the ability of individuals to change race— powerfully indicates race's chosen nature. Not infrequently someone Black through the social construction of their ancestry is physically indistinguishable from someone White.[181] Consider Richard Wright's description of his grandmother in *Black Boy:* "My grandmother was as nearly white as a Negro can get without being white, which means that she was white."[182] Given the prevalent presumption of essential, easily recognized phenotypical differences, light-skinned Blacks exist at an ambiguous and often unacknowledged racial border between White and Black.[183] Those in this liminal space often respond along a range from some few who cross the established color line by "passing" to those who identify strongly with their Black status.[184]

For most people, the pervasive social systems of meaning that attach to morphology ensure that passing is not an option.[185] Moreover, for those who do jump races, the psychological dislocations required—suspending some personal dreams, for example childbirth; renouncing most family ties, for instance foregoing weddings and funerals; and severing all relations with the community, for example, ending religious and civic affiliations—are brutal and severe.[186] In addition, because of the depth of racial animosity in this society, passing may only succeed in distancing one from her community, not in gaining her full acceptance among Whites. In this sense, recall the words of Thomas's father: "I noticed how a cold rejection turned into an indifferent acceptance when they heard my exaggerated accent."[187] Nevertheless, some people do choose to jump races, and their ability to do so dramatically demonstrates the element of choice in the micromechanics of race.

It also demonstrates, however, the contingency of the choices people make, and reinforces the point that choices are made in specific contexts. Choices about racial identity do not occur on neutral ground, but instead occur in the violently racist context of American society. Though the decision to pass may be made for many reasons, among these the power of prejudice and self-hate cannot be denied. Thomas's younger brother José reveals the racist hate within him in the same instant that he claims to be White. José shouts at Piri: "I ain't black, damn you! Look at my hair. It's almost blond. My eyes are blue, my nose is straight. My motherfuckin' lips are not like a baboon's ass. My skin is white. White, goddamit! White!"[188] José's comments are important, if painful to repeat, because they illustrate that a person's choice in the matter of race may be fatally poisoned by ambient racist antipathies. Nevertheless, notice that the context in which passing occurs constantly changes. For example, it may be that in the contemporary context passing as White increasingly does not in fact require that one *look* White. Recently, many Anglos, committed to the pseudo-integrationist idea that ignoring races equals racial enlightenment, have seemingly adopted the strategy of pretending that the minorities they are friendly with are White. Consider the words of a White Detroit politician: "I seldom think of my girlfriend, Kathy, as black....A lot of times I look at her and it's as if she is white; there's no real difference. But every now and then, it depends on what she is wearing and what we're doing, she looks very ethnic and very Black. It bothers me. I don't like it. I prefer it when she's a regular, normal, everyday kind of person."[189] Even so, passing may be far less common today than it was a hundred years ago. One observer estimates that in the half-century after the Civil War, as many as 25,000 people a year passed out of the Black race.[190] The context in which passing occurs constantly changes, altering in turn the range of decisions individuals face.

Despite the dramatic evidence of choice passing provides, by far the majority of racial decisions are of a decidedly less epic nature. Because race in our society infuses almost all aspects of life, many daily decisions take on racial meanings. For example, seemingly inconsequential acts like listening to rap and wearing hip hop fashions constitute a means of racial affiliation and identification. Many Whites have taken to listening to, and some to performing, rap and hip hop.[191] Nevertheless, the music of the inner city remains Black music.[192] Rapping, whether as an artist or audience member, is in some sense a racial act. So too are a myriad of other actions taken every day by every person, almost always without conscious regard for the racial significance of their choices. It is here, in deciding what to eat, how to dress, whom to befriend, and where to go, rather than in the dramatic decision to leap races, that most racial choices are rendered. I do not suggest that these common acts are racial choices because they are taken with a conscious awareness of their racial implications. Rather, these are racial choices in their overtones or subtext, because they resonate in the complex of meanings associated with race. Given the thorough suffusion of race throughout society, in the daily dance of life, we cannot avoid making racially meaningful decisions.

Notes

[Notes 24, 92, 120, 129 are included here because they are referred to in subsequent notes.]

[24] Masatoshi Nei & Arun K. Roychoudhury, "Genetic Relationship and Evolution of Human Races", in 14 EVOLUTIONARY BIOLOGY 1, 11 (1982)

[92] For a powerful critique of the model minority line, see RONALD TAKAKI, IRON CAGES: RACE AND CULTURE IN 19TH CENTURY AMERICA 298–302 (1990). If Asians are held up to Blacks as indictments by comparison, then for Latinos, Cubans serve that role. Cubans, particularly those who arrived here prior to the 1981 Marielos exodus, are relatively prosperous, well-educated, and politically powerful. The success of Cubans as recent immigrants, therefore, is often brandished as evidence of community guilt or cultural shortcomings in debates on the economic plight of Chicanos, Puerto Ricans, and Central Americans. On occasion, those who tout Cuban success concede that as immigrants they often possessed considerable education, business experience, professional training, and wealth, prior to their arrival in the United States. Far less frequently mentioned is that the federal government, in its ideologically inspired desire to embarrass Fidel Castro, undertook to ensure the economic well-being of Cuba's emigres by providing them with $957 million in aid in the years between 1961 and 1974. See GASTON FERNÁNDEZ, BEVERLY NAGEL, & LEON NARVÁEZ, HISPANIC MIGRATION TO THE UNITED STATES 80 (1987). See also Lisa Otero & Juan Zúñiga, *Latino Identity and Affirmative Action: Is There a Case for Hispanics* (1992) (unpublished manuscript, on file with author); *see generally* ELEANOR ROGG, THE ASSIMILATION OF CUBAN EXILES: THE ROLE OF COMMUNITY AND CLASS (1974). This aid took the form of resettlement

assistance, job training, professional recertification, job search assistance, special research and teaching grants for Cuban scholars, funding for public school bilingual education programs, and assistance to the public schools for the extra costs incurred by the rapid influx of Cuban children. FERNÁNDEZ ET AL., at 80. *See also* Migration and Refugee Assistance Act, Pub. L. No. 87-510 (1962). I await, though in vain, a similar commitment to other Latinos, and all racial minorities generally.

[120] Notice that the racial and sexual construction of Mexican women as European, refined, and eligible for marriage differs markedly from the construction historically accorded Black women, which has emphasized sexual availability and condoned rape while stigmatizing marriage. It should be emphasized that this view of Mexican women applied only to some, in particular to those of the elite class with significant European antecedents, and began to wane towards the end of the 19th century as more Anglo women moved into the Southwest. Nevertheless, the different social-sexual-racial identity accorded Mexican and Black women at virtually the same historical and geographical moment is remarkable. This may reflect the absence of a rule of racial construction as applied to Mexicans similar to the one-drop rule prevalent in the reigning U.S. mythology concerning Blacks. *See* F. JAMES DAVIS, WHO IS BLACK: ONE NATION'S DEFINITION 168 (1991). (Davis argues, perhaps overbroadly, that "racially visible minority groups other than blacks in the United States...are not subject to a one-drop rule, and those persons whose ancestry is one-fourth or less from one of those groups are able to become fully assimilated by intermarrying with whites.")

[129] Because the identities of Whites and Blacks (and other minorities) are constructed in dualistic opposition to each other, the rehabilitation of minorities implies a more honest appraisal of the characteristics of Whites. More pointedly, challenging the stereotype that Blacks are evil challenges the myth that Whites are innocent.

> [The] three unarmed Black men [who became lost in Howard Beach] threatened to undo the very concept of white that so occupies the imagination of Europe and America that it blots out everything else. The threat that the Black Other brings to white space is not that more houses will be robbed but that the crime rate will *not* rise with their presence—that they will actually come and go peacefully and without incident. This would be the greatest catastrophe because then it would be inescapably revealed that whites rob the homes of other whites, that white men rape white women, that the evils of white society are attributable to whites, and ultimately that whites do not exist because the defining characteristics of whiteness—innocence and purity—is a phantasm.

Richard Ford, *Urban Space and the Color Line: The Consequences of Demarcation and Disorientation in the Postmodern Metropolis*, 9 HARV. BLACKLETTER J. 117, 138 (1992) (citation omitted).

[150] Black literature is replete with powerful examples. For two classic considerations of race by Black authors, see RALPH ELLISON, INVISIBLE MAN (1947) and JAMES WELDON JOHNSON, AUTOBIOGRAPHY OF AN EX-COLORED MAN (1960). For important explorations of race and identity by Asian authors, *see*, e.g., CARLOS BULOSAN, AMERICA IS IN THE HEART (1943); CYNTHIA KADOHATA, THE FLOATING WORLD (1989); and DAVID MURA, TURNING JAPANESE; MEMOIRS OF A SANSEI (1991). On Asian American literature, *see generally* READING THE LITERATURES OF ASIAN AMERICA (Shirley Geok-lin Lim & Amy Ling eds., 1992). For investigations of these same themes by Latino authors, *see*, e.g., JULIA ALVÁREZ, HOW THE GARCÍA GIRLS LOST THEIR ACCENT (1992); JOSÉ ANTONIO VILLAREAL, CLEMETE CHACÓN (1984). For first-rate commentary on Chicano literature, *see* JUAN BRUCE-NOVOA, RETROSPACE: COLLECTED ESSAYS ON CHICANO LITERATURE (1990). For a Native American's literary reflections on identity in modern America, *see* JIM NORTHRUP, WALKING THE REZ ROAD (1993).

[151] PIRI THOMAS, DOWN THESE MEAN STREETS (1967).

[152] The reformulation of questions of identity into questions of race is a common theme in Latino literature, though often the conflict plays out in nationalistic terms. *See, e.g.,* OSCAR ACOSTA, THE AUTOBIOGRAPHY OF A BROWN BUFFALO (2d ed. 1989) and THE REVOLT OF THE COCKROACH PEOPLE (2d ed. 1989) (author rejects an individually American or Mexican identity before embarking on a journey of self-creation as a Chicano).

[153] THOMAS, *supra* note 151, at 90.

[154] *Id.* at 91.

[155] I say what Piri "saw" as moral hypocrisy because for my part I want to warn against facile condemnations of those who, in the context of a violently racist society, strive to envelop themselves and their loved ones in the protective mantle of Whiteness. *See, e.g.,* JOHNSON, *supra* note 150. Johnson's ex-colored man chose to pass as White in order to spare his children the depredations of being Black in the United States.

[156] THOMAS, *supra* note 151, at 145.

[157] For an enlightening discussion of the politics of hair among African Americans, as well as a trenchant analysis of the unfortunate and ill-conceived distinction in antidiscrimination jurisprudence between "immutable" and "cultural" characteristics—where employers can discriminate on the basis of the latter but not the former—*see* Paulette Caldwell, *A Hair Piece: Perspectives on the Intersection of Race and Gender,* 1991 DUKE L.J. 365.

[158] For a compilation of interesting but poorly analyzed anecdotes concerning the politics of appearance in the Black community, *see* KATHY RUSSELL, MIDGE WILSON & RONALD HALL, THE COLOR COMPLEX: THE POLITICS OF SKIN COLOR AMONG AFRICAN AMERICANS (1992). It bears mention that not only Blacks seek to whiten their features. Eyelid surgery among Asians and blue contact lenses and bleached hair among Latinos are all too common.

[159] *Id.* at 51.

[160] "So we rub ointments on our skin and pull our hair and wrap our bodies in silk and gold. We remake and redo and we sing and we pray that the ugliness will be hidden and that our beauty will shine through like light and be accepted. And we work and we work and we work at ourselves. Against ourselves. In spite of ourselves, and in subordination of ourselves." Patricia J. Williams, *The Obliging Shell: An Informal Essay on Formal Equal Opportunity,* 87 MICH L. REV. 2128, 2141 (1989).

[161] KARL MARX, THE EIGHTEENTH BRUMAIRE OF LOUIS BONAPARTE (1963), *quoted in* RENATO ROSALDO, CULTURE AND TRUTH: THE REMAKING OF SOCIAL ANALYSIS 105 (1989).

[162] As Law Professor Deborah Waire Post relates: "People are often misled by the context in which they find me, and I find their confusion funny. When I worked for Margaret Mead, students who asked me ['What are you?'] always assumed the answer would be 'Samoan.' When I lived in Texas, there were those who assumed the answer would be 'Hispanic' and others who just knew I had to be Creole from Louisiana." Deborah Waire Post, *Reflections on Identity, Diversity and Morality,* 6 BERKELEY WOMEN'S L.J. 136 (1991).

[163] *See* Melvin M. Tumin & Arnold Feldman, *Class and Skin Color in Puerto Rico,* in COMPARATIVE PERSPECTIVES ON RACE RELATIONS 197 (Melvin M. Tumin ed., 1969).

[164] FRANTZ FANON, BLACK SKIN, WHITE MASKS 44–45 (1967).

[165] THOMAS, *supra* note 151, at 108.

[166] Thomas might have agreed with Adrian Piper's sense that "[w]hat joins me to other blacks, then, and other blacks to another, is not a set of shared physical characteristics, for there is none that all blacks share. Rather, it is the shared experience of being visually or

cognitively *identified* as black by a white racist society, and the punitive and damaging effects of that identification." Adrian Piper, *Passing for White, Passing for Black,* 58 Transition 30, 31 (1992).

[167] Thomas, *supra* note 151, at 187–88.

[168] The role of spatial demarcation in determining racial identity produces strange results: "Persons in Virginia who are one-fourth or more Indian and less than one-sixteenth African black are defined as Indians while on the reservation but as blacks when they leave." Davis, *supra* note 148, at 9 (citing Brewton Berry, Race and Ethnic Relations 26, 3d ed., 1965). For a first-rate discussion of the spatial elements of race, see Ford, *supra* note 129.

[169] Richard Griswold Del Castillo, The Los Angeles Barrio, 1850–1890: A Social History 141 (1979).

[170] Takaki, Iron Cages, *supra* note 92, at 217.

[171] *Id.*

[172] *Id.* at 218.

[173] *Id.* at 221.

[174] 22 Stat. 58 § 14 (1882).

[175] The Chinese Exclusion Case: *Chae Chan Ping* v. *United States*, 130 U.S. 581, 595 (1889). The Chinese, the Court wrote, "were generally industrious and frugal. Not being accompanied by families, except in rare instances, their expenses were small; and they were content with the simplest fare, such as would not suffice for our laborers and artisans. This competition between them and our people was for this reason altogether in their favor, and the consequent irritation, proportionately deep and bitter, was followed, in many cases, by open conflicts, to the great disturbance of the public peace." *Id.*

[176] "The erection of racial classification in man based upon certain manifest morphological traits gives tremendous emphasis to those characters to which human perceptions are most finely tuned (nose, lip and eye shapes, skin color, hair form and quantity), precisely because they are the characters that men ordinarily use to distinguish individuals." Richard C. Lewontin, *The Apportionment of Human Diversity,* 6 Evolutionary Biology 381, 382 (1972).

[177] Thomas, *supra* note 151, at 152.

[178] Henry Louis Gates, Jr., Loose Canons: Vol. 101 Notes on the Culture Wars (1992).

[179] Angela Harris, *Race and Essentralism in Feminist Legal Theory,* 42 Stan L. Rev. 581, 614 (quoting T. J. Jackson Lears, *The Concept of Cultural Hegemony: Problems and Possibilities,* 90 Am. Hist. Rev. 567, 570 (1985).

[180] Consider as an example of racial choice exercised in the full recognition of context Deborah Waire Post's self-identification as Black:

> My decision to identify myself as black person is not exclusively a matter of descent, although my father's grandfathers were a runaway slave and a free black man who fought in the Civil War. Nor is it simply a matter of residence, although the fact that I grew up in a black neighborhood surely played a part in the creation of my sense of identity. It is not a matter of skin color, although there has never been a question about the fact that I am a person of color. Some might argue that I am black because whites will not let me be anything else. I prefer to believe I am who I am, a black woman, because I made an ethically and morally correct choice with respect to my identity.

Post, *supra* note 162, at 137.

[181] Notice, of course, that under the prevalent social rules governing racial identity the opposite is not true. Any Black ancestry makes one Black. The "one-drop rule" or the "rule of hypodescent," as this phenomenon is sometimes called, is discussed in Neil Gotanda, *A Critique of "Our Constitution is Color-blind,"* 44 STAN. L. REV. 1, 24–26 (1991). *See also,* DAVIS, *supra* note 120, at 4–16 (explaining the "one-drop rule"). There may be light-skinned Blacks, but there are no dark-skinned Whites.

[182] RICHARD WRIGHT, BLACK BOY 48 (1966). Nei and Roychoudhury state that "about 20 percent of the gene pool of American Negroid is known to have been derived from Caucasoid by recent racial admixture." Nei & Roychoudhury, *supra* note 24 at 11 (citing T. Edward Reed, *Caucasian Genes in American Negroes,* 165 SCIENCE 762 (1969)). Notice that again Nei and Roychoudhury, by referring to the "gene pool" of the "American Negroid" and "Caucasoid" populations, cannot free themselves from language that strongly insinuates the existence of distinct biological races. We can presume that Nei and Roychoudhury are in fact referring to the gene pool of those peoples socially defined as Black, which reveals intermixture with those peoples socially defined as White. This intermingling occurs despite pronounced social taboos. Opposition to miscegenation remains very strong among Whites. In 1972, nearly two out of five Whites (39 percent) not only objected to interracial marriage, but thought such marriages should be illegal. In 1991, a sad and startling 17 percent of Whites continued to support the criminalization of interracial marriage. *See* RUSSELL ET AL., *supra* note 158, at 116.

Nei & Roychoudhury are not the first to recognize the small proportion of genetic difference attributable to race. Richard Lewontin reached similar conclusions in 1972. *See* Richard C. Lewontin, *The Apportionment of Human Diversity,* 6 EVOLUTIONARY BIOLOGY 381, 397 (1972). *See generally,* L. L. Cavalli-Sforza, *The Genetics of Human Populations,* 231 SCI. AM. 80 (Sept. 1974). Lewontin argued that biologists should abandon all talk of biological races. "Since such racial classification is now seen to be of virtually no genetic or taxonomic significance…no justification can be offered for its continuance." Lewontin at 397. Nei & Roychoudhury agree that talk of biological races should be abandoned, but point out that there remains statistically significant differences between smaller population groups that justify the continued scientific division of humans by gene type. Nei & Roychoudhury, *supra* note 24 at 41.

> The key prerequisite for differentiation of any animal population into races is some kind of separation of groups that prevents interbreeding. In man's development separation must have been achieved mainly by geography…Geographic distance favors local differentiation even where there are no major barriers to movement. Unless there are strict barriers of some kind, however, the differences are not sharp but gradual, continuous rather than discontinuous. This kind of gradation is characteristic of most human racial differentiation.

In *Human Races,* Nei & Roychoundhury present their findings in dendrograms, horizontal branching trees that compare genetic variation among populations. The "Dendrogram for representative human populations of the world" demonstrates the gradual gene frequency shifts as one moves through the following groups: Lapp, English, Italian, Iranian, Northern Indian, Malay, Chinese, Japanese, Polynesian, Micronesian, South Amerind (American Indian), Eskimo, Alaskan Indian, Australian Aborigine, Papuan, Nigerian, Bantu, and Bushman (Khoi). Nei & Roychoudhury, *supra* note 24, at 38.

Unfortunately, in presenting their evidence Nei and Roychoudhury seem to reinscribe racial hierarchies. They present nine separate dendrograms. Because the dendrogram is horizontal, the compared populations appear listed vertically at the ends of the branches. Of the nine dendrograms, eight roughly but unquestionably list the different populations in a literal hierarchy ranging downward from the most fair-skinned groups. For example, the hierarchy of African populations places Italians at the top of the tree, "as a reference population," and then starts down: North African, Beja, Sandawe, Bantu, Yoruba, Dama, Pygmy, Bushman, and Hottentot. *Id.* at 22. At the top are the Italians, followed by the North Africans, who are "Caucasoids," *Id.* at 18, below them are the Beja, who "seem to have had gene admixture with eastern Mediterranean Caucasoids," *Id.* at 19. Skipping the Sandawe, the next major group includes the Bantu, Yoruba, and Dama. The Bantu "are morphologically similar to the Yoruba"; the Yoruba "are classic Negroes"; and the Dama are similar to the Bantu and Yoruba. Finally, the hierarchy reaches the pygmies (who call themselves Babinga), the Bushman (San), and the Hottentot (Khoi), all of whom are "short-statured" or "middle-sized." This ordering is not dictated by geographic proximity, nor does it reflect a simple, North-South bias. While the North African and Beja populations are from the North, the Sandawe from Tanzania are ranked above the Yoruba from Nigeria, and the Bantu and the Dama from South Africa are listed above the Babinga of Central Africa and the Khoi and San of Namibia. Nor is the ranking dictated by genetic closeness. Because a dendogram measures genetic distance among populations, there is little scientific advantage to start with any one particular group. For examples of dendrograms that do not reflect racial hierarchies, see Cavalli-Sfroza, at 87. Nei and Roychoudhury install Italians at the apex and arrange the ranking of African populations so that the fairest-skinned groups are at the top, and the "classic" African populations below, but still above—literally and figuratively—the shorter Babingas, San, and Khoi. Nei and Roychoudhury reflexively fall into the comfortable habit of White supremacy in science.

[183] Looking White but being Black comes with a host of painful experiences. For a law professor's take on the confusions induced by white skin and Black identity, see Judy Scales-Trent, *Commonalities: On Being Black and White, Different and the Same,* 2 YALE J.L. & FEM. 305 (1990). *See also* Piper, *supra* note 166.

[184] Some prominent Black leaders have had predominantly White ancestors. Walter White, for example, served as president of the National Association for the Advancement of Colored People (NAACP) from 1931 to 1955 and clearly identified himself as Black, though at least one scholar estimates that he was likely not more than one-sixty-fourth African by ancestry. DAVIS, *supra* note 120, at 7. Interestingly, White did occasionally pass as White, but only in order to investigate lynchings in the South. *Id.* at 56. Adrian Piper evokes the choice between being White or Black in the title of her piece on passing, *Passing for White, Passing for Black.* Piper, *supra* note 166.

[185] "There are groups to which we belong or, perhaps more descriptively, into which we are thrown. A mere act of will cannot disaffiliate us from these groups. Even our attempt to hold ourselves apart merely reconfirms our membership." Gerald Torres, *Critical Race Theory: The Decline of the Universalist Ideal and the Hope of Plural Justice—Some Observations and Questions of an Emerging Phenomenon,* 75 MINN. L. REV. 993, 1005 (1991).

[186] *See* DAVIS, *supra* note 120, at 143. ("Those who pass…must give up all family ties and loyalties to the black community in order to gain economic and other opportunities.")

[187] THOMAS, *supra* note 151, at 152. *See supra* note 177.

[188] THOMAS, *supra* note 151, at 144.

[189] RUSSELL ET AL., *supra* note 158, at 120. For a collection of essays on racial assimilation, *see* LURE AND LOATHING: ESSAYS ON RACE, IDENTITY, AND THE AMBIVALENCE OF ASSIMILATION (Gerald Early ed., 1993).

[190] Davis, *supra* note 120, at 22. ("The peak years for passing as white were probably from 1880 to 1925, with perhaps 10,000 to 25,000 crossing the color line each year, although such estimates are most likely inflated. By 1940 the annual number had apparently declined to no more than 2,500 to 2,750.... At least since the 1920s, apparently, most mulattoes who could pass have remained in the black population.")

[191] *See* Ford, *supra* note 129, at 128 (commenting on the "refreshing if at the same time disquieting subversion of racial identity" implicit in the emergence of White rappers).

[192] Some commentators read a bit more into rap. For example, one suggests that "rap is the voice of alienated, frustrated, and rebellious black youth who recognize their vulnerability and marginality in post-industrial America." Clarence Lusane, *Rhapsodic Aspirations: Rap, Race and Politics,* 23 THE BLACK SCHOLAR 37 (1993). My claim is more limited. I posit only that rap has a racial character to it, and that that character is Black.

"Indian" and "Black" as Radically Different Types of Categories

JACK D. FORBES

◇◆◈◆◇

Study Question

Summarize Forbes' argument that the categories "Indian" and "Black" are treated as radically different.

One of the strange things about the Americas is that ethnic and racial categories are extremely arbitrary and are unevenly applied. The same North American white writer who might regard every person with some degree of African ancestry as being "black" will *not* see every part-American as an "Indian" (as "red"). Of the 20 to 30 million persons in the United States who probably have American ancestry, only 1 to 2 million are regarded as "Indians."

But one who seeks to comprehend must first confront these strange mysteries: how can Africans always remain African (or black) even when they speak Spanish or English and serve as cabinet secretaries in the United States government or as trumpet players in a Cuban *salsa* group; yet "Indians" seem to be reclassified as "mestizos" (or "hispanics," etc.) the moment they leave a traditional way of life, with very few exceptions.

In short, "blacks" are always "blacks" even when mixed with white or American Indian. "Indians," however, exist as a sort of *cultural* category (or as a caste). They must remain unchanged in order to be considered "Indian."

Perhaps, then, in contrasting the two categories (in a loose way at first), we must bear in mind that "real Indians" are seen not exclusively or even primarily as a racial or ethnic category but as something more fluid, subject to change as the way of life changes. I am reminded of a Dutch book on "The Last Indians" featuring pictures *only* of traditional South American people still living a way of life which is stereotypically "Indian." Not a single picture of soldiers, factory workers, or cowboys is presented, as if "the last Indians" will disappear when they put on pants (if they do) and thereby become less "exotic."

Blacks, on the other hand, are not seen *only* as traditional villagers in Africa. No one would dare to write a book on "The Last Blacks," with pictures of "tribesmen" in ceremonial costumes. So the category of "black" has a different quality than has that of "Indian," or so it would seem.

Of course, many anthropologists and historians are more sophisticated than is the popular media and are aware that "Indians" can change and still be "Indians." But even they do not equate the category "Indian" with that of "black." A "black" person may be an isolated individual, integrated into a white context, and still be "black," but an integrated "Indian" (having lost his "tribe" and language) is seldom regarded as an

"Indian." He will be considered a "Ladino," "cholo," "mestizo," "caboclo," "Mexican," "Chicano," or whatever, but seldom will he be seen as an "Indian."

And with the mixture of bloods the "Indian" disappears. He is "blanched" out, becoming "white," or is darkened, becoming "black," or he is placed in a "Half-breed," non-Indian category.

Now, of course, this latter statement must be qualified for the United States, since mixed-bloods are sometimes regarded as "Indians" there, but usually only if they meet the same cultural criteria as are applied to unmixed "Indians."

The results of all of this are rather startling. One is told, for example, that there are no "Indians" left in most of the Caribbean, an assertion which leaves one rather surprised when people from Puerto Rico, Cuba, or the Dominican Republic—of obvious American ancestry—are met with.

One is told that the Sandinistas of Nicaragua are opposing the Miskito "Indians," and yet one looks in vain for any sharp racial differences between most "Nicaraguans" and Miskitos. Why aren't the Nicaraguans also called "Indians?"

Reports state that only about 250,000 "Indians" (or fewer) are left in Brazil; yet, one also reads of tens of millions of people starving in the dry northeast who are supposed to have been of "Indian" blood a little while back; one even reads of the *Mamalucos* (mamelucos) of southern Brazil and wonders where they have all disappeared to, after being so important not so very long ago.

Argentina is a "white" country we are told, with no "Indians" (or just a few thousands); yet, there were plenty of brown people there in 1890 (and no one mentions the "cabecitas negras" in the working class of Buenos Aires).

One can go on and on: One meets people who look "Indian" or part-"Indian," but they come from places where there are no reported "Indians." The "blacks" never have that problem! White writers are *always finding "blacks"* (even if they look rather un-African), and they are *always losing "Indians."*

Of course, all of the above is an oversimplification because North American and British-Canadian usage is somewhat different from that found in Francophone, Spanish-speaking, and Brazilian areas. No doubt North American racism has so thoroughly distorted discourse that one should not expect "logic" to operate there. The obsession with "blackness" *as a genetic evil,* a product largely of the post-Civil War period and the early 20th century (but also found in the Iberian empires to some degree) has created a peculiar situation. American ancestry, on the other hand, has been viewed more as a *social* or *cultural evil.*

The "Indian," in short, is culturally a "savage" (or a backward rustle), but his blood can be "purified" by mixture with whites. It might have taken one or two generations in some areas, or four generations in others, but ultimately the "stain" could be removed. But African ancestry, while treated similarly in some cases, gradually came to be seen as "irredeemable" in significant parts of North America, at least.

The various barriers to interracial marriage, etc., which reflect the above, have been partially discussed in my recent book. In general, they tended to become evermore restrictive (and genetic) with the passage of time, but remained less restrictive for white-Native American marriages (in general). Doubtless this partially reflects the fact that many Native Americans are generally closer in appearance to Europeans than are West Africans, and that very few persons of less than one-quarter American ancestry can be distinguished from Europeans. However, some half-West Africans can also appear to be "white," and many one-quarter and, even more, one-eighth West Africans can "pass" as Europeans. Thus, the phenotypes of mixed-bloods do not entirely explain the differential treatment.

Known Ancestries and Race

Photos by Ray Elfers

How do these photographs and information about known ancestries relate to Jack D. Forbes idea that "Blacks" are always "Black" even when mixed with white or American Indian [or Asian]?

Known ancestries: Native American, African

Known ancestries: Japanese and African

Known ancestries: Native American, German, Norwegian, African

Known ancestries: African, Native American, Canadian

Known ancestries: Cherokee, European-American, African American, Blackfoot, French

Known ancestries: Native American, German, Norwegian, African

Getting Recognized

L. WADE BLACK AND ROBERT THROWER

◇◆◇◆◇

Study Questions

1. Why do Wade Black and Robert Thrower believe it is important to make a film about "Getting Recognized"?
2. Identify the issues that make getting recognized a controversial and complicated process.
3. Historically, what kinds of conditions have encouraged people to self-identify as Indian? To suppress, deny, or lose interest in their Indian Identity?

Introduction

For most Americans, "getting recognized" is a subject given little thought, usually involving nothing more than continuity of appearance among friends and acquaintances. It might involve some slight awkwardness if the interval since last encounter has been great, or if one's appearance has changed—different clothes, a new hairstyle. But it is an informal transition, individual and momentary, with few important consequences, since it simply re-establishes a relationship that has already been acknowledged to exist.

For the Native American, "getting recognized" is an entirely different matter. It is a formal and sometimes arduous process, imposed by forces outside oneself, with major implications that involve the acknowledgement of one's culture, one's history, and one's heritage. For the Native American, "getting recognized" is the process by which one's community—national, tribal, or peer group—determines whether within that community one is permitted to "be" Native American. It is a formal process demanded of no other American citizens. Every other American is permitted to self-identify—for

employment purposes, to qualify for government benefits, to assume certain formal roles within the community. Only Native Americans must formally apply to have their cultural heritage acknowledged. They, alone among all Americans, must "get recognized."

For the Creek Indians in south Alabama, "Getting Recognized" has always been a consideration of great personal and interpersonal significance. For almost 150 years, the pressures to assimilate into the dominant white culture were enormous, determining where one stood within the local community in terms of access to privilege, the personal experience of prejudice, and the opportunities available to oneself and one's children. The process of getting recognized was an informal one, but one with important implications. To be recognized as Indian meant a lifetime of second-class citizenship and a similar future for one's children. Inferior schools. Limited education. Restricted opportunities for employment. Minimal participation in the power structure of the community. Everyday encounters with prejudice. The arguments for self-identifying as white were compelling. The arguments for self-identifying as Indian were virtually non-existent. Much of the Native American community assimilated, either by inter-marriage or by obscuring one's cultural background.

Between 1900 and 1955, federal "Indian Money" twice became available in the Southeast. Suddenly there was a financial incentive to "be Indian." Each time, for a short period of time, a flurry of "Indians" came forward in the white community. Each time, after the Indian monies were distributed, there was re-assimilation into the white community. By the mid-50s, virtually all distinctive qualities of traditional culture had been lost in south Alabama, and the Creek community existed only as small isolated pockets of [mainly] low-income housing identified by the white community as "Indian." A few members of these communities continued to self-identify with pride, but for most it simply meant a status which they had not been able to escape.

During the 1940s, the Poarch Creeks under Chief Calvin McGhee began protesting their second-class status with roadblocks, meetings with local and state officials, and community gatherings. Renewed interest in Native culture during the 1950s and 1960s became a national movement felt even in such rural and isolated communities as Poarch, Alabama. The Civil Rights movement of the 60s accelerated Native protest. By the mid 70s, the local Creek community had reorganized as The Creek Nation East of the Mississippi (CNEM), which demanded and eventually received formal status as an Indian "band," qualifying it for federal and state programs. Tribal elders reestablished ties with the Creek community in Oklahoma and brought in Creek cultural specialists to help restore Creek cultural traditions. CETA projects in the late 70s focused on Native Ameri-

can culture (tribal documentation and traditional crafts). An annual fall Pow Wow was begun, at first strongly influenced by Western Indian traditions but gradually re-introducing more traditional Eastern Creek culture. Crafts persons from the Creek community began to travel outside the local area to fairs, folk life festivals, and other community celebrations. Meanwhile, CNEM continued to pursue tribal recognition. Finally, in1984 , the Creek community around Poarch, Alabama, received formal recognition as a tribal unit, tribal lands were restored as reservation property, and the community formally reorganized as the Poarch Band of Creek Indians (PBCI). They "got recognized."

Suddenly, for both whites and Indians in south Alabama, there was again value in identification as Native American. A new problem was posed. Members of the "white" community began to self-identify as "Creeks." The process of assimilation reversed. Tribal membership assumed increasing financial, social service, and employment benefits, and individuals now had to come to PBCI offices to "get recognized" as Creek. Ironically, a local community that had once self-identified almost entirely as white seemed to become a community that self-identified almost entirely as Native American. Many individuals who had once avoided identification as Creek had to establish ties to a traditional Creek community they had previously shunned. This double meaning of "getting recognized" has played a complex role in the Creek community of south Alabama. For years, the need to meet formal criteria for federal recognition provided cohesion and solidarity for a small, proud community that continued to self-identify as Native American. Then, after tribal recognition was granted, the tribal roll swelled with new members whose interest in tribal membership was in many cases more economic than cultural. Tribal elections have become a complicated struggle for leadership by two competing community groups. Among the Creeks in south Alabama, tribal membership has grown dramatically, but tribal cohesion and sense of direction has become much less clear.

This film will look at the issues surrounding recognition within a national context while it focuses on the complicated history of "getting recognized" in Native American south Alabama. The long struggle for Poarch Creek recognition, and the tensions and conflicts that arose as a result of that process, parallel continuing national struggles over Native American recognition, especially in the resurgence of Native and tribal identification east of the Mississippi. Using archival footage, stills, interviews, written and recorded oral histories, location videotaping, and historical records, and by comparing the Poarch experience with that of the MOWA Choctaws and the Florida Tribe of Eastern Creeks, two nearby Native communities that have been unable to secure federal recognition, Getting Recognized will look at the complex issues surrounding tribal and individual identity, the pressure to assimilate, differing perceptions concerning what it means to be Native American, and the tensions that arise as economic issues compete with cultural identity to determine the future of a Native American community.

Native American history remains a national subject of fascination, but contemporary Native issues are still a minor topic in the national media. Despite extensive coverage of Native gaming in Connecticut, Minnesota, and South Dakota, virtually no one outside the Indian community can explain the legal and cultural issues involved in "being Indian." This is especially true for Native cultures east of the Mississippi River, particularly in the Southeast. When coverage of eastern tribes exists, it almost always focuses directly or indirectly on recognition rights, but it

rarely provides the critical historical and legislative background that makes understanding these rights possible. Instead, it is almost always focused on gambling, an economic issue intricately connected to inter-tribal and native/white conflicts over recognition.

Recognition conflicts are widespread in the East, most visibly in New England, but in Alabama alone there are eight tribal communities recognized by the state but denied federal recognition. In Florida, five state-recognized Creek communities are seeking federal recognition. If the Lumbees in South Carolina achieve recognition, they will immediately become one of the largest tribal bodies in the country. The Catawbas in South Carolina were formally recognized only recently, restoring a status taken from them in 1959, and qualifying them for $50 million in federal reparation funds for treaty violations. Legislative recognition of the MOWA Choctaws passed the U.S. Senate in March, 1994, but failed to pass the U.S. House of Representatives. Other tribal communities in the Southeast appear close to recognition. Self-identification as Native American on the U.S. census has more than tripled since 1960. In Alabama, self-identification as Native increased 118 percent between 1980 and 1990. Title V Indian Education programs are exploding throughout the South.

This is a national story important to both white and Native communities. It applies to every Native American community in which pressures to assimilate and prejudices against tribal peoples have divided and fragmented the history, culture, and sense of self that once united tribal groups. It has also pitted tribal communities against one another as both recognized and unrecognized groups of self-identified Native Americans compete for limited resources, treaty rights, tribal rights, economic self-interest, and formal federal and state recognition. Whether we are talking about conflicts between Navajo and Hopi in the Southwest, fishing rights among the Menominee in the Upper Midwest, or admission to tribal membership among the Pequod and Lene Lenape in the East, "getting recognized" is a major issue in Native American culture as tribal communities continue to struggle with what it means to be Native American.

The Poarch Creeks were the first "new" Native American community in the Southeast to receive formal recognition since the nineteenth century. Their story is a case study in the national recognition struggle, recent enough that it is still contemporary community memory, yet long enough ago that it demonstrates the stresses that recognition introduces within the Native community and between the Native and white communities. This project will focus on Poarch Creeks to provide a historical, legislative, and culture examination of recognition issues as they affect the national community.

Audience Development and Local Support

This project has its roots in the late 1970s, when the Poarch Creeks used CETA funds to establish a tribal media center for self-documentation of tribal community history. Wade Black was one of the CETA instructors and temporarily the Tribal Media Center Director, and Robert Thrower was one of the original CETA students. Changes in federal funding policies during the 1980s eventually forced the closing of this center, but in 1993 the Poarch Creeks resumed efforts to re-establish their media center. A 1993 proposal for documentation funding was declined by the National Park Service, but the Tribal Council used tribal funds to purchase basic equipment and used JTPA funds to begin re-training tribal personnel. In September 1993, Research and Development

funding for "Getting Recognized" was granted by the Native American Public Broadcasting Consortium (NAPBC). Project personnel have worked with Elizabeth Weatherford (Museum of the American Indians), Roberta Grossman (500 Nations), and Paul Steckler (Last Stand at Little Bighorn, Eyes on the Prize) for research and to identify additional Native crew members for participation in the project. In July, 1994, the project completed negotiations to work cooperatively with the Center for Public Television (CPT) at the University of Alabama, a state of the art broadcast production facility. This will permit use of CPT field equipment, crew personnel, and online facilities, and will reduce production costs for this project considerably. CPT is the producer of the award-winning documentary series "The Alabama Experience," a weekly documentary series for Alabama Public Television, and such long-form documentaries as the recently completed 90-minute biography of Carl Elliott, the first recipient of the Robert F. Kennedy Award for courage in politics. This arrangement will be the first time CPT has agreed to work cooperatively with an independent outside producer and it opens the door for future cooperative productions. In addition, Robert Thrower has begun working with the Department of Broadcasting at the University of West Florida (UWF) in Pensacola to provide production training to tribal personnel in Poarch. The arrangements with both CPT and UWF will greatly increase the involvement of public broadcasting in the Southeast with Native subjects and Native production personnel.

We feel extremely encouraged by our success in negotiating these agreements, since they will also provide low-cost access to high quality broadcast equipment and facilities in a region where equipment access remains a serious problem for independent producers.

The Memoirs of Madison Hemings

MADISON HEMINGS

◇◆◈◆◇

Study Questions
1. Highlight the various "interracial relationships" Madison Hemings describes.
2. How does the case of Madison Hemings illustrate the role of choice, context, and chance in affecting racial classification.

I never knew of but one white man who bore the name of Hemings; he was an Englishman and my great grandfather. He was captain of an English tracking vessel which sailed between England and Williamsburg, Va., then quite a port. My great grandmother was a fullblooded African, and possibly a native of that country. She was the property of John Wales, a Welchman. Capt. Hemings happened to be in the port of Williamsburg at the time my grandmother was born, and acknowledging her fatherhood he tried to purchase her of Mr. Wales, who would not part with the child, though he was offered an extraordinarily large price for her. She was named Elizabeth Hemings. Being thwarted in the purchase, and determined to own his own flesh and blood he resolved to take the child by force or stealth, but the knowledge of his intention coming to John Wales' ears, through leaky fellow servants of the mother, she and the child were taken into the "great house" under their master's immediate care. I have been informed that it was not the extra value of that child over other slave children that induced Mr. Wales to refuse to sell it, for slave masters then, as in later days, had no compunctions of conscience which restrained them from parting mother and child of however tender age, but he was restrained by the fact that just about that time amalgamation began, and the child was so great a curiosity that its owner desired to raise it himself that he might see its outcome. Capt. Hemings soon afterwards sailed from Williamsburg, never to return. Such is the story that comes down to me.

Elizabeth Hemings grew to womanhood in the family of John Wales, whose wife dying she (Elizabeth) was taken by the widower Wales as his concubine, by whom she had six children—three sons and three daughters, viz: Robert, James, Peter, Critty, Sally, and Thena. These children went by the name of Hemings.

Williamsburg was the capital of Virginia, and of course it was an aristocratic place, where the "bloods" of the Colony and the new State most did congregate. Thomas Jefferson, the author of the Declaration of Independence, was educated at William and Mary College, which had its seat at Williamsburg. He afterwards studied law with Geo. Wythe, and practiced law at the bar of the general court of the Colony. He was afterwards elected a member of the provincial legislature from Albemarle county. Thos. Jefferson was a visitor at the "great house" of John Wales, who had children about his own age. He formed the acquaintance of his daughter Martha (I believe that was her name, though I am not positively sure,) and intimacy sprang up between them which ripened into love, and they were married. They afterwards went to live at his country seat Monticello, and in course of time had born to them a daughter whom they named Martha. About the time she was born my mother, the second daughter of John Wales and Elizabeth Hemings was born. On the death of John Wales, my grandmother, his concubine, and her children by him fell to Martha, Thomas Jefferson's wife, and consequently became the property of Thomas Jefferson, who in the course of time became famous, and was appointed minister to France during our revolutionary troubles, or soon after independence was gained. About the time of the appointment and before, he was ready to leave the country his wife died, and as soon after her interment as he could attend to and arrange his domestic affairs in accordance with the changed circumstances of his family in consequence of this misfortune (I think not more than three weeks thereafter) he left for France, taking his eldest daughter with him. He had sons born to him, but they died in early infancy, so he then had but two children—Martha and Maria. The latter was left home, but afterwards was ordered to follow him to France. She was three years or so younger than Martha. My mother accompanied her as a body servant. When Mr. Jefferson went to France Martha was just budding into womanhood. Their stay (my mother's and Maria's) was about eighteen months. But during that time my mother became Mr. Jefferson's concubine, and when he was called back home she was *enciente* by him. He desired to bring my mother back to Virginia with him, but she demurred. She was just beginning to understand the French language well, and in France she was free,

while if she returned to Virginia she would be re-enslaved. So she refused to return with him. To induce her to do so he promised her extraordinary privileges, and made a solemn pledge that her children should be freed at the age of twenty-one years. In consequence of his promise, on which she implicitly relied, she returned with him to Virginia. Soon after their arrival, she gave birth to a child, of whom Thomas Jefferson was the father. It lived but a short time. She gave birth to four others, and Jefferson was the father of all of them. Their names were Beverly, Harriet, Madison (myself), and Eston—three sons and one daughter. We all became free agreeably to the treaty entered into by our parents before we were born. We all married and have raised families.

Beverly left Monticello and went to Washington as a white man. He married a white woman in Maryland, and their only child, a daughter, was not known by the white folks to have any colored blood coursing in her veins. Beverly's wife's family were people in good circumstances.

Harriet married a white man in good standing in Washington City, whose name I could not give, but will not, for prudential reasons. She raised a family of children, and so far as I know they were never suspected of being tainted with African blood in the community where she lived or lives. I have not heard from her for ten years, and do not know whether she is dead or alive. She thought it to her interest, on going to Washington, to assume the role of a white woman, and by her dress and conduct as such I am not aware that her identity as Harriet Hemings of Monticello has ever been discovered.

Eston married a colored woman in Virginia, and moved from there to Ohio, and lived in Chillicothe several years. In the fall of 1852 he removed to Wisconsin, where he died a year or two afterwards. He left three children.

As to myself, I was named Madison by the wife of James Madison, who was afterwards President of the United States. Mrs. Madison happened to be at Monticello at the time of my birth, and begged the privilege of naming me, promising my mother a fine present for the honor. She consented, and Mrs. Madison dubbed me by the name I now acknowledge, but like many promises of white folks to the slaves she never gave my mother anything. I was born at my father's seat of Monticello, in Albemarle county, Va., near Charlottesville, on the 19th day of January, 1805. My very earliest recollections are of my grandmother Elizabeth Hemings. That was when I was about three years old. She was sick and upon her death bed. I was eating a piece of bread and asked if she would have some. She replied: "No, granny don't want bread any more." She shortly afterwards breathed her last. I have only a faint recollection of her.

Of my father, Thomas Jefferson, I knew more of his domestic than his public life during his life time. It is only since his death that I have learned much of the latter, except that he was considered as a foremost man in the land, and held many important trusts, including that of President. I learned to read by inducing the white children to teach me the letters and something more; what else I know of books I have picked up here and there till now I can read and write. I was almost 21½ years of age when my father died on the 4th of July, 1826.

About his own home he was the quietest of men. He was hardly ever known to get angry, though sometimes he was irritated when matters went wrong, but even then he hardly ever allowed himself to be made unhappy any great length of time. Unlike Washington he had but little taste or care for agricultural pursuits. He left matters pertaining to his plantations mostly with his stewards and overseers. He always had mechanics at work for him, such as carpenters, blacksmiths, shoemakers, coopers, &c. It was his mechanics he seemed mostly to direct, and in their operations he took great interest. Almost every day of his later years he might have been seen among them. He occupied much of the time in his office engaged in correspondence and reading and writing. His general temperament was smooth and even; he was very undemonstrative. He was uniformly kind to all about him. he was not in the habit of partiality or fatherly affection to us children. We were the only children of his by a slave woman. He was affectionate toward his white grandchildren, of whom he had fourteen, twelve of whom lived to manhood and womanhood. His daughter Martha married Thomas Mann Randolph by whom she had thirteen children. Two died in infancy. The names of the living were Ann, Thomas Jefferson, Ellen, Cornelia, Virginia, Mary, James, Benj. Franklin, Lewis Madison, Septemia and Geo. Wythe. Thos. Jefferson Randolph was Chairman of the Democratic National Convention in Baltimore last spring which nominated Horace Greeley for the Presidency, and Geo. Wythe Randolph was Jeff. Davis' first Secretary of War in the late "unpleasantness."

Maria married John Epps, and raised one son—Francis.

My father generally enjoyed excellent health. I never knew him to have but one spell of sickness, and that was caused by a visit to the Warm Springs in 1818. Till within three weeks of his death he was hale and hearty, and at the age of 83 years walked erect and with a stately tread. I am now 68, and I well remember that he was a much smarter man physically, even at that age, than I am.

When I was fourteen years old I was put to the carpenter trade under the charge of John Hemings, the youngest son of my grandmother. His father's name was Nelson, who was an Englishman. She had seven children by white men and seven by colored men—fourteen in all. My brothers, sister Harriet and myself, were used alike. We were permitted to stay about the "great house," and only required to do such light work as going on errands. Harriet learned to spin and to weave in a little factory on the home plantation. We were free from the dread of having to be slaves all our lives long, and were measurably happy. We were always permitted to be with our mother, who was well used. It was her duty, all her life which I can remember, up to the time of father's death, to take care of his chamber and wardrobe, look after us children and do such light work as sewing, &c. Provision was made in the will of our father that we should be free when we arrived at the age of 21 years. We had all passed that period when he died but Eston, and he was given the remainder of his time shortly after. He and I rented a house and took mother to live with us, till her death, which event occurred in 1835.

In 1834 I married Mary McCoy. Her grandmother was a slave, and lived with her master, Stephen Hughes, near Charlottesville, as his wife. She was manumitted by him which made their children free born. Mary McCoy's mother was his daughter. I was about 28 and she 22 years of age when we married. We lived and labored together in Virginia till 1836, when we voluntarily left and came to Ohio. We settled in Pebble township, Pike County. We lived there four or five years and during my stay in the county I worked at my trade on and off for about four years. Joseph Sewell was my first employer. I built for him what is now known as Rizzleport No. 2 in Waverly. I afterwards worked for George Wolf Senior and I did the carpenter work for the brick building now owned by John J. Kellison in which the Pike County Republican is printed. I worked for and with Micajab Hinson. I found him to be a very clever man. I also reconstructed the building on the corner of Market and Water Streets from a store to a hotel for the late Judge Jacob Row.

When we came from Virgina we brought one daughter (Sarah) with us, leaving the dust of a son in the soil near Monticello. We have born to us in this State nine children. Two are dead. The names of the living besides Sarah, are Harriet, Mary Ann, Catharine, Jane, William Beverly, James Madison, Ellen Wales. Thomas Eston died in the Andersonville prison pen, and Julia died at home. William, James and Ellen are unmarried and live at home in Huntington township, Ross County. All the others are married and raising families. My post office address is Pee Pee, Pike County Ohio.

Litigating Whiteness:
Trials of Racial Determination
in the Nineteenth-Century South

◇◆◆◇

ARIELA J. GROSS

Study Questions
1. In the trial of Abby Guy what kinds of criteria were used to "prove" Guy's race.
2. Identify and briefly describe the five ways of talking about race.

Jurors had before them both the evidence of their own eyes and many reasons not to trust their own eyes; both common sense and the fear of racial unknowability. To compound the difficulty, no matter who assumed authority to determine race, there was no single discourse of "race" shared by all witnesses or litigants in the courtroom at any time in the nineteenth-century South, and certainly no agreement about what constituted the "essence" of race. As the lawyer for an Alabama free person of color argued in *Thurman* v. *State*, "A mulatto is to be known, not solely by color, kinky hair, or slight admixture of negro blood, or by a greater admixture of it not amounting to one-half, but by reputation, by his reception into society, and by the exercise of certain privileges."[65] While the "scientific" language of the distinction between the "African and caucasian races" filtered into the courtroom, it by no means dominated everyone's understanding of what it meant to be black or white.

Among whites, and among people whose racial identity was in question, there were instead shifting "essences" of whiteness and blackness, hard to grasp and yet, paradoxically, also commonsensical and self-evident to those who proclaimed knowledge of them.

Categorizing these "evidences" and "essences" of race is, to some extent, an artificial exercise. Through the story of Abby Guy, I hope to show how they worked together, on both sides of a legal dispute. I will also, however, briefly outline five ways of talking about race at trial, certain of which increased in frequency and persuasive power over the course of the nineteenth century, but especially between 1800 and 1865. Race as a physical marker, as already noted, was considered unreliable. Nevertheless, physical description remained an important part of these trials, along with physical inspection. Witnesses described the appearance of people who were not present in court, painting visual pictures that sometimes markedly contradicted one another. Race as documented ancestry, the sort of evidence one might expect in a statutory regime defining race in terms of ancestry, was important in early cases but was consistently less important in later cases. Race as ascriptive identity, or reputation in society, and race as performance overlapped to some extent, but I believe they are analytically distinct.[66] Here, reputation refers to acceptance in society, others' beliefs about one's identity, and one's social associations, whereas performance refers to one's acts. Finally, race as a scientific category, interpreted by medical experts or others who used the new language of physiology and ethnology, began to appear in the courtroom in the late 1840s.

1. Abby Guy

In the trial of *Guy* v. *Daniel*, a variety of criteria were discussed on both sides to prove Guy's race. Along with the evidence of inspection and medical experts, the jurors heard from a large number of neighbors of Guy and Daniel. Guy's lay witnesses focused on her social identity, her associations with white people, and her having performed tasks that white people quintessentially performed. Richard Stanley testified that she visited among white folks, and went to church, parties, etc."[67] Keightly Saunders, a fifty-seven-year-old farmer who owned four slaves, one a mulatto, in 1850, testified that Guy "visited among the whites as an equal."[68] Saunders was "locally known as quite a character"[69] a drinker and storyteller, free with "curse words which flowed in his conversation like water from a spring."[70] Nevertheless, he commanded respect in the neighborhood and was a friend of Judge Hawkins, who was considered the leader of the bar in the region.[71] Saunders's testimony for Guy must have carried considerable weight. Jeremiah Oats, a farm laborer with no slaves or land of his own in 1850,[72] had done work for Guy, and he testified that she had been competent to contract and pay her bills herself.[73] William M.

Drucker, Sheriff of Ashley County, himself a slaveholder, explained that he did not tax Guy because she was a widow, whatever her racial status.[74]

William Daniel emphasized documentary evidence of Abby Guy's slave origins. He produced his father's will, which did not free Guy but devised her to James Condra, Daniel's brother-in-law, as well as Daniel's receipt for Guy from Condra.[75] Daniel admitted that Guy had been of little value to him as a slave and so he had "permitted her to go when and where she pleased, for several years past"[76] but when she left the State of Arkansas for Louisiana, he brought her and her children home and asserted his right of ownership over them.[77]

He argued, in effect, that as a slave, she must be black, because only blacks are slaves. There was another dimension to his argument: He should not have to prove her racial identity because status was enough. If he could prove that she was rightly his slave, she should not be free, whatever her degree of blood, whatever her racial identity. Abby Guy, on the other hand, having no credible evidence of a right to freedom in previous free status, no documentation of "that previous Right"[78] had to make her case in her own person. Her right to freedom inhered in her whiteness. Her success at trial rested on her ability to shift the ground of argument to that question.

On behalf of William Daniel, Thomas S. Thompson, a relatively wealthy farmer with six slaves, told the jury that he had known both Guy and her mother Polly as slaves, although they were both "bright mulatto."[79] Thompson betrayed some confusion over the exact determination of their racial status—Polly "was a yellow woman, darker than white.... Could not say whether Polly was of African or Indian extraction. I have seen some only of half blood who would probably be as white as Polly was."[80] But he was much more confident about their slave status. Polly "always held herself as a slave and acted as such. She and Guy always labored and conducted themselves as slaves in the family, with the exception that they took more care of themselves perhaps than others."[81]

On cross-examination, Thompson admitted that he was Daniel's brother-in-law and that he "had never studied Physiology nor the distinction of races."[82] He also admitted that he had seen white persons who worked in the fields become as dark as Guy and her mother, and he had seen white persons with hair as curly as theirs.[83]

Several other farm laborers testified about Guy and Polly's slave status, but they acknowledged the difficulty of determining their racial status.[84] As James Barnett noted, he "had seen persons recognized as white, who were as dark as Polly."[85]

William Daniel's witnesses made no strong claims about Guy's racial identity. Indeed, implicit in their acknowledgment that people of ambiguous appearance fell on both sides of the line between white and "negro" was a claim that status should decide race, or at least that race could not decide status; what mattered was how people recognized Guy and her mother, which depended on whether they were slaves or free. Abby Guy, on the other hand, made a strong claim to a whiteness that should overwhelm all evidence of slave status or ancestry in slavery. She asked the jury to consider her white because she acted white, because she looked white, and because doctors found her to be white.

After the testimony closed, the lawyers for both Guy and Daniel proposed instructions for Judge Sorrels to give the jury. The judge gave all of the instructions drafted by Abby Guy's lawyers, which charged the jury to follow a "one-fourth rule" with one wrinkle: Guy and her children could only be proved slaves if they had more than one-fourth "negro blood" or if they were descended in the maternal line from a slave who was one-fourth negro or more. Furthermore, "every presumption, consistent with reason, should be indulged in favor of freedom."[86] The judge refused to give most of William Daniel's proposed instructions, including an instruction to ignore "all evidence on Physiology, [which] is irrelevant"[87] and several to the effect that evidence that Guy had been held in slavery should be evidence of her status as a slave.[88]

The Ashley County jury gave a verdict for Abby Guy and her children in favor of freedom. The jury list for *Daniel* v. *Guy* no longer exists, save for the name of the foreman, Ambrose Bull, a forty-nine-year-old farmer who owned six slaves and property worth $1,000 in 1850.[89] William Daniel won his appeal to the Arkansas Supreme Court, which rejected the one-fourth rule propounded by the trial court in favor of a rule of maternal descent (implicitly, a one-drop-of-blood-rule, as one could be held "negro" with only a tiny fraction of African ancestry so long as it passed through the maternal line).[90] Daniel succeeded in having the case retried in neighboring Drew County, where he thought he would find a more sympathetic jury. That case also ended in a verdict for Guy.[91]

This time, Daniel appealed on the ground that the jury had based their verdict on an improper exhibition of Guy's feet, for which she had been required to remove her shoes and stockings in court, as well as the more general ground that "there was a total want of evidence to support the verdict."[92] The Arkansas Supreme Court, however, thought it quite appropriate to inspect a person's feet in order to detect "negro blood," and it refused to disturb the jury verdict.[93] Chief Justice English, who had also delivered the opinion establishing the one-drop rule, nevertheless expressed his own skepticism about the jury's decision, remarking in dictum that "it is possible that the jury found against the preponderance of evidence, through reluctance to sanction the enslaving of persons, who, to all appearance, were of the white race, and, for many years before suit, had acted as free persons and been treated as such."[94] So, in 1861, it affirmed the verdict in *Daniel* v. *Guy*, setting Guy and her children free on the eve of the Civil War.[95]

The trials of *Daniel* v. *Guy* and their appeals differed widely in the issues that animated dispute. At trial, the racial identity of Abby Guy and her children was disputed on the ground of physical appearance, social acceptance, and reputation "as an equal," and exercise of the rights of free persons. Abby Guy may have won because the jurors were reluctant to remove rights to which she had a "prescriptive" claim by virtue of having exercised them for some years; because the jurors believed from their own observations that she was white, regardless of her ancestry; because the jurors did not want to risk the horror of "white slavery"; or because Abby Guy's medical experts and other witnesses were more credible, or carried more weight, than did William Daniel's. But the jury outcome almost certainly did not depend on a determination of a precise fraction of the "African blood" in Abby Guy's veins. The legal issue that moved Chief Justice English to overturn the trial court—whether one-fourth negro blood defined "negro" or whether any fraction passed through the maternal line would suffice—did not decide the actual case left to the juries of Ashley or Drew County.

Guy's lay witnesses made little effort to describe her physically. Most of their testimony focused on her social identity: her passing among whites "as an equal"; her living and working on her own; her ability to form contracts; and so on. On the other hand, the witnesses for William Daniel turned their attention at trial to Guy's ancestry, in particular to her mulatto mother, Polly, her shade of color and curly hair. The jury in *Daniel* v. *Guy* could view Guy and her children directly and listen to Guy's experts, who talked about what happened to "negro blood" after several generations. Thus, they could choose among several grounds for racial determination: Guy's appearance; her reputation in the community; science; and the discourse that equated whiteness with freedom and the exercise of legal rights. Guy asked the jury to consider her white on the grounds that she was free, because she looked white, and because doctors found her to be white. William Daniel asked the jury to consider her a slave that she had always been a slave and that he could trace "negro blood" in her ancestry. Not only was there no consensus about whether Guy was white, but there was also no consensus about the conjunction between status and race—about whether she should be free if white or whether she must be enslaved if black.

2. Race as Physical Marker

If "race" was a question for the jury, then the easiest way for jurors to determine a person's race would be to see for themselves. As the Mississippi Supreme Court ruled in 1876, one's identity as a "colored person" may be "brought to [the jurors'] attention of proof by ocular demonstration," because sometimes "jurors may use their eyes as well as their ears."[96] Inspection allowed the jury to circumvent the opinions of experts. As the North Carolina court noted in the same year, "[t]he eyes of the members of the jury must be presumed to be as good as those of medical men."[97] In Abby Guy's case, she and her children "were personally presented in Court," and the judge instructed the jury to "treat their observation and inspection of plaintiffs' persons as evidence," applying their own "knowledge of the distinction between the negro and the white races" and whatever rules might apply for discerning "negro blood."[98] Litigants seeking to prove a person's whiteness almost always sought to exhibit her to the jury, in the hope that the presumption raised by light skin would be enough.[99] In William Daniel's second appeal to the Arkansas Supreme Court, when his counsel objected "with much warmth of expression" to the exhibition of Abby Guy's naked feet to the jury, Chief Justice English rejected his appeal, noting that it did not take an expert to recognize the value of an inspection of the feet to a determination of racial status: "The experience of every intelligent observer of the race...will doubtless attest the truth.... No one, who is familiar with the peculiar formation of the negro foot, can doubt, but that an inspection of that member would ordinarily afford some indication of the race...."[100]

Yet despite its visual power, exhibition did not take place in every case, and even in those where it did, jurors were given many reasons not to believe their own eyes. Twenty of sixty-eight case records referred explicitly to inspections; in only two of these was that the only evidence before the jury, and in only one other case was testimony about appearance the only other evidence.[101]

Far more ubiquitous in trials of racial determination were witnesses' descriptions of appearance: color, hair, eye color, and features. Often in the courtroom, a certain physical description of the person at issue became a mantra repeated by innumerable witnesses. In *Ulzere* v. *Poeyfarre*, at least fifteen witnesses described the woman P as "plus blanche que rouge...les cheveux noirs et lisses [more white than red...black straight hair]."[102] Most physical descriptions centered on a few features considered to be characteristic of racial difference: curly or straight hair; dark or light skin; flat or thin nose; and thick or thin lips.[103] From these descriptions, witnesses often made the jump to "blood." Jesse Turner testified that Susan is of very light complexion, has straight hair, is slightly swarthy, and has rather thick lips and coarse features. From her appearance, [Turner] is of the opinion that she has a small amount of African blood in her veins—what amount impossible to say, but [he] thinks not more than an eighth or a sixteenth. Her mouth and features, generally, indicate the African blood....[104]

Often physical descriptions referred to ancestors of the person in question, mothers and grandmothers who were not in the courtroom, or fathers and grandfathers whose identity was not even assured. *State* v. *Watters* was a miscegenation case involving a white woman and a man accused by the state of being a mulatto, although he "contended that he was descended from Portuguese, and not from Negro or Indian ancestors."[105] William Watters's witnesses testified, however, that his grandmother was a negro "not as black as some negroes they had seen, and had thin lips."[106] The court rejected testimony by one of the witnesses that the grandmother had told him that the father of her child, Watters's mother, was a white man. The state's witness, by contrast, swore that "he knew the grandfather and grandmother...and they were coal black negroes."[107] Similarly, Whitmell Dempsey, who was indicted as a free negro for carrying a firearm, objected to testimony on behalf of the state by a witness who claimed to have heard from someone now dead that Dempsey's great-grandfather was "a coal-black negro," but the court allowed it.[108] Dempsey's witnesses, on the other hand, testified that the mother of Dempsey's great-grandfather was white, that the great-grandfather "was a reddish copper colored man, with curly red hair and blue eyes," and that every succeeding generation of Dempsey men married white women.[109]

Litigants recognized the power of physical description when the person was unavailable for inspection. For example, in *State* v. *Chavers*, the defendant objected that the trial judge had allowed a witness to assert "that the defendant's father was a man of dark colour, and had kinky hair, that he was a shade darker, than the defendant himself, and his hair was about as much kinked." The state argued that "as a negro is almost entirely known by his external marks, for example, his colour, his kinky hair, his thick lips...the nearer the defendant approached the appearance of a negro in these marks he was consequently by so much the farther from a white person."[110]

Yet even when the person at issue was available for inspection, witnesses offered their own physical descriptions of her. They called attention to those features that might have gone unnoticed by the observer, or those that might have fooled the juror. For example, even witnesses appearing on behalf of a litigant trying to prove someone's blackness and slave status might have described the person as white in appearance, while emphasizing the trickery involved in making that person appear white. In *Williamson* v. *Norton*,[111] in which a man named Robert had passed as a white man

on a steamboat but was claimed as a slave by Alexander Norton, Alexander Martin described him as "a shade lighter than a new saddle, with...hair dark, but straight."[112] Rufus Blanchard would never "have suspected him of having any african blood. I should have thought that he was of Spanish origin. He was a man of clear skin and of dark complexion. His dress was adapted to setting off his complexion to good advantage."[113] Several witnesses in this case mentioned the way Robert dressed to make himself look whiter.[114] In *State* v. *Jacobs*, a North Carolina criminal case, the state introduced a witness to testify that "the Defendant was of yellow complexion—had kinky hair though his hair on the day of the trial was much straighter than usual."[115] Ultimately, what made race as a physical marker so inadequate as a basis for decision was its contestable, and seemingly mutable, nature. Often witnesses appeared to see the same person quite differently[116], or, as in Jacobs, they insisted that the person had made himself look different on prior occasions. In short, like any form of evidence, racial appearances could be manipulated.

3. Race as Documented Ancestry

Before the Civil War, determinations of race were necessarily intertwined with questions of status as slave or free. In the first decades of the nineteenth century in particular, race determination cases centered more on the documentation of a person's inherited status and "pedigree," and less on other kinds of evidence of racial identity.[117] Many of these early cases reached the issue of race not as a question of black or white, but as one of black or Indian. "Red" complexion, unlike "negro" appearance, gave rise to a presumption of freedom.[118] Some of the fluidity that characterized these early cases results from the greater permeability of the border between Indian and white[119], the conflation of "race" and "nation" in the definition of "Indian"[120], and the lesser stigma attached to the Indian "race" by whites.[121] After Indian removal and the Cherokee cases, there were few Indians in the southeastern United States to pose problems of racial identification, and fewer questions to be resolved about Indian status. The Indians who remained were absorbed either into white society or communities of "people of color."[122]

A telling example of an early suit for freedom that raised questions of racial identity was *Phoebe v. Vaughan*.[123] Phoebe and her two sons, Davy and Tom, brought suit against Abraham Vaughan of Wilson County, Tennessee, claiming their descent from an American Indian in Dinwiddie County, Virginia. Vaughan was a Revolutionary soldier who settled in Wilson County in the first decade of the nineteenth century.[124] Phoebe and her sons enlisted the help of John Bonner, a member of the Methodist and Quaker Humane Society, sympathetic to the plight of the enslaved. Bonner was a Virginia-born farmer who had also been a Minuteman during the Revolution.[125]

In many ways, Vaughan was an unlikely defendant in a suit for freedom. Several people testified to having heard Vaughan say that all men of all colors should be free.[126] Indeed, Vaughan's defense to the claim that he had acknowledged Phoebe's right to freedom was that Vaughan only meant that all negroes had the right to be free! This antislavery sentiment, however, extended only to the abstract family of slaves, and not to his own. When Phoebe and her sons took him to court, Vaughan not only fought the suit, but swore before witnesses that he would "have Davy's hide" and "kill him or his arm would rot off."[127] This suit seemed to Vaughan the worst sort of betrayal by one whom the family had known as "moms" and whom his children had called "mother."[128] (Vaughan also claimed that when he spoke of Phoebe's right to freedom he had been "in a passion" and had been drinking the day before.)[129] In April 1822, he brought Davy and Tom before two magistrates at John Telford's house, in a rage, accusing them of various crimes.[130] According to several white witnesses at the house, Davy and Tom were acquitted, but Vaughan, enraged, proceeded to whip them both so severely that most of the other whites left the room in disgust or distress, and Davy lost most of the flesh on his back.[131] Phoebe, with the help of John Bonner and her attorneys, deposed witnesses in Virginia to prove that she was the daughter of an Indian woman named Beck, raised in slavery by Thomas Hardaway. Beck's sister Tabb had won her freedom in Prince George's County, Virginia, by proving that Indians enslaved after 1691 were wrongly held in slavery, and other relatives had won their freedom as well. In order to identify her as the same enslaved woman who now appeared in Tennessee, Phoebe's witnesses testified that she had lost an eye to ringworm. Phoebe also called witnesses from Wilson County who testified that they had heard Abraham Vaughan declare Phoebe's right to freedom in the past. Her star witness was Seth P. Pool, a Wilson County man who claimed acquaintance with Beck in Virginia and corroborated the testimony of the Virginia witnesses. Pool apparently did not bear enough of a grudge against John Bonner, who had assaulted him several years earlier, to affect his testimony on Phoebe's behalf.[132]

Vaughan, on the other hand, called witnesses who impugned Seth Pool's veracity[133], and who claimed that Phoebe was bought not from Thomas Hardaway but from a man named Edmund Cooper. Vaughan's witnesses had never heard Phoebe claim her freedom; they had only heard her express the hope that her free husband, Glasgow Hope, might buy her.[134]

Although witnesses for Phoebe mentioned her "copper complexion," suggesting Indian descent, and witnesses for Vaughan talked about her as "tolerably bright and freckled when young," Phoebe's appearance did not become a central issue in the case. No experts testified as to Phoebe's "Indian-ness" or blackness; indeed, there was a peculiar absence of concern about whether Phoebe was in fact of Indian or African origin. Vaughan, despite his professed belief in freedom for all, did not seem overly concerned that an Indian might be held in slavery, if it could be shown, for example, that her ancestors were enslaved when it was still legal to do so. On the whole, the attitude of the defense witnesses seemed to be that if Phoebe was a slave, and had been a slave when brought to Tennessee, then she must be black. Status determined color.

Phoebe's suit was tried before Judge Thomas Stewart in neighboring Sumner County, just north of Wilson County. Most of the jurors and witnesses in Phoebe's case were farmers who owned a handful of slaves. Nevertheless, they gave a verdict for Phoebe's freedom, suggesting that even slaveholders were willing to set someone free.[135] The question of Phoebe's racial identity was a question both about her status (was Phoebe born free?) and her literal identity (was she the same Phoebe?) as much as it was a question of her Indian or black race. The question of racial determination was not hotly contested. Although it was an issue in court whether Phoebe was black, Indian, or white, race was recognized as an imperfect referent for status, rather than the focal point of the controversy. The evidence witnesses gave differed from later cases like *Daniel* v. *Guy*[136]: Not only were there no expert witnesses to discuss the "science" of race, but there was also little evidence about Phoebe's social performance of race.

The political climate at the time of Phoebe's case also was less contentious concerning the slavery question than it became after 1830. John Bonner, the agent of Phoebe and her children, made no secret of his antislavery inclinations. Indeed, he belonged to a religious society devoted in part to helping slavery's victims. In later cases, those who testified for slaves seeking their freedom, or helped them in any way, had to declare their freedom from abolitionism and insist that only philanthropy motivated them. But in Phoebe's case, even Vaughan himself had made antislavery statements in the past. The "proslavery argument" that enslaved status was the best of all possible conditions for people of African blood had not yet fully flowered. Nat Turner's 1831 rebellion had not yet made free blacks seem so dangerous. Furthermore, in the "pioneer" communities of Middle Tennessee, where the events and the trying of this case took place, there was still some room for people of marginal status to live as free men and women.[137] Despite their increasing reliance on slave labor, the possibility of freeing a slave did not seem to threaten inordinately the slaveholding men who sat on Phoebe's jury in 1823.

Although appellate courts' preferred documentary evidence to "reputation" testimony (for which there was a hearsay exception in racial determination cases)[138], juries found reputation at least as persuasive as documents. For example, in the slander case of *Cauchoix* v. *Dupuy*, Cauchoix claimed to be pure white, and he produced marriage and baptismal certificates going back to the seventeenth century without a trace of evidence of color.[139] Although he won the case, the jury awarded him only $250 in damages, when he had requested $6000.[140] Likewise, documentary evidence frequently gave way to "scientific" evidence, even in cases where a person's slave status seemed quite certain. For example, in *Gaines* v. *Ann*[141], a Texas jury found whiteness, despite heavy documentary and testamentary evidence that Ann, her mother, and her grandmother were slaves. The jury made this finding based on "evidence of her being pure white blood" given by two doctors who "had examined her and could not detect any of the indicia of the existence of African blood in her."[142] In spite of this jury finding, however, an appellate court reversed.[143]

4. Race as Ascriptive Identity: Reputation, Associations, and Reception in Society

What nineteenth-century judges and lawyers commonly called "reputation evidence" drew on a variety of kinds of evidence or criteria for racial determination. Here, I shall use the term "reputation evidence" to refer to testimony about a person's acceptance in the community, including the person's associations with blacks or whites and the racial status his neighbors assigned to him—what he "passed for." I shall consider separately testimony about self-presentation and about what I shall call "performance," but these categories necessarily overlap. One's social activities and one's associations are not always distinct; one's acceptance by others and self-presentation depend on one another. Furthermore, part of acceptance in the community involved rumors about ancestry. In testifying about a person's reputation, witnesses revealed the complicated

connections between community memory of a family's racial identity and their sense of an individual's racial identity. The translation into practice of rules based on "blood" required an inquiry into each family member's status, balanced against the present status of the person in question. And in practice, testimony about a family's social identity and reputation served to combat documentary evidence of slave, free negro, or Indian status.

A good example of the use of reputation testimony is the case of *Boullemet* v. *Phillips*[144], a Louisiana slander case. Slander, of course, is all about rumor, so much of the testimony was bound to center on rumors and reputation. The lawsuit arose when a Mr. Murphy refused to serve in the Louisiana militia with Stephen Boullemet, "saying he was a colored man," and Boullemet's friends traced the rumor to Alexander Phillips.[145]

In two trials held in quick succession in the spring of 1840, witnesses for Stephen Boullemet insisted that he had lived his life as a white man, that he had been accepted into white society, and that his mother was reputed to be, if not white, then Indian, but certainly not "colored." Francis Oboyd testified that Boullemet was "received in good circles of society—he was received as a white man."[146] William Emerson testified that Boullemet was "always considered a white boy at school...[and] was a kind of favorite at school."[147] Thomas Spear testified that Boullemet's children played with his children, although he had heard the rumor that Boullemet's mother was a colored woman.[148] Several witnesses from Santo Domingo confirmed that the Boullemets had been a respectable white family on that island, and that "if a white person was to unite to a coloured woman he was immediately considered as degraded."[149] The Santo

Domingo witnesses testified that Boullemet and his mother were "descendants of Indians (descendants de Sauvages)."[150] Mrs. Lavigne had seen Boullemet's father, on the other hand, "at Lafayette Balls and at Mr. Mackay's balls...Mr. Boullemet visited Mrs. Brennan, Mrs. Benvist, Mr. Baptiste, Mrs. Legalle, Mrs. Chapion, Mrs. Mouchon...."[151]

By contrast, witnesses for the defendant described Boullemet's mother as the mulatto housekeeper of his father, the "menagere" who kept his grog shop.[152] Norbert Vaudry, for example, explained on cross-examination that while Boullemet's father was indeed "a very respectable man," his mother "never associated with white ladies."[153] Accordingly, Vaudry "always took her for a coloured woman."[154] Another witness from Santo Domingo claimed that "the mother of the woman who calls herself Mrs. Boullemet she had no more the appearance of an Indian than witness himself has that of a broom stick (l'air d'un Indian comme mien d'un manisse a balet)."[155] Furthermore, "her complexion was more that of a grenadier than that of a woman....[T]he children might have been considered as interesting children but not as white children."[156] At the second trial, the defendant's Santo Domingo witnesses emphasized that they had never known of Indians in the West Indies[157], that Mrs. Boullemet, who was called Fillette, was known "as coloured," although several of the witnesses did not know whether she was "descended from an Indian or negro race."[158] As Thomas Bausy said, "the fact is he never gave it a thought."[159] Mr. Barnett testified that many boarders left Boullemet's father's boarding house after he married Fillette.[160] Several defense witnesses tried to explain the racial practices of Santo Domingo in the years leading up to the slave revolt, in which mulattoes were accepted on an equal footing in certain realms—in the military and in public office, but not in private

white society and certainly not in marriage.[161] Boullemet called several rebuttal witnesses (and recalled some who had testified before) to deny that Fillette and his mother were the same person. The housekeeper, whom they claimed was known as Mrs. Julie, was about forty when Mrs. Boullemet arrived at the age of eighteen.[162]

Late nineteenth-century cases similarly relied on reputation evidence. In *Hare* v. *Board of Education,* James Hare's children were kept out of the public school in Gates County on the ground that they were negroes.[163] The Board of Education called J. H. Ellis to testify that James Hare's mother (admitted to be "a pure-blood white woman") was living with Charles Jones, "a yellow man," when James was born.[164] When asked, "From your knowledge of the plaintiff, from your observation of him and his associations, do you say he is a white man or a negro?"[165] Ellis answered, "I say he is a colored man. He associated with colored people until they would not have him."[166] Similarly, Morgan averred, "From my knowledge of him I say he is a colored man. He has associated with the colored race."[167] A "colored man," William Eason, also testified for the Board that Hare had associated with people of color: "[Hare] was at our church at the mourners' bench for a week. He courted my wife; she is a colored woman."[168] On the other hand, Hare made the case that his father was not Charles Jones, who was "about three-fourths white," but Elbert Matthews, who was "a white man, dark-coloured."[169]

The neighbors of both Stephen Boullemet and James Hare judged their racial status by the company they kept. Acceptance in the white community could signify white identity, and certain kinds of associations with "colored" people almost certainly meant blackness. In court, witnesses remembered whether the person at issue had inhabited churches, schools, and other spaces that were designated white or black.

5. The Rise of Race as Science and Performance

Trials in the early nineteenth century, like *Phoebe* v. *Vaughan*, often revolved around documentary evidence, status, and ancestry. During the 1850s, however, as the question of race became more central and more hotly contested, courts began to consider "scientific" knowledge of a person's "blood" as well as the ways she revealed her blood through her acts. The mid-nineteenth century saw the development of a scientific discourse of race that located the essence of racial difference in physiological characteristics such as the size of the cranium and the shape of the foot, and attempted to link physiological, moral, and intellectual difference.

This section will show the domestication and popularization of "racial science" by lawyers, doctors, and laypeople at trials. It will also suggest some reasons for the heightened focus on racial identity in the courtroom in the decades preceding the Civil War. The following part will focus on the performance of whiteness, arguing that racial science, despite its rising importance as a way of understanding "race," shared the stage with a discourse of race as social performance.

Numerous developments between 1830 and 1850 help explain the rise in litigation over racial determination in the pre-Civil War years. The final decades before the Civil War were increasingly difficult times to live on the "middle ground" between slavery and freedom, black and white. First, the threat posed to slavery by abolitionism and slave revolts beginning in the 1830s led

proslavery Southerners to develop a new explicit defense of slavery in racial terms: The "necessary evil" became the "positive good." The proslavery argument rested on the racial inferiority and fitness for slavery of African Americans. The development of this ideology made the status of free black people, an increasingly anomalous liminal group, more and more precarious. If black people fulfilled their highest purpose in slavery, and freedom was an attribute of whiteness, then how could there be free black people? The 1840s and 1850s saw a tightening of manumission laws, making it increasingly difficult to free a slave voluntarily, and a corresponding rise in the restrictions on free blacks' freedom of movement and other civil rights.[170] This trend culminated in the self-enslavement laws of the 1850s, which gave free blacks a choice between leaving the state or choosing a master and enslaving themselves.[171] (Needless to say, the latter option had no takers.)[172]

People who crossed racial boundaries—"mulattoes"—like free blacks, threatened efforts to make slave status more congruent with blackness and freedom more congruent with whiteness. Although most states had bans on interracial marriage and fornication before the Civil War, Alabama had no barrier to interracial marriage until 1852[173], and Mississippi's statute provided only that ministers and officials were authorized to celebrate marriages between free whites.[174] In prewar Tennessee, interracial marriage was punishable by a fine; by 1870, it was a felony for which one could be imprisoned for five years.[175] White Southern perceptions that the mulatto population was growing, as well as the increasing domestic slave trade from the Upper South to the Lower South, and rising geographic mobility in Southern society, were making it harder to determine who was white or black, and who was a slave.[176] These developments fed white Southerners' anxieties about the possibilities of knowing and determining racial identities.

The growing urgency surrounding racial identity and the higher stakes attendant on drawing racial boundaries manifested themselves in an upswing in litigation after 1850.[177] In the cases themselves, the effort to align slavery and racial status more closely made it considerably more difficult for a litigant to convince a jury or a judge that she was white.[178] But most striking in the cases of racial determination was the new fervor with which the trials were conducted. The 1850s saw the clamor around race rise to a fever pitch. The trials of racial determination not only garnered local attention because of the often salacious subject matter, but they also became the objects of national political discourse because they fed into abolitionist claims about white slavery and "tragic octoroons." Suits for freedom were politicized in the newspapers and in retellings by abolitionists and fugitive slaves. Litigants became more invested in the search for the true essence of race, but despite the rhetoric suggesting that common sense could help distinguish between whites and blacks, that essence was elusive. Increasingly, documentation of status gave way to two arguments for whiteness or blackness: science and performance. In the postbellum years, the stakes in these courtroom battles changed somewhat, but the shape of the conflict retained important continuities with the disputes of the 1850s.

The first of these developments, the introduction of a "scientific" discourse about race into the courtroom, traces its roots to the well-documented rise of "racial science" among phrenologists and medical doctors during this period. Although there is some debate about when scientific racism came to

dominate American racial ideology, most historians date its beginnings to the mid-nineteenth century.[179] By drawing the contrast between nineteenth-century biological essentialism and early twentieth-century anthropological theories, which saw racial differences as the product of social and cultural construction, these historical accounts make "science" appear to have been the monolithic language of race in the nineteenth century.[180] The evidence from courtroom battles over racial determination, however, suggests that, at least before the Civil War, racial science was not the predominant way of understanding racial identity.

Only nine cases appear to have relied on expert scientific testimony about racial differences.[181] The discourse of racial science, of course, was not limited to medical experts. In reviewing the cases, it is often hard to distinguish the testimony of a medical expert from that of a layperson, because the "racial science expert" was typically a local doctor whose testimony highlighted the same aspects of physical appearance that other witnesses did. For example, Abby Guy's lawyer called two local doctors to inform the jury about the "distinguishing marks between the negro and the white race."[182] Dr. Isaac Newton, an elderly physician who owned substantial land holdings as well as a young mulatto woman slave with two children, qualified as an expert because he "had read Physiology."[183] Dr. Newton testified that curly hair and flat noses "remain observable for several descents [from the negro]," implying that Abby Guy, who lacked these features, must have been far removed from "the negro."[184] Dr. M. C. Comer, who owned thirty slaves of his own,[185] corroborated Dr. Newton's testimony.[186]

Medical experts, however, were more likely than lay people to be seen as capable of hypothesizing about the trajectory of "negro blood" in one's family tree. For example, three doctors testified on behalf of Thomas Gary, a slave suing for his freedom.[187] Dr. Brown "could discover no trace of the negro blood in his eyes, nose, mouth, or jaws."[188] While Dr. Brown was unwilling to conclude firmly that Gary had not a drop of negro blood, he explained that he "[s]hould suppose it would take at least twenty generations from the black blood to be as white as complainant."[189] Dr. Wilcox could "discover no evidence of negro blood in him" by examination, having known Gary seven or eight years;[190] and Dr. Dibbrell had examined Gary and guessed that he had approximately one-sixteenth negro blood, although he cautioned that there was "no definite rule."[191] The only signs of negro blood were "upper lip rather thicker than in the white race" and "temperament sanguine."[192]

In *Sullivan* v. *Hugly*[193], Justice Lyon of the Georgia Supreme Court articulated an explanation for why medical testimony should count more than lay testimony. In that case, the plaintiff in an inheritance dispute questioned the paternity of Amos Hugly, claiming that he should lose the right to inherit from his father, because he was really the child of his mother's adulterous affair with a black man.[194] Dr. Dudley Hammond testified that "this child differed from the pure white race in several particulars... [Dr. Hammond] was indelibly impressed with those [developments] pertaining to the negro variety...skin dark...eyes large and prominent, nose short, and hair black, the facial angle deficient."[195] Justice

Lyon noted that "[n]either of these [other] witnesses are experts, or profess any skill in physiology, genealogy, or ethnology....The testimony of Dr. Hammond is to the same purport, but is much stronger and more important, from the fact, that he is a scientific and learned gentleman on the subject of the races, and examined the child at different times closely, for the purpose of ascertaining whether it was a white child or a mulatto."[196]

Nevertheless, the court noted that none of these opinions were "infallible." Dr. Hammond's testimony "should have been corroborated by that of others skilled like himself...."[197] Furthermore, Justice Lyon continued, in matters of racial determination, higher courts should not second-guess juries, and this jury had seen fit to decide that Amos Hugly was white, or at any rate, to give his mother's husband the benefit of the presumption of paternity.[198]

Conversely, lay witnesses were encouraged by lawyers to put their testimony in "scientific" terms. In Abby Guy's case, her lawyers asked several of Daniel's witnesses whether they had studied "Phisiology or the difference in distinctions of races."[199] Although the trial judge in this case allowed the witnesses to testify even if they made no claim of expertise[200], in others, laypersons were excluded from testifying about racial descent.[201] Witnesses, then, had an incentive to don the mantle of science when they gave physical descriptions. Despite these incentives, racial science dominated the cases far less than one might expect, and it was almost entirely absent before the 1850s.

Notes

[65] 18 Ala. 276, 277 (1850).

[66] Martha Hodes employs the distinction between reputation and self-presentation. See Hodes, supra note 20, at 103. Although the individuals at issue did not speak for themselves

at trial, witnesses reported on the way they held themselves out in society. Most often, however, witnesses did not distinguish between the way people held themselves out and the way they were perceived, or what they "passed for."

[67] Transcript of Trial, *Daniel* v. *Guy*, supra note 1, at 20 (bill of exceptions).

[68] Id. at 23–24.

[69] Etheridge, supra note 36, at 84.

[70] Id. at 85.

[71] See id. at 84–85.

[72] He had managed to acquire $1,400 worth of property by 1860. See Census of 1850, supra note 35; Census of 1860, Manuscript Population Schedules, Ashley County, Ark. [hereinafter Census of 1860].

[73] See Transcript of Trial, *Daniel* v. *Guy*, supra note 1, at 23 (bill of exceptions).

[74] See id. at 21.

[75] See id. at 32–34 (exhibits A and B).

[76] Id. at 65–67 (answer of William Daniel).

[77] See id.

[78] Id. at 3 (petition of Abby Guy).

[79] *Daniel* v. *Guy*, 19 Ark. 121, 126 (1857).

[80] Transcript of Trial, *Daniel* v. *Guy*, supra note 1, at 25 (bill of exceptions). In the statement of facts in the state supreme court report, this was summarized as "Had seen half-breeds as white as she was." Daniel, 19 Ark. at 125.

[81] Transcript of Trial, *Daniel* v. *Guy*, supra note 1, at 28 (bill of exceptions)

[82] Id. at 27.

[83] See id. at 28.

[84] See, e.g., id. at 29–30 (testimony of James Kates); id. at 30 (testimony of K. B. Thompson).

[85] Id. at 29 (testimony of James Barnett) (emphasis added). In 1860, J. D. Barnett was a 47-year-old farmer from Georgia, with $1,200 worth of real property and $3,000 worth of personal property. See Dwelling 700, Census of 1860, supra note 72.

[86] Daniel, 19 Ark. at 129.

[87] Id.

[88] See id.

[89] See Transcript of Trial, *Daniel* v. *Guy*, supra note 1, at 16; Census of 1850, supra note 35.

[90] See Daniel, 19 Ark. at 131-32.

[91] See *Daniel* v. *Guy*, 23 Ark. 50, 51 (1861).

[92] Id. at 54.

[93] See id. at 52, 55. The headnote to the case emphasized that it was, "as often held, [the] province of the jury to pass upon the weight of the evidence." Id. at 51.

[94] Id. at 54–55.

[95] See id. This was not the end of the story for Abby Guy and William Daniel. In June 1863, Abby Guy, now Abby Roper, was back in the Ashley County Circuit Court, trying to recover the horses, oxen, and cart Daniel had taken from her when he brought her back from the bayou in 1856. Daniel claimed, first, that Guy could not sue in trover because she was a slave, and second, that the statute of limitations had run out on her suit. The court, in

chancery, gave Guy a preliminary injunction against Daniel's interposition of a plea of the statute of limitations. Daniel took that as a final judgment and appealed it to the Arkansas Supreme Court, where he lost. See *Daniel* v. *Roper*, 24 Ark. 131 (1863). There is no record of the outcome of Guy' s trover suit.

[96] *Garvin* v. *State*, 52 Miss. 207, 209 (1876).

[97] *Warlick* v. *White*, 76 N.C. 175, 179 (1877).

[98] Transcript of Trial, *Daniel* v. *Guy*, supra note 1, at 21.

[99] See, for example, *Chancellor* v. *Milly*, Transcript of Trial, *Chancellor* v. *Milly* (Ky. Mason County Cir. Ct. Fall 1838) (collection of Ky. State Archives, Lexington, Ky., Supreme Court Files), rev'd, 39 Ky. (9 Dana) 23 (1839), in which Milly's lawyer exhibited her to the jury to prove her whiteness, and she won her freedom from slavery. The appellate court found error in the trial judge's refusal to admit testimony to rebut the presumption of freedom raised by her white looks. See Milly, 39 Ky. (9 Dana) at 24.

[100] *Daniel* v. *Guy*, 23 Ark. 50, 51 (1861). In *Warlick* v. *White*, Transcript of Trial, *Warlick* v. *White*, No. 11,775 (N.C. Catawba County Super. Ct. Aug. 1876) (collection of N.C. Dep't of Archives & History, Raleigh, N.C., Supreme Court Records), rev'd, 76 N.C. 175 (1877) [hereinafter Transcript of Trial, *Warlick* v. *White*], the race of 11–year-old Sarah Carpenter was at issue. The plaintiffs, seeking to prove that she had black blood, "proposed to exhibit Sarah J. Carpenter to the jury and for that purpose to place her upon the witness stand." Id. at 4. The defendant (Sarah's mother) objected to the jury's inspection of Sarah, raising concerns about delicacy and decency in 12 men's inspection of a young girl. The trial court "declined to have the child subjected to the inspection of the jury," Id., but the appellate court remanded the case for a new trial to allow the inspection to take place, in an opinion addressing the issue of jury inspections for the purpose of racial determination, see Warlick, 76 N.C. at 179–80. The court noted the concern that some, including Sarah's mother, had raised—that such an inspection would be "indecent or indelicate." Id. at 178. The court distinguished this case from one in which a woman's pregnant condition was displayed to the jury, implying that Sarah's race would be immediately more evident without disrobing before the jury, and thus an unseemly display would not be required. See Id. And yet, although the details of this inspection do not appear in the record, it is clear that many jury inspections involved just such a disrobing. Indeed, as Walter Johnson has suggested, these disrobings reenacted the inspections of the slave trader's yard. See Johnson, supra note 20, at 18. In order to prove whiteness, one often had to perform whiteness through the rituals of the slave market. Thus, Johnson suggests the contradictions inherent in finding these women "white." After all, what good white woman would submit herself to such indelicate inspection? If she were truly, purely white, what good white man would look at her disrobed? Rather, he suggests, these women represented "enslaved whiteness," the tantalizing, hypersexualized, and commodified whiteness of the "fancy girls" sold as concubines—white in beauty but not in social status. "Fancy girls" in the slave market and women suing for their freedom underwent the same "inspections." Id.

[101] See infra Appendix.

[102] *Ulzere* v. *Poeyfarre*, No. 468 (La. New Orleans Parish Ct. May 1820) (collection of Earl K. Long Library, Special Collections & Archives, Univ. of New Orleans, New Orleans, La., Supreme Court Records), rev'd, 8 Mart. (o.s.) 155 (La. 1820).

[103] See, e.g., Transcript of Trial, *State* v. *Chavers*, supra note 27.

[104] *Gary* v. *Stevenson*, 19 Ark. 580, 584-85 (1858).

[105] Transcript of Trial, *State* v. *Watters*, No. 3540 (N.C. Ashe County Super. Ct. Feb. 1842) (collection of N.C. Dep't of Archives & History, Raleigh, N.C., Supreme Court Records), aff'd, 25 N.C. (3 Ired.) 455 (1843).

[106] Watters, 25 N.C. (3 Ired.) at 456.

[107] Id.

[108] See Transcript of Trial, *State* v. *Dempsey*, No. 4723 (N.C. Bertie County Super. Ct. Mar. 1849) (collection of N.C. Department of Archives & History, Raleigh, N.C., Supreme Court Records), aff'd, 31 N.C. (9 Ired.) 384 (1849).

[109] Dempsey, 31 N.C. (9 Ired.) at 385. The court instructed the jury that even one black great-great-grandfather was enough to make a person black. See id.

[110] Transcript of Trial, *State* v. *Chavers*, supra note 27.

[111] Transcript of Trial, *Williamson* v. *Norton*, No. 2427 (La. New Orleans Dist. Ct. 1850) (collection of Earl K. Long Library, Special Collections & Archives, Univ. of New Orleans, New Orleans, La., Supreme Court Records), aff'd in part and rev'd in part, 7 La. Ann. 393 (1852) [hereinafter Transcript of Trial, *Williamson* v. *Norton*].

[112] Williamson, 7 La. Ann. at 394.

[113] See Transcript of Trial, *Williamson* v. *Norton*, supra note 111, at 56 (deposition of Rufus Blanchard).

[114] See id. at 48–50, 54–59 (depositions of Rufus Blanchard and Lyman Cole). Lyman Cole noted that Robert "had more the appearance of the gentleman than the plebeian." Id. at 49.

[115] Transcript of Trial, *State* v. *Jacobs*, No. 7915 (N.C. Brunswick County Super. Ct. Mar. 1859) (collection of N.C. Dep't of Archives & History, Raleigh, N.C., Supreme Court Records), aff'd, 51 N.C. (6 Jones) 284 (1859).

[116] See *Bryan* v. *Walton*, 14 Ga. 185 (1853) [Bryan I].

[117] See, e.g., *Davis* v. *Wood*, 14 U.S. (1 Wheat.) 6 (1816) (involving a suit for freedom that turned on the plaintiff's mother's descent from an Englishwoman); *Gregory* v. *Baugh*, 25 Va. (4 Rand.) 611 (1827) (involving a suit for freedom that turned on whether the plaintiff's mother was descended from an Indian woman who was entitled to her freedom); *Pegram* v. *Isabell*, 12 Va. (2 Hen. & M.) 193 (1808) (involving a suit for freedom that turned on the plaintiff's descent from her Indian ancestor in her maternal line).

[118] See *Hudgins* v. *Wrights*, 11 Va. (1 Hen. & M.) 134 (1806).

[119] In general, Indian status, like slave status, followed that of the mother. This was in sharp contrast, however, to racial identity, as "negro"; it was possible to be considered white with half Indian "blood." See, e.g., *United States* v. *Sanders*, 27 F. Cas. 950, 950–51 (C.C.D. Ark. 1847) (No. 16,220) ("[T]he child of a white woman by an Indian father, would...be deemed of the white race; the condition of the mother, and not the quantum of Indian blood in the veins, determining the condition of the offspring.").

[120] Membership in one of the Indian "nations" could be gained by intermarriage more easily than an Indian racial identity could. See, e.g., Transcript of Trial, *State* v. *Melton*, No. 6431 (N.C. Stanley County Super. Ct. Dec. 1852) (collection of N.C. Dep't of Archives & History, Raleigh, N.C., Supreme Court Records), aff'd, 44 N.C. (Busb.) 49 (1852) (holding that "Indian" racial identity, for the purposes of a statute prohibiting intermarriage, meant one-eighth Indian ancestry, or Indian "blood...to the third degree"); Transcript of Trial, *Tuten's Lessee* v. *Martin* (collection of Tenn. State Archives, Nashville, Tenn., Supreme Court Records), rev'd, 11 Tenn. (3 Yer.) 452 (1832) (noting that because Tuten had married Rachel

Coody of the Cherokee nation, lived within the territory of the Cherokees, and followed their practices and habits, he was "the head of an Indian family" for the purposes of land ownership).

[121] The lesser stigma attached to the Indian race by whites can be seen in racial determination trials in the ways witnesses discussed someone interchangeably as "Indian" and "white," in contrast to "colored" and "black" or "negro." In *Boullemet* v. *Phillips*, Transcript of Trial, *Boullemet* v. *Phillips*, No. 4219 (La. New Orleans Parish Ct. Feb. 1840) (collection of Earl K. Long Library, Special Collections & Archives, Univ. of New Orleans, New Orleans, La., Supreme Court Records), rev'd, 2 Rob. 365 (La. 1842) [hereinafter Transcript of Trial, *Boullemet* v. *Phillips*]. French witnesses who had come to Louisiana from Santo Domingo and from New Orleans testified both that Mr. Boullemet's mother was Indian and that she was white. Jean Fauchet testified on direct examination that the Boullemets "were considered as a respectable family, they were considered as white." Id. at 13. On cross-examination, he explained that he had heard that Mr. Boullemet's mother "was a descendant of an Indian race...that [her] mother...was of a dark colour like the Indians (elle etait brune comme les Indiens)...that he knew many white persons who had the same complexion and who had no African or Indian blood in their veins." Id. at 14. Suzanne Mouchon testified that "Mrs. Boullemet was considered as a white person....[S]he appeared to be of an Indian race she was of a dark white color (Blanche Brune)." Id. at 28–29. Characterizing her as Indian, or having Indian blood, did not prevent them from also seeing her as white. Mrs. Lavigne even noted, in one breath, that "Mr. Boullemet's wife she was considered as white she was an Indian she did not look like a negro or colored person—she visited nobody but was always hunting in the woods." Id. at 32. Of course, in Mrs. Lavigne's story, Mrs. Boullemet may have been considered to be white but still not have been white.

[122] In *State* v. *Belmont*, 35 S.C.L. (4 Strob.) 445, 449 (1850), Amelia Marchant's witnesses claimed that she was Indian and Portuguese. Witnesses for Ambrosio Belmont, who sought to disqualify her from testifying against him in a criminal trial, produced witnesses who claimed she was the daughter of a "colored man." Whereas the trial court charged the jury that Indians were included in the same class as other people of color, the South Carolina Supreme Court distinguished "free Indians in amity with this government," even if the person in question no longer lived with the tribe in a separate national existence but had become a resident of the state and intermarried with whites.

McMillan v. *School Committee*, Transcript of Trial, *McMillan* v. *School Comm.*, No. 16,384 (N.C. Robeson County Super. Ct. Fall Term 1889) (collection of N.C. Dep't of History & Archives, Raleigh, N.C., Supreme Court Records), aff'd, 12 S.E. 330 (N.C. 1890), reveals the difficulty of drawing legal distinctions between Indians and blacks, even after slavery, given the social history of "colored" communities of Indians and free blacks. The Croatan Indians were by legend considered to be survivors of the last Roanoke colony. Yet Nathan McMillan, suing the School Committee of the "Croatan" District in 1888 to gain his children's entry into school, claimed that "[t]he people or class now called Croatans were reputed to be and were called Mulattoes before the Croatan Act [of the North Carolina legislature] was passed." Id. at 19. Before the Civil War, they "were always a separate race to themselves—attended their own churches and some schools of their own and would not associate with the negroes." Id. at 26–27 (testimony of J. C. M. Eachin). No one disputed that Nathan's wife was a "Croatan," but Nathan's racial status was contested.

[123] Transcript of Trial, *Butcher* v. *Vaughan*, No. 5626 (Tenn. Sumner County Cir. Ct. Aug. 1823) (collection of Tenn. State Library and Archives, Nashville, Tenn., Sumner County Court Records, Roll A-5083), rev'd sub nom. *Vaughan* v. *Phebe* [sic], 8 Tenn. (Mart. & Yer.) 4 (1827) [hereinafter Transcript of Trial, *Butcher* v. *Vaughan*].

[124] See Thomas E. Partlow, Wilson County, Tennessee, Deed Books C–M, 1793–1829, at 353 (1984) [hereinafter Partlow, Wilson County Deed Books C–M] (deed book E); Thomas E. Partlow, Wilson County, Tennessee, Deed Books N-Z, 1829–1853, at 105 (1984) [hereinafter Partlow, Wilson County Deed Books N-Z] (deed book P); Thomas E. Partlow, Wilson County, Tennessee Miscellaneous Records, 1800–1875, at 95–100, 151, 159 (1982) [hereinafter Partlow, Wilson County Miscellaneous Records].

[125] See Partlow, Wilson County Deed Books C–M, supra note 124, at 329 (deed book H); Partlow, Wilson County Miscellaneous Records, supra note 124, at 147.

[126] See Transcript of Trial, *Butcher* v. *Vaughan*, supra note 123 (depositions of Rachel Bowers and James Weir).

[127] Id. (depositions of Joseph Davenport and Nancy Davenport).

[128] Id. (deposition of Rachel Bowers).

[129] Id. (depositions of Rachel Bowers, Nancy Davenport, and James Weir).

[130] John Telford was a native of the region, son of one of the first settlers, and a large landowner. See Partlow, Wilson County Miscellaneous Records, supra note 124, at 95–100, 124, 159.

[131] See Transcript of Trial, *Butcher* v. *Vaughan*, supra note 123. With Bonnet's assistance as "agent," Davy and Tom also sued Vaughan for assault. Although suits for freedom were often formally filed as writs of trespass, using the traditional language of assault and battery, this suit appears to have been genuine. John Bonner also described in an affidavit to the Sumner County Court Vaughan's further efforts to rid himself of the freedom suit. First, he tried to bribe Bonner with a Lodge membership to convince Phoebe to drop the suit. He then pursued a change of venue from Wilson County to Sumner County for purposes of delay. Bonner also asserted that Vaughan had prohibited Phoebe and her sons from attending depositions in the suit, effectively preventing them from taking place. At that point, the court shifted control over the plaintiffs from Vaughan to Bonner.

[132] Bonner had been found guilty in the Wilson County Court in 1815 for assault and battery against Seth P. Pool. See Thomas E. Partlow, The People Of Wilson County, Tennessee, 1800–1899, at 3 (1983). Phoebe's other witnesses included James McDonald, Vaughan's son-in-law, and Booth Warren, a slaveholder who had been indicted for assault and battery just a year before.

[133] The 1815 jury that found Bonner guilty of assaulting Pool had fined Bonner only one cent. It may have been that Pool had something of a bad reputation in Wilson County. Matthew Figures, a miller and justice of the peace, one of the oldest and most prosperous landowners in the county, and William Steele, a trustee of the biggest church in town, a second major in the militia, and a major landowner, however, both vouched for Pool's character on Phoebe's behalf. Character witnesses against Pool were Charles Locke, a small landowner, Elizabeth Sanders, and Booth Warren. See Frank Burns, Wilson County 17, 18 (1983); Partlow, supra note 132, at 25, 89; Thomas E Partlow, Wilson County, Tennessee, Circuit Court Records 182 (1988); Partlow, Wilson County Deed Books C–M, supra note 124, at 15, 283 (deed books C and G); Partlow, Wilson County Deed Books N–Z, supra note 124, at 285 (deed book Q); Thomas E. Partlow, Wilson County, Tennessee, Deeds, Marriages, And Wills, 1800–1902, at 160, 162, 176, 187, 190 (1987) [hereinafter Partlow, Wilson County: Deeds]; Partlow, Wilson County Miscellaneous Records, supra note 124, at 84, 94, 99, 103; Census of 1820, Manuscript Population Schedules, Wilson County, Tenn.

[134] See Transcript of Trial, *Butcher* v. *Vaughan*, supra note 123 (depositions of Benjamin Bennett, Judith Bennett, Nancy Hicks, and Rebecca Yeargin).

[135] Ten of the jurors in the Sumner County trial appeared in the 1820 census, and of these, five had remained in the county when the census taker returned ten years later. In 1820, all but one of the jurors listed their occupation as "agriculture," and the median number of slaves owned by jurors was four. The one juror who owned more than a handful of slaves, George D. Blackmore, one of the earliest settlers in Sumner County, had twenty-six in 1820, but only ten slaves in 1830. On the other hand, the four other slaveholders appearing in the 1830 census all increased their slaveholding in the ten-year period. Compare Census of 1820, Manuscript Population Schedules, Sumner County, Tenn., with Census of 1830, Manuscript Population Schedules, Sumner County, Tenn.

Although all were farmers, their circumstances varied considerably. Josiah Walton, who was also a stock dealer, was the chairman of the county court for several years and private secretary to Andrew Jackson in 1818. He was born in Sumner County to a large slaveowning family. See Goodspeed's General History Of Tennessee, at 924 (C. & R. Elder Booksellers 1973) (1887). John Parsons, on the other hand, was of meagre enough means that he specified a bequest of $25 to one of his sons in his will. See Shirley Wilson, Sumner County, Tennessee Bond Book, 1787–1835, at 14 (1994). William Chapman's family had been in Sumner County for at least three generations, whereas Artemus Tufts moved there from Massachusetts by way of Charleston, South Carolina. See Carol Wells, Sumner County, Tenn. Court Minutes, 1787–1805 and 1808–1810, at 107 (1995).

[136] For a discussion of *Daniel* v. *Guy*, see supra Subsection II.B.1.

[137] For the history of the Middle Tennessee frontier, see generally Thomas Perkins Abernethy, From Fontier To Plantation In Tennessee: A Study In Frontier Democracy (University of Ala. Press 1967) (1932); Stephen V. Ash, Middle Tennessee Society Transformed, 1860–1870: War And Peace In The Upper South (1988); and Robert Tracy McKenzie, One South Or Many? Plantation Belt And Upcountry In Civil War-Era Tennessee (1994.).

[138] See *Davis* v. *Wood*, 14 U.S. (1 Wheat.) 6 (1816) (holding that hearsay and general reputation are admissible to prove pedigree but not status); *Pegram* v. *Isbell*, 12 Va. (2 Hen. & M.) 193 (1808) (holding that prior litigation deciding the status of a woman is not conclusive evidence of the status of the woman's offspring).

[139] Transcript of Trial, *Cauchoix* v. *Dupuy*, supra note 30; see also Transcript of Trial, *Lange* v. *Richoux*, No. 2491 (La. New Orleans Dist. Ct. May 1833) (collection of Earl K. Long Library, Special Collections & Archives, Univ. of New Orleans, New Orleans, La., Supreme Court Records), aff'd, 6 La. 560 (1833) (involving the elaborate genealogy of a family of free people of color).

[140] See Cauchoix, 3 La. at 207. This case was unusual. In the vast majority of cases, record evidence was on the side of the party asserting someone's blackness or slave status. Whiteness was an argument in itself, expected to stand outside and beyond documentary evidence. Documentation of status as a slave or free person of color was the best available evidence of African ancestry, and it was the source most commonly resorted to by those trying to prove a person's blackness.

[141] 17 Tex. 211 (1856).

[142] Id. at 215.

[143] See id.

[144] Transcript of Trial, *Boullemet* v. *Phillips*, supra note 121. Some of the circumstances under which questions of racial determination arose underscore both the financial benefit that accompanied white status in the 19th-century South, which Cheryl Harris has eloquently described, see Harris, supra note 18, at 1715–45, and the honor attached to whiteness.

[145] Transcript of Trial, *Boullemet* v. *Phillips*, supra note 121 at 9 (testimony of Francis Oboyd).

[146] Id.

[147] Id. at 36 (testimony of William Emerson).

[148] See id. at 11 (testimony of Thomas Spear).

[149] Id. at 12 (testimony of Jean Chaillot); see also id. at 24 (testimony of Jean Chaillot); id. at 14, 26 (testimony of Jean Fauchet).

[150] Id. at 24 (testimony of Jean Chaillot). On cross-examination, he explained that he "knew that the mother of Mr. Boullemet was a descendent from Indians because she told him so. She told him so without being asked." Id. at 25; see also id. at 14, 28, 29, 32 (testimony of Mrs. Louis Engelhim, Jean Fauchet, Mrs. Lavigne, and Suzanne Mouchon). At the second trial, Jean Fauchet testified that he could not "state if they were Indians but heard that they descended from zinguies (Bohemions)." Id. at 69 (testimony of Jean Fauchet).

[151] Id. at 31 (testimony of Mrs. Lavigne).

[152] Id. at 18 (testimony of Norbert Vaudry).

[153] Id. at 19–20.

[154] Id.

[155] Id. at 41 (testimony of Joseph P. Baude-[illegible]).

[156] Id. at 42–43.

[157] See id. at 41,45 (testimony of Joseph P. Baude-[illegible] and Norbert Vaudry).

[158] Id. at 48 (testimony of P. D. Henry); see also id. at 49, 50 (testimony of Barthelemy Bacas and Thomas Bausy).

[159] Id. at 50 (testimony of Thomas Bausy).

[160] See id. at 52 (testimony of Mr. Barnett).

[161] See id. at 62–63, 75–76 (testimony of Franois Carlon and deposition of Madame Verine Laplante).

[162] See id. at 68–69 (testimony of Mrs. Preaux). The first jury in this case could not reach a verdict. The second jury gave a verdict for Stephen Boullemet, showing that they believed he was a white person. The trial judge indicated that he disagreed with their reading of the facts of the case but felt that he could not disturb the verdict. The Louisiana Supreme Court, however, finding the verdict "contrary to the evidence," overturned it and remanded the case for a new trial. *Boullemet* v. *Phillips*, 2 Rob. 365., 366–67 (La. 1842).

Similarly, in *Cauchoix* v. *Dupuy*, Transcript of Trial, *Cauchoix* v. *Dupuy*, supra note 30, the plaintiff sued for slander because his impending marriage had been scuttled by the rumor that his aunt was a woman of color in New York. Witnesses on both sides reported that they had known Mr. Cauchoix and his family in Havana and had known his aunt, Madame Allien, in New York, but they gave completely conflicting views of their racial status. See id. Some witnesses said that they had never even heard it rumored in Havana that the Cauchoix had colored blood; others claimed to have known them as colored people. See id. Similarly, one witness said that Madame Allien "was invited by a great many ladies of the City of New York," and another noted that "there was current report there in Circulation that [Madame Allien] was a colored woman." Id.

[163] Transcript of Trial, *Hare* v. *Board of Educ.*, No. 17,552 (N.C. Gates County Super. Ct. June 1893) (collection of N.C. Dep't of Archives & History, Raleigh, N.C., Supreme Court Records), aff'd, 18 S.E. 55 (N.C. 1893).

[164] Id. at 14.

[165] Id. at 15.

[166] Id.

[167] Id.

[168] Id. at 16.

[169] Id. at 17. The court instructed that marriage was prohibited between whites and people with up to the "third degree" of African ancestry (a black ancestor within three generations). Id. at 18. Thus, if Hare's father was Charles Jones, then Hare would have been considered to have one-eighth "negro blood," enough to make him "negro."

For an example of a late 19th-century slander case, see *Spotorno v. Fourichon*, Transcript of Trial, *Spotormo v. Fourichon*, No. 18,349 (La. New Orleans Civ. Dist. Ct. 1888) (collection of Earl K. Long Library, Special Collections & Archives, Univ. of New Orleans, New Orleans, La., Supreme Court Records), aff'd, 4 S. 71 (La. 1888), which involved the blackmailing of a grocer at the St. Maurice Benevolent Society. Fourichon was a grocer who kept a store at the corner opposite Spotorno's and had often used the rumor of Spotorno's color in business competition. For example, he told a black customer that "his negro friend across the street keeps a grocery" and asked a white customer why he did not "buy from a white man instead of buying from a negro." The plaintiff, Spotorno, testified that his children played with all the other children in the neighborhood, except on one occasion when "I told my child go tell Mr. Senac that his children are calling you a nigger. I want it stopped, I want it to stop or I will stop it, I will go and see him and stop it." The lawyer prompted Spotorno, "Well, what did Mr. Senac do?" and he answered, "Mr. Senac gave a good lamming to his child, that was the end of it." Id.

[170] On the developments of the 1840s and 1850s, see Berlin, supra note 38, at 343–80; and Morris, supra note 33, at 371–423.

[171] See, e.g., An Act to Remove the Free Negroes and Mulattoes from this State, 1859 Ark. Acts 175.

[172] According to Ira Berlin, "In 1860, only 144 mostly elderly free Negroes remained in [Arkansas]." Berlin, supra note 38, at 374; see also MORRIS, supra note 33, at 30–36.

[173] See Peter Wallenstein, Race, Marriage, and the Law of Freedom: Alabama and Virginia, 1860s–1960s, 70 Chi.-Kent L. Rev. 371,373 (1994).

[174] See 1838 Miss. Digest of Laws Ch. 75, [sections] 1, at 560.

[175] See 1857–1858 Tenn. Code [subsections] 2437, 2445–2447, at 481–82; 1870 Tenn. Laws, ch. 39. For discussions of bans on interracial sex and marriage, see Peter W. Bardaglio, *Reconstructing the Household: Families, Sex, and the Law in the Nineteenth-Century South* 48–64 (1995); and Johnston, supra note 25, at 165–216.

[176] On the slave trade, see Michael Tadman, *Speculators and Slaves: Masters, Traders, and Slaves in the Old South* (1989). On social and geographic mobility, see James Oakes, *The Ruling Race: A History of American Slaveholders* 69–95 (1982); Richard C. Wade, *Slavery in the Cities: the South* 1820–1860, at 243–81 (1964); and Johnson, supra note 20, at 6–7. During the 1850s, according to the federal census, mulatto slavery rose by 66.9 percent, to 10.4 percent of the total slave population. See Bureau of the Census, Negro Population in the United States, 1790–1915, at 220–21 (1918).

[177] There was a rise in appellate cases of racial determination from seven per decade before 1850 to 24 per decade between 1850 and the first year of the Civil War. See infra Appendix.

[178] Before 1850, 58 percent of the 68 trials in which race was an issue ended in a finding of whiteness; after 1850, only 25 percent of trials ended in a finding of whiteness. See infra Appendix.

[179] See, e.g., George M. Fredrickson, *The Black Image in the White Mind: the Debate on Afro-American Character and Destiny,* 1817–1914, at 74 (1971) (dating scientific racism to the emergence of the "American school of ethnology" in the 1840s and 1850s). For the history of scientific racism, see generally Reginald Horsman, *Race and Manifest Destiny: The Origins of American Racial Anglo-Saxonism* (1981); and Bruce R. Dain, A Hideous Monster of the Mind: American Race Theory, 1787–1859 (1996) (unpublished Ph.D. dissertation, Princeton University) (on file with the Princeton University Library).

[180] For a summary of this literature, see Pascoe, supra note 10, at 46.

[181] Eight of these took place after 1848. See infra Appendix.

[182] See *Daniel* v. *Guy,* 19 Ark. 121, 136 (1857). The Arkansas Supreme Court commented that this was appropriate, "[i]f they were skilled in the natural history of the races of men." Id.

[183] Transcript of Trial, *Daniel* v. *Guy,* supra note 1, at 31 (bill of exceptions).

[184] Id.

[185] See Census of 1850, supra note 35.

[186] See Transcript of Thai, *Daniel* v. *Guy,* supra note 1, at 32 (bill of exceptions).

[187] See Gary v. Stevenson, 19 Ark. 580, 583–84 (1858).

[188] Id. at 583.

[189] Id.

[190] Id.

[191] Id. at 584.

[192] Id.

[193] 32 Ga. 316, 322–23 (1861).

[194] See id. at 317; see also HODES, supra note 20, at 108–16 (discussing Sullivan).

[195] Sullivan, 32 Ga. at 319.

[196] Id. at 322–23.

[197] Id. at 323.

[198] See id. at 324.

[199] Transcript of Trial, *Daniel* v. *Guy,* supra note 1. at 27 (cross-examination of Thomas S. Thompson).

[200] See id.

[201] See, e.g., Transcript of Trial, *Hopkins* v. *Bowers,* No. 16,598 (N.C. Orange County Super. Ct. Mar. 1890) (collection of N.C. Dep't of Archives & History, Raleigh, N.C., Supreme Court Records), rev'd on other grounds, 12 S.E. 984 (N.C. 1891). In this property dispute, one of the plaintiffs, John Hopkins, testifying to Ann Bowers's mixed blood, was asked by the plaintiff's counsel, "what degree of African descent, in his opinion, was Ann." Id. at 21 (testimony of John Hopkins). After the defendant objected, the judge asked Hopkins "if he had ever given any attention to, or had any experiences in the admixture of races." Id. When Hopkins said he had not, "[h]is Honor adjudged him not to be an expert in this matter and excluded the question." Id. at 21–22.

Invoking Ancestors

LAURA L. LOVETT

Study Questions

1. Explain the following statement: "Remembering Native American and African ancestry became part of a way of resisting a simplistic legal definition of themselves as 'Colored.'"
2. What are some of the themes characteristic of the WPA slave narratives with regard to their Indian relatives?

In her book about her family, writer Kathryn Morgan resisted any singular definition of racial identity when she noted that her great-grandmother, great-uncles, and great-aunt were "white by nature, black by law, African and Cherokee by choice. They called themselves the "children of strangers."[12] Labeling themselves "African and Cherokee by choice" allowed her relatives to reconstruct for themselves and others the racial categories assigned them "by law" as residents of legally segregated Lynchburg, Virginia. Remembering Native American and African ancestry became part of a way of resisting a simplistic legal definition of themselves as "Colored."

Kathryn Morgan's account of her family's negotiation of their racial identity falls within a tradition of African American autobiography, where writers used their personal experiences to address the larger social, political, and economic context for their place in a segregated society.[13] While scholars often associated this tradition with African American intellectuals, I want to examine how other accounts of Native American ancestry addressed the context of segregation.

The Federal Writers' Project of the Works Progress Administration (the WPA) sought to create work for up to five thousand writers in a year by commissioning travel guides, historical markers, and projects like interviews with millworkers, immigrants, and former slaves. Although interviewers were often given racist guidelines for representing southern Black dialect, these materials offer a unique glimpse into popular perception of scientific ideas about race and racial inheritance.[14] In the same way that Morgan's anecdote revealed an acceptance of the categories of science and law as creating parameters within which her family reconstructed its identity, the WPA narratives offer a way to gauge the effects of the project of biracial classification that was inherent in segregation.[15]

Many of the former slaves interviewed as part of the WPA Writer's Project remembered legacies of Native American ancestry. My survey of 2,193 narratives revealed that nearly 12 percent of the narratives contained some reference to the interviewee being related to or descended from a Native American.[16] While not all of these individuals elaborated on what significance these relations held for them, the fact that so many testified to such a heritage suggests that it was an important element in many family histories. The body of work written by historians Jack Forbes, R. Halliburton, Daniel Littlefield, and Theda Perdue speaks to the empirical evidence confirming the long history of interrelations and the probability that these family memories are rooted in historical realities.[17]

Underlying this effort to recall Native American kinship was the popularly held assumption that racial characteristics were biological and passed on from one generation to the next. Immediately prior to the challenge to racial classification launched by social scientists in the early twentieth century, Americans—Black, White and Indian—commonly understood race differences to be a matter of fact. For many of the informants of the WPA ex-slave narratives, this meant that any Native American blood conveyed to its recipient those racial characteristics thought to be innate in Native Americans. In the last quarter of the nineteenth century, those stereotypic racial characteristics most commonly associated with Native Americans by African Americans were those of the "noble savage." To many people at the turn of the century, then, any claim to Native American ancestry could be construed as a claim to the possession of some of the features of the noble savage, including a heroic (sometimes savage) commitment to liberty, a connection to the land, or an aristocratic if doomed opposition to "progress." Persons making such claims often saw themselves as the inheritors of those traits they found distinctively Native American and desirable because of this.[18]

For Anna Baker, an ex-slave from Monroe County, Mississippi, the knowledge of her grandfather's Native American blood was even more significant to her than his name. Close to eighty when she was interviewed, Baker explained that her mother had left the family when she was very young and that all she knew of her maternal grandparents was that her grandfather had been a "full-blood" Indian.[19] His exploits, according to family legend, had included standing up to the overseer. It seems that he agreed to relinquish part of his freedom and work for the man who owned Baker's grandmother in order to be near the woman he loved. There were limits to what he would tolerate while in this position, though. When the overseer tried to beat him, the grandfather retreated to his home and barred his door. In turn, the overseer, with others, threatened to break open the door, whereupon the grandfather responded by throwing "a shovel full of red hot coals" at them, and then running away while the overseer screamed in pain.[20] The outcome of the tale served as both a moral to whites and a legacy of resistance for the teller: Though the man had disappeared, his granddaughter claimed that those "White folks" learned that if they were going to whip an Indian, as they had done so many of their slaves, they had better kill him or he would kill them.[21]

Anna Baker's narrative is fairly typical. Often in the WPA narratives the Indian relative has disappeared, leaving a legacy of resistance to coercion and injustice. This particular narrative implies that the patrimony of freedom-loving manifested itself in the actions of Baker's mother, who, like her father, left familial connections behind. Yet the story does not end there. The White interviewer had noted at the beginning of her report that Baker's "high forehead and prominent cheek bones indicate that there is a strain of other than the pure African in her blood." Baker herself directly attributes her "brown color" to her maternal grandfather. The imprint of his physical characteristics, she implies, mirror those of his less visible ones. The threat of the lesson for the overseer might well reside in Baker's own self.[22]

The explicit threat of such Indian forebears was often presented not only as a part of the individual giving the oral history but as a separable element of that person's makeup. Rebecca Hooks typifies one way of perceiving blood and racial character. Hooks noted with some pride that her former mistress blamed her tendency to resist directions on the "cursed Cherokee blood in her." This phrasing, so common it is almost cliched, suggests that the Native American kinship bestowed separable platelets, each imbued with whatever stereotypically Indian qualities were advantageous to the situation. Hooks could not help her need to assert herself as someone not entirely at the whim of her capricious mistress; it was her "Indian blood."[23]

In his WPA interview, Frank Berry of Jacksonville, Florida, identified himself as a grandson of Osceola, "the last fighting chief of the Seminole tribe."[24] His grandmother had been kidnapped by the Seminole who, as Berry recalled, often intermarried with captured or escaped slaves. Although eventually retaken by her former slave master, she passed on to her son a characterization of his Native American heritage that celebrated the bravery of the people on his father's side of the family. "The red men," he is quoted as noting, "were credited with inciting many uprisings and wholesale escapes among the slaves."[25]

This direct claim to the legacy of Native American resistance and "Indian royalty," as Osceola is presented, may have influenced the interviewer's perception of Berry. Pearl Randolph's report identifies Berry as holding numerous offices in the Radical Reconstruction Government in the South following the Civil War. An experiment in biracial government which for a time offered the hope of an eventual move toward political and civil equality, Radical Reconstruction was short-lived and not well supported while in effect. During that brief interlude, Frank Berry had served as a state and federal government contractor, a registration inspector in 1879, and a U.S. marshall in 1881. As Randolph commented, Berry, "who in spite of reduced circumstances manages still to make one think of top hats and state affairs," reminded her of "the old days of black aristocracy when Negroes held high political offices in the state of Florida, when Negro tradesmen and professionals competed successfully and unmolested with the whites."[26] There is an implicit equation made in Randolph's account between Berry's Indian ancestry, as the grandson of Osceola, and as a member of what she called the "black aristocracy" of Reconstruction. Both are rendered in her narrative as tragically, and inevitably, disappearing. Yet this does not jibe with the way Berry presents his Indian kinship. His version suggests that the same qualities that inspired "uprisings and wholesale escapes" lives on in his veins.

Often the Native Americans who appear in the WPA narratives, whether as relations or simply as people living near the ex-slaves, are described in terms of how they differ from Whites. This is exactly the image of "the White Man's Indian" that Robert Berkhofer Jr. characterizes as a "separate and single other…always alien to the White."[27] The context here is important, though, because the image is offered in the narratives as both a critique of Whites and as a celebratory record of familial attributes, many of them an integral part of the individuals' self-construction.

This kind of laudatory representation can be seen in narratives depicting Indians as living outside of the economic control of plantation society. Black interviewees remembered Indian kin who preferred living in the woods or who possessed remarkable naturalist skills, as well as attributes like innate fierceness. Martha Richardson's father, a Native American, like the "general run of Indians," loved to hunt.[28] She claimed that he passed on his family legacy, telling her many times about the "great Catawba Indians," who made all of their own medicines and killed bears, wearing their skins after roasting the flesh for a feast.[29] She was known locally for her mastery of Indian medical lore. For Millie Ann Smith, her grandfather's stories of running off to stay with his relatives at the nearby Native American camp for weeks at a time seemed to be related to his skill at hunting the deer, wild hogs, turkeys, and raccoons that fed his master's family when they first moved to Texas.[30] The image Robert Scott had of his Native American mother was that she could "row a boat, shoot a bird on the wing, and perform wondrous feats of strength and skill."[31]

All of these images of Native Americans share the memory of resistance to "civilization" as embodied by the slave plantation system. Passed down through the family for generations, these images were remembered as a viable part of their identity in the midst of a cultural project undertaken by scholars, newspaper editors, and government policymakers to claim that Native Americans in the West had been entirely subdued and they would soon "vanish," as they had already done in the East.[32] Historian Rayna Green suggests that this context is particularly important because the pervasive American cultural practice of what she calls "playing Indian" by non-Indian people depends upon the "physical and psychological removal,

even the death, of Indians." It is possible to interpret the WPA stories as genealogical "performances," since so many of the representations echo the stereotypic images of Indians available in cultural forums like novels, pageants, medicine shows, and paintings. Jeffrey Steele, for example, identifies the features most often ascribed to Indians in nineteenth-century advertising as codifying the four most prevalent images in the WPA narratives: Indian ancestors as vanishing royalty, as possessing a special affinity for nature, as doomed by an innately noble character in the face of White progress, and as possessing an unchangeable savagery. The context of racial ideology at the time, however, prevents these images from functioning merely as performative. The Blacks invoking these images indicate that, in light of scientific arguments about racial inheritance, those characteristics ran through their blood. Indian traits flowed through their veins.[33]

Claiming kinship with Native Americans provided African Americans in the late nineteenth and early twentieth century with a way of rebelling against a system of segregation, discrimination, and "civilization" imposed on them by White society. This can be considered a route of resistance, because White and Black Americans with the aid of cultural images, science, and governmental policy, defined Indians as living outside of White society. They perceived Indians to be dangerous for having fought the encroachment of society at virtually every step. Native American ancestors could thus be empowering insofar as the Native American embodied the potential in Blacks themselves to disrupt social order and White civilization.

Notes

[12] Kathryn L. Morgan, *Children of Strangers: The Stories of a Black Family* (Philadelphia: Temple University Press, 1980), 7.

[13] P. Franklin, *Living Our Stories, Telling Our Truths: Autobiography and the Making of the African American Intellectual Tradition* (Oxford: Oxford University Press, 1995).

[14] "Memorandum from Henry Bennett to Mrs. Wharton, Dated Febuary 21, 1941," reprinted in the appendix to the general introduction, *The American Slave: A Composite Autobiography*, 19 vols., ed. George P. Rawick (Westport, CT: Greenwood Press, 1977), supplement series 1, vol. 6, Mississippi Narratives, pt. 1, lxii–lxiii.

[15] Similar interviews conducted by the American Freedmen's Inquiry Commission sixty years earlier do not present the same kind of concerns or categories. No one describes themselves in terms of their racial ancestry.

The operative categories for these individuals were "slave" or "free." Because the WPA narratives were conducted in the 1930s, they reflect the post–Civil War scientific project of racial classification that, I argue, works in conjunction with legalized segregation. For a reprint of some of the American Freedmen's Inquiry Commission interviews, see John Blassingame, *Slave Testimony: Two Centuries of Letters, Speeches, Interviews, and Autobiographies* (Baton Rouge: Louisiana State University Press, 1977).

[16] While many of the narratives discussed memories of Indians living near the interviewees, for the purposes of this project, I considered only those narratives that claimed some kind of kinship relation to Native Americans. See especially the Oklahoma volumes for representations of Native Americans not claimed as kin: Rawick, ed., *The American Slave*, vol. 7 and supplement series 1, vol. 12.

[17] See especially Jack D. Forbes, *Black Africans and Native Americans: Color, Race and Caste in the Evolution of Red-Black Peoples* (Oxford: Basil Blackwell Ltd., 1988); R. Halliburton Jr., *Red Over Black: Black Slavery Among the Cherokee Indians* (Westport, CT: Greenwood Press, 1977); Daniel F. Littlefield Jr., *The Cherokee Freedmen: From Emancipation to American Citizenship* (Westport, CT: Greenwood Press, 1978); Theda Perdue, *Slavery and the Evolution of Cherokee Society, 1540–1866* (Knoxville: University of Tennessee Press, 1979.

[18] See Robert F. Berkhofer Jr., *The White Man's Indian: Images of the American Indian from Columbus to the Present* (New York: Vintage Books, 1978); Roy Harvey Pearce, *Savagism and Civilization: A Study of the Indian and the American Mind* (1953; revised, Baltimore: Johns Hopkins Press, 1977); S. Elizabeth Bird, ed., *Dressing in Feathers: The Construction of the Indian in American Popular Culture* (Boulder, CO.: Westview Press, 1996); and Richard Drinnon, *Facing West: The Metaphysics of Indian-Hating and Empire-Building* (Minneapolis: University of Minnesota Press, 1980).

[19] Rawick, ed., *The American Slave*, supplement series 1, vol. 6, Mississippi Narratives, 92.

[20] Ibid, 99.

[21] Ibid, 99–100.

[22] Ibid, 92.

[23] Rawick, ed., The American Slave, vol. 17, Florida Narratives, 175.

[24] Ibid, 27.

[25] Ibid, 28. On the significance of the legacy and popular perception of Osceola and the Seminole, see Jay Mechling, "Florida Seminoles and the Marketing of the Last Frontier," in Bird, ed., *Dressing in Feathers*.

[26] Ibid, 29.

[27] Berkhofer, *The White Man's Indian*, xv.

[28] Rawick, ed., *The American Slave*, vol. 3, South Carolina Narratives, pt. 4, 19.

[29] Ibid.

[30] Rawick, ed., *The American Slave*, vol. 5, Texas Narratives, pt. 4, 41.

[31] Langhorne, "Robert Scott, the Albemarle Minstrel," 165.

[32] The report of the Indian Commissioner of 1901, based on the census of the previous year, was the first to contradict the popularly held belief that Indians were disappearing. Though some tribes were reported to be dying out, others were increasing. "Report of the Indian Commissioner," *The Southern Workman* 30, no. 1 (January 1901): 748–49.

[33] Rayna Greene, "The Tribe Called Wannabee: Playing Indian in America and Europe," Folklore 99, no. 1 (1988): 30–55; Jeffrey Steele, "Reduced to Images: American Indians in Nineteenth-Century Advertising" in Bird, ed., *Dressing in Feathers,* 45–64.

Race Relations in Black and White

Angelo N. Ancheta

Study Questions

1. Anchetta argues that the binary black-white model of race relations is a problematic one. Why is this the case?
2. The "histories of all racial minorities include extensive violence" but the themes for each group are unique. What are some of the unique themes surrounding anti-Asian violence?
3. Ancheta argues that people classified as Asian have been classified as "near-black" in the past and "near-white" in the present. Why?

Race Relations in Black and White

"Are you black or are you white?" For Asian Americans the obvious answer would seem to be "neither." Yet, when questions of race relations arise, a dichotomy between black and white typically predominates. Formed largely through inequities and conflicts between blacks and whites, discourse on race relations provides minimal space to articulate experiences independent of a black-white framework. The representation of Asian Americans is especially elusive and often shifts, depending on context, between black and white.

Popular works on race suggest that expositions of Asian American experiences are peripheral, more often confined to the footnotes than expounded in the primary analyses. Studs Terkel's *Race* frames race relations through a dialogue about blacks and whites, confined almost entirely to the opinions of blacks and whites. Andrew Hacker's *Two Nations: Black and White, Separate, Hostile, Unequal* contains, as its subtitle implies, extensive discussions of inequality between blacks and whites, but only a minimal analysis of inequality among other racial groups.

The controversial books *The Bell Curve* by Charles Murray and Richard Herrnstein, and *The End of Racism,* by Dinesh D'Souza, go to considerable length to expound arguments that blacks as a group are less intelligent than whites and suffer from cultural pathologies that inhibit advancement to the level of whites. When discussed at all, Asian Americans are offered as a " model minority" group, to be contrasted with blacks and likened to whites because of their higher IQ scores and cultural values stressing family, hard work, and educational achievement.

News media portrayals of racial minorities suffer from the same tendency to reduce race relations to a simple black-white equation. Popular television news shows such as ABC's *Nightline* offer recurring programming on race relations, but confine their analysis to black-white relations. Public opinion polls on race and civil rights usually exclude Asian Americans as subjects or as participants, or reduce them to the category of "Other." News coverage of racially charged events is most often framed by black versus white antagonisms. The murder trial of O. J. Simpson, for instance, provoked extensive dialogue on the impact of race and racism on the criminal justice system, but excluded for the most part any perspectives from Asian Americans or Latinos, which is ironic for a trial held in Los Angeles, a city where half of the population is Asian American and Latino.

Public policies that reflect and reinforce race relations also approach race in terms of black and white. Historically, the major landmarks denoting both racial subordination and progress in racial rights have been measured through the experiences of African Americans. Slavery and its abolition, the black codes and the Reconstruction-era constitutional amendments, Jim Crow laws and the desegregation cases culminating in *Brown* v. *Board of Education,* the struggles of the civil rights movement and the federal legislation of the 1960s—these are the familiar signs that have dominated the landscape of civil rights in the United States. Debates on affirmative action have occasionally shone the spotlight on Asian Americans, but almost exclusively as unintended victims of affirmative action in higher education. Problems of ongoing racial discrimination and inequality among Asian American communities are largely ignored.

Not that focusing on black experiences is unjustified. African Americans have been the largest racial minority group in the United States since the country's birth, and continue to endure the effects of racial subordination. By any social or economic measure, African Americans suffer extensive inequality because of race. In describing the African American experience, the statement of the Kerner Commission resonates as strongly today as it did in 1968: "Our nation is moving toward two societies, one black, one white—separate but unequal." But to say that our nation is moving toward two separate and unequal societies, however disconcerting is fundamentally incomplete. Underlying the Kerner Commission's statement is the assumption that our nation's cities are divisible along a single racial axis. Cleavages between black and white persist but American race relations are not an exclusively black-white phenomenon and never have been. The civil unrest in Los Angeles in 1992 is just one example of the intricacy of contemporary racial dynamics, shedding light on a host of race-based and class-based conflicts, as well as an array of racial and ethnic groups—blacks, whites, Asians, Latinos—who were both victims and victimizers.

Black and White by Analogy

Dualism is a convenient lens through which to view the world. Black or white, male or female, straight or gay—the categories help us frame reality and make sense of it. In matters of race, a black-white dichotomy has been the dominant model, based primarily on the fact that African Americans, have been the largest and most conspicuous nonwhite racial group in the United States. But the legal history of the United States is punctuated by the abridgement of rights among other racial and ethnic groups such as Asian Americans, and the country's changing demographics are mandating new perspectives based on the experiences of immigrants. Still, the black-white model is the regnant paradigm in both social and legal discussions of race.

How can Asian Americans fit within a black-white racial paradigm? Historian Gary Okihiro poses the question this way: "Is yellow black or white?" Okihiro suggests that Asian Americans have been "near-blacks" in the past and "near-whites" in the present, but that "[y]ellow is emphatically neither white nor black." Recognizing the dominance of the black-white paradigm in the law, Frank Wu adopts a similar view proposing that Asian Americans have been forced to fit within race relations discourse through analogy to either whites or blacks. He posits that American society and its legal system have conceived of racial groups as whites, blacks, honorary whites, or constructive (legal jargon for "implied") blacks.

For most of the nation's history, Asian Americans have been treated primarily as constructive blacks. Asian Americans for decades endured many of the same disabilities of racial subordination as African Americans—racial violence, segregation, unequal access to public institutions and discrimination in housing, employment, and education. The courts even classified Asian Americans as if they were black. In the mid-nineteenth century, the California Supreme Court held in *People* v. *Hall* that Chinese immigrants were barred from testifying in court under a statute prohibiting the testimony of blacks, by reasoning that "black" was a generic term encompassing all non-whites, including Chinese: "[T]he words 'Black person'...must be taken as contradistinguished from White, and necessarily excludes all races other than the Caucasian."

Similarly, in *Gong Lum* v. *Rice*, decided twenty-seven years before *Brown* v. *Board of Education,* the United States Supreme Court upheld the constitutionality of sending Asian American students to segregated schools. Comparing its earlier rulings on the "separate but equal" doctrine, the Court stated: "Most of the cases cited, arose it is true, over the establishment of separate schools as between white pupils and black pupils, but we can not think that the question is any different or that any different result can be reached ...where the issue is as between white pupils and the pupils of the yellow races." In the eyes of the Supreme Court, yellow equaled black, and neither equaled white.

In more recent years, the inclusion of Asian Americans in civil rights laws and race-conscious remedial programs has relied on the historical parallels between the experiences of Asian Americans and African Americans. The civil rights protections available to Asian Americans are most often contingent upon the rights granted to African Americans. Civil rights laws that apply to Asian Americans, as constructive blacks, can usually trace their origins to a legislative intent to protect African Americans from racial discrimination.

The treatment of Asian Americans as "honorary whites" is more unusual. In the Reconstruction-era South, Asian Americans were initially afforded a status above blacks for a period of time during the nineteenth century; Louisiana, for example, counted Chinese as whites for census purposes before 1870. The status was short-lived: the Chinese were soon reduced to constructive black status under systems of racial segregation. More contemporary race relations controversies appear to have elevated Asian Americans to the status of honorary whites, particularly in the minds of those who oppose race-conscious remedies such as affirmative action. Asian Americans are often omitted from protection in affirmative action programs as a matter of course, lumped with whites even in contexts where Asian Americans still face racial discrimination and remain underrepresented.

The rigidity of the legal system's treatment of race as either black or white is evident in civil rights litigation filed by Asian Americans plaintiffs in the earlier half of this century. Unlike the fictional grocer in Spike Lee's *Do the Right Thing*, Asian Americans sought to be classified, quite unsuccessfully, as white under the law, in recognition of the social and legal stigmas attached to being categorized as black. Gong Lum, for example, argued that his daughter Martha should not have to attend school for colored children in Mississippi because "'[c]olored' describes only one race, and that is the negro." Because his daughter was "pure Chinese." Gong Lum argued that she ought to have been classified with whites rather than blacks. The Court rejected this reasoning and held that yellow was black when it came to segregation.

During the late-nineteenth and early-twentieth centuries, Asian Americans sought to be classified as white in attempts to become naturalized citizens. Congress enacted naturalization legislation in 1790 to limit citizenship to "free white persons." After the Civil War, the law was amended to allow persons of "African nativity" or "African descent" to naturalize, but Congress rejected extending naturalization to Asian immigrants. Asian immigrants sought relief through the courts, but had little success arguing that they were white: Burmese, Chinese, Filipino, Hawaiian, Japanese and Korean plaintiffs were all held to be nonwhite; mixed-race plaintiffs who were half-white and half-Asian were also held to be nonwhite. The United States Supreme Court laid to rest any questions about the racial bar in *Ozawa* v. *United States,* ruling that Japanese immigrants were not white, and in *United States* v. *Thind,* ruling that Asian Indian immigrants were not white. Asian immigrants were prohibited by statute from naturalizing through the 1940s, and the racial bar on naturalization was not repealed until 1952.

From today's vantage point, these attempts by Asian immigrants to be classified as white seem absurd and even subordinative, because they symbolically pushed blacks down the social ladder relative to whites and Asians. But when the legal paradigm limits options to black or white and nothing else, curious and unseemly choices inevitably arise. The solution, of course, is to develop and rely on theories that comprehend the complexity of race relations, which includes discerning that the experience of Asian Americans are not the same as the experiences of African Americans.

Racism in Context: Anti-Asian Violence

To better understand the experiences of Asian Americans, consider how racial subordination operates within a specific context: anti-Asian violence. Racial violence is not a new phenomenon, and the histories of all racial minorities include extensive violence, whether it is the genocide of Native American tribes during the expansion of the United States, the terrorism against blacks in the South, the military conquest and ongoing border violence against Latinos in the Southwest, or the attacks on Asian immigrant laborers in the West. Incidents of anti-Asian violence reveal unique themes of prejudice and discrimination that illustrate the dynamics of racism against Asian Americans.

Chronicling the growth of anti-Asian violence is recent years, a 1986 report by the United States Commission on Civil Rights concluded that "anti-Asian activity in the form of violence, harassment intimidation, and vandalism has been reported across the nation." The National Asian Pacific American Legal Consortium has measured anti-Asian violence during the 1990s and has tracked a wide variety of crimes, including graffiti, vandalism, cross burnings, property damage, arson, hate mail, intimidation, physical assaults, homicides, and police misconduct. Calculating figures is difficult because of underreporting—many immigrants face language barriers or are fearful of the police—and because of major weaknesses in law enforcement's compilation of statistics. The numbers that are available are sobering. Nationally, the number of incidents of anti-Asian violence reported by the National Asian Pacific American Legal Consortium grew from 335 in 1993 to 452 in 1994, 456 in 1995, and 534 in 1996—a 59 percent increase from 1993 to 1996.

The most notorious episode of recent anti-Asian violence was the killing of Vincent Chin in 1982. Chin, a twenty-seven-year-old Chinese American, was celebrating his upcoming wedding at a Detroit bar when he was approached by Ronald Ebens and Michael Nitz, two white automobile factory workers. Ebens and Nitz thought Chin was Japanese and blamed him for the loss of jobs in the automobile industry. After calling Chin a "jap," the two men chased him out of the bar. They eventually caught Chin and proceeded to beat him repeatedly with a baseball bat. Chin died from his injuries a few days later. Ebens and Nitz each pleaded guilty to manslaughter but received only probation and a fine. Ebens was later convicted of federal civil rights violations, but his conviction was overturned on appeal and he was acquitted on retrial. Neither Ebens nor Nitz spent any time in prison for the killing.

A similar incident occurred in 1989 in Raleigh, North Carolina. Jim (Ming Hai) Loo had been playing pool with several friends when he was approached by Robert Piche and his brother Lloyd Piche, who began calling Loo and his friends "chinks" and "gooks" and blaming them for the death of American soldiers in Vietnam. Once outside, Robert Piche pistol-whipped Loo on the back of the head, causing Loo to fall onto a broken bottle that pierced his brain. Loo died from his injuries two days later. Robert Piche was convicted and sentenced to thirty-seven years in prison; Lloyd Piche was sentenced to six months in prison by a state court, and sentenced to four years in prison for federal civil rights violations.

Another tragic illustration of anti-Asian violence is the multiple killings of Asian American children at the Cleveland Elementary School in Stockton, California, in 1989. Patrick Purdy used an AK-47 assault rifle to spray bullets into a crowded schoolyard, killing five children and wounding over twenty others before turning the gun on himself. Although initially labeled the product of a disturbed mind obsessed with guns and the military, the shootings were later proved to be motivated by racial hatred. A report issued by the California attorney general's office found that Purdy targeted the school because it was heavily populated by Southeast Asian children.

Perpetrators who are affiliated with hate groups have been responsible for many anti-Asian crimes. During the early 1980s, when tensions erupted between Vietnamese immigrant fishermen and native-born fishermen in several coastal states, the Ku Klux Klan engaged in extensive harassment and violence against Vietnamese fishermen along the Gulf Coast of Texas. Federal litigation was required to end a pattern of threats, cross burnings, arsons, and shootings. In 1990, Hung Truong, a fifteen-year-old Vietnamese boy living in Houston, was attacked by two men who were later identified as white supremacist "skinheads." After following Truong and his friends as they walked down the street, the two assailants jumped out of their car, one wielding a club, and shouted "White power." They chased Truong and proceeded to kick and beat him, even as he pleaded for his life. the two men admitted at trial that they attacked Truong because he was Vietnamese.

More common, however, are incidents that do not involve formal hate groups and that occur in day-to-day interactions among people at work in schools, at home, and on the street. Here are some examples, all of which occurred during a ten-month period in California during 1995 and 1996:

- A Chinese American high school student was physically attacked in the parking lot of a fast-food restaurant in the Northern California suburb of Novato by several other students, who shouted "Go back to China where you belong" and "chink, gook, chinaman."
- While walking her dog in a San Francisco park, a Japanese American woman was assaulted by a white woman who grabbed her by the arm, threw dog feces at her, and cried out "Go home! Go home!" and "Hiroshima!"
- A Chinese American man was stabbed repeatedly in the parking lot of a Northern California supermarket by a white male assailant who later admitted to the police that he wanted to kill a "chinaman" because they "got all the good jobs."
- A Vietnamese man was killed while he was skating on a high school tennis court in the Southern California city of Tustin. The assailant boasted about the killing in a letter to a friend in which he graphically described the attack and wrote offhandedly, "Oh I killed a jap a while ago."

Even the virtual world of computer networks has been the site of anti-Asian intimidation. In September 1996, a threatening electronic message was sent to about sixty students at the University of California, Irvine—a college campus whose undergraduate student population is approximately one-half Asian American—accusing Asians of being responsible for all crimes on campus, ordering them to leave the university, and threatening to hunt them down and kill them if they did not leave. The e-mail was signed "Asian-hater."

Many incidents of anti-Asian violence arise from conflicts among racial minorities. During the 1990s, Asian American tenants in San Francisco's public housing projects—primarily Southeast Asian refugees and their families—were subjected to harassment and violence by African American tenants. Inadequate institutional policies, including poor overall security and a flawed racial integration strategy, aggravated cultural differences and tensions among the tenants, resulting in intimidation and numerous assaults. Many families feared for their lives and became prisoners in their own homes, while others moved out of public housing altogether.

Anti-Asian violence is even linked to political rhetoric and public policy making. During the 1994 campaign for California's Proposition 187, the ballot initiative designed to restrict the rights of undocumented immigrants, racial rhetoric and literature abounded. In Los Angeles, for example, mailboxes were stuffed with flyers that supported the passage of Proposition 187 and stated: "WE NEED A *REAL* BORDER. FIRST WE GET THE SPICS, THEN THE GOOKS, AND AT LAST WE GET THE NIGGERS. *DEPORTATION.* THEY'RE ALL GOING HOME." Other flyers pointed to the "invasion" of the "Gooks," stating "they had to go"; references to genocide and "taking back America" were also common.

Attempting to solve anti-Asian violence is as difficult and troubling an exercise as reading the graphic reports of the violence itself. The National Asian Pacific American Legal Consortium has identified several problems on both the national and local level that remain unaddressed by government and policy makers: incomplete reporting and monitoring mechanisms among law enforcement; the weakness or absence of hate crimes laws; inadequate training of law enforcement personnel; insufficient funding for civil rights agencies; and major barriers to reporting, including the absence of bilingual services for limited-English-speaking immigrants.

Even where reporting mechanisms and laws are in place, prosecuting hate crimes is problematic: inadequately trained officers may not collect relevant evidence, and prosecutors may be reluctant to press charges because of the difficulty of proving intent on the part of the perpetrator. The problem is compounded when the victims are recent immigrants who may speak little English and may be reluctant to report the crimes because of their distrust of law enforcement. In some areas of the country, such as New York City, police relations are so poor that police misconduct is itself a major source of anti-Asian violence. At its base, addressing anti-Asian violence means developing explanations and solutions to racial subordination against Asian Americans in general; violence is the most pernicious variation on several general themes.

Racial Themes

Without question, the examples of anti-Asian violence demonstrate that overt racism is still a serious problem for Asian Americans, just as it has been for African Americans and other racial minorities. Some types of anti-Asian violence can thus be explained by treating violence against Asian Americans and other racial minority groups as expressions of white racism. Anti-Asian violence committed by white supremacists targeting anyone who is not white fits within a binary model of race that places all racial minorities in the same category of "nonwhite."

But many incidents of anti-Asian violence suggest that more complex dynamics are at work. Members of one Asian ethnic group are often mistaken for being members of other Asian ethnic groups. Racial and ethnic slurs are interlaced with nativist anti-immigrant rhetoric.

Resentment about economic competition, both foreign and domestic, is often implicated. Even hostility rooted in the United States' previous military involvement in Asian countries may be a factor. And a white-nonwhite framework cannot explain racial violence in which members of one nonwhite group victimize members of another nonwhite group. Several basic themes can be gleaned from these and other examples of violence against Asian Americans.

Racialization

One theme is the importance of *racial* categorizing in anti-Asian violence. The killing of Vincent Chin is an example of how anti-Asian violence is realized: based on his physical appearance, Chin, a Chinese American, was taken to be a Japanese national by his killers, who had made him the focus of their anger and frustration toward Japanese competition in the automobile industry. A perpetrator who makes the race-based generalization that all Asians look alike puts every Asian American at risk, even if the specific antagonisms are targeted against a smaller subset of people.

The attribution of specific ethnic characteristics to anyone falling within the racial category of "Asian" is common anti-Asian violence. For example, when Luyen Phan Nguyen, a Vietnamese premedical student, was killed in Coral Springs, Florida, in 1992, he was taunted with slurs at a party and later chased down by a group of men who beat and kicked him repeatedly. Among the epithets directed at Nguyen during the beating were "chink," "vietcong," and "sayonara"— three separate and distinct ethnic slurs.

Nativism and Racism

Another theme manifested by anti-Asian violence is the centrality of nativism, which John Higham defines as "intense opposition to an internal minority on the ground of its foreign (i.e., 'un-American') connections." Asian Americans are equated with foreigners, or they are at least presumed to be foreign-born. Race and nativism thus intersect to produce a distinctive form of subordination of Asian Americans—what Robert Chang labels "nativistic racism."

In many incidents, Asian American victims are perceived and categorized as foreigners by their assailants: Vincent Chin was transformed into a Japanese national; Jim Loo became a Vietnamese adversary; immigrant merchants were remade as foreign investors and capitalists. Anti-immigrant epithets such as "Go home!" or "Why don't you go back to your own country?" frequently accompany anti-Asian violence, along with specific racial and ethnic slurs. And under the rubric of foreign outsider, Asian Americans fall into an array of unpopular categories: economic competitor, organized criminal, "illegal alien," or just unwelcome immigrant.

Patriotic racism is a peculiar and especially deep-seated form of nativist racism. American military conflicts against the Japanese during World War II, against Koreans and Chinese during the Korean War, and against the Vietnamese during the Vietnam War have generated intense animosity against Asian Americans. During World War II, the federal government's internment of Japanese Americans, most of whom were United States citizens, reflected patriotic racism at its worst, as a formal governmental policy. Intimidation and violence against Asian Americans is still common on December 7 because of the hostility that arises on the anniversary of the bombing of Pearl Harbor by Japan.

Racial Hierarchies and Interracial Conflict

A related theme made evident by anti-Asian violence revolves around the intermediate position that Asian Americans appear to occupy on a social and economic ladder that places whites at the top and blacks on the bottom. Black-on-Asian hate crimes often contain strong elements of cultural conflict and nativism—blacks, like whites, treat Asians as foreigners. But black-on-Asian crimes also have strains traceable to resentment over the economic achievements of Asian Americans, particularly their entrepreneurial success in the inner cities. The destruction of Korean immigrants' businesses in 1992, many located in the historically black residential area of South-Central Los Angeles, reflected a growing anger against Asian American prosperity.

In this context, the "model minority" stereotype of Asian Americans becomes a two-edged sword, breeding not only incomplete and inaccurate images of Asian American success but resentment and hostility on the part of other racial groups. Racial differentiation often places Asian Americans in a middle position within the racial hierarchy of the United States—neither black nor white, and somewhere between black and white.

The Limits of Black and White

Hate violence is the most extreme form of racial subordination against Asian Americans but it sheds light on important differences between the subordination of Asian Americans and African Americans. A binary model of race based on relations between blacks and whites cannot fully describe the complex racial matrix that exists in the U.S. In terms of representation, a black-white model ignores or marginalizes the experiences of Asian Americans, Latinos, Native Americans, Arab Americans, and other groups who have extensive histories of discrimination against them. A black-white model discounts the role of immigration in race relations and confines discussion on the impact race has had on anti-immigrant policies that affect the nation's growing Asian American and Latino populations. A black-white model also limits any analysis of the relations and tensions between racial and ethnic groups, which are increasingly significant in urban areas where racial "minorities" are now becoming majorities.

In essence a black-white model fails to recognize that the basic nature of discrimination can differ among racial and ethnic groups. Theories of racial inferiority have been applied, often with violent force, against Asian Americans, just as they have been applied against blacks and other racial minority groups. But the causes of anti-Asian subordination can be traced to other factors as well, including nativism, differences in language and culture, perceptions of Asians as economic competitors, international relations, and past military involvement in Asian countries. Recent immigration from Asian countries is elevating culture and language to prominent places on the race relations landscape, challenging even the integrity of the racial category "Asian American." And the promotion in recent years of a "model minority" racial stereotype, based on the high education levels and incomes of some Asian Americans, represents a curious and distorted form of racism, denying the existence of Asian American poverty and inequality. All of these considerations point to the need for an analysis of race that is very different from the dominant black-white paradigm.

Asian Americans and the Civil Rights Laws

Racial discourse finds expression in the civil rights laws—the sections of the federal Constitution and the anti-discrimination statutes designed to address racial discrimination. Hate crime laws, for instance, create special crime based on racial violence or augment the punishment for violent crimes when there is finding of racially discriminatory intent. Asian Americans are protected by these laws and other antidiscrimination laws from racial discrimination. But, like other manifestations of race, the antidiscrimination laws define most rights within a black-white framework, and the laws contain significant limitations in accommodating the full array of Asian American experiences. When questions of civil rights move beyond a black-white dichotomy, rights and remedies become problematic and Asian Americans are often left without the full protection of the law.

The laws fail to recognize the intersection of race and nativism found in anti-Asian discrimination. When United States-born Asian Americans suffer discrimination as perceived immigrants, antidiscrimination laws may provide relief, but only if the facts permit a finding of discrimination based on categories of race or national origin, and not on the basis of being perceived as a foreigner. Laws such as the Immigration Reform and Control Act of 1986, which requires employers to verify the immigration status of all newly hired employees, have actually caused more discrimination against Asian Americans because of the common perception that all Asian Americans are immigrants and are therefore more likely to be undocumented.

Governmental ambivalence toward anti-immigrant discrimination is a significant weakness in the system of civil rights enforcement. Most antidiscrimination laws protect immigrants from discrimination based on race or national origin, but they lack specific protections for immigrants as immigrants.

Attempts to expand civil rights legislation to protect immigrants have been rebuked in the past. In California, for instance, legislation to protect immigrants from intimidation and hate violence was introduced and passed twice by the state legislature during the mid-1990s, but was vetoed each time by Governor Pete Wilson.

Some laws, such as California's Proposition 187, openly discriminate against undocumented immigrants. Federal laws discriminating against immigrants have gone even further, because the federal laws related to immigration enjoy special constitutional status arising from deference to national sovereignty. Welfare reform legislation enacted in 1996 not only discriminated against undocumented immigrants but against lawful permanent residents—"green card" holders—by stripping many permanent residents of eligibility for entitlement programs such as Food Stamps and Supplemental Security Income, which remained available to citizens. The impact of anti-immigrant policies falls most heavily on Asian Americans and Latinos because of the large numbers of immigrants within their communities and because of the linkage between nativism and race.

Characteristics inherent to immigrants are often ignored in the law. Forms of language-based discrimination dealing with accent and the ability to speak a second language at work are problematic under the civil rights laws, which generally lack explicit protections for language minority groups. Language may serve as a proxy for race, but the nexus between language and race is usually absent in statutes and in judicial interpretations of the law. In addition, the ability to access important government services such as police and fire, emergency health care, and public education is often compromised because of the narrowness of rights related to language and ethnicity.

Within the broader race relations landscape, where Asian Americans are ignored or, increasingly, where they occupy a racial middle ground, civil rights laws are not well equipped to recognize variations in both discrimination and the remedies for discrimination. The "model minority" image often leads to the exclusion of Asian Americans from corrective civil rights programs; Asian Americans are even labeled, along with whites, as victims of affirmative action. The image also leads to antagonisms between Asian Americans and members of other racial groups because of the perceptions of relative inequality and the resentment arising from those perceptions. In the area of interethnic relations, as in other areas, the antidiscrimination laws do not go far enough in recognizing and addressing the problems of Asian Americans.

How to Tell Your Friends From the Japs

TIME, DECEMBER 22, 1941

◇◆◆◇

Study Questions

1. The fact sheet "How to Tell Your Friends From the Japs" was published December 22, 1941. Why would such a fact sheet be published at this time?
2. How does this reading help you understand some of the racial issues Asian Americans face as outlined in "Race Relations in Black and White?"

...There is no infallible way of telling [Chinese and Japanese] apart, because the same racial strains are mixed in both. Even an anthropologist, with calipers and plenty of time to measure heads, noses, shoulders, hips, is sometimes stumped. A few rules of thumb—not always reliable:

- Some Chinese are tall (average: 5 ft. 5 in.). Virtually all Japanese are short (average 5 ft. 2 1/2 in.).
- Japanese are likely to be stockier and broader-hipped than short Chinese.
- Japanese—except for wrestlers—are seldom fat; they often dry up and grow lean as they age. The Chinese often put on weight, particularly if they are prosperous (in China, with its frequent famines, being fat is esteemed as a sign of being a solid citizen).
- Chinese, not as hairy as Japanese, seldom grow an impressive moustache.
- Most Chinese avoid horn-rimmed spectacles.

- Although both have the typical epicanthic fold of the upper eyelid (which makes them look almond-eyed), Japanese eyes are usually set closer together.
- Those who know them best often rely on facial expression to tell them apart: the Chinese expression is likely to be more placid, kindly, open; the Japanese more positive, dogmatic, arrogant.

  In Washington, last week, Correspondent Joseph Chiang made things much easier by pinning on his lapel a large badge reading "Chinese Reporter—NOT *Japanese*—Please."
- Some aristocratic Japanese have thin, aquiline noses, narrow faces and, except for their eyes, look like Caucasians.
- Japanese are hesitant, nervous in conversation, laugh loudly at the wrong time.
- Japanese walk stiffly erect, hard-heeled. Chinese, more relaxed, have an easy gait, sometimes shuffle.

PART 3

◇•◆•◇

Ethnic Classification

Because of the problematic nature of the concept of "race" and the difficulties associated with racial classification, many social scientists have suggested that the term *race* be abandoned. They argue that "ethnicity" is a concept which more meaningfully captures important human attributes and that it should be used instead. In this section, we examine the concept of ethnicity and the system used in the United States for ethnic classification. In addition, we ask whether it is possible to classify people according to ethnicity.

Social scientists use the term *ethnicity* very broadly. It can refer to people who share (or believe they share) a national origin; a common ancestry; a place of birth; distinctive and visible social traits such as religious practice, style of dress, body ornaments, or language; and/or socially important physical characteristics such as skin color, hair texture, and/or physical build. This broad definition suggests that a person's ethnicity can be based on almost countless numbers of traits.

The U.S. Bureau of the Census asks respondents at least six questions to determine their ethnicity. It asks about race, Hispanic origin, ancestry, place of birth, and language, including a self-rating of ability to speak English (see the reading "Questions Related to Ethnicity"). These questions tell us nothing about the meaning a specific ethnicity holds for respondents, about the forces that have shaped respondents' senses of their ethnic identities, or the importance of ethnicity to their lives.

Federal Statistical Directive No. 15 (see the reading in Part 2) names two official ethnic categories into which all people in the United States must be placed: (1) Hispanic/Spanish origin and (2) non-Hispanic/Spanish origin. The directive defines a Hispanic/Spanish person as a person from Mexican, Puerto Rican, Cuban, Central American, South American, or other Spanish culture or origin, regardless of race (see Table 3.1). Although

Table 3.1   United States: Hispanic Origin by Race

NOT OF HISPANIC ORIGIN	NUMBER OF PEOPLE
White	188,424,773
Black	29,284,596
American Indian, Eskimo, or Aleut	1,866,807
Asian or Pacific Islander	69,943
Other race	239,306
HISPANIC ORIGIN	**NUMBER OF PEOPLE**
White	11,402,291
Black	645,928
American Indian, Eskimo, or Aleut	148,336
Asian or Pacific Islander	232,684
Other race	94,708

Source: U.S. Bureau of the Census (1996a).

federal agencies may collect information on other ethnic groups, those groups must ultimately fall under the two official categories.

In determining whether someone is Hispanic or non-Hispanic, Census Bureau coders consider the answers respondents give to the six ethnicity questions. If respondents give inconsistent answers to these questions, coders are directed to assign the "correct" ethnic identity. In many cases, census coders assigned an ethnicity that did not match the respondents' answers. For example, 40 percent of those whom the Census Bureau classified as "Hispanic" on the basis of their answers to the place of birth, ancestry, and language questions answered "no" to the Hispanic origin question.

Census coders and other researchers blamed these inconsistencies on "response error"—on respondent misunderstanding, ignorance, ambivalence about their "real" ethnic identity, or a desire to hide their "true" ethnic identity (Gimenez 1989). Figure 3.1 shows the flowchart Census Bureau interviewers and coders use to make decisions about the category in which to place respondents who give complex answers to the ethnicity questions. Notice how the flowchart directs interviewers to classify the "problem" respondents as belonging to one ethnic group.

Sociologist Martha Gimenez (1989) argues that the source of inconsistencies in answers given to the six ethnicity questions lies not with the respondents but with the concept of Hispanic/Spanish origin. It "forces respondents to agree to having 'Spanish/Hispanic' origin; something which for a substantial number of people makes no sense, both in terms of their actual ancestry and/or in terms of their historical sense of who they are and/or (in the case of Latin Americans) their nationalistic allegiance to their country of origin" (p. 566).

Figure 3.1 Procedures for Recording Ethnic Origin for Problem Cases

This flowchart offers several if-then scenarios to guide Census Bureau interviewers when they encounter "problem cases" with regard to ethnicity. If respondents answer ethnicity questions in ways that indicate both Hispanic and non-Hispanic identity, they are asked a series of questions to "help" them identify with one ethnic category.

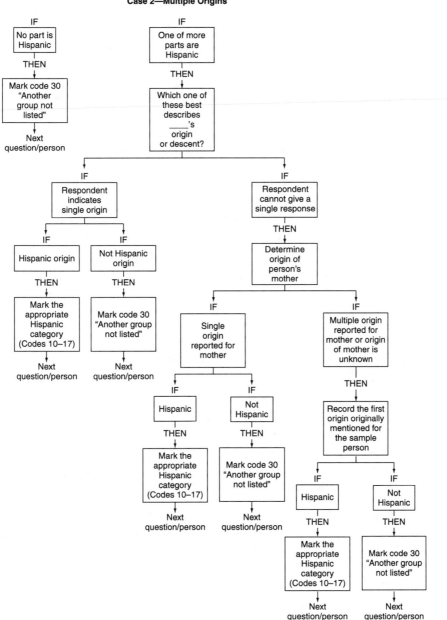

Case 2—Multiple Origins

Source: U.S. Bureau of the Census (1994:C3–17).

In the reading "Directive No. 15 and Self-Identification" by Luis Angel Toro (1995), we gain insights about why the label "Hispanic" is confusing to the many people the U.S. government eventually labels as such. As background information consider that the countries labeled Latin American are lands of immigrants just like the United States. In fact, the history of Latin America is intertwined with that of Asia, Europe, the Middle East, and Africa. As a result of this interconnected history, the countries of Latin America are not populated by a homogeneous group known as "Hispanics," but by native- and foreign-born persons, immigrants and nonimmigrant residents, and persons from every conceivable ancestry (not just Spanish ancestries). Toro offers four case studies of people whose lives reflect the history of intermixing. These cases show that for many people "answering the racial and ethnic identity questions involves considerable guesswork as to what the government is asking" (Toro 1995:1260). In spite of the confusing facts, many people continue to use "Hispanic" to describe themselves or others, as if the label provides meaningful information about a person. (See the box **"When Is Ethnicity Relevant in a Case Report?"**) We fail to realize that the category "Hispanic" is an artificial population—"a statistical construct formed by aggregates of people who differ greatly in terms of national origin, language, race, time of arrival in the United States, culture, minority status, social class, and socioeconomic status" (see the reading "What's in a Name?"; Gimenez 1989:559).

The difficulties associated with simply defining and determining who is of "Hispanic/Spanish" ethnicity leave us with the following nagging questions about the nature of ethnicity:

- Who belongs to an ethnic group?
- What characteristics distinguish one ethnic group from others? (E.g., Is eating rice for breakfast a behavior which makes someone Japanese? Is the ability to speak French a behavior that makes someone French?)
- Is it possible to describe what it means to be a member of a particular ethnic group?

Cynthia K. Mahmood and Sharon Armstrong's (1989) research shows that these questions are not easy to resolve. For their research, Mahmood and Armstrong traveled to Eastermar, a village in the Netherlands province of Friesland, to study the Frisian people's reactions to a book published about them. They found that the Frisian people were unable to agree on a single "truth" about them as described in that book. At the same time, Frisian villagers could not come up with a list of features that would apply to all Frisian people and distinguish them from other people living in

When Is Ethnicity Relevant in a Case Report?

To the Editor:—With reference to a recently published case report of a 29-yr-old woman with a bronchial trifurcation at the carina, we fail to understand the medical or epidemiologic relevance of describing the patient as "Hispanic"[1] The term Hispanic refers to a cultural group, not a racial group. Hispanics may be white, black, Asian, or any other race.[2] The 1990 census considers persons to be of Spanish Hispanic origin if the person's origin or ancestry is Mexican, Mexican-American, Chicano, Puerto Rican, Cuban, Argentinean, Colombian, Costa Rican, Dominican, Ecuadorian, Guatemalan, Honduran, Nicaraguan, Peruvian, Salvadoran; from other Spanish-speaking countries of the Caribbean or Central or South America; or from Spain.[3] In fact, the only real prerequisite for being Hispanic is self-identification. For federal data collection purposes, Hispanic persons are those who say they are Hispanic. A large number of Hispanics in the United States are bilingual. Thus, this classification does not necessarily mean that the individual cannot speak English. The term Hispanic has caused controversy in the past and has been associated with derogatory remarks. A number of alternative terms have been used by Hispanic-Americans to name themselves, including Spanish or Latino.

Our comments should not be interpreted as excessive sensitivity nor to suggest that the term "Hispanic" should not be used. We suggest avoiding labeling patients in a scientific publication, unless the description adds relevant, pertinent, and useful information.

Rafael Ortega, M.D.
Assistant Professor of Anesthesiology

Marcelle M. Willock, M.D.
Professor and Chairman
Department of Anesthesiology
Boston University Medical Center
88 East Newton Street
Boston, Massachusetts 02118

References

1. Stene R, Rose M, Weinger MB, Benumof JL, Harrell J: Broch trifurcation at the carina complicating use of a double-lumen tracheia tube. ANESTHESIOLOGY 80:1162–1164, 1994.

2. Garwood AN: Hispanic Americans: A Statistical Source Book. Boulder, Numbers and Concepts, 1991.

3. Schick FL, Schick R: Statistical Handbook on U.S. Hispanics. Phoenix, The Oryx Press, 1991.

(Accepted for publication June 26, 1994.)

Anesthesiology
81:1082, 1994

In Reply:—Ortega and Willock make several excellent and thoughtful points. The use of the adjective "Hispanic" has no useful medical or epidemiologic purpose in our article that I know of. I thank Ortega and Willock for their culturally sensitive comments.

Jonathan L. Benumof, M.D.
Professor of Anesthesia
Department of Anesthesiology, 0801
University of California, San Diego
9500 Gilman Drive
La Jolla, California 92093

Eastermar. Yet, the Frisians were "convinced of their singularity," and the villagers reacted emotionally to any suggestion that perhaps they did not constitute a distinct culture.

The Frisian situation captures the conceptual challenges associated with the idea of identifying an ethnic group: the paradox of recognizing an ethnic group but being unable to define its *boundaries,* the characteristics which mark some people off from others as unified and distinct. In other words, there is no easy formula that can be used to clearly classify people into distinct ethnic categories (Nathan 1993).

To further illustrate the difficulties of conceptualizing ethnicity and placing people into ethnic categories, consider that when Raymond Breton and his colleagues (1990) studied ethnicity in Toronto, they asked respondents 167 questions to determine their ethnicity. They found no single question could be used as a mark of membership in an ethnic group. Likewise, when Mary C. Waters (1990) studied the process by which people reach an answer to the question "What is your ethnic origin (ancestry)?", she asked subjects at least 83 follow-up questions to determine how they came up with an answer.

Breton and Waters asked such a large number of questions because membership in an ethnic group involves more than sharing a language, a national origin, or distinctive physical features. Membership involves social demands. Consider Merry White's (1988) discussion about what it means to be Japanese in Japan.

> The simplest definition of being Japanese is to be born in Japan, to be of Japanese parents, to live in Japan, and to speak Japanese. As we have seen, a person is Japanese not only because he or she speaks Japanese, likes raw fish, and carries a Japanese passport, but because he or she is an active participant in relationships with clearly drawn lines of responsibility and loyalty. (p. 110)

Breton and Waters' research challenges the common practice of using the most visible biological markers such as eye shape and color, hair texture and color, and skin color to determine ethnicity. The problem with biological markers is that our genetic endowment gives us human and physical traits, not an ethnic culture or identity.

One reason there are no markers that can be used to clearly classify people into distinct ethnic categories is that most people have mixed ancestry and possess a blend of physical and cultural traits. The case of culinary artist and chef Jeannette Holley, featured in *American Visions,* shows that ethnic categories can never be clear-cut.

The 37-year-old chef is thin and tall, with taffy-colored skin and sculptured black hair. Her deep, almond eyes allow only momentary glimpses into her private world of inner connections. Her father is African-American, her mother, Japanese, and Holley has spent much of her life in Asia, first outside Tokyo and later in Seoul, Korea. "I was raised an American. I lived in Asia for 17 years. I spoke English at home, although it wasn't my first language. Language itself becomes a property of who you are. The less Japanese I speak, the less Japanese I feel." (Burns 1993:36)

Depending on the marker one chooses to use—skin color, national origin, territory, ancestry, eye structure, language—Jeannette Holley could be classified as a member of any number of ethnic groups. Yet, because Holley has no single ethnic identity, we cannot say that she lacks an ethnicity.

The Holley case suggests that if we try to determine objectively what constitutes membership in an ethnic group, we must confront the fact that there are many ways one can demonstrate ethnicity. Salman Rushdie (1991) makes this point about Indians living in England.

England's Indian writers are by no means the same type of animal. Some of us, for instance, are Pakistani. Others Bangladeshi. Others West, or East, or even South African...This word "Indian" is getting to be a pretty scattered concept. Indian writers in England include political exiles, first-generation migrants, affluent expatriates whose residence here is frequently temporary, naturalized Britons, and people born here who may never have laid eyes on the subcontinent. Clearly nothing that I say can apply across all these categories. (pp. 16–17)

Charles Hirschman (1993) points out that there is no such thing as mutually exclusive or clear-cut ethnic categories. There has always been *ethnic blending*—"inter-ethnic unions (interbreeding) and shifts in ethnic affiliation" (p. 549)—such that "most ethnic communities are either amalgams of different peoples or have absorbed significant numbers of other groups through conquest, the expansion of national boundaries, or acculturation" (p. 550). The reading "The Mingling of Alaska Natives with 'Foreigners': A Brief Historical Overview" by Julie E. Sprott (1994) illustrates Hirschman's point.

If people possessed complete information related to their ancestry, practically everyone in any society would belong to multiple ethnic categories. Hirschman suggests that the ambiguity of ethnicity would seem to minimize the importance of ethnicity in people's lives. Yet, based on a casual reading and viewing of the news, exactly the opposite seems to be true. Hirschman believes this is the case because in most societies the politics of ethnicity are based on notions of inclusion and exclusion (or the idea that clear boundaries separate outsiders from insiders), which discourage people from claiming multiple ethnic identifications. Thus Hirschman argues that the questions we ask about ethnicity should reflect a social and political reality in the United States which assumes that *one* ethnicity dominates.

Hirschman's argument may be true with regard to the politics of ethnicity. It does not seem to apply to self-identification. The majority of respondents who participated in the 1990 Census, when asked about their ancestry or ethnic origin, listed multiple ancestries.

Because there are no clear markers which can be used to classify people into ethnic groups, perhaps the best way to determine someone's ethnicity is to rely on self-identification. Self-identification can prove to be problematic because people's sense of ethnic identification "can range from nonexistent to levels so high that the fate of the group is experienced as the fate of the self" (Verkuyten 1991:286). In addition, everyone has different criteria—some more stringent than others—for claiming membership in an ethnic group. For example, as sociologist Anny Bakalian (1991) remarks in her research on Armenian identity, "One can say he or she is an Armenian without speaking Armenian, marrying an Armenian, doing business with Armenians, belonging to an Armenian church, joining Armenian voluntary associations, or participating in the events and activities sponsored by such organizations" (p. 13). The basis for such a claim may be "a nostalgic allegiance to the culture of the immigrant generation, or that of the old country; a love for and pride in a tradition that can be felt without having to be incorporated in everyday behavior" (Nagel 1994:154).

Then there are those who simplify their ethnicity by a process sociologist Mary C. Waters (1990) calls "selective forgetting." In the reading "Choosing an Ancestry," Waters describes how people she interviewed chose to reorganize only some of their ancestries and to forget or discount the others, and who are uncertain about whether they actually belong to a particular ethnic group, in what respect they belong, and to what degree (see also Infield 1951). The uncertainty may stem from a wide range of experiences. For example, people may become uncertain about their ethnic identity when the professed identity does not correspond to what others believe someone claiming that identity should be. Conversely, what others believe a person should be may not fit with that person's conception of himself or herself. For example, novelist and critic Ilan Stavans (1995), grew up "in Mexico's capital, [in] a secure, self-imposed Jewish ghetto" (p. 195). He spoke Spanish, took vacations to Disney World in Florida, went to Texas on shopping sprees, watched "Star Trek" on television, ate junk food, and yet considered himself Mexican. "What makes me Mexican? It's hard to know: language and the air I breathed" (p. 195). As a foreign student on scholarship in the United States, Stavans "ceased to be Mexican and became, much to my surprise, a Latino—what's worse, a white Latino, something most people have difficulty understanding" (p. 196).

It is important to recognize that self-identification is not simply a matter of individual choice but it is affected by larger societal, historical, and political constraints. Some kinds of people have more freedom than others in claiming an ethnic identity. For example, people classified in racial terms as white have a great deal of freedom in determining their ethnic identity; those defined as nonwhite, especially those defined as black, have much less choice. Black Americans, whether they be native born or immigrants from Haiti, Jamaica, Trinidad, Germany, or Kenya experience considerable social pressure to identify as black "even when they know or believe they have many 'nonblack' ancestors" (Waters 1994, 1990). Then there is the phenomenon of *involuntary ethnicity*. In this situation, a dominant group defines others in racial and ethnic terms, thus forcing the latter to become, appear, and/or feel more ethnic than they might otherwise be. Some ethnic groups, such as Hispanic, are an artificial product of government classification. Other ethnic groups such as the Punjabi Mexicans emerge as a result of immigration laws, the system of racial and ethnic classification, and anti-miscegenation laws. Pujabi Mexicans are the offspring of unions between Mexican women, who immigrated to the United States in the wake of the Mexican Revolution, and Pujabi men, who immigrated without wives from India to the United States at the turn of the twentieth century. At that time, U.S. immigration laws established an annual quota allowing only 100 men from India into the country each year and preventing those men from bringing wives. The Pujabi men's "choice of wives was strongly affected by the anti-miscegenation laws in effect at the time. Asian Indians were technically Caucasians, but [because of their skin color] they were not generally regarded as 'white' and this meant that they were prohibited from marrying 'white' women" (Leonard 1993:4).

Even when people are free to define their ethnicity, we must remember that people's sense of their ethnic identity is not static. It may shift over time. Joane Nagel (1995b) writes about the phenomenon of ethnic renewal on an individual and collective level. On an individual level, *ethnic renewal* occurs when a person takes on or asserts a new ethnic identity. Ethnic renewal can take many forms, including reclaiming a discarded identity (as when an adopted child learns about and identifies with biological relatives), discovering a new side of the family, or learning about and reviving lost traditions. (See the box **"Juntos Como Hermanos: A Study of a Spanish-speaking Catholic Church"** for an example of a "Hispanic"

Juntos Como Hermanos:[1]
A Study of A Spanish-Speaking Catholic Church

Since 1998 St. Mathews has been the home base for the Hispanic Catholic Community in the area. Before that, the home base was St. Josephs Church, a few miles away. As the Hispanic community grew in size it moved to St. Mathews, which offers more physical space. Mass is conducted in Spanish on Sunday at 11:30 A.M. Mass is also conducted in English, Monday through Friday at 8:00 A.M. The church pastor, Padre Jose, explained that these English-language masses were attended primarily by long-time residents of the immediate neighborhood. Many who attend the English-language masses are elderly and Padre Jose did not want them to have to go to another church that was further away and more difficult for them to get to. There is little to no interaction between "weekday" members and the Spanish-speaking members.

Padre Jose is the pastor of St. Mathews. He conducts mass every Sunday and is responsible for most of the administrative duties. There are two other priests, Hermano David and Hermano Anthony, who also minister at St. Mathews. The church employs two office assistants, Lois and Margaret, who organize church-sponsored meetings and programs. The priests and employees at St. Mathews speak fluent Spanish, although only Margaret is a native speaker.

There are about fifty "core families," as Padre Jose refers to them, who attend Mass every week. The rest of the community is made up of families and individuals who attend less regularly. Involvement in the church can be gauged by attendance. Members who attend on a regular basis are more

likely to be involved in the programs and activities of St. Mathews. The families who attend St. Mathews are scattered all over the area.

The congregation is made up primarily of families; either a mother, father, and their children; or a mother and her children; or couples. I have never seen a man alone with children and I rarely saw men carrying or holding children. It is also rare to see women alone. They are almost always with men or children. A few women arrive with other women, usually, their mothers, or their grown daughters.

Children are everywhere at St. Mathews. They run up and down the aisles, play in the pews, or sit outside the church. The ages range from tiny infants to children eleven years old. According to Padre Jose, families are encouraged to bring their children and involve them in church-sponsored activities at an early age. Babies are often heard crying during the mass and children are often seen carrying or leading younger children around. Although a "crying room" is available, parents or family members rarely use it. Most children are allowed to cry without being shushed or scolded. This shows that St. Mathews welcomes and accepts children. Teenagers are largely absent from church services and activities. I have observed only a handful of families with teenagers attending mass. During one mass, a group of teens were invited to the ceremony, but these teens were not regular members. In my interview with Padre Jose, he told me that the church was working to attract this age group.

A few men between the ages of 20 and 40 come to services alone. These men usually arrive early and are dressed poorly, often wearing jeans, T-shirts, and gym shoes or work boots. They sit in the back (usually the last three pews.) They do not take communion and few sing hymns. These men stand out in contrast to the great family presence in the church. I speculate that these men are migrant workers with family members living elsewhere.

[1]My title refers to one of the hymns often sung in the church "Juntos Como Hermanos." The translation of this title is "Together Like Brothers and Sisters," which wonderfully expresses the church and its values. The church is for many an extended family. It is a place to come together with people who have similar experiences and concerns. Their shared language and values create a strong sense of community.

Continued

Juntos Como Hermanos *(Continued)*

When I began my study I assumed that people attended St. Mathews as a way of preserving their culture and language. What I found at St. Mathews surprised me. While St. Mathews is a setting that preserves culture, it also encourages assimilation. The church offers programs and services, aimed at helping members gain the skills they need to adapt to Midwestern U.S. society.

The church provides classes for those who need help improving their English-language skills. It also helps with job placement. The church bulletins list jobs requiring Spanish-speaking skills and list scholarship opportunities for both Catholics and Spanish-speaking people. During tax season, St. Mathews organized workshops to help people file their tax forms. The church also sponsors activities for adults and children such as basketball teams and Bible study classes. The church has created a library housing Spanish-language books and videos for adults and children.

The church works to protect the rights of members. It organizes and participates in boycotts against companies exploiting Hispanic and migrant labor. In 1999, it organized a boycott against a produce-packing plant in a nearby state. Church members distributed fliers and fact sheets about the company. In addition, the church sponsors speakers to lecture on topics such as racism. The church also attempts to educate the general public about Hispanic culture and heritage. As part of the outreach it holds a Hispanic culture festival every summer, which raises money for the church while informing patrons about the variety of traditions encompassed by the Spanish-speaking world.

The idea of family at St. Mathews goes beyond ones immediate family. Efforts are taken to treat everyone in the community as kin. People are very affectionate and warm towards one another. During the "peace" portion of the mass, many people embrace or kiss. It seems that each member seeks to connect with everyone within reaching distance. I have observed people reaching across several pews to shake hands and even exit the pew to greet someone across the aisle.

Aid or assistance is available for anyone who needs it. Special collections are taken for members who have health problems or who are in the hospital. Transportation is provided for those who have no way to get to church. Members of the church work together to meet the needs of fellow members.

People arrive throughout the ceremony. Many do not arrive until about 12:30 P.M., an hour after mass starts. The church is rarely full by 11:30 A.M., when mass is scheduled to begin, but is full by about 12:15 or 12:30 P.M. People arrive constantly throughout the ceremony. About as many people arrive after mass starts as do those arriving "on time." This may have to do with the Hispanic tradition regarding arrival times. In Spain and many other Spanish-speaking countries, specified arrival times are thought of as suggestions rather than as an exact time to arrive. It is often customary to arrive late. It may be that the "tardiness" at St. Mathews is a reflection of this custom. Late arrivers are not expressing disrespect to the church or an inability to get somewhere on time. In time conscious America, the church is likely to be one of the few places where the members can feel comfortable expressing this tradition without adverse consequence.

St. Mathews plays two important roles in the lives of its members. It offers both opportunities for assimilation and for culture preservation. St. Mathews provides assistance for those who need help adjusting to life in the Midwest, while at the same time using and teaching the Spanish language and values. This creates a bicultural community whose members have both adapted to so-called American customs and values while preserving many traditional values.

Sara Fair, Northern Kentucky University student, class of 2000 church that seeks to help its members adjust to American culture and preserve their culture and tradition.)

Ethnic renewal can also be a collective phenomenon as when an organization forms or plans strategies to restore and/or revive institutions, culture, history, or traditions. One striking example of ethnic renewal can be found by comparing the 1980 and 1990 census findings on the number of Native American ethnic groups. In Table 3.2, we see that overall the

Table 3.2 Top 25 American Indian Tribes in the United States: 1990 and 1980 (Data are based on a sample).

	1990 Census		1980 Census	
TRIBE	NUMBER	PERCENT	NUMBER	PERCENT
All American Indians	1,937,391	100.0	1,478,523	100.0
Cherokee	369,035	19.0	232,080	15.7
Navajo	225,298	11.6	158,633	10.7
Sioux[1]	107,321	5.5	78,608	5.3
Chippewa	105,988	5.5	73,602	5.0
Choctaw	86,231	4.5	50,220	3.4
Pueblo[2]	55,330	2.9	42,552	2.9
Apache	53,330	2.8	35,861	2.4
Iroquois[3]	52,557	2.7	38,218	2.6
Lumbee[4]	50,888	2.6	28,631	1.9
Creek	45,872	2.4	28,278	1.9
Blackfoot[2]	37,992	2.0	21,964	1.5
Canadian and Latin American	27,179	1.4	7,804	0.5
Chickasaw	21,522	1.1	10,317	0.7
Tohono O'Odham	16,876	0.9	13,297	0.9
Potawatom	16,719	0.9	9,715	0.7
Seminole[2]	15,564	0.8	10,363	0.7
Pima	15,074	0.8	11,722	0.8
Tlingit	14,417	0.7	9,509	0.6
Alaskan Athabaskans	14,198	0.7	10,136	0.7
Cheyenne	11,809	0.6	9,918	0.7
Comanche	11,437	0.6	9,037	0.6
Paiute[2]	11,369	0.6	9,523	0.6
Osage	10,430	0.5	6,884	0.5
Puget Sound Salish	10,384	0.5	6,591	0.4
Yaqui	9,838	0.5	5,197	0.4

	CHANGE FROM 1980 TO 1990	
TRIBE	NUMBER	PERCENT
All American Indians	458,868	31.0
Cherokee	136,955	59.0
Navajo	66,665	42.0

Table 3.2   (Continued)

CHANGE FROM 1980 TO 1990

TRIBE	NUMBER	PERCENT
Sioux[1]	28,713	36.5
Chippewa	32,386	44.0
Choctaw	36,011	71.7
Pueblo[2]	12,778	30.0
Apache	17,469	48.7
Iroquois[3]	14,339	37.5
Lumbee[4]	22,257	77.7
Creek	17,594	62.2
Blackfoot[2]	16,028	73.0
Canadian and Latin American	19,375	248.3
Chickasaw	11,205	108.6
Tohono O'Odham	3,579	26.9
Potawatomi	7,004	72.1
Seminole[2]	5,201	50.2
Pima	3,352	28.6
Tlingit	4,908	51.6
Alaskan Athabaskans	4,062	40.1
Cheyenne	1,891	19.1
Comanche	2,400	26.6
Paiute[2]	1,846	19.4
Osage	3,546	51.5
Puget Sound Salish	3,793	57.5
Yaqui	4,641	89.3

[1]Any entry with the spelling "Siouan" in the 1990 census was miscoded to Sioux in North Carolina.
[2]Reporting and/or processing problems in the 1980 census have affected the data for this tribe.
[3]Reporting and/or processing problems in the 1990 census have affected the data for this tribe.
[4]Miscoding of entries in the 1980 census for "Lummee," "Lummi," "Lumbee," or "Lumbi" have affected the data for this tribe.

The data in this table are consistent with those published in 1990 CP-3-7, *1990 Census of Population,* "Characteristics of American Indians by Tribe and Language," issued July 1994. The report is available from the Government Printing Office (GPO) for $51.00. The GPO stock number for the report is 003-024-08700-6. The GPO telephone number is (202) 512-1800.

The Subject Summary Tape File (SSTF) 13, "Characteristics of American Indians by Tribe and Language," can be ordered from the Census Bureau's Customer Service Office, (301) 457-4100 or FAX (301) 457-3842. Also, a CD-ROM presenting these data is available from the Customer Services Office.

Source: U.S. Bureau of the Census (1996; 1994).

number of Native Americans increased by 458,868 or 31 percent, an increase that cannot possibly be explained by new births alone. For one Native American ethnic group, the numbers increased by as much as 248 percent.

The point is that ethnicity cannot be accommodated by simply marking a box on a census form. As Mary C. Waters (1990) argues in *Ethnic Options: Choosing Identities in America,* "[k]nowledge of one's ethnic ancestry is the result of sifting, simplifying, and distorting the knowledge one has about it in interaction with the labels others attach to it" (p. 26). In fact one might argue that the individual process Waters describes mirrors the popular sifted, simplified, distorted versions of U.S. history many people hold, which assumes every ethnic group has a separate history and that the most important story is the settling of the frontier or westward migration of English-speaking people. In "Reflections on American Ethnicity" David Steven Cohen (1991) argues that "ethnicity has been an important factor from the beginning. In a sense ethnicity is a better explanation than the frontier of the shaping of American culture" (p. 320). But the ethnicity Cohen describes is dynamic, emerging, changing, not static, unvarying, or constant.

Ethnicity, then, is not a simple concept. It is a complex multidimensional concept. In "Theories of Ethnicity: An Overview and Assessment" by Yen Le Espiritu, we learn that ethnic consciousness can be a product of shared ancestry, sentimental attachment, and/or a product of political and social processes. It is something that can be chosen, imposed, created, recreated, or denied.

The reading "Are Italian Americans Just White Folks?" by Rudolph J. Vecoli examines the Italian experience in the United States. People who claim Italian descent constitute the fifth largest ancestry group in the United States. However, like any ethnic experience, the meaning of "Italian" varies depending on a variety of factors including "geography, generation, gender, social class, and political disposition." The meaning of a particular ethnicity has also been affected by social and political forces. In the case of Italians in America, their experience has been shaped by "urban 'renewal,' highway construction, and changing population patterns." That experience has also been shaped by academic theories of race/ethnicity and by government policies defining the official race and ethnic categories.

The "peopling of America is one of the great dramas in all of human history" (Sowell 1981:3). It involved the conquest of the native peoples, the annexation of Mexican territory along with many of its inhabitants (who lived in what is now New Mexico, Utah, Nevada, Arizona, California, and parts of Colorado and Texas), and the influx of millions of people (voluntarily and by force) from practically every country in the world. The United States is a country "marked by exceptional ethnic diversity." At the same time it is a country where a "majority of Americans [share] a same conception of who they are, what they believe in, and how they are different from people of other nations" (Salins 1997:103). In the reading "Americans United by Myths," Peter D. Salins addresses two important questions: What is this common identity Americans share and how did this identity emerge? In a nutshell, Salins argues that "the American identity emerged from a compelling national mythology." Salins defines *myths* as "exaggerated or simplified representations of human traits and situations, paradigms of society and morality, that are based on some underlying truth." Salins argues that in the United States there are several essential and unifying ideas and images that have been elevated to the status of myth. The unifying power of these myths is reflected in the fact that aggrieved individuals and groups appeal to these myths even as they seek to change the society.

Questions Related to Ethnicity

The U.S. Bureau of the Census

Study Question

Look over the questions from the U.S. Bureau of the Census that are related to ethnicity." Think of three scenarios in which respondents would be classified as "Hispanic," but in which that classification does not capture the complexity of respondents' "ethnic" backgrounds.

1. Race (Question 4 was asked of all respondents).
   Instructions for Question 4
   If you fill the "Indian (Amer.)" circle, print the name of the tribe or tribes in which the person is enrolled. If the person is not enrolled in a tribe, print the name of the principal tribe(s).
   If you fill the "Other API" circle [under Asian or Pacific Islander (API)], only print the name of the group to which the person belongs. For example, the "Other API" category includes persons who identify as Burmese, Fijia Hmong, Indonesian, Laatian, Bangladeshi, Pakistani, Tongan, Thai, Cambodian, Sri Lankan, and so on.

Figure 1 Race Question for the 1990 Census

4. Race Fill ONE circle for the race that the person considers himself/herself to be. If Indian (Amer.), print the name of the enrolled or principal tribe.→	○ White ○ Black or Negro ○ Indian (Amer.) (Print the name of the enrolled or principal tribe.)
	○ Eskimo ○ Aleut
	Asian or Pacific Islander (API)
If Other Asian or Pacific Islander (API), print one group, for example: Hmong, Fijian, Laotian, Thai, Tongan, Pakistani, Cambodian, and so on. →	○ Chinese ○ Japanese ○ Filipino ○ Asian Indian ○ Hawaiian ○ Samoan ○ Korean ○ Guamanian ○ Vietnamese ○ Other API↓
If Other race, print race.→	○ Other race (Print race.)↑

Figure 2   Hispanic Question for the 1990 Census

7. **Is this person of Spanish/Hispanic origin?** Fill ONE circle for each person.	○ No (not Spanish/Hispanic) ○ Yes, Mexican, Mexican-Am., Chicano ○ Yes, Puerto Rican ○ Yes, Cuban ○ Yes, other Spanish/Hispanic (Print one group, for example: Argentinean, Colombian, Dominican, Nicaraguan, Salvadoran, Spaniard, and so on.) ↓
If **Yes, other Spanish/Hispanic,** print one group. →	

If you fill the "Other race" circle, be sure to print the name of the race.

If the person considers himself/herself to be "White," "Black or Negro," "Eskimo," or "Aleut," fill one circle only. Do not print the race in the box.

The "Black or Negro" category also includes persons who identify as African-American, Afro-American, Haitian, Jamaican, West Indian, Nigerian, and so on.

All persons, regardless of citizenship status, should answer this question.

2. Hispanic origin (Question 7 was asked of all respondents).

Instructions for Question 7

A person is of Spanish/Hispanic origin if the person's origin (ancestry) is Mexican, Mexican-Am., Chicano, Puerto Rican, Cuban, Argentinian, Colombian, Costa Rican, Dominican, Ecuadoran, Guatemalan, Honduran, Nicaraguan, Peruvian, Salvadoran; from other Spanish-speaking countries of the Caribbean or Central or South America; or from Spain.

If you fill the Yes, other Spanish/Hispanic circle, print one group.

A person who is not of Spanish/Hispanic origin should answer this question by filling the No (not Spanish/Hispanic) circle. Note that the term "Mexican-Am." refers only to persons of Mexican origin or ancestry.

Figure 3   Ancestry Question for the 1990 Census

13. **What is this person's ancestry or ethnic origin?** ↓ (See instruction guide for further information.)
(For example: German, Italian, Afro-Amer., Croatian, Cape Verdean, Dominican, Ecuadoran, Haitian, Cajun, French Canadian, Jamaican, Korean, Lebanese, Mexican, Nigerian, Irish, Polish, Slovak, Taiwanese, Thai, Ukranian, etc.)

Figure 4   Place of Birth Question for the 1990 Census

> **8. In what U.S. state or foreign country was this person born?** ↓
>
> ```
> [                                        ]
> ```
>
> (Name of state or foreign country; or Puerto Rico, Guam etc.)

All persons, regardless of citizenship status, should answer this question.

3. Ancestry (Question 13 was asked of a sample of the population).

   Instructions for Question 13

   Print the ancestry group. Ancestry refers to the person's ethnic origin or descent, "Roots," or heritage. Ancestry also may refer to the country of birth of the person or the person's parents or ancestors before their arrival in the United States. All persons, regardless of citizenship status, should answer this question.

   Persons who have more than one origin and cannot identify with a single group may report two ancestry groups (for example, German-Irish).

   Be specific. For example, print whether West Indian, Asian Indian, or American Indian. West Indian includes persons whose ancestors came from Jamaica, Trinidad, Haiti, etc. Distinguish

Figure 5   Language and Ability to Speak English Questions for the 1990 Census

---

> **15a. Does this person speak a language other than English at home?**
>
> ○ Yes   ○ No - Skip to 16
>
> **b. What is this language?** ↓
>
> (For example: Chinese, Italian, Spanish, Vietnamese)
>
> **c. How well does this person speak English?**
>
> ○ Very well   ○ Not well
> ○ Well   ○ Not at all

Cape Verdean from Portuguese; French Canadian from Canadian; and Dominican Republic from Dominica Island.

A religious group should not be reported as a person's ancestry.

4. Place of Birth (Question 8 was asked of a sample of the population).

Instructions for Question 8

For persons born in the United States:

Print the name of the State in which this person was born. If the person was born in Washington, D.C., print District of Columbia.

If the person was born in U.S. territory or commonwealth, print Puerto Rico, U.S. Virgin Islands, Guam, American Samoa, or Northern Marianas.

For persons born outside the United States:

Print the name of the foreign country or area where the person was born. Use current boundaries, not boundaries at the time of the person's birth. Specify whether Northern Ireland or the Republic of Ireland (Eire); East or West Germany; North or South Korea; England, Scotland or Wales (not Great Britain or United Kingdom). Specify the particular country or island in the Caribbean (not, for example, West Indies).

5. Language (Question 15 was asked of a sample of the population).

Instructions for Question 15

Mark Yes if the person sometimes or always speaks a language other than English at home.

Do not mark Yes for a language spoken only at school or if speaking is limited to a few expressions or slang.

Print the name of the language spoken at home. If this person speaks more than one non-English language and cannot determine which is spoken more often, report the first language the person learned to speak.

Directive No. 15 and Self-Identification

Luis Angel Toro

◇•◆•◇

Study Question

What do the four examples in this reading say about the category "Hispanic"?

Heavy public criticism of Directive No. 15 reveals another primary consideration when thinking about governmental racial and ethnic classification schemes: the issue of self-identification. Persons with many different cultural identifications find that Directive No. 15 badly misconceptualizes their identity.[1] The poor fit between Directive No. 15 and the society it attempts to describe has practical as well as ethical implications. As a practical matter, confusing, indecipherable, or inaccurate classifications will result in an inaccurate picture of the population being measured. Ethically, it is difficult to justify imposing a racial classification system reflecting theoretically discredited white supremacist ideals[2] on the very people whom civil rights laws were meant to protect and assist. For most Chicanos,[3] Directive No. 15 presents no right answer. Instead, Chicanos must choose some formula that misstates their identity or be forced into the statistical limbo of the "Other" classification.[4]

While Directive No. 15 purports to embrace the idea that people should be allowed to declare their own identity, it permits such expression only within the confines of the racial worldview it embodies. For persons whose upbringing did not inculcate them with the view of race embodied in the Directive, answering the racial and ethnic identity questions involves considerable guesswork as to what the government is asking. Consider these hypothetical examples of its application. These are not likely to be hypothetical in a strict sense; evidence suggests that all of the examples in the following sections have actually occurred.

Two Chicano Examples

A Mexican couple immigrates to the United States and has children. They receive a Census form in the mail and set about determining their own and their children's racial identity. Looking at the racial categories, the couple sees none that describe them. They do not view themselves as American Indians but as *mestizos,* persons of mixed European and indigenous heritage. They are not enrolled members of a recognized tribe, nor are they identified as Indians in the community in which they live.[5] By the same token, neither are they identified as whites.[6] In the "Hispanic origin" question, the couple sees "Mexican, Mexican-American, or Chicano" specifically listed as a "Hispanic" group. They identify themselves as part of that group and as being of "Other" race on the race question.

This couple might identify their children in the same manner. Alternatively, they might believe that a "Mexican or Mexican-

American" is only someone who was born in Mexico. As immigrants, they may not be familiar with the north of the border term "Chicano." Since their children were born in the United States, they answer the Hispanic origin question in the negative. Knowing that there are millions of people like their children in this country, and believing that there must be some place on the Census form for them, they think again about the race question. Obviously, their children are not white: Every day they face the avoidance behaviors and "microaggressions" exhibited by whites, designed to remind them that they are not part of that group.[7] They do not believe that their children are part of the "Black" or "Asian/Pacific Islander" groups, so they think again about the American Indian category. Perhaps aware of the one drop rule that, at least culturally, defines as Black any person with any known African ancestor or trace of apparent African ancestry,[8] they conclude that "community recognition" as Indian means being treated as nonwhite on the basis of apparent indigenous ancestry. Therefore, they mark their children as members of the "American Indian or Alaskan Native" race.[9]

Now, suppose that a fourth generation Chicano is filling out a Census form. Spiritually uplifted by the cultural pride inherent in the concept of Aztlán, he identifies himself racially as "American Indian" but answers "yes" to the Hispanic origin question, marking the "Mexican, Mexican-American, or Chicano" box. To the respondent, this seems like a decent reflection of his *mestizo* identity. To the Census Bureau, it is a wrong answer.

Suppose now that this same fourth generation Chicano is responding to a question under the combined race/ethnic short format permitted under Directive No. 15. Choosing between the selections, "White, Hispanic" and "American Indian" is easy. The respondent selects "American Indian" as the response, because he has never been treated as a white person in his community, because "Hispanic" seems an inaccurate description of a Chicano culture that has a strong indigenous influence,[10] and because in physical appearance, i.e., "racially," the respondent is far closer to being a Native American than a European.

Two Filipino Examples

Now, let us imagine that a Filipina with a Spanish surname is filling out the Census form. She was born to parents who moved to the United States shortly after World War II. She is aware that "Spanish surname" used to be the name of today's "Hispanic" classification, and that the Philippines were a Spanish colony for centuries before becoming a U.S. dependency after the Spanish-American War in 1898.[11] She is a Catholic, but neither she nor any member of her family speaks Spanish. She knows some Chicanos at work, but her close friends are all Filipino.

Examining the "race" question, she faces little difficulty. The Philippines are Pacific islands, and "Filipino" is specifically listed as a subgroup of the designation "Asian/Pacific Islander." She identifies herself "racially" as "Filipino." The next question asks her if she is of "other Spanish origin or culture." She seems to fit under this broad categorization. Her name, like that of many Filipinos, is Spanish, and the Roman Catholic religion was brought to the Philippine Islands by Spanish conquistadors.[12] She feels that this satisfies the "other Spanish culture or origin" criterion, so she indicates that she is also of "Hispanic origin," selecting the "Other Hispanic" box.

Her brother lives nearby and receives a Census form. He works at a place with many Chicanos and spends a great deal of time socializing with them. Like his sister, he identifies himself as "racially" Filipino. Turning to the "Hispanic origin" question, he perceives that this question is designed to capture persons like his co-workers, who identify as Mexican-American, and not persons from the Philippines. He therefore answers "no" to the Hispanic origin question.

This hypothetical is not offered to imply that Filipinos are responsible for the gap between "Hispanic" and Chicano achievement.[13] Certainly Filipinos are a racialized minority group in the United States with a long history of oppression.[14] This hypothetical does reveal, however, that the decision whether to answer the "Hispanic origin" question affirmatively may not relate at all to the question of whether the person is a member of one of the groups the classification is meant to capture. For both Chicanos and Filipinos, responding to Directive No. 15 requires guessing how a white person would classify them rather than exercising the power of self-definition.

Even for a Filipino, however, the decision whether or not to claim "Hispanic origin" might be tactical under the combined format. If the person feels that being identified as "Hispanic" might be more advantageous than being identified as an "Asian/Pacific Islander," for example, because affirmative action is being used as an excuse to cap Asian/Pacific Islander admissions to a university,[15] the decision to claim "Hispanic origin" might allow the person a competitive advantage, secured, of course, at the expense of the Chicano community. At least in this instance, the person could claim that switching categories did not detract from the overall goal of affirmative action—to assist racially subordinated minorities in a racist society. The same cannot be said of whites who employ the same device to help their careers and defeat the goals of affirmative action as they relate to the Chicano community.

Notes

[1] In a series of hearings in Boston, Denver, San Francisco, and Honolulu, OMB officials heard criticisms from, among others, Native Hawaiians who felt they should be grouped as indigenous Americans rather than as a subgroup of the Asian/Pacific Islander classification; children of mixed-culture marriages who resented being forced to select one cultural identity; Arab-Americans who felt that being described as part of the white majority inaccurately reflected their position in society; and persons, including this author, who criticized the "Hispanic" classification on a number of grounds. *See* Tony Bizjak, *Speakers Voice Varied Views on Race Classification,* SACRAMENTO BEE (July 15, 1994, at B4); Steven A. Holmes, *U.S. Urged to Reflect Wider Diversity In Racial and Ethnic Classifications,* N.Y. TIMES (July 8, 1994, at 18); Gregory Lewis, *Census Racial Designations Slammed in S.F.,* SAN FRANCISCO EXAMINER (July 15, 1994, at A-1).

[2] *See supra* notes 70 and 141–43 and accompanying text.

[3] I use the terms "Mexican-American" and "Chicano" interchangeably, recognizing that a considerable difference of opinion exists within the community about the appropriateness of either term. As one historian has noted, the terms used to describe members of this group have varied over time and have depended largely on who was doing the describing. *See*

Rodolofo Acuña, *Occupied America: A History of Chicanos,* ix (3d ed. 1988). I also do not assume that immigrants from Mexico form a distinct community from Chicanos. To the contrary, I argue that immigrants merge into the existing community. *See infra* notes 148–95 and accompanying text.

[4] *See* Richard Reinhold, *Others (Among Others) Play Havoc With Census,* N.Y. Times (Oct. 11, 1981, at 8).

[5] Directive No. 15, *supra* note 11, at 19.269.

[6] *Id.*

[7] *See* Peggy Davis, *Law as Microaggression,* 98 Yale L.J. 1559, 1565–68 (1989).

[8] While most likely the one-drop rule was accepted in the lives of most white Americans, it rarely constituted the legal definition of Blackness. Finkelman, *Crime of Color, supra* note 4, at 2110 n. 240.

[9] A significant number of households had parents who marked themselves as "Hispanics," or Mexicans or "Other" race, while listing their children as racially American Indian. Hearings, *supra* note 146, as 10 (statement of Harry A. Scarr, Acting Director, Bureau of the Census).

[10] *See* Anzaldúa, *supra* note 115, at 1–6, 27–39, 65–91.

[11] *See* The Diamond Rings, 183 U.S. 176, 178 (1901).

[12] *See* Phillipines: A Country Study 5–6 (Ronald E. Dolan ed., 1993).

[13] Some 57,000 persons described themselves in the 1990 Census as "Hispanic, Asian/Pacific Islander." Alternative Comparison Groups, *supra* note 30, at 3.

[14] See Chang, *supra* note 18, at 1291–92 (noting that despite early efforts to portray themselves as more "Western" than other "Asian-American" groups, Filipinos have been treated as part of a "yellow peril").

[15] On the use of affirmative action as a method to secure a permanent majority quota of white men, *see* Derrick Bell, *And We Are Not Saved: The Elusive Quest for Racial Justice* 140–61 (1987); Richard Delgado, *Affirmative Action as a Majoritarian Device: Or, Do You Really Want to be a Role Model?* , 89 Mich. L. Rev. 1222 (1991).

What's in a Name?

HIMILCE NOVAS

◇◆◇

Study Questions
1. What is the origin of the term "Hispanic"?
2. Do people in Latin American countries self-identify as "Hispanic"?
3. Why do many "Hispanic" writers and artists object to the term?
4. Is "Latino" preferable to "Hispanic"?

When it comes to the term "Hispanic," you can say a great deal. "Hispanic" comes from *España,* Spain, the country that led the conquest (as in *conquistadors*) of the New World. The many different native peoples, known generally as Amerindians, whom the Spanish discovered, eventually adopted or incorporated the Spanish language, culture, and religion and, to a large extent, intermarried or interbred with their conquerors. Add to that all the African peoples brought as slaves to the Americas by the end of the fifteenth century, who later also intermarried or interbred with the Spanish settlers and *conquistadors,* as well as with the native Amerindians, and you get the whole enchilada defined in the United States as "Hispanic."

Perhaps no other ethnic group in the United States is as diverse in its culture, physical appearance, and traditions as the Hispanics. The reason is that whereas all other ethnic groups have been categorized by their country of origin—the Irish from Ireland, the Germans from Germany, and so on—Hispanics are classified by their own or their ancestors' mother tongue, Spanish, and not by their specific culture, racial makeup, or even geographic background—which encompasses no fewer than twenty-one separate republics, each with its own distinct culture and history, including indigenous languages, religions, foods, and individual philosophies!

In Latin America, the homeland of most of the people known in the United States as Hispanics, no one defines himself or herself as Hispanic. The Mexicans call themselves Mejicanos, the Puerto Ricans Puertorriqueños, the Cubans Cubanos, the Colombians Colombianos, the Dominicans Dominicanos, and so on.

For Latin Americans, who like North Americans fought hard to win their independence from European rule, identity is derived from their native lands and from the heterogeneous cultures that thrive within their borders. Each Latin American country views itself as the curator of multiethnic, diverse cultures that cannot be totally embraced by the term "Hispanic." In fact, many peoples of Latin America speak ancient native languages and use Spanish merely as their official language.

To the recent immigrant, the realization that she or he is no longer Nicaraguan, Mexican, or Colombian, but now belongs to a new, homogenized group called "Hispanic," often serves as the bridge toward assimilation into a new country. It is, ironically, the first American word that applies to her or him.

In the United States, many Hispanics consider the word "Hispanic" merely a bureaucratic government census term, and call themselves "Latinos" or else use the terms "Mexican-American," "Dominican-American," and so on. Many Latinos, particularly writers and artists, strongly object to "Hispanic" and prefer to be called "Latinos" or "Latinas" (depending on gender).

Novelist Sandra Cisneros, author of *Woman Hollering Creek and Other Stories,* goes as far as refusing to let her work appear in anthologies that use the word "Hispanic" because, she says, it smacks of colonization. "It's a repulsive slave name," she declared in an interview for *The New York Times.* John Leguizamo, the part-Colombian, part–Puerto Rican writer and actor, creator of the one-man show *Spic-O-Rama,* says he simply used to call himself "Spanish" (the term used for Puerto Ricans in New York until recently), but that he now prefers "Latino," although he does not consider "Hispanic" offensive. "Now 'wetback, greasy spic,' that's derogatory," he told an interviewer.

Many others have embraced the term "Hispanic" as a means to bolster solidarity among the various groups and gain political power. Raul Yzaguire, president of the National Council of La Raza, and former congressman Herman Badillo both believe that "Hispanic" is a name that promotes unity. Enrique Fernández, editor of *Más,* a Spanish-language entertainment magazine, believes that he speaks for many when he says that "Hispanic" is preferable to "Latino," since "Latino," taken back to its roots, refers to an even older empire—the one that took over Spain.

In recent elections, Latinos, united under that single "Hispanic" banner, have demonstrated unprecedented influence and have been responsible for much landmark legislation.

Are Brazilian-Americans Hispanic?

No. Brazilian-Americans speak Portuguese and are of Portuguese, not Spanish, descent.

On April 22, 1500, a Portuguese navigator named Pedro Alvares Cabral landed at Porto Seguro, Brazil. Spanish navigators had also seen Brazil's coast for the first time that year. But Portugal had won the rights to Brazil from the Pope in 1494, under the Treaty of Tordesillas with Spain, and thereafter ruled Brazil for more than three hundred years.

There are approximately 1,153,154 Americans of Portuguese descent in the United States. Most live in Rhode Island and Massachusetts and elsewhere along the Northeast Corridor. According to the 1990 census, 94,023 Brazilian-born and 218,525 Portuguese-born Americans reside in the United States.

What Makes Latinos So Difficult to Count?

Hispanics are defined as residents of the United States who belong to Spanish-speaking ethnic groups. Most are U.S. citizens, but others are legal resident aliens with green cards. Still others are undocumented—mostly workers who entered the country illegally in search of a better life for themselves and their families.

The Immigration Reform and Control Act of 1986 granted amnesty and the opportunity to obtain American citizenship to thousands of undocumented workers. However, because of stiff penalties imposed on U.S. employers who knowingly hired undocumented workers, many Hispanics who would have qualified for amnesty and legal status were unable to do so, since the new law required them to show proof that they had been living and working in the United States before

January 1, 1982. In many instances, their employers were reluctant to come forward on their behalf for fear of government reprisal. It was one of those damned-if-you-do and damned-if-you-don't cases that creep up in our history from time to time.

According to U.S. government estimates, Americans of Hispanic origin numbered 22,354,059 (or 9 percent of the population) in 1990. That count was up from 16,940,000 in 1985. This sharp increase in population, combined with the fact that the median age of Hispanics in 1988 was below thirty, makes Latinos the most rapidly growing ethnic minority in the United States.

The Mingling of Alaska Natives with "Foreigners": A Brief Historical Overview

JULIE E. SPROTT

⬧◆⬥◆◇

Study Questions

1. What three characteristics define the history of contact between groups of white Russo-Euro-American origin and Alaska natives?
2. Make a chart showing the major waves of migration and the motivating factors behind each wave.

Mixed-blood ancestry for some Native groups of Alaska has a long history. Before the modern era, population admixture took place within specific locales where foreign visitors were concentrated. Today the process is more nearly ubiquitous, played out largely through migration of Natives to urban centers. In some situations, a great power imbalance in favor of the visitors tempered the intimate interaction of the foreign men with Native women, characteristic, for example, in the early Russian period. What admixture "meant" for identity or social status of Natives has been variably depicted in the literature as a negative influence, an advantage, or without social significance.

For the purposes of this article, I will ignore the intermingling of Alaska Natives with other ethnic populations and concentrate on relationships between Alaska Natives and groups of white Russo-Euro-American origin. Three features of the history of contact are pertinent: (1) the vast majority of visitors were male; (2) foreigners typically came to Alaska in cycles or "waves"; (3) the motivation for new arrivals involved exploitation of one or more natural resources that afforded monetary or strategic advantage. Once those resources fell in price, became depleted, or lost strategic edge, the bulk of the visitors left. There were, on the other hand, many examples of non-Natives, such as trappers and traders, who stayed to work and raise families in rural regions. Some were missionaries who attempted to convert the Natives to Christianity, to provide medical care, and to educate the populace (VanStone 1964). Though not properly depicted as coming in "waves," traders and missionaries were significant agents of sociocultural change, a topic that falls outside the scope of this article.

Another caveat to the idea of recurring waves of migration is the phenomenon of "bureaucratization of the north" that has accelerated in the most recent period. Jobs have burgeoned as a result of federal, state, and local government-related activities in Alaska, particularly since World War II and the enactment of statehood in January 1959. This trend is shown, for example, in census data. In 1939, the distribution of the population between Natives (45 percent) and non-Natives (54 percent) was almost equal: by 1950, close to a decade later, whites consisted of 72 percent of the population (Levin 1991:17). At present, 36.1 percent of

Alaska's work force is employed in government-sector jobs, including military personnel (ADL 1993a, 1993b).

The date usually cited for the official arrival of foreigners to Alaska and the beginning of colonization is 1741, the year of the Russian Vitus Bering's sighting of the southern coast of Alaska and his crew's wintering over on Bering Island (Fisher 1990:17). In the first 50 years of contact, Russians brutalized peoples of the southwest and south-central areas of Alaska, populated by Aleut, Koniaq, and Chugach Natives (summarized by VanStone 1984). Military men and traders who followed the early explorers virtually enslaved the population and compelled Native men to hunt for seal and otter pelts; many Native women became wives or concubines of the intruders (Oleska 1990:178). Population decline among Natives in the southwest during that time has been estimated between 80–90 percent (Smith and Barnett 1990:14; Veltre 1990:181). A class designation for mixed-blood children called Creoles developed in subsequent generations.

The Russians expanded their range of influence further to the south, founding a fur-trading post that later became the colonial capital of Sitka in 1806. Tlingit, who lived nearby, showed their displeasure by attacking the fort several times (Antonson 1990:165) and were never fully subdued by the Russians (Fedorova 1975:17). By 1799, a gentler, less interfering policy toward Natives was adopted after the Russian-American Company began administering the territory through an Imperial Charter, renewed twice until the sale of Alaska to the United States in 1867.

Contact with the more northerly and interior Native groups was effected primarily through fur trading, fishing, and mission activities that accompanied the establishment of outposts by the Russian-American Company. From the early 1800s, these efforts were concentrated around Bristol Bay, the Yukon-Kuskokwim Delta, the Copper and Nushagak River regions, and Norton Sound. The Inupiat, residents of the northern coastal regions, had minimal contact until the search for the Franklin expedition and whaling began in the 1840s (Arndt 1990; Fortuine 1989:25). Most of the more interior-dwelling Athapaskan Indians encountered few outsiders until the end of the nineteenth century.

The Creoles—An Historical Example of a Socially Recognized Mixed-Blood Class

By the time of the signing of the Second Charter for the Russian-American Company in 1821, mixed-blood Natives were common, although they never exceeded an estimated 1,900 (Black 1990:152). Both the second and third charters specified a status estate for the new Creole class. Creoles received the right to obtain a formal education in exchange for service to the Company, becoming free men when this service ended (Fedorova 1975:12–13).

Not all of Creole status were mixed bloods, because some "islanders" who pledged political allegiance to Russia were also joined to the Creole class (Oleska 1990:185). Nevertheless, the enumeration of Creoles is considered a fair indication of the numbers born to intermixed couples in the region (Black 1990:146). It is well documented that many Creoles held respected positions as explorers, traders, priests, and health care personnel (Arndt 1990:95, Fortuine 1990:127–128). For example, as many as half the Company ships in the 1860s were under the command of Creoles (Fedorova 1975:14).

What the Creole estate meant in relation to ethnic identity compared to other status groups in Russian America is difficult to discern from the literature, as mentioned earlier. Some historians argue that Creoles maintained their aboriginal cultural identity and embraced the best of both worlds (Oleska 1990), but others voice the opposite—that they belonged to neither culture and were despised by both (Fedovora 1975:14). Oleska (1987, 1990) contends that Creoles became key culture-bearers in the region, because it was through literary traditions of the Creole Russian Orthodox priests that aspects of Aleut culture survived to the present. No other Native groups in Alaska suffered as great a population loss and deprivation as did the early contacted groups, and in no other region was there a formally recognized mixed-blood class like the Creoles.

Other "Waves" of Contact: Whalers, Gold Seekers, the Military, and Oilmen

The whaling enterprise in the latter half of the nineteenth century and the brief but intensive Gold Rush of 1898 and 1899 massively impacted Eskimo populations of the Bering Strait and north coast, bringing them into contact with men from many different countries. As many as 232 vessels came in search of whales in that region in 1854 (Ray 1975:198). Seventy ships were seen in Point Hope alone in 1884 (Milan 1978). It has been estimated by Foote (1964:18) that "from 1848 to 1885 about 3,000 American whaling ships carrying approximately 90,000 men passed northward through Bering Strait." During the wintering-over period that became common later in the whaling era, Natives were hired as cabin boys, cooks, hunters, and seamstresses. Whole

families set up residence close to the ships and, as a result, increased the potential of intercourse between whalers and Native women (Stefansson 1913:202–203). An observer at Saint Michael in 1898, for example, wrote that mixed bloods outnumbered full bloods in the village (Ray 1975:245).

The Gold Rush of 1898–1899 created more disruption, particularly in the Saint Michael and Nome areas. Each region received "from ten to twelve times the population of the entire Bering Strait in the space of a year"; some 30,000 non-Natives flocked to the Seward Peninsula (Ray 1975:204, 246, 251). Following the initial rush, less intense, but nevertheless ongoing mineral exploration took miners into the interior via major routes along the Yukon and Kuskokwim Rivers up through the 1920s (Oswalt 1990:100–106). Oswalt relates that there was a general silence in the newspapers of the time about the interaction of goldseekers with Natives, though some missionaries wrote of their concerns, and one in particular from Bethel was found by Oswalt (1990:106) to have written: "It is gravely true that many of the white men now here do create serious difficulties in the uplift of the natives. Profanity and basest animal lust are either openly practiced or hidden beneath a much scratched veneer of politeness." Jenness (1957:165) said of the North Slope region that "by 1914 half or more of the Eskimos around Barrow and Point Barrow were of 'foreign' extraction; and twenty years later not more than fifteen Mackenzie natives could claim descent from the original population." As Ray (1975:159, 170–171) indicates, many non-Native men took Native women as wives, and often the white man who became a permanent resident was viewed positively by villagers, although this attitude is largely undocumented in the literature. Similar to Burch's opinion cited in the introduction of this article, Ray (1975:252) depicts a predominance of Native cultural values and norms in the village setting:

> When a white man remained, he became a member of the Eskimo community. If he married an Eskimo woman, his children were looked upon as Eskimo; and though he usually did not learn the language, he often preferred to adopt Eskimo values and way of life...Life resolved culturally and genetically to the Eskimo.

The next large influx of non-Natives to Alaska occurred during the Second World War and subsequent Cold War period with the construction and maintenance of the DEW Line radar stations dotting the Arctic Circle. The Aleuts again suffered extreme hardship and population losses, this time as a result of relocation away from their natal villages during the War. For other Native groups living near military installations, the effect of the military presence was a double-edged sword—more money flowed into villages as jobs increased, but culture change intensified as well. Hughes (1960) outlined changes that accompanied the military base on Saint Lawrence Island, including electrification of the village, construction of mainland-style housing, and considerable out-migration during the mid-1940s to mid-1950s. Men joined the National Guard and were trained or served in the "Lower 48." He noted that at least six women in the village married whites and moved to the mainland; a number of other young women said they wished to do likewise (Hughes 1960:284).

Oil exploration in the Cook Inlet and the North Slope regions and subsequent construction of the TransAlaska oil pipeline in the 1960s and 1970s brought a new wave of migrants from the Lower 48. Resulting oil revenues to Alaska transformed its politics, economics, and sociocultural milieu, all of which is beyond the scope of this article to detail. Changes accompanying the oil wealth have not all been positive. For example, in a household survey of residents of North Slope villages completed in 1977, more than one-third of adults were ambivalent about their quality of life. Some saw development from oil revenues as "good" and cited increases in available jobs; others decried development, citing the ill effects on the environment (Kruse, Kleinfeld, and Travis 1980:80). Jorgensen (1990) suggests that windfalls from oil development have resulted in a deepening of economic dependence in Native villages. During 1982–1987, the years of his study, he noted an increase in the cost of living and more reliance on welfare by families (Jorgensen 1990:305).

The literature yields few clues about the interaction of Native families with oil workers. The north coast Prudhoe Bay facilities are remote, and staff rotate work in shifts for several weeks at a time. Contact could perhaps take place between workers who maintain the pipeline along its corridor and Natives living nearby, but whatever the effects of this interchange, the vastly greater impact has occurred indirectly as a byproduct of the oil wealth. Purchasing power has effected increased intrusion of popular culture, as, for example, through the medium of television. Practically every village home contains a television set and many homes are connected to cable TV. Desire for amenities of the city, and education and job opportunities account in part for the increasing out-migration of villagers to the city. As a concomitant circumstance, many date and marry non-Natives.

Indicators of Admixture and Intermarriage in the Contemporary Era

The history of contact for Alaska Natives has varied by region and Native subgroup. Population admixture began intensively more than 200 years ago. Contemporary empirical research offers little information about this melding, with a few exceptions. Research conducted by the International Biological Program in the late 1960s used a genealogical methodology to estimate admixture among adults of five north coastal villages. Results showed that 25–37 percent of the population pool had non-Eskimo genes, primarily of western European origin, with additional heritage from Africans, Asians, and Polynesians (Milan 1978; Szathmary 1984).

Another study determined the extent of European-related genetic markers in red blood cells and sera of Saint Lawrence Islanders and residents of Wales. No greater than 9 percent of admixture was found for any village group, touted by the authors as evidence for geographic isolation even to the near present (Crawford, et al. 1981), although the discussion by Hughes (1960) presented earlier suggests that this low percent of admixture was probably a function of significant out-migration of ethnically mixed couples.

These studies aside, little is known about the current ancestral makeup of Alaska Native subgroups as a whole. According to the 1990 Census, 85,698 Alaska Natives comprised 15.6 percent of the state's population (ADL 1991:9). About 44 percent of Alaska Natives live in urban settings, with a little less than 40 percent of this group residing in Anchorage, dubbed "the largest Native village." The Alaska data mirror trends in the Lower 48: approximately 49 percent of Native Americans lived in cities in 1980 (Thornton 1987:227).

Migration away from rural villages in Alaska has steadily increased since the 1950s, with more women leaving villages than men (Bureau of the Census 1983; Kruse and Foster 1986). Urban-based studies on Alaska Natives that contain marital data show high percentages of Native women married to non-Native men, 47 percent from a sample in Anchorage (Dubbs 1975), and 40 percent from a Fairbanks sample (Milan and Pawson 1975). Extrapolating from 1980 census data, Levin (1991:141) found that regardless of residential location, Athapaskan women and Southeast Indian women were more likely to marry non-Native men than Native men. A 1988–89 survey study of 1,237 households of North Slope Inupiat showed a similar trend. Forty percent of the 25 married women between 18 and 24 years of age had non-Native spouses (Kruse 1991:323). Moreover, according to birth records of Native infants born in Anchorage in 1977, only 85 of the 430 births were of a Native father and mother; 144 were of a Native mother and white father, and 81 had a white mother and Native father (Ender 1980). Data on marriages in 1990 for Alaska residents indicate that about 50 percent of Native brides married white men; a third of the brides of Native men were white (ABVS 1993:132). Taken together, these data confirm significant increases in intermarriage and a rise in the number of Alaska Native infants of multiple ancestry in the most recent era.

Choosing an Ancestry

MARY C. WATERS

Study Questions
1. How did Mary Waters come to learn about "hidden ancestries"?
2. Why do you think many people selectively forget or dismiss some parts of their ethnic heritage?

In my interviews I explored the issue of how people decide how to answer a question about ethnic origin in a census or survey. I began each interview by showing people the census ancestry question and asking how they would answer it. Then I immediately asked the reason for that particular answer. The ways in which people described their family histories and the ways in which they came to their answers reveal just how much sifting and sorting occurs *even* before they consider the question. The complex interplay among the different aspects of an individual's ethnic identification was an overriding theme in the interviews.

Very often over the course of an interview, individuals remembered an ancestry that was not even consciously a part of what they believed their ethnic origins to be. This selective forgetting is illustrated in the case of Laurie Jablonski, a 29-year-old social worker. Laurie reported at the beginning of the interview that she was fourth-generation Polish-German. Her great-grandparents on her mother's side had been German immigrants, her father's grandmother was German, and her father's grandfather was Polish. Laurie discussed at length the various elements that she thought made up her Polish and German heritage. Even though culturally her family observes many German customs and is very German-identified, Laurie often gives her ethnic identity simply as Polish when asked. She said this was because her last name was Polish, and that is often how others identify her. Thus though her self-identification in private and with her family is German-Polish, and she believes that her origin is more than three-quarters German, her self-identification to others is often only Polish.

However, a much more extreme example of simplification and "selective forgetting" became clear at the end of the interview. At the end of an hour-and-a-half interview, when the tape recorder was turned off, Laurie said that she had just remembered that she had some English in her too, that her grandmother had told her five years ago that one of her ancestors, she does not know which one, had been married to an English person. She recalled being really annoyed when her grandmother told her this and remembered thinking, "I am already this mishmash, don't tell me that I am anything else too."

Ted Jackson, a 27-year-old office worker, also reported feeling annoyance when he discovered that he really had more ancestral elements in his background than he had originally thought. He said he was of Irish, French, German, English, and Scottish ancestry: "I didn't even know I was Scottish until I got interested in my roots and I went over to my grandmother's. I didn't know I was English. I thought I was only a couple of things, but then she really made me feel like a dirt ball—throw everything else in there too."

Further probing in many of the interviews revealed ancestries in the histories of these people that were just deemed too inconsequential to mention. A respondent who seemed on the verge of forgetting an ancestry was Mike Gold, a 54-year-old lawyer, who reported that he would have answered English and French on the census form, and that he was fourth-generation American. When I asked why he would have answered English and French, he answered:

A: Well, my mother was English and my father was French and Polish.

Q: Then why would you not answer English, French, and Polish?

A: I don't know. I guess I just never think about the Polish.

The unimportance of certain ancestries to people is clear in the ways in which they naturally describe these ancestries as part of their origin immediately after giving themselves an ethnic label that does not include them. For instance, Bill Kerrigan, a 19-year-old college student:

Q: What is your answer to the census question?

A: I would have put Irish.

Q: Why would you have answered that?

A: Well, my dad's name is Kerrigan and my mom's name is O'Leary, and I do have some German in me, but if you figure it out, I am about 75 percent Irish, so I say I am Irish.

Q: You usually don't say German when people ask?

A: No, no, I never say I am German. My dad just likes being Irish…I don't know, I guess I just never think of myself as being German.

Q: So your dad's father is the one who immigrated?

A: Yes. On this side it is Irish for generations. And then my grandmother's name is Dubois, which is French, partly German, partly French, and then the rest of the family is all Irish. So it is only my maternal grandmother who messes up the line.

Thus in the course of a few questions Bill labeled himself Irish, admitted to being part German but not identifying with it, and then as an afterthought added that he was also part French. His identification as Irish was quite strong, both culturally and socially, which explains his strong self-labeling. Further in the interview, however, he described a strong German influence as he was growing up. His mother's first husband, who died before she married his father, had been a German immigrant, and he had spoken German with her. Bill's half brothers and sisters from that marriage were apparently quite German-identified, and Bill himself was quite knowledgeable about his German maternal grandmother. He reported that his mother was strongly committed to her German ancestry and would definitely have mentioned it along with her Irish ancestry on the census form. He said he never thought of himself as German, however.

Another example is a 46-year-old manager, Rose Peters, who chose between her Italian and Irish ancestries based on the ideas she got about both from her parents:

Q: When you were growing up did you consider yourself ethnic?

A: Yes, I was very strongly Italian, because the Irish…whenever I was in a bad mood, that was the Irish in me. So I always related the Irish with the bad things and the Italian with all of the good things.

Q: Why?

A: I guess because every time I would do something bad, my mother would say, "Oh, that's those Irish eyes. That's the Irish from your father." The good things, like if I cleaned my room, she would say, "Oh, look, you are a Rosio," which was the Italian. So I thought all the Irish were hotheads and all the Italians had clean houses and good food.

People contradicted themselves frequently in the interviews because they had become so used to the simplifications of their ancestors' backgrounds that they did not even notice that their first answer to the question was incomplete. Notice how Betty O'Keefe, a 60-year-old housewife, did not even notice that she was telling me about a French part to her ancestry:

Q: Ancestry?

A: Irish.

Q: Why?

A: Because the majority, the great majority, of my ancestors were Irish.

Q: Do you know anything about the immigrants?

A: It wasn't my father and it wasn't my grandfather. I met my great-grandmother, and she didn't have an Irish accent, so it must have been like in the 1840s with the famine Irish, I presume. That's my father's side. They have a branch that were French too, but mostly Irish.

There were many other cases in which other ancestries would "pop up" in the course of an interview. And these "hidden ancestries" were often present in people who had very strong identifications with only those parts of their identities they "claimed" or recognized. Of course, the selective identification described here is not just the choice of the individual. A large part of this simplification occurs when parents decide what they will tell their children about who they are and who their ancestors were.

Reflections on American Ethnicity

DAVID STEVEN COHEN

◇◆◈◆◇

Study Question
List some of the popular misconceptions about the role of ethnicity in shaping U.S. history. Explain why these ideas can be classified as misconceptions.

...**E**thnicity has been an important factor from the beginning. In a sense, ethnicity is a better explanation than the frontier of the shaping of American culture. The frontier, conceived as either a line moving westward or as an area of supposed free land, is ethnocentric to a fault. It is limited to an Anglo-American perspective on history. The frontier may more accurately be seen as the place where Europeans, African-Americans, and Native Americans came into contact in the Americas. Many of the cultural traits associated with the frontier were in fact ethnic culture traits. Three examples are the log cabin, the covered wagon, and the cowboy. Research by folklorists and cultural geographers has shown that the log cabin was not an indigenous product of the American frontier. It was an adaptation of Scandinavian and German log construction techniques to floorplans that were English and Scotch-Irish. First introduced in the Delaware Valley, this construction technique diffused throughout the Appalachian Valley and into the Trans-Appalachian West, following the routes of migration.[1] The covered wagon, or Conestoga wagon, as it was sometimes called, is derived from northern European freight and farm wagons found in western Germany and the Netherlands. The English adopted these wagons from the Netherlands. Thus, there were

German, Dutch, and English prototypes for these wagons that became the famed "prairie schooners" of the American West.[2] And what could be more American than the cowboy? But, the cowboy was in fact an Anglo-American adaptation of ranching techniques introduced to the Americas by the Spaniards. The cowboy was known by different names in different countries—the *gauchos* of Argentina, the *llaneros* of western Venezuela and eastern Colombia, and the *vaqueros* of Mexico—but they were all part of the same Spanish ranching complex.[3]

Instead of viewing the settling of North America in the ethnocentric terms of the western migration of English-speaking people, the frontier may better be visualized as the boundary between settlements of several European ethnic groups (the French in Canada, the Spaniards in New Spain, the Dutch in New Netherland, the Swedes in New Sweden, the English in the British colonies), several Native American culture groups (the eastern woodland, the southeastern, the plains, the southwestern, and the Pacific northwestern), and several West African culture groups (the Yoruba, the Kongo, the Dahomean, the Mande). The interaction among these peoples resulted, in the words of one historian, in a "Columbian exchange" that reshaped the diet, the

249

language, the music, the dance—not just of America, but of the world.[4]

Before proceeding, we might distinguish between immigration and ethnicity. Immigration is one of several ways that an ethnic group comes to reside in a particular place. It refers to the voluntary act of leaving one's country of birth and moving to another country to live and work. The immigration model does not apply to most African-Americans and Native Americans. With the exception of those people of African ancestry who have immigrated from South America, the Caribbean, or Africa (whom the census incidentally lists as black, but not African-American) most African-Americans were brought to America involuntarily as slaves. Native Americans, of course, were here when the first Europeans arrived. The current theory is that their ancestors migrated from Asia to the Americas about 15,000 years ago across a land bridge that once spanned the Bering Straits. Thus, Native Americans exemplify two other processes by which an ethnic group might come into existence; that is, by migration and by conquest.

There are those who argue that African-Americans and Native Americans should not be considered ethnic groups, but racial groups. Through the 1930s sociologists continued to use the terms "race" and "immigrant" synonymously, it wasn't until World War II, in reaction to Nazi racial theories about the so-called Aryan master race, that scholars began to distinguish between race, linguistic group, and ethnic group.[5] Furthermore, the *Harvard Encyclopedia of Ethnic Groups* includes within its definition of ethnicity, regional groups (Southern Appalachian Mountain People, Southerners, Yankees) as well as religious groups (Jews, Eastern Catholics, Eastern Orthodox, Mormons, Muslims).[6] I would argue that race,

language, region, or religion may help define an ethnic group, but they are not synonymous with ethnicity. Blacks may be African-American, Afro-Cuban, Jamaican, or Haitian; Southern Mountain People may be German, Scotch-Irish, or English; Jews may be Sephardic or Ashkenazic; Hispanics may be Cuban, Colombian, or Puerto Rican; and so on.

Ethnicity is dynamic. Ethnic identities emerge and change. Immigrants become ethnics, a process which is manifested in the emergence of a sense of group identity. Many nineteenth-century immigrants identified with the town or region from which they came, not the country. In fact, the country may not have existed when they left. The Poles identified with Warsaw or Galicia, the Italians with Sicily or Naples, the Germans with Hanover or Bavaria. Once they settled in America, the group identity emerged. For some, like the Ukrainians, the name of the ethnic group did not even exist until the twentieth century. Previously, they were known as Ruthenians or Little Russians, terms which they dislike today. Often the identity that emerged in this country was a composite of traits from different regions of the old country. For example, the Ukrainian-American ethnic identity combines the woodcarving tradition from the Carpathian Mountains, the music and dance tradition of the Cossacks, and the embroidery and costumes of the eastern province of Poltava.[7] Ethnic boundaries have not been water-tight. Some individuals and groups have changed their ethnic identity. My own research indicates that more than half the Dutch settlers in New Netherland were not from the Netherlands. But they became Dutch, because this was the dominant culture in the region. And my work with the Ramapo Mountain People underlines the fact that a group that originated as free blacks who were culturally Dutch is in the process of becoming recognized by their neighbors and the newspapers, if not the Bureau of Indian Affairs, as an Indian tribe.[8]. . .

Some historians and sociologists see ethnic groups as subcultures in a predominantly White Anglo Saxon Protestant America. They use the term ethnic to mean "minority" as distinct from a vague construct called "mainstream" American culture. While it is true that there is a popular culture that cuts across regional, class, religious, racial, and ethnic divisions, this popular culture is not necessarily the culture of a single ethnic group, even though certain individuals have tried to define American culture in terms of their own region, class, religion, or ethnic group. For example, the frontier thesis may be considered the result of Frederick Jackson Turner's effort to define America in terms of the region from which he came.

It has been customary to refer to the United States as predominantly WASP, because American institutions were derived from our experience as British colonies. Historian David Hackett Fischer argues that the population of the United States in 1790 was also predominantly British.[9] There are two problems with this notion. First, it is derived from the total white population, excluding African-Americans, who constituted approximately 19.3 percent of the population in 1790. Second, it presumes that the English, the Scots, and the Irish were a single ethnic group. When you factor out these non-English people who also came from the British Isles, but who had different languages and cultures, the English population of the United States in 1790 was only about 49.2 percent of the total population, including African-Americans. Thus, the English were the largest single ethnic group—as

compared to African-Americans (19.3 percent), Irish, both Ulster and Eire (7.8 percent), Germans (7 percent), Scots (6.6 percent), and Dutch (2.6 percent)—but they were a plurality rather than a majority of the total population.[10] This is an important point in understanding American ethnicity.

Some historians also persist in distinguishing between the so-called "old" immigrants (that is, the Irish, Germans, and Chinese who came to the United States in great numbers between 1840 and 1880) and the "new" immigrants (the eastern and southern Europeans who came between 1880 and 1930).[11] There are several problems with this periodization, but most notable is defining what constitutes "new" immigration. To term an immigration that ended in 1930 as "new" may have made sense at one time, but certainly not today. The period since World War II has seen a whole new wave of immigration from different parts of the world. The immigrants who have come since the immigration act of 1965 may be the real "new" immigrants, but so may those who have come since 1980, which also represents a shift in countries of origin. The problem will not go away as long as the terms "old" and "new" are used.

I would like to suggest a different periodization, one not based solely on immigration, but which deals with the "peopling" not just of *British* North America, but of North America in general.[12] I suggest four major periods: (1) the pre-Columbian migration of the ancestors of Native Americans across the Bering Straits and their dispersal throughout North America; (2) the migration of Europeans and Africans, mostly as indentured servants and slaves, during the colonial period from about 1500 to the end of the slave trade in the United States in 1808; (3) the period between 1820 and 1930, during which European immigrants were attracted to the United States by the related developments of industrialization and urbanization; and (4) the period between World War II and the present, during which suburbanization and a post-industrial economy combined with a shift in immigration sources to Latin America, the Caribbean, and Asia....

Ethnicity has had an important impact on the local, regional, and national levels of American culture and society. The ethnic neighborhood is one of the most visible signs of ethnicity in America, as was noted by Robert E. Park, his students, and colleagues at the University of Chicago during the 1920s. They noted that immigrants in Chicago tended to cluster together in "colonies" or "ghettos," which were segregated, residential enclaves. These ethnic neighborhoods underwent a process which the University of Chicago sociologists termed "succession," as more recent immigrant groups replaced earlier immigrant groups.[13] However, as historian Humbert S. Nelli has shown, despite the high visibility of one ethnic group in these neighborhoods, rarely was the neighborhood the residence of a single ethnic group nor did a single ethnic group even constitute a majority of the population. Often remnants of earlier immigrant groups that resided in the neighborhood remained. One or two of the largest ethnic groups composed a plurality of the population and stamped its identity on the neighborhood.[14]

This pattern can be seen in the Ironbound or Down Neck neighborhood of Newark, New Jersey. The names derive from the fact that the neighborhood is bounded by railroad trestles and by a necklike curve in the Passaic River. In 1860, 37 percent of its population was born in Ireland, 20 percent in Germany, and 23 percent in other foreign countries. By 1910, the population makeup of the neighborhood had changed. In that year, 11.7 percent of the population was born in Italy, 11.3 percent in Russia, and 7.7 percent in Austria. The 1980 census, which listed ethnic identity rather than foreign birth, showed that 36.6 percent of the population was Portuguese, 14.7 percent Spanish, and 9.8 percent Puerto Rican. There were still small Italian and Polish populations, 8 percent and 4.4 percent, respectively.[15]

The one major exception to this pattern is African-Americans. For them, residential segregation in northern urban neighborhoods has been increasing progressively.[16] In the city of Newark, in 1850 blacks constituted only 5 percent of the population of the Third Ward. By 1940, in the midst of the Great Migration of African-Americans from the South to northern cities, which commenced during World War I, blacks constituted 63.2 percent of the population of the Third Ward. By the 1980 census, in 15 of Newark's census tracts, blacks constituted 75 percent or more of the population, and in 7 census tracts they were 90 percent or more of the total population. This unprecedented degree of urban, residential segregation is unmatched by any other ethnic group, including Hispanics.[17]

Not only are different ethnic groups clustered within cities, cities have different ethnic makeups, which is one factor that has given these cities their distinct identities. For example, the largest foreign-born population in Milwaukee in 1920 was German (33.1 percent of the total foreign-born population); in Boston it was Irish (23.5 percent of the foreign-born); and in New York it was Russian and Lithuanian (24 percent), approximately 80 percent of which was Jewish.[18] Thus, the association of Boston with the Irish, Milwaukee with the Germans, and New York with the Jews, has some basis in the distribution of ethnic populations.

Ethnicity is not solely an urban phenomenon. One of the lesser explored dimensions of American ethnic history has been rural ethnicity. In 1911, the report of the United States Senate's Immigration Commission on *Recent Immigrants in Agriculture* noted that in 1900, 21.7 percent of all foreign-born breadwinners were employed in agriculture. The largest number of foreign-born farmers were German, but there were also Norwegians, Swedes, Italians, Poles, Portuguese, Bohemians, and Japanese. In New Jersey alone, there were significant South Jersey agricultural populations of Germans in Egg Harbor City, Italians in Vineland, and eastern European Jews in the so-called Jewish agricultural colonies.[19] Many Italians continue to be engaged in agriculture in South Jersey.

Contrary to the positions of some sociologists, such as Herbert J. Gans and Will Herberg, who argued in the 1950s and 1960s that class or religious identities eclipsed ethnic identity in the suburbs, the overall pattern that has emerged since then clearly shows that ethnicity continues strong in suburbia.[20] The 1980 census shows that, like urban ethnic neighborhoods, certain suburban communities have become associated with particular ethnic groups. For example, in New Jersey the largest suburban concentration of Italians was in Belleville (a suburb of Newark), where people of Italian and Italian mixed with some other ancestry constituted 52 percent of the total population. The largest suburban concentration of Poles was in South River with a total Polish and Polish mixed with other ancestry constituting 31 percent of the population. In the Jersey Shore resort community of Spring Lake, Irish and Irish mixed with other ancestry constituted 48.3 percent. Middle-class

blacks also have moved out of the inner cities into the suburbs. The largest suburban black concentration in 1990 was in Plainfield, where they constituted 63 percent of the total population 18 years or older. In the post–World War II suburban community of Willingboro, which was the Levittown studied by Herbert Gans, blacks constituted 52.4 percent of the 18-or-older population in 1990.[21]

The differential distribution of ethnic groups has also influenced regional identities. In 1860, two-thirds of the Irish in the United States lived in New England or the Mid-Atlantic States, mostly in cities, and about half the Germans in the country lived in the Midwest, mainly on farms. The 1980 census showed that 79 percent of Poles lived in the Northeast and Midwest in what some people have termed the "Polka Belt," 53 percent of African-Americans live in the South, 77 percent of the Japanese in the West, and 73 percent of Puerto Ricans live in the Northeast.[22]

On the national level, changes in the sources of immigration have changed the overall make-up of the American population. According to the 1990 census, the total population of the United States was 248.7 million. Of this total, 12.1 percent listed themselves as black, 9 percent as Hispanic, 2.9 percent as Asian or Pacific Islander, and 0.8 percent as American Indian, Eskimo, or Aleut. At this time the breakdown of the white European population by ethnic group is not yet available for the 1990 census, but in 1980 was as follows: of a total population of 226.5 million, only 21.9 percent listed themselves as English, 21.7 percent as German, 17.7 percent as Irish, and 4.4 percent as Scottish.[23] Thus, American pluralism continues to mean that no one ethnic group composes more than a plurality of the population.

Certain ethnic traits have become part of our national popular culture. I already have mentioned the log cabin, the covered wagon, and the cowboy, all of which have ethnic origins. Much of the American diet has ethnic origins as well. Consider such Native American foods as corn (maize), the tomato, chili peppers, the German sausage (which became the American hot dog), the Italian pizza, the Jewish bagel, and the Mexican taco, all of which have been adopted into the American diet, as seen by their appearance on the menus of franchise restaurants around the country. The American language has incorporated words and expressions from the great variety of languages spoken by American ethnic groups. Consider the African-American expressions "boogie-woogie," "jive," "jazz," "rock and roll," "rap"; the Dutch "stoop," "cookey," and "hook" (for a point of land); the Spanish "vamoose," "calaboose," "buckeroo" (from *vaquero*); the German "kindergarten," "delicatessen," and "nix" (for veto); the Chinese "kow-tow"; the Yiddish "klutz," and so on.[24] American music has also been shaped by ethnic traditions, from the African-American blues and spirituals to the Scotch-Irish ballads and fiddle tunes, which together represent the twin fountainheads of American popular music. To this mix have been added Cajun, Tex-Mex, polka, salsa, and zydeco music, all of which are ethnic. In dance, there is African-American buck dancing, Celtic-American step dancing (which is the grandparent of square dancing and clog dancing), as well as the numerous dance traditions that have come from Latin America (tango, samba, mambo, cha-cha, and conga). And finally, there are the ethnic festivals, including both single group festivals like Saint Patrick's Day, which is celebrated by Irish and non-Irish alike, and the ubiquitous multi-ethnic festivals that have become so popular since the ethnic revival of the 1970s.

I am not suggesting that ethnicity is the only, or even the most important, factor in American history. It is only one factor—along with race, class, religion, gender, and region—all of which are related to ethnicity, yet are independent from it. Certain topics in American history, such as the Civil War, for example, may best be explained by factors other than ethnicity, such as race or region.

Whether or not one approves of ethnic diversity, it is a fact of life in America and has been from the beginning. But what is the future of ethnicity in America? As the world enters a post–Cold War era, and ethnic conflict in eastern Europe and the Middle East seems to be tearing nations apart, what will be the effect of ethnic diversity in the United States? I don't adhere to the Pollyanna view of cultural pluralists who think that all one has to do is to attend a multi-ethnic festival and everyone will get along with one other. There has been too much ethnic conflict in the United States to think that ethnic diversity is always a force for peace and understanding. However, what makes ethnicity different in the United States from some other countries is that no ethnic group constitutes more than a plurality of the total population and that, despite the clustering of ethnic populations, no ethnic group completely dominates any particular state or region. In the last analysis, James Madison's insight about American government applies to American ethnicity; namely, that this nation is sufficiently large and sufficiently diverse that no one ethnic group can have its way all the time. To rephrase Madison's dictum, in America we behold a pluralistic remedy for the diseases most incident to pluralistic society.

Notes

[1] Henry Glassie, "The Types of the Southern Mountain Cabin," in Jan Harold Brunvand, *The Study of American Folklore: An Introduction* (New York: W. W. Norton, 1968), 338–370; Henry Glassie and Fred Kniffen, "Building in Wood in the Eastern United States: A Time-Place Perspective," *The Geographical Review* 56 (1966), 40–66; Harold R. Shurt-leff, *The Log Cabin Myth* (Gloucester, Mass.: Harvard University Press, 1939); C. A. Weslager, *The Log Cabin in America, From Pioneer Days to the Present* (New Brunswick, N.J.: Rutgers University Press, 1969).

[2] J. Geraint Jenkins, *The English Farm Wagon: Origins and Structure* (Lingfield, England: The Oakwood Press for the Museum of English Rural Life, 1961); John Omwake, *The Conestoga Six-Horse Bell Teams of Eastern Pennsylvania* (Cincinnati: Ebbert and Richardson, 1930); George Schumway and Howard C. Frey, *Conestoga Wagon, 1750–1850: Freight Carrier for One Hundred Years of America's Westward Expansion* (n.p.: George Schumway, 1968).

[3] Charles Julian Bishko, "The Peninsular Background of Latin American Cattle Ranching," *The Hispanic American Historical Review* 32 (1952), 491–515; Fred Kniffen, "The Western Cattle Complex: Notes on Differentiation and Diffusion," *Western Folklore* 12 (1953), 179–185; Peter Riviere, *The Forgotten Frontier: Ranchers of Northern Brazil,* Case Studies in Cultural Anthropology (New York: Holt, Rinehart, & Winston, 1972).

[4] Andrew W. Crosby, Jr., *The Columbian Exchange: Biological and Cultural Consequences of 1492.* Contributions in American Studies, no. 2 (Westport, Conn: Greenwood Press, 1972).

[5] Ruth Benedict, *Race, Science, and Politics* (New York: Viking Press, 1945), 11–12.

[6] Stephen Thernstrom, ed., *Harvard Encyclopedia of American Ethnic Groups* (Cambridge, Mass., and London: Belknap Press of Harvard University Press, 1980).

[7] Robert B. Klymaaz, "Ukrainian Folklore in Canada: An Immigrant Complex in Transition" (Ph.D. diss., Indiana University, 1971); Robert B. Klymaaz, *Continuity and Change: The Ukrainian Folk Heritage in Canada* (Ottowa: Canadian Centre for Folk Culture Studies, the National Museum of Man, and the National Museums of Canada, 1972); Paul Robert Magocsi, "Ukrainians," in Thernstrom, *Harvard Encyclopedia of American Ethnic Groups,* 200–210; David S. Cohen, *Ukrainian-Americans: An Ethnic Portrait,* photographs by Donald P. Lokuta (Trenton: New Jersey Historical Commission, 1982).

[8] Fredrik Barth, ed., *Ethnic Groups and Boundaries* (London and Bergen-Oslo: George Allen & Unwin, Universitets Forlager, 1969); David S. Cohen, "How Dutch Were the Dutch of New Netherland?" *New York History* 62 (1981), 43–60; David S. Cohen, *The Romapo Mountain People* (New Brunswick, N.J.: Rutgers University Press, 1974).

[9] David Hackett Fischer, *Albion's Seed: Four British Folkways in America* (New York: Oxford University Press, 1989).

[10] Thomas J. Archdeacon, *Becoming American: An Ethnic History* (New York and London: Macmillan, 1983), 25. These figures computed by Archdeacon are based on estimates in American Council of Learned Societies, "Report of the Committee on Linguistic and National Stocks in the United States," *Annual Report of the American Historical Association for the Year 1931* (Washington: Government Printing Office, 1932). These figures have been slightly revised by Thomas L. Purvis, "The European Ancestry of the United States Population, 1790," *William and Mary Quarterly* 41 (1984), 85–135.

[11] Leonard Dinnerstein and David M. Reimers, *Ethnic Americans: A History of Immigration and Assimilation* (New York: Dodd, Mead and Co., 1975), 10–55.

[12] Bernard Bailyn, *The Peopling of British North America: An Introduction* (New York: Alfred A. Knopf, 1986).

[13] Robert E. Park, Ernest W. Burgess, and Roderick D. McKenzie, *The City* (London: University of Chicago Press, 1967), 9–12, 50–53, 142–155.

[14] Humbert S. Nelli, *Italians in Chicago, 1880–1930: A Study in Ethnic Mobility* (New York: Oxford University Press, 1970), 22–54.

[15] Raymond Michael Ralph, "From Village to Industrial City: The Urbanization of Newark, New Jersey, 1930–1860" (Ph.D. diss., New York University, 1978), 157; U.S. Census, 1910. Population, 3: 152; U.S. Census, 1980. Newark SMSA. Tracts 68–79.

[16] William Julius Wilson, *The Truly Disadvantaged: The Inner City, the Underclass, and Public Policy* (Chicago and London: University of Chicago Press, 1987).

[17] Ralph, "From Village to Industrial City," 157; Clement A. Price, "The Beleaguered City as Promised Land: Blacks in Newark, 1917–1947," in William C. Wright, ed., *Urban New Jersey Since 1870* (Trenton: New Jersey Historical Commission, 1975): U.S. Census, 1980. Newark SMSA, PHC 80-2-261, P-7.

[18] U.S. Census, 1920. Population, 2: 738, 745, 747, 1008–1009. The figure of 80 percent of the New York City population born in Lithuania and Russia as Jewish is based on the relative numbers of Lithuanian, Russian, and Yiddish, and Hebrew speakers in the city's population.

[19] U.S. Senate Immigration Commission, *Immigrants in Industries,* Part 24: *Recent Immigrants in Agriculture* (1911), 1: 3–9, 47 ff.; 2: 89ff; Emily Fogg Meade, "The Italian on the Land: A Study in Immigration." U.S. Bureau of Labor, *Bulletin* no. 70 (1907), 473–533; Dieter Cunz, "Egg Harbor City: New Germany in New Jersey," New Jersey Historical Society, *Proceedings* 73 (1955), 89–123; Joseph Brandes, *Immigrants to Freedom: Jewish Communities in Rural New Jersey Since 1882* (Philadelphia: University of Pennsylvania, 1971); Rita Zorn Moonsammy, David S. Cohen, and Lorraine E. Williams, eds.

[20] Herbert J. Gans, *The Levittowners: Ways of Life and Politics in a New Suburban Community* (New York: Random House, 1967); Will Herberg, *Protestant, Catholic, Jew: An Essay in American Religious Sociology* (1955: Reprint, Garden City, N.Y.: Doubleday, 1960).

[21] U.S. Census, 1990. Reapportionment/Redistricting Data. PL-94, 171.

[22] Leonard Dinnerstein and Frederic Cople Jaher, *Uncertain Americans: Readings in Ethnic History* (New York: Oxford University Press, 1977), 72; U.S. Bureau of the Census. *Statistical Abstract of the United States* (1989), 41.

[23] "Census Shows Profound Changes," *New York Times,* March 11, 1991, pp. A1, B4: U.S. Census, 1910. Supplementary Report, Ser. PC80-S1-10.

[24] H. L. Mencken, *The American Language: An Inquiry into the Development of English in the United States* (New York: Alfred A. Knopf, 1921), 51–55, 100–109, 197–205.

Theories of Ethnicity:
An Overview and Assessment

YEN LE ESPIRITU

◇◆◇

Study Questions

1. What is panethnicity? Give examples of panethnic movements.
2. Distinguish between the primordialist and instrumentalist theory of ethnicity.
3. What is categorization? How is it related to panethnicity?
4. Define internal ethnicity.
5. Explain the following statement: "In some cases, culture is used to define a boundary; in others, it is ultimately the product of a boundary."
6. What are some structrual conditions that lead to the construction of ethnic boundaries?
7. Explain the following statement: "Panethnic groups in the United States are products of political and social processes, rather than of cultural bonds."

Theories of Ethnicity: An Overview and Assessment

Ethnic consciousness continues to thrive in contemporary societies, despite Marxist and functionalist predictions that modernization and industrialization will bring about a decrease in the importance of ethnic ties (Park 1950; Lipset and Rokkan 1967). As Edna Bonacich and John Modell (1980: 1) put it, "Almost every society in the world has some degree of ethnic diversity and for most, ethnicity appears to be a pivotal point of division and conflict." In the United States, the civil rights movement of the 1950s and 1960s and the subsequent radical minority movements (Black, Brown, Red, and Yellow Power) reawakened sociologists and others to the continuing importance of cultural and racial divisions in defining lines of social order. A variety of theories have sought to explain the tenacity of ethnic boundaries. Two divergent approaches dominate this literature: the primordialist focus on "communities of culture" and the instrumentalist emphasis on "communities of interests."

Primordialism: Communities of Culture

Primordialists focus on culture and tradition to explain the emergence and retention of ethnicity. Ethnic cohesion is deemed sentimental; that is, people form ethnic groups because they are or regard themselves as bound together by a "web of sentiment, belief, worldview, and practice" (Cornell 1988b: 178). Scholars taking this approach claim that this "intuitive bond" originated in the primordial past—at the beginning (Connor 1978:

257

377; also Isaacs 1975: 45; van den Berghe 1981: 80). This "beginning" gives ethnicity a special tenacity and emotional force. In other words, the meaningfulness of ethnic identity derives from its birth connection; it came first. Capturing the emotive aspects of ethnicity, primordialism offers a plausible reason for the durability of such attachments.

Nonetheless, primordialism has several shortcomings. First, primordial ties do not always lead to ethnic solidarity. For example, the strained relationship between Canadian-born Chinese and Vietnamese-born Chinese in Canada suggests that groups sharing the same ancestry do not necessarily fraternize (Woon 1985). Second, primordial explanations of ethnicity cannot readily account for variations in the intensity of ethnic awareness. As Ivan Light (1981: 55) observed, these variations "indicate that living people are making a lot or a little of their 'primordial' ties according to present convenience."

Finally, in the primordialist literature, issues of economic and political inequalities are often treated as epiphenomenal (McKay 1982:399). Focusing on the psychological origin of ethnicity, simple primordialism overlooks the economic and political interests that are so tightly bound up with ethnic sentiment and practice (Glazer and Moynihan 1963; Greenberg 1980). Because conscious ethnic identity emerges and intensifies under situations of intergroup competition, what need to be addressed are the structural conditions that produce ethnic groups—not only the cultural variables themselves.

Instrumentalism: Communities of Interest

Unlike primordialists, who assume that participation within the confines of one's ethnic group is valuable in and of itself (Oal 1990), instrumentalists treat ethnicity as a strategic tool or resource. Scholars taking this approach argue that populations remain ethnic when their ethnicity yields greater returns than other statuses available to them. The functional advantages of ethnicity range from "the moral and material support provided by ethnic networks to political gains made through ethnic bloc voting" (Portes and Bach 1985: 24). In other words, ethnic groups are not only sentimental associations of persons sharing affective ties but also interest groups.

The most extreme variant of the instrumentalist approach takes whatever attributes are associated with particular ethnic groups to be primarily situational, generated and sustained by members' interests. Thus membership in one group is only for the sake of obtaining comparative advantage vis-à-vis membership in another. As Orlando Patterson (1975: 348) stated, "The strength, scope, viability, and bases of ethnic identity are determined by, and are used to serve, the economic and general class interests of individuals." A more moderate version combines an analysis of the external activators of ethnic behavior with their specific cultural form and content. For example, Abner Cohen (1969: 3) argued that because ethnic groups are culturally homogeneous, they can more effectively organize as interest groups. In either case, rational interests are assumed to play an important role in the retention or dissolution of ethnic ties (Glazer and Moynihan 1963; Bonacich and Modell 1980).

Rethinking Primordialism and Instrumentalism

Whatever their differences, primordialists and instrumentalists both assume that ethnic groups are largely voluntary collectivities defined by national origin, whose members share a distinctive, integrated culture. The phenomenon of panethnicity challenges these assumptions, calling attention instead to the coercively imposed nature of ethnicity, its multiple layers, and the continual creation and recreation of culture.

Voluntary and Imposed Ethnicity

Focusing on sentimentality and rational interests, primordialists and instrumentalists posit that ethnicity endures because individuals derive psychological or material support from their ethnic affiliations. But the obverse is also true: once sentimental and economic ties disappear, ethnics will vanish into the acculturated mainstream. These propositions imply that ethnicity is largely a matter of choice—in the sense that individuals and groups can choose to keep or discard their ethnicity according to their changing psychological and material needs.

However, to conceptualize ethnicity as a matter of choice is to ignore "categorization," the process whereby one group ascriptively classifies another. Categorization is intimately bound up with power relations. As such, it characterizes situations in which a more powerful group seeks to dominate another, and, in so doing, imposes upon these people a categorical identity that is defined by reference to their inherent differences from or inferiority to the dominant group (Jenkins 1986: 177–178). Thus, while ethnicity may be an exercise of personal choice for Euro-Americans, it is not so for nonwhite groups in the United States. For these "visible" groups, ethnicity is not always voluntary, but can be coercively imposed. As Mary Waters (1990: 156) concluded, "The ways in which identity is flexible and symbolic and voluntary for white middle-class Americans are the very ways in which it is not so for nonwhite and

Hispanic Americans." Her conclusion echoes the internal colonialism perspective, which maintains that white ethnics differ from nonwhites in the reduced severity of oppression they experience (Blauner 1972: 60–66).

Panethnicity—the generalization of solidarity among ethnic subgroups—is largely a product of categorization. An imposed category ignores subgroup boundaries, lumping togethr diverse peoples in a single, expanded "ethnic" framework. Individuals so categorized may have nothing in common except that which the categorizer uses to distinguish them. The Africans who were forcibly brought to the United States came not as "blacks" or "Africans" but as members of distinct and various ethnic populations. As a result of slavery, "the 'Negro race' emerged from the heterogeneity of African ethnicity" (Blauner 1972: 13; also Cornell 1990: 376–379). Diverse Native American tribes also have had to assume the pan-Indian label in order to conform to the perceptions of the American state (Keyes 1981: 25; Nagel 1982: 39). Similarly, diverse Latino populations have been treated by the larger society as a unitary group with common characteristics and common problems (Moore and Pachon 1985: 2). And the term Asian American arose out of the racist discourse that constructs Asians as a homogeneous group (Lowe 1991: 30). Excessive categorization is fundamental to racism because it permits "whites to order a universe of unfamiliar peoples without confronting their diversity and individuality" (Blauner 1972: 113).

When manifested in racial violence, racial lumping necessarily leads to protective panethnicity. Most often, an ethnic group is sanctioned for its actual or alleged misconduct, as when middleman minorities are attacked for their own entrepreneurial success (Bonacich 1973). But minority groups can also suffer reprisal because of their externally imposed membership in a larger grouping. Because the public does not usually distinguish among subgroups within a panethnic category, hostility directed at any of these groups is directed at others as well. In 1982, for example, as detailed in Chapter 6, a Chinese American was beaten to death by two white men who allegedly mistook him for Japanese. Under the force of necessity, ethnic subgroups put aside historical rivalries and enroll in a panethnic movement. According to Tamotsu Shibutani and Kian Kwan (1965: 210), groups often join forces when they recognize that the larger society does not acknowledge their differences.

That is not to say that panethnicity is solely an imposed identity. Although it originated in the minds of outsiders, today the panethnic concept is a political resource for insiders, a basis on which to mobilize diverse peoples and to force others to be more responsive to their grievances and agendas. Referring to the enlarged political capacities of a pan-Indian identity, Stephen Cornell (1988a: 146) stated that "the language of dominant-group categorization and control has become the language of subordinate-group self-concept and resistance." Thus, group formation is not only circumstantially determined, but takes place as an interaction between assignment and assertion (Ito-Adler 1980) In other words, panethnic boundaries are shaped and reshaped in the continuing interaction between both external and internal forces.

Multiple Levels of Ethnicity

In general, primordialists and instrumentalists have used national origin to designate ethnic groups (Parsons 1975: 56). This approach ignores the range of ethnicity—from small, relatively isolated kin groups to large categories of people bound together by symbolic attachments (Yinger 1985: 161). Addressing this oversight, recent studies of ethnicity have been more attentive to internal ethnicity, or ethnic differences within a national origin group (Bhachu 1985; Desbarats 1986). At the other end of the spectrum is panethnicity, in which groups of different national origins merge into new larger-scale groupings (Nagel 1982; Padilla 1985; Cornell 1988a).

Although prevalent, the movement from small-scale to large-scale organization is by no means unilinear (Horowitz 1985: 64–65). Among Native Americans, ethnic organization occurs along three boundaries: subtribal, tribal, and supratribal (Nagel 1982; Cornell 1988a). Similarly, in a study of Latino politics in Chicago, Felix Padilla (1985) reported a shifting of identity between Cuban or Mexican American on the one hand, and Latino American on the other, based on the political context. In the Asian American case, researchers have noted both the rise of pan-Asian organization and the increase in conflict among constituent populations (Trottier 1981). The ebb and flow of panethnic tendencies indicates that ethnic organization is multitiered, situational, and partly ascribed.

Ethnic Group and Cultural Group

Primordialists and instrumentalists agree that a distinctive, integrated culture is the principal antecedent and defining characteristic of ethnic groups (Horowitz 1985: 66). This assertion ignores the emergent quality of culture: culture not only is inherited but can also be created and re-created to unite group members (Roosens 1989: 12). As Lisa Lowe (1991: 27) points out, "Culture may be a much 'messier' process than unmediated vertical transmission from one generation to another, including practices that are partly inherited, partly modified, as well as partly invented."

According to Susan Olzak (1985: 67), the majority of ethnic groups in contemporary societies are fundamentally new, making claims to cultural traditions that are symbolic or mythical, or that no longer exist. With the changing positions of groups within society, old forms of ethnic cultures may die out, but new forms may also be generated (Yancey, Ericksen, and Juliani 1976: 391). Calling attention to the emergent quality of culture, Abner Cohen (1981: 323) reported that when different cultural groups affiliate themselves in opposition to other groups, their differences quickly disappear. As group members borrow customs from one another, intermarry, and develop a common lifestyle, a common culture emerges. Donald Horowitz (1985: 69) similarly concluded that "culture is more important for providing *post facto* content of group identity than it is for providing some ineluctable prerequisite for an identity to come into being."

The above discussion suggests that, in some cases, culture is used to define a boundary; in others, it is ultimately the product of a boundary. Hence, objective cultural differences need to be distinguished from the socially constructed boundaries that ultimately define ethnic groups (Hechter 1975: 312–326). Cultural differences are merely *potential* identity markers for the members of those groups. When this potential is taken up and mobilized, a cultural group—a group of people who share an identifiable set of meanings, symbols, values, and norms—is transformed into an ethnic group, one with a conscious group identity (Barth 1969: 15; Patterson 1975: 309–310).

Because panethnic groups are new groups, any real or perceived cultural commonality cannot lay claim to a primordial origin. Instead, panethnic unity is forged primarily through the symbolic reinterpretation of a group's common history, particularly when this history involves racial subjugation. Even when those in subordinate positions do not initially regard themselves as being alike, "a sense of identity gradually emerges from a recognition of their common fate" (Shibutani and Kwan 1965: 208). Drawing on the experiences of blacks, Robert Blauner (1972: 140–141) argued that cultural orientations not only are primordial but can also be constructed from a shared political history: "The centrality of racial subjugation in the black experience has been the single most important source of the developing ethnic peoplehood" and "the core of the distinctive ethnic culture." Similarly, Lowe (1991: 28) maintains that "the boundaries and definitions of Asian American culture are continually shifting and being contested from pressures both inside and outside the Asian origin community." Thus the study of panethnicity suggests that culture is dynamic and analytic rather than static and descriptive.

Ethnic Change: The Construction of Panethnicity

In moving away from cultural explanations of ethnicity, the study of panethnicity directs research and theoretical debate to those structural conditions that lead to the construction of ethnic boundaries in the first place. For the most part, structural theorists have focused on the effects of economic conditions on ethnic solidarity such as the existence of a cultural division of labor or a split labor market (Bonacich 1972; Hechter 1978; Nielsen 1985). While important, economic explanations of ethnic solidarity are incomplete because they largely ignore the similarly paramount role played by political organization and processes. Noting the important role of the polity in modern societies, Daniel Bell (1975: 161) suggested that "competition between plural groups takes place largely in the political arena."

Ethnic groups are formed and changed in encounters among groups. To interact meaningfully with those in the larger society, individuals have to identify themselves in terms intelligible to outsiders. Thus, at times, they have set aside their national or tribal identities and accept the ascribed panethnic label. Since the central government is the most powerful ascriptive force in any state, "there is a strong political character to much modern ethnic mobilization" (Nagel 1986: 96). According to Joane Nagel (1986: 98–106), ethnic resurgences are strongest when political systems structure political access along ethnic lines and adopt policies that emphasize ethnic differences. When the state uses the ethnic label as a unit in economic allocations and political representations, ethnic groups find it both convenient and necessary to act collectively. In other words, the organization of political participation on the basis of ethnicity provides a rationale for, and indeed demands, the mobilization of political participation along ethnic lines. As Jeffrey Ross (1982: 451) suggested, ethnic groups are most likely to exist where multiple access points into the political systems are available. Thus instead of declining, ethnicity is politicized and legitimized in modern states.

One possible explanation for the development of panethnicity in modern states is the competitive advantage of large-scale identities. The formation of larger ethnic units "gives people more weight in playing ethnic politics at the higher level" (van den Berghe 1981: 256; also Hannan 1979: 271).

While valid, this ecological perspective is incomplete. Panethnic coalition is not only an efficacious organizational strategy but also a response to the institutionally relevant ethnic categories in the political system. When the state uses a unitary panethnic label— rather than numerous national or tribal designations—to allocate political and economic resources, it encourages individuals to broaden their identity to conform to the more inclusive ethnic designation. Over time, these individuals may see themselves as more than just an artificial state category, but rather "as a group which shares important common experiences: oppression, deprivation, and also benefits" (Enloe 1981: 134). Thus, shifts in ethnic boundaries are often a direct response to changes in the political distribution system.

To conceptualize panethnicity as a political construct is not to deny its economic function. On the contrary, panethnic organization is strongest when given economic reinforcement by the politically dominant group. The state's recognition of "legitimate" groups directly affects employment, housing, social program design, and the disbursement of local, state, and federal funds (Omi and Winant 1986: 3–4). According to Paul Burstein (2985: 126), "Politics revolves around economic issues more than anything else."

Another economic dimension is the constraint of social class on panethnic solidarity. In general, similar class position enhances the construction of panethnic consciousness whereas intense class stratification works against it (Lopez and Espiritu 1990: 204). Ironically, class divisions are often most evident within the very organizations that purport to advance panethnic unity: the leaders and core members of these organizations continue to be predominantly middle-class professionals (Padilla

1985 156–157). This class bias undercuts the legitimacy of the organizations and the use of panethnicity as their organizing principle. As argued in Chapters 3 and 4, however, the dominance of the professional class in panethnic organizations is rooted in the very way the state has responded to minority demands. Because the political and funding systems require and reward professionalism, the ability to deal effectively with elected officials and public agencies has become a desirable qualification for leadership—a development that favors more politically sophisticated, articulate, and well-educated persons (Espiritu and Ong 1991). Thus, once again, economics is linked to the politics of panethnicity.

The emphasis on the political nature of panethnicity does not ignore culture either. While panethnic groups may be circumstantially constructed, they are not simply circumstantially sustained (Cornell 1988*b*). Once established, the panethnic group—as a result of increasing interaction and com-

munication among its members—can produce and transform panethnic culture and consciousness. As persons of diverse backgrounds come together to discuss their problems and experiences, they begin to develop common views of themselves and of one another and common interpretations of their experiences and those of the larger society (Cornell 1988*b*: 19). In other words, they begin to create a "political history," which then serves as the core of the emerging panethnic culture—and a guide to action against the dominant groups (Blauner 1972: 141). Culture building is essential in consolidating ethnic boundaries because it promotes group consciousness, reminding members constantly "of the disproportionate importance of what they shared, in comparison to what they did not" (Cornell 1990: 377). In so doing, it levels intergroup differences and inspires sentiments conducive to collective action. Excellent examples may be found in the recent history of the United States.

Are Italian Americans Just White Folks?

RUDOLPH J. VECOLI

◇◆◈◆◇

Study Questions
1. What is "symbolic ethnicity"? (Include the ideas of Gans and Waters in your answer.) According to the Vecoli, how had this concept shaped the meaning of Italian ethnicity?
2. Why is the author critical of the choices (boxes) available on forms asking a person's race/ethnicity?
3. How does Vecoli view ethnicity?
4. Why is Vecoli critical of the "most extreme" versions of multiculturalism?
5. Why study the Italian-American experience?

Although Chicago is not my hometown, the Windy City holds a special significance for me, personally and as a scholar. Chicago was my first big-city experience, coming into town on liberty from the Great Lakes Naval Training Station in 1945. But that is another story. I want to tell you about my experience when I was researching my dissertation on Italians in Chicago during the fifties.[1] Over a period of several years, I witnessed the death of Chicago's Litle Italies. The old neighborhoods were under siege from urban "renewal," highway construction, and changing population patterns; but when I first arrived, they were still there. Halsted Street was still the heart of the West Side colony, lined with *fruttistendi, grosserie,* and *stori.*[2] Hull House was still a functioning institution, not a museum.

As my research stretched over several years, I witnessed the destruction of that neighborhood. Images remain etched in my memory: a vast desolate area (like the bombed-out cities of wartime Europe) where houses and stores had been bull-dozed; finally, the only building standing was the Italian Church of the Guardian Angel (La Chiesa dell'Angelo Custode). One day, as I watched from a distance, a procession emerged from the church and paraded through the empty streets with the statue of the patron saint—a Felliniesque vision. On the Near North Side was Little Sicily (also called Little Hell), where Father Luigi Giambastiani had presided over the parish of St. Philip Benizi for fifty years. Though the church still stood, the houses of his parishioners had been leveled to make way for public housing. Padre Luigi was a bitter man, his parishioners scattered and his church soon to be destroyed. Many Italians I spoke with during those years were bitter. Their lives were literally reduced to heaps of rubble.

I tell you this not to indulge in nostalgia about life in the old neighborhoods but to remind us that the death of the Little Italies in the fifties (a subject that deserves a book and a film), not only in Chicago but across the country, marked the end of the first chapter of the history of the Italians in America. At the time I thought it was the end of the story. The old immigrants were dying; their children were headed for the suburbs, hellbent on becoming 100 percent American. My own research was driven by the fear that they (including part of me) would disappear without a trace. Oblivion is the worst thing that can happen to a people.

In the fifties there was no American Italian Historical Association (AIHA); there was no field of Italian American studies. The last substantial work, Robert Foerster's *The Italian Emmigration of Our Times,* had been published in 1919. The assumption dominating the public culture, including history and the social sciences, was that the European nationalities (the term *ethnicity* did not come into currency until the sixties) were rapidly disappearing from the American scene. Israel Zangwill's "melting pot," it seemed, had worked its magic.

Of course, today we know that was not the case. For varied and complex reasons, the sixties brought an explosion of repressed identities that erupted through the surface of Anglo-American hegemony and revealed the true pluralism of this society. And lo an behold, the Italian Americans had not disappeared after all; here they were tarantella-ing in public, staging protest rallies, and writing books about themselves. By and large those were not the old *paesani,* but second- and third-generation Italian Americans. As part of this phenomenon, the founding of the AIRA in 1966 signified the emergence of a mature scholarship on the Italian American experience, one that was to yield a bountiful harvest of monographs, dissertations, articles, novels, poems, films, and plays. The decades of the sixties and seventies also witnessed a revitalization of Italian American communal life. While

the old *società di mutuo soccorso* became less and less pervasive, new cultural, political, and social organizations sprang up. And the voices of Italian Americans could be heard in the public dialogue about the character and future of this "new pluralism," as it was called. Italian America was alive and well, or so it seemed.

Then came the eighties and nineties, and suddenly we are told it was all a mirage, that we don't really exist, that we are in the "twilight of Italian American ethnicity." What happened? In the parlance of football, we were blindsided; we were hit high and low. In the late seventies, neonationalists began decrying what they termed the excesses of ethnic "tribalism" that threatened the ungluing, the fragmenting of America, what Arthur M. Schlesinger Jr. has described in his shrill polemic *The Disuniting of America.* At the same time, they sneered that the "ethnic revival" was nothing more than a pipedream of would-be ethnic demagogues and called for a return to the melting pot.

If the neonationalists/assimilationists perceived European American ethnicity in general (and Italian American ethnicity in particular) as annoying distractions that did not need to be tolerated, as did ethnicity among "people of color," neo-Marxists dismissed "white ethnicity" as a smokescreen for racism. While the ethnic nationalism of people of color could be accommodated under their model of indigenous resistance to colonial oppressors, Americans of European ancestry who affirmed their ethnicities were simply reactionary fascists.

Much of the intellectual underpinnings for this attack on the "new ethnicity" has come from sociologist Herbert Gans and his followers. Gans's theory of symbolic ethnicity is based on the assumption of straight-line, inevitable assimilation; Gans argued that what had been perceived by some as an "ethnic revival" was really a form of ac-culturation and assimilation.[3] What was new was that the "symbolic ethnicity" of Euro-pean Americans consisted of subjective identity that was not based in lived culture or social networks. Gans recognized that Italian Americans still ate spaghetti, attended religious *feste,* and might on occasion dance the tarantella, but he dismissed those as leisure-time activities, simply hobbies like collecting stamps or butterflies. In serious matters, Italian Americans were becoming indistinguishable from their suburban, mid-dle-class European American neighbors.

In recent years, Richard Alba and Mary Waters have buttressed the theory of sym-bolic ethnicity with their sociological stud-ies. They have particularly sought to resolve the contradiction that they perceive be-tween high levels of ethnic identity and alleged low levels of actual ethnic involve-ment. It is Alba who condemned Italian Americans to the "twilight of ethnicity."[4] Seconding Gans, he concluded that particu-larly for the third and fourth generations, ethnicity had become muted, voluntary, and private. What some thought was an ethnic revival was really an expression of receding ethnicity. But Alba has further argued that a new ethnic group is emerging from the melting pot, the European Americans, in part a result of extensive intermarriage but also as a response to African American mili-tancy. In her book *Ethnic Options,* Waters distinguished between the ethnicity of people of color, which is due to oppression and thus real and involuntary, and that of whites, which is symbolic and voluntary and she adds, "contentless."[5] Further, white ethnics oppose removing barriers for eth-nics of color because they do not under-stand the difference between the two forms of ethnicity. Waters describes traditional European ethnic groups as sexist, racist,

clannish, and narrow-minded. Obviously, I disagree vigorously with Gans et al. For rea-sons I hope to make clear.

First, however, a word about multicultural-ism.[6] In the seventies we thought that persons who shared a common identity (a sense of peoplehood) constituted an ethnic group and that pluralism described a society in which there were a number of such ethnic groups. Now we are told that the appropriate term is multiculturalism, a word I first encountered when the Canadian government adopted a policy of inclusive multiculturalism in 1971. However, in the American version of multi-culturalism, certain "preferred minorities" are to be nurtured by the benign rays (and funds) of multiculturalism while "others" are con-demned to the eternal night of nongroup-ness. Race, Gender, and Class became the trinity worshipped by the cult of multicultur-alism; however, social class is assigned a minor role, and biological differences stem-ming from skin pigmentation and sexual organs are regarded as the significant sources of group identity.

Drawing eclectically upon postmodern, semiotic, and feminist theories, American multiculturalism in its more extreme forms has as its agenda the radical transformation of the polity and curriculum of American universities—and other institutions as well. Given their project of deconstructing patri-archy, racism, and capitalism, which are identified with European American male domination, multiculturalists privilege (to use one of their favorite terms) the litera-tures, histories, and cultures of "people of color" and of the third world. Meanwhile, the ethnicities of European Americans are suspect as an ideological cover for racial and sexual exploitation.

If radical theories of postmodernism and feminism have provided the intellectual fire-power behind the multicultural movement, strangely enough, the political clout has come from the federal government. While the Civil Rights Act of 1964 mandated equal opportunity "regardless of race, color, religion, sex, or *national origin*" (emphasis added), its subsequent implementation specified particular racial/ethnic populations, as well as women, as the beneficiaries of affirmative action programs. In 1977 the Equal Employment Opportunity Commission's Directive No. 15: *Race and Ethnic Standards for Federal Statistics and Administrative Reporting,* established the following categories for compliance purposes: "White, not of Hispanic Origin; Black, not of Hispanic Origin; Hispanic, regardless of race; American Indian or Alaskan Native; and Asian or Pacific Islander."

Those categories, of course, have no basis in biology or ethnology, mixing egregiously racial, cultural, and geographic criteria and lumping together populations that have wildly divergent histories and cultures—and, be it noted, totally ignoring class as a determinant of disadvantage. Yet this bureaucratic formula has legitimated the five-part division of the American people; university administrators, educators, foundation officers, and the like have embraced those categories as designating distinctive peoples. Private-sector as well as governmental programs in ethnic studies, institutes on pluralism, diversity curricula, fellowships, and multicultural workshops and conferences legally restrict their scope to those "protected classes" to the exclusion of persons of European, North African, and Middle Eastern origins, who are classified as "white."

How often have you been confronted with forms in which you are asked to indicate your "race and ethnicity" by checking a box for "White" (or the totally dehumanizing "Other") as the only alternative to American Indian or Alaskan Native, Asian or Pacific Islander, black or Hispanic? Does this upset you? It upsets me, not only because the "white" option automatically excludes me from the multicultural umbrella with all its perks but even more because of the impudence of those who would deny me my history, my culture, and my identity and relegate me to the realm of nonbeing.

The Office of Management and Budget held hearings this past summer on the revision of the race and ethnic standards for federal statistics. The hearings make fascinating reading. Forceful objections were voiced by several witnesses to the "white" category on the grounds that the term did not describe either a race or an ethnicity. A number argued for a European American category, but others demanded specific recognition of their groups as Arab Americans, Hawaiians, or German Americans. I was disappointed that no one appeared to protest the submergence of Italian Americans into the white pool.[7]

Perhaps you can understand my personal chagrin in finding myself (and my people) consigned to the shadowlands of peoplehood just as we were forty years ago! As in the fifties, the public and academic cultures deny the validity of Italian American claims to a place in the country's ethnic spectrum. Perhaps I was witnessing the last chapter of Italian American history in the fifties. But I think not. I am persuaded that this is not the twilight of Italian American ethnicity, for several reasons. First, my conception of ethnicity as a dynamic, evolving form of adaptation is the antithesis of the Gans et al. notion that it is a static quantity, a commodity, which once dissipated is gone forever. In my conception, ethnicity is protean, capable of taking a variety of forms, of being expressed in a range of behaviors, and of being revived. Does one need to speak the mother tongue, live in a particular neighborhood, worship in a specific church, or even eat spicy foods to be ethnic? I think not. What is essential now, as it always has been, is a subjective sense of peoplehood based in common memories and manifested in symbols that evoke those memories (a flag, a ritual, a song, a fig tree).[8]

Second, I believe in my own experience as a participant in and student of Italian American life more than I do in the charts and tables of sociologists.[9] That experience teaches me that, while the context and content of Italian American identity have been drastically altered over the past half century, that identity persists in significant ways for many. For how many? I am suspect of statistics and cite them sparingly. But the fact that the 1990 U.S. census reported almost fifteen million persons, identifying themselves to be of Italian ancestry (making them the fifth-largest ancestry group) cannot be dismissed offhandedly. While the census report does not tell us what that response meant, the fact that they were willing to claim Italian ancestry means something—as does the fact that only 5 percent of all respondents reported their ancestry as just "American" and less than 1 percent answered "white."

Beyond statistics, I spy abundant evidence of vitality and creativity in Italian American life, which, compared to its moribund status in the fifties, tempts me to speak of a *rinascimento*. What is this evidence? Certainly not a revitalization of the Little Italies, except as tourist attractions. But in this age of faxes and e-mail, group affiliation does not depend on physical proximity. In recent years, old organizations such as the Order of the Sons of Italy in America (OSIA) and UNICO have taken a new lease on life, and new organizations, devoted to cultural and heritage activities, have proliferated. A new generation of Italian American

publications has seen the light of day: community newspapers like Chicago's excellent *Fra Noi* and scholarly journals such as *VIA* and *Italian Americana*. And of particular importance, more than ever before Italian Americans are articulating their experiences through fiction, poetry, films, theater, and exhibits. Meanwhile, in their search for roots, many journey to ancestral *paesi,* scour archives and cemeteries, and reestablish ties with long-lost cousins. If you know genealogists, you would not demean their passionate quest for ancestors by dismissing it as simply a hobby.

What distinguishes this interest in Italy today from the philofascism of the 1930s is tht it is not inspired by politics. Rather, it increasingly takes the form of a reaffirmation of specific regional or local origins. Associations based on such ties are burgeoning: Figli di Calabria, Piemontesi nel Mondo, Trentini nel Mondo, Cuore Napoletano, Lucchasi nel Mondo, for example. Noting this trend, the late Robert Harney commented that this revival of *regionalismo* and *campanilismo* was the "undoing of the Risorgimento."[10] Indeed, it reflects the growing regionalism in Italy since the devolution of authority and funds to the regions in 1970. Of course, the regions and provinces promote contacts with their far-flung emigrants and descendants for reasons of tourism and commerce. But my experience suggests that genuine interest in distant *paesani* also animates these initiatives. For myself, I find my Lucchese American identity, based on specific cultural traditions personally more satisfying than the abstract idea of being Italian American. Since I abhor the idea of all melting pots, I applaud this revival of localized dialects and traditions.

By now you probably have guessed my answer to the question posed by the title of this essay. If Italian Americans are not just plain white folks, what are they? I have elsewhere presented my ideas about Italian American ethnicity, and rather than recapitulate them here, I refer you to those writings.[11] Suffice it to say that to be an Italian American today obviously means something very different from what it meant fifty or seventy-five years ago. We have learned from our AIHA conferences that the meaning varies according to geography, generation, gender, social class, and political disposition. We would be hard pressed to define what it is that we share as Italian Americans today, but of one thing I am certain: we are once again in the process of reinventing our ethnicity.

In the meantime, how do we position ourselves in this increasingly diverse and contentious American society? If we reject being lumped together as white European Americans, what are our options? Could we pass as African Americans or Latinos? I don't think our black or Chicano brothers would have us—which brings us to the subject of race and Italian Americans. In the years of massive immigration, the racial classification of Italians was in doubt. Many Anglo-Americans questioned that those swarthy sons of sunny Italy were really white. Employers and labor leaders referred to them as "black labor," while the color line was invoked to keep them out of certain neighborhoods, schools, and organizations. Nor was this peculiar to the South. I recently discovered the charter of the Washington League of Knights and Ladies of Minneapolis, established in 1902, which specifically excluded Negroes and Italians.

I need not remind you of the animus of racial nativists towards southern and eastern Europeans—and Italians in particular. The current controversy swirling about *The Bell Curve* reminds me that, in the 1920s, IQ scores were cited to prove the inferiority

(and thus undesirability) of Italians.[12] Innocent of the racial code in this "free country," newly arrived immigrants often worked with and lived among African Americans. Such association was itself taken as confirmation of the Italians' ambiguous racial status. Once they became aware of the terrible price to be paid for being "black," they hastened to distance themselves from African Americans and to be accepted as white. The historic relationships of Italian Americans and African Americans are, of course, much more complex than that; they would require a big book, a book that needs to be written.[13]

Let me tell you where I stand. As an unreconstructed pluralist, I believe that true multiculturalism must be inclusive of the full range of ethnic groups that compose the society and that ethnicity is a cultural, not a biological, phenomenon. Races, as discrete populations sharing unique hereditary qualities (common gene pools), have not and do not exist; in this conclusion, I am in the company of geneticists and anthropologists. But race as a cultural construct and racism as an ideology have played a powerful and pernicious role in the history of the past two hundred years. The source of peoplehood is not blood but shared history and culture. On that basis, we Italian Americans have as much a claim to our peoplehood as any other segment of society.

Since ethnicity is not transmitted to the next generation through germ plasm, it has to be learned from parents, teachers, clergy, community leaders, the media. How good a job have we been doing of teaching our children about their Italian American heritage? Despite my earlier upbeat remarks, we have reason for concern about the future of Italian America. In part, this is because the mainstream institutions—the schools, films, press, television—either omit

Italian Americans or portray them in an ugly, distorted fusion. An irony is that persons of Italian ancestry who fill important positions in such institutions, either because they are de-ethnicized or because of ethnic self-hatred, acquiesce in or even propagate such stereotypes. I applaud the work of the Commission on Social Justice of the OSIA, the National Italian American Foundation, and the Joint Civic Committee of Italian Americans in Chicago. But we need to do more, and we need more muscle to put an end to such group defamation.

Yet we must admit that the transmission of cultural heritage within families and by Italian American institutions is often done poorly, if at all. The result is that we are raising a generation of lost souls. As other groups adopt militant forms of ethnic assertion, young people without a clear and strong identity are at a disadvantage. We encounter them in our classrooms—kids with Italian names but without an inkling of the history those names carry with them. Some hunger to be Italian American but don't know how. Some adopt as their role models the mafiosi of the gangster films. Or they take on the dress, music, and behavior of other ethnics; they become Latinos or Wiggers; yet others become skinheads.[14] I am not faulting the youth; *it is we who have failed them.*

To quote Lenin: "What is to be done?" I have no panacea, but I think that we who are the self-chosen custodians of Italian American heritage have a special role and responsibility. Ethnicity is a form of memory, and many Italian Americans are suffering from amnesia. Freud observed that forgetting is "the avoidance of the pain of remembering." And there was much that was painful in the Italian American experience. I don't believe that we should connive in those silences; our job is to bring to the surface the painful memories of bigotry, repression, and conflict. In addition to writing our books and articles, we need to connect with Italian Americans where they live. Exhibits, oral history projects, films, family histories—those are the means of engaging Italian Americans in the process of recovering often traumatic but also inspiriting memories. As we deal with our real history, I think we will engage the imaginations of our young people. Let me share with you a letter I recently received from an aspiring fourth-generation student: "I have a strong attachment to my ethnic roots and am eager to learn more about the true story of Italian Americans—not the stereotypical, thin version presented by the media and so widely believed. The Italian experience…is complex and varied and I hope to further flesh out, in my small way, the incomplete story of my ancestors."

The AIHA, which from its inception has been dedicated to the purpose of disseminating understanding of the Italian American experience, has made enormous contributions to a reawakening of Italian American consciousness. What too often has been lacking has been the political and economic support of Italian American organizations and individuals whose resources could have amplified manyfold the work of the AIHA. A long-rooted tradition of anti-intellectualism among Italian Americans has restricted the essential linkage of wealth and power with intellect and creativity.

But you may ask, why bother? Why invest our time, energy, and money in revitalizing Italian American ethnicity when there are so many other urgent matters to attend to? Why not simply submerge ourselves in the vanilla frosting and enjoy the perks of being "white" in a racist society? Replies will vary, but I have a couple of answers for myself. First, let me say I am not into ethnic chauvinism. I am as opposed to Italocentrism as I am to Anglocentrism or Afrocentrism. Beyond the personal significance of the Italian American experience in which I am willy-nilly a participant, as a humanist I argue for the intrinsic significance of that experience. It is an epic story of a disapora, the story of the tragedies and triumphs of millions, the story of generations struggling to reconcile the old and the new. It is neither grander nor meaner than the story of other migrant peoples, *but it is our story.* Knowledge of that story can enrich and inspire our lives; it can provide us with a center and a compass in these turbulent times.

But the Italian American experience has a larger significance, which transcends its meaning for us as individuals. Over the past century we have collectively comprised a considerable segment of the American population; there is no sphere of life in which our presence has not been manifest. To delete that experience is to omit a big slice of American history. Further, we need to ponder what meaning that experience has for understanding the character of this society and the critical issues that confront it today. Sheldon Hackney, the chairman of the National Endowment for the Humanities, has called for a "national conversation" about our sources of diversity and of unity. What makes us different? What makes us American? Italian American voices used to be heard in that conversation. Based on our historic experience, I think we have something to contribute to it. Of course, we would not speak with one voice; there have been a variety of Italian American experiences subject to a variety of interpretations.

I would argue that our experience has taught us firsthand of the evils of racism and nativism. Guido Calabresi was recently sworn in as a judge of the Second U.S. Circuit Court of Appeals (on the fifty-fifth anniversary of the arrival of his family from Italy). Speaking of American history, Judge Calabresi observed: "Our tragic moments—for which we are still paying and will long pay—are those times when our laws furthered bigotry and discrimination." We, as Italian Americans, should resonate to those words, particularly in these times when the latest arrivals in this Promised Land are the object of nativist attacks. We, the descendants of *contadini,* should not tolerate those who say, "Oh, but our immigrant ancestors were different. They suffered hardships, but because they were hardworking, self-reliant, honest, etc., they made it."[15] Anyone who has studied Italian American history knows that this is a gross oversimplification, if not falsification, as well as a slander on the new immigrants.

Our experience has taught us the fallacy of the very idea of race and the mischief of racial labels. It has taught us that both total assimilation and total separatism are will-o'-the-wisps, unachievable and undesirable if they were achievable. It has taught us that a healthy ethnicity is compatible with, indeed essential to, a healthy America. For these reasons, we Italian Americans have something important to contribute to the national dialogue.

Finally, we must say no to both the neonationalists and the multiculturalists who would deny us the right to define our own identities as Italian Americans. We must say no to the xenophobes and bigots whether we or others are their targets. Neither white nor black nor brown nor red nor yellow, we are distinguished by our unique experience in these United States. Let us claim our rightful inheritance as Italian Americans.

Notes

[1] "Chicago's Italians Prior to World War I: A Study of Their Social and Economic Adjustment" (University of Wisconsin, 1963).

[2] For a superb study of the linguistic adaptation of the Italian immigrants, see Hermann W. Haller, *Una lingua perduta e ritrovata: L'italiano degli italo-americani* (Florence: La Nuova Italia, 1993).

[3] Herbert Gans, "Symbolic Ethnicity: The Future of Ethnic Groups and Cultures in America," in *On the Making of Americans: Essays in Honor of David Riesuan* (Philadelphia: University of Pennsylvania Press, 1977), 193–220.

[4] Richard D. Alba, *Italian Americans: Into the Twilight of Ethnicity* (Englewood Cliffs, N.J.: Prentice-Hall, 1985). See also Alba, *Ethnic Identity: The Transformation of White America* (New Haven, Conn.: Yale University Press, 1990).

[5] Mary C. Waters, *Ethnic Options: Choosing Identities in America* (Berkeley: University of California Press, 1990).

[6] The literature relating to the controversies swirling about multicultural is extensive, but for a critical review of its extreme form, I recommend Richard Bernstein, *Dictatorship of Virtue: Multiculturalism and the Battle for America's Future* (New York: Alfred A. Knopf, 1994).

[7] Ramona Douglass, however, did testify before the House Subcommittee on the Census on behalf of establishing a "multiracial/multiethnic category." Ms. Douglass, who is president of the Association of MultiEthnic Americans, identified herself as Sicilian American on her mother's side, while her father is of Ogalala Indian and African American ancestry.

[8] For an elaboration of this view I refer you to Kathleen Neils Conzen, David A. Gerber, Ewa Morawska, George E. Pozzetta, and Rudolph J. Vecoli, "The Invention of Ethnicity: A Perspective frrom the U.S.A.," *Journal of American Ethnic History* (fall 1992): 3–41.

[9] For an attempt to articulate the influence of personal experience on the writing of history, see Rudolph J. Vecoli, "Italian Immigrants and Working-Class Movements in the United States: A Personal Reflection on Class and Ethnicity," *Journal of the Canadian Historical Association,* 4 (1993), 293–305.

[10] "Undoing the Risorgimento: Emigrants from Italy and the Politics of Regionalism," in *If One Were to Write a History . . . : Selected Writings by Robert E. Harney,* ed., Pierre Anctil and Bruno Ramirez (Toronto: Multicultural History Society of Ontario, 1991), 201–26. In a personal communication, Andrew Canepa confirmed by impression of the resurgence of regional and local associations, citing a lengthy list of such organizations in California.

[11] "The Search for an Italian American Identity: Continuity and Change," in *Italian Americans: New Perspectives in Italian Immigration and Ethnicity,* ed. Lydio Tomasi (New York: Center for Migration Studies, 1985), 88–112; "The Coming of Age of the Italian Americans," *Ethnicity* 5 (1978): 11947.

[12] William McDougall, professor of psychology at Harvard College, presented essentially the same argument regarding the hereditary and racial basis of intelligence in *Is America Safe for Democracy?* (New York: Charles Scribner's Sons, 1921). McDougall (p. 64) reported that Italians scored 84, and colored scored 83, as compared with the score of 106 of "all Americans." He noted, however, that "the recent Italian immigrants are not probably a fair sample of the population of Italy."

[13] For provocative discussions of the ambiguous racial status of Italian immigrants, see Robert Orsi, "The Religious Boundaries of an Inbetween People: Street *Feste* and the Problem of the

Dark-Skinned Other in Italian Harlem, 1920–1990." *American Quarterly* 44 (September 1992): 313–47; and David R. Roediger, *Towards the Abolition of Whiteness* (London: Verso, 1994), particularly chap. 11, "Whiteness and Ethnicity in the History of 'White Ethnics' in the United States."

[14] Donald Tricarico, "Guido: Fashioning an Italian American Youth Style," *Journal of Ethnic Studies* 19 (spring 1991): 41–66, is a fascinating account of an Italian American youth culture.

[15] Anna Quindlen, "Hypocrisy from a Nation of Immigrants," *Star Tribune* (Minneapolis). Quindlen's maternal grandparents were immigrants from Italy. A leading proponent of Proposition 187 in California, Sally Vaughn, who also had Italian grandparents, declared: "I resent them [current immigrants] comparing themselves to my grandparents, who came here legally, worked hard, learned to speak English and tried to be good citizens." *Star Tribune,* November 6, 1994.

Americans United by Myths

Peter D. Salins

◇◆◆◇

Study Questions

1. Salins argues that "the American identity emerged from a compelling national mythology. Describe that mythology in terms of master and subsidiary myths.
2. How are these myths perpetuated? Give examples.
3. How does Salins handle movies and books that highlight the contradictions and imperfections of American society (and its mythology)?
4. Salins identifies popular movies that help to perpetuate these myths. Identify five movies since 1995 that operate to perpetuate American mythology.

America is a memory—a memory of the lives and actions, the beliefs and efforts, of millions of human beings who have lived in American spaces participated in an American social world, and died Americans. The memory is contained in American names—of people, of places, of events and institutions. The memory is contained in stories Americans tell one another—in poems and histories, in speeches and broadcasts, in shows and pictures, in jokes and obituaries. It is contained in the ways Americans behave and in their expectations of behavior; it is contained in the rituals Americans perform and in the games they play; it is contained in American social groupings, and in the political, economic, and religious institutions Americans maintain.

In the American memory are contained many of the truths which are self-evident to Americans, which help them understand their country, and to explain their lives.

James Oliver Robertson, 1980

Assimilation in the United States depends on all Americans—immigrants and natives and members of all ethnic groups—sharing a strong and unified national identity. In other countries people acquire a shared identity from ethnic and historical bonds—tribalism elevated to the level of the nation state. (Or they don't, as in Yugoslavia, Lebanon, and even Canada, and the result is tribal warfare, hot or cold, within the confines of the nation state.) In the United States, a country marked by exceptional ethnic diversity and a relatively brief history, national unity is grounded, instead, in a majority of Americans sharing the same conception of who they are, what they believe in, and how they are different from the people of other nations. America is, perhaps, unique in the intensity and eagerness with which its people have been psychically invested in a singular national mission and a singular collective self-image.

At first glance, it would seem unlikely that the citizens of the United States should have come by a shared identity. Ours is a vast continental nation, with enormous regional variations in topography, climate, and economic conditions and with strong regional traditions. Its population, one of the largest in the world, encompasses members of innumerable occupations, religions, and ethnicities living in every conceivable setting, from teeming cities and leafy suburbs to rural villages and isolated farms. Clearly, Americans are too varied and numerous to have achieved their shared identity by negotiation, as if such a thing could ever be negotiated anywhere. In some countries, like Britain, a national identity is derived from a monarchy and the traditions of a powerful elite, but the American people have always been far too egalitarian and pluralistic to submit to a shared identity imposed from above. Yet, almost miraculously, the shared identity is there, and it has been an essential ingredient in the maintenance of national harmony and the overcoming of national differences for over two hundred years.

The American identity emerged from a compelling national mythology. Since independence, the most essential ideas and images that unify Americans have been elevated to the status of myths. Myths are not mere fantasies or untruths. Myths are exaggerated or simplified representations of human traits and situations, paradigms of society and morality, that are based on some underlying truth. The word *myth* is often used in a narrower and more superficial sense to disparage a commonly held view and to dismiss it as false or mistaken, as in the common formulation "the myth and reality of. . . ." I even used the word that way in Chapter 5, when I discussed the *myth* of the WASP. In this chapter, however, I refer to myths in their deeper and broader meaning, as popular images that help to unify a society by creating, in the words of this chapter's epigraph, the ingredients of a collective memory and a collective self-

image. Most people believe them to represent if not actual reality, then a kind of idealized reality.

What distinguishes myths from mere propaganda is that they are communicated and diffused throughout society in an entirely natural, un-self-conscious way. They have no single source or any particular venue; rather, they infiltrate a vast cross section of institutions and media. Whenever and wherever they crop up, people just presuppose their inherent validity. Even the sophisticated and the skeptical do not reject myths outright; they accept them as metaphors, reflections of reality. The only explicit antagonism to societal myths comes from individuals and groups that reject the myths' fundamental premises and wish to replace them with their own countermyths.

America's myths have been essential to the country's great project of assimilating its immigrants and maintaining social harmony. They made it easier for native Americans to accept the arrival of immigrants, to live sociably with them, and even to feel a kinship with people so radically different from themselves. They made it easier for immigrants to feel at home in their new country, to accept the legitimacy of its institutions, and to understand their new countrymen's mores and values. Myths made it possible for native-born Americans and immigrants to share lands and resources, laws and institutions, even ancestors and traditions.

Americans are especially well disposed to share a national mythology. As I discussed in Chapter 4, Americans attained high (and standardized) levels of mass literacy and education sooner than just about any other national population. Already by the middle of the nineteenth century, 90 percent of the American population could read and write and three-quarters had some formal education. And they have been plugged in longer to a more extensive and redundant network of communication than have citizens of any other nation: The United States was the home of the first mass-market newspapers and magazines, the first mass-market cinema and the first mass-market radio and television broadcasts. It was easy for ideas and concepts with popular appeal to spread quickly across the United States and to acquire a transcendent mythical status.

The mythic poems of Henry Wadsworth Longfellow and Walt Whitman and the mythic novels of James Fenimore Cooper, Bret Harte, Mark Twain, Horatio Alger, and Zane Grey became bestsellers. Normal Rockwell's covers on the *Saturday Evening Post* became emblems of harmonious and egalitarian small-town life from coast to coast. Political heroes like George Washington and Abraham Lincoln and inventors like Alexander Graham Bell and Thomas Edison were mythologized in elementary school texts read by a majority of American schoolchildren. American values were mythologized in the editorials of mass-circulation newspapers, political speeches, religious sermons, and commencement addresses. Notions and symbols of American myths were expropriated by commercial products and widely disseminated in their advertisements. But perhaps the most powerful generators of myth were the twentieth-century innovations of radio, television, and the movies. Hollywood, especially from the 1930s through the 1950s, was self-consciously dedicated to mythmaking on a grand scale.

While the myths of other countries revolve around ethnic bonds, ancient traditions, triumphs of the battlefield, or the universal dilemmas and paradoxes of human existence, America's are obsessed with articulating the ingredients of a unique American identity. While the myths of other countries have no comprehensive focus, America's originate in a few basic ideas, beginning with America's master myth: *America as the land of the new beginning*. When the sociologist Seymour Martin Lipset called the United States "the world's first new nation," he gave voice to a conviction that Americans, from colonial times to the present, have fervently held about their country. In one way or another, all the ingredients of American mythology come back to that single powerful concept. America was not simply *there*, it was *created*. It was created by men and women who turned their backs on the wicked and backward *Old* World (Europe) and who were determined to make the *New* World (America) a far better place. America was to be an exemplar to the rest of the world of what a free people (in many senses of that word) could accomplish: The place where the most just principles of social organization and political governance would reign, where the most useful products of human ingenuity would be applied, and where the noblest traits of human character and the highest aspirations of the human spirit would flourish. As Oscar Handlin, the leading historian of immigration, noted, "The image of the city on the hill persisted since the days of the first settlers; and the events of the revolutionary period only confirmed the certitude that a great destiny awaited the Republic." Americans especially enjoyed having their mythic self-conception confirmed by Europeans, hence the enthusiastic reception in the United States of Alexis de Tocqueville's *Democracy in America*. But few Europeans expressed the myth more lyrically than did the English poet Percy Bysshe Shelley:

> That land [America] is like an Eagle, whose young gaze
> Feeds on the noontide beam, whose golden plume
> Floats moveless on the storm, and in the blaze

Of sunrise gleams when Earth is wrapped
   in gloom;
An epitatph of glory for the tomb
Of murdered Europe may thy fame be
   made,
Great People! as the sands shalt thou become;
Thy growth is swift as morn, when night
   must fade;
The multitudinous Earth shall sleep beneath thy shade.

Immigrants were always central characters in this master myth, and their assimilation was always one of its central premises.
As the land of the new beginning, America
had no choice but to be made up of immigrants. That was the whole idea. People
would leave their old, unsatisfactory homelands and join together to create this more
perfect nation. As social commentator James
Oliver Robertson put it: "The society immigrants left behind was corrupt, decadent,
tyrannical, or at least inferior. American
society is new and superior." Woodrow
Wilson expressed the immigrant's aspiration
more grandly: "America lives in the heart of
every man everywhere who wishes to find a
region where he will be free to work out his
destiny as he chooses." Seen in this light,
the ethnic heterogeneity of the immigrants
was a positive—even essential—feature because if the immigrants were merely a nation transplanted, they would find it harder
to abandon their discredited institutions,
anachronistic customs, and invidious status
distinctions. Better yet, people from many
lands would complement each other as they
harvested the best traits of each constituent
culture and discarded the worst. The notion
of immigrants creating the New World is enshrined in two of the most familiar and
compelling American mythological stories
(each celebrated by a national holiday):
Christopher Columbus's voyage of discovery
and the Pilgrims' flight from persecution to
establish a free and moral society in the
New England wilderness.

There was another way in which immigrants were essential to America's master
myth. A steady flow of immigrants served to
validate America's superiority. From the beginning, Americans have been firm believers
in markets, and immigration has been the
supreme market test of national superiority.
Each new wave of immigrants attested to
America's enduring desirability. America
was a club (or a religion) that was perpetually pleased to enroll new members. Under
this formulation, it was not immigrants who
were privileged to be allowed to settle in
America; it was America that was privileged
because it was chosen by immigrants, from
among all the nations of the world, to be
their new homeland. As the historian Henry
Steele Commager noted: "The American
cherished an uncritical and unquestioning
conviction that his was the best of all countries, and every emigrant who crossed the
Atlantic westward—few went the other
way—confirmed him in his assumption that
this fact was everywhere acknowledged."[8]
Even today, practically the first question a
native American asks of a newly encountered immigrant is: "How do you like the
United States?" If the answer, as expected, is
enthusiastic, the American feels fulfilled; if it
is critical, the American is crushed.

Assimilation, American style follows naturally from this conception of the immigrant
in the land of the new beginning. In the traditional view of assimilation (assimilation,
European style) there is an established society to which immigrants must assimilate.
Under such circumstances, immigrants are
expected to shed all their "alien" cultural
features and conform as closely as possible
to the characteristics of their adopted country. In the land of the new beginning, there

is no firmly established society. A new society is being created, and it is being created by immigrants. American society and American culture are works in progress, and immigrants are the artisans who are fashioning those works. Thus, the ethnicity of immigrants and any cultural baggage the immigrants bring along as a result of that ethnicity are irrelevant to their new status as Americans. By virtue of the act of immigration itself, immigrants have enrolled in the project of building their new nation and have turned their backs permanently on the imperfect societies they left behind. Whatever cultural habits immigrants may want to retain from their former homelands are thus viewed by "natives" as mere idiosyncratic vestiges, markers of individual differences in a new society that, among its many unique values, is supremely tolerant of individual differences. In Robertson's words:

> Americans were people who came here and committed themselves to America, or they were people who were born here and belonged here. They were not Creoles or colonials, or provincials; they were not exiles, not English or Scots or Irish or German; nor were they "natives." [America] made them free of all such identities.

The most assimiliationist aspect of America's master myth is the conviction that in the process of creating a new country, the immigrants have re-created themselves. In other words, the new land is populated by a "new man." Few passages of American social history have been as frequently reprinted as this excerpt from Hector St. John de Crevecoeur's *Letters from an American Farmer*:

> What, then is the American, this new man? . . . He is an American, who, leaving behind him all his ancient prejudices and manners, receiving new ones from the new

mode of life he has embraced, the new government he obeys, and the new rank he holds. He becomes an American by being received in the broad lap of our great Alma Mater. Here individuals of all nations are melted in a new race of men, whose labors and posterity will one day cause great changes in the world. . . . The American ought, therefore, to love this country better than that wherein either he or his forefathers were born.

This concept of Americans constituting an entirely "new race" distinct from any particular ethnic stock is the bedrock of assimilation because it so completely contradicts the ethnic particularism that is assimiliationism's great enemy. If the mere act of joining the American nation makes immigrants, regardless of where they come from, members of the American "race," then ethnicity (including race), in its traditional sense of connoting some immutable biological or otherwise hereditary state, is explicitly superseded. Two hundred years after de Crevecoeur, this idea is alive and well. Few Americans would disagree with Patrick J. Buchanan's assertion during the 1995–96 Republican presidential primary campaign, apropos America's troubled black-white relations, that "there is only one race in this country, the American race."

America's master myth has, since indepence, inspired the unique institutions, activities, and personality traits that characterize Americans, which, in turn, have generated a host of subsidiary myths that keep reminding Americans of who they are, what makes them different from the peoples of other nations, and the scope and grandeur of their shared national project. Only a few of these myths revolve around immigration per se, but most have some particular relevance to the status of immigrants.

The American Idea is the oldest and most powerful of these mythic concepts, and rightly so. As the ideological foundation on which national unity rests, it has generated a mythical idiom from which most other national myths derive. John Gunther said, "Ours is the only country deliberately founded on a good idea." The substance of the American Idea is enshrined in three universally revered texts: the Declaration of Independence, the Constitution, and Lincoln's magnificent Gettysburg Address. Although the Constitution, specifically its first ten amendments (the Bill of Rights), is the living, breathing official document that transforms the American Idea from myth into concrete reality, it is the soulstirring language of the Declaration of Independence and the Gettsyburg Address that gives the American Idea its mythic status:

We hold these truths to be self-evident; that all men are created equal; that they are endowed by their Creator with certain inalienable rights, that among these are life, liberty, and the pursuit of happiness; that, to secure these rights, governments are instituted among men, deriving their just powers from the consent of the governed.

* * *

Fourscore and seven years ago our fathers brought forth on this continent a new nation, conceived in Liberty, and dedicated to the proposition that all men are created equal.

Now we are engaged in a great civil war, testing whether that nation or any nation so conceived and so dedicated can long endure....

...We here highly resolve that this nation under God shall have a new birth of freedom; and that government of the people, by the people, for the people, shall not perish from the earth.

These words, memorized by every American schoolchild (as well as by millions around the world) form the inspirational seal of the American people. Indeed, I was deeply moved myself as I committed them to paper. Here we find all the key precepts of the American Idea: the supremacy of the individual, the equality of men, the guarantee of liberty and other fundamental human rights, the rule of law, and government by consent of the people. What lifts the American Idea from the plane of reigning political orthodoxy to that of mythology are three things: its moral grandeur, its presumed immutability, and its function as the great unifier of the American people. It is mainly the American Idea that makes America and Americans different from all other people on earth (even if an increasing share of that polity is cribbing important parts of it). It is mainly the American Idea that vanquishes ethnic particularism and ethnic prejudice. It is mainly the American Idea that places the United States on the moral high ground that has allowed it to dominate world geopolitics. It is mainly the American Idea that enables Americans to resolve the recurring conflicts and challenges of modern society. Beyond its symbolic manifestations, the American Idea, in its full mythological majesty, has been continually invoked since independence to inspire and motivate Americans to feel good about themselves and to do the right thing. Politicians wrap their own personae and programmatic ideas in its precepts. The correct resolution of every philosophical controversy among Americans is adduced from it. All aggrieved individuals and groups—above all, black Americans—appeal to its guaranteed civil rights and liberties. It is the American Idea that, from the beginning, has given Americans their most precious gift: a sense of moral superiority over the people of every other nation. It is this moral superiority that led labor leader Meyer London to say: "To me Americanism means . . . an imperative duty to be nobler than the rest of the world." As Commager put it:

> The moral superiority of his country was . . . axiomatic to the American. The assumption of superiority was accompanied by a sense of destiny and mission. . . . Successive generations were equally eager to spread the American idea over the globe and exasperated that foreign ideas should ever intrude themselves into America.

Just as the American master myth—America as the land of the new beginning—is assimilationist to the core, so is the American Idea, its purest submyth. The American Idea furnishes the philosophical rationale for admitting immigrants. More important, it offers the moral justification for treating them as equals after they arrive. It provides a noble and stirring platform for a shared national identity. Its rules and concepts offer a basis, both idealistic and pragmatic, for resolving disputes among immigrants and natives and among members of diverse ethnic constituencies. In other words, if you believe in the American Idea, then assimilation is easy.

All myths need human incarnations, especially heroes. The American Idea is personified by the heroic Founding Fathers: the simple men of incomparable wisdom who devised it and who fought the War of Independence against great odds to make it the charter of the land of the new beginning. And looming heroically above the rest of the Founding Fathers is the Father of Our Country, George Washington. Much of the mythology of the American Idea is wrapped up in the larger-than-life portrayals—in schoolbooks, children's literature, plays, and movies—of George Washington and the other revolutionary heroes: Thomas Jefferson, Benjamin Franklin, Alexander Hamilton, John Adams, James Madison, and others. The other key mythic figure of American history is Abraham Lincoln, the martyred president who arose providentially from the most humble beginnings to keep his countrymen true to the American Idea and who had to fight a war to make it prevail against the dark forces of sectionalism and immorality. Lincoln has sparked an even richer and more voluminous mythological literature than the somewhat distant heroes of the revolutionary era.

The American Idea has depended heavily, for its mythic promotion, on the efforts of public institutions. Schools have been its primary marketplace, backed up by museums, libraries, public events, monuments, and, of course, holidays. The American Idea is celebrated directly on the Fourth of July and on Washington's and Lincoln's Birthdays (recently combined in Presidents' Day) and indirectly on Veterans Day and Memorial Day (honoring those who fought and died for the American Idea). The American Idea is the staple of political speeches and schools' commencement addresses. But it has not lacked for fictional validation. A few movie classics like *Abe Lincoln in Illinois* (1939), *State of the Union* (1948), and *1776* (1972) engaged it directly, and it forms the implicit subtext in political movies like *The Best Man* (1964), *Seven Days in May* (1964), and the musical *Of Thee I Sing* (1931). In *Mr. Smith Goes to Washington* (1939), a classic of this genre, Jimmy Stewart saves the American Idea, as embodied in the day-to-day workings of congressional politics, from the subversive forces of political cynicism. Many war movies, especially like those made about the two world wars, such as *Sergeant York* (1941), *Sands of Iwo Jima* (1949), and *Command Decision* (1948), revolve around the American Idea as the raison d'être for American involvement in the conflicts and the selfless heroism of the main protagonists.

As the American Idea gives Americans a way to view their society, the other myths give Americans a way to view themselves, especially in comparison with the lesser mortals of other societies. These myths persuade Americans that they are pioneers, rugged individualists, people who rise by achievement, people in the vanguard, people of justice and principle, and people of tolerance. And just as the American Idea provides the larger rationale for the United States being perpetually a nation of immigrants, these subsidiary myths give natives and immigrants the day-to-day rationale for living together. The mythic celebration of the individualist makes it easier for natives to tolerate newcomers, however strange. The mythic celebration of achievement makes it easier for them to tolerate immigrant competitors in the workplace. The mythic celebration of progress and enlightenment makes it easier for both immigrants and natives to accept change, to abandon traditional customs and occupations, and to move on to common new ones.

As the American Idea itself has been mythologized mainly in the public arena of textbooks, museums, holidays, and speeches, its subsidiary myths have been conveyed mostly in the world of fiction: novels, plays, movies, and television.

One of the richest troves of American mythology is the most popular of American fictional genres, the Western. Stories about the settlement of the West (every place west of the Mississippi) have loomed large in both popular and serious literature: James Fenimore Cooper's *The Prairie* (1827), Bret Harte's *The Luck of Roaring Camp* (1868) and *The Outcasts of Poker Flat* (1869), Owen Wister's *The Virginian* (1902), Zane Grey's

Riders of the Purple Sage (1912), and Willa Cather's *O Pioneers!* (1913). But most Americans have been steeped in the mythology of the Westerns by the movies—hundreds of them. Westerns may span a variety of subgenres, but each shares certain paradigmatic plot structures and characters. The main protagonist is a heroic figure, who comes out of nowhere and rides into a newly settled town on horseback. (Subtext: The hero is an immigrant, an American "new man.") He comes by himself, usually without family or friends. (Subtext: He is a rugged individualist.) He either has a specific mission that brings him to this place or is passing through and discovers a mission. The most common mission is to save the townspeople from some greedy and immoral villains. Here we have a profusion of mythic subtexts. The townspeople represent the faces of American progress. They, too, are immigrants, at least figuratively, sometimes literally, dedicated to building a modern society in the prairie or the wilderness. They are extending American civilization and the values of the American way, but as a collectivity they are weak. They need our hero, the rugged individualist, the superior American, to secure their new world. The villains, usually corrupt local businessmen or marauding lawless bands, represent the Old-World forces of darkness. They are the un-Americans, the ever-present agents of anti-democracy against whom true Americans must continually do battle with steadfast courage and vigilance. Americanism in a wicked world is under constant attack.

Beneath the surface of their main plots and key characters, Westerns illustrate a host of American mythical ideas. One evident idea is the categorical rejection of class distinctions. The hero is always classless, perhaps even uncouth. He is often romantically linked with a local woman (often the person who is the most directly endangered), who is invariably better educated—but this does not matter. Any people in the frontier town with class pretensions are ridiculed or come to grief. The good guys and the bad guys are judged only by their actions and achievements, not by their wealth or breeding.

Nevertheless, in the classless society of the West, the pursuit of wealth, if undertaken honestly, is admirable. In spite of the surface turbulence of good guys fighting bad guys, there are enormous opportunities for economic advancement and upward social mobility, which illustrate another staple of American mythology. Messy as they are, the frontier territories of the West are booming. Formerly penniless settlers get rich operating ranches; panning for gold; and opening general stores, hotels, and even saloons and brothels. It is the job of the hero to protect this spirit of enterprise. The saloons and brothels, and their owners and patrons, are usually portrayed indulgently, illustrating the uneasy tension between what today would be called "family values" and a libertarian tolerance of poetty vice. This tension itself is built into American mythology. Free men (and women) are presumably free to do anything, even to sin, if others are not harmed in the process. But the libertarianism of the American Idea is implicitly grounded in a higher morality that demands that Americans display personal virtue and self-restraint. Just as real-world American society has never resolved this tension, neither have the mythical Westerns.

The Western mythologizes the irrelevance of ethnicity in American life. Neither American nativity nor national origin make any difference with regard to the characters, both good and bad, although ethnicity may show up as a mark of picturesque individuation, for example, in portrayals of "the Frenchie" or "the Swede." Even blacks are usually portrayed with respect in Westerns and are generally found in the entourage of the good guys. The case of the Indian is problematical, but in a way that does not really contradict the mythic paradigms. There are good Indians and bad Indians. The familiar Western slogan—"the only good Indian is a dead Indian"—is not really an accurate statement of the way Indians are perceived. There *are* good Indians; they are the ones who throw in their lot with the good Americans, serving as workers, scouts, or allies. Perhaps the most famous good Indian is the Lone Ranger's sidekick, Tonto. By abandoning their ethnic compatriots, Indians, like all other immigrant "new men," are on their way to becoming Americans. The bad Indians—the ones who can be killed with impunity—are the ones who insist on maintaining not so much a separate ethnic identity as a national one. (In a popular Lone Ranger joke, Tonto says, in response to the Lone Ranger's description of some presumably shared danger, "What do you mean 'we,' white-man?") In the mythology of American identity, this is the unforgivable sin.

What I have described is the classic, pre–1960s Western. Like assimilation itself, the Western genre has been subject to revisionism, a revisionism explicitly aimed at overturning the classical American myths and replacing them with countermyths. The best movies of this revisionist genre include *Hang 'Em High* (1967), *McCabe and Mrs. Miller* (1971), and *Unforgiven* (1992). In these films and many others, the hero, although still a loner, is a man of highly ambiguous character. (Subtext: America has a dark past.) He still arrives alone, but he regrets his solitude. (Subtext: Individualism is lonely and unsatisfactory.) The townspeople are also portrayed much more ambiguously. The lawmen—

legitimate lawmen, not to be confused with the explicitly wicked ones in some classic Westerns—dispense arbitrary and unfair justice. (Subtext: The American Idea is often perverted.) The town's development is chaotic and unsatisfactory; the ranches are ruining the unspoiled natural environment. (Subtext: Capitalism and progress are not all they are made out to be.) Movies like *Little Big Man* (1970) and *Dances with Wolves* (1990) introduce the most radical revisionist idea, one that most subverts the myth of ethnic universalism: recasting the status of Indians. Not only is the oppression of Indians now seen as profoundly immoral, the good Indians are the ones who stick by their independent nationhood, and the bad ones are the ones who betray their tribes and join the white man. And the best white men are the ones who throw in their lot with the Indians. (Subtext: Indians should not assimilate and the officially sanctioned ethnic federalism built into the Indian treaties and reservations is a model for ethnic relations in the larger society.)

If American mythical concepts have been amply illustrated in the realm of popular culture by the Western genre, they have been reinforced by parallel works of literature and drama appealing to middle- and highbrow tastes. Just about every giant of American literature has touched on one or another of these mythic themes. James Fenimore Cooper, in *Leatherstocking Tales: The Deerslayer* (1841), *The Last of the Mohicans* (1826), and *The Pathfinder* (1840), was the first major author to chronicle the lonely frontiersman bringing civilization to the wilderness. His hero, Natty Bumppo, or "Leatherstocking, anticipating the Western hero by half a century, is a classless individualist. His mission is to be a herald—a pathfinder—of modernity. Mythical themes animated the works of the transcendentalists, whether essayists like Ralph Waldo

Emerson and Henry David Thoreau or novelists like Nathaniel Hawthorne and Herman Melville, as they celebrated individualism and rationality (a surrogate for modernity). And in his poems, Whitman was directly engaged in advancing American mythology, as in this passage from *Leaves of Grass* (1855):

> How America is the continent of glories,
>   and of the triumph of freedom and
> of the Democracies, and of the fruits of so-
>   ciety, and of all that is begun,...
> Of seeds dropping into the ground, of
>   births,
> Of the steady concentration of America, in-
>   land, upward, to impregnable and
> swarming places, ...
> Of mighty inland cities yet unsurvey'd and
>   unsuspected,
> Of the new and good names, of the mod-
>   ern developments, of inalienable home-
>   steads,
> Of a free and original life there, of simple
>   diet and clean and sweet blood,
> Of litheness, majestic faces, clear eyes, and
>   perfect physique there,
> Of immense spiritual results future years
>   far West, each side of the Anahuacs,
> Of these songs, well understood there....

These works have lent plausibility and nuance to the myths of the migrant, the pioneer, the principled individualist, the rugged capitalist, the classless society, the march of progress, the evil of racism, and the nobility of immigrants. Immigration and assimilation are addressed explicitly in only a limited corner of this literature. But they are addressed implicitly in much of the rest because the mythical traits and institutions these works glorify, advertently or not, flatter immigrants and support assimilation. The works that romanticize Americans who migrated across the continent implicitly romanticize those who migrated across the world. The works that glorify the lonely individual making his own way implicitly glorify immigrants who were determined to be masters of their own destiny. The works that satirize snobbery and class pretensions implicitly legitimate the status of lower-class immigrants. The works that celebrate upward mobility implicitly endorse the economic success of immigrants.

Important as American literature has been in developing the tapestry of American mythology, no medium has been so instrumental to this purpose as film. As the pop artist Andy Warhol put it:

> It's the movies that have really been running things in America ever since they were invented. They show you what to do, how to do it, when to do it, how to feel about it. Everybody has their own America, and then they have the pieces of a fantasy America tht they think is out there but they can't see.

Given the seminal importance of movies in solidifying American mythology, it is noteworthy that most movies, especially those of the 1930s, 1940s, and 1950s—the ones with the greatest mythical resonance—have been made by immigrants or the recent descendants of immigrants, notably Jewish Americans. Not only were owners of the great studios of the mythmaking era immigrants or, at best, first-generation natives, so were most of the directors, screenwriters, and actors. So here we come full circle. American mythology secures a place for immigrants at the American social table. Immigrants repay the debt by becoming the most effective promoters and disseminators of that mythology.

A cursory review of the Academy Award winners since 1930 imparts the flavor of American mythology as portrayed in film. Not every award-winning film has had mythic significance, and many of the mythic messages have been muddled or blurred, but through it all, certain themes pertaining to American identity and the collective American self-image have appeared again and again. In the 1930s, a period of great economic hardship and great inequality of income and wealth, movies like the "screwball" comedies of such directors as Frank Capra, Preston Sturges, and George Cukor painted a mythic picture of class relations and class attitudes. Typical of these movies were *It Happened One Night* (1934), *Holiday* (1938), and *The Philadelphia Story* (1940), in which dashing, impecunious, highly individualistic male heroes woo and win spoiled rich girls. The rich girls' wealthy families are the heavies, not because they are rich, but because they are stuffy and snobbish. The hero either comes from a modest background or rejects his wealthy one. In addition to his romantic appeal, he is a man of boldness, vision, and accomplishments. He pries the heroine loose from her stifling upper-class roots and gets her to join him in the pursuit of his own quintessentially American dream. Several myths come together here: America as basically egalitarian and classless despite its vast income disparaties (but also tolerant of those wealth and income disparities); the lonely, but ultimately triumphant, individualist hero; his dogged upward mobility; and the bridging of class (and, implicitly, ethnic) barriers. Other Oscar-winning movies of the period, like *You Can't Take It With You* (1938), developed similar themes.

After World War II, when prosperity had returned and Americans needed to ponder the significance of the war, movies turned their mythic lens on reaffirming the universalism of the American Idea. *The Best Years of Our Lives* (1946) mythologized this universalism, both in celebrating the heroism of American soldiers who fought for it in the war and in depicting the painful postwar adjustment that allowed Americans to live and work together despite their class and ethnic differences. *Gentleman's Agreement* (1947) was a hard-hitting attack on "un-American" ethnic discrimination (in this case, anti-Semitism), made all the more universal an American issue because the crusading hero was a Gentile.

In the 1950s and early 1960s, movies like *On the Waterfront* (1954), *Marty* (1955), and *A View from the Bridge* (1962), made in the then fashionable mode of gritty social realism, for the first time tackled the significance of immigration and assimilation directly as they portrayed first- and second-generation immigrants' painful—but ultimately successful—adjustment to American society. They presented a naturalistic image of life in America's urban ethnic enclaves in stories that pit the protagonists' aspirations for upward mobility and social assimilation against the un-American and antiassimilationist forces holding them back, namely, corrupt unions (read un-American socialism) and tradition-bound families and friends.

Since the late 1960s, Academy Awards have been given to movies that have taken cinematic mythology sharply off its historic trajectory into revisionist countermythology. *Midnight Cowboy* (1969) stood many earlier myths on its head. The two individualist protagonists, a drifter from the Southwest (the locale of the former Western hero) and a derelict in New York, are no longer heroes; they are losers. The message seems to be that individualism definitely does not pay. New York City, the movie's setting, is no longer a site for upward economic and social mobility with some understandable urban rough edges but a swamp of irredeemable pathology; thus, if you live in New York City, you can forget about the American Dream. The Oscar-winning *Godfather* movies (1972 and 1974) discredited New York as well, and by glorifying the Mafia, they cynically discredited Americans' mythic assumptions about upward mobility, the virtue of the entrepreneur, and the justice of the American civic order. *One Flew Over the Cuckoo's Nest* (1975) parodied American myths: The heroic individualist was really mentally ill, and the societal establishment (the management of a mental institution) was evil. *The Deer Hunter* (1978) portrayed the injustice of the Vietnam War, puncturing Americans' mythic pretensions regarding the universalist values driving its foreign policy, and depicted life in ethnic Pittsburgh as singularly bleak. No upward mobility or assimiliation was to be found there.

And so it goes. *Ordinary People* (1980) showed the hollowness of the American Dream, even for Americans who have achieved it. *Dances with Wolves* (1990) and *Unforgiven* (1992) were textbook examples of the revisionist Western, in which American soldiers and men on horseback were the villains while the Indians who maintained a separate tribal identity and women were the victims. *Pulp Fiction* (1994) satirized and inverted the typical crime adventure story; the "heroes" were two thugs who literally got away with murder but were supposed to engage our sympathy as they contemplated their unsatisfactory lives with mock-maudlin philosophizing. Almost without exception, the Oscar-winning movies after the late 1960s not only have repudiated Americans' cherished myths, but they have pessimistic and cynical endings. The happy endings of American movie classics (as well as most mythic fiction) were not mere concessions to the tastes of an immature and naïve audience, they were metaphors of general societal optimism. Americans fighting for American values and displaying American virtues always faced tough fights against cunning and determined adversaries, but they always prevailed, meaning that American values and American virtues prevailed. In the more recent countermythology, corrupted or disillusioned Americans, pursuing unworthy and selfish objectives, either overcome their blameless victims or lose out against adversaries even more wicked than themselves; either way, injustice triumphs and American society stinks.

This critique of cinematic mythological revisionism does not mean to suggest that traditional American mythology was insensitive to America's manifest contradictions and imperfections. On the contrary, the best of America's mythological fiction, whether in the works of its great novelists or in the best of its plays and movies, clearly recognized all the betrayals of American values and inconsistencies in American behavior that accompanied the pursuit of American ideals. Cooper's classical mythical individualist pioneer, Natty Bumppo, clearly understood the tragic dimension of the American settlers' confrontation with the Indians, that American progress and civilization were being imposed at the expense of an ancient and worthy culture, and he was troubled and ambivalent about it. Novels set in America's rapidly industrializing and urbanizing post–Civil War era, such as those of William Dean Howells, Frank Norris, and Theodore Dreiser, may have portrayed the daring and ingenuity of America's quintessential self-made men, but they also depicted their cruelty and ruthlessness; they presented a panorama of rising prosperity and general upward mobility, but also the harsh and unforgiving attributes of urban and industrial life. The finely nuanced novels of social behavior by Henry James and Edith Wharton

presented their American characters in a profoundly ambivalent light: on the one hand, innocent, optimistic, venturesome, and idealistic but on the other hand, naive, crude, and unsophisticated. James and Wharton seemed never quite sure whether Europeans were, in the end, a far superior and more civilized breed. Sinclair Lewis portrayed the paradigmatic successful middle American of the 1920s as a blinkered Philistine and the quintessentially wholesome American small town as a wasteland. Novelists of twentieth-century urban life like John Farrell, Henry Roth, and Saul Bellow, writing about the children of turn-of-the-century immigrants in their ethnic ghettos, painted a decidedly mixed picture of American locales as full of pitfalls as they were of promise.

Nevertheless, even as they presented American life as it was, warts and all, America's serious novels, plays, and movies contributed to American mythology in two important ways. First, their heroes and heroines often embodied, in relatively unequivocal terms, mythic American virtues: rugged individualism, devotion to progress and modernity, and aspirations of personal advancement and mobility. Also, their story contexts usually exemplified paradigmatic American settings and themes: the frontier, the developing city, the modern workplace, the ethnic ghetto, or the mythic farm or small town. Second, like the ancient myths grounded in human frailty, the very complexity and ambivalence of their portrayals deepened, rather than undercut, their mythic resonance. By highlighting America's flaws, this literature developed a profoundly mythic paradigm: Americans seek desperately to build their new world in the land of the new beginning and to build it on the new and idealistic American principles—the American Idea and its subsidiaries—but as they do so, they often lose their way. They lose their way either because many American ideals are inherently contradictory (liberty and virtue, equality and merit, the natural and the modern, country and city) or because Americans are only human. But their attempts are nevertheless heroic; there is nobility in trying, in pursuing the vision and the ideals, even if they must often be betrayed.

These powerful ideas anticipate the angry charges of hypocrisy that have been leveled against the American belief system by the young and the disillusioned since the 1960s, poisoning the national dialogue, including its dialogue about assimilation. The best works of America's mythology supply an answer to those who claim that tradi-tional American aspirations are all a fraud. American aspirations are not a fraud, but in an imperfect world they can only be imperfectly realized, and it is far better to dedicate onself and one's society to an ideal, even if it cannot be achieved, than to accept an imperfect world cynically and fatalistically. Without their myths, Americans can never remain a truly unified people, no matter how common their consumer culture. Without their continued mutual dedication to a unified national mission and a unified national self-image, Americans will not only be unable to bring the newest immigrants into the national fold, they will no longer be able to get along with each other.

PART 4

⬥•◆•⬥

The Persistence, Functions, and Consequences of Social Classification

In Part 4, we address the broad question of why the idea of race, and formal and informal efforts to categorize and classify people by "race," persist and continue when they have no logical scientific basis. In particular, attention is given to the manner in which the legal system supports classification, the relationship between classification schemes and educational theory and practice, and how each of these components reinforce each other. The prefaces and readings so far make the point that the categories created in the past appear logical even today because they match what people already think and believe.

There are several related answers to the question of why the idea of "race" and racial classification persists. One answer is that the schemes reflect the desires, interests, and needs of people who have the power to make laws that define the self and others. Legal rulings, in turn, legitimate the exploitation and control of less powerful groups by more powerful ones (Bell n.d.). Consider the following cases that have made classification schemes an integral and enduring part of social relations in the United States.

- In 1830, the Congress of the United States authorized the negotiated removal of Native Americans to what was then Oklahoma territory. "The Indian Removal Act" was supposedly based on consent, but in fact many groups were forcibly removed by the military (Hazel 1985). What was at work was the power of the people who made the laws to enforce them. In this case, the law restricted most Native Americans to life on a reservation and made them, in essence, wards of the federal government. This third-class citizenship status is a condition from which many Native Americans have still not been able to extricate themselves.

- In *People* v. *Hall,* 1854, the California Supreme Court legally defined the meaning of the terms black, Mulatto, Indian, and white. It declared that the phrase "white person" applied to a single, fixed category. The other terms applied in a generic sense to all categories of persons labeled nonwhite regardless of their specific features. The effect of the decision was to add people of Asian descent to the list of persons legally barred from testifying against whites in court.

  > ...In using the words, "No Black, or Mulatto person, or Indian shall be allowed to give evidence for or against a White person," the Legislature, if any intention can be ascribed to it, adopted the most comprehensive terms to embrace every known class or shade of color, as the apparent design was to protect the White person from the influence of all testimony other than that of persons of the same caste. The use of these terms must, by every sound rule of construction, exclude every one who is not of white blood.... (cited in Rothenberg 1988:202)

- In 1636, Colonists in the Caribbean declared that Indians and Negroes could be sold for life. In 1640, four years later, the colony of Virginia sentenced a black indentured servant who had runaway along with two whites to "serve his said master or his assigns for the rest of his natural life here or else where" (Jordan 1974:42). The two white servants were sentenced to serve an additional four years each. These decisions signaled the beginning of the association of the color "black" with the status "slave" and the color "white" with "privileged status" in the United States.

What is to be noted about these cases is that there is no attempt to hide the intent here. The language speaks directly to the prejudice of white lawmakers as they created color/race-based classification systems to their advantage and to the disadvantage of everyone else. How does one group come to possess the kind of power that allows it to categorize other people and to construct legal systems to support what they do?

A necessary condition for the emergence of groups with varying degrees of wealth, power, and unequal privilege is a society characterized by extreme inequality. Sociologists have identified four patterns of contact between different groups that seem to lead to conditions of dominance and subordination. In each of these cases, inequality is a significant factor in the initial contact phase and tends to intensify over time. Martin Marger (1991:54–56) have labeled the four patterns as follows:

1. *Annexation.* A process that leads to the incorporation of all or part of one nation into an adjacent, more powerful nation. The annexation may be negotiated (as in the Louisiana Purchase by the United States from the French) or attained through military action (as in the ceding of the Southwestern Territories to the United States at the close of the war with Mexico). Mexicans living in these annexed areas immediately took on a subordinate status and were set apart by their physical features, language, and traditions.

2. *Voluntary Immigration.* The process whereby people living in one country elect to move to another country. Push factors (economics, political conditions, natural disasters) and pull factors (political and religious freedom, more jobs, higher pay) induce people to emigrate. Voluntary immigration is well known and is the most common pattern of contact. The best example is the voluntary movement of thousands of people from Ireland to the United States in the 1840s and 1850s, motivated in part by a potato famine in Ireland. The low social standing given the Irish by European society followed them to the United States where they found themselves on the bottom of the white class structure.

3. *Involuntary Immigration.* This involves the forced transfer of people from one society to another. The best known example is the transfer of millions of Africans to the Americas over a period of more than 400 years. They were set apart by their physical features, language, religion, and cultural traditions. All these factors, in the minds of their captors, caused them to exhibit the greatest divergence from the norms of the Europeans and made them ideal candidates for slavery. Indentured servants also fit into the category of involuntary immigrants, although most of these were poor whites, who eventually became free men.

4. *Conquest/Colonialism.* This is a form of domination in which an external country imposes its political, economic, social, and cultural institutions on an indigenous people. Using superior military force, the European countries controlled parts of Asia, Africa, Australia, and the Americas for hundreds of years. Puerto Rico and the Virgin Islands are present-day examples of American colonies. A special case of colonialism is termed *internal colonialism.*

5. *Internal Colonialism.* When relations that mirror those in classical colonialism exist among ethnic groups in the same country, this situation is called *internal colonialism.* The concept is normally used to explain the situation of disadvantaged groups involuntarily subjugated in newly independent nations that emerged following the

era of European colonialism. The relations of African, Asian, Hispanic, and Native Americans to white Americans in the United States is an example of this.

Bonnie C. Freeman (1978) defined the following characteristics as "essential to a colonial relationship, and especially to the colonial educational process":

1. The colonized group is assumed to be intellectually, morally, and physically inferior.
2. The colonial educational system is controlled by the dominant group and is detached from the culture of the colonized and colonizer as well.
3. The history of the colonized is either denied or reinterpreted in such a fashion that colonial education constitutes a fundamental assault on the identity of the colonized group.
4. The substance of the colonial education is different from that given the colonizer.
5. A plausible outcome of the colonial situation is that the colonized begin to identify with their oppressor, to assume the superiority of his values and knowledge, to see themselves as weak and ignorant, and, finally, to depend on the colonizer for a definition of the situation, "protection," and other resources. (208–209)

Conflict emerges as a central and defining feature in the relationships between "racial and ethnic" groups in all of the above contact patterns. As dominant groups take steps to make permanent and institutionalize their advantage, they develop an ideology of "difference," or "classification" to rationalize and justify their treatment of less-powerful groups, hence, "the Other." The first public school in the country opened its doors exclusively to white males in 1821 (Pulliam 1968). The privileged status of white males in America today is due almost exclusively to the fact that they alone benefited from this early access to education. In societies like the United States where inequality was/is the foundation of its construction, it should not be surprising that classification schemes that function to maintain differences (Kozol 1992) would be an integral part of the formal education system.

It has been emphasized that categories which are illogical or without biological foundation maintain significance because powerful people benefit materially from their existence. The words "the other" appear repeatedly in legal documents constructed by ruling-class whites in a system devised to control, dominate, and exploit nonwhite peoples. A 1712 South Carolina law used the term in a legal document enslaving African Americans, Native Americans, and their descendants.[1] This law no doubt served as a partial model for the inclusion of the phrase in the Constitution of the United States.

> Representatives and direct Taxes shall be apportioned among the several States which may be included within this Union, according to their respective Numbers, which shall be determined by adding to the whole Number of free Persons, including those bound to Service for a Term of Years, and excluding Indians not taxed, three fifths of all other Persons.[2]

"Those bound to Service" is a reference to indentured servants. The words "three-fifths of all other persons" included all those persons legally declared slaves (chattel property). This is known as the "three-fifths compromise." Slaves, of course, were not allowed to vote. Nevertheless, they could be counted as three-fifths of a person, which had the effect of increasing the number of representatives from slave-holding states in the Congress. The ratification of the Constitution had the effect of raising "inequality" to the level of a formal value in a society supposedly based on an unswerving commitment to "equality."

The idea that Africans were only three-fifths of a human being is reflected in the popular characterization of them as "mules" in Southern culture. Judy Scales-Trent (1995) addresses this question in the reading "On Being Like a Mule." Whites used the term *mulatto* to classify the offspring of a "white" and a "black" person. The word *mulatto* is full of symbolisms that help whites to rationalize the classification and abuse of "the Other"; in this case, the Negro slave, who is, somehow "less than a human being." And "Negro slaves and their descendants" are "chattel property—as, that is to say, an automatically inferior form of humanity, a kind of two-legged domestic animal" (Pope-Hennesy 1969:47). Under this system, you do not have to treat an animal the way you would treat a full human being.

A mule is a work animal. It is used to carry heavy burdens and as a draft (plow) animal in farming. To liken enslaved Africans to a mule then is to objectify and give concrete meaning to the often-heard expression among white Southerners that the slaves were "beasts of the field." Scales-Trent also suggests that the analogy is intended to make the case for "racial purity" since the mule is a sterile animal and cannot reproduce. This is an interesting argument because during and after slavery most children with African and European ancestry were born to white fathers and African or Native American mothers. And, in fact, throughout colonial America, classification systems were devised that were intended to specify the exact proportion of African blood a person carried (Marger 1991). As Scales-Trent makes clear, the mule analogy represents the extreme form of "the Other."

Many states, as one part of the effort to control slaves, made it illegal to teach them to read and write. The primary purpose of such laws was to prevent slaves from reading and understanding abolitionist newspapers, and in general, knowing too much.[3] A North Carolina law had the following title: "An Act to Prevent All Persons from Teaching Slaves to Read and Write, the Use of Figures Excepted." Why do you think it was acceptable to teach slaves elementary arithmetic but not other forms of literacy? The answer is simply that plantation owners wanted to be sure that their slaves could keep an accurate count of the number of bales of cotton and barrels of rice being shipped to market. The denial of the right to an education along with that of the right to vote, more so than their actual enslavement, explains the lack of educational achievement of African Americans. The legacy of these forms of legal discrimination was to relegate the slaves and their descendants to a lower-than-average standard of living.

The reading "Article XIX, Chinese: Constitution of the State of California" exemplifies several aspects of the purpose and function of classification and how dominant groups use it to their advantage. For example, Asian-Americans, like African and Native Americans, are treated like an internally (Blauner 1969, 1972) colonialized group. The Ruling states the following:

1. *Set limits on nonwhite voluntary immigration.* Asian immigration was always very rigidly controlled. The major restrictions were not removed until the 1960s. Most Hispanics became U.S. citizens by virtue of the annexation of what had been parts of Mexico. African voluntary immigration has been virtually nonexistent.

2. *Legally protected jobs for whites by limiting opportunities for nonwhite employment.* This has been a constant feature of American society since the end of the Civil War. Nonwhites could be used as slaves or as forced laborers as needed. In all other instances they were not wanted.

3. *Reinforced in the popular mind (socialization) the idea of the significance of color classification in American society.*

4. *Highlighted the fact that "race" in the United States is defined by the legal system in the absence of any clear biological basis for doing so.* This is another example of "racial" ideology being confused with what is assumed to be fact.

5. *Stigmatized Asian-Americans and assigned them to the status of "the Other," while institutionalizing and upholding white supremacy.*

The important thing to understand about all these policies is that they were never intended to reduce group boundaries (classification/categories) leading to the full integration of various ethnic groups into the mainstream of society. The purpose of these policies has always been to maintain existing relations of inequality (Altbach and Kelly 1987, Carnoy 1974). The first objective of classification is social control; another is to produce docile, hardworking categories of persons (indentured servants, Asian coolies, black sharecroppers, Hispanic farm workers) who know their place and stay in it (Altbach and Kelly 1978).

In the reading "Persons of Mean and Vile Condition," Howard Zinn offers insights into the "origin of the color line" and the manner in which classification schemes functioned to control people in the early history of the United States. For the elite in the American colonies, the greatest fear was that discontented whites, especially indentured servants who were treated like slaves, would join blacks and overthrow the existing order. Laws were passed to segregate and encourage animosity between blacks and whites. For example, if a white servant and a slave escaped together and were captured, the white servant would have to serve additional time as an indentured servant beyond that of his contract. The black slave would be beaten and dismembered in some way. There were also laws forbidding interracial marriage (whites were banished; blacks beaten) and laws preventing blacks from striking whites (blacks could have their ears cut off for retaliating in this way).

Other strategies colonial officials used to promote white-black division included (1) monopolizing the eastern seaboard land, thereby forcing landless whites to move into the frontier, placing the frontiersman in direct conflict with the Indians; (2) passing laws prohibiting free blacks from traveling through Indian country; (3) signing treaties with Indians requiring them to return fugitive slaves; and (4) declaring all "interracial" children "black," thereby reducing the number of persons labelled "white" and, therefore, privileged.

The idea of "race" and the belief that people can be classified according to "racial" schemes finds support in the work of educators and scientists precisely because they profess objective and disinterested neutrality in the outcomes they report. In other words, what they report supposedly reflects the application of the scientific method to whatever is being studied. In fact, more often than not, what they conclude, report, and teach is not without ideological bias. Educators and scientists appear to the general public as all-knowing experts, committed to understanding and explaining cultural and physical reality. Because basic scientific and research principles are either not taught very well or are not sufficiently retained, most people are not prepared to critically assess and analyze what researchers report.

Further, scientists and educators are not immune to ideological currents that are of long-standing duration and have powerfully impacted the values, norms, and social arrangements of a society. Too often science simply reflects and reinforces popular opinion. Science, to be sure, is a powerful tool when properly applied. But much of it is still largely trial and error and one cannot declare 100 percent confidence in the research methods being employed. What is considered a tentative conclusion by most researchers is too often taken as an absolute truth by the general public. In their urge to classify people, for example, scientists have generally ignored those persons they label "mixed race." In fact, the classification schemes they use follow the popular opinion that there are clear-cut "racial" categories. These same popular views, when embraced by scientists, receive official sanction and are used by the federal government as guidelines for "racial" classification.

Stephen Jay Gould (1981a) has described several instances in which so-called scientists have misused science to claim that the "racial" classification schemes they use are valid and accurate. In one instance, Gould (1981b) describes how the census of 1840 was used to justify the institution of slavery. Dr. Edward Jarvis, a medical statistician, reviewed census tables for that year and showed that "one in 162 blacks was insane in free states, but only one in 1,558 in slave states" (Gould 1981b:20). Taken on face value, the census tables showed that insanity among blacks increased as one moved from the North to the South. Location, however, did not impact insanity among whites. The implication of the census figures was that "the slaves actually benefitted from not having many of the hopes and responsibilities which the free, self-thinking and self-acting enjoy and sustain, for bondage saves him from some of the liabilities and dangers of active self-direction" (Gould 1981b:20). Upon further investigation, Jarvis was actually able to show that there were many errors in collecting the data. In one case, it was reported that 133 out of 156 blacks were insane. It turned out that the figure actually referred to the number of whites in the local state mental hospital. Despite Jarvis's efforts, he was unable to have the data corrected, and it was allowed to stand as fact. As recently as 22 years ago, social scientists like Eugene Genovese (1974) were still using racist ideology to argue that blacks actually benefited from what he described as the paternalistic nature of American slavery.

The reading "Science and Jewish Immigration" by Stephen Jay Gould (1983) is yet another example of the misuse of science. Traditionally, immigration officials with the support of scientists had been able to use general measures of dullness and lack of intelligence to exclude Italians, Greeks, Turks, and Slavic immigrants from the United States. When they found that these measures could not be used to exclude most Jews, they decided to make the test "more sophisticated." A study by H. H. Goddard, one of the leaders of the Eugenics movement in the United States, and one by Karl Pearson, an English scientist and Eugenicist credited with having invented statistics, were used to make the claim that Jews, too, were stupid.

Goddard claimed, at first, that he could identify mentally defective people simply from their facial features. He later turned to a form of the IQ test developed at Stanford University. Pearson claimed that his use of a biased "cold statistic" controlled for bias and thus proved the mental inferiority of Jews. To measure and predict intelligence, he used such variables as cleanliness of hair and teachers' judgments to try to predict Jewish intelligence. In this case, the statistical technique (correlation) proved only as good as the data it was used to analyze. Both researchers used faulty operational definitions of intelligence, violating basic research principles.

This example is a classic case of the use of the self-fulfilling prophecy and the misuse of science to support what the researchers had already concluded. As a result of these highly biased studies by "reputable" researchers, immigration restrictions were put in place in 1924. The quotas resulting from this act reduced Eastern European and Jewish immigration to the United States to a trickle.

In the reading "Remarks on the First Two Volumes of *Sex and Race*," world historian (usually labeled as a black historian) J. A. Rogers describes how mainstream scholars and others "who didn't want the present knowledge in their heads disturbed" (1972:6), dismissed his work as biased and irrelevant without, in most cases, reading what he had written. Rogers' experiences offer insights into how certain accounts of the past do not become part of the school curriculum. It does not seem to matter that Rogers loathes "racial propaganda" and was committed to avoiding it. Likewise, it does not matter that Rogers' historical accounts are the result of tens of thousands of miles of travel at home and abroad and that he has

> consulted books and printed matter so vast in number that were I to try to say how many I would sound like a Munchausen; visited the leading museums of many of the civilized lands, and engaged in research in their libraries and ever going to great pains to get my facts as humanly correct as possible. In short, I felt I have looked into books and dug up buried knowledge that many college professors or doctors of philosophy do not know exist, because just as there is a life in the deeper depths of the ocean of which the average fisherman knows nothing so there are depths in the ocean of research of which some of the most learned have never dreamed. (Rogers 1972:vi)

What Rogers does in the three-volume work entitled *Sex and Race* is effectively destroy the "myth" of "racial purity," an idea which serves as the cornerstone of social relations in colonial and ex-colonial societies.

"Why 'Race' Makes No Scientific Sense: The Case of Africans and Native Americans" by Prince Brown, Jr. illustrates why the idea of "racial purity" is a myth. The article is an historical account of unions and relationships between Native Americans and African slaves and the emergence of a people known as the "Black Indians." As you read this article, consider that by social convention the people we call Indians are classified as Mongoloid and that the people we call African Americans are classified as belonging to the Negroid/Negro[4] "race." Brown reminds us that when slaves ran away, they often ran to Native American villages where they formed unions with those who took them in. Exposure to this historical fact leaves us with many questions and highlights the weaknesses of the various classification schemes employed in the United States: To which "racial" category do the offspring of Native Americans and Africans belong? How do we describe the American experience so that it reflects the contributions of Native Americans and African Americans? How does the fusion of African and Native American culture affect our ideas of "American culture?"

We are now ready to offer a sociological explanation to the following question: Why do classification schemes persist given the numerous critiques of them that undermine their validity? "The ideology of race is a system of ideas which interprets and defines the meaning of racial differences, real or imagined, in terms of some system of *cultural values*"[5] (Nash 1962:285). One way in which sociologists study cultural values in society is by using what is called the *functionalist perspective*. Sociologist Richard T. Schaefer writes:

> In the view of a functionalist, a society is like a living organism in which each part contributes to the survival of the whole. Therefore, the *functionalist perspective* emphasizes how the parts of society are structured to maintain its stability. According to this approach, if an aspect of social life does not contribute to a society's stability or survival—if it does not serve some identifiably useful function—it will not be passed on from one generation to the next. It would seem reasonable to assume that bigotry between races offers no such positive function, and so why, we ask, does it persist? The functionalist, although agreeing that racial hostility is hardly to be admired, would point out that it does serve some positive functions from the perspective of racists. (1995:13)

What powerful whites in the United States (who are able to define and label others and to have their definitions become widely accepted) understand is that (racial) classification serves their purposes and interests; albeit, at the expense of others. Much widespread discrimination in the United States is rationalized as just good business practice.

Based on his review of the research literature Manning Nash formulates "four functions that racial beliefs [values] have for the dominant group":

1. Racist ideologies provide a moral justification for maintaining a society that routinely deprives a group of its rights and privileges. Southern whites justified slavery by believing that Africans were physically and spiritually subhuman and devoid of souls.
2. Racist beliefs discourage subordinate people from attempting to question their lowly status, for to do so is to question the very foundations of the society.
3. Racial beliefs provide a cause for political action and focus social uncertainty on a specific threat. Racial ideologies not only justify existing practices but serve as rallying points for social movements, as seen in the rise of Nazi party.
4. Racial myths encourage support for the existing order by introducing the argument that if there were any major societal change, the subordinate group would suffer even greater poverty and the dominate group would suffer lower living standards. (1962:286–87)

Thus a racial ideology evolves when a set of values, such as those which support a system of oppression, is challenged or threatened (Nash 1962). According to functionalist theory, classification schemes persist because they function to help support and preserve arrangements which benefit powerful people in society. Dysfunctional aspects of classification are harmful to both the dominant and subordinate groups but have the greatest negative impact on the subordinate groups. Arnold Rose (1951:19–24) has identified some of the dysfunctional factors.[6] They continue to be the source of major social problems in the United States.

We shall now turn to brief introductions of the other articles in Part 4. They were selected to help make clearer how classification schemes were created, what their functions are, and how they were institutionalized. "We must be prepared to find that discrimination is in part sustained by a socialized reward system" (Merton 1976:201).

The term *institutionalization* means that beliefs and behaviors that reflect the values of a society's dominant group have become widely accepted, and have become a part of the personality of the majority of persons as they are socialized into that society. Further, social arrangements/structures within the society are organized in accordance with the society's values, and societal behavior reflects these beliefs. The values, beliefs, and behaviors exist at the center of the cultural ethos[7] of the society. Once people came to accept racial categories as meaningful, they instituted rules, regulations, and policies that were presented and justified as logical extensions of racial categories.

For example, after African Americans were declared slaves, and along with Native Americans labeled "the Other" in the U.S. Constitution, parallel but unequal social institutions such as segregated schools were created to reflect the fact of these definitions. In order to justify these behaviors, white Americans argued that persons of African descent lacked the intellect for formal education and that it would be a waste of resources to attempt to educate them. Also, rules that called for separate public drinking fountains for blacks and whites were largely followed by members of both groups. Both segregated schools and drinking fountains represent a stage in the process of the institutionalization of an idea/practice that sociologists call *accommodation* (Park 1950).[8] Violation of the rules resulted in mild social rebuke for whites (from other whites) and severe legal sanctions for blacks (many were actually charged with a crime). Thus, something is institutionalized when it is the (sometimes unconscious) normal, everyday, expected mode of interaction between individuals in a society. "Racial" tension arises, and conflict erupts when subordinate group individuals challenge the institutionalized conventions and attempt to change them. This last point (nonwhite challenges to institutionalized white privilege) is forcing many whites to deal with the question: "What does it mean to be white?"

As transformative academic awareness (Banks 1993) ever so slowly begins to penetrate the educational canon, whites are being forced to reexamine the assumption that "whiteness" was/is sacrosanct. They are having to deal with charges of racism every day of their lives, a situation from which they have been shielded by the historical segregation in American society. They are frustrated by the fact that now that integration has been forced upon them, they cannot totally control the nature of the interaction. Witness the white student complaints about blacks segregating themselves on university campuses, which necessarily means in turn that whites are also segregating themselves—but this fact does *not* lead to complaints.

Many white students still, mistakenly so, believe that the United States is a "colorblind" society; most say that they believe the maxim "all men are created equal." They also just happen to believe that most black students are admitted to the university because of affirmative action, and that most others are admitted based on merit. Many white students feel threatened by the new multicultural and Afrocentric perspectives, and are beginning to circle the wagons and demand "white studies and white holidays," never comprehending that this is what they have always had. People classified as white are beginning to consciously develop a "white identity." As members of the dominant group, they have not had to think about the meaning assigned to their racial category as nonwhites have lacked the power to force whites to consider who they are and why as a group they are more socially, economically, and politically privileged than other racial groups.

Unlike blacks, white students have no experience being asked such questions, let alone having to try to answer them. As Toni Morrison writes: "The trauma of racism is, for the racist and the victim, the severe fragmentation of the self" (1989:16). Given their normative socialization—more specifically their mis-education in a racist culture—some whites do not perceive or understand institutionalized racism. White students are being forced to endure the mental and psychological turmoil that has always been the lot of subordinate peoples, and they do not like it. Being classified "white" no longer guarantees ones safe passage through America's troubled "racial" waters.

The reading "Taking Back the Center," by Trina Grillo and Stephanie M. Wildman, builds further on this theme of White angst resulting from the nonwhite challenge to white dominance in all aspects of American institutional life. According to these authors, white supremacy has resulted from their expectation that they and their concerns will occupy center stage in any and all discussions. People who benefit from white privilege perceive it as normative and implicit. Their socialization has not prepared them to have this assumption challenged by its nonwhite victims.

Many whites resent, and respond with anger and disrespect, when they are not the main presenters or the subjects of presentations. They do not know how to deal with the fact that they have not had to compete for the center stage. That is, until the 1950s and 1960s white privilege was protected by law, and since that time by custom and tradition. This resentful behavior is evident even when nonwhite scholars are interpreting their own history and planning their self-help efforts. Toni Morrison explains why the African Americans' reach to share center stage is so bothersome to some whites:

> Now that Afro-American artistic presence has been "discovered" actually to exist, now that serious scholarship has moved from silencing the witnesses and erasing their meaningful place in and contribution to American culture, it is no longer acceptable merely to imagine us and imagine for us. We have always been imagining ourselves...We are the subjects of our own narrative, witnesses to and participants in our own experience, and, in no way coincidentally, in the experience of those with whom we have come in contact. We are not, in fact, "other." We are choices. (1989:8–9)

Whites rightly perceive that African Americans are transforming the academic canon and redistributing the privilege and power that has been associated with the white monopoly of it.

Plessy v. *Ferguson* (1896) is the best-known, and perhaps the most infamous, legal decision rendered by the U.S. Supreme Court in the post-slavery period. In 1891, Homer A. Plessy challenged a Louisiana law that required him to ride in a segregated railway car. In 1896, the U.S. Supreme Court ruled against him, making segregation in public places the law of the land. Interestingly, segregation emerged as a general feature of American society as a way of controlling African Americans after slavery was declared illegal. The first article we present about this case is the actual text of the decision rendered by the Court. Speaking for the majority, Mr. Justice Brown puts forth the "rationale" offered to assert and legally institutionalize white supremacy—a rationale being a reason or list of reasons that does not have to be consistent with any facts. Mr. Justice Harlan's dissenting opinion is, on the other hand, a "rational" act consistent with or based on reason or fact. The decision of the majority shows how classification schemes were used to rationalize inequality—even when information existed that should have dictated another outcome.

"Plessy," the second reading by Cheryl I. Harris, is a law review essay that makes several noteworthy points about the *Plessy* case. Usually not reported when this case is cited is the fact that Plessy's physical features were such that he easily could, and often did, pass for "white." The fact that he had "African blood" had to be brought to the attention of the court. So, one of the things that the court was deciding was Plessy's "race." Again, "race" is not a self-evident biological fact. Nevertheless, the court's decision carried consequences for Plessy that he would not have had to endure had the court not been informed of his African ancestry.

A second point made by Harris is that the court gave voice to the idea that "whiteness" was an implicit quality, a property, that had "an actual pecuniary value" (Harris 1993). This was not true for "blackness" and therefore, whites and blacks could not ride in the same railroad car since this would have the effect of equating the two and not recognizing the privilege that was implicit in being white. At the same time, the court decided that requiring segregated railroad cars did not amount to discrimination against blacks, it was only that blacks chose to interpret it that way. The effect of the ruling was to legalize what had become the custom of white supremacy and to uphold "race" subordination.

We have argued the scientific view that "racial" classification is not possible and has a hard time competing with the popular (ideologically constructed) view of "race." The experience of one teacher dramatizes this reality. Eloise Hiebert Meneses, who teaches a class on anthropology of race and ethnicity, explains that

...I spend three weeks providing students with the scientific data on biological interrelatedness and discover, in the end, that I have convinced very few of them that race (as a set of discrete biological characteristics)

does not exist. Their daily experience of interaction with people of other "races" convinces them I have some abstract, nitpicking theory that doesn't fit the real evidence, easily obtained by their own eyes. Furthermore, it is clear that neither I nor other scientists are going to find it easy to convince people anywhere that "there is no such thing as race." If those in the biological sciences are right, whence this firm commitment to folk theory of race?" (Meneses 1994:139)

Dr. Meneses' perception is confirmed by another astute observer, "You can just look around and see how the world is split up—black people sitting over there at that table, white people walking down the hall, maybe a table with black people and white people sitting together. Our eyes tell us the truth" (Scales-Trent 1995:2). These views make clear how difficult it is to change beliefs resulting from socialization that are centered at the core of the personality. The reading "The Declaration of Athens," is intended to help people understand the difference between (what Nash [1962] has labeled) "race and the ideology of race." It is the ideology of and not the fact of race that drives society's preoccupation with the concept.

Further, as Nash and Jacquard make clear, while researchers may continue to study what some call "race," it is not possible to show any relationship between it and traits like intelligence and morality. Such traits are heavily influenced by the cultural experiences that people have.

The readings reflect the consequences of social classification. They do not, as some would argue, reflect the objective practice of science or rational, logical thought. Science can tell us how to perform an abortion; it cannot, and does not, tell us whether we should do so. That decision reflects the general social situation and prevailing values. We must address not only *what* value will prevail but also *whose* values. The values at work when some people are oppressed are those of the people who have the power to impose their will on others. They do so by dominating and controlling mainstream societal institutions (political, legal, economic, military, educational, political, etc.), and by socially creating and misusing specious and nonscientific classification systems.

Notes

[1] Thomas Cooper and David J. McCord, eds., *Statutes at Large of South Carolina* (10 vols., Columbia, 1836–1841), VII, 352–7.

[2] The U.S. Constitution, Article I, Section 2. P5 in *The United States Government Manual 1996/1997*. Washington, DC: United States Government Printing Office.

[3] Laws such as these expose the contradictory nature of much proslavery logic. If, as one of the arguments go (an argument made by no less an American personage than Thomas Jefferson), slaves were biologically incapable of learning and thinking abstractly, why the great concern about them reading, understanding, and acting on it?

[4] A term, by the way, that means absolutely nothing to continental Africans and has been largely rejected by diasporan Africans. The word was coined and used almost exclusively by Europeans as a negative and derogatory term for Africans. *See* John B. Opdycke, 1950. Pp. 241–42 in *The Opdycke Lexicon of Word Selection*. New York: Funk & Wagnalls.

[5] *Italics* added for emphasis.

[6] (1) A society that practices discrimination fails to use the resources of all individuals. Discrimination limits the search for talent and leadership to the dominant group. (2) Discrimination aggravates social problems such as poverty, delinquency, and crime, and places the financial burden of alleviating these problems on the dominant society. (3) Society must invest a good deal of time and money to defend its barriers to the full participation of all members. (4) Goodwill and friendly diplomatic relations between nations are often undercut by racial prejudice and discrimination. (5) Communications between groups is restricted. Little accurate knowledge of the minority and its culture is available to the society at large. (6) Social change is inhibited since it may contribute to assisting the minority. (7) Discrimination promotes disrespect for law enforcement and the peaceful settlement of disputes (Rose 1951:19-24).

[7] The disposition, character, or fundamental values peculiar to a specific people, culture, or movement. *The American Heritage Dictionary,* 2nd College Edition, 1985.

[8] While all such laws were declared unconstitutional in the mid-1960s, it should be understood that changing a law does not change attitudes and only changes public behavior that can readily be observed and monitored. Today, African Americans are still refused service in some public facilities in the United States.

On Being Like a Mule

JUDY SCALES-TRENT

◇◆◆◇◆

Study Questions

1. Given that the person labeled a "mulatto" has one white and one black ancestor, how would you classify him or her? What would be the basis of your classification of that person?
2. How do you think European Americans who parented children with African Americans perceived themselves and their children since it was their direct offspring who were labeled as "mules"?
3. What is "gained" by labeling those with ancestors from Europe and Africa a "mule?"

It is impossible to look on a man and pretend that this man is a mule. It is impossible to couple with a Black woman and describe the child you have both created as a mulatto—either it's your child, or a child, or it isn't.

—James Baldwin

It wasn't until very recently, as I was looking up the spelling of the word "mulatto" in the dictionary, that I inadvertently discovered its derivation: "From the Spanish 'mulato,' young mule." Transfixed by those words on the page, I looked slowly down the column of words to find the definition of "mule":

"(MYÖÖL), *n.*

1. The sterile offspring of a female horse and a male donkey, valued as a work animal, having strong muscles, a body shaped like a horse, and donkeylike large ears, small feet, and sure-footedness....
2. Any hybrid between the donkey and the horse.

3. *Informal.* A very stubborn person.
4. *Bot.* any sterile hybrid...."

"Sterile hybrid." What a ghastly term to apply to a person. It describes the result of a sexual union so unnatural, by species so unlike, that this creature is unable to meet one of the basic criteria of a species—the ability to reproduce. It describes a creature that will, happily, *not* be able to continue its unnatural line—a being that will die without offspring, so that the categories "horse" and "donkey" ("white," "black") will return to their former state of purity.

Sexual license across boundaries, with no social consequences—this is the dream of America.

I struggle to get a feeling for my namesake, the mule. My first thought is of Zora Neale Hurston's description of the black woman as "de mule uh de world"—the one who has to pick up the load and carry it for everyone else, white people and black men alike. I think of the mules in the Arizona copper mines who walked slowly down

305

into the pitch-black mines, then slowly back up, laden with ore, year after year, never seeing the world outside of the mine, never seeing the light, until they went blind. A beast of burden. Slave-like. And stupid enough to accept slave treatment.

It is hard to think of anything positive about mules. They are not noble like horses, loyal like dogs, elegant like the lion. It was not mules who crossed the Alps to win a war for Hannibal. Mules are just there, stolid and stupid, strange-looking horses with ill-fitting ears.

Names are important. What people call us is important. Sometimes, when we name ourselves, the name says something about the person wearing the name. But, more often, we are named by others, and the name tells us something valuable about the namer.

In this case, the namer, America, calls me "mulatto"—"like a mule." What does this tell us about America? What is gained by comparing those with ancestors from both Europe and Africa to a mule, a "sterile hybrid"? Actually, quite a lot. First of all, it makes clear that people from Africa and people from Europe are two different animal species, species that should lead separate lives, species that cannot be family. It also emphasizes the notion of hierarchy, for it seems obvious to me that our culture values horses more than donkeys. There are legends, poems, movies about horses; they are swifter, more lovely than donkeys. It is horses that are the superior creature in this unnatural couple. And what happens when this superior animal violates the normal order of things, transgresses strict boundaries to have sexual union with an inferior being, a creature of another species? Nature herself is offended, and condemns this union by presenting it with a deformed offspring—one that cannot reproduce.

Thus, the image of the "sterile hybrid"—the mule, the mulatto—has enormous value. It teaches the lesson that America wants us all to remember. It reminds us of concepts of difference and opposition between African American and European American. It reinforces our understanding of the hierarchy of racial power and the importance of racial purity. And it tells us once again that sexual union between the two groups will not go unpunished.

In a country that considered it important to divide people by ancestry, in a country that decided to create a special name for those children born of the union of people from different lands, think of all the *other* words that could have been used! Imagine what new name could have been created if, instead of seeing this union as an attack on the dream of racial purity, America saw it as an opportunity to join two groups, much as royalty has used marriage to symbolize and consolidate the union of different groups of people. America could have then created a name to celebrate this union:

"people-who-link-us-together"
"people-who-join-our-families"
"people-who-bind-us-in-friendship"

Or, America could have seen these people as the forerunners of a new world, a world where all are linked through kinship:

"new people"
"people-of-the-future"

Or indeed, America could have looked at all the new, glorious skin colors created through the union of so many different kinds of people and celebrated this display of beauty:

"people-of-the-rainbow"

It would make me think of Joseph's coat of many colors. It would make me think of children returning home. It would make me think of God.

But no, we have only the mule, and the word "mulatto." We have only messages of opprobrium, disdain, ridicule—images of stupidity, slavery, and powerlessness. The young woman startled me with her rage. A European American with an African American child, she rejected the term out-right. "I *hate* that word! It is so ugly. I will *not* use it for my child." She's right, of course. She doesn't have to use that word. Ever. None of us do.

I recently attended a conference at which African American scholars from many disciplines came together to discuss issues of ethnicity, color, and gender as they pertain to African American identity. How exciting to be part of a group that finally wanted to address these hard, hard questions within our community! Because the discussion concerned color, there was some debate during the sessions about the use of the word "mulatto." Some refused to use it, noting its insulting connotations. Others used it, but pointed out that they did so only because it was an important historical word

that had been used extensively in the literature of race and color: they could not address that literature without using that term. This all seemed thoughtful and well reasoned to me.

But it was there, for the first time, that someone named me "a hankety-haired yellow heifer." Well, no—not me directly, but it *felt* direct, because the dark-skinned scholar who made the reference in her presentation was angry when she made it. She was angry because a white black woman—a nineteenth-century writer—had made derogatory comments in her writing about black Americans with dark skin. Now this scholar laughed when she said the words, as if to diminish their force. She also apologized before using it, and called it "a phrase from my youth," as if it was really not her using those words that day. But it was. It was a phrase she used to wound, and she meant it for that moment and for the pain she felt that day.

I have decided not to travel down the path of trying to figure out all that she meant by naming me after yet another farm animal: a heifer, a "hankety-haired yellow heifer." I know enough. It sure wasn't good.

Article XIX, Chinese: Constitution of the State of California (1872; Repealed November 4, 1952)

STATE OF CALIFORNIA

◇◆◆◇◆◇

Study Question

Codes enacted in 1872 to the California Constitution placed tight controls on Asian Americans living in that state. Describe these controls.

Historical Note: Article XIX was repealed at the general election of November 4, 1952. Prior to its repeal, the article read as follows:

Section 1. Undesirable aliens; protection from. The Legislature shall prescribe all necessary regulations for the protection of the State, and the counties, cities, and towns thereof, from the burdens and evils arising from the presence of aliens who are or may become vagrants, paupers, mendicants, criminals, or invalids afflicted with contagious or infectious diseases, and from aliens otherwise dangerous or detrimental to the well-being or peace of the State, and to impose conditions upon which persons may reside in the State, and to provide the means and mode of their removal from the State, upon failure or refusal to comply with such conditions; provided, that nothing contained in this section shall be construed to impair or limit the power of the Legislature to pass such police laws or other regulations as it may deem necessary.

Section 2. Corporations; employment of Chinese prohibited. No corporation now existing or hereafter formed under the laws of this State, shall, after the adoption of this Constitution, employ directly or indirectly, in any capacity, any Chinese or Mongolian. The Legislature shall pass such laws as may be necessary to enforce this provision.

Section 3. Public work; employment of Chinese prohibited. No Chinese shall be employed on any State, county, municipal, or other public work, except in punishment for crime.

Section 4. Foreigners Ineligible to citizenship; coolieism; segregation of Chinese. The presence of foreigners ineligible to become citizens of the United States is declared to be dangerous to the well-being of the State, and the Legislature shall discourage their immigration by all the means within its power. Asiatic coolieism is a form of human slavery, and is forever prohibited in this State, and all contracts for coolie labor shall be void. All companies or corporations, whether formed in this country or any foreign country, for the importation of such labor, shall be subject to such penalties as the Legislature may prescribe. The Legislature shall delegate all necessary power to the incorporated cities and towns of this State for the removal of Chinese without the limits of such cities and towns, or for their location within prescribed portions of those limits, and it shall also provide the necessary legislation to prohibit the introduction into this State of Chinese after the adoption of this Constitution. This section shall be enforced by appropriate legislation.

Persons of Mean and Vile Condition

Howard Zinn

Study Question

1. Is it accurate to define indentured servants as *voluntary* immigrants? Explain.
2. How did the colonial elite control the lives of indentured servants?
3. How does Howard Zinn's presentation of the interaction among Europeans, Native Americans, and Africans add to your understanding of race relations and the origin of the "color line" in colonial America? Does it cause you to reexamine what you believed before reading the article? Explain.

In the 1600s and 1700s, by forced exile, by lures, promises, and lies, by kidnapping, by their urgent need to escape the living conditions of the home country, poor people wanting to go to America became commodities of profit for merchants, traders, ship captains, and eventually their masters in America. Abbot Smith, in his study of indentured servitude, *Colonists in Bondage,* writes: "From the complex pattern of forces producing emigration to the American colonies one stands out clearly as most powerful in causing the movement of servants. This was the pecuniary profit to be made by shipping them."

After signing the indenture, in which the immigrants agreed to pay their cost of passage by working for a master for five or seven years, they were often imprisoned until the ship sailed, to make sure they did not run away. In the year 1619, the Virginia House of Burgesses, born that year as the first representative assembly in America (it was also the year of the first importation of black slaves), provided for the recording and enforcing of contracts between servants and masters. As in any contract between unequal powers, the parties appeared on paper as equals, but enforcement was far easier for master than for servant.

The voyage to America lasted eight, ten, or twelve weeks, and the servants were packed into ships with the same fanatic concern for profits that marked the slave ships. If the weather was bad, and the trip took too long, they ran out of food. The sloop *Sea-Flower,* leaving Belfast in 1741, was at sea sixteen weeks, and when it arrived in Boston, forty-six of its 106 passengers were dead of starvation, six of them eaten by the survivors. On another trip, thirty-two children died of hunger and disease and were thrown into the ocean. Gottlieb Mittelberger, a musician, traveling from Germany to America around 1750, wrote about his voyage:

> During the journey the ship is full of pitiful signs of distress—smells, fumes, horrors, vomiting, various kinds of sea sickness, fever, dysentery, headaches, heat, constipation, boils, scurvy, cancer, mouth-rot, and similar afflictions, all of them caused by the age and the high salted state of the

food, especially of the meat, as well as by the very bad and filthy water....Add to all that shortage of food, hunger, thirst, frost, heat, dampness, fear, misery, vexation, and lamentation as well as other troubles.... On board our ship, on a day on which we had a great storm, a woman about to give birth and unable to deliver under the circumstances, was pushed through one of the portholes into the sea....

Indentured servants were bought and sold like slaves. An announcement in the *Virginia Gazette,* March 28, 1771, read:

> Just arrived at Leedstown, the Ship Justitia, with about one Hundred Healthy Servants, Men, Women & Boys....The Sale will commence on Tuesday the 2nd of April.

Against the rosy accounts of better living standards in the Americas one must place many others, like one immigrant's letter from America: "Whoever is well off in Europe better remain there. Here is misery and distress, same as everywhere, and for certain persons and conditions incomparably more than in Europe."

Beatings and whippings were common. Servant women were raped. One observer testified: "I have seen an Overseer beat a Servant with a cane about the head till the blood has followed, for a fault that is not worth the speaking of...." The Maryland court records showed many servant suicides. In 1671, Governor Berkeley of Virginia reported that in previous years four of five servants died of disease after their arrival. Many were poor children, gathered up by the hundreds on the streets of English cities and sent to Virginia to work.

The master tried to control completely the sexual lives of the servants. It was in his economic interest to keep women servants from marrying or from having sexual relations, because childbearing would interfere with work. Benjamin Franklin, writing as "Poor Richard" in 1736, gave advice to his readers: "Let thy maidservant be faithful, strong, and homely."

Servants could not marry without permission, could be separated from their families, could be whipped for various offenses. Pennsylvania law in the seventeenth century said that marriage of servants "without the consent of the Masters...shall be proceeded against as for Adultery, or fornication, and Children to be reputed as Bastards."

Although colonial laws existed to stop excesses against servants, they were not very well enforced, as we learn from Richard Morris's comprehensive study of early court records in *Government and Labor in Early America.* Servants did not participate in juries. Masters did. (And being propertyless, servants did not vote.) In 1666, a New England court accused a couple of the death of a servant after the mistress had cut off the servant's toes. The jury voted acquittal. In Virginia in the 1660s, a master was convicted of raping two women servants. He also was known to beat his own wife and children; he had whipped and chained another servant until he died. The master was berated by the court, but specifically cleared on the rape charge, despite overwhelming evidence.

Sometimes servants organized rebellions, but one did not find on the mainland the kind of large-scale conspiracies of servants that existed, for instance, on Barbados in the West Indies. (Abbot Smith suggests this was because there was more chance of success on a small island.)

However, in York County, Virginia, in 1661, a servant named Isaac Friend proposed to another, after much dissatisfaction with the food, that they "get a matter of Forty of them together, and get Gunnes & hee would be the first & lead them and cry as they went along, 'who would be for Liberty, and free from bondage,' & that there would enough come to them and they would goe through the Countrey and kill those that made any opposition and that they would either be free or dye for it." The scheme was never carried out, but two years later, in Gloucester County, servants again planned a general uprising. One of them gave the plot away, and four were executed. The informer was given his freedom and 5,000 pounds of tobacco. Despite the rarity of servants' rebellions, the threat was always there, and masters were fearful.

...Escape was easier than rebellion. "Numerous instances of mass desertions by white servants took place in the Southern colonies," reports Richard Morris, on the basis of an inspection of colonial newspapers in the 1700s. "The atmosphere of seventeenth-century Virginia," he says, "was charged with plots and rumors of combinations of servants to run away." The Maryland court records show, in the 1650s, a conspiracy of a dozen servants to seize a boat and to resist with arms if intercepted. They were captured and whipped.

The mechanism of control was formidable. Strangers had to show passports or certificates to prove they were free men. Agreements among the colonies provided for the extradition of fugitive servants— these became the basis of the clause in the U.S. Constitution that persons "held to Service or Labor in one State...escaping into another...shall be delivered up...."

Sometimes, servants went on strike. One Maryland master complained to the Provincial Court in 1663 that his servants did "peremptorily and positively refuse to goe and doe their ordinary labor." The servants responded that they were fed only "Beanes and Bread" and they were "soe weake, wee are not able to perform the imploym'ts hee

puts us uppon." They were given thirty lashes by the court.

More than half the colonists who came to the North American shores in the colonial period came as servants. They were mostly English in the seventeenth century, Irish and German in the eighteenth century. More and more, slaves replaced them, as they ran away to freedom or finished their time, but as late as 1755, white servants made up 10 percent of the population of Maryland.

What happened to these servants after they became free? There are cheerful accounts in which they rise to prosperity, becoming landowners and important figures. But Abbot Smith, after a careful study, concludes that colonial society "was not democratic and certainly not equalitarian; it was dominated by men who had money enough to make others work for them." And: "Few of these men were descended from indentured servants, and practically none had themselves been of that class."

...By the years of the Revolutionary crisis, the 1760s, the wealthy elite that controlled the British colonies on the American mainland had 150 years of experience, had learned certain things about how to rule. They had various fears, but also had developed tactics to deal with what they feared.

The Indians, they had found, were too unruly to keep as a labor force, and remained an obstacle to expansion. Black slaves were easier to control, and their profitability for southern plantations was bringing an enormous increase in the importation of slaves, who were becoming a majority in some colonies and constituted one-fifth of the entire colonial population. But the blacks were not totally submissive, and as their numbers grew, the prospect of slave rebellion grew.

With the problem of Indian hostility, and the danger of slave revolts, the colonial elite had to consider the class anger of poor whites—servants, tenants, the city poor, the propertyless, the taxpayer, the soldier and sailor. As the colonies passed their hundredth year and went into the middle of the 1700s, as the gap between rich and poor widened, as violence and the threat of violence increased, the problem of control became more serious.

What if these different despised groups—the Indians, the slaves, the poor whites—should combine? Even before there were so many blacks, in the seventeenth century, there was, as Abbot Smith puts it, "a lively fear that servants would join with Negroes or Indians to overcome the small number of masters."

There was little chance that whites and Indians would combine in North America as they were doing in South and Central America, where the shortage of women, and the use of Indians on the plantations, led to daily contact. Only in Georgia and South Carolina, where white women were scarce, was there some sexual mixing of white men and Indian women. In general, the Indian had been pushed out of sight, out of touch. One fact disturbed: whites would run off to join Indian tribes, or would be captured in battle and brought up among the Indians, and when this happened, the whites, given a chance to leave, chose to stay in the Indian culture. Indians, having the choice, almost never decided to join the whites.

Hector St. Jean Crevecoeur, the Frenchman who lived in America for almost twenty years, told, in *Letters from an American Farmer,* how children captured during the Seven Years' War and found by their parents, grown up and living with Indians, would refuse to leave their new families. "There must be in their social bond," he said, "something singularly captivating, and far superior to anything to be boasted among us; for thousands of Europeans are Indians, and we have no examples of even one of those Aborigines having from choice become Europeans."

But this affected few people. In general, the Indian was kept at a distance. And the colonial officialdom had found a way of alleviating the danger: by monopolizing the good land on the eastern seaboard, they forced landless whites to move westward to the frontier, there to encounter the Indians and to be a buffer for the seaboard rich against Indian troubles, while becoming more dependent on the government for protection. Bacon's Rebellion was instructive: to conciliate a diminishing Indian population at the expense of infuriating a coalition of white frontiersmen was very risky. Better to make war on the Indian, gain the support of the white, divert possible class conflict by turning poor whites against Indians for the security of the elite.

Might blacks and Indians combine against the white enemy? In the northern colonies (except on Cape Cod, Martha's Vineyard, and Rhode Island, where there was close contact and sexual mixing), there was not much opportunity for Africans and Indians to meet in large numbers. New York had the largest slave population in the North, and there was some contact between blacks and Indians, as in 1712 when Africans and Indians joined in an insurrection. But this was quickly suppressed.

In the Carolinas, however, whites were outnumbered by black slaves and nearby Indian tribes; in the 1750s, 25,000 whites faced 40,000 black slaves, with 60,000 Creek, Cherokee, Choctaw, and Chickasaw Indians in the area. Gary Nash writes: "Indian uprisings that punctuated the colonial period and a succession of slave uprisings and insurrectionary plots that were nipped in the bud kept South Carolinians sickeningly aware that only through the greatest vigilance and through policies designed to keep their enemies divided could they hope to remain in control of the situation."

The white rulers of the Carolinas seemed to be conscious of the need for a policy, as one of them put it, "to make Indians & Negros a checque upon each other lest by their Vastly Superior Numbers we should be crushed by one or the other." And so laws were passed prohibiting free blacks from traveling in Indian country. Treaties with Indian tribes contained clauses requiring the return of fugitive slaves. Governor Lyttletown of South Carolina wrote in 1738: "It has allways been the policy of this government to create an aversion in them [Indians] to Negroes."

Part of this policy involved using black slaves in the South Carolina militia to fight Indians. Still, the government was worried about black revolt, and during the Cherokee war in the 1760s, a motion to equip five hundred slaves to fight the Indians lost in the Carolina assembly by a single vote.

Blacks ran away to Indian villages, and the Creeks and Cherokees harbored runaway slaves by the hundreds. Many of these were amalgamated into the Indian tribes, married, produced children. But the combination of harsh slave codes and bribes to the Indians to help put down black rebels kept things under control.

It was the potential combination of poor whites and blacks that caused the most fear among the wealthy white planters. If there had been the natural racial repugnance that some theorists have assumed, control would have been easier. But sexual attraction was powerful across racial lines. In 1743, a grand jury in Charleston, South Carolina, denounced "The Too Common Practice of Criminal Conversation with Negro and other Slave Wenches in this Province." Mixed offspring continued to be produced by white-black sex relations throughout the colonial period, in spite of laws prohibiting interracial marriage in Virginia, Massachusetts, Maryland, Delaware, Pennsylvania, the Carolinas, Georgia. By declaring the children illegitimate, they would keep them inside the black families, so that the white population could remain "pure" and in control.

What made Bacon's Rebellion especially fearsome for the rulers of Virginia was that black slaves and white servants joined forces. The final surrender was by "four hundred English and Negroes in Armes" at one garrison, and three hundred "freemen and African and English bond-servants" in another garrison. The naval commander who subdued the four hundred wrote: "Most of them I persuaded to goe to their Homes, which accordingly they did, except about eighty Negroes and twenty English which would not deliver their Armes."

All through those early years, black and white slaves and servants ran away together, as shown both by the laws passed to stop this and the records of the courts. In 1698, South Carolina passed a "deficiency law" requiring plantation owners to have at least one white servant for every six male adult Negroes. A letter from the southern colonies in 1682 complained of "no white men to superintend our negroes, or repress an insurrection of negroes...." In 1691, the House of Commons received "a petition of divers merchants, masters of ships, planters and others, trading to foreign plantations... setting forth, that the plantations cannot be maintained without a considerable number of white servants, as well to keep the blacks in subjection, as to bear arms in case of invasion."

A report to the English government in 1721 said that in South Carolina "black slaves have lately attempted and were very near succeeding in a new revolution...and therefore, it may be necessary...to propose some new law for encouraging the entertainment of more white servants in the future. The militia of this province does not consist of above 2,000 men." Apparently, two thousand were not considered sufficient to meet the threat.

This fear may help explain why Parliament, in 1717, made transportation to the New World a legal punishment for crime. After that, tens of thousands of convicts could be sent to Virginia, Maryland, and other colonies. It also makes understandable why the Virginia Assembly, after Bacon's Rebellion, gave amnesty to white servants who had rebelled, but not to blacks. Negroes were forbidden to carry any arms, while whites finishing their servitude would get muskets, along with corn and cash. The distinctions of status between white and black servants became more and more clear.

In the 1720s, with fear of slave rebellion growing, white servants were allowed in Virginia to join the militia as substitutes for white freemen. At the same time, slave patrols were established in Virginia to deal with the "great dangers that may...happen by the insurrections of negroes...." Poor white men would make up the rank and file of these patrols, and get the monetary reward.

Racism was becoming more and more practical. Edmund Morgan, on the basis of his careful study of slavery in Virginia, sees racism not as "natural" to black-white difference, but something coming out of class scorn, a realistic device for control. "If freemen with disappointed hopes should make common cause with slaves of desperate hope, the results might be worse than anything Bacon had done. The answer to the problem, obvious if unspoken and only gradually recognized, was racism, to separate dangerous free whites from dangerous black slaves by a screen of racial contempt."

There was still another control which became handy as the colonies grew, and which had crucial consequences for the continued rule of the elite throughout American history. Along with the very rich and the very poor, there developed a white middle class of small planters, independent farmers, city artisans, who, given small rewards for joining forces with merchants and planters, would be a solid buffer against black slaves, frontier Indians, and very poor whites.

The growing cities generated more skilled workers, and the governments cultivated the support of white mechanics by protecting them from the competition of both slaves and free Negroes. As early as 1686, the council in New York ordered that "noe Negro or Slave be suffered to work on the bridge as a Porter about any goods either imported or Exported from or into this Citty." In the southern towns too, white craftsmen and traders were protected from Negro competition. In 1764, the South Carolina legislature prohibited Charleston masters from employing Negroes or other slaves as mechanics or in handicraft trades.

Science and Jewish Immigration

STEPHEN JAY GOULD

Study Questions

1. Who was H. H. Goddard? Describe his general theories on identifying morons. What kind of "scientific" measures did he develop as a way of identifying morons?
2. Who was Karl Pearson? Describe one of Karl Pearson's measures of worthiness.
3. Why were Jews a particular focus of Goddard's and Pearson's research?
4. How does the article "Science and Jewish Immigration" help you to understand that the practice of science is a social process and that attitudes and values effect the outcome of research?
5. What impact did Goddard's and Pearson's research have on immigration policy?

In April 1925, C. B. Davenport, one of America's leading geneticists, wrote to Madison Grant, author of *The Passing of the Great Race,* and the most notorious American racist of the genteel Yankee tradition: "Our ancestors drove Baptists from Massachusetts Bay into Rhode Island, but we have no place to drive the Jews to." If America had become too full to provide places of insulated storage for undesirables, then they must be kept out. Davenport had written Grant to discuss a pressing political problem of the day: the establishment of quotas for immigration to America.

Jews presented a potential problem to ardent restrictionists. After 1890, the character of American immigration had changed markedly. The congenial Englishmen, Germans, and Scandinavians, who predominated before, had been replaced by hordes of poorer, darker, and more unfamiliar people from southern and eastern Europe. The

catalog of national stereotypes proclaimed that all these people—primarily Italians, Greeks, Turks, and Slavs—were innately deficient in both intelligence and morality. Arguments for exclusion could be grounded in the eugenic preservation of a threatened American stock. But Jews presented a dilemma. The same racist catalog attributed a number of undesirable traits to them, including avarice and inability to assimilate, but it did not accuse them of stupidity. If innate dullness was to be the "official" scientific rationale for excluding immigrants from eastern and southern Europe, how could the Jews be kept out?

The most attractive possibility lay in claiming that the old catalog had been too generous and that, contrary to its popular stereotype, Jews were stupid after all. Several "scientific" studies conducted between 1910 and 1930, the heyday of the great immigration debate, reached this devoutly desired conclusion. As examples of distorting facts to match expectations or of blindness to obvious alternatives, they are without parallel. This essay is the story of two famous studies, from different nations and with different impact.

H. H. Goddard was the director of research at the Vineland Institute for Feebleminded Girls and Boys in New Jersey. He viewed himself as a taxonomist of mental deficiency. He concentrated upon "defectives of high grade" who posed special problems because their status just below the borderline of normality rendered their identification more difficult. He invented the term "moron" (from a Greek word for "foolish") to describe people in this category. He believed at the time, although he changed his mind in 1928, that most morons should be confined to institutions for life, kept happy with tasks apportioned to their ability, and above all, prevented from breeding.

Goddard's general method for identifying morons was simplicity itself. Once you had enough familiarity with the beast, you simply looked at one, asked a few questions, and drew your evident conclusions. If they were dead, you asked questions of the living who knew them. If they were dead, or even fictitious, you just looked. Goddard once attacked the poet Edwin Markham for suggesting that "The Man with the Hoe," inspired by Millet's famous painting of a peasant, "came to his condition as the result of social conditions which held him down and made him like the clods that he turned over." Couldn't Markham see that Millet's man was mentally deficient? "The painting is a perfect picture of an imbecile," Goddard remarked. Goddard thought he had a pretty good eye himself, but the main task of identifying morons must be given to women because nature had endowed the fair sex with superior intuition:

After a person has had considerable experience in this work, he almost gets a sense of what a feeble-minded person is so that he can tell one afar off. The people who are best at this work, and who I believe should do this work, are women. Women seem to have closer observation than men.

In 1912, Goddard was invited by the U.S. Public Health Service to try his skill at identifying morons among arriving immigrants on Ellis Island. Perhaps they could be screened out and sent back, thus reducing the "menace of the feebleminded." But this time, Goddard brought a new method to supplement his identification by sight—the Binet tests of intelligence, later to become (at the hands of Lewis M. Terman of Stanford University), the Stanford-Binet scale, for the conventional measure of IQ. Benet had just died in France and would never witness the distortion of his device for identifying children who needed special help in school into an instrument for labeling people with a permanent stamp of inferiority.

Goddard was so encouraged by the success of his preliminary trials that he raised some money and sent two of his women back to Ellis Island in 1913 for a more thorough study. In two and a half months, they tested four major groups: thirty-five Jews, twenty-two Hungarians, fifty Italians, and forty-five Russians. The Binet tests produced an astounding result: 83 percent of the Jews, 87 percent of the Russians, 80 percent of the Hungarians, and 79 percent of the Italians were feebleminded—that is, below mental age twelve (the upper limit of moronity by Goddard's definition). Goddard himself was a bit embarrassed by his own exaggerated success. Weren't his results too good to be true? Could people be made to believe that four-fifths of any nation were morons? Goddard played with the numbers a bit, and got his figures down to 40 or 50 percent, but he was still perturbed.

The Jewish sample attracted his greatest interest for two reasons. First, it might resolve the dilemma of the supposedly intelligent Jew and provide a rationale for keeping this undersirable group out. Second, Goddard felt that he could not be accused of bias for the Jewish sample. The other groups had been tested via interpreters, but he had a Yiddish-speaking psychologist for the Jews.

In retrospect, Goddard's conclusions were far more absurd than even he allowed himself to suspect in anxious moments. It became clear, a few years later, that Goddard had constructed a particularly harsh version of the Binet tests. His scores stood well below the rankings produced by all other editions. Fully half the people who scored in the low, but normal, range of the Stanford-Binet scale tested as morons on Goddard's scales.

But the greater absurdity arose from Goddard's extraordinary insensitivity to environmental effects, both long-term and immediate, upon test scores. In his view, the Binet tests measured innate intelligence by definition, since they required no reading or writing and made no explicit reference to particular aspects of specific cultures. Caught in this vicious circle of argument, Goddard became blind to the primary reality that surrounded his women on Ellis Island. The redoubtable Ms. Kite approaches a group of frightened men and women—mostly illiterate, few with any knowledge of English, all just off the boat after a grueling journey in steerage—plucks them from the line and asks them to name as many objects as they can, in their own language, within three minutes. Could their poor performance reflect fear, befuddlement, or physical weakness rather than stupidity? Goddard considered the possibility but rejected it:

What shall we say of the fact that only 45 percent can give sixty words in three minutes, when normal children of 11 years sometimes give 200 words in that time! It is hard to find an explanation except lack of intelligence....How could a person live even 15 years in any environment without learning hundreds of names of which he could certainly think of 60 in three minutes.

Could their failure to identify the date, or even the year, be attributed to anything other than moronity?

Must we again conclude that the European peasant of the type that immigrates to America pays no attention to the passage of time? That the drudgery of life is so severe that he cares not whether it is January or July, where it is 1912 or 1906? Is it possible that the person may be of considerable intelligence and yet, because of the peculiarity of his environment, not have acquired this ordinary bit of knowledge, even though the calendar is not in general use on the continent, or is somewhat complicated as in Russia? If so what an environment it must have been!

Goddard wrestled with the issue of this moronic flood. On the one hand, he could see some benefits:

They do a great deal of work that no one else will do....There is an immense amount of drudgery to be done, an immense amount of work for which we do not wish to pay enough to secure more intelligent workers....May it be that possibly the moron has his place.

But he feared genetic deterioration even more and eventually rejoiced in the tightening of standards that his program had encouraged. In 1917, he reported with pleasure that deportations for mental deficiency had increased by 350 percent in 1913 and 570 percent in 1914 over the average for five preceding years. Morons could be identified at ports of entry and shipped back, but such an inefficient and expensive procedure could never be instituted as general policy. Would it not be better simply to restrict immigration from nations teeming with morons? Goddard suggested that his conclusions "furnish important considerations for future actions both scientific and social as well as legislative." Within ten years, restriction based upon national quotas had become a reality.

Meanwhile, in England, Karl Pearson had also decided to study the apparent anomaly of Jewish intelligence. Pearson's study was as ridiculous as Goddard's, but we cannot attribute its errors (as we might, being unreasonably charitable, in Goddard's case) to mathematical naïveté, for Pearson virtually invented the science of statistics. Pearson, the first Galton Professor of Eugenics at University College, London, founded the *Annals of Eugenics* in 1925. He chose to initiate the first issue with his study of Jewish immigration, apparently regarding it as a model of sober science and rational social planning. He stated his purpose forthrightly in the opening lines:

> The purport of this memoir is to discuss whether it is desirable in an already crowded country like Great Britain to permit indiscriminate immigration, or, if the conclusion be that it is not, on what gounds discrimination should be based.

If a group generally regarded as intellectually able could be ranked as inferior, then the basic argument for restriction would be greatly enhanced, for who would then defend the groups that everyone considered as stupid? Pearson, however, loudly decried any attempt to attribute motive or prior prejudice to his study. One can only recall Shakespeare's line, "The lady doth protest too much, methinks."

There is only one solution to a problem of this kind, and it lies in the cold light of statistical inquiry.... We have no axes to grind, we have no governing body to propitiate by well advertised discoveries; we are paid by nobody to reach results of a given bias. We have no electors, no subscribers to encounter in the market place. We firmly believe that we have no political, no religious and no social prejudices.... We rejoice in numbers and figures for their own sake and, subject to human fallibility, collect our data—as all scientists must do—to find out the truth that is in them.

Pearson had invented a statistic so commonly used today that many people probably think it has been available since the dawn of mathematics—the correlation coefficient. This statistic measures the degree of relationship between two features of a set of objects: height versus weight or head circumference versus leg length in a group of humans, for example. Correlation coefficients can range as high as 1.0 (if taller people are invariably heavier to the same degree) or as low as 0.0 for no correlation (if an increase in height provides no information about weight—a taller person may weigh more, the same, or less, and no prediction can be made from the increase in height alone). Correlation coefficients can also be negative if increase in one variable leads to decrease in the other (if taller people generally weigh less, for example). Pearson's study of Jewish immigration involved the measurement of correlations between a large array of physical and mental characters for children of Jewish immigrants living in London.

Pearson measured everything he imagined might be important in assessing "worthiness." He established four categories for cleanliness of hair: very clean and tidy, clean on the whole, dirty and untidy, and matted or verminous. He assessed both inner and outer clothing on a similar scale: clean, a little dirty, dirty, and filthy. He then computed correlation coefficients between all measures and was generally disappointed by the low values obtained. He could not understand, for example, why cleanliness of body and hair correlated only 0.2615 in boys and 0.2119 in girls, and mused:

> We should naturally have supposed that cleanliness of body and tidiness of hair would be products of maternal environment and so highly correlated. It is singular that they are not. There may be mothers who consider chiefly externals, and so press for tidiness of hair, but it is hard to imagine that those who emphasize cleanliness of body overlook cleanliness of hair.

Pearson concluded his study of physical measures by proclaiming Jewish children inferior to the native stock in height, weight, susceptibility to disease, nutrition, visual acuity, and cleanliness:

> Jewish alien children are not superior to the native Gentile. Indeed, taken all round we should not be exaggerating if we asserted that they were inferior in the great bulk of the categories dealt with.

The only possible justification for admitting them lay in a potentially superior intelligence to overbalance their physical shortcomings. Pearson therefore studied intelligence by the same type of short and subjective scale that had characterized his measures of physical traits. For intelligence, he relied upon teachers' judgments rated from A to G. Computing the raw averages, he found that Jewish children were not superior to native Gentiles. Jewish boys ranked a bit higher, but the girls scored notably lower than their English classmates. Pearson concluded, with a striking analogy:

> Taken on the average, and regarding both sexes, this alien Jewish population is somewhat inferior physically and mentally to the native population....We know and admit that some of the children of these alien Jews from the academic standpoint have done brilliantly; whether they have the staying power of the native race is another question. No breeder of cattle, however, would purchase an entire herd because he anticipated finding one or two fine specimens included in it; still less would he do it, if his byres and pastures were already full.

But Pearson realized that he was missing one crucial argument. He had already admitted that Jews lived in relative poverty. Suppose intelligence is more a product of environment than inborn worth? Might not the average scores of Jews reflect their disadvantaged lives? Would they not be superior after all if they lived as well as the native English? Pearson recognized that he had to demonstrate the innateness of intelligence to carry his argument for restricted immigration based on irremediable mediocrity.

He turned again to his correlation coefficients. If low intelligence correlated with measures of misery (disease, squalor, and low income, for example), then an environmental basis might be claimed. But if few or no correlations could be found, then intelligence is not affected by environment and must be innate. Pearson computed his correlation coefficients and, as with the physical measures, found very few high values. But this time he was pleased. The correlations produced little beyond the discovery that intelligent children sleep less and tend to breathe more through their nose! He concluded triumphantly:

> There does not exist in the present material any correlation of the slightest consequence

between the intelligence of the child and its physique, its health, its parents' care or the economic and sanitary conditions of its home.... Intelligence as distinct from mere knowledge stands out as a congenital character. Let us admit finally that the mind of man is for the most part a congenital product, and the factors which determine it are racial and familial.... Our material provides no evidence that a lessening of the aliens' poverty, an improvement in their food, or an advance in their cleanliness will substantially alter their average grade of intelligence.... It is proper to judge the immigrant by what he is as he arrives, and reject or accept him then.

But conclusions based upon negative evidence are always suspect. Pearson's failure to record correlations between "intelligence" and environment might suggest the true absence of any relationship. But it might also simply mean that his measures were as lousy as the hair in his category 4. Maybe a teacher's assessment doesn't record anything accurately, and its failure to correlate with measures of environment only demonstrates its inadequacy as an index of intelligence. After all, Pearson had already admitted that correlations between physical measures had been disappointingly small. He was too good a statistician to ignore this possibility. So he faced it and dismissed it with one of the worst arguments I have ever read.

Pearson gave three reasons for sticking to his claim that intelligence is innate. The first two are irrelevant: teachers' assessments correlate with Binet test scores, and high correlations between siblings and between parents and children also prove the innateness of intelligence. But Pearson had not given Binet tests to the Jewish children and had not measured their parents' intelligence in any way. These two claims referred to other studies and could not be transferred

to the present case. Pearson appreciated this weakness and therefore advanced a third argument based upon internal evidence: intelligence (teachers' assessment) failed to correlate with environment but it did correlate with other "independent" measures of mental worth.

But what were these other independent measures? Believe it or not, Pearson chose "conscientiousness" (also based on teachers' assessments and scored as keen, medium, and dull), and rank in class. How else does a teacher assess "intelligence" if not (in large part) by conscientiousness and rank in class? Pearson's three measures—intelligence, conscientiousness, and rank in class—were redundant assessments of the same thing: the teachers' opinion of their students' worth. But we cannot tell whether these opinions record inborn capacities, environmental advantages, or teachers' prejudices. In any case, Pearson concluded with an appeal to bar all but the most intelligent of foreign Jews:

> For men with no special ability—above all for such men as religion, social habits, or language keep as a caste apart, there should be no place. They will not be absorbed by, and at the same time strengthen the existing population; they will develop into a parasitic race.

Goddard's and Pearson's studies shared the property of internal contradictions and evident prejudice sufficient to dismiss all claims. But they differed in one important respect: social impact. Britain did not enact laws to restrict immigration by racial or national origin. But in America, Goddard and his colleagues won. Goddard's work on Ellis Island had already encouraged immigration officials to reject people for supposed moronity. Five years later, the army tested 1.75 million World War I recruits with a set of examinations that Goddard helped write and that were composed by a committee meeting at his Vineland Training School. The tabulations did not identify Jews per se but calculated "innate intelligence" by national averages. These absurd tests, which measured linguistic and cultural familiarity with American ways, ranked recent immigrants from southern and eastern Europe well below the English, Germans, and Scandinavians who had arrived long before (Gould 1981a). The average soldier of most southern and eastern European nations scored as a moron on the army tests. Since most Jewish immigrants arrived from eastern European nations, quotas based on country of origin eliminated Jews as surely as collegiate quotas based on geographical distribution once barred them from elite campuses.

When quotas were set for the Immigration Restriction Act of 1924, they were initially calculated at 2 percent of people from each nation present in America at the census of 1890, not at the most recent count of 1920. Since few southern and eastern Europeans had arrived by 1890, these quotas effectively reduced the influx of Slavs, Italians, and Jews to a trickle. Restriction was in the air and would have occurred anyway. But the peculiar character and intent of the 1924 quotas were largely a result of propaganda issued by Goddard and his eugenical colleagues.

What effect did the quotas have in retrospect? Allan Chase, author of *The Legacy of Malthus,* the finest book on the history of scientific racism in America, has estimated that the quotas barred up to six million southern, central, and eastern Europeans between 1924 and the outbreak of World War II (assuming that immigration had continued at its pre-1924 rate). We know what happened to many who wanted to leave but had no place to go. The pathways to destruction are often indirect, but ideas can be agents as surely as guns and bombs.

Remarks on the First Two Volumes of *Sex and Race*

J. A. ROGERS

◇◆◇◆◇

Study Questions

1. What is the central message in J. A. Rogers' remarks on Volumes I and II of *Sex and Race*?
2. Given the problems described by Rogers, what would you suggest be done to ensure that a wide variety of views are included in school curriculum?

Our race is essentially slavish; it is the nature of all of us to believe blindly in what we love, rather than that which is most wise. We are inclined to look upon an honest, unshrinking pursuit of truth as something irreverent. We are indignant when others pry into our idols and criticize them with impunity, just as a savage flies to arms when a missionary picks his fetish to pieces....

—Sir F. Galton III

Certain orthodox scholars, white and colored, have not liked the history as given in the two preceding volumes of "Sex and Race," as well as in my earlier books. One English editor after reading the "100 Amazing Facts About the Negro," wrote me that it made him feel as if the white race had never accomplished anything. Others said that I claim everybody who has ever done anything as Negro, nevertheless, I had never said, or dreamed of saying, that Homer, or Pericles, or Aeschylus, or Julius Caesar, or Alfred the Great, Shakespeare, Milton, Michael Angelo, Bach, Handel, Wagner, Washington, Lincoln, Edison, Franklin D. Roosevelt, Einstein, or thousands of other noted white men were of Negro ancestry; nor did I attribute to Negroes any role of any importance in Europe, itself, from say the sixteenth century onwards. Yet because I mention a few individuals, whom they had all along believed to be of unmixed white strain, I have been called "fantastic" and "credulous!"

And I have been ridiculed not on the result of research, not on examination of the sources which I have given abundantly, but on sheer belief. These scholars did not happen to run across such facts in their reading; in a word, the research I had done was off the beaten track of the college curriculum, therefore, it did not exist.

Perhaps I exaggerate, perhaps I am really being fantastic when I say this of the orthodox scholars; well, I shall give a not uncommon illustration and let the reader judge for himself.

In 1943, Gunnar Myrdal, noted economist of the University of Stockholm, Sweden, aided by 75 experts, working for five years, completed for the Carnegie Corporation at a cost of $209,000, a work on the race problem entitled "An American Dilemma" and published by Harper and Brothers. On page 1393 of this book (1st ed.), I am listed as an example of those who write "pseudo-history, fantastically glorifying the achievements of Negroes."

On what grounds was this judgment arrived at? On anything I had written? No, I was judged on a nonexistent book—a book that no mortal could ever have seen.

Here are the facts: In 1927, I finished a manuscript entitled "This Mongrel World, A Study of Negro-Caucasian Mixing In All Ages and All Countries." At about that time I was asked to fill out a blank for "Who's Who in Colored America," and intending to publish the manuscript soon I listed it as being published. However, circumstances prevented my doing so. Thirteen years later, due to the much greater research I had done on the subject, I changed the title to "Sex and Race." Parts of the manuscript I used in Volumes One and Two of that work and discarded most of the rest. In short, when "An American Dilemma" was published not even the manuscript of "This Mongrel World" existed. Nevertheless this *nonexistent manuscript* is listed as a *published book* in Myrdal's bibliography. What had happened? In reading through my biographical sketch in "Who's Who in Colored America," Myrdal, or some of his assistants, saw the title and on that alone condemned me. Not a word was said of any of my published books. They probably didn't take the trouble to look into any of them.

Now what is the difference between an attitude of this sort and that of any uneducated man, or any bigot, who would similarly condemn Myrdal's work, or that of any other scientist in such off-hand manner? So far as I am concerned, none whatever.

Furthermore, though I have no philanthropist or foundation, or staff of experts behind me, I go to as great pains as any of the most conscientious of these experts to get my facts straight, checking and rechecking, and travelling hither and yon to see with my own eyes whenever possible what I am writing about; and quoting only from the original sources and from those I have reason to believe are the most reliable. One can do no more. Of course, there will always be errors, but when seventy-six experts, working with unlimited funds as in "An American Dilemma," make errors surely a lone worker, like myself, might be forgiven a few.

Another reason why some object to the facts as given in my books is that they feel that their own learning is being impeached. If such facts were true, why, they certainly would have known them. One able Negro musician, who had a fine education in England, admitted to me later that when he heard me say for the first time that Beethoven was colored, he was "offended." Had he not long been acquainted with Beethoven?

In 1930 while I was carrying in the Negro press a series of articles on great Negroes, an Aframerican, studying in Germany, and now a college professor, wrote the *Pittsburgh Courier,* leading Negro weekly, that my stories were dubious even though I had included Bilal, Dumas, Pushkin, General Dodds, Chevalier de St. George, Henri Diaz, and others who are very plainly mentioned in biographies as being of Negro ancestry. The simple truth is that he didn't know the first thing of the true ancestry of these individuals but never having heard it, why, that alone made what I said false. As for my statement that the Virgin Mary and Christ were once worshipped as black and that at the present time pilgrimages are made to the shrines of the Black Virgins in France, Spain, and even in Germany, that seemed a veritable Munchausen tale. One Negro columnist, a Catholic, actually resented the idea that the Madonna could have been black. Had he not all his life seen her depicted as white?

Still another reason for their rejecting my researches is that they didn't want the present knowledge in their brains disturbed. They had been taught that the Negro's position in history had been that of a slave and it was much more pleasant to go on believing that than to investigate.

Race prejudice is responsible too, in part. There are those who at the merest mention that this or that noted person was, or might have been, of Negro ancestry, at once set their backs up like an angry cat. So racial are such people that when one attributes Negro ancestry even to an ancient Greek or Egyptian it is "social equality"—a lowering of their own personal dignity. One white woman angrily resented the idea that Alexander Dumas, the great novelist, could possibly have been of Negro ancestry.

The classic example of this sort, however, is Mary Preston, a Southern white woman, whose readings on Shakespeare were popular in her day. Miss Preston twisted "Othello" to suit herself. While admitting that Shakespeare did make Othello "black," that was positively not what Shakespeare meant so far as she was concerned. She said (italics hers): "In studying the play *Othello* I have always *imagined* its hero a *white man*. It is true the dramatist paints him black, but this shade does not suit the man. It is a stage decoration which *my taste discards;* a fault of color from an artistic point of view. I have, therefore, as I before stated in my *readings* of this play, dispensed with it. Shakespeare was too correct a delineator of human nature to have colored Othello *black* if he had personally acquainted himself with the idiosyncracies of the African race. We may regard, then, the daub of black upon Othello's portrait as an *ebullition* of fancy, a *freak* of imagination—

the visionary concept of an ideal figure.... Othello *was a white* man."[1]

Wherein we ask does such an attitude differ from that of any blind believer in revealed religion?

Of course this attitude is hugely amusing. It is one of a piece, too, with the feeling of certain Gentiles when they take up a book on Jewish biography and see for the first time that this or that great pioneer, scientist, or soldier whom they had all along fancied to be non-Jewish was a Jew.

The result of this attitude toward "Negro" history is that the better-known historians, sociologists, and anthropologists, with few exceptions, have been great claimers of Negroid peoples as white. The idea has been to maintain white supremacy. Pick up any national or world history and you'll find even the Ethiopians, who such early writers as Xenophanes, Aristotle, Herodotus and Strabo, tell us were black and wooly-haired, that is, the type now called Negro, are white. They still say the Ethiopians are white though they are uniformly blacker and more wooly-haired than the American Negroes.

Whenever, too, Negroes are mentioned as having appeared anywhere, whether in prehistoric America, the Caucasus, or Albania, they are invariably spoken of as "slaves." For instance, Ignatius Donnelly in trying to prove that the so-called New World was known to the people of the Old reproduces from the ancient Mexican monuments certain portraits of Negroes which he calls "idols."[2] But in the same breath he says they were "slaves" who "were brought to America at a very remote epoch." (Please note the contradiction: "slaves" who were "idols!") His reason for saying they were slaves is that "Negroes have never been a sea-going race," for which statement he hasn't a shred of evidence. Of course, the "slave" had to be brought in to square with white imperialism and the exploitation of the darker peoples even though what he mentions occurred in prehistoric times. The Negro must always be marked down so that his labor can be had in the cheapest market.

The motive for this twisting of history is that white imperialism must be shown as being of old, aristocratic ancestry. This imperialism was built upon the backs of the darker races. A noted example was the British empire, of whose 500,000,000 people, eighty percent are colored. Now some of these colored people as the Ethiopians, Egyptians, East Indians, and Moors were the originators of Western civilization; they were highly civilized when the Europeans were savages[3]—a fact that cannot be denied as long as the works of Julius Caesar and Tacitus exist. But it would never do to show that the lord and master once had very humble beginnings so it must be shown that the originators of civilization were white— that the white has always been on top. Therefore, for the purposes of adding lustre to white imperialism, the Ethiopians, Egyptians and the others are called "white," but for the purposes of profit they are treated as colored. Thus the white imperialist eats his cake and has it too.

It is a blow to the pride of certain white Americans, Englishmen, and Germans to hear it said that peoples and individuals they had all along fondly believed to be "pure" white were not so. Because I said on the testimony of white people who knew Beethoven, as well as on reports of his ancestry by German scholars, that he showed evidence of Negro strain, I have received letters as cross as if I had attacked the writers themselves.

Any talk of Negro progress angers many. If the blacks advance who will they have to be better than? There will go their splendid isolation of fancied superiority. Even worse, they already see themselves losing out, a state of mind expressed by Bacon when he said, "Men of noble birth are noted to be envious towards new men when they arise for the distance between them is altered and it is like a deceit of the eye that when others come on they think themselves go back."

So thorough has been the penetration of white imperialist propaganda that only a small percentage of the white or the colored in any part of Western civilization today have any idea that any other than white people had a hand in the origin of civilization. Although I had been an omnivorous reader from my earliest years, I was well past twenty before it began to dawn upon me that the darker peoples could have had a part in it. Even now I can recall my astonishment when this occurred to me.

Even as the white manufacturers have bleached out our salt, sugar, flour, so the white historian has bleached out world history. The dark or mineral portion has been rejected. Of course this process has produced a product beautifully pleasing to the eyes of those who have been psychologized to admire it, but which, nevertheless, is constipative and harmful to the mental digestion.

But as there are those who, realizing the value of the minerals that have been rejected from our foods, have placed them in again, thereby increasing the health value, as say how bran has been restored to the bleached, starved-out white bread, so in like manner I have attempted to gather up the Negro, or dark, rejected portion of history in the hope that some day they will be restored to world history, thereby permitting a less clogging effect on the mind.

Such being my purpose I do not ever claim that I am writing world or national history. Call it the bran of history if you will.

As for those who will regard this "bran" as proving that the white race has never accomplished anything and that the Negro did everything, I can do nothing about it.

I can say, in addition, that I dislike too much the whitening of history; I have too great a loathing for racial propaganda, even knowingly to indulge in it. Moreover, the facts I have given have been culled nearly always from white writers, some of them very ancient, who related facts as they saw them, and who did not worship at the shrine of white imperialism, or did not think of the effect of what they said would have in later years.

To get those little known facts I have travelled tens of thousands of miles in many lands; consulted books and printed matter so vast in number that were I to try to say how many I would sound like a Munchausen; visited the leading museums of many of the civilized lands, and engaged in research in their libraries and ever going to great pains to get my facts as humanly correct as possible. In short, I felt I have looked into books and dug up buried knowledge that many college professors or doctors of philosophy do not know exist, because just as there is a life in the deeper depths of the ocean of which the average fisherman knows nothing, so there are depths in the ocean of research of which some of the most learned have never dreamed. For instance, it is estimated that in the National Library of France alone there are 8,000,000 books and pieces of printed matter. How much does the most educated man now alive know of the totality of knowledge in these books? Very, very little. One is ever learning. Truly, as Sir Isaac Newton once said, as he looked out on the ocean, that there he was picking up pebbles on the beach, as it were, while the vast ocean of unexplored knowledge lay before him.

Those who will forget their orthodoxy for a while and read my books might not find them so fantastic after all. And even should they reject them they might still profit to the extent of knowing the arguments on the other side and thus be able to refute them, not by denunciation, but in a manner more compatible with common sense.

I hasten to add that I am not accusing all the leading historians of catering to white imperialism. Some, as H. G. Wells, Hendrik Van Loon, and Arnold J. Toynbee, have made striking utterances against race prejudice. I believe that these latter accepted the popular white view of history without thinking that there was another side. As the New World was not on the charts of the scholars prior to Columbus so the achievements of the Negro and Negroid peoples were not on theirs.

Furthermore, there are white writers as Volney, Godfrey Higgins, Gerald Massey, Henry M. Stanley, David Livingstone, and Frobenius, greatest of all the Africanologists, who gave a perspective of Negro history that is increasingly found to be the truth. Why, we ask, were the works of these men by-passed by Wells and Toynbee? Were what they said of the Negro in history too fantastic to be considered?

For instance, Toynbee, who is one of the most unprejudiced of historians, attributes a civilization even to the Polynesian but denies any to the Negro. He says,

> "When we classify Mankind by color, the only one of the primary races...which has not made a creative contribution to any of our twenty-one civilizations is the Black Race...
>
> "The Black Race has not helped to create any civilization while the Polynesian White Race has helped to create one civilization, the Brown Race two, the Yellow Race three, the Red Race and the Nordic White Race four apiece, the Alpine White Race nine, and the Mediterranean White Race ten."[4]

What is the Polynesian White Race? There is no such people. The Polynesians, prior to the migration of white people to their islands, were chiefly of mixed Negro and Mongolian strain, with probably a slight admixture of white strain from Asiatic Russia. The Paris Museum of Ethnology in the Jardin des Plantes has what is, without a doubt, the most comprehensive collection of casts of Polynesian types from nearly all the islands, and they are shown to be what would be loosely called Negroes in the United States. Of course, much white "blood" has been mixed in with the South Sea islander since these casts were made over a century ago. Gobineau calls the Polynesians black and he was right at the time he wrote.

Let me express here once again my theory of so-called race. It is this: There is a single human race, which by imperceptible degrees shades from the blond of the Scandinavian to the blackness of the Senegambian or the Solomon Islander with the Sicilian or the Maltese somewhere in the centre. Some peoples as the Portuguese are nearer to the blond, while others as those of Mauretania or Southern India are nearer to the black, therefore, when I see anywhere, no matter where, an individual whose appearance is Negroid, that it, if his facial contour, his lips, nose, hair, present what a lifetime of observation has taught me are signs of Negro inheritance, I say that that person had a Negro ancestor near or distant according to the Negroid signs he presents. One's ancestry, I know, does not come out of the air, but is a reality of realities.

Similarly, if I see anywhere an individual whose appearance is Caucasian, that is, his lips, nose, hair, etc., present what a lifetime of observation has taught me are signs of "unmixed" Caucasian inheritance, I set that person down as white. If it is logical to speak of Caucasian strain among Negroes it is just as logical to speak of Negro strain among Caucasians. In this latter respect the Nazi anthropologists are at least right.

For instance, I once attended a reception given to an American Negro publisher and his wife in London. The latter was very fair and in her evening gown looked whiter in skin and more regular in profile than some of the Englishwomen present. If I attributed Negro ancestry to the publisher's wife, whose mother was undoubtedly colored, what should I have said of these Englishwomen who were more colored than she is in appearance?

One may sometimes find Negro ancestry where one least expects it. Take Colette, France's leading woman writer. She is blonde and to all appearances a European. Only a very experienced eye would discover signs of a strain not "pure" Nordic in her. Yet she had a Negro ancestor. When I said that in 1930, I was again charged with claiming all noted white persons as Negroes. But who said it first? Colette, herself.[5] The European, unlike the American, is not inclined to hide his Negro strain, if any. Also J. Larnac in his biography of her says that she inherited some Negro strain from her grandfather ("tenant de son grandpère un peu de sang coloré"). Her mother, "Madame Colette," he says, "is the daughter of Sophie Celeste Chatenay and a colored man with violet fingernails, who manufactured chocolates in Belgium, Henri Marie Landay."[6] If Colette, who is so blonde, has a Negro strain, I fail to see where the same would be impossible in the case of Beethoven, who did show Negro ancestry.

Again, there are those dear souls who will say that I exaggerate when I call these apparently white persons "Negroes." Would such kindly address themselves to the United States Census Bureau which decrees that if one has a known Negro ancestor, he is a Negro. The wife of the Negro editor mentioned above, was listed as a Negro. And the unwritten law is that if one is known to be of such ancestry, however distant, he is at once marked down. As long as this "one drop" theory remains refutation of alleged Negro inferiority must follow the arbitrary lines set by the Bureau of the Census.

However, no one can possibly know what so-called racial elements enter into his make-up. O. A. Wall estimated that the total number of one's ancestors since the time of Christ was around 144 quadrillions, and said that if one did not count the intermarriage of relatives the figure would be 288,230,376,151,711,742.[7] Thus since life goes back at least a million years, the ancestors of any individual would be as many as the sands of the sea or the stars of the firmament.

Talk of a pure race after that!

I, furthermore, visualize changes in human types as I visualize changes in cosmography, that is, as land that was once at the bottom of the sea now rears lofty peaks among the Alps and the Himalayas and vice versa; and as lands that were once tropical are now frigid, all due to the eternal change in Nature, so peoples who were once black are now white, and the opposite. Or to use a symbol: As parts of the earth are white or black or intermediate tints depending on whether such parts are facing, or are behind, or are sideways to the sun, so, in cosmic time it is with the coloring of the human race.

That humanity is one, that the earliest human beings were of a single color, is evident to even the Australian Bushman, supposedly the lowest in intelligence on earth. Dr. Berkeley Hill says they believe "that a white man is only one of themselves reborn." "Tumble-down black fellow, jump up

white fellow," is the common phrase among them "to express this belief," he says.

There are two principal sides to every question both of which when mixed together go to form the truth as oxygen and hydrogen to form water. My aim is to glean from both sides, using experience and an open mind as my guide. Because one is definitely opposed to our theory, he is not necessarily wrong, and because one favors us, neither does that make him right.

Everything that is, is truth by sheer force of its existence. Therefore by truth I mean that principle, which, at every moment, upholds the right of each individual, regardless of whoever or whatever he may be, to equality of dignity and opportunity, in short, equal justice.

As regards the term, Nature, I use it in no anthropomorphic sense. I do not think of it as a deity but as meaning the totality of all things—that unknown Force which is forever being unfolded, and within which lies the destiny of all things. The term, Nature, is inadequate of course, but since it is impossible to find a correct name that seems to me as good as any other.

I have also tried to get away from the crass materialism of Western civilization, which because of its eagerness to get hold of material things is forever rending itself and bringing untold misery on itself and all mankind. Three appallingly catastrophic wars in a quarter of a century!

Happily, there is a certain trend in the West today towards the animism of the East and of Africa, to explore into and to make one's self a part of the great inner forces of Nature. For the really cultured Western thinker of today, a bit of board is no longer just board but a segment of the universe seething with the life of the atom; trees are no longer just trees but breathing organisms, marvellous with their own psychology, their own loves and aversions; bees, insects, spiders, animalculae are discovered to have histories almost as intricate and hardly less interesting than those of man; cats, dogs, apes, elephants are discovered to have intelligence which has been cut out of the same cloth, so to speak, as man's. Though its reach is far lower, it operates essentially the same, all intelligence, human and animal, being but a part of the Great Whole.

Finally, as regards human beings, we are getting farther and farther away from the old "science" of physiognomy, and are appraising individuals, not on their looks, but on their acts. We are learning that to gauge intelligence by skull measurement, size of brain, skin color and hair are the sheerest infantilism, no matter how high the reputation of the scientist who advances such theories.

Let not those who think they are up be jealous of those who have been down and are rising. Let them rather rejoice that the human race, of which we are all part, is advancing. Let the thrill of feeling superior come not as the result of looking down on others but in seeing them rise, and in knowing that we are in a position to help them to do so.

To love one's fellow-man is the beginning of all true wisdom and the end of war, the greatest of all insanities.

In the better days that are coming it will be immaterial what color or what race of human beings did this or that great thing. This insanity of color fastened on us by the Virginia slaveholder and the New England slave-dealer will pass as other fantastic theories have passed. In the meantime the reciting of Negro accomplishment, past and present, will be necessary to counteract anti-Negro propaganda even as the reciting of Jewish accomplishment is a foil to anti-Semitism.

Notes

[1] *Studies in Shakespeare,* p. 71, 1869. Apropos of this a noted psychoanalyst once objected to my saying during a discussion period that when Shakespeare said, "Black men are pearls in beauteous ladies eyes," he actually meant black men. No, he said, there were no Negroes in England in Shakespeare's time, and he was positive about it. I informed him that there was not only Negro slavery in England at the time but that G. B. Harrison, an Elizabethan authority, thinks that Shakespeare, himself, had a Negro sweetheart. (For sources see *Sex and Race,* Vol. I, p. 201, 1941, and Vol. II, p. 400.)

[2] Donnelly, I. *Atlantis,* pp. 174–5, 1882.

[3] Julian Huxley and A. C. Haddon say, "It is asserted vociferously in certain quarters that the Nordic 'race' is gifted above all others with initiative and originality and that the great advances in civilization have been due to Nordic genius.

"What are the facts? The fundamental discoveries on which civilization is built are the art of writing, agriculture, the wheel and building in stone. All these appear to have originated in the Near East, among peoples who by no stretch of the imagination could be called Nordic or presumed to have but the faintest admixture of Nordic or proto-Nordic genes." (*We, Europeans,* p. 94, 1935.)

[4] Toynbee, A. J. *A Study of History,* Vol. I, p. 234, 1934.

[5] *La Maison de Claudine,* p. 99, 1922.

[6] *Colette,* pp. 11, 17, 18, 1927. See also *Sex and Race,* Vol. I, p. 240, 1941.

[7] *Sex and Sex Worship,* pp. 304–06, 1992. I do not see, however, where the intermarriage of relatives would affect the computation of one's ancestors except in the cases of those who are the product of incest, and that only in the case of where brother weds sister. Even if a man cohabited with his mother and had children by her as the ancient Britons used to do (at least that is what I infer from Caesar when he said that fathers and sons had the same wives), it seems to me something else would enter into the ancestry of the child. And there is no doubt of it when first cousin marries first cousin. The uncle or the aunt of the latter would have wed someone not related to the family, thus creating new combinations of genes. One has, it is true, only eight great-grandparents but we must not forget that behind each one of these stood enough millions of ancestors probably to go around the world several times. Truly, as Einstein has said, the number of one's ancestors is "astronomical."

Caesar's statement on incest among the ancient Britons reads, "Groups of ten or twelve men have wives together in common and particularly brothers along with brothers and fathers with sons." (*Gallic Wars,* Bk. V, 14.)

Why "Race" Makes No Scientific Sense: The Case of Africans and Native Americans

PRINCE BROWN, JR.

◇◆◈◆◇

Study Questions

1. Who is the "Father of Native American Slavery"?
2. Explain the following statement: "The history of the relationship between Africans and Native Americans is long, deeply intertwined, and largely unwritten."
3. Based on the information presented in "Why 'Race' Makes No Scientific Sense: The Case of African and Native Americans," why do you think scientists and other researchers have ignored the complex biological reality in favor of the idea that people can be classified in a single racial category?

In the futile efforts to create "racial" classification schemes, people born to the combination of African and Native American parents have been overlooked. Examining this particular case of the fusion of biology and culture assists understanding of human variation and makes clear that fixed, distinct, and exclusive categories for races never have existed and do not now exist.

Everywhere ships anchored in the Americas, Asia, Africa, and the various islands there was immediate exchange and sharing of human genes. In the case of Africans and Native Americans, this process was set in motion more than 500 years ago and continues unabated. Hence, many persons labeled African American have Native American ancestry, and the reverse is true. According to the African-American historian Carter G. Woodson, the history of the relationship between Africans and Native Americans is long, deeply intertwined, and largely unwritten (Woodson 1920, p. 45).

In this reading the term *Native American* shall be used to refer to the native inhabitants of North, Central, and South America and the Caribbean Islands. *African* shall be used to refer to people descendant from the African continent; *European* shall, in the same manner, be used to reference people from Europe.

Conventional history teaches that Native American–African contact commenced with Columbus's arrival in the Americas in 1492. We may start then by calling attention to the physical characteristics of the Spanish and Portuguese sailors making up the crews of the first voyages of exploration (1492–1520). Many of them can be labeled "mulatto," which, according to Forbes (1993, p. 140), may have derived from the Arabic, translated as half-caste, mestizo, hybrid, half-breed, or half-blood (that is, any person with one Arabic and one non-Arabic parent). The European inhabitants of Spain and

Portugal had known many dark-complected North African Moors (CKSSG 1989, p. 403), as well as Africans from south of the Sahara as conquerors for more than 800 years. Thus, the first contact between Native Americans and part-Africans (Portuguese and Spanish sailors) occurred in the Caribbean with the arrival of Columbus's ships. It is safe to assume that some of the sailors may have been unmixed Africans as well since many were brought to Spain and Portugal as slaves after about 1440.

Immediately upon the arrival of Spanish ships in the Caribbean the enslavement of Native Americans began. Columbus's disdain of the natives, his disregard for their humanity, and his perception that their mere existence signaled their availability as objects to be used in furthering his ambitions earned him the title "Father of Native American Slavery." It was he who suggested to the Spanish monarchs that the docile Native Americans who welcomed his crew would make ideal slaves (Forbes 1993, pp. 21–25). It is not well known that thousands of Native Americans were shipped to Europe as slaves and in subsequent years served as soldiers for the Portuguese and Spanish in their wars for control of the West African slave trade (Forbes 1993). Thus, African–Native American interbreeding occurred in Europe and Africa as well as in the Americas.

It was, on the other hand, Columbus's contemporary Bartolome de la Casas whose concern over the high rate of death among enslaved Native Americans led to his suggestion that Africans be used in that capacity instead. La Casas was a priest who observed firsthand the appalling treatment of Native Americans.

We know that almost as soon as they arrived, Africans started to run away and join Native Americans (Forbes 1993), establishing joint communities (Katz 1986; Forbes

1993) and independent ones (Campbell 1990). They clearly preferred to face the unknown rather than live as slaves. These runaways were called "Cimarrons" in South America and "Maroons" in the Caribbean. Women of Native American ancestry were the first mothers of children born to European and African men in the initial phase of settlement (Forbes 1993), because there were no European women and few African women present. As the slave trade grew in scope, more and more African women were brought in (Rogers 1984). It was not until Europeans were able to create secure zones containing permanent housing that they were joined by sizable numbers of women from Europe.

Forbes argues that, given the initial absence of European women and the fact that the number of imported slaves continued to grow, people of African and Native American descent made up the majority of the population in the colonial territories (Forbes 1993). The situation was only slightly different in the United States. Relative to the rest of the Americas, it was settled much later and European women were among the early colonists.

Keep in mind that many of the first African slaves brought in to the colonies that later became the United States had been slaves in the Caribbean. Therefore, many were already mixed biologically with Native Americans. As the number of African slaves continued to grow, population ratios changed quickly. In fact, by 1765 a Massachusetts census showed more Africans than Native Americans in some counties. The increase in the slave population led to more runaways and, consequently, increased absorption of Native Americans into the African population.

Africans took advantage of the presence of nearby Native American settlements as primary destinations when they decided to run away from their owners. This process started very early and continued until the end of slavery. It does not appear that Native Americans made any strong effort to return slaves, and Europeans were apparently too busy establishing the colony to invest much time in slave retrieval. Massachusetts passed the first laws enslaving Africans (initially they were free persons) between 1639 and 1661. This followed the failed effort to enslave Native Americans, who were held in joint bondage with Africans for a while. Prior to the passage of laws enslaving them, Africans (the majority of whom were males) could, of their own volition, choose to join Native American communities. It is logical to assume that they would have taken wives primarily from the Native American community.

Native Americans and Africans shared a number of social traits and values that facilitated their absorption into each other's culture. The recognition of kinship traced matrilineally (on the female side) and the practice of polygyny (multiple wives) constituted common forms of social organization. Other shared views centered on a spirituality that celebrated the mutual dependency of humans and animals. This belief was manifested through the social structure known as the clan and represented by an animal icon. Africans and Native Americans possessed a reverence for the earth, which they considered sacred. These shared traits made the social acceptance of one group by the other easier than it otherwise might have been. Also helpful was the fact that the subtropical setting, as found in the southeastern United States, was one with which both groups were familiar.

Africans brought to Native American communities an intimate knowledge of Europeans, skilled farming techniques acquired in their former slave roles, and a spirit of resistance to domination, evidenced by their status as runaways. They emerged as important political and military leaders in the communities in which they settled (Katz 1986). Europeans frequently expressed fear of African-inspired revolts with Native American support (Porter 1932, Forbes 1993, Mullin 1992). These hybrid communities were the centers of the most successful defenses against European domination. The Seminoles of Florida provide an outstanding example of successful autonomy. This group of Africans and Native Americans engaged in protracted military struggle with the United States army. Though outnumbered and less well armed, they defended their community with tenacity to avoid being resettled in Indian Territory (what later became Oklahoma). After the Civil War, many Seminoles served as guards on the Mexican border and as scouts for the same army that they had fought in Florida.

The widespread interbreeding between Native Americans and Africans led to a number of efforts by writers and legislators to develop terms that specify different biological combinations. But, in fact, terms like *mulatto, mustee,* and *colored* (terms that were later adopted by social scientists) were not used consistently within or between societies. They carried no more specificity than the expression "people of color," which has been applied to Native American–African, European-African, European–Native American, and Asian peoples. *Mustee* evolved in the United States to refer to persons of African–Native American ancestry (Johnston 1929).

In South America the terms *mulatto, zambo,* and *zambaigo* have been used for the same purpose at different times (Forbes 1993). Likewise, the term *negro* has not always been used to refer only to African ancestry. Therefore, it cannot be assumed that the literature on the subject specifying ancestry carries the definition assigned by the reader. Paul Cuffee, a well-known "free person of color," is often presented as being of African extraction when, in fact, he is of African–Native American ancestry. Off the reservation, persons of African–Native American ancestry are commonly perceived and spoken of as African. On the reservation, those same persons are Native Americans.

Classification laws determining the legal status of people of color changed with each event that Europeans defined as a threat. Depending on location and time, a person could be legally free if born to a Native American mother, or a slave if born to an African mother. Thus, it was an advantage for persons so labeled to be born to a Native American mother.

On the several occasions between 1869 and 1902 when the state of Massachusetts reallocated lands assigned to Native Americans, many persons who were compensated with small pensions were more African than Native American in appearance (Woodson 1920, p. 57). Katz reports the existence of "Black Indian" societies (1986, p. 129) in almost every seaboard state between the American Revolution and the Civil War.

Europeans in King William County, Virginia, petitioned the legislature to take away the land deeded to the Pamunkies because "these people had become Negro and hence had no claim to the rights of the Indians" (Johnston 1929, p. 29). The charge against another group of Native Americans, the Gingaskin, in 1784 was that their "land is at present an asylum for free Negroes and other disorderly persons, who build huts thereon and pillage and destroy the timber without restraint to the great inconvenience of the honest inhabitants of the vicinity, who have ever considered it a den of thieves and a nuisance to the neighborhood" (p. 32). The Gingaskin were successfully removed from their lands by a court order in 1812.

Legislative actions demonstrate but one of the ways in which "racial" classification schemes are used to subordinate less powerful groups. This pattern of removing Native Americans from land formally ceded to them by treaty was one that was repeated many times in the United States.

The slave-based colonial culture literally pushed Africans and Native Americans together. In fact, some Native American groups adopted the European practice of enslaving Africans. But if benign slavery were ever the case in the United States, it occurred among the Five Civilized Tribes (so labeled because of their adoption of European customs) of the Southeast. The Cherokee, Chickasaw, Choctaw, Creek, and Seminole were centered in Florida, Georgia, Alabama, and Mississippi. The first two did display some color-prejudice toward Africans. For the most part, however, researchers are agreed that relations between these masters and slaves involved minimum supervision and often approached equality as they struggled against a common enemy.

The emulation of the European practice of slavery did not prevent the removal of these groups, with their slaves, to Indian Territory (which later became Oklahoma) after the passage of the Indian Removal Act of 1830. With the implementation of this act (during which more than 60 different Native American ethnic groups were forced to move), Oklahoma became known as an "Indian" state (Strickland, 1980). Perhaps a more accurate description may be that it became an "Indian and African" state. Further north and west (Minnesota) some of the first pioneers to live with and marry Native Americans were of African descent (Katz 1987).

The extensive biological mixing of Africans and Native Americans clearly demonstrates the compatibility of human genes deriving from groups and individuals where some aspects of their physical appearance are different. The process of absorption of Native Americans into the African population largely accounts for the fact that there is such a small population of people labeled Native Americans on the East Coast of the United States. Jack D. Forbes contends that the view that indigenous peoples in the Americas were replaced [killed off or died out] and the area repopulated by Europeans and Africans is erroneous. Rather, he suggests that

> [Native] American survivors and African survivors (because huge numbers of Africans also died in the process) have merged together to create the basic modern populations of much of the Greater Caribbean and adjacent mainland regions. (1993, p. 270)

The case of African and Native Americans makes clear that the label *race,* when assigned to a particular set of observable human features, is socially derived. The categories widely used to denote "race" are inappropriate since they do not capture "real" biological distinctions (Levin, 1991) but rather reflect social and cultural conventions. The point is that it is not possible to identify biological ancestry simply by referencing physical features. Indeed, from the perspective of evolutionary biology we are all Africans—sharing common ancestors who evolved first in Africa.

References

Campbell, Mavis. 1990. *The Maroons of Jamaica 1655–1796.* Trenton, NJ: Africa World Press.

CKSSG: S. Chodorow, M. Knox, C. Schirokauer, J. Strayer, and H. Gatzke. 1989. *The Mainstream of Civilization to 1715.* Orlando, FL: Harcourt Brace Jovanovich.

Forbes, Jack D. 1993. *Africans and Native Americans.* Urbana and Chicago: University of Illinois Press.

hooks, bell. 1992. *Black Looks: Race and Representation.* Boston: South End Press.

Johnston, James H. 1929. "Documentary Evidence of the Relations of Negroes and Indians." *Journal of Negro History* Vol. 14 (1).

Katz, William L. 1986. *Black Indians.* New York: Macmillan.

———. 1987. *The Black West.* Seattle, WA: Open Hand Publishing.

Levin, Michael D. 1991. "Population Differentiation and Racial Classification." *Encyclopedia of Human Biology* Vol. 6. Academic Press.

Mullin, Michael. 1992. *Africa in America.* Chicago: University of Illinois Press.

Porter, Kenneth W. 1932. "Relations Between Negroes and Indians Within the Present Limits of the United States." *Journal of Negro History* Vol. XVII, No. 3 (July).

Rogers, J. A. 1984. *Sex and Race,* Vol. 2. St. Petersburg, FL: Helga M. Rogers.

Strickland, Rennard. 1980. *The Indians in Oklahoma.* Norman, OK, and London: University of Oklahoma Press.

Woodson, Carter G. 1920. "The Relations of Negroes and Indians in Massachusetts." *Journal of Negro History* Vol. 5 (1).

Taking Back the Center

Trina Grillo and Stephanie M. Wildman

Study Questions
1. What is the "center-stage" problem?
2. What does "stealing the center" mean? Give examples.

White supremacy creates in whites the expectation that issues of concern to them will be central in every discourse. Analogies serve to perpetuate this expectation of centrality. The center-stage problem occurs because dominant group members are already accustomed to being on center-stage. They have been treated that way by society; it feels natural, comfortable, and in the order of things.

The harms of discrimination include not only the easily identified disadvantages of the victims (such as exclusion from housing and jobs) and the stigma imposed by the dominant culture, but also the advantages given to those who are not its victims. The white, male, heterosexual societal norm is privileged in such a way that its privilege is rendered invisible. As Kimberlé Crenshaw explained:

> According to the dominant view, a discriminator treats all people within a race or sex category similarly. Any significant experiential or statistical variation within this group suggests...that the group is not being discriminated against....Race and sex, moreover, become significant only when they operate to explicitly *disadvantage* the victims; because the *privileging* of whiteness or maleness is implicit, it is generally not perceived at all.[1]

Because whiteness is the norm, it is easy to forget that it is not the only perspective. Thus, members of dominant groups assume that their perceptions are the pertinent perceptions, that their problems are the problems that need to be addressed, and that in discourse they should be the speaker rather than the listener.[2] Part of being a member of a privileged group is being the center and the subject of all inquiry, in which people of color or other non-privileged groups are the objects.[3]

So strong is this expectation of holding center-stage that even when a time and place are specifically designated for members of a non-privileged group to be central, members of the dominant group will often attempt to take back the pivotal focus. They are stealing the center[4]—usually with a complete lack of self-consciousness.[5]

This phenomenon occurred at the annual meeting of Law and Society, where three scholars, all people of color, were invited to speak to the plenary session about how universities might become truly multicultural. Even before the dialogue began, the views of many members of the organization were apparent by their presence or absence at the session. The audience included nearly every person of color who was attending the meeting, yet many whites chose not to attend.

When people who are not regarded as entitled to the center move into it, however briefly, they are viewed as usurpers. One reaction of the group temporarily deprived of the center is to make sure that nothing remains for the perceived usurpers to be in the center of. Thus, the whites who did not attend the plenary session, but who would have attended had there been more traditional (i.e., white) speakers, did so in part because they were exercising their privilege not to think in terms of race, and in part because they resented the "out groups" having the center.

Another tactic used by the dominant group is to steal back the center, using guerilla tactics where necessary. For example, during a talk devoted to the integration of multicultural materials into the core curriculum, a white man got up from the front row and walked noisily to the rear of the room. He then paced the room in a distracting fashion and finally returned to his seat. During the question period he was the first to rise, leaping to his feet to ask a lengthy, rambling, question about how multicultural materials could be added to university curricula without disturbing the "canon"—the exact subject of the talk he had just, apparently, not listened to.

The speaker answered politely and explained how he had assigned a Navajo creation myth to accompany St. Augustine, which highlighted Augustine's paganism and resulted in each reading enriching the other. He refrained, however, from calling attention to the questioner's rude behavior during the meeting, to his asking the already-answered question, or to his presumption that the material the questioner saw as most relevant to his own life was central and "canonized," while all other reading was peripheral, and, hence, dispensable.

Analogies offer protection for the traditional center. At another gathering of law professors—the annual meeting of the American Association of Law Schools—issues of racism, sexism, and homophobia were the focus of the plenary session for the first time in the organization's history. Again at this session, the number of white males present was far fewer than would ordinarily attend such a session. After moving presentations by an African-American woman, an Hispanic man, and a gay white man who each opened their hearts on these subjects, a question and dialogue period began.

The first speaker to rise was a white woman, who, after saying that she did not mean to change the topic, said that she wanted to discuss another sort of oppression—that of law professors in the less elite schools. As professors from what is perceived by some as a less-than-elite school, we agree that the topic is important and it would have interested us at another time, on another day. But this questioner had succeeded in depriving the other issues of time devoted (after much struggle) specifically to them, and turned the spotlight once again onto her own concerns. She did this, we believe, not out of malice, but because she too had become a victim of analogical thinking.

The problem of taking back the center exists apart from the issue of analogies; it will be with us as long as any group expects, and is led to expect, to be constantly the center of attention.

Notes

[1] Crenshaw, *supra* note 7, at 150–51.

[2] *See* Wildman, *The Question of Silence: Techniques to Ensure Full Class Participation,* 38 J. LEGAL EDUC. 147, 149–50 (1988).

[3] *See* HOOKS, *supra* note 3, at 43 (discussing liberation struggles initiated when people seen as objects "assert that they are subjects").

[4] Parents of young children who try to have a telephone conversation will easily recognize this phenomenon. At the sound of the parent's voice on the phone, the child materializes from the far reaches of the house to demand attention.

[5] For an interesting discussion of how law contributes to our vision of reality and our self-consciousness, *see* Reich, *Law and Consciousness,* 10 CARDOZO L. REV. 77 (1988).

PLESSY V. FERGUSON
May 18, 1896, 163 U.S. 537 (1896)

THE U.S. SUPREME COURT

Study Questions
1. One of Plessy's attorneys, Albion Tourgee, argued "Probably most white persons if given a choice, would prefer death to life in the United States *as colored persons.*" What does this say about the status "white" relative to the status "color/black" in the United States in 1896?
2. What do you think other people should think and understand when they learn that Plessy's African heritage (physically he appeared to be white) had to be brought to the attention of the court?

MR. JUSTICE BROWN, after stating the case, delivered the opinion of the court.

This case turns upon the constitutionality of an act of the General Assembly of the State of Louisiana, passed in 1890, providing for separate railway carriages for the white and colored races. Acts 1890, No. 111, p. 152.

The first section of the statute enacts "that all railway companies carrying passengers in their coaches in this State, shall provide equal but separate accommodations for the white, and colored races, by providing two or more passenger coaches for each passenger train, or by dividing the passenger coaches by a partition so as to secure separate accommodations: *Provided,* That this section shall not be construed to apply to street railroads. No person or persons, shall be admitted to occupy seats in coaches, other than, the ones, assigned, to them on account of the race they belong to."

By the second section it was enacted "that the officers of such passenger trains shall have power and are hereby required to assign each passenger to the coach or compartment used for the race to which such passenger belongs; any passenger insisting on going into a coach or compartment to which by race he does not belong, shall be liable to a fine of twenty-five dollars, or in lieu thereof to imprisonment for a period of not more than twenty days in the parish prison, and any officer of any railroad insisting on assigning a passenger to a coach or compartment other than the one set aside for the race to which said passenger belongs, shall be liable to a fine of twenty-five dollars, or in lieu thereof to imprisonment for a period of not more than twenty days in the parish prison; and should any passenger refuse to occupy the coach or compartment to which he or she is assigned by the officer of such railway, said officer shall have power to refuse to carry such passenger on his train, and for such refusal neither he nor the railway company which he represents shall be liable for damages in any of the courts of this State."

The third section provides penalties for the refusal or neglect of the officers, directors, conductors and employés of railway companies to comply with the act, with a proviso that "nothing in this act shall be construed as applying to nurses attending children of the other race." The fourth section is immaterial.

The information filed in the criminal District Court charged in substance that Plessy, being a passenger between two stations within the State of Louisiana, was assigned by officers of the company to the coach used for the race to which he belonged, but he insisted upon going into a coach used by the race to which he did not belong. Neither in the information nor plea was his particular race or color averred.

The petition for the writ of prohibition averred that petitioner was seven eighths Caucasian and one eighth African blood; that the mixture of colored blood was not discernible in him, and that he was entitled to every right, privilege and immunity secured to citizens of the United States of the white race; and that, upon such theory, he took possession of a vacant seat in a coach where passengers of the white race were accommodated, and was ordered by the conductor to vacate said coach and take a seat in another assigned to persons of the colored race, and having refused to comply with such demand he was forcibly ejected with the aid of a police officer, and imprisoned in the parish jail to answer a charge of having violated the above act.

The constitutionality of this act is attacked upon the ground that it conflicts both with the Thirteenth Amendment of the Constitution, abolishing slavery, and the Fourteenth Amendment, which prohibits certain restrictive legislation on the part of the States.

1. That it does not conflict with the Thirteenth Amendment, which abolished slavery and involuntary servitude, except as a punishment for crime, is too clear for argument. Slavery implies involuntary servitude—a state of bondage; the ownership of mankind as a chattel, or at least the control of the labor and services of one man for the benefit of another, and the absence of a legal right to the disposal of his own person, property and services. This amendment was said in the *Slaughter-house cases,* 16 Wall. 35, to have been intended primarily to abolish slavery, as it had been previously known in this country, and that it equally forbade Mexican peonage or the Chinese coolie trade, when they amounted to slavery or involuntary servitude, and that the use of the word "servitude" was intended to prohibit the use of all forms of involuntary slavery, of whatever class or name. It was intimated, however, in that case that this amendment was regarded by the statesmen of that day as insufficient to protect the colored race from certain laws which had been enacted in the Southern States, imposing upon the colored race onerous disabilities and burdens, and curtailing their rights in the pursuit of life, liberty and property to such an extent that their freedom was of little value; and that the Fourteenth Amendment was devised to meet this exigency.

So, too, in the *Civil Rights cases,* 109 U.S. 3, 24, it was said that the act of a mere individual, the owner of an inn, a public conveyance or place of amusement, refusing accommodations to colored people, cannot be justly regarded as imposing any badge of slavery or servitude upon the applicant, but only as involving an ordinary civil injury, properly cognizable by the laws of the State, and presumably subject to redress by those laws until the contrary appears. "It would be running the slavery argument into the ground," said Mr. Justice Bradley, "to make it apply to every act of discrimination which a person may see fit to make as to the guests he will entertain, or as to the people he will take into his coach or cab or car, or admit to his concert or theatre, or deal with in other matters of intercourse or business."

A statute which implies merely a legal distinction between the white and colored races—a distinction which is founded in the color of the two races, and which must always exist so long as white men are distinguished from the other race by color— has no tendency to destroy the legal equality of the two races, or reestablish a state of involuntary servitude. Indeed, we do not understand that the Thirteenth Amendment is strenuously relied upon by the plaintiff in error in this connection.

2. By the Fourteenth Amendment, all persons born or naturalized in the United States, and subject to the jurisdiction thereof, are made citizens of the United States and of the State wherein they reside; and the States are forbidden from making or enforcing any law which shall abridge the privileges or immunities of citizens of the United States, or shall deprive any person of life, liberty or property without due process of law, or deny to any person within their jurisdiction the equal protection of the laws.

The proper construction of this amendment was first called to the attention of this court in the *Slaughter-house cases,* 16 Wall. 36, which involved, however, not a question of race, but one of exclusive privileges. The case did not call for any expression of opinion as to the exact rights it was intended to secure to the colored race, but it was said generally that its main purpose was to establish the citizenship of the negro; to give definitions of citizenship of the United States and of the States, and to protect from the hostile legislation of the States the privileges and immunities of citizens of

the United States, as distinguished from those of citizens of the States.

The object of the amendment was undoubtedly to enforce the absolute equality of the two races before the law, but in the nature of things it could not have been intended to abolish distinctions based upon color, or to enforce social, as distinguished from political, equality, or a commingling of the two races upon terms unsatisfactory to either. Laws permitting, and even requiring, their separation in places where they are liable to be brought into contact do not necessarily imply the inferiority of either race to the other, and have been generally, if not universally, recognized as within the competency of the state legislatures in the exercise of their police power. The most common instance of this is connected with the establishment of separate schools for white and colored children, which has been held to be a valid exercise of the legislative power even by courts of States where the political rights of the colored race have been longest and most earnestly enforced.

One of the earliest of these cases is that of *Roberts* v. *City of Boston,* 5 Cush. 198, in which the Supreme Judicial Court of Massachusetts held that the general school committee of Boston had power to make provision for the instruction of colored children in separate schools established exclusively for them, and to prohibit their attendance upon the other schools....

Similar laws have been enacted by Congress under its general power of legislation over the District of Columbia, Rev. Stat. D.C. §§ 281, 282, 283, 310, 319, as well as by the legislatures of many of the States, and have been generally, if not uniformly, sustained by the courts. *State* v. *McCann,* 21 Ohio St. 198; *Lehew* v. *Brummell,* 15 S. W. Rep. 765; *Ward* v. *Flood,* 48 California, 36; *Bertonneau* v. *School Directors,* 3 Woods, 177;

People v. *Gallagber,* 93 N.Y. 438; *Cory* v. *Carter,* 48 Indiana, 327; *Dawson* v. *Lee,* 83 Kentucky, 49.

Laws forbidding the intermarriage of the two races may be said in a technical sense to interfere with the freedom of contract, and yet have been universally recognized as within the police power of the State. *State* v. *Gibson,* 36 Indiana, 389.

The distinction between laws interfering with the political equality of the negro and those requiring the separation of the two races in schools, theatres and railway carriages has been frequently drawn by this court. Thus in *Strauder* v. *West Virginia,* 100 U.S. 303, it was held that a law of West Virginia limiting to white male persons, 21 years of age and citizens of the State, the right to sit upon juries, was a discrimination which implied a legal inferiority in civil society, which lessened the security of the right of the colored race, and was a step toward reducing them to a condition of servility. Indeed, the right of a colored man that, in the selection of jurors to pass upon his life, liberty and property, there shall be no exclusion of his race, and no discrimination against them because of color, has been asserted in a number of cases. *Virginia* v. *Rives,* 100 U.S. 313; *Neal* v. *Delaware,* 103 U.S. 370; *Bush* v. *Kentucky,* 107 U.S. 110; *Gibson* v. *Mississippi,* 162 U.S. 565. So, where the laws of a particular locality or the charter of a particular railway corporation has provided that no person shall be excluded from the cars on account of color, we have held that this meant that persons of color should travel in the same car as white ones, and that the enactment was not satisfied by the company's providing cars assigned exclusively to people of color, though they were as good as those which they assigned exclusively to white persons. *Railroad Company* v. *Brown,* 17 Wall. 445.

Upon the other hand, where a statute of Louisiana required those engaged in the transportation of passengers among the States to give to all persons travelling within that State, upon vessels employed in that business, equal rights and privileges in all parts of the vessel, without distinction on account of race or color, and subjected to an action for damages the owner of such a vessel, who excluded colored passengers on account of their color from the cabin set aside by him for the use of whites, it was held to be so far as it applied to interstate commerce, unconstitutional and void. *Hall* v. *De Cuir,* 95 U.S. 485. The court in this case, however, expressly disclaimed that it had anything whatever to do with the statute as a regulation of internal commerce, or affecting anything else than commerce among the States.

In the *Civil Rights* case, 109 U.S. 3, it was held that an act of Congress, entitling all persons within the jurisdiction of the United States to the full and equal enjoyment of the accommodations, advantages, facilities and privileges of inns, public conveyances, on land or water, theatres and other places of public amusement, and made applicable to citizens of every race and color, regardless of any previous condition of servitude, was unconstitutional and void, upon the ground that the Fourteenth Amendment was prohibitory upon the States only, and the legislation authorized to be adopted by Congress for enforcing it was not direct legislation on matters respecting which the States were prohibited from making or enforcing certain laws, or doing certain acts, but was corrective legislation, such as might be necessary or proper for counteracting and redressing the effect of such laws or acts. In delivering the opinion of the court Mr. Justice Bradley observed that the Fourteenth Amendment "does not invest Congress with power to legislate upon subjects that are within the domain of state legislation; but to provide modes of relief against state legislation, or state action, of the kind referred to. It does not authorize Congress to create a code of municipal law for the regulation of private rights; but to provide modes of redress against the operation of state laws, and the action of state officers, executive or judicial, when these are subversive of the fundamental rights specified in the amendment. Positive rights and privileges are undoubtedly secured by the Fourteenth Amendment; but they are secured by way of prohibition against state laws and state proceedings affecting those rights and privileges, and by power given to Congress to legislate for the purpose of carrying such prohibition into effect; and such legislation must necessarily be predicated upon such supposed state laws or state proceedings, and be directed to the correction of their operation and effect."

Much nearer, and, indeed, almost directly in point, is the case of the *Louisville, New Orleans & c. Railway* v. *Mississippi,* 133 U.S. 587, wherein the railway company was indicted for a violation of a statute of Mississippi, enacting that all railroads carrying passengers should provide equal, but separate, accommodations for the white and colored races, by providing two or more passenger cars for each passenger train, or by dividing the passenger cars by a partition, so as to secure separate accommodations. The case was presented in a different aspect from the one under consideration, inasmuch as it was an indictment against the railway company for failing to provide the separate accommodations, but the question considered was the constitutionality of the law. In that case, the Supreme Court of Mississippi, 66 Mississippi, 662, had held that the statute applied solely to commerce within the State, and, that being the construction of the state statute by its highest court, was accepted as conclusive. "If it be a matter," said the court, p. 591, "respecting commerce wholly within a State, and not interfering with commerce between the States, then, obviously, there is no violation of the commerce clause of the Federal Constitution....No question arises under this section, as to the power of the State to separate in different compartments interstate passengers, or affect, in any manner, the privileges and rights of such passengers. All that we can consider is, whether the State has the power to require that railroad trains within her limits shall have separate accommodations for the two races; that affecting only commerce within the State is no invasion of the power given to Congress by the commerce clause."

A like course of reasoning applies to the case under consideration, since the Supreme Court of Louisiana in the case of the *State ex rel. Abbott* v. *Hicks, Judge, et al.,* 44 La. Ann. 770, held that the statute in question did not apply to interstate passengers, but was confined in its application to passengers travelling exclusively within the borders of the State. The case was decided largely upon the authority of *Railway Co.* v. *State,* 66 Mississippi, 662, and affirmed by this court in 133 U.S. 87. In the present case no question of interference with interstate commerce can possibly arise, since the East Louisiana Railway appears to have been purely a local line, with both its termini within the State of Louisiana. Similar statutes for the separation of the two races upon public conveyances were held to be constitutional in *West Chester &c. Railroad* v. *Miles,* 55 Penn. St. 209; *Day* v. *Owen,* 5 Michigan, 520; *Chicago & c. Railway* v. *Williams,* 55 Illinois, 185; *Chesapeake &c. Railroad* v. *Wells,* 85 Tennessee, 613;

Memphis &c. Railroad v. *Benson,* 85 Tennessee, 627; *The Sue,* 22 Fed. Rep. 843; *Logwood* v. *Memphis &c. Railroad,* 23 Fed. Rep. 318; *McGuinn* v. *Forbes,* 37 Fed. Rep. 639; *People* v. *King,* 18 N.E. Rep. 245; *Houck* v. *South Pac. Railway,* 38 Fed. Rep. 226; *Heard* v. *Georgia Railroad Co.,* 3 Int. Com. Com'n, 111; S.C., 1 Ibid. 428.

While we think the enforced separation of the races, as applied to the internal commerce of the State, neither abridges the privileges or immunities of the colored man, deprives him of his property without due process of law, nor denies him the equal protection of the laws, within the meaning of the Fourteenth Amendment, we are not prepared to say that the conductor, in assigning passengers to the coaches according to their race, does not act at his peril, or that the provision of the second section of the act, that denies to the passenger compensation in damages for a refusal to receive him into the coach in which he properly belongs, is a valid exercise of the legislative power. Indeed, we understand it to be conceded by the State's attorney, that such part of the act as exempts from liability the railway company and its officers is unconstitutional. The power to assign to a particular coach obviously implies the power to determine to which race the passenger belongs, as well as the power to determine who, under the laws of the particular State, is to be deemed a white, and who a colored person. This question, though indicated in the brief of the plaintiff in error, does not properly arise upon the record in this case, since the only issue made is as to the unconstitutionality of the act, so far as it requires the railway to provide separate accommodations, and the conductor to assign passengers according to their race.

It is claimed by the plaintiff in error that, in any mixed community, the reputation of belonging to the dominant race, in this instance the white race, is *property,* in the same sense that a right of action, or of inheritance, is property. Conceding this to be so, for the purposes of this case, we are unable to see how this statute deprives him of, or in any way affects his right to, such property. If he be a white man and assigned to a colored coach, he may have his action for damages against the company for being deprived of his so-called property. Upon the other hand, if he be a colored man and be so assigned, he has been deprived of no property, since his is not lawfully entitled to the reputation of being a white man.

In this connection, it is also suggested by the learned counsel for the plaintiff in error that the same argument that will justify the state legislature in requiring railways to provide separate accommodations for the two races will also authorize them to require separate cars to be provided for people whose hair is of a certain color, or who are aliens, or who belong to certain nationalities, or to enact laws requiring colored people to walk upon one side of the street, and white people upon the other, or requiring white men's houses to be painted white, and colored men's black, or their vehicles or business signs to be of different colors, upon the theory that one side of the street is as good as the other, or that a house or vehicle of one color is as good as one of another color. The reply to all this is that every exercise of the police power must be reasonable, and extend only to such laws as are enacted in good faith for the promotion for the public good, and not for the annoyance or oppression of a particular class. Thus in *Yick Wo* v. *Hopkins,* 118 U.S. 356, it was held by this court that a municipal ordinance of the city of San Francisco, to regulate the carrying on of public laundries within the limits of the municipality, violated the provisions of the Constitution of the United States, if it conferred upon the municipal authorities arbitrary power, at their own will, and without regard to discretion, in the legal sense of the term, to give or withhold consent as to persons or places, without regard to the competency of the persons applying, or the propriety of the places selected for the carrying on of the business. It was held to be a covert attempt on the part of the municipality to make an arbitrary and unjust discrimination against the Chinese race. While this was the case of a municipal ordinance, a like principle has been held to apply to acts of a state legislature passed in the exercise of the police power. *Railroad Company* v. *Husen,* 95 U.S. 465; *Louisville & Nashville Railroad* v. *Kentucky,* 161 U.S. 677, and cases cited on p. 700; *Daggett* v. *Hudson,* 43 Ohio St. 548; *Capen* v. *Foster,* 12 Pick. 485; *State ex rel. Wood* v. *Baker,* 38 Wisconsin, 71; *Monroe* v. *Collins,* 17 Ohio St. 665; *Hulseman* v. *Rems,* 41 Penn. St. 396; *Orman* v. *Riley,* 15 California, 48.

So far, then, as a conflict with the Fourteenth Amendment is concerned, the case reduces itself to the question whether the statue of Louisiana is a reasonable regulation, and with respect to this there must necessarily be a large discretion on the part of the legislature. In determining the question of reasonableness it is at liberty to act with reference to the established usages, customs and traditions of the people, and with a view to the promotion of their comfort, and the preservation of the public peace and good order. Gauged by this standard, we cannot say that a law which authorizes or even requires the separation of the two races in public conveyances is unreasonable, or more obnoxious to the Fourteenth Amendment than the acts of Congress requiring separate schools for colored children in the District of Columbia, the constitutionality of which does not seem to have been questioned, or the corresponding acts of state legislatures.

We consider the underlying fallacy of the plaintiff's argument to consist in the assumption that the enforced separation of the two races stamps the colored race with a badge of inferiority. If this be so, it is not by reason of anything found in the act, but solely because the colored race chooses to put that construction upon it. The argument necessarily assumes that if, as has been more than once the case, and is not unlikely to be so again, the colored race should become the dominant power in the state legislature, and should enact a law in precisely similar terms, it would thereby relegate the white race to an inferior position. We imagine that the white race, at least, would not acquiesce in this assumption. The argument also assumes that social prejudices may be overcome by legislation, and that equal rights cannot be secured to the negro except by an enforced commingling of the two races. We cannot accept this proposition. If the two races are to meet upon terms of social equality, it must be the result of natural affinities, a mutual appreciation of each other's merits and a voluntary consent of individuals. As was said by the Court of Appeals of New York in *People* v. *Gallagher,* 93 N.Y. 438, 448, "this end can neither be accomplished nor promoted by laws which conflict with the general sentiment of the community upon whom they are designed to operate. When the government, therefore, has secured to each of its citizens equal rights before the law and opportunities for improvement and progress, it has accomplished the end for which it was organized and performed all of the functions respecting social advantages with which it is endowed." Legislation is powerless to eradicate racial instincts or to abolish distinctions based upon physical differences, and the attempt to do so can only result in accentuating the difficulties of the present situation. If the civil and political rights of both races be equal one cannot be inferior to the other civilly or politically. If one race be inferior to the other socially, the Constitution of the United States cannot put them upon the same plane.

It is true that the question of the proportion of colored blood necessary to constitute a colored person, as distinguished from a white person, is one upon which there is a difference of opinion in the different States, some holding that any visible admixture of black blood stamps the person as belonging to the colored race (*State* v. *Chavers,* 5 Jones, [N.C.] 1, p. 11); others that it depends upon the preponderance of blood (*Gray* v. *State,* 4 Ohio, 354; *Monroe* v. *Collins,* 17 Ohio St. 665); and still others that the predominance of white blood must only be in the proportion of three fourths (*People* v. *Dean,* 14 Michigan, 406; *Jones* v. *Commonwealth,* 80 Virginia, 538). But these are questions to be determined under the laws of each State and are not properly put in issue in this case. Under the allegations of his petition it may undoubtedly become a question of importance whether, under the laws of Louisiana, the petitioner belongs to the white or colored race.

The judgment of the court below is, therefore, *Affirmed.*

MR. JUSTICE HARLAN dissenting.

By the Louisiana statute the validity of which is here involved, all railway companies (other than street-railroad companies) carrying passengers in that state are required to have separate but equal accommodations for white and colored persons, "by providing two more passenger coaches for each passenger train, or by dividing the passenger coaches by a partition so as to secure separate accommodations." Under this statute, no colored person is permitted to occupy a seat in a coach assigned to white persons; nor any white person to occupy a seat in a coach assigned to colored persons. The managers of the railroad are not allowed to exercise any discretion in the premises, but are required to assign each passenger to some coach or compartment set apart for the exclusive use of his race. If a passenger insists upon going into a coach or compartment not set apart for persons of his race, he is subject to be fined, or to be imprisoned in the parish jail. Penalties are prescribed for the refusal or neglect of the officers, directors, conductors, and employees of railroad companies to comply with the provisions of the act.

Only "nurses attending children of the other race" are excepted from the operation of the statute. No exception is made of colored attendants traveling with adults. A white man is not permitted to have his colored servant with him in the same coach, even if his condition of health requires the constant personal assistance of such servant. If a colored maid insists upon riding in the same coach with a white woman whom she has been employed to serve, and who may need her personal attention while traveling, she is subject to be fined or imprisoned for such an exhibition of zeal in the discharge of duty.

While there may be in Louisiana persons of different races who are not citizens of the United States, the words in the act "white and colored races" necessarily include all citizens of the United States of both races residing in that state. So that we have before us a state enactment that compels, under penalties, the separation of the two races in railroad passenger coaches, and makes it a crime for a citizen of either race to enter a coach that has been assigned to citizens of the other race.

Thus, the state regulates the use of a public highway by citizens of the United States solely upon the basis of race.

However apparent the injustice of such legislation may be, we have only to consider whether it is consistent with the Constitution of the United States....

In respect of civil rights, common to all citizens, the Constitution of the United States does not, I think, permit any public authority to know the race of those entitled to be protected in the enjoyment of such rights. Every true man has pride of race, and under appropriate circumstances, when the rights of others, his equals before the law, are not to be affected, it is his privilege to express such pride and to take such action based upon it as to him seems proper. But I deny that any legislative body or judicial tribunal may have regard to the race of citizens when the civil rights of those citizens are involved. Indeed, such legislation as that here in question is inconsistent not only with that equality of rights which pertains to citizenship, national and state, but with the personal liberty enjoyed by every one within the United States....

The white race deems itself to be the dominant race in this country. And so it is, in prestige, in achievements, in education, in wealth, and in power. So, I doubt not, it will continue to be for all time, if it remains true to its great heritage, and holds fast to the principles of constitutional liberty. But in view of the Constitution, in the eye of the law, there is in this country no superior, dominant, ruling class of citizens. There is no caste here. Our Constitution is color-blind, and neither knows nor tolerates classes among citizens. In respect of civil rights, all citizens are equal before the law. The humblest is the peer of the most powerful. The law regards man as man, and takes no account of his surroundings or of his color when his civil rights as guarantied by the supreme law of the land are involved. It is therefore to be regretted that this high tribunal, the final expositor of the fundamental law of the land, has reached the conclusion that it is competent for a state to regulate the enjoyment by citizens of their civil rights solely upon the basis of race.

In my opinion, the judgment this day rendered will, in time, prove to be quite as pernicious as the decision made by this tribunal in the *Dred Scott* case.

It was adjudged in that case that the descendants of Africans who were imported into this country, and sold as slaves, were not included nor intended to be included under the word "citizens" in the Constitution, and could not claim any of the rights and privileges which that instrument provided for and secured to citizens of the United States; that, at the time of the adoption of the Constitution, they were "considered as a subordinate and inferior class of beings, who had been subjugated by the dominant race, and, whether emancipated or not, yet remained subject to their authority, and had no rights or privileges but such as those who held the power and the government might choose to grant them" 17 How. 393, 404. The recent amendments of the Constitution, it was supposed, had eradicated these principles from our institutions. But it seems that we have yet, in some of the states, a dominant race,—a superior class of citizens,—which assumes to regulate the enjoyment of civil rights, common to all citizens, upon the basis of race. The present decision, it may well be apprehended, will not only stimulate aggressions, more or less brutal and irritating, upon the admitted rights of colored citizens, but will encourage the belief that it is possible, by means of state enactments, to defeat the beneficent purposes which the people of the United States had in view when they adopted the recent amendments of the

Constitution, by one of which the blacks of this country were made citizens of the United States and of the states in which they respectively reside, and whose privileges and immunities, as citizens, the states are forbidden to abridge. Sixty millions of whites are in no danger from the presence here of eight millions of blacks. The destinies of the two races, in this country, are indissolubly linked together, and the interests of both require that the common government of all shall not permit the seeds of race hate to be planted under the sanction of law. What can more certainly arouse race hate, what more certainly create and perpetuate a feeling of distrust between these races, than state enactments which, in fact, proceed on the ground that colored citizens are so inferior and degraded that they cannot be allowed to sit in public coaches occupied by white citizens? That, as all will admit, is the real meaning of such legislation as was enacted in Louisiana.

The sure guaranty of the peace and security of each race is the clear, distinct, unconditional recognition by our governments, national and state, of every right that inheres in civil freedom, and of the equality before the law of all citizens of the United States, without regard to race. State enactments regulating the enjoyment of civil rights upon the basis of race, and cunningly devised to defeat legitimate results of the war, under the pretense of recognizing equality of rights, can have no other result than to render permanent peace impossible, and to keep alive a conflict of races, the continuance of which must do harm to all concerned. This question is not met by the suggestion that social equality cannot exist between the white and black races in this country. That argument, if it can be properly regarded as one, is scarcely worthy of consideration; for social equality no more exists between two races when traveling in a passenger coach or a public highway than when members of the same races sit by each other in a street car or in the jury box, or stand or sit with each other in a political assembly, or when they use in common the streets of a city or town, or when they are in the same room for the purpose of having their names placed on the registry of voters, or when they approach the ballot box in order to exercise the high privilege of voting....

The arbitrary separation of citizens, on the basis of race, while they are on a public highway, is a badge of servitude wholly inconsistent with the civil freedom and the equality before the law established by the Constitution. It cannot be justified upon any legal grounds.

If evils will result from the commingling of the two races upon public highways established for the benefit of all, they will be infinitely less than those that will surely come from state legislation regulating the enjoyment of civil rights upon the basis of race. We boast of the freedom enjoyed by our people above all other peoples. But it is difficult to reconcile that boast with a state of the law which, practically, puts the brand of servitude and degradation upon a large class of our fellow citizens,—our equals before the law. The thin disguise of "equal" accommodations for passengers in railroad coaches will not mislead any one, nor atone for the wrong this day done....

I am of opinion that the statute of Louisiana is inconsistent with the personal liberty of citizens, white and black, in that state, and hostile to both the spirit and letter of the Constitution of the United States. If laws of like character should be enacted in the several states of the Union, the effect would be in the highest degree mischievous. Slavery, as an institution tolerated by law, would, it is true, have disappeared from our country; but there would remain a power in the states, by sinister legislation, to interfere with the full enjoyment of the blessings of freedom, to regulate civil rights, common to all citizens, upon the basis of race, and to place in a condition of legal inferiority a large body of American citizens, now constituting a part of the political community, called the "People of the United States," for whom, and by whom through representatives, our government is administered. Such a system is inconsistent with the guaranty given by the constitution to each state of a republican form of government, and may be stricken down by congressional action, or by the courts in the discharge of their solemn duty to maintain the supreme law of the land, anything in the Constitution or laws of any state to the contrary notwithstanding.

For the reason stated, I am constrained to withhold my assent from the opinion and judgment of the majority.

Plessy

CHERYL I. HARRIS

✧◆❖◆✧

Study Question
How does knowing Plessy's physical appearance change your thinking about and understanding of the court case *Plessy* v. *Ferguson?*

Plessy arose at a time of acute crisis for Blacks. The system of legalized race segregation known as Jim Crow[1] and heightened racial violence[2] had reversed the minimal gains attained by Blacks during Reconstruction.[3] Against a background of extreme racial oppression, the Supreme Court's opinion in *Plessy* rejecting Thirteenth and Fourteenth Amendment challenges to state enforced racial segregation was consonant with the overall political climate.

The case arose in 1891, as one of a series of challenges to a Louisiana law that required racial segregation of railway cars, and was brought after Homer A. Plessy attempted to board a coach reserved for whites and was arrested for violating the statute.[4] Because, according to the plea filed on Plessy's behalf, "the mixture of African blood [was] not discernable in him,"[5] it is evident that Plessy's arrest was arranged as part of a strategy that included the tacit cooperation of railway officials, many of whom were displeased with the separate car law due to the increased expense of operation.[6] The Court dismissed Plessy's claim that legalized racial separation produced racial subordination because

[T]he underlying fallacy of the plaintiff's argument consists in the assumption that the enforced separation of the two races stamps the colored race with a badge of inferiority. If this be so, it is not by reason of anything found in the act but solely because the colored race chooses to put that construction on it.[7]

Plessy's claim, however, was predicated on more than the Equal Protection Clause of the Fourteenth Amendment. Plessy additionally charged that the refusal to seat him on the white passenger car deprived him of property—"this reputation [of being white] which has an actual pecuniary value"—without the due process of law guaranteed by the amendment.[8] Because phenotypically Plessy appeared to be white,[9] barring him from the railway car reserved for whites severely impaired or deprived him of the reputation of being regarded as white.[10] He might thereafter be regarded as or be suspected of being not white[11] and therefore not entitled to any of the public and private benefits attendant to white status.

The brief filed on Plessy's behalf advanced as its first argument that, because "the reputation of belonging to the dominant race...is property, in the same sense that a right of action or inheritance is property," empowering a train employee to arbitrarily take property away from a passenger violated due process guarantees.[12] Because of white supremacy, whiteness was not

351

merely a descriptive or ascriptive characteristic—it was property of overwhelming significance and value. Albion Tourgée, one of Plessy's attorneys, pointedly argued that the property value in being white was self-evident:

> How much would it be *worth* to a young man entering upon the practice of law, to be regarded as a *white* man rather than a colored one? Six-sevenths of the population are white. Nineteen-twentieths of the property of the country is owned by white people. Ninety-nine hundredths of the business opportunities are in the control of white people....Probably most white persons if given a choice, would prefer death to life in the United States *as colored persons*. Under these conditions, is it possible to conclude that *the reputation of being white* is not property? Indeed, is it not the most valuable sort of property, being the master-key that unlocks the golden door of opportunity?[13]

Moreover, Tourgée noted that, in determining who was white, not only were there no national standards, there were also conflicting rules that, by definition, incorporated white domination:

> There is no law of the United States, or of the state of Louisiana defining the limits of race—who are white and who are "colored"? By what rule then shall any tribunal be guided in determining racial character? It may be said that all those should be classed as colored in whom appears a visible admixture of colored blood. By what law? With what justice? Why not count everyone as white in whom is visible any trace of white blood? There is but one reason to wit, the domination of the white race.[14]

The Court ignored Tourgée's argument, and asserted simply that, although the statute obviously conferred power on the train conductor to make assignments by race, no deprivation of due process had resulted because the issue of Plessy's race did not "properly arise on the record."[15] Because there was nothing to indicate that Plessy had been improperly classified under any operative racial definition, no claim for a lack of judicial process in reviewing an improper classification would lie.

The opinion, however, inexplicably proceeded to consider whether Plessy had suffered damage to his property in the form of his reputation, a question dependent on the issue of racial classification that the Court had previously declined to address. The Court simply concluded that, if Plessy were white, any injury to his reputation would be adequately compensated by an action for damages against the company, given that counsel for the state had conceded that the statute's liability exemption for conductors was unconstitutional.[16] The Court stated:

> If he be a white man and assigned to a colored coach, he may have his action for damages against the company for being deprived of his so-called property. Upon the other hand, if he be a colored man and be so assigned, he has been deprived of no property, since he is not lawfully entitled to the reputation of being a white man.[17]

At one level, the Court's opinion amounted to a wholesale evasion of the argument that, as a matter of federal constitutional law, Plessy's assignment to a railway car for Blacks, in the absence of a clear standard defining who was white, was an arbitrary and unauthorized taking of the valuable asset of being regarded as white. At another level, the Court's decision lent support to the notion of race reputation as a property interest that required the protection of law through actions for damages. It did not specifically consider any particular rule of race definition, but it protected the property interest in whiteness for all whites by subsuming even those like Plessy, who phenotypically appeared to be white, within categories that were predicated on white supremacy and race subordination. Officially, the court declined to consider whether Plessy met any statutory definition of whiteness, but deferred to state law as the legitimate source of racial definitions.[18] Although the opinion rhetorically signaled some qualifications about the existence of the property right in whiteness,[19] in fact, the Court protected that right by acknowledging that whites could protect their reputation of being white through suits for damages and by determining that Plessy would be subject to rules that continued white privilege. *Plessy* demonstrated the Court's chronic refusal to dismantle the structure of white supremacy, which is maintained through the institutional protection of relative benefits for whites at the expense of Blacks. In denying that any inferiority existed by reason of de jure segregation, and in denying white status to Plessy, "whiteness" was protected from intrusion and appropriate boundaries around the property were maintained.

Notes

[1] *See generally* C. Vann Woodward, *The Strange Career of Jim Crow passim* (1974) (describing the American system of legally mandated race segregation).

[2] Lynching, an extreme form of social control designed to contain or obliterate potential economic and political challenges posed by Blacks, rose during the ten-year period between 1890 and 1900. In 1892 alone, over 255 Black men, women, and children were lynched. *See* Giddings, *supra* note 37, at 26.

[3] Some historians have argued that the actual material conditions of Blacks deteriorated in the last two decades of the nineteenth century as they were squeezed out of the core of the labor force. *See* Myrdal, *supra* note 4, at 222 (arguing that, after Emancipation, "no...proprietary interest [of slaveowners] protected negro laborers from the desire of white workers to squeeze them out of skilled employment[,] [t]hey were gradually driven out and pushed down into 'Negro jobs', a category which has been more and more narrowly defined").

[4] *See* Charles Lofgren, *The Plessy Case* 41 (1987).

[5] *Id.* at 41.

[6] *See id.* at 32.

[7] *Plessy* v. *Ferguson,* 163 U.S. 537, 551 (1896).

[8] Brief for Plaintiff in Error at 8, *Plessy* (No. 210) [hereinafter Brief for Homer Plessy].

[9] *See* Lofgren, *supra* note 173, at 41.

[10] Albion Tourgée, attorney for Plessy, had specifically sought a fair-skinned plaintiff in order to raise this argument, over vigorous opposition from organized Black leadership. Although Tourgée was seeking a narrower ground for the Court to rule upon, as he was very pessimistic about overturning Jim Crow in the hostile political climate, Black leadership objected that such a strategy, even if successful, would mitigate conditions only for those Blacks who appeared to be white. Legally sanctioning the privilege of fair skin over dark would only serve to reinforce the legitimacy of the race hierarchy that kept white over Black. Nevertheless, Tourgée prevailed in his efforts to pursue this strategy and Homer A.

Plessy was chosen because phenotypically he appeared to be white. *See* JACK GREENBERG, *Litigation for Social Change: Methods, Limits and Role in Democracy* 13–15 (1974). Greenberg notes that one of the benefits of Tourgée's approach was that, had it been accepted by the Court, it might have, in time, made Jim Crow laws extremely difficult to administer. Thus, states might simply have abandoned them. *See id.* at 14.

[11] *See* Brief for Homer Plessy, *supra* note 177, at 9–10.

[12] *Id.* at 8.

[13] *Id.* at 9.

[14] *Id.* at 11. Although from a very different perspective and analysis, Tourgée's attack on the arbitrariness of racial categories presaged the full-blown assault on the illusion of colorblindness offered by Neil Gotanda's insight that recognition of race in this society involves race subordination. Gotanda states:

> Under hypodescent [the rule governing race in the United States], Black parentage is recognized through the generations.... Black ancestry is a contaminant that overwhelms white ancestry. Thus, under the American system of racial classification, claiming a white racial identity is a declaration of racial purity and an implicit assertion of racial domination....
>
> ...[T]he moment of racial recognition is the moment in which is *reproduced* the inherent asymmetry of the metaphor of racial contamination and the implicit impossibility of racial equality.

GOTANDA, *supra* note 24, at 26–27 (footnotes omitted).

[15] *Plessy* v. *Ferguson,* 163 U.S. 537, 549 (1896). The information filed against Plessy had failed to specify his race. *See* LOFGREN, *supra* note 173, at 154. However, Plessy's petition for writs of prohibition and certiorari had alleged that he was seven-eighths white. *See id.* at 55. Attached to the petition was the affidavit of the arresting officer who had identified Plessy as a "passenger of the colored race." *Id.* Notwithstanding the court's demurral, there was thus little doubt that the record contained facts pertaining to Plessy's race.

[16] *See Plessy,* 163 U.S. at §49.

[17] *Id.*

[18] The Court validated, as acceptable norms, state law requirements including, presumably, all common law regarding the proportion of "colored blood necessary to constitute a colored person." The Court stated:

> It is true that the question of the proportion of colored blood necessary to constitute a colored person, as distinguished from a white person, is one upon which there is a difference of opinion in the different states.... But these are questions to be determined under the laws of each state and are not properly put in issue in this case.

[19] *Id.* at 552 (citations omitted).

Obviously, state law also would control the federal due process claim. This fact invites speculation that had Plessy been on a train in a different state with different laws defining whiteness, the case might have gone the other way, although on the narrower basis of the deprivation of due process.

The Declaration of Athens: Scientists Speak Out Against Racism

Unesco Courier

◇◆◈◆◇

Study Questions

1. List at least two reasons why "race" is not a biological reality.
2. What is racism?
3. Which recommendations in this declaration apply to scientists and the uses to which they put their research?

Organized by UNESCO at the invitation of the Foundation for Human Rights of Athens, a symposium devoted to a critical review of the pseudo-scientific theories invoked to justify racism and racial discrimination was held in the Greek capital from 30 March to 3 April 1981.

Since those who attempt to impose the notion that some kind of "natural hierarchy" exists between different populations or between different individuals often invoke science in support of their theories, it was necessary for UNESCO to clarify the situation by making the true standpoint of scientists widely known. Twenty-three distinguished personalities from eighteen countries, representing the various disciplines involved—geneticists, biologists, anthropologists, sociologists, psychologists, historians, etc.—spent a week analysing the most up-to-date findings of science and drawing from them the arguments with which to counter the affirmations of the neo-racists. The collective statement of their conclusions is known as The Declaration of Athens.

The scientists brought together by UNESCO appeal to the peoples of the world and to all individuals everywhere to base their attitudes, behaviour, and statements on the following conclusions, which represent the present state of scientific knowledge on the racial question.

1. The latest anthropological discoveries confirm the unity of the human species.

2. The geographical dispersion of the human species has favoured its racial differentiation but has not affected its basic biological unity.

3. All attempts to classify the human species so as to give objective content to the concept of race have been based on visible physical characteristics. In fact, the concept of race can only be based on transmissible characteristics, that is to say, not on visible physical features but on the genetic factors that govern them.

4. Modern biological techniques have made it possible to study these factors. They reveal a far greater genetic diversity than had been imagined.

5. It has been found that the difference between the genetic structures of two individuals belonging to the same population group can be far greater than the differences between the average genetic structures of two population groups. This finding makes it impossible to arrive at any objective and stable definition of the different

races and consequently deprives the word "race" of much of its biological meaning.

6. Whatever the differences observed, biology can in no way serve as the basis for a hierarchy between individuals or population groups, since no human group possesses a consistent genetic inheritance. In any event, one is never justified in proceeding from observation of a difference to the affirmation of a superiority-inferiority relationship.

7. In fact, each human being possesses a genetic combination that is unique among the countless possible combinations.

8. Man has developed culture, which has enabled the human race to adapt itself to different ecological environments and to transform them according to its needs.

9. The pre-eminence of culture makes the human species unique and invalidates any explanations of human behaviour based solely on the study of animal behaviour. There are no grounds for explaining variations in group behaviour in terms of genetic differences.

10. Intellectual activity constitutes one of the most striking characteristics of man. Certain disciplines have developed techniques for measuring this activity.

11. These techniques are designed to compare individuals within a given population group and cannot, by definition, be used for the purpose of comparing different population groups.

12. It follows, *a fortiori,* that any value judgement on the intellectual capacities of a given group based on such measurements is completely without foundation.

13. Indeed, the complexity of the interaction between biological and cultural factors makes any attempts to establish the relative importance of innate and acquired characteristics completely meaningless.

14. It is unacceptable and scientifically unjustifiable to use the results of psycholog-ical tests and the intelligence quotient in particular to promote social ostracism and racial discrimination.

15. The social sciences provide no support for the view that racism is a collective form of behaviour that inevitably arises when certain kinds of social relationship predominate between different ethnic groups. On the other hand, the plurality and coexistence of cultures and races that characterize many societies constitute the most felicitous form of mutual enrichment between peoples.

16. Racism, which takes a number of forms, is in reality a complex phenomenon involving a whole range of economic, political, historical, cultural, social, and psychological factors. Effective action to combat racism must necessarily address itself to all these factors.

17. Racism is generally a tool used by certain groups to reinforce their political and economic power, the most serious cases being those involving apartheid and genocide.

18. Racism also takes the form of denying that certain peoples have a history and of underrating their contribution to the progress of mankind.

19. While the quantitative analysis of social phenomena can help to elucidate sociological and economic issues, it can also be used to promote exclusion and segregation. The application of quotas, tolerance thresholds and numerical stipulations for educational purposes based on ethnic or racial criteria should be denounced when it violates the basic principles of human rights. However, legitimate measures can be taken to redress the wrongs inflicted on certain underprivileged groups.

20. Those engaged in scientific activity bear a major responsibility for the social future of their contemporaries. Where racism is concerned, this responsibility involves political and ethical choices. Scientific re-

search, particularly in the field of the human and social sciences, should always be based on respect for human dignity.

21. Recognition of the risks to mankind implicit in certain applications of science should lead not to a rejection of science but rather to the fostering among the public at large of a genuinely scientific attitude, that is, an attitude based not on an accumulation of certainties but on the cultivation of a critical spirit and the continual challenging of accepted views. The struggle against racism in all its forms calls for the extensive involvement of scientists in the fostering of these attitudes, making use in particular of education systems and the media.

22. There is a need therefore for scientists, whatever their differences or divergencies of viewpoint, to strive to maintain the objectivity that will ensure that their work and conclusions cannot be used as the basis for falsifications and interpretations detrimental to mankind.

Signatories

A. C. Bayonas (Greece), historian and philosopher;

T. Ben Jelloun (Morocco), philosopher and writer;

J. Björnebye (Norway), philologist;

A. Bouhdiba (Tunisia), sociologist;

H. Condamine (France), geneticist;

E. Czeizel (Hungary), geneticist;

M. Diabate (Ivory Coast), ethno-sociologist;

C. A. Diop (Senegal), anthropologist;

R. Droz (Switzerland), psychologist;

M. Fraginal (Cuba), ethnologist;

S. Genoves (Mexico), anthropologist;

A. Jacquard (France), geneticist and mathematician;

J. Ki-Zerbo (Upper Volta), historian;

C. B. Krimbas (Greece), geneticist;

E. Nevo (Israel), geneticist;

H. Tawa (Lebanon), historian and mathematician;

D. Trichopoulos (Greece), professor of medicine;

T. Tsunoda (Japan), professor of medicine;

P. Vegleris (Greece), lawyer and professor of law;

L. P. Vidyarthi (India), anthropologist;

G. Wald (U.S.A), Nobel Prize winner for medicine;

A. Yotopoulos Marangopoulos (Greece), President of the Athens Human Rights Foundation;

I. M. Zolotareva (USSR), anthropologist.

PART 5

◇◆◈◆◇

Toward a New Paradigm: Transcending Categories

I am not under the illusion that changing habits and emotions is easy. Even when one has been persuaded by reason and swears off the practice of race-thinking, one must be continually on guard against betrayal by words and especially by thought-clichés. The power of superstition is that it speaks in the tones of common sense.

—JACQUES BARZUN
Race: A Study in Superstition (1965:XVII)

In this book, we have presented evidence to support the argument that there is no such thing as race. We have shown that racial classification is based on at least two false assumptions: (1) that people can be divided into clear-cut categories so that everyone fits into one category only and (2) that each category tells us something meaningful about the people assigned to it that differentiates them from people assigned to other categories. As stated in the "Introduction," our goal in critiquing classification schemes was not to create "better" categories with clearer dividing lines but to show the futility of trying to classify people in this manner. Our goal was to explore how people come to define arbitrary categories as clear-cut and the mechanisms by which they maintain the illusion of independent or pure categories.

If we have succeeded in showing there is no such thing as race, it would seem that the only logical recommendation we can make is to abandon the practice of classifying people by race. Such a solution, however, ignores a critical moral question: How do we deal with the legacy of racial classification? Keep in mind that the racial categories in place today did not come into being because multiracial people chose to identify with one particular racial group over others. The system of racial classification is the result of more than 200 years of laws and practices enforcing categorization (Knepper 1995), beginning with the nineteenth-century vision of a hierarchy of the races with Europeans on top, supported by the assumption that physical, mental, moral, and aesthetic attributes are biologically determined.

This ranking and classification system was used to justify colonialism, slavery, and other forms of imperialism "as a moral necessity because the original inhabitants were seen as less than human and did not deserve the land they inhabited" (Mirza and Dungworth 1995:347).

The idea of "race" and, by extension, racial classification have been challenged for some time. As one example, consider that *Race: A Study in Modern Superstition* by Jacques Barzun was published in 1937 and reissued in 1965. In the preface to the 1965 edition, Barzun states "This book is coming back into print because the idea [of race] it treats of, although repeatedly killed, is nevertheless undying" (p. ix). However, it is only recently that these challenges have begun to reach mainstream audiences. Hundreds of articles and books were written in the 1990s on this subject. As well, a significant number of authors have written autobiographical accounts describing what it means to fit no one racial category. Examples include *Life on the Color Line: The True Story of a White Boy Who Discovered He Was Black* by Gregory Howard Williams (1995), *Notes of a White Black Woman* by Judy Scales-Trent (1995), *The Color of Water: A Black Man's Tribute to His White Mother* by James McBride (1996), *Caucasia* by Danzy Senna (1998), and *Divided to the Vein: A Journey into Family and Race* by Scott Minerbook (1996). In addition, the U.S. Bureau of Census reviewed the literature and research findings related to racial classification and evaluated the adequacy of current racial and ethnic categories specified in Federal Statistical Directive No. 15. Beginning with the 2000 census respondents will be given the opportunity to self-identify with one or more racial categories. All of this attention to the meaning of race suggests that we are in the midst of a paradigm shift. Still, as the comments from students in a recent Race and Gender class at Northern Kentucky University make clear, the process by which the old paradigm loosens its grip on thinking is a slow one (see Box **"Conversations About the Meaning of Race"**).

Thomas Kuhn (1975) wrote about paradigm shifts in *The Structure of Scientific Revolutions*. According to Kuhn, paradigms are the dominant and widely accepted theories and concepts which are used to comprehend and explain events in the world. In the reading "The Anthropology of Race: A Study of Ways of Looking at Race," Vivian J. Rohrl (1995) offers a brief historical overview of the so-called scientific paradigms related to race, beginning with those of the late eighteenth and early nineteenth century (phase 1), which assumed for the most part the existence of clear-cut racial categories. She ends with the 1960s and early 1970s (phase 6)—the years in which the anthropologist Ashley Montagu (a person ahead of his time) puts forth the paradigm that "there is no such thing as race." Rorhl traces how the meaning of race has evolved from clear-cut divisions of humanity to "a way in

Conversations About the Meaning of Race

Students in my "Race and Gender" class report trying to tell a relative, friend, or acquaintance that "there is no such thing as race." A sample of their experiences are listed below.

- I mentioned to a friend of mine when a golf tournament was on that Tiger Woods was not "black." My friend looked at me blankly and said "he looks black to me." I tried to explain that each of his parents were "mixed race," so therefore Tiger could not be one race. I don't think my friend was convinced.

- I tried to discuss this idea with my parents. They were open to the idea that people of different "races" can have children. Yet they still believe that if a baby looks "black" (or Asian, or Native American, or Hispanic) it is black regardless of its genetic heritage. The conversation seemed very futile because they had no real concept of different ethnic groups among the races. They are educated people but these ideas didn't seem to make sense to them.

- I had a short conversation with a person classified as "black." I kept it short because I didn't want to offend him. But now that I know him a little bit better, I don't think he would be offended since I learned that he grew up among whites most of his life. He pretty much knew where I was coming from on this issue. I can't quite remember exactly what specific issues we talked about but I do remember that he was very open-minded about it.

- I have discussed these ideas with my parents and husband. The immediate reaction from my husband was "that's why I hate those classes, they try to brainwash you to socialist thinking." Now, my husband is not racist, but he could not understand the concept of race as a myth. I gave up on him. My parents laughed and thought it was a waste of time to study such matters, and I gave up trying to convey the message. Actually, I had the same kind of reaction on the first day of class, but after studying the readings, viewing photographs, and discussing these ideas everything seemed to make sense.

- I have discussed this class with many people. I actually talked about Tiger Woods to my parents as we were watching a golf tournament. I told them he wasn't "black." They said, "Well, what is he?" I tried to tell them and they did not believe me. This topic came up the following Sunday only this time with my parents and grandparents. One of my parents announced to everyone there, "Kim said Tiger Woods isn't black." I tried to explain it again but everyone said, "He looks black to me and so do his parents." Then I used examples to explain how physical characteristics do not tell the whole genetic story. After I explained this idea, they believed me a little bit but not fully.

- I have tried several times to try and explain the idea of racial classification to my boyfriend John. I told him that race doesn't really exist. Our conversations did not last very long because he couldn't understand what I was trying to say. I tried to tell him about the articles we read and that helped a little. He basically said that I was probably right that people created the idea of race, but there was nothing we could do about it now. I think he wanted to understand, but did not know how to make himself.

- Since I started this class, I've discussed some of the ideas with my parents. My parents are golfers, so I told them about Tiger Woods. They are very open-minded and are just as intrigued by this "new" interpretation of race as I am. This is a topic people need to know about. Ignoring it will only cause more problems.

- I have discussed the idea that race doesn't exist with a friend at work. At first she thought I was really strange, but as I spoke more on the subject she started to understand and get the meaning of what I was saying. I gave several examples of how the idea of race has been embedded in our minds from a very young age, and even in our textbooks at school. It didn't take too much convincing on my part to get my friend to understand what I was saying.

- I have talked about the idea of "race" with my district manager at work for about five hours. I told him

Continued

Conversations About the Meaning of Race *(Continued)*

how I used to believe in race, but that I no longer do. At first he was very surprised by my comments, but as I explained the different things we have learned in class he somehow started to believe me. He very much enjoyed talking about "race," because his mother is "black" and his father is "white."

- I told my great-uncle, who is racist, that I was taking this course and about the ideas we were learning. He asked me why I was taking such a course. At first, I considered saying "because I have to" but instead I said "it seemed interesting." He asked me more questions about the content of the course. He seemed to think it was some kind of plot against America's youth. I asked why, and he said, "Everyone knows that niggers are different."

- A friend of mine and I spent probably two hours talking about this topic. She seemed very receptive to the idea. It wasn't that hard to get my point across to her. On the other hand, I tried discussing it with my parents, and they looked at me like I was crazy.

They were not very interested in even trying to understand. I think they are set in their ways and don't want to be open to new ideas. I really think it is a generation thing. I think it is so hard for them to be open-minded because of the way they were raised to see race. They don't understand me when I talk about it. I told my dad, an avid golfer, about Tiger Woods. He seemed to understand that Tiger's genetic heritage is complex, but he still refers to him as the "black golfer."

- I was at work [at United Parcel Service] one night when management asked us to fill out an employee survey. One of the questions was, "What race are you?" There were four choices (Black, White, Asian/Pacific Islander, and Native American), but there was also a fifth choice—"Hispanic." I told my co-workers that Hispanic wasn't a race, but they asked me "How come?" I tried to explain that Hispanics can be of any race, but it wasn't getting through. We talked about it for at least five minutes.

---

which one group designates itself as 'insider' and other groups as 'outsiders' to reinforce or enforce its wishes and/or ideas in social, economic, and political realms" (p. 96).

Paradigms gain their status not because they explain everything, but because they seem to be the "best" way of looking at the world for the time being. On the one hand, paradigms are important because they serve a unifying function offering a common vocabulary people draw upon to think about the world, themselves, and others. For example, most people in the United States, even "mixed-race" people, think of themselves and others in terms of race. "[T]hey go along with the idea that they are members of one of the races recognized by the government. In fact, they often identify with a traditional race that represents only a small fraction of their genetic heritage" (Earnest 1989:182). While paradigms impose an order on the world and people's relationships with each other, they act as blinders, severely limiting the kinds of questions that people ask, the observations they make, and the actions they take.

The explanatory value, and hence the status, of a paradigm is threatened by *anomaly,* an observation or observations that it cannot explain.

Anomalies confront us with the fact that the "old" paradigm is not relevant. In the case of the idea of race, those persons who are products of sexual unions between two individuals classified as belonging to different races are the anomalies who challenge a paradigm directing us to think about race in terms of clear boundaries and distinct differences. Obviously, the existence of anomalies alone is not enough to cause people to abandon a particular paradigm. Otherwise, racial classification would have been abandoned long ago, and we would laugh and shudder at the thought that people once believed in the idea of race (Barzun 1965). Consider that W. E. B. Du Bois alerted us to this anomaly at the turn of the twentieth century.

Du Bois was preoccupied with the "strange meaning of being black here in the dawning of the Twentieth Century."[1] His preoccupation was no doubt affected by the fact that his father was a Haitian of French and African descent and his mother was an American of Dutch and African descent (Lewis 1993). Historically, in the United States a "black" person is a black even when their parents are of different "races." In order to accept this idea, we have acted as if white and blacks do not marry and/or produce offspring, and we have acted as if one parent, the "black" one, contributes a disproportionate amount of genetic material—so large a genetic contribution that it negates the genetic contribution of the other parent. In *The Philadelphia Negro: A Social Study,* originally published in 1899, Du Bois wrote about popular ideas of race and reality. Ironically, almost 100 years after this book was published the flaws of the U.S. system of racial classification are just now becoming a standard topic in many sociology texts. Yet, Du Bois documented that blacks and whites married and paired off, despite laws prohibiting marriage, and that they did have children. He reminded us that race amalgamation took place "largely under the institution of slavery and for the most part, though not wholly, outside the bonds of legal marriage" (1996 reprint: 359). It is this kind of data which Du Bois painstakingly collected that is used today to discredit the idea of race as a valid way of categorizing humanity and to remind us that a "multiracial" people is not a recent phenomenon.

We have learned, however, that even when the evidence supporting the myth of race is right before our eyes, we have glossed over the stubborn facts and dismissed them or explained them away. The reading "Letter from Thomas Jefferson" shows how Jefferson processed the fact of race-mixing. Instead of acknowledging that the existence of "multiracial" offspring destroyed the logic of racial classification, Jefferson devised complex formulas to determine when someone was "cleared of Negro blood" and became white. Barzun (1965) wrote about this resistance "to the facts before our eyes" in the preface to *Race: A Study in Modern Superstition:*

The present book attempted a modest beginning of persuasion, having in view the adult educated reader to whom it showed in some detail the inconsistent racial fantasies developed in civilized Europe during the last 180 years. Men of good will, men of honor, scholars and scientists in the several branches of learning, have been the authors of these theories and the apologists of this superstition. They have argued on every conceivable premise of physique, language, temperament, moral character, coloring, shape of skull, and political belief, to establish the reality and the ranking of dozens, of hundreds, of supposed races. To each race they have ascribed traits that explained why the world was as it was and whither it was going. They have struggled to gloss over stubborn facts or to dismiss them; they have argued with the fanatics of rival theories or despised them. Encased in verbal armor, they have fought sham fights with real emotions and on real issues within and across national boundaries. Their labor has been great, and in the aggregate self-destructive, for their "facts" cancel one another and their habits of thought only prove to the detached observer that here are men of one culture, cast in the same intellectual mold, and unfortunately not graced with simple judgement. (pp. xx–xxi)

In the face of such resistance, under what conditions do paradigms shift? According to Kuhn, before people abandon old paradigms, someone must articulate an alternative paradigm that accounts convincingly for the anomaly. A scientific revolution occurs when enough people in the community *hear* the critique, break from the old paradigm, and change the nature of their research or thinking in favor of a new paradigm. The new paradigm "changes some of the field's most elementary theoretical generalizations" (Kuhn 1975:85). The new paradigm causes converts to see the world in an entirely new light and to wonder how they could possibly have taken the old paradigm seriously. "[W]hen paradigms change, the world itself changes with them" (p. 111). The story of how people come to hear the ideas which discredit dominant paradigms is obviously a complicated one. Clearly, most people have failed to hear ideas expressed by Du Bois and Barzun.[2]

Law professor Cruz Reynoso (1992) offers some insights about the slow process by which many people in the United States have come to change their views about race and ethnicity. In the reading "Ethnic Diversity: Its Historical and Constitutional Roots," Reynoso describes some major events and court cases which show that the United States has struggled to accommodate diversity and has made fundamental changes in thought and practice. He does not argue that the changes have been perfect or fast. In fact, history shows that change has been slow and laborious, but it has occurred.

The struggle we face today can be stated in question form: How do we begin to dismantle racial classification without abdicating a responsibility to correct its legacy? This is an especially difficult question for several reasons. First, today the major justification for collecting data on race and ethnicity is to monitor and enforce civil rights laws. If we abandon racial classification, we lose an important mechanism through which we can appraise the success or failure of efforts to combat discrimination. A second reason this question is difficult relates to responsibility for the past: Who should be held responsible for correcting the legacy of racial classification? In "Making Good Again," Erich H. Loewy asks who is responsible for the Nazi Holocaust? In answering the question, he explores the meaning of responsibility especially as it applies to those who were not alive at the time and explains why it is important to "make good again." In view of these dilemmas, we offer some modest suggestions to continue the process of change.

Suggestion 1. Carefully consider every situation where racial classification occurs and ask this question before making a decision about whether to abandon classification in that setting: Is this instance of racial classification satisfying an obligation to correct past injustices or is it contributing to further injustice? In the reading "Perceptions and Misperceptions of Skin Color" by Stephen H. Caldwell and Rebecca Popenoe (1995a), the authors give us one example of a situation where knowing someone's race is of limited value to accomplishing the task at hand. Caldwell and Popenoe argue that clinicians should consider dropping any reference to the race of their patients during case presentations because, in most cases, knowing their race does not improve diagnostic and therapeutic decisions. In fact, knowing someone's race can introduce bias and even obscure an accurate appraisal of a patient's genetic and cultural background. Caldwell and Popenoe (1995b) maintain that the clinicians must recognize the limited scientific meaning of the terms "black" or "white" "Indian" and "Asian."[3] They suggest that clinicians drop references to race and ask patients about their ethnic history when they suspect that cultural factors or geographic origin may offer clues about the diseases to which a patient may be inherently prone and about the ways in which he or she may react to both illness and treatment (1995b).

While it might be useful to limit references to race and ethnicity in case presentations and epidemiological research, keeping track of the race and ethnicity of patients is essential to monitoring whether equality exists with regard to access to health and treatment outcomes. If people classified as "black" or "Native American" have less access to certain treatments (i.e., organ transplants or kidney dialysis) or if they have less favorable health outcomes than people classified as "white," then we have an obligation to investigate the possibility that people may have been treated differently because of their race or because of the race others perceive them to be. The reading "Selected Discrimination Cases Handled by the U.S. Department of Justice in 1999" shows that both individual and institutional discrimination exist and must be held in check.

Individual discrimination is any overt action by an individual that depreciates someone from the outgroup, denies outgroup opportunities to participate, or is violent toward others' lives and property. *Institutionalized discrimination*, on the other hand, is the established and customary way of doing things in society—the challenged and unchallenged rules, policies, and day-to-day practices that impede or limit minority members' achievements and keep them in a subordinated and disadvantaged position. It is "systematic discrimination through the regular operations of societal institutions" (Davis 1978:30). Institutional discrimination can be overt or subtle. It is overt when laws and practices are designed with the clear intention of keeping minorities in subordinate positions, as in the 1831 Act Prohibiting the Teaching of Slaves to Read. Institutionalized discrimination is subtle when the discriminatory consequences of a practice are neither planned nor intended.

Suggestion 2. Develop the intellectual discipline to recognize *race-thinking,* a habit of thought where "people permit themselves to think of human groups without the vivid sense that groups consist of individuals and that individuals display the full range of human differences" (Barzun 1965:ix). We engage in race thinking because most of what the general public knows about racial groups "is gradually acquired over time in the form of metaphors, images, or stereotypes" (Peroff 1997:5). In the reading "Indianness," Nicholas Peroff argues that most people's idea of Indianness does not come from first-hand experiences with American Indians. Rather their idea of Indianness comes from such things as movies, literature, the media, team logos, automobile names, and beer commercials. Peroff uses the term "indianness" with a small "i" to designate the popular image of "indianness" most people hold in their head.

Race-thinking is evident when people engage in *selective perception,* a thought process in which people notice only those behaviors or events that support their stereotypes about a race or ethnic group. For example, while watching the Olympics a spectator notices that "blacks" are concentrated in sports such as basketball and certain track events (sprints). He or she uses this observation to support a belief that blacks dominate in these sports because extraordinary speed, agility, and strength is part of their genetic makeup. At the same time, our hypothetical spectator fails to draw the same kind of conclusion about white athletes concentrated in sports such gymnastics and platform diving (i.e., that the genetic heritage of "whites" also gives them extraordinary speed, agility, and strength to dominate these different sports).

As a second example of selective perception, many people see crime as primarily a "black" problem. They point to "the facts" supporting their generalization, such as the data gathered by the U.S. Department of Justice estimating that 28.5 percent of men classified as black will be admitted to prison during their lifetime compared to 4.4 percent of men classified as white (see Table 5.1). They fail to realize that the prison population is made up of those who got caught, as well as the falsely accused. The prison population does not include secret deviants (people who have broken laws but whose violation goes unnoticed, or, if it is noticed, no one has reacted to enforce the law). Sociologist Howard Becker (1963) maintains that "no one really knows how much of this phenomenon exists, but [he is] convinced that the amount [of secret deviants] is very sizable, much more than we are apt to think"(1963:20). For example, a 1998 U.S. Department of Justice survey of crime victims documented that 31 million violent and property crimes were committed against U.S. residents of 12 years of age and older. Of these 31 million crimes, only about 38 percent were reported to police. This means that police were never alerted to 62 percent of crimes. As one example of how some groups are more likely to be noticed and caught than other groups consider the information in Table 5.2.

The reading "Brain's Use of Shortcuts Can Be a Route to Bias" by K. C. Cole shows us that perception is an active mental process by which people impose their expectations on how they perceive a person or situation and that people "do not so much believe what they see as see what they believe" (Cole 1995: A-18). Cole concludes that people have to understand that wanting to be fair is not enough to ensure they will be fair. People must also recognize the unconscious forces (the cognitive weakspots) that affect understanding and judgments. For example, consider the data in Figure 5.1 which shows the kinds of cases filed with the Equal Employment Opportunity Commission and awaiting resolution.

Note that of the 121,230 cases, 34,074 cases were "race-related," and 742 were "color-related." If you assume that these 34,074 cases are "blacks" filing complaints against "whites," you have failed to consider the possibility that a significant, yet unknown, number of these cases are "reverse discrimination" claims by whites. In addition, you have failed to consider that there are other categories of persons in the United States, in addition to the two mentioned, who might choose to use the EEOC to address perceived

Table 5.1 Percentage of U.S. Males Likely to Ever Go to Prison, Based on Constant 1991 Rates of First Incarceration, by Age, Race, and Hispanic Origin

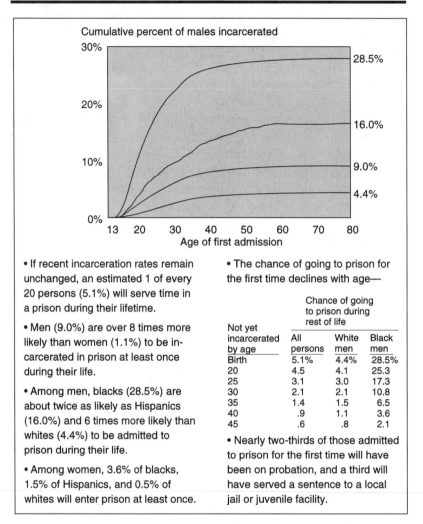

• If recent incarceration rates remain unchanged, an estimated 1 of every 20 persons (5.1%) will serve time in a prison during their lifetime.

• Men (9.0%) are over 8 times more likely than women (1.1%) to be incarcerated in prison at least once during their life.

• Among men, blacks (28.5%) are about twice as likely as Hispanics (16.0%) and 6 times more likely than whites (4.4%) to be admitted to prison during their life.

• Among women, 3.6% of blacks, 1.5% of Hispanics, and 0.5% of whites will enter prison at least once.

• The chance of going to prison for the first time declines with age—

Not yet incarcerated by age	Chance of going to prison during rest of life		
	All persons	White men	Black men
Birth	5.1%	4.4%	28.5%
20	4.5	4.1	25.3
25	3.1	3.0	17.3
30	2.1	2.1	10.8
35	1.4	1.5	6.5
40	.9	1.1	3.6
45	.6	.8	2.1

• Nearly two-thirds of those admitted to prison for the first time will have been on probation, and a third will have served a sentence to a local jail or juvenile facility.

wrongs. Understanding this possibility is critical since many whites would see the data as unfounded accusations of discrimination against white employers by unqualified blacks. Many blacks, equally uninformed, would see the data an overwhelming evidence of institutionalized white discrimination against them. Recent published disclosures regarding Avis Car Rental Agency's failure to rent automobiles to black customers, Denny's Restaurant chain's systematic policy of refusing to serve black customers, and Texaco Oil Company's failure to promote qualified minority employees would give

Table 5.2   Who Gets Caught?

Between January 1995 and September 1996, Maryland state highway patrol officers assigned to a stretch of highway known as I-95 stopped 823 drivers for traffic violations and then searched the cars for drugs. Use the information in Chart 1 to answer the questions below.

Chart 1
Illegal Substances Found in Cars of those Motorists
Stopped for Traffic Violations and Searched

Drugs Found

CLASSIFIED AS	YES	NO	TOTAL SEARCHED
Minority	188	473	661
White	47	115	162
Column Total	235	588	823

Looking only at the raw numbers in the Yes column, which group is more likely to have illegal substances in their cars?

What percentage of all the cars stopped and searched is "minority?"

What percentage of all the cars stopped and searched is "white?'"

Maryland highway patrol officers assigned to this section of I-95 were accused of *racial profiling,* the practice of using race as a basis for making some decision such as stopping drivers for traffic violations and/or searching cars for drugs. These numbers alone do not necessarily mean that the patrol officers[1] are guilty of this practice. Perhaps minority drivers make up _____ percent of all drivers on I-95 and are being pulled over in proportion to their actual numbers. Or perhaps minority drivers violate speeding laws more than "white" drivers do and thus deserve to be pulled over in greater numbers. Social Psychologist John Lamberth designed a study to determine if this was the case. Actual data was supplied and/or collected by the Maryland State Police and the (American Civil Liberties Union) ACLU. The researchers were asked to

✓ determine the percentage of cars driven by whites and nonwhite groups
✓ determine the percentage of cars speeding by race of driver

Chart 2
Percentage of Drivers Speeding by Racial Classification

Speeding Violations

CLASSIFIED AS	YES	NO	ROW TOTAL
Black	938	35	973
White	4000	341	4341
Other	232	9	241
Unknown	184	2	186
Column Total	5354	387	5741

[1]We do not know the race of the highway patrol officers. But it is unlikely that they were all "white." The point is that we are *all* socialized to view some racial groups as more "deviant" than other racial groups.

(continued)

Table 5.2 Who Gets Caught? (*continued*)

Use information in Charts 1 and 2 to answer the questions below.

Fill in the percentage of drivers on the I-95 that were classified as "black" _____, "white" _____, "Other" _____, and "Unknown" _____.

What percentage of *all* drivers speed?

What percentage of *"black"* drivers speed?

What percentage of *"white"* drivers speed?

What percentage of drivers' classified as *"Other"* speed?

What percentage of drivers classified as *"Unknown"* speed?

Fill in the percentage of all speeders that are "black" _____, "white" _____, "Other" _____, and "Unknown" _____.

What conclusions can you draw about race classification and speeding?

If racial profiling were not being used, what percentage of drivers stopped for traffic violation should have been minority (based on information in Chart 2)? _____

If racial profiling were not being used, what percentage of all the cars stopped and searched should have been "white?"' (based on information in Chart 2)? _____

In what percent of all minority cars searched were illegal substances found? _____

In what percent of all "white" cars searched were illegal substances found? _____

Do Maryland State Police stop and search black motorists at a rate disproportionate to their numbers on the highway? Explain.

What conclusions can we draw about race and possession of illegal substances? (Can we say that minorities are more likely to use drugs than whites? Or is there some other explanation for the 188 minority people versus the 47 white people shown in Chart 1?)

Source: Lamberth, John. 1996. "Report of John Lamberth, Ph.D." *http://www.aclu.org/court/lamberth.html.*
Answers to questions can be found in Appendix A.

much credence to their claim. Before drawing conclusions about the meaning of this data, it would also be important to consider the characteristics of those filing other kinds of cases. How many people claiming age bias are classified as white, black, Native American, Asian/Pacific Islander, or Hispanic? The point is that this vague way of presenting data leaves people

Figure 5.1   Kinds of Cases Awaiting Action by the Equal Employment Opportunity Commission[1]

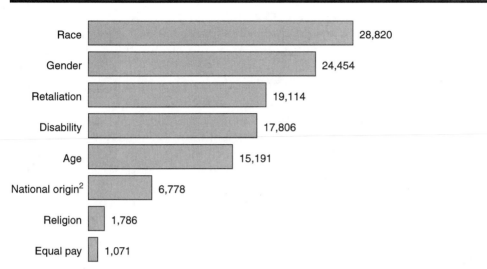

[1]Some complaints may be filed in multiple categories.
[2]Most English-only cases fall under national origin.
Source: Equal Employment Opportunity Commission (1999).

free to interpret it in ways that are consistent with their biases. When this happens, people lose sight of the fact that affirmative action and other civil rights programs are designed to ensure equal opportunity for all people.

Suggestion 3. Make a concerted attempt to understand differences and to see similarities as well. Anthropologist Mary Catherine Bateson (1968) observed that when people first make contact with others whom they perceive as different, their first reaction is usually ethnocentric. That is, people usually notice only those attributes that are different from the ones they possess, and they generally describe the differences in negative and highly oversimplified terms. "They" (whoever they are) have no conception of individuality, have no sense of privacy, have no emotion, are money-driven, are not creative, are stuck in the past, have no sense of responsibility, do not know how to be genuine, have no work ethic, and so on. Even when differences are perceived as positive, they are described in oversimplified terms, as in the claim that "Native Americans" love the earth and have never behaved in ways to spoil it, or when Japanese tell white Americans, "You don't hold things in like we do. You express how you really feel. You don't have to hide your true feelings" (Berry 1995:8). In any event, whether differences are described in positive or negative terms, one of the parties is described as lacking in some quality in relation to the other.

If one is serious about understanding differences, the first step is to talk to those seen as different and listen to what they say. Investigators should not assume that they know the truth. As a rule of thumb, one should avoid making judgments and recommendations that affect others when they are based on superficial knowledge and/or derived from ethnocentric thinking. With regard to education, for example, Iranian education critic, reformer, and scholar Samad Behrangi maintains that "unless we have seen the school's environment and surrounding community, unless we have lived among the people, unless we have been friends with the people, we have not heard their voice and have not known their desires, it is not even proper to have sympathy for the environment, or impose unrelated educational policies, or even to write stories or textbooks for them" (Behrangi 1994:28).

In the reading "Talking Past One Another" by Richard T. Schaefer (1996), we learn that whites and nonwhites tend to have different views about the extent to which discrimination still exists and about the amount of progress that has been made in this area. This difference of opinion can lead to heated debate with members of both groups talking past one another. The difference of opinion can be traced in large part to differences in the way each side defines a central term of the debate—racism. As a specific case in point, consider the controversy over sport teams named the "Redskins," "Braves," and "Chiefs," and their mascots.

On one side of the controversy are those who say, "What's the big deal? Stop being so overly sensitive." On the other side are those who argue that these names and images are degrading to Native Americans. In the reading "Let's Spread the 'Fun' Around," Ward Churchill argues that we need to recognize and acknowledge the big picture. He shows how "negative images and stereotypes" are casually but unconsciously taught and perpetuated through team names and images. Most Atlanta Brave fans (who by the way are predominantly "white"), engaging in the "Tomahawk Chop" at baseball games, are so accustomed to socially defining less powerful groups that they fail to see such action as equivalent to the public taunting of Native Americans.

In addition to understanding differences, we must also strive to understand similarities across groups. In this regard it is important to recognize that we all share a common history. That common history has been obscured by the language of racial classification. As one example consider that W. E. B. Du Bois is labeled a "black" sociologist in spite of the fact that he was American-born and of Dutch, French, and African ancestries.

Du Bois's classification camouflages shared histories and interconnected experiences. Although we look to Du Bois's writing to help us understand the "black" experience, a study of how his ancestors connected (and broke those connections) with one another can also help us to understand the French, Dutch, and ultimately the American experience. Likewise the existence of the so-called black golfer, Tiger Woods, is a story of shared history of interconnections and disconnections among African, Native American, Thai, and white people.

Shared histories—both interconnections and disconnections—among peoples classified as distinct and different races can be found in decisions to pass into the white race. Lawrence Otis Graham (1999) lists the rules of passing which explain how to "disconnect" with one race and "connect" with another (see the reading "The Rules of Passing"). The second reading is an excerpt from "Childhood and Sexual Identity Under Slavery" by Anthony S. Parent, Jr. and Susan Brown Wallace. Here we learn that relationships between slave owners and slaves were emotional, intimate, and complex. Sexual liaisons (usually forced, sometimes willing) between masters and slave women were commonplace. These sexual relationships produced not only "mixed-race" offspring, but sons and daughters, half-brothers and half-sisters, grandsons and granddaughters. "Often mistresses who felt threatened by the relationships that their husbands had with black women took out their frustration and anger on the resulting children" (p. 50). Some of the offspring were given special privileges, others penalized. Depending on their physical characteristics some passed into the white race; others remained slaves.

Suggestion 4. Learn to identify the oppressor within. "The true focus of revolutionary change is never merely the oppressive situations which we seek to escape, but that piece of the oppressor which is planted deep within each of us" (Lorde 1984:123). The reading "Toward a New Vision" by Patricia Hill Collins challenges us to think of oppression as not an "either/or" phenomenon (someone is either oppressed or not oppressed) but as a "both/and" phenomenon allowing people to be both oppressed and oppressor. She offers a framework and a vocabulary to help us understand the various dimensions of oppressive structures, and she encourages us to recognize that the interlocking categories of race, class, and gender structure all situations and "vests everyone with varying levels of power and privilege." Collins also offers a framework to help us identify the oppressor within, which includes learning (1) to recognize that differences in power and privilege frame relationships among people; (2) to build empathy for others (who are both more privileged and less privileged) by taking an interest in the facts of their lives; and (3) to identify which catalysts foster group solidarity and bring people from different groups together.

Suggestion 5. Remember that the idea of race as a social construction does not mean that the experience of race should be equated with illusion, fallacy, or cognitive error. To make such an association ignores the fact that the experience of race is real and that it effects life chances, lived experiences, perceptions, or judgments. In the reading "White-Blindness," Bruce N. Simon argues that once we learn that race is a social construction we cannot draw a conclusion that "race doesn't matter." Simon uses the O. J. Simpson trials as a vehicle for showing the problem with taking a "color-blind" position that "race doesn't/shouldn't matter" or other variations of that position (e.g., "we all belong to one race—the human race" or "we shouldn't notice skin color"). He offers an alternative version of color-blindness that entails the recognition and rejection of white privilege. The final two readings, "White Privilege Shapes the U.S." and "More Thoughts on Why the System of White Privilege Is Wrong" by a white university professor, Robert W. Jensen, tackle the very difficult task of having whites acknowledge "white privilege" without being saddled with guilt feelings. White society, especially its more privileged sectors, rationalize its acceptance of white privilege by asserting that it is based solely on their hard work. That is, they merit it. The unspoken and implied assertion is equally clear: non whites are disadvantaged because they lack the ambition to work hard, or the ability to achieve like successful whites. Here, a culturally constructed mythology of "merit" is used to deny the fact that most people do not have *complete* control over their fate and that this lack of control is more so the case for non whites than for whites. This denial persists despite the fact that every six-grader is aware of this country's past legal discrimination against non whites and most teenagers and every adult have personal knowledge of discrimination against non whites. It is precisely this kind of knowledge that produces the white sense of guilt. While deep down the more privileged whites know that they benefit disproportionately from past and present policies, they rightly claim that they are not responsible for what happened in the past. This leads some whites to the specious contention that it should not matter how they became privileged. It also leads to the unfounded argument that efforts to make up for past discriminations penalize whites. Ironically, the issue of white guilt stems from their own lack of critical reflection about the meaning of racial classification and its consequences. Guilt is not what most nonwhites want whites to feel. Rather, nonwhites want whites to take responsibility for their conscious and unconscious participation in a discriminatory social system—a system in which whites as a group are the primary economic, social, educational, and political beneficiaries. Once people grasp fully the profound significance of a three-hundred-year-long effort to classify people by race and they understand the causes and consequences of that effort, society is then in a better position to begin to dismantle that system and its legacy on the present and future.

Notes

[1] The strange meaning of being black in America includes a *double consciousness,* which Du Bois defined as "this sense of always looking at oneself through the eyes of others, of measuring one's soul by the tape of the world which looks on in amused contempt and pity." The double consciousness includes a sense of two-ness—"an American, a Negro; two souls, two thoughts, two unreconciled strivings; two warring ideals in one dark body, whose dogged strength alone keeps it from being torn asunder." Another element of the strange meaning of being black in the United States can be found in its system of racial classification, which asks us to believe that people can be classified into clear-cut racial categories.

[2] Du Bois (1868–1963) was not confident that his ideas would be heard or taken seriously as is clear from what he wrote in "The After-Thought" to his book *The Souls of Black Folk:* "Hear my cry, O God the Reader; vouchsafe that this my book fall not still-born into the world wilderness. Let there spring, Gentle One, [1] from out leaves vigor of thought and thoughtful deed to reap the harvest wonderful."

[3] Caldwell and Popenoe point out that often the kind of work a person does is more relevant than race and ethnicity in determining a diagnosis and treatment.

The Anthropology of Race: A Study of Ways of Looking at Race

Vivian J. Rohrl

Study Questions
1. Briefly summarize the "scientific" and "nonscientific" attempts to understand human differences. How did these theories help to justify oppression?
2. Explain the following statement: The "range of self-labels reflects the fact that we all tend to think of our own nature as human nature."

First of all, I would like to make clear that, as far as contemporary scientific anthropology is concerned, there is no set of scientific racial categories (Lasker 1976). Furthermore, one premise of anthropology is that science, rather than reaching absolute truth in a vacuum, progresses and selects what and how we study on the basis of who we are and what we believe and assume about life and relationships. This means that, if the concept of race once existed, it was the product and result of ways in which groups of people thought about other groups. The fact that our scientists are now dismantling the idea of race reflects aspects of our North American version of such things as equal rights under the law, an extension of the earlier Euroamerican "melting pot" tradition. Having said that, in the rest of this discussion I will explore with you the ways in which the concept has been used in the past and the implications of this word "race" in modern times.

Last November, during a talk at the American Anthropological Association in Washington, D.C., French anthropologist Hervé Varenne (1993) commented on the marked absence of references to race and ethnicity in current books by American social scientists about the United States. He noted, for example, that Bellah's (1985) book *Habits of the Heart,* as well as more recent books, described many aspects of culture and community with only tangential reference, if any, to ethnicity or race. Does this imply that America is not an "ethnically structured society"? he asks. Yet, as a social scientist, he has made his own observations of our newspapers and news broadcasts, which, he finds, bear numerous "unmarked" markers of race or ethnicity. In one article, for example, he finds reference to New York's Cardinal O'Connor as a man over 55; in another, H. R. McCall, a new State Controller in New York, is described as an African-American, without reference to his age. This, claims Varenne, brings identifiers to the minds of the viewers; men of 55 and older may feel they understand O'Connor better; "others" may not do so. Similar structures occur in the minds of the "natives," or American viewers, with regard to Mr. McCall. Further, many will identify the Cardinal as of Irish descent; news telecasts, which emphasize appearances and printed names, enhance this phenomenon of identification, even if it's understated. Anthropologist Varenne calls himself and the rest of us to task for not investigating the *idea* or image of race and ethnicity in our culture. He, and we, are not interested so much in describing what will prove to be nonexistent races. Rather, it is important to see how such ideas and notions operate within society, consciously or unconsciously, and where these ideas come from. It is important to trace the scientific unreality of the concept and the embeddedness of the *idea,* however imprecise and changing, in social reality.

In order to better understand the idea of race, we should realize that there is no one overall definition of it. Even in scientific literature, we see it used in many different ways. For example, Jane Goodall (1985), in the book *In the Shadow of Man,* refers to chimpanzees as a species, then compares them to our human "race." Some anthropologists identify hundreds of human races. If scientists differ and disagree about how we use the term "race," there are even more differences in everyday usage. And not just in our own country; others use "race" with still other meanings. There are so many ways in which people have used the word "race," ranging from the statement that there is no such thing as race to describing a very large number of races for people who live and interact within a very narrow area. The word has had emotional loads of so many kinds. Even in our schools, so-called minorities may receive certain treatment or quotas, depending on somewhat self-determined identifying markers. In some public schools, children are allowed one chance to change their self-chosen category of ethnic identification if it proves more advantageous in terms of school placement. Thus, for example, some children from India may place themselves either in the "Asian" or the "Caucasian" category. In the attempt to move children of different backgrounds into the same schools, which frequently means away from their neighborhood schools, "Asian" or "Caucasian" may be a sought-after minority or may represent an overly high proportion to be balanced with members of other ethnic groups. In many ways, the concept of "race" becomes blended with politics, ethnicity or culture patterns, economics, geography, and other factors, even though the concept came into anthropology through biology and the supposedly scientific results of observations and measurements. What, then, is race? How and why do we talk about it? Is the concept of any use? What should we do about it? These are all good questions. I will first present some related definitions, then a brief history of studies of race, followed with some remarks about race in relation to ethnicity, intelligence, and related muddles in the models. Before talking about race, it is necessary to look at ourselves and our fellow humans in terms of [the following]:

A Few Definitions

A *species* is a population that can interbreed and produce fertile offspring. What people used to sometimes refer to as the human "race" is really, biologically speaking, one species. All of the so-called races are able to interbreed with all others to produce viable offspring. All living humans are therefore members of the same species, *Homo sapiens* (Garn 1974). While many features of human beings, such as blood type, are biologically inherited through genetic mechanisms, what makes humans human is our capacity for *culture,* defined as patterned, shared, *learned* behavior, much of which is handed down or transmitted through various methods of learning, including instruction, rewards and punishments, and imitation; it is not biological. Culture is transmitted largely through language, a learned system of symbols and meanings characteristic of all members of our species. Technically speaking, a *race* is a subgroup of a biological species. Unlike the idea of ethnic group or culture, the word "race" usually implies that the features of the group are at least partially inborn or biologically inherited. However, especially in modern times, these distinctions can be blurred.

Modern scientists are not the only people who have tried to learn more about groups of human beings. Curiosities and classifications go back in recorded history, for example to the ancient Greeks. Herodotus, a historian of the fifth century B.C., described people of various colors and shapes, as well as with differing customs, in his travels, including some who, he had been told, had umbrella-shaped feet and who stood upside-down for their protection from the sun and the rain. Aristotle, a century after Herodotus, described essential created forms, and this was related to the Judaeo-Christian tradition in which God's creations were seen as immutable or unchangeable, and people didn't question why. It was simply in their "essence" (Shanklin 1994). Beginning with the ancient Greeks, scholars believed that four "humours," or types of bodily fluids, were related to environment and affected behavior. Thus, people of "choleric" temperament or humor had an excess of bile, were easily angered, and had yellowish faces. Supposedly, a balanced temperament had an equal distribution of the "four humours." Surprisingly, strange as it may seem, a lot of this reasoning is with us today, as we will discuss later. And I mean more than simply the expression "to be in good humour," which is a survival of such beliefs. To continue with the ancients, European explorers of unknown continents brought back written accounts and drawings of humans and not-so-human creatures, some with fantastic shapes and even devil-

ish tails. Later Columbus and other explorers brought back descriptions of other human beings who were docile people of handsome, graceful build. The so-called savages were, however, frequently seen as naked or half-naked cannibals. Their humanity was questioned (Shanklin 1994). This was the result of Europeans encountering what we now call "culture shock." The newly discovered customs caused uncertainties and the shaking of beliefs and assumptions with which Europeans had been living. Then, in 1537, Pope Paul III announced in his document *Sublimis Deus,* or "The Transcendent God," that these American "savages" were, indeed, human, and thus could be invited to join the Church. This coincided with a period of exploitation, colonization, conversion, and redrawing of human knowledge about humanity. During the seventeenth and eighteenth centuries, Europeans began to seek scientific speculations and interpretations about varieties of living creatures, including humans.

The Swedish naturalist Linnaeus, during the eighteenth century, created a catalogue-like classification of all living creatures, including humans. He assumed some connections between appearance, environment, and temperament, for example, categorizing Asians as "melancholy," and somewhat reminiscent of the "four humours." The French naturalist Buffon determined that all humans differed from other creatures with respect to the ability to reason. He believed at first that all types of people and animals became smaller and weaker the further they strayed from the original Garden of Eden, which he thought was near Paris (of course); this is why, he thought, American animals and natives were smaller and weaker. Then, Thomas Jefferson took skins of large American mammals, including moose, to France with him, to explain to Monsieur Buffon that, as to the natives, the weaker ones simply had a different diet and other habits of living. When Buffon saw the huge moose and deer skins, he then decided that the further the creatures got from the Garden of Eden, the more gigantic they become. In 1775, Blumenbach, a German scholar, made detailed classifications of human physical types, observing that "the innumerable varieties of mankind run into each other by innumerable degrees." During this period there were differing ideas about newly discovered "natives." Some believed that they had "strayed from Eden" and fallen from "God's Grace." Others believed that with a little training and instruction, these "savages," who once were, "on a lower rung of the ladder" leading up to progress, could be elevated to "civilized" living. It was during this period that the French philosopher and writer Jean-Jacques Rousseau coined the phrase "noble savage." He asserted that these people are the true nobility, untouched by the artificial affectations of "civilized" aristocracy. It was the work of Rousseau that helped to spark the French Revolution of 1789. All these studies reflect the human need to understand, make sense of, and classify or categorize our natural and social environment.

Scientific Exploration and Explanation of Race

Phase 1. Late eighteenth and early nineteenth centuries. In addition to monogenists, people who believed in one common origin for all varieties of human beings, there were polygenists, people who believed in basic original races with different points of origin. Others believed in long-term immutable unchanging races and sometimes referred to analogies to the Tower of Babel and different human types

developing as a punishment for humans. Mostly, they assumed that biological heredity forms behaviors, including the ability to shape the mouth to make certain linguistic sounds. So, scientists of that period believed that you were born with the ability to make the sounds of your language.

Phase 2. Paul Broca, the mid–nineteenth-century French scholar considered by some to be the father of physical anthropology, shaped studies of race for the late 1800s. He limited the study of race to visible characteristics including skin color and body types, and above all, head form. Thus, some scientists posited three main races of mankind—today we would prefer the term humankind: Caucasoid (known as "white"—predominantly of European origins), Mongoloid (known as "yellow"—predominantly of Asian origins), and Negroid (known as "black"—predominantly of African origins). Further, there were three main head forms: Dolicocephalic (narrow-headed) characterizing the Negroid; Bracycephalic (broad-headed, more easily visualized as wide-faced, characterizing the Mongoloid); and Meso-cephalic (Middle-headed, characterizing the Caucasoid). That raises the question: Was there a connotation of "middle-of-the-road" or "The Golden Mean" or "just right"? These categories were based on a set of measurements acquired by means of measuring people's heads with instruments called calipers and noting the proportion of width (side-to-side) to length (back to front). The formula was width over length times 100—the cephalic index. Without going much into the background of colonialism and its consequences and prejudices, in the sense of prejudgments of temperament and of other features based on misperceived physical features, I will say here that there were a lot of ideas with no scientific or empirical basis that were floating around accounting for popular versions of race. One result of the age of colonialism that followed exploration was the idea of cultural evolution, of progress from simple savagery to complex civilization, of nature worship to monotheism—worship of one God—, of "inferior" to "superior," and so on. As another example of this kind of thinking, some of the "nonwhite" races had been considered closer to the apes in physical characteristics or appearance—maybe even a missing link! In reality, it could be seen that alleged members of the so-called white race were more apelike in the sense of having more hair than any of the other races as they were described at that time. In this period, culture was confounded with or considered attributable to physically ascertainable racial features. Brain size was considered correlated to intelligence, and that, too, is a fallacy, as will be seen. A nineteenth-century physician, Morton, measured aboriginal and European skulls in North America. The quantitative data show that the cranial or skull capacities of the different racial or ethnic groups were similar, but his own biases led him to believe that Euro-Americans have greater cranial capacity than Native North Americans (Gould 1981). Our Neanderthal relatives, now extinct, had a bigger skull than most modern-day humans, and yet, Neanderthals were not so "brainy." Charles Darwin, with his theory of biological evolution, went past the notion of that almost mystical or foreordained progress believed to be inherent in humanity to the idea of minute adaptations to local environmental features, and thus began the demystifying of the prevalent view of social progress that was in its most highly developed form during colonial times, that is into the late nineteenth century.

Phase 3. Early in the twentieth century. Franz Boas, the anthropologist at Columbia University considered to be the father of modern scientific anthropology, did extensive studies measuring the head form and other bodily features of immigrants to the United States, and he discovered that shortly after immigrating, their measurements, including the cephalic index, and more so the measurements of their children, became closer to the typical measurements of people born and raised in the United States. Boas proved conclusively that there is no relationship between race, language, and culture. A baby born of Asian parents brought into an English family would grow up speaking perfect English and acquiring other customs of British culture. In the 1940s, Sherwood Washburn, anthropologist at the University of Chicago, and later at the University of California, studied the behavior of monkeys and apes who were given different diets. He discovered that even bone shapes were not constant but changed according to what the primates ate. If they chewed on a lot of hard food, this increased the mass of their jaw (masseter) muscles which, in turn, caused the supporting structure, or jawbones (mandible and maxilla), to grow to larger proportions. Thus, even bone structure in the *head* of one person is variable during a lifetime. So much for the cephalic index! This discovery, that head form and other skeletal features vary according to nutrition and other environmental factors led to:

Phase 4. Mid–twentieth-century anthropology. Anthropologists selected features known to be determined by only one gene. Thus, the genotype would correspond to phenotype, or what we can see and measure as a visible manifestation of gene activity. For those of us not familiar with these terms: *Genotype* refers to strictly inherited features contained in the genes that are combined within pairs of chromosomes located in our body cells that can be transmitted physically, or genetically, from one generation to another. *Phenotype* is the way in which this gene or (biological) genetic composition expresses or manifests itself in appearance in other physiological characteristics, including variations in bone structure, skin color, and blood groups. Phenotype is the variable appearance resulting from the gene's variable expression, affected by external features such as nutrition and environment. Blood type factors, including A,B,O, Rh, Diego, and the like were determined to be instances in which the genetic mechanism was simple and the phenotype or appearance in the blood was always the same and could be traced back to one genetic structure or gene; thus, here, the phenotype invariably corresponds to the genotype, regardless of environmental or other changes. Other examples of such correspondence include the sickle-cell trait and thalassemia genes, which are related to immunity to malaria and are found in malaria-infested areas, and also a lactase-deficiency gene, which can cause improper digestion of milk and milk products. We'll come back to that. By the 1940s, when anthropologist Robert Redfield, at the University of Chicago, was asked, "What is the Negroid race?" He replied, "The Negroid race is an invention of the Caucasoid race." This phase led quickly, in anthropology, to:

Phase 5. Limitation of "race" study to populations, and not individuals. Thus, American Indians were seen as a subrace that has a large proportion of O blood type and virtually zero percent of B blood type. The advantage of population studies was that you could not point to one individual and name him or her as a typical member of a specific race. Rather, the word was limited to descriptions of populations with statistically measur-

able known genetic features, such as blood type. Race was then described as an interbreeding isolated or semi-isolated population. As long as the population was not totally isolated, there could always be some variability within it, partly due to interbreeding or intermarriage among different types of people and partly due to chemical changes in the genes themselves, called mutations, which can be passed on to the offspring and in this manner spread changes within a population, and would affect even the most isolated of groups. This leads to the description of microraces, small populations with a number of predominant genetic features in common. Sherwood Washburn, mentioned earlier, said that the study of race was a scientific study for scientific purposes and that the "races" varied according to what you wanted to study. Thus, the study of sickle-cell isolates a trait that, when it is found in one chromosome, is a protection against malaria, conferring immunity, and is more predominant in tropical populations where there is more likelihood of being inoculated by the malaria-carrying mosquito (*Anopheles*). These identifying features represent physical traits that once were excellent adaptations to certain environments (Shanklin 1994).

Phase 6. Ashley Montagu, anthropologist at Rutgers University, was perhaps a little ahead of his time when he wrote his books, in the 1960s and 1970s, proving that there was no such thing as race. Ever since prehistoric times, he says, human populations have been mingling, interbreeding, and changing, so that there are no "original races." Even in ancient human remains, we find great variability among skeletal materials of individuals occupying the same site. Montagu proposed that, instead of race, we substitute the term "ethnic group," which designates a society with a shared, learned identity (Montagu 1964; Montagu 1971; Montagu 1982).

"Race" and Reality

Indeed, "ethnic group" covers a large number of features by which a group of people distinguishes itself, including language or way of speaking, dress, and other behaviors. It should also be mentioned that some groups of people refer to themselves with a word that could be translated as "race"—for example, the Latin-American Spanish "raza"—which really refers to *no* necessarily visible or genetically transmittable physical features. In parts of Latin America, whether a person is "Indian" or "Spanish" or some other category could not be ascertained physically but only by looking at what they are wearing and how they are talking. A number of studies conducted among Brazilians reveal about 40 different categories of people. These categories are supposedly based partially on skin color and partially on such factors as occupation and education. As a result, two children in the same Brazilian family can be classified in different "racial" categories from their parents and from each other. Furthermore, Brazilians don't completely agree on the features in their categories, for example, whether *moreno claro* was lighter or darker than *mulato blanco*. Thus, there is no segregation of races in Brazil, and there is no concept of *hypodescent* such as exists in the northern hemisphere. What this means is that in the United States, if a person was known to have a drop of African blood, that person was considered African, while in Brazil people were put on a continuum, in which one group graded into the next. Thus, social definitions have nothing to do with genes. It is easy to attribute significance on a physiological feature when one wants to (Alland 1967; Mead 1971).

In the United States, there are at least three ways of claiming American Indian, or Native American, ancestry. There is the legal Indian, a reservation member, who maintains this identity as long as she or he lives on the reservation. Secondly, there is the person with the Indian phenotype, who may not be considered Indian in certain times and places. Thirdly, there is the person who claims Indian ancestry (Alland 1967). All of these classifications may not have much to do with genetic composition of the person.

What About Race and Intelligence?

Although some scientists have tried to correlate race with intelligence, there is no such thing as fixed races or immutable intelligence. Among most anthropologists, and many other persons, this almost doesn't need to be said. In order to explore this further, let us actually see what "intelligence" consists of. Scales that we use in our society, including the Stanford-Binet 60, the Wechsler scales, and the Guilford model of intellect, use such concepts as "verbal," "memory," "spatial relations," and "abstractive abilities" as partial measures of intelligence. So, if a group of people emphasizes abilities associated with reading and modern mathematics, we might see abstractive abilities valued and exercised, while in cultures without a written tradition, memory-related tasks would make the people seem superior to the average as measured in Anglo-American tests of memory. Among societies that do not emphasize verbal or rhetorical skills and where the children learn by watching and copying, spatial relations abilities may be more highly developed. And this survey of test elements does not even take into account the effect on the brain of good nutrition and emotional well-being, both of which, in an urban environment, are usually accessible to privileged socioeconomic groups and raise performances on intelligence measures (Rohrl 1979).

Intelligence tests measure culturally patterned experience. Thus, for young elementary school children, a test was devised in which the children were asked to write the first letter of a word that describes a given picture. Needless to say, when seeing a picture of snow for the first time, California children proved "dumber" than their more northerly counterparts.

There are also cultural differences in the way people react to test-taking. For example, when Porteus, a psychologist, in the early 1900s, gave his Porteus Maze Test—a pencil-and-paper maze—to Australian aborigines, they were unaccustomed to paper and pencil and unaccustomed to answering questions alone as individuals rather than as a group. Consequently, they fared less well "intelligence"—wise than a comparable group of Europeans or Anglo-Americans, while, on the other hand, the aborigines in a real situation could find their way around the woods much faster than the average Western "civilized" person (Porteus 1931).

There is also no correlation between brain size and intelligence. The Neanderthals, as I already mentioned, had, on the average, a larger head and brain case than many modern humans. Culture itself, being learned behavior, is not correlated with size or shape of the brain or any other physiological feature (Boas 1940; Montagu 1965). Our measures of intelligence tell us more about our own culture—the measurers and creators of tests—than about the people we are measuring. Now, let's talk about:

The Trouble with Ethnicity

These days, all too frequently, people confuse race and culture, even after the strictures of Boas and his students, colleagues, and followers. Just to add to the confusion, I will briefly take us back to earlier days, before industrialization, to see how human groups thought of themselves, as reflected in what they called themselves. Some groups of human beings had either never seen outsiders or didn't associate much with them, had lived in small bands that were accustomed to one familiar territorial range and had a culture, a lifestyle, in common. Their name for their own people frequently translates simply as "people" or "human beings." Thus, the Navajo Indians, of the American Southwest, called themselves *diné,* which means "people." The Cheyenne Indians of the American Central Great Plains called themselves, in their own language, *Tsis-tsis-tas,* which also means "people." The Ojibwa of the North Central Lakes region of North America called themselves *Anish-a-nah-be,* which also means "the original people" (Rohrl 1981).

This range of self-labels simply reflects the fact that we all tend to think of our own nature as human nature. On seeing other cultural types, we tend to assume that we have reached the best style of living and adapting. The best way to express this would be by describing the encounter between the governor of Virginia and the Six Nations Indians who resided there in 1744 (Franklin 1784): "the Government of Virginia has made an offer to the Indian Chiefs that if they would send six youths from the Six Nations to Williamsburg, the college there would take care of them, feed and provide for them, and instruct them in all the learning of the white people." The Indian spokesman replied:

> We know that you highly esteem the kind of learning taught in those colleges, and that the maintenance of our young men, while with you, would be very expensive to you. We are convinced, therefore, that you mean to do us good by your proposal and we thank you heartily.
>
> But you, who are wise, must know that different nations have different conceptions

of things; and you will not therefore take it amiss, if our ideas of this kind of education happen not to be the same with yours. We have had some experience of it; several of our young people were formerly brought up at the colleges of the northern provinces; they were instructed in all your sciences; but when they came back to us, they were bad runners, ignorant of every means of living in the woods, unable to bear either cold or hunger, knew neither how to build a cabin, take a deer, nor kill an enemy, spoke our language imperfectly, were therefore neither fit for hunters, warriors, nor counselors; they were totally good for nothing.

We are however not the less obligated by your kind offer, though we decline accepting it; and to show our grateful sense of it, if the gentlemen of Virginia will send us a dozen of their sons, we will take care of their education, instruct them in all we know, and make men of them.

Not only did these eighteenth-century Indians of the Six Nations have a well-developed style of living, they also were aware of the bicultural standards, the standard of the "sciences" and the standards of the well-adapted hunter and food-grower. If we return to the origin of the definition of "intelligence," meaning the ability to understand relationships and differentiate or choose between the forms and styles around us to enhance our survival, the Six Nations of the eighteenth century possibly demonstrated more of it.

Even the most well-meaning policies can overlook the large variability of people within one designated group. In one instance, the (ethnic) category "Asian" designated who would live in a government-assisted housing project for newly arrived immigrants to the United States. Immediately, differences arose between two Southeast Asian neighbors, a Laotian and a Cambodian family, who spoke different languages and had different—in some ways, almost opposite—social and family structures (Rohrl, n.d.).

Conclusion

Getting back to our main subject, examples of the bicultural or multicultural encounters illustrate that intelligence and culture are not determined by any biologically inherited features. If the native Indian youths had accepted the offer of the Virginian government, they would simply have acquired a new language and culture adapted to an alien lifestyle. So, the questions really get down to "ours and yours" or the differences between "selves" and "others." Race is simply a way in which one group designates itself as "insiders" and other groups as "outsiders" to reinforce or enforce its wishes and/or ideas in social, economic, and political realms. Furthermore, even "scientifically determined" microraces are not constant and are related to ecological and cultural factors. This is why most physical anthropologists no longer use even the concept of "microrace." In fact, for the past twenty years, the concept of races has been considered no longer valid in anthropology. Anthropologists do study individual genetic mechanisms for specific studies, for example adaptability to certain ecological environmental features, such as the sickle cell that is found mainly in populations that carry a large potential for malarial infection, in Africa south of the Sahara, especially in a belt of agricultural societies including the Central Sudan, Nigeria, Ghana, and Gambia. The sickling gene increases where malaria is widespread. However, currently, with hardly any threat of malaria in the United States, the number of African Americans with the sickle cell trait in this country is much smaller than in malaria-infested areas of Africa. Thus, human populations are, even biologically, in constant flux. This is why in physical/biological anthropology the concept of human variation replaces the former idea of "race" as a biological entity (Lasker 1976). The variability within any one so-called race is greater than the variability between the specified ethnic groups or races. These are some reasons why the concept of "race" is at best controversial, and why most social scientists of the 1990s believe that, in general, the concept has neither usefulness nor validity (Wolf 1994). Perhaps in the future we will look back at the ways in which people have used the term "race" as just another step in our continuing enlightenment. At the moment, the conflation of community with heredity is still one of the most dangerous fallacies of modern times.

References

Alland, A. 1967. *Evolution and Human Behavior.* New York: Natural History Press.

Bellah, R. N., R. Madsen, W. M. Sullivan, A. Swidler, and S. M. Tipton. 1985. *Habits of the Heart: Individualism and Commitment in American Life.* New York: Harper & Row.

Boas, F. 1940. *Race, Language, and Culture.* New York: The Free Press.

Franklin, B. 1784. "The Indian's Refusal," in *Remarks Concerning the Savage of North America.*

Garn, S. M. 1974. "Races of Mankind" in *The New Encyclopædia Brittannica.* Chicago: Encyclopædia Brittanica, Vol. 15, pp. 348–357.

Gould, S. J. 1981. *The Mismeasure of Man.* New York: W. W. Norton.

Lasker, G. W. 1976. *Physical Anthropology.* New York: Holt, Rinehart & Winston.

Mead, M. and J. Baldwin. 1971. *A Rap on Race.* Philadelphia: J. B. Lippincott.

Montagu, A., Editor, 1964. *The Concept of Race.* New York: The Free Press.

———. 1965. *The Idea of Race.* Lincoln, Nebraska: University of Nebraska Press.

———. 1971 (1951). *Statement on Race.* New York: Oxford University Press.

———. 1982 (1964). *Man's Most Dangerous Myth: The Fallacy of Race.* Cleveland: World.

Porteus, S. D. 1931. *The Psychology of a Primitive People.* New York: Longmans, Green.

Rohrl, V. 1979. "Culture, Cognition, and Intellect: Towards a Cross-cultural View of 'Intelligence'" in *The Journal of Psychological Anthropology,* Vol. 2 No. 3, pp. 337–364.

———. 1981. *Change for Continuity: The People of a Thousand Lakes.* Washington, D.C.: University Press of America.

———. n.d. "Field Notes of a Community Mediator," unpublished manuscript.

Shanklin, Eugenia. 1994. *Anthropology and Race.* Belmont, Ca: Wadsworth.

Stocking, G. W. 1982. *Race, Culture, and Evolution.* Chicago: University of Chicago Press.

Varenne, Herve. 1993. "American Race Through the News," paper presented at the annual meetings of the American Anthropological Association, Washington, D.C.

Wolf, Eric. 1994. "Perilous Ideas: Race, Culture, People," in *Current Anthropology,* Vol. 35 (1), pp. 1–12.

Letter from Thomas Jefferson: Virginia's Definition of a Mulatto

Thomas Jefferson

Study Questions
1. Reread Jacques Barzun's account on page 360 of one way in which the myth of race is perpetuated. How does Thomas Jefferson's equation for determining "race" support Barzun's argument?
2. Now that it has been shown through DNA testing that Thomas Jefferson fathered children with a woman he owned, does this letter take on added significance? Explain.

March 4, 1815   *Monticello*

You asked me in conversation, what constituted a mulatto by our law? And I believe I told you four crossings with the whites. I looked afterwards into our law, and found it to be in these words: "Every person, other than a Negro, of whose grandfathers or grandmothers anyone shall have been a Negro, shall be deemed a mulatto, and so every such person who shall have one-fourth part or more of Negro blood, shall in like manner be deemed a mulatto"; L. Virgà 1792, December 17: the case put in the first member of this paragraph of the law is *exempli gratiâ*. The latter contains the true canon, which is that one-fourth of Negro blood, mixed with any portion of white, constitutes the mulatto. As the issue has one-half of the blood of each parent, and the blood of each of these may be made up of a variety of fractional mixtures, the estimate of their compound in some cases may be intricate, it becomes a mathematical problem of the same class with those on the mixtures of different liquors or different metals; as in these, therefore, the algebraical notation is the most convenient and intelligible. Let us express the pure blood of the white in the capital letters of the printed alphabet, the pure blood of the Negro in the small letters of the printed alphabet, and any given mixture of either, by way of abridgment in MS. letters.

Let the first crossing be of a, pure Negro, with A, pure white. The unit of blood of the issue being composed of the half of that of each parent, will be $a/2 + A/2$. Call it, for abbreviation, h (half blood).

Let the second crossing be of h and B, the blood of the issue will be $h/2 + B/2$ or substituting for $h/2$ its equivalent, it will be $a/4 + A/4 + B/2$ call it q (quarteroon) being ¼ Negro blood.

Let the third crossing be of q and C, their offspring will be $q/2 + C/2 = a/8 + A/8 + B/4 + C/2$, call this e (eighth), who having less than ¼ of a, or of pure Negro blood, to wit ⅛ only, is no longer a mulatto, so that a third cross clears the blood.

From these elements let us examine their compounds. For example, let h and q cohabit, their issue will be $h/2 + q/2 = a/4 + A/4 + a/8 + A/8 + B/4 = {}^3a/8 + {}^3A/8 + B/4$ wherein we find ⅜ of a, or Negro blood.

Let b and e cohabit, their issue will be $b/2 + e/2 = a/4 + A/4 + a/16 + A/16 + B/8 + c/4 = {}^5a/16 + {}^5A/16 + B/8 + c/4$, wherein ⁵⁄₁₆ a makes still a mulatto.

Let q and e cohabit, the half of the blood of each will be $q/2 + e/2 = a/8 + A/8 + B/4 + a/16 + A/16 + B/8 + C/4 = {}^3a/16 + {}^3A/16 + {}^3B/8 + C/4$, wherein ³⁄₁₆ of a is no longer a mulatto, and thus may every compound be noted and summed, the sum of the fractions composing the blood of the issue being always equal to unit. It is understood in natural history that a fourth cross of one race of animals with another gives an issue equivalent for all sensible purposes to the original blood. Thus a Merino ram being crossed, first with a country ewe, second with his daughter, third with his granddaughter, and fourth with the great-granddaughter, the last issue is deemed pure Merino, having in fact but ¹⁄₁₆ of the country blood. Our canon considers two crosses with the pure white, and a third with any degree of mixture, however small, as clearing the issue of the Negro blood. But observe, that this does not reestablish freedom, which depends on the condition of the mother, the principle of the civil law, *partus sequitur ventrem,* being adopted here. But if e emancipated, he becomes a free *white* man, and a citizen of the United States to all intents and purposes. So much for this trifle by way of correction.

Photo of newly freed slaves. Based on their physical characteristics many in this photograph would not be labeled "black." Yet because of their mixed biological ancestry and the classification rules of the time they all suffered slave status.

Ethnic Diversity: Its Historical and Constitutional Roots

CRUZ REYNOSO

Study Questions
1. List the various historical and constitutional events that show the struggle in the United States to accommodate diversity.
2. Evaluate the process of change.

I want to talk with you about the law and ethnic diversity in our country. Since the birth of our nation, we Americans have been in an evolutionary process of defining who we are as Americans, what the American community is, and who belongs to it. In that regard, the American experience has been a great historical experiment, successful sometimes, but not successful other times. The experience we have had as a people is intertwined with our Constitution and the principles that the Constitution has established. The basic question we have to ask ourselves is the following: How can we as a people, or as peoples of diverse religions, races, and ethnicities, live together and prosper together?

Before the birth of our nation, and sadly it continues today, some of the great wars in this world have come about due to the hatred toward those who are different—by religion, race, or ethnicity. We see what is happening in the former Soviet Union, Eastern Europe, the Middle East, Africa, and even such places as South America. These hatreds are live issues, traumatic issues that have brought a great deal of suffering to the human family. When we as Americans came together to form our nation, I think we

asked the same basic question: Can we have a nation, can we have a people, who can live together and consider themselves as one, and yet be as different as the peoples of this world?

One of America's experiments was in religion. Even though the Constitution declares that the federal government shall not establish religion, we understood early that the essence of that constitutional mandate was a concern about our right, as individual Americans, to practice our own religion. Those who penned the Constitution had in mind the great wars of Europe and the Middle East which had killed so many and had brought so much suffering. So they concluded that the new country had to be one in which folk of different religions could live together. The living together by those who practice different religions has not been all that easy. Books have been written about the "other Americans," Americans who were not of European, Protestant ancestry. Fred Hart, former Dean of the University of New Mexico, and still a professor there, tells that his dad remembers when they were growing up in Boston. Signs in some establishments that hired workers would read something like, "Help wanted:

Irish and Dogs need not apply." That reaction of prejudice and hatred by some of the owners of those plants was based on religion as well as ethnicity. Indeed, it was not until John Kennedy's presidential campaign that the nation said, "We have matured enough that we can see a Catholic in the White House." That is a long time—from the inception of our country until 1960.

We have succeeded in creating an American culture wherein folk of different religions can live together and consider themselves one people. We appear to have reached a relatively satisfactory solution, at least for a while, because the issue of religion does not come up all the time. There is a fellow you may have heard of by the name Pat Buchanan. He is described by some as a conservative, a right-winger, a racist, and by others as a great American. Never is he described as "the Catholic candidate." Yet he is a Catholic, and he often cites his Catholicism to reject the accusation that he is a racist. To me, it is an evolution in the public life of our country that we have a person running for president whose Catholicism hardly gets mentioned.

Others have also suffered. Non-Christians, particularly Jewish people, as well as Hindus and Native Americans have suffered from exclusion. A few years ago, the Alaska Supreme Court issued, I thought, a moving opinion about the rights of a Native American to kill a moose because it was part of the religion of that particular tribe.[1] The Alaska Supreme Court was balancing the right of the state to protect the environment with the right of that particular tribe to exercise its own religion, and, in a sensitive opinion, tried to balance those interests. Thus, the historic process continues.

Issues of religion will always be with us, because who we are religiously is so important to each of us. Yet, we have made so much progress. That is our success story. In America we have been able to live together and consider ourselves as one people, though a people of great religious diversity.

The next area in which we as a nation have worked so hard has been that of race, particularly pertaining to African-Americans. We succeeded so poorly that we experienced here what had happened in other countries—a great war, a great civil war. A larger percentage of Americans were killed and maimed during that war than any other war, over something called race. The Civil War is just a reminder of how important and divisive issues of diversity can be. But from the suffering of this nation in that great war, which pitted brother against brother and sister against sister, came an important amendment to the Constitution—the Fourteenth Amendment. Some post–Civil War amendments, like the Thirteenth, are easily understood. The more difficult Fourteenth Amendment provided the source for a redefinition of who we are as Americans. The constitutional notions of equality and due process found within the pre–Civil War Fifth Amendment were incorporated into the post–Civil War amendments. With the Fourteenth Amendment our country was saying, "We meant what we said in the original Ten Amendments." We redefined ourselves as a people to include African-Americans, including former slaves. While many African-Americans had lived as freed men and women before the Civil War, we had not previously succeeded in dealing with the issue of race.

You recall that in the Lincoln-Douglas debates, Abraham Lincoln argued that the Constitution set forth the ideal of equality. Those who signed the Constitution understood that we would not meet that ideal immediately, but that we as Americans had a duty to work day in and day out to get the reality of our country a little bit closer to that ideal. To me, and this may sound strange to you, we reached a new public understanding of the reality that we as Americans are of many races, when we built the Vietnam Veterans Memorial in Washington, D.C., and included a black soldier among the soldiers represented. I think we recognized publicly that all races have sacrificed to make this nation great.

Native Americans, like African-Americans, have suffered because of race. Our country originally dealt with Native Americans through the War Department. We viewed Native Americans as the enemy—they were to be killed or captured. Since then American history has evolved to a better understanding between the Indian and non-Indian.

In recent years, the issue of ethnicity and language has come into the forefront. Ethnicity and language, like religion and race, define us. Are we as Americans, or should we be, a people of one language and one ethnicity? In many states there is what is called the English-only movement. A friend of mine from New England, with whom I have served on several committees of the American Bar Association, came up to me one day and said, "Cruz, I know an elderly couple, friends of mine, who went from New England to Florida, and when they came back they said that they were taken aback. They found portions of Miami where everybody spoke Spanish. Only when the couple explained that they did not speak Spanish was English spoken." My friend said, "Cruz, we must do something about this; we must have one language for all of us." I responded: "You are absolutely right. When are you learning Spanish?"

We have struggled with the issue of language and ethnicity throughout our national life. I do not think that we have yet decided what our national ideal is in that regard. My own view is that we Americans are now, and have historically always been, a people of many languages and many ethnic groups. I mentioned the Native Americans, who were here before the European-Americans, and who enjoyed great civilizations and who created marvelous works of art. Somehow we look at the Native Americans of Mexico and the Latin Americans as being those who created great civilizations and great art. The reality is that Native Americans who have lived in what we now call the United States also had that great creativity. We can look to the great irrigation system constructed in New Mexico, or we can look to the political organization of the Navajo nation. Other ethnic groups, such as the Spanish-speaking, came to this land over a hundred years before the English-speaking. Travel in New Orleans or Florida, certainly in Puerto Rico and the Southwest, demonstrates their influence. Sante Fe, New Mexico, claims to be the longest standing city that has been a seat of government in what is now the United States. It goes back to the mid-sixteenth century. So folk of different languages and different ethnics groups have been here for a long time.

In the seventeenth century, when the English-speaking Europeans came to the eastern shores of the United States, so did those who spoke French and German and other languages. Indeed, in his autobiography, Benjamin Franklin spoke about how the United States Constitution was translated into the German language during the political debates about whether or not the Constitution should be approved by the people of this country. It seems to me that we have always recognized the importance of people who are of different ethnic groups and tongues.

Take a look at the history of my own state of California. While I spent four years in New Mexico, and I tell folks that I consider myself part manito (a New Mexican is a manito), I was born in California. First came the Native Americans, then the Mexicans and Spaniards who came and settled that land well before the Americans got there. Then came groups from South America, particularly the Chilean community in San Francisco, in large part because they were fishermen and traders who sailed up and down the Pacific coast. In the middle of the last century, the Americans came to California, and about the same time came many Chinese, followed by Japanese and Filipinos. Currently we have great influxes of people from Southeast Asia and Central America. In Los Angeles, I see whole communities change in a matter of few years. I used to stay in a certain part of Los Angeles which a few years ago was mostly Mexican-American (Chicano) and Anglo-Americans. Now it is mostly Central Americans.

We have seen these great historical changes in our country. It seems to me that we have the political foundation and the ideals of our Constitution to help us meet those realities. Those ideals will help us craft a country in which we consider ourselves as one people, while continuing to enjoy the strength which comes from different religions, races, languages and ethnicities.

We start with basics. The Constitution states that all of us, all the "persons" in this country, enjoy constitutional protections; it is not "citizens," the "English-speaking" or the "Spanish-speaking," who are protected, but all of us as "persons." The United States Supreme Court had occasion to deal with the issue of ethnicity and language in a case that came before it in 1923. You may have read about it in your Constitutional Law classes, *Meyer* v. *Nebraska*.[2] You may remember that it is a case that dealt with a state statute enacted around 1919 during the First World

War.[3] There was a strong anti-German feeling during that time in America. I recall older persons I knew, who were adults during that war, telling me that in their schools, German books and music were destroyed. If they were German, they could not be good. At the time, the Nebraska legislature enacted a criminal statute that prohibited the teaching of German to youngsters before they had graduated from the eighth grade.[4] There was a parochial school in Nebraska called the Zion Parochial School where youngsters were taught in English and in German.[5] A young teacher by the name of Meyer, despite the law, continued to teach in German. He was arrested and convicted.[6] Here is what the statute said:

No person individually or as a teacher, shall, in any private, denominational, parochial or public school, teach any subject to any person in any language other than the English language.... Languages, other than the English language, may be taught as languages only after a pupil shall have attained and successfully passed the eighth grade as evidenced by a certificate of graduation issued by the county superintendent of the county in which the child resides.[7]

Meyer appealed his conviction, but the courts in Nebraska upheld the constitutionality of the statute.[8] Interestingly, court decisions in Nebraska excluded the "dead languages,"—Latin, Greek, and Hebrew—from this statute.[9] The legislature, according to the state supreme court, did not mean that students could not study dead languages, only that they could not study certain "live" languages.[10] Eventually the case reached the United States Supreme Court, and the Court looked at the facts and asked itself whether the statute could be constitutional. The Court tried to define what "liberty" meant under the Fourteenth Amendment.[11]

Although the Justices did not talk about it, I think they were also concerned about the Ninth Amendment. When the first Ten Amendments were introduced, an important political debate took place regarding the question of whether those protections that we receive from the first ten amendments were exclusive. In many states, many people said, "No, we want to make clear that those protections are by way of description, for there are many other rights that we have as Americans that government does not have the right to take away." That conclusion was echoed in the *Meyer* case:

> While this Court has not attempted to define with exactness the liberty thus guaranteed [by the Fourteenth Amendment], the term has received much consideration and some of the included things have been definitely stated. Without a doubt, it denotes not merely freedom from bodily restraint but also the right of the individual to contract, to engage in any of the common occupations of life, to acquire useful knowledge, to marry, to establish a home and bring up children, to worship God according to the dictates of his own conscience, and generally to enjoy those privileges long recognized at common law as essential to the orderly pursuit of happiness by free men.[12]

Notice that none of these protections mentioned are found in the Constitution. The Court was saying that surely the right to marry, the right to have children, the right to bring up your family have to be so fundamental that Congress and the states cannot monkey around, if you will, with those rights. Those unstated rights include the right to worship God according to the dictates of a person's own conscience, and generally to enjoy those privileges long recognized at common law as essential to the orderly pursuit of happiness by free men

and women. The Court then went on to discuss the importance of language to an individual.[13] The Court ruled that the Nebraska statute was unconstitutional, and that the state had to have an overwhelmingly important reason to prohibit a youngster from learning German, or a teacher from teaching German.[14] The state, the Court wrote, clearly may go very far in order to improve the quality of its citizens, physically, mentally, and morally.[15] The individual, however, has certain fundamental rights which must be respected and that includes the right of languages.[16] It seems to me that such a right includes the right of ethnicity. The right to one's own language was recognized as fundamental within our Constitution.

The Court had another occasion to look at the issue of ethnicity in a case from the state of California. We produce a great deal of constitutional law from the state of California. A case came up in 1947, if I remember correctly, called *Oyama* v. *California*.[17] California had passed a statute that prohibited aliens from owning land in California.[18] The breadth of the statute had been narrowed by court decisions; by the 1940s the statute had been interpreted to mean that Japanese could not own land in California. A Japanese immigrant had bought and paid for some land and then put the title in the name of his son, so the son was the legal owner.[19] The father then filed in court to become the guardian, and, in fact, was the child's actual guardian.[20] The statute declared that if a person, who could not legally become a citizen, paid for the land, it would be presumed that such payment was an effort to get around the statute.[21] In that event, the land would escheat to the state.[22] Interestingly, it was the Attorney General of California who brought the action against Mr. Oyama. The only person who testified was the person in charge of the land.[23] The Oyamas did not testify because the hearing took place during the Second World War, when the Oyamas were confined in a concentration camp.[24]

The trial court decided against the Oyamas, and the case was appealed in the California courts.[25] The courts found that the father had paid for the land, and that the Oyamas were clearly trying to get around the statute, and, therefore, the land properly escheated to the state.[26]

The United States Supreme Court looked at the case from the point of view of the little boy, Fred Oyama, and said, "Wait a minute. We are looking at the rights of a citizen, Fred Oyama."[27] Another contemporaneous statute in California permitted parents to make a gift of land to a child by paying for the land.[28] The Court underscored that an American citizen, the child, was being treated differently because of who his parents were.[29] This case presented a conflict between a state's right to formulate a policy in land-holding within its boundaries and the right of American citizens to own land anywhere in the United States.[30] The Court concluded that when these two rights clash, the rights of a citizen may not be subordinated merely because of his father's country of origin (that is, the ethnicity of the citizen).[31]

So we start to see a constitutional pattern which protects persons from discrimination on the basis of ethnicity. And I just want to remind us that the Constitution so often deals in the negative, that is, "You can't do A, B, and C," but what it really means is that people have certain rights. While the Court ruled that the Constitution provided protection from discrimination, it really was defining the right of Americans to their own language and ethnicity.

When I was a youngster in Orange County, California, we still had segregated schools. For several years I was sent to a public grammar school referred to as "The Mexican School." There were other schools called "The American Schools." I was born in the then-little town of Brea; Orange County was rural in those pre-Disneyland days. I had gone to school in Brea for a couple years and then my family moved to the nearby community of La Habra. There were a lot of folks in La Habra of Mexican ancestry. When September came, we looked for a school and found a place that looked like a school we were used too—it was built with bricks, it was two stories and had a playground in the back. My brothers and I went there to sign up, and the school officials said, "No, you don't go to this school, you go to another, the Wilson School." So we went to Wilson School. We noticed that all the youngsters there were Latinos and Chicanos, and we asked why we were being sent to this school. We were told that we were being sent to this school to learn English. Since my brothers and I already knew English, we were a little bit suspicious that maybe that was not the reason. After a few months a black family with two youngsters moved into our barrio. They did not speak a word of Spanish; they only spoke English. Nonetheless, they were sent to our school. So we got doubly suspicious. Incidentally, educationally speaking, it was not a lost cause at all. You may have heard of the "immersion system" of learning a language other than your own; those black youngsters were speaking Spanish as well as we in about six months. Meanwhile, we noticed that there were Anglo-American families whose houses literally abutted on Wilson School, and they were being sent to distant schools. After a while we recognized that, in fact, ours was a segregated school.

A few years after I "graduated" from Wilson (grades kindergarten through sixth), the school was integrated. A lawsuit was filed challenging the segregation of Mexican-American school children in a nearby school district. A federal judge ruled that under California law, school segregation was unlawful.

Related issues reached the United States Supreme Court. It was in a different context that the case of *Hernandez* v. *Texas*[32] came before the high Court in 1954. A Texan who was Mexican-American had been convicted of murder and appealed.[33] He was unhappy that there had been no Latinos, Chicanos, or Mexican-Americans on the jury.[34] The county in Texas where he was tried was 14 percent Mexican-American, yet for twenty-five years there had not been one Latino on a jury commission, a grand jury, or a petit jury.[35] During that time apparently 6,000 persons had been called to serve on one of those commissions or juries and not one had a Spanish surname.[36] Indeed, the Court also pointed out that there were some suspicious matters in that community. In the courthouse, there were two bathrooms, one unmarked, and the other with a sign that read "Colored Men" and then below it "Hombres Aqui" (Men Here). That made the Court a little bit suspicious.[37] There was at least one restaurant in town, the Court said, that had a sign in front that read, "No Mexicans Served." Until very recently the public schools had been segregated.[38] There was extensive testimony in the record by the authorities arguing that they had never discriminated against Latinos; all they tried to do was to find the best possible people to serve.[39] The Supreme Court concluded that despite the generalized denial, it was very difficult to believe that out of 6,000 people, they had not been able to find one qualified Latino.[40] The Court noted that "[t]he state of Texas would have us hold that there are only two classes—white and Negro—within

the contemplation of the Fourteenth Amendment,"[41] even as late as 1954. Incidentally, you will find *Hernandez* v. *Texas* reported just before a case that may sound familiar to you, *Brown* v. *Board of Education of Topeka*.[42] The Court was busy in those days. The Court rejected the Texas notion out of hand. "The Fourteenth Amendment," the Court said, "is not directed solely against the discrimination due to a 'two-class theory'— that is, based upon differences between 'white' and Negro."[43] The Court went on to say that the Constitution indeed protects everybody:

> The exclusion of otherwise eligible persons from jury service solely because of their ancestry or national origin is discrimination prohibited by the Fourteenth Amendment. The Texas statute makes no such discrimination, but the petitioner alleges that those administering the law do.[44]

And, in fact, the Court was convinced that that is exactly what had happened. So again we have a confirmation by the Court that ethnicity is protected.

For those of you who might be concerned about the current Supreme Court, I just want to tell you that the following is written by a distinguished observer of the court:

> Even Justice Rehnquist, the modern Justice who takes the least interventionist view of equal protection and who is the strongest opponent of the expansion of "suspect classification" jurisprudence, acknowledged in *Trimble* v. *Gordon*...that classifications based on "national origin, the first cousin of race"...were areas where "the Framers obviously meant [equal protection] to apply."[45] So apparently even those who take lightly the post–Civil War amendments are convinced that in this area, in the area of ethnicity, there is no question that it is protected by the Constitution.

Finally, I want to mention a case decided by the California Supreme Court called *Castro* v. *California*.[46] It is one of my favorite cases, maybe because I was the director of a legal services group called California Rule Legal Assistance (CRLA), which filed this action on the behalf of its clients. The challenged California constitutional provision read: "[N]o person who shall not be able to read the Constitution in the English language, and write his or her name, shall ever exercise the privileges of an elector in this State."[47] That constitutional provision was passed in 1891, and I will come back to that fact in a few minutes.[48]

Our clients were able to show that in Los Angeles County where they lived, there were seventeen newspapers published in Spanish, eleven magazines, many radio and television stations, and through these, they were able to know exactly what the public issues of the day were and were able to cast a vote that was educated.[49] The California Supreme Court, analyzing the state constitutional provision by the standards of the federal Constitution, said, in essence, "It cannot stand. We consider the right of citizens. The right to vote is very important." The court determined that the state could not take away the right to vote unless there was a very important reason to do so, and here the court simply did not find that reason. These voters, by reading and hearing, could, in fact, educate themselves.[50] Then, at the end of the opinion, the court added one of my favorite paragraphs in American jurisprudence. Writing for the court, Justice Raymond Sullivan said:

> We add one final word. We cannot refrain from observing that if a contrary conclusion were compelled it would indeed be ironic that petitioners, who are the heirs of a great and gracious culture, identified

with the birth of California and contributing in no small measure to its growth, should be disenfranchised in their ancestral land, despite their capacity to cast an informed vote.[51]

So we have come a long way—in California and in the nation.

In *Castro,* the court reviewed the history of constitutional and statutory changes in California, and in one of the footnotes it cited to a case called *People v. Hall.*[52] It is one of my favorite cases in California jurisprudence for a reason opposite that of *Castro* v. *California.* Let me tell you about the *Hall* case. When California was first formed into a state, the English-speaking and the Spanish-speaking worked cooperatively. They got together in the constitutional convention of 1849 and agreed upon a constitution, even though some who were at that convention spoke no English, and others spoke no Spanish. Yet they got together and created a constitution that was published in both English and Spanish.

But then, sadly, the atmosphere started changing in California, and the case of *People v. Hall,*[53] decided in 1854, gives you a sense of how much change had come about. The legislature had passed a statute that prohibited any testimony against a white person in court if the testimony came from a black, mulatto, or an American Indian.[54] A white man was convicted of murder by the testimony of a Chinese man.[55] At that time we had no intermediate court, so the lawyers for the convicted appealed directly to the California Supreme Court.

The California Supreme Court was composed of three members at that time, and it wrote an opinion that is great fun to read in its historical context. The court pointed out that the Native Americans are part of the Mongoloid races and that eons ago, the

Mongoloid races from Asia had travelled over the Bering Straits and through Alaska. In the course of many thousands of years these migrants ended up in the lands we now call the United States. The Indians and the Chinese were of the Mongoloid race. When the legislature said Indians could not testify, it obviously meant to include anybody of the Mongoloid race.[56] Since Chinese belong to the Mongoloid race, the court reasoned, they obviously cannot testify against a white man, and so the court reversed the murder conviction.

The *Hall* court described the Chinese people as a "distinct people...whose mendacity is proverbial; a race of people whom nature has marked as inferior, and who are incapable of progress or intellectual development beyond a certain a point, as their history has shown...."[57] This quote does not include another discussion in which the court noted that if allowed to testify against a white person, the Chinese would soon want to vote, want to be lawyers, and would even want to sit on the bench.[58] The court ruled on the basis of clear statutory construction. The court seemingly asked, "How could anybody disagree that Indian means Chinese." Indeed, the court wrote: "[E]ven in a doubtful case we would be impelled to this decision on the grounds of public policy."[59]

Sadly, just a few years thereafter, Manuel Dominguez, who had been at the California constitutional convention, and had signed the constitution, was not permitted to testify in a court of law in San Francisco in 1857 because he was of Indian ancestry. That is part of the history of California. To look at the *Castro* decision and see how the law has evolved is a matter of great satisfaction to me.

Incidentally, I have always been interested in Los Angeles. If you visit Los Angeles, go down to the area where Los Angeles was first founded, La Placita (the little plaza). There is a plaque there which has the names of all of the people who helped found Los Angeles. The Spaniards were great record keepers. The records identify people by race and by occupation as well as other characteristics. That plaque identifies the race of the original settlers. I have a book here[60] which published a census taken about the time Los Angeles was founded. Let me just go down the line; you will see the great variety of people that founded California. The reality contrasts with the early romanticized movies that came out of Hollywood portraying Spanish vaqueros as typical. Here are the real Californios: Josef de Lara, Spaniard; his wife Maria, india sabina; Josef Navarro, mestizo; his wife Maria, mulata; Basil Rosas, indian; a husband, indian; his wife, indian; another husband Alejandro Rosas, indian; his wife Juana, coyote indian—mixture of pure Indian and mestizo; Pablo Rodriguez, indian; wife Maria Rosalia, indian; Manuel Camero, mulato; his wife Maria Tomasa, mulata; Luis Quintera, negro; his wife Maria Petmulata; Jose Moreno, mulato; Antonio Rodriguez, chino (Chino—a person who has negroid features, but was born of white parents).[61] That is the real mixture of Los Angeles from whence many of us come.

Let me just read you a passage from that same book. A very distinguished early Californio, Pablo de la Guerra, who was late as state senator, is quoted. The title of the book was *Foreigners in Their Native Land*, taken from a speech he delivered in the California legislature in 1856:

> It is the conquered who are humble before the conqueror asking for his protection, while enjoying what little their misfortune has left them. It is those who have been

sold like sheep—it is those who were abandoned by Mexico. They do not understand the prevalent language of their native soil. They are *foreigners in their own land*. I have seen seventy- and sixty-year-olds cry like children because they have been uprooted from the lands of their fathers. They have been humiliated and insulted. They have been refused the privilege of taking water from their own wells. They have been denied the privilege of cutting their own firewood.[62]

This is our history.

Yet we have struggled. As the cases from the California and the United States Supreme courts indicate, we have indeed made a great deal of progress. The struggles continue. Issues like education and political empowerment create conflict. As we all know, progress does not come overnight. My hope is that as we struggle with these issues, we will also struggle with that notion of how can we be diverse and yet be one people.

For myself, I have enjoyed that diversity. I have a friend by the name of Bill Ong Hing, a professor at Stanford. He invited my family and me to go to his church where a Chinese play was presented. We enjoyed tremendously seeing a culture that my family and I had not seen before. I remember walking down the streets of San Francisco and a gentleman coming up to Bill. The two of them chatted for a couple of minutes in Chinese and then spoke in English. I did not feel that they were talking about me during that time. So often we reject folk who speak a language other than our own, because we think, "Well, they must be talking about me." I never thought that any one person was that important. I would hope that we learn to enjoy the reality that other people are different and that they have a language, a cultural richness, if you will,

that we can enjoy. Indeed, I really do give thanks for the fact that we have people in this country who speak different languages and come from different cultures who will make our country far stronger economically and far stronger politically.

I always think of the advertising that we as Americans do. I am told that there was a time when General Motors was advertising in Latin America for their then-new car called the Nova. Apparently nobody had told them that "Nova" in Spanish is "Nova," which means "It won't go." It was not a successful advertising campaign. Or another time when my former colleague, Justice Joseph Groden of the California Supreme Court, came back from a long trip in China, and he told me there were Coca-Cola signs all over China. I asked about Pepsi-Cola because I had read that Pepsi had a contract with the Chinese government. At that time Pepsi-Cola had a little ditty, you may remember many years ago, that went something like, "Pepsi, come alive with Pepsi." Unfortunately, it had been mistranslated in Chinese to read, "Pepsi brings your ancestors back to life," and the Chinese, with their respect for their ancestors, were not amused. Pepsi apparently lost its contract.

I also remember reading an article by a German industrialist who said basically, "You know, I speak English, and I go to all of these gatherings where folk come from all over the world selling their high-tech equipment. I go and look at all that and I see that the Americans make very good equipment, and the Japanese have very good equipment, as do other nationals. They all look very good. Then afterwards, though I speak English, I socialize with folks generally in the German language, because I feel more comfortable in German. All I can tell you is that in Germany, you'll sell in the German language."

I think that our diversity will indeed bring strength to us, and I think that we can profit from it. But more importantly, we need to continue working with the reality that we are a very diverse people, ethnically and linguistically. Despite those differences, as with differences of race and religion, we ought to look at what unites us, what makes us all Americans. We need to look at our history, at the land, at the suffering we have been through as a people. We need to examine the ideals that we find in the Constitution, those very ideals that have brought the California and the United States Supreme courts to declare that there are those rights so important that government can not take them away from us. If nobody can take those rights away from us, we need to rejoice in those rights, to rejoice in our differences, to appreciate those differences, and to profit one from another.

Notes

[1] *Frank* v. *State of Alaska,* 604 P.2d 1068 (Ala. 1979).

[2] 262 U.S. 390 (1923).

[3] *Id*. at 397, citing NEB. LAWS 1919, ch. 249, entitled "An act relating to the teaching of foreign languages in the State of Nebraska" (approved April 9, 1919).

[4] *Id*. (citing NEB. LAWS 1919, ch. 249, § 2).

[5] *Id*. at 396–97.

[6] *Id*. at 396.

[7] *Id*. at 397 (quoting NEB. LAWS 1919, ch. 24, §§ 1–2).

[8] *Id*.

[9] *Id*. at 400–01.

[10] *Id*. at 401.

[11] The Fourteenth Amendment states, in pertinent part: "No State shall…deprive any person of life, liberty, or property, without due process of law; nor deny to any person within its jurisdiction the equal protection of the laws." U.S. CONST. amend. XIV, § 1.

[12] *Meyer,* 262 U.S. at 399.

[13] *Id*. at 400–03.

[14] *Id*. at 402–03.

[15] *Id*. at 402.

[16] *Id*. at 400–01.

[17] 332 U.S. 633 (1948).

[18] *Id*. at 635–36 & nn. 1 & 3, citing Alien Land Law, 1 CAL. GEN. LAWS, Act 261 (Deering 1944 & Supp. 1945).

[19] *Id*. at 636–37.

[20] *Id*.

[21] *See id*. at 636, citing Alien Land Law, 1 CAL. GEN. LAWS, Act 261, § 9(a).

[22] *Id*.

[23] *Id*. at 638. The witness, John Kurfurst, had been left in charge of the Oyama property when the Oyama family was evacuated in 1942 as part of the evacuation of persons of Japanese descent during World War II. *Id*. at 637–38.

[24] *See id.* at 638.

[25] *See id.* at 639.

[26] *Id.* at 639–40.

[27] *See id.* at 640.

[28] *Id.* at 640 & n. 16, citing CAL. PROB. CODE ANN. § 1407.

[29] *Id.* at 640–41.

[30] *Id.* at 647.

[31] *See id.* at 646–47.

[32] 347 U.S. 475 (1954).

[33] *Id.* at 476.

[34] *Id.* at 476–77.

[35] *Id.* at 480–81 & n. 12.

[36] *Id.* at 482.

[37] *Id.* at 479–80.

[38] *Id.* at 479.

[39] *Id.* at 481.

[40] *Id.* at 482.

[41] *Id.* at 477.

[42] 347 U.S. 483 (1954).

[43] *Hernandez,* 347 U.S. at 478.

[44] *Id.* at 479.

[45] CONSTITUTIONAL LAW 624 n.3, Gerald Gunther ed., 11th ed. (1985), citing *Trimble* v. *Gordon,* 430 U.S. 762, 777 (1977) (Rehnquist, J., dissenting).

[46] 466 P. 2d 244 (Cal. 1970).

[47] *Id.* at 245 (quoting CAL. CONST. art. 2, § 1).

[48] *Id.* The English literacy requirement was proposed in 1891 by a California state assemblyman, A. J. Bledsoe, who in 1886 had been part of a committee that expelled all persons of Chinese ancestry from Humboldt County, California. *Id.*

[49] *Id.* at 254–55.

[50] *See, e.g., id.* at 254–57.

[51] *Id.* at 259.

[52] *Id.* at 248 n.11, citing *People* v. *Hall,* 4 Cal. 399 (1854).

[53] 4 Cal. 399 (1854).

[54] *Id.* at 399, quoting Act of April 16, 1850 (regulating California criminal proceedings).

[55] *Id.*

[56] *Id.* at 400–04.

[57] *Castro,* 466 P.2d at 248 n.11, quoting *Hall,* 4 Cal. at 404–05.

[58] *Hall,* 4 Cal. at 404–05.

[59] *Id.* at 404.

[60] *Foreigners in Their Native Land* 33 (David J. Weber ed., 1st ed. 1973).

[61] *Id.* at 34–35.

[62] *Id.* at vi, quoting Pablo de la Guerra, Speech to the California Senate (1856).

Making Good Again

Erich H. Loewy

◇•◆•◇

Study Questions
1. Outline the various levels of responsibility for the Holocaust.
2. Are German people the only group who should be held responsible? Explain.
3. Why do Germans living today have an obligation "to make good again"?
4. What historical events must the United States come to terms with?

A little while ago I was discussing the trials of some of the former members of the Stasi (the East German secret police) with a German friend and colleague of mine. The whole question of guilt and punishment naturally came up. My friend felt that digging out the truth about the Stasi outrages and bringing those guilty to a speedy, full, and public trial was of great importance for Germany, especially, he said, since Germany had never really come to terms with or fully acknowledged its involvement in the atrocities of the Nazi period. He felt that it was essential for a people to confront the evil committed and to assess the questions of involvement, guilt, and eventual rectification.

Christian Pross's book, published in Germany in 1988 as *Wiedergutmachung: Der Kleinkrieg Gegen die Opfer,* is a work that has ramifications far beyond recounting a shameful (indeed outrageous) episode of history. It is a work that inevitably raises not only historical but also profound social and ethical questions. The remaining historical questions concerning the issues Dr. Pross describes in Germany are only marginally questions of fact: the facts as related in Dr.

Pross's book speak quite sufficiently and eloquently for themselves. The historical questions go beyond these facts. They ask, among other things, how people could have done better and why they didn't; whether and where such Nazi influence continues to prevail; and who, besides those named, were involved. They also ask how we can apply what we have learned to the future. Indeed, the future is upon us: the current concern in Germany with some of the outrages committed by the Stasi, the question of involvement and collusion from sometimes unexpected quarters, and the way such information will ultimately be dealt with hearkens back to the immediate post-Nazi period; recent events in the former Yugoslavia, and atrocities that continue to go largely unexamined and almost entirely unpunished, cry out to heaven. The historical questions, just like the ethical questions that arise from them, are however not purely questions one can relate to the German or to the Yugoslav experience. They go far beyond what happened in Germany or Yugoslavia.

The ethical questions are, of course, profound. Grappling with them raises a whole host of related issues, issues that are hardly confined to Germany and the Nazis' treatment of the Jews or Gypsies. Nor are the ethical questions strictly questions of the twentieth century, although the twentieth century has certainly seen some of the worse outrages in history. they are, however, ethical questions that, for many reasons, have been more explicitly and more urgently addressed in this century than ever before. The events provoking such questions are events involving all of us: all of us, in one way or another, have been party to them. Our being "party" to them may be as victims, as active or even as passive members of a society victimizing others, or simply as bystanders watching from afar. Our involvement, furthermore, may, at different times and in different places, be both as victim and as oppressor: aptly so, the prayer "let not the oppressed become the oppressor" is central to every Yom Kippur service. Its lesson, unfortunately, often remains unlearned, even by those praying.

It is not difficult to find the victims this century has produced. Some of them have been continued from other centuries (for victimization is a process as old as history): Native Americans, blacks in America, and women. Others are new victims created by the particular events of this particular century: Armenians in Turkey, victims of Stalinism, Japanese-Americans, Cambodians, Haitians, Palestinians, Central and South Americans, Kurds—there is almost no end! Still others have been recurrent victims; not only the Jews but blacks, Gypsies, and many others. Among the victims, the economic victims of a capitalist society (a society in which profit and individual enterprise have become the highest good) must also be counted.

The word *Wiedergutmachung* is not easy to translate: *rectification, reparation,* and *res-titution* all fail to convey the flavor of the verb *Wiedergutmachen* ("to make good again"), which, among other things, and most important, implies a healing process. It is a healing process that, while it cannot eliminate the scars could, by reestablishing lost trust, go far in making these scars almost (but not quite) an unpleasant remembrance of things past. Such a healing process is necessary if societies that have historically harmed or disadvantaged groups within or outside their borders are to live internally and externally in peace, and, perhaps equally important, if they are to regain or maintain their own self-respect.

Wiedergutmachung is not quite restitution: returning wrongfully obtained property is restitution. But returning such property does not reestablish trust, does not truly heal. *Wiedergutmachen* goes beyond restitution. As a necessary condition of "making good again," *Wiedergutmachen* includes an element of restitution: one cannot "make good again" or heal without, where possible, giving back what one has wrongfully taken. But beyond this, to heal or to "make good again" recognizes that specific material goods taken and returned often cannot make up for the damage done. Giving back the material goods that were taken from them to people who have been imprisoned in concentration camps or have had their lives shattered can hardly be considered to be "making good again." Making good again must do all it can to show compassion for the victim, must show the victim that the individual or society has come to realize and now truly feels that "there but for the grace of God (or the accident of genetics) go I."

It is often said that money cannot rectify what was done. There is no question that this is true: one cannot compensate the murdered; one cannot compensate those whose physical and psychological existence was shattered or whose lives were uprooted and distorted. The truth of such a statement does not, however, mean that monetary compensation cannot at least help ameliorate the pain and suffering, nor that those who are responsible are not obligated to do their utmost to provide fair compensation. While monetary compensation hardly "rectifies" the situation and certainly does not heal, it nevertheless helps in both material and, perhaps of even greater importance in the long run, in symbolic ways. Trying to give just compensation permits those whose lives were seriously affected to at least (and that necessarily only to a limited extent) recoup their material losses. Furthermore, and most important, trying to give just compensation, when properly done, helps in the healing process. When those responsible for causing the damage (or those historically associated with causing it) are themselves willing to apply balm to the wounds they caused, healing will proceed more easily. Scars, often deep and disfiguring scars, will be left; but such scars will be firmer and better healed. It is here, especially, that German *Wiedergutmachung* has (probably irremediably) missed its opportunity: the story Dr. Pross relates is one of a forced and grudging process, a process engaged in, not to truly heal, but so that an "unpleasant problem" could once and for all be gotten out of the way. And just as is the case with the Japanese-American victims of incarceration in the United States during World War II, time and the death of the victims has served to make most (but not yet quite all) of the problem moot.

Fundamentally, restitution or rectification needs to be a worldwide issue if healing is to take place. It would be easy to see the problem as an isolated event: a merely and specifically historical problem that concerns the survivors (both the victims and those who were somehow involved in the victimizing) of the Nazi era while ignoring the wider lessons that this book can teach us. If these wider lessons are not recognized, internalized, and acted upon, then nations and societies that have committed flagrant injustices to their own or to weaker populations over whom they exerted control cannot expect to live in peace.

Survivors of the Nazi era on both sides (victims and perpetrators) are inevitably linked by a common history. It is necessarily, and on both sides, an uneasy linkage. The question of responsibility is often brought up here: after all, there were not only many Germans who looked with horror at these outrages (and some, even if but a few, who actively tried to oppose them) but also others who, while not opposing them, "took no part"; and there are today many more (indeed, the majority) who were either small children or not even born at the time. Responsibility needs to be defined before the question of restitution to the victims of Nazism by the present German state can be answered. It is not a unique question, one confined to the results of the Nazi era. Rather, questions of this sort need to be raised throughout the world: the question of affirmative action in the United States and in South Africa, the Palestinian question, Yugoslavia, and a multitude of other issues. In a broader sense, the same question appropriately needs to be asked when it comes to what exploiting nations owe those whom they have historically and devastatingly exploited.

To hold all Germans (either all Germans who lived during the Nazi period or who are alive today) personally responsible for the outrages that occurred during the Nazi era is obviously absurd. Persons who were not even born, persons who actively opposed the Nazis, persons who were appalled but who did nothing, and even those who simply closed their eyes and refused to see, cannot be thrown into the same historical pot with those who ordered, carried out, or actively condoned the evil.

There are several senses in which the word *responsibility* can be used. I may be causally responsible by having played a greater or lesser role in a causal chain. Responsibility, in this sense, may or may not be culpability. Being involved in a causal chain does not mean willing participation. I may be the driver of a car that skids or whose brakes fail and that, therefore, kills a child. My involvement in the causal chain is beyond doubt, but to hold me culpable under circumstances truly beyond my control is absurd. On the other hand, I may be driving a car and deliberately kill the child, or I may be driving recklessly, drunk, or knowingly with faulty brakes. In that case, I am causally responsible as well as (albeit perhaps to a variable degree) culpable.

To be responsible not only in the sense of causal responsibility but of culpability implies a possible alternative: something I could have done no matter how difficult the doing might have been to break the causal chain. When I could have done things differently or when I could have opposed an action, we can begin to speak of responsibility in the sense of culpability. In that sense, a three-year-old living in Nazi Germany cannot be thought "culpable"; an adult who knew what was going on (and most did) and who failed to in some way oppose it could, in some sense, be held culpable. Even here, matters are far from clear: culpability may or may not be different depending upon the degree of involvement or the proximity of the actor to the act. The person repairing the rails when he knows that, among other trains, the trains to Auschwitz roll over this track may, in the

sense of being culpable, be co-responsible with the person who scheduled the trains and the one who operated the gas chambers: but while all bear some responsibility, assigning the same degree of guilt to all hardly seems fair. One could, perhaps, argue that part of the difference here is similar to the difference between freedom of action and freedom of will: it is the person who wills the action (in the original German Kantian sense of *Wille* as *Gesetzgebender Wille,* or law-giving will: the will that then determines the person's action) who could be argued to be the most culpable. Such a distinction hardly frees from personal guilt those who did not will the action but who more or less freely participated, but it does state that assigning guilt is hardly an easy matter. Inasmuch as persons knew what was going on and could have done otherwise than they did, they are in some sense implicated not only in acting but in willing such an action.

Responsibility as culpability may be active or passive. The person who knew about Auschwitz and who repaired the rails over which the trains to Auschwitz passed: the person who, knowing about Auschwitz, drew up the train schedule; and the person who operated the gas chambers, all were actively involved. To a different degree in each, they "willed the action." Others, who knew of Auschwitz or who at least knew of the rounding up of Jews, of concentration camps, and of the misery caused by the Nazi regime and who failed to protest even when they themselves were not directly involved in the causal chain, may (and in a different sense) be culpable. Here culpability is culpability for not interfering when interference was possible.

Germans who lived as adults in Nazi Germany and failed to in some way resist Nazi atrocities known to them (even if only by speaking out) inevitably made themselves a party to such atrocities, just as Americans who know about racism in America and who fail to speak out or to act make themselves a party to injustice. Germans living in Nazi Germany who actively spoke out took grave risks: they endangered life, limb, and freedom, as well as those of their families. Speaking out against racism in the United States may, at times, be risky: but it is not of the same order of risk as was speaking out in the Nazi state.

If we acknowledge that the Germans living after the war (or those living today) have a responsibility to rectify past historical evils, then the stories recounted in Dr. Pross's work speak eloquently that this responsibility has been largely evaded. It would appear that many government officials implicated in forging or carrying out Nazi policy were the very ones who played a major role in setting the policies that controlled rectification; likewise former Nazi physicians, some actively involved in causing the damage they were now to judge, played a major role in deciding who would and who would not be entitled to help. This resulted in a charade that, far from helping the healing process, rubbed salt into the wounds.

The atrocities committed in Germany by the Nazis were not committed out of context with Germany's history, social setting, and economic realities. Neither the claim that those living there for the most part "knew nothing about what was going on" nor the claim that all those living at the time "were guilty of participating" can be sustained. At the end of the war, the initial attempt to investigate, assign culpability, and digest the monstrous crimes committed was begun, but it was soon deflected by the fear of communism and the beginning and soon the escalation of the Cold War.

Forces similar to those that helped propel Hitler to power served to help hide much of the evil done and even to spirit some of the perpetrators into hiding. Just as Western capital helped build Nazism as a hedge against the perceived threat of communism, Western influence and at times direct intervention helped guide greater and lesser criminals into secure hiding. It is well known that U.S. authorities, in collusion with, at the very least, members of the Catholic church, if not indeed with the Vatican, and often working through safe houses set up in monasteries, actively participated in the escape of some of the more odious Nazis, sometimes through what came to be known as the "rat line" running from Germany via Austria and Italy and sometimes via Spain and Portugal. The ultimate destination was South America, especially Paraguay and Argentina. A number of such Nazis, men who had actively participated in, and some of whom had been responsible for, the barbarism of that era, were used as U.S. agents or, at times, worked for the U.S. scientific establishment. They were placed on U.S. payrolls and enjoyed U.S. protection. A pervasive and often paranoid fear of communism, or of anything conceived as possibly not entirely hostile to communism, helped Hitler gain and initially consolidate power and later helped those guilty of some of the most heinous atrocities to escape. The story of Klaus Barbie, the "Butcher of Lyon," is not unique in this respect.

In the Nazi period itself, the nations of the world largely stood idly by while Hitler persecuted and eventually exterminated Jews, Gypsies, and any other population group that he saw as opposing him. Despite lofty international pronouncements, little assistance was given to these persecuted people. The League of Nations through its High Commissioner for Refugees in 1934 announced that "governments had been induced to postpone or soften admission regulations...and some countries of potential permanent residence had been persuaded to lessen restrictions on immigration." But this was pure window dressing: nothing substantial was ever accomplished. The Evian Conference, purportedly called to find a solution to the problem of Jewish refugees and attended by most Western nations, took place in 1938 as the curtain was ready to fall. It, too, not only failed to produce concrete results but, as an article in *Newsweek* stated, the case resulted in "most governments promptly slamming their doors against Jewish refugees." Historically, the Evian Conference showed that: (1) the world was hardly unaware of the deplorable conditions in Nazi Germany and the threat hanging over the Jewish population, and (2) beyond pious platitudes, and although it could have done so, the world was not only quite unwilling to interfere but also quite unwilling to help.

Western nations used every excuse possible to refrain from accepting refugees (especially Jewish refugees) trying to escape. I personally remember consulates telling my family and friends that American "quotas were full," only to find out many years later that the U.S. quota had never been filled except for one year: in fact, from 1933 to 1942, only 45 percent of the quota was actually used. During this entire time, except for regular quota admissions with their families, the United States allowed only 240 children into the country, and those were charged to the quota. Individual consuls had the ultimate power of deciding who would receive visas. Many used their power to keep out as many refugees as they possibly could, or to drag their feet until those trying to enter vanished. Some consuls, unfortunately often in key consulates, were at the very least suspect of being antiforeign if not outright anti-

Semitic. Many, many lives were lost because of this maximization of red tape.

Those refugees from Nazi terror who were grudgingly allowed to enter the United States often found hostility and pervasive anti-Semitism rather than welcome: the term "refu-Jew" was coined and much used during this period. Pelley's Silver Shirts, members of the German American Bund, and the Coughlinite Christian Front movement were vocal and active throughout the United States. Persons dressed very similarly to storm troopers, wearing swastika armbands, railed in the streets against the Jewish threat and sometimes engaged in fights with passersby. Father Coughlin, the much-listened-to-radio priest who was also the publisher of the rabidly anti-Semitic tabloid *Social Justice,* cleverly used economic fears to rouse latent anti-Semitism. In this he was supported by, among others, the Brooklyn Catholic diocese's weekly paper *Tablet.* The Protestant *Defender* magazine played essentially the same tune. Surveys as late as 1940 showed that one-third of Americans favored anti-Jewish legislation, one-third disapproved, and the rest were neutral. Despite extensive evidence to the contrary, some newspapers and some speeches by many members of Congress continued to warn of the alleged economic threat posed by allowing refugees to enter this country.

I can state from personal experience (fortified by the pertinent literature on the subject) that arriving and living as a refugee in America was a not altogether pleasant experience. Escaping from the Nazis only to watch the rising tide of American Nazism, to be goaded by thugs with swastika armbands, or to read and hear the distorted railings of the right-wing press and radio was bad enough; to be avoided, if not indeed ostracized socially, was worse. It was not, however, merely social isolation. The

government itself became suspect when, in 1939, the German ship *St. Louis,* carrying over nine hundred people, was not allowed to discharge passengers in the United States. Almost all of the *St. Louis's* passengers were refugees from Nazi Germany, and 734 of them would have visas to the United States the moment the quota cleared a few months from then. The passengers on board the *St. Louis,* who were bound for Cuba, where they were to find intermediate sanctuary before being allowed into the United States, were refused entrance even though they held valid transit visas at departure. Despite the pleadings of the German captain, the United States refused to grant temporary asylum to these refugees so that they could subsequently legally enter the country.

Suspicion of the U.S. government's stance deepened when, during the war, the railroad spur into Auschwitz was never bombed and the traffic into the extermination camps was never effectively interfered with, even though the West controlled the air and what was going on was well known. Intervention would have been easy.

When the United States became involved in the war, American citizens of Japanese origin were imprisoned in detention camps while their sons fought gloriously in the U.S. Army. American concentration camps were hardly the same as those of Nazi Germany: people were not beaten, starved to death, or exterminated. Nevertheless, what happened in Nazi Germany and what occurred at the same time in the United States are frighteningly similar. Japanese were imprisoned merely because of their racial heritage: being Japanese, these were suspected of being enemies of the state.

There are many parallels between Germany's experience with making restitution to its victims and the story of the Japanese incarcerated in the United States during World War II. The Japanese in the United States were either Issei or Nisei. Issei were the first generation, born in Japan, who, even when they had been in the United States for a decade, could not become citizens. Nisei were the second generation, born in the United States and citizens by virtue of birth. Most Japanese-Americans lived on the West Coast. The outbreak of the war brought with it a wave of anti-Japanese feeling in this country—not feeling against Japan but hatred of all Japanese on a racial basis. The Japanese suffered insult, assault, and indignity at the hands of the U.S. population. While this persecution was not carried to the extreme of anti-Jewish persecution in Germany, it was based on the same blind hatred of what was labeled as a different race. Newspapers and the airways carried a stream of racial attacks urging America to "herd 'em up, pack 'em off and give 'em the inside room in the badlands. Let 'em be punched, hurt, hungry and dead up against it." Government propaganda intimating sabotage at Pearl Harbor and suggesting that the Japanese in California were ready to sabotage the U.S. war effort did not help ease America's hysteria. Although the Japanese both in the continental United States and in Hawaii were repeatedly accused of disloyalty, sabotage, and spying, no proof of these charges was ever forthcoming; nor were weapons discovered in their homes or on their property except for those used in hunting, or dynamite used for routine earth moving for farming purposes. In the midst of this hysteria, the decision to intern not only the Issei but also their children (who had been born in the United States) swiftly followed.

It was not until 1988 that Congress, against considerable opposition, finally decided that perhaps some *Wiedergutmachung* was in order for the Japanese-Americans: a *Wiedergutmachen* that took the form of giving $20,000 and an apology to each internee left alive. Many internees, of course, had died in the intervening years. And even for those who were still alive, payment was delayed for a few years. Germany is not the only nation in which *Wiedergutmachung* was obfuscated and delayed!

Another historically persecuted group in the United States are African-Americans. Before, during, and for some time after the war, blacks in many areas of the United States lived under a restrictive system of near-apartheid. And elsewhere in this country, blacks were treated far from equally to whites. Educational opportunities and jobs were often not open to them and when open, were not open on an equal basis. Blacks could not live where they wanted and were discriminated against in a multitude of tacit and overt ways. During the war a black fighter squadron was finally established, largely to show that "Negroes" couldn't effectively serve in this capacity. Pilots not only served effectively but went on to form a squadron escorting bombers over Germany. They set a record of not losing a single one of their charges. Despite being highly decorated pilots (officers in one of the U.S. Army Air Corps's top fighter squadrons), they could not enter the Officers' Club when they were rotated back "home" to their base for rest: they were, after all, black! Although the U.S. armed forces were grudgingly integrated after the war, it was not until the 1960s that any real attempt was made to end overt segregation in civilian life throughout the nation. Today, while legal equality theoretically exists, ghettoization continues and opportunities for blacks remain relatively sparse. Affirmative action, an American attempt at *Wiedergutmachen,* was resisted (and resisted often quite successfully) with a tenacity that equals the German obfuscation of justice. Today it is being steadily dismantled.

Victimization and exploitation are hardly limited to political situations. In the United States today, as well as in the nations that have recently emerged from behind the Iron Curtain, the rate of poverty and homelessness is not only appalling but, at least in the United States, getting worse. This has created a large number of economic victims of a crassly market-oriented system that gives to the wealthy while increasingly denying the poor. It is a state of affairs in which the affluent have gained and maintained their affluence largely by first exploiting and then ignoring those who have been exploited. It is a state of affairs that also cries out for *Wiedergutmachung,* for restitution and for healing.

Neither are victimization and exploitation limited to nations victimizing population groups within their borders. Those of us who live in the more prosperous areas of the world, for example, do so, at least in part, at the expense of those who have been and continue to be exploited. Governments can only pursue policies and carry out programs with the tacit approval of the citizenry. While this holds particularly true in truly democratic societies, it is to a lesser extent (and especially in the long run) true even of dictatorships. No power structure can, over the long haul, pursue policies diametrically opposed to the general will without collapsing. The citizenry, while it need not actively embrace the government's policies, must either not oppose or not really care about them. Among others, it is this truth that underwrites historical guilt, be it in Germany, the United States, the Far East, or anywhere.

One suspects that the population of Germany (like the population of the United States when it comes to affirmative action or restitution for the illegally incarcerated Japanese of World War II) either did not care about or was basically hostile to *Wiedergutmachung.* Not caring, however, easily turns into active opposition when persons, justifiably or not, believe that they will have a price to pay. Many Americans are neutral about (or even pay lip service to) seeing justice done to their fellow citizens; when, however, "doing justice" might involve them in paying a price (be it a money price through increased taxes or a more personal price by giving special opportunities to the historically disadvantaged), their opinions quickly change. In order to be willing to pay a price, not only must one be convinced of the justice of a given course of action, but likewise one must be willing to acknowledge responsibility. This "responsibility" does not have to be culpability; it can be personal, communal, historical, or simply human: if community is to have any meaning, undoing a wrong and healing a wound is a human responsibility. One must, in other words, recognize, acknowledge, and then come to terms with one's own and one's community's history.

It is this that—at least when it comes to the issues that Dr. Pross has so carefully researched and written about—Germany and my native Austria have only lately begun to do. In Germany, this process, and the entire process of "coming to terms" with what has been done, is far more vigorously pursued than it is in Austria. The reasons for this are beyond the scope of this chapter, but they include the incredible fact that following the war, Austria was declared to be an occupied nation, a *victim* of the German Nazis!

In drawing analogies between Germany's guilt and the guilt of other nations, I am hardly relativizing or exculpating either the Nazis or the Germans. The action of the Nazis and the complicity of many Germans cry out to heaven, as does Western complicity with Nazi deeds. I am in no way attempting to justify these actions or to lessen the guilt of the Nazis or of those who went along. My robbing a store is not in any sense justified by my neighbor's holding up

a bank. My obligation to try to "make good again" by returning what I made off with, as well as attempting to undo other damage I caused, is not lessened by my neighbor's evasion of this responsibility.

Germans living today have an obligation to "make good again" as far as this is still possible, and this process has lately been gaining momentum. Such a process does not end with material restitution: German attempts to remember the Holocaust by fitting memorials, days of remembrance, and other symbolic actions have gone far in advancing this process. The fact that Germany has advanced this process both materially and symbolically owes much to German historians, journalists, and many others, including the author of this book, who have appealed and continue to appeal to the German conscience. They have appealed successfully in part because they have appealed to a new generation. Germany since the end of World War II has had three distinctly different generations: (1) the generation of the perpetrators, those who, in one way or another, witnessed it—a generation one might call the generation of actors; (2) the generation of their children, a generation one might, with notable exceptions, as a whole classify as one of silence; and (3) the generation of *their* children, a generation one might look upon as that of inquiry. It is this generation on whose ready ears these appeals have fallen. But beyond the German experience, we all must confront the evil committed and the sad fact that each of us is capable of similar actions. We must come to terms with the question of our own national and personal involvement, guilt, and eventual rectification. And we must do what little we personally can do to advance the process of "making good again." Ultimately, the world's peace and prosperity depend upon this process.

Perceptions and Misperceptions
of Skin Color

Stephen H. Caldwell and Rebecca Popenoe

◇•◈•◇

Study Question
Explain why knowledge of a patient's race has little diagnostic or therapeutic utility.

Case presentations are part of many clinicians' daily routines. The format for such presentations often involves stating the age, sex, and race of the patient in the opening description. However, although single-word racial labels such as "black" or "white" are of occasional help to the clinician, they are of limited diagnostic and therapeutic help in many routine cases. Because of their broad scope and lack of scientific clarity, these terms often poorly represent information—for example, about genetic risks and perceptions of disease—that they are supposed to convey. In many instances, they are superficial and potentially misleading terms that fail to serve the patient's medical needs. Demoting these terms from the opening line of routine case presentations shows a recognition of their limitations as scientific labels. Our patients will be better served by more detailed explorations of ethnicity, when germane, in the History of Present Illness or Social History sections of the case presentation in question.

The presentation of a case history has a traditional format that has evolved over centuries (1). In many institutions, medical students are routinely taught to begin their case presentations with a statement describing the age, sex, and "race" of the patient. In regions of the United States such as ours, where the population is predominantly of European-American or African-American descent, the description of race is often distilled down to "black" or "white." Thus, in our institution and in those with similar demographics, the fourth spoken word of many case presentations broadly describes the patient as black or white. Exactly when and how this form of introduction became common is unclear. French physician Louis Martinet (1795–1875) described the importance of stating "the name, sex, age, and occupation of the patient....In some cases it becomes necessary to state the country or district from which the patient comes and the diseases which prevail there" (2). In the United States, the format of the opening line seems to have been established a priori in case reports in the early and mid-twentieth century. Since then, the actual utility or validity of these terms has seldom been discussed. We hope to show that the diagnostic and therapeutic utility of the terms "black" and "white" is limited. We contend that the use of these terms in the opening statements of routine, day-to-day case presentations implies that the terms have an importance and a scientific validity beyond their real merit. If ethnicity is thought to be pertinent to the case in question, the patient

409

will be better served if the physician replaces these terms with more detailed comments in the History of Present Illness, the Social History, or the Physical Examination sections of the report. When broadly and routinely applied, as they often are, racial labels such as "black" and "white" can actually obscure an accurate appraisal of a patient's genetic and cultural backgrounds, both of which may significantly affect the patient's health risks and outcomes for various diseases. A similar argument may be made for other traditional racial terms, such as Hispanic, Asian, or Native American. Because most of our experience has been with patients of European-American and African-American descent, we focus primarily on this area.

Case Presentations

Several examples will serve to illustrate the superficiality of racial divisions in day-to-day medical parlance. Recently, a 24-year-old "white" female presented in our clinic with, among other problems, α-thalassemia trait. A thorough social history later revealed that one of the patient's parents was of Mediterranean ancestry, a point obscured by the patient's married name and fair complexion and the clinician's use of the label "white." Similarly, a middle-aged, "white" male presented with recurring fever and abdominal pain. He was eventually diagnosed with familial Mediterranean fever. A careful social history revealed the patient's Greek ancestry. In short, the term "white" encompasses a diversity of genetic backgrounds that the term poorly represents.

The label "black" may also be misleading in predicting diagnoses among African-American patients. Although we are not aware of any studies of specific prevalences,

autoimmune hepatitis is perceived to be more common in patients of European descent than in others, and indeed it may be more common because it is associated with inherited histocompatibility antigens. However, we have encountered the disorder not infrequently in patients of African-American descent. A recent published case report described a "black" female with autoimmune hepatitis and a poor response to steroid therapy that may have been due to carriage of α-1-antitrypsin (3), which has also been reported to occur less frequently in patients of African descent (4). As in the cases of "white" patients mentioned above, the notation "black" in the opening description of this patient was potentially misleading if her diagnoses were to be based on suspected prevalences. The authors of the report were obviously unimpressed with the likelihood of either disorder based on the patient's stated race, and they rightly pressed ahead to arrive at their diagnosis.

The terms "race" and "ethnicity" are often used interchangeably, but they are in fact far from synonymous: "Race" refers to differences of biology, "ethnicity" to differences of culture and geographic origin. We contend that ethnic differences, rather than distinctions between black and white, more accurately convey information potentially relevant to a particular case. For instance, a Kenyan, a Haitian, and an African-American would be considered racially identical— "black"—according to current practice, but they do not share nutritional habits, attitudes, and beliefs about medical care, or even biological inheritance.

Webster's Dictionary defines race as "any of the major biological divisions of mankind, distinguished by color and texture of hair, color of skin and eyes, stature, bodily proportions, etc." But are the crucial differences among human beings really those of superficial appearance? Is it scientifically justified to assume that these outer traits indicate inner biological differences among humans?

By using the terms "black" and "white," the medical community purports to refer to real biological divisions within our species, and yet a closer look at the data shows that these divisions do not fall as neatly as our terms for skin color suggest. For instance, persons from Papua New Guinea, although "black-skinned," are genetically more closely related to Asians than to "black" Africans.

In addition, numerous studies (5) of human physical variation within populations show that traits that are often lumped together as definitive of a race do not in fact vary as a group. When population geneticist Richard Lewontin measured the degree of population differences in gene frequencies for 17 polymorphic traits, he found that only 6.3 percent of all variation could be accounted for at the level of major geographic race (6). The visible characteristics of "race" were unreliable indicators of genotypic variation.

This is not to argue that regional genetic variation does not exist. As Pat Shipman has recently pointed out (7), the fact that the lines of classification are so difficult to draw and necessarily so imprecise (one reason for this is constant mating across established group lines) does not refute the existence of regional variants of our species. Future researchers could explore more medically relevant differences among groups of *Homo sapiens* that have occupied different regions over time. At the present stage of knowledge, however, the division of the world's population into perceived races lacks scientific clarity and legitimacy.

Anthropologists have long recognized that the racial lines drawn by a society are cultural rather than scientific constructions (8, 9). Within the international medical community, therefore, racial divisions may not even be perceived in the same way. What is black to someone from the United States, for example, may be white to a Brazilian or a Caribbean Islander. The terms "black" and "white" say more about how U.S. society has been structured than about medically relevant, biological realities.

Webster's Dictionary defines the term "ethnic" as "designating any of the basic divisions or groups of mankind, as distinguished by customs, characteristics, language, etc." Social scientists accept "ethnicity" as a term that refers to the cultural distinctions that persons make themselves—their identities. Reductionist racial labels often obscure rather than illuminate ethnic differences. Ideas about medical care, nutrition, and disease that bear on treatment are better provided by giving information about ethnic identity and background in the Social History section of the case presentation.

The medical community is increasingly aware of the ways in which cultural practices influence a person's health (10). The various persons grouped as black and white, however, are often widely divergent in beliefs, habits, reactions to illnesses, and perceptions of the medical community. The terms "black" and "white" do not impart the type of information implied by their continued use in the introductions to routine case presentations.

Genetic Background of the U.S. Population

In the United States, 350 years of interaction has led to considerable mixing between persons of various geographic origins (11). Although the evidence of such diverse ancestry is at least implicitly acknowledged in the African-American community by attention to gradations of skin color, it is less frequently acknowledged that many "whites" have African and other "nonwhite" ancestors. However, a recent highly acclaimed autobiography by Shirlee Taylor Haizlip (12), a "black" woman, calls attention to the prevalence of such cases. Haizlip recounts her discovery of her own "white" relatives who had split off from the "black" side of her family a generation earlier. As for the African-American population in the United States, geneticist Luigi Cavalli-Sforza (13) has estimated that 30 percent of their genes derive from "white" sources.

These facts suggest that the traditional racial divisions used in the United States are of questionable utility and accuracy. This issue has recently earned the attention of U.S. government demographers. According to news accounts (14), the current official categories used in the U.S. Census and other documents are presently being reviewed by the Office of Information and Regulatory Affairs in the Office of Management and Budget. The debate within the government treats issues of ethnic and racial identity that are beyond the scope of this paper, but it supports our contention that the use of racial labels is burdened by inaccuracies. This seems especially true at the level of the routine case presentation.

Does Bias Become an Issue?

Numerous reports about the course and optimal treatment of many diseases have been based on perceived racial groupings. We do not dispute that racial or ethnic categories sometimes have important epidemiologic implications. However, the division into "black" and "white" in routine, day-to-day presentations is often irrelevant and potentially misleading.

Do these terms engender bias? One study (15), which examined the way in which "black" and "white" patients are presented at morning report, suggests that they do. Black patients were far more likely than whites to be identified by a racial label, and yet that label was considered relevant in only 2 of 18 cases. The authors perceived the presentations of black patients to be unflattering more often than the presentations of white patients.

To the extent that the terms "black" and "white" often needlessly separate persons in a clinical setting, their use may sometimes be construed as pejorative, whether this is intended or not. In most cases, racial monikers simply represent a long-followed tradition. We submit that many clinicians who work in settings in which these terms are routinely used may be surprised at their own reactions when the terms are deleted from day-to-day presentations.

Published Case Reports and Current Practice

Although our emphasis is on the routine "workday" oral case presentation, we reviewed case reports or clinical pathological conference reports from current and past issues of nine medical journals to assess the ways in which these reports have been presented over the past 10 years. Overall, most of the journals varied considerably in their use of racial labels in the opening lines of case reports. In general, this seemed to be less the result of editorial policy than of individual authors' styles (Table 1).

In addition, we informally surveyed the clerkship directors of 48 U.S. medical schools using a brief written questionnaire that asked specifically whether medical students were taught by oral or written example to use the terms "black" or "white" in

Table 1 Statements of Case Reports or Clinical Pathologic Conference Reports Published in Medical Journals*

JOURNAL	TYPE OF REPORT	RACIAL DESCRIPTION USED IN 1994	RACIAL DESCRIPTION USED IN 1984
American Journal of Cardiology	Case	Varied	No
American Journal of Gastroenterology	Case	No	Varied
American Journal of the Medical Sciences	Case	No	Varied
Chest	Case	Varied	Varied
Circulation	CPC	Yes	No reports available
Gastroenterology	Case	Yes	No reports available
Mayo Clinic Proceedings	Case	No	No
Medicine	Case	Varied	Varied
New England Journal of Medicine	CPC	No	No

*The May or June issues of the journals were reviewed. Most issues had more than one case report; two issues had one clinical pathologic conference report each. CPC=clinical pathologic conference reports.

the introductory statements of routine case presentations. Four responses were possible ("yes," "no," "variable," and "don't know") and allowance was made for qualifying comments.

Thirty-seven (77 percent) clerkship directors responded (7 from the Northeast, 15 from the South, 12 from the Midwest, and 3 from the West). Twenty-two of the 37 (59 percent) answered "yes" and 12 (32 percent) answered "variable." Only one answered "no," and he added that students are expressly taught to not use the terms unless they think them relevant. Two directors answered "don't know," and occurs by "osmosis" from the resident housestaff to the students.

Many of those who responded with "yes" or "variable" also commented that this practice is taught to students passively, by the oral example of residents. Thus, as experience with residents and clinicians from numerous medical schools might suggest, describing race in the opening line seems to be common in U.S. medical schools. This practice is either passed along as oral tradition or formally taught. We could not detect a significant regional variation in this small survey (6 of 7 directors from the Northeast and 9 of 15 directors from the South answered "yes" and the remainder from these regions answered "variable" or "don't know").

Conclusions

Most physicians would agree that both the genetic constitution and the cultural background of a person predisposes him or her to various diseases and may modulate responses to certain therapies. An accurate social history can, in many cases, provide invaluable information about a patient's ethnic background and possible risks for certain diseases. However, labels such as "black" or "white" in the opening line of case histories poorly represent this important information. The same may be said of other broad, superficial terms, such as Hispanic or Asian, that inadequately address attributes that should be dealt with in a more meaningful way when thought to be pertinent to patient care.

In many routine cases, such terminology serves as little more than a "jog" to the memory of busy clinicians. The costs, however, may be to engender the perception of bias, to miss clinically relevant information, and to assume the presence or absence of genetic or cultural factors that, in fact, may or may not be present. Demoting these labels from the opening line of our day-to-day presentations shows a recognition of their limitations as scientific terms and a commitment to representing pertinent ethnic variations in an accurate, relevant, and ultimately more helpful manner.

References

1. Stoeckle JD, Billings JA. A history of history-taking: the medical interview. *J Gen Intern Med*. 1987;2:119–27.

2. Walker HK. The origins of the history and physical examination. In: Walker HK, Hall DW, Hurst JW, eds. *Clinical Methods: The History, Physical, and Laboratory Examinations*. Boston: Butterworths; 1990:17.

3. Lok AS, Ghany MG, Gerber MA. A young woman with cirrhosis: autoimmune hepatitis vs. alpha 1-antitrypsin deficiency [Clinical Conference]. *Hepatology*. 1994;19:1302–6.

4. Wulfsberg EA, Hoffmann DE, Cohen MM. Alpha 1-antitrypsin deficiency. *JAMA*. 1994;271:217–22.

5. Molnar S. *Human Variation: Races, Types, and Ethnic Groups*. 2d ed. Englewood Cliffs, NJ: Prentice-Hall; 1983:128–46.

6. Lewontin RD. Human diversity. In: Nelson H, Jurmain R, eds. *Introduction to Physical Anthropology*. St. Paul: West Publishing; 1982:203.

7. Shipman P. *The Evolution of Racism: Human Differences and the Use and Abuse of Science*. New York: Simon and Schuster; 1994.

8. Boas F. The Mind of Primitive Man: A Course of Lectures Delivered before the Lowell Institute, Boston, Mass., and the National University of Mexico, 1910–1911. New York: Macmillan; 1911.

9. Gould SJ. *The Mismeasure of Man*. New York: W. W. Norton; 1981.

10. Pachter LM. Culture and clinical care. Folk illness beliefs and behaviors and their implications for health care delivery. *JAMA*. 1994;271:690–4.

11. Buckley TE. Unfixing race. *The Virginia Magazine of History and Biography*. 1994;102:349–80.

12. Haizlip ST. *The Sweeter the Juice*. New York: Simon and Schuster; 1994.

13. Shipman P. Facing racial differences together. *The Chronicle of Higher Education*. 3 Aug 1994;40:B-1.

14. Holmes SJ. Federal government is rethinking its system of racial classification. *New York Times* 1994 8 July.

15. Finucane TE, Carrese JA. Racial bias in presentation of cases. *J Gen Intern Med*. 1990;5:120–1.

Selected Discrimination Cases Handled by the U.S. Department of Justice in 1999

U.S. DEPARTMENT OF JUSTICE

Study Questions
1. Determine whether each case is an example of institutional discrimination or individual discrimination.
2. List some of the ways discrimination is institutionalized.

Three Indicted for Civil Rights Attack on Hispanics in Idaho

WASHINGTON, D.C.—A federal grand jury in Boise, Idaho, has indicted three Nampa, Idaho, men for physically assaulting Hispanic residents last summer, and chasing Hispanic children through the street while yelling racial slurs, the Justice Department announced.

The six count indictment, presented yesterday and unsealed today, charges Scott Brooke, 18, Jack David Carter, 18, and Chris Maurer, 19, with violating federal civil rights laws as well as conspiracy and using a sawed-off shotgun to commit a crime of violence.

"This administration is firmly committed to putting an end to racial violence," said Attorney General Janet Reno. The indictment stems from a series of alleged racially motivated attacks against several Hispanic men, women, and children in Nampa last summer. Three youths were also charged with committing acts of juvenile delinquency in connection with the same civil rights offenses. Federal law prohibits the release of names or photographs of persons charged as juveniles. "Hate crimes reflect a cancer of the soul and have no place in our society," said Acting Assistant Attorney General for Civil Rights Bill Lann Lee. "Our constitution and laws protect the right of all people to go about their daily lives free from intimidation and racial assaults. We will always be vigilant in our efforts to prosecute those who use hatred and violence in an effort to divide our communities."

Count one of the indictment alleges that from December 1996 through August 1, 1997, the defendants and others conspired to interfere with the fair housing rights of Hispanic residents of Nampa. Among other things, the conspiracy count alleges that the individuals: physically assaulted Hispanics at or near their homes on five occasions in the summer of 1997, including on two occasions by striking their victims with firearms; chased a 14-year-old and a 9-year-old Hispanic child through the streets of the children's Nampa neighborhood, yelling racial slurs; and, attacked two Hispanic men as they arrived to visit Hispanic friends at their home in Nampa, yelling racial slurs and telling their victims that they should go back to Mexico.

"I can think of nothing more important to the people of Idaho than protecting their basic right to live peacefully in their neighborhoods," said Betty Richardson, U.S. Attorney in Idaho. "We need to ensure that all members of our community are safe, regardless of their race, color, religion, or ethnicity."

Counts two, three, and four of the indictment charge the six individuals with specific instances of using force or the threat of force to interfere with Hispanic residents' housing rights, including a July 4, 1997, assault on an Hispanic man and woman as they were moving in with the man's parents in Nampa.

Count five of the indictment charges the defendants with using or carrying a firearm during a crime of violence.

Count six of the indictment alleges that the firearm used by the defendants to strike their victim during a July 13, 1997, assault was an illegal and unregistered sawed-off shotgun.

If convicted on the four criminal civil rights charges, the adult defendants each face a maximum of 10 years imprisonment and a $250,000 fine per count. If convicted on the federal weapons offenses, the adult defendants each face an additional mandatory 10 years imprisonment.

An indictment is only a charge, and is not evidence of guilt. The defendants are presumed innocent until proven guilty beyond a reasonable doubt.

"The people of Canyon County simply will not tolerate criminal conduct based on racial hatred," stated Canyon County Prosecuting Attorney David L. Young. "Where, as here, federal law and procedure provide the best forum for prosecution, we will do all that we can to ensure that a prosecution in federal court is successful."

The Nampa Police Department and Federal Bureau of Investigation worked together over the last year in conducting the investigation. The Canyon County Prosecuting Attorney's Office is assisting the United States Attorney's Office and the Civil Rights Division of the U.S. Department of Justice in prosecuting the case.

"The investigation was a model of cooperation between state and federal law enforcement agencies," said Betty Richardson, the U.S. Attorney in Idaho.

Tom Kubic, FBI Special Agent in Charge of the Salt Lake Field Division, which covers Idaho, also praised the investigative efforts. "This investigation and prosecution demonstrate that on cases of utmost urgency to our community the FBI and local law enforcement, such as the Nampa Police Department, will combine their resources to conduct the most thorough examination of the evidence possible. The FBI is committed to working in partnership with local law enforcement to pursue this kind of crime."

Last year, Attorney General Reno launched a Justice Department initiative to fight hate crimes across the country. As part of that initiative, regional task forces were created to focus on hate crimes. Next Wednesday, lead prosecutors from each task force will participate in a conference in Washington, D.C. to coordinate their efforts nationwide.

No trial date has been set.

Justice Department Moves to Resolve Indian Land Dispute Involving Madison and Oneida Counties in New York

WASHINGTON, D.C.—The Justice Department intervened Friday in a private federal lawsuit brought by the Oneida Indian Nation of New York, the Oneida Indian Nation of Wisconsin, and the Thames Band of Canada over Indian land in Madison and Oneida Counties in New York. The lawsuit alleges that in the eighteenth and nineteenth century, New York State illegally obtained land that belongs to the Oneida Nation.

"The Oneida Nation has an historical and federally protected interest in this land," said Lois Schiffer, Assistant Attorney General in charge of the Justice Department's Environment Division. "New York State violated federal law when it purchased the land without Congressional approval in the late eighteenth and early nineteenth century. It is time to right this wrong and compensate those who have been injured."

On Friday, the Justice Department intervened in a similar case involving the Seneca Nation and disputed land in Allegany County, New York.

According to the Department's papers filed Friday in U.S. District Court in Syracuse, New York State tried to buy land from the Oneidas on twenty-two occasions from 1795 through 1846, without the consent of the United States Congress. A 1790 federal statute prohibits the purchase of land from Indian tribes without Congressional consent.

The Oneida's suit, originally filed in 1974 in U.S. District Court in Syracuse, challenges the validity of the sale of approximately 246,000 acres, all located in Madison and Oneida Counties, from the Oneida to the State of New York. The complaint involves only approximately 2800 acres of that area that are currently owned by the two defendant counties.

Interior Secretary Bruce Babbitt said, "Although we are intervening and are willing to litigate the case, we are also willing to engage in serious settlement discussions with the state and the Oneidas."

Similar Indian land claims in other states have been resolved through negotiation. In those claims, the tribes, the state, and the federal government have reached agreements that have compensated tribes and eliminated questions about the land title of present-day owners. In some of these settlements, tribes bought land from willing sellers to create or expand a reservation.

The U.S. Supreme Court has ruled that no time limitation applies to this type of Indian land claim.

Sixteen Indicted for Recruiting Mexican Women into the United States and Forcing Them into Prostitution

Attorney General Announces Worker Exploitation Task Force

WASHINGTON, D.C. —Sixteen individuals who orchestrated an elaborate scheme to lure young female Mexican nationals to the United States by promising them legitimate employment, and instead forcing them into prostitution, were indicted today, the Justice Department announced.

The 52-count indictment, handed down in U.S. District Court in Ft. Pierce, Florida, charged six members of the Cadena family of Veracruz, Mexico, and ten associates with violating federal civil rights, immigration, sexual exploitation, and extortion statutes. According to the indictments, between the fall of 1996 and February of this year, the family operated an organization that recruited Mexican women to come to America. The women, some as young as 14, were smuggled into Texas, transported to Florida and South Carolina, and, instead of being given legitimate work as promised, were forced to become prostitutes to pay back their smuggling debt.

"Every person, rich or poor, citizen or noncitizen, has a right to be free," said Acting Assistant Attorney General for Civil Rights Bill Lann Lee. "The allegations in today's indictments are shocking and reflect a cruel exploitation of women on a systemic basis."

Earlier today, Attorney General Janet Reno announced an interagency federal task force to combat the serious problem of modern-day slavery and worker exploitation in the United States.

"We must get these modern day slavery cases off the front pages of the newspapers and into the history books," said Reno.

The task force, co-chaired by Mr. Lee and the Solicitor of the Labor Department, will utilize the resources of the Civil Rights Division, the FBI, INS, and the Department of Labor to create a coordinated effort to investigate and prosecute these so-called cases of indentured servitude.

Today's indictment alleged that the Cadena family and others operated an organization which used "recruiters" to interest young women into coming to the United States. The recruiters promised the women domestic, restaurant, landscaping, and health care jobs. The organization paid professional smugglers to bring the women across the border in Texas and harbored them in safehouses until they could be transported to Florida and South Carolina.

Once transported, the women were told to perform acts of prostitution in order to pay off smuggling fees, and were subjected to violence and force if they refused to do so. Many worked six days a week, and none were permitted to return home. Most of those who attempted to escape were tracked down, brought back and subjected to physical and sexual assault.

The women worked as prostitutes in brothel houses in Orlando, Tampa, Avon Park, Ft. Myers, Haines City, Lake Worth, Ocoee, Okeechobee, and Zolfo Springs, Florida, and Lake City and John's Island, South Carolina. The brothels were operated by "ticketeros" who collected the money earned by the prostitutes by selling tickets, which were actually condoms, to be exchanged for sexual encounters. These ticketeros also routinely threatened the women to ensure that they continued to work.

The women only retained a small fraction of their earnings while the rest went to their smuggling debt and other debts. Many women who became pregnant at the brothels were forced to have abortions.

"The defendants lured underage Mexican women with promises of opportunity and a better life," said U.S. Attorney Thomas E. Scott in Miami. "Instead, they received a one-way ticket to a life of prostitution."

Over the past three years alone, the Justice Department has brought ten indentured servitude cases involving more than 150 victims.

If convicted, the 16 defendants face up to life in prison. Eight defendants are in custody. Eight others are at large.

Fourteen women are referenced in the indictment, three of whom are minors. The victims, who have been declared material witnesses by the court, have been released on bond and granted temporary legal status for one year while the case is pending. The Justice Department is working with social service providers in South Florida who are ensuring the victims are housed, fed, and clothed, and can obtain work.

This case was jointly investigated by the Border Patrol and the FBI, with the assistance of the Florida Department of Law Enforcement, Okeechobee County Sheriff's Office, and the Lake Worth Police Department. The case is being prosecuted by the Justice Department's Civil Rights Division and the U.S. Attorneys office in the Southern District of Florida. It is the second major slavery case investigated by the Miami sector of the Border Patrol in the past two years.

Largest Real Estate Company in Alabama Settles Racial Discrimination Case with the Justice Department

WASHINGTON, D.C.—The largest real estate company in Alabama will no longer steer prospective African American homeowners to homes in minority neighborhoods, under an agreement reached today with the Justice Department, two private citizens and a civil rights organization.

The agreement, filed together with a complaint in U.S. District Court in Birmingham, resolves complaints that First Real Estate Corporation engaged in unlawful discriminatory conduct that violated the Fair Housing Act.

In the complaint, the Justice Department alleged that African American clients were steered toward predominantly minority neighborhoods while white clients were directed to white neighborhoods. It also alleged that potential customers were steered to company sales agents based on race, and that properties located in areas with a high minority population were advertised differently from properties in other areas.

"We are pleased that First Real Estate has chosen to work cooperatively with the United States and the private plaintiffs to assure that the guarantees of the Fair Housing Act are a fact of life in our community," said G. Douglas Jones, the U.S. Attorney in Birmingham. "The decree should serve as a model for all realtors."

Under the agreement, First Real Estate will not consider the race of a prospective homeowner and neighborhood in deciding where to show a home; assign customers to agents without regard to race; modify its advertising so the availability of homes that it has listed for sale is provided to everyone; educate agents and employees of their responsibilities under the Fair Housing Act; and, establish a $100,000 fund to compensate persons who may have been injured as a result of the company's alleged discriminatory practices.

First Real Estate also has agreed to promote fair housing in the Birmingham metropolitan area by sponsoring clinics for prospective home buyers and by developing a marketing plan to promote all communities in the metropolitan area as open to all races and nationalities.

The Justice Department first became involved in the matter after learning about a private civil suit that was filed in November 1995 by two African American former sales agents. The agents alleged the company only referred African American customers to them, and discouraged them from showing homes in white areas.

In December 1997, the Fair Housing Center of Northern Alabama, a private organization, filed a private civil suit raising similar allegations. The Center will assist First Real Estate in its efforts to promote fair housing in Birmingham.

Today's settlement resolves the two private suits as well as the Justice Department suit. "The Justice Department is firmly committed to making fair housing a reality for all Americans," said Joan Magagna, Acting Chief of the Housing Section of the Civil Rights Division. "No one should ever be denied the right to live where they choose simply because of the color of their skin."

The monetary fund will be paid to victims identified through a claims process conducted by the Justice Department and the private plaintiffs. Any person who believes that he or she has been a victim of race discrimination by First Real Estate should contact the Civil Rights Division at 1-800-896-7743 or the Fair Housing Center of Northern Alabama at 205-324-0111.

Arkansas Residents Plead Guilty to Racially Motivated Church Arson

WASHINGTON, D.C.—Two Arkansas residents pleaded guilty today to setting fire to a Christian school operated by an interracial church in Shirley, Arkansas, under a plea agreement announced by the Justice Department. The case was investigated by the National Church Arson Task Force.

Michelle Leigh Dunn, 22, and Robert Marion Treece, 25, both of Shirley, pleaded guilty in U.S. District Court in Little Rock, admitting that they set fire to the school run by the Universal Church of God in Shirley, on May 21, 1995.

"No community should have to experience racially motivated arsons," said James E. Johnson, Treasury Undersecretary for En-

forcement, and Bill Lann Lee, Acting Assistant Attorney General for Civil Rights, Co-chairs of the National Church Arson Task Force. "We will continue to stomp out the flames of racial hatred wherever they may burn."

Dunn and Treece admitted to charges alleging that they conspired to intimidate, prevent, and discourage African-Americans in Shirley, by setting fire to the school. The charge carries a maximum penalty of 10 years imprisonment or a $250,000 fine, or both. In addition to the conspiracy charge, Treece, who actually set the fire, pleaded guilty to the use of fire to commit a felony. The charge carries a mandatory year term of imprisonment.

Under the plea agreements, all remaining charges against Dunn and Treece would be dismissed.

A third man, Jerry Lynn Jones, 25, of Shirley, entered a guilty plea in connection with the case on August 14, 1998. Jones, who drove Treece to the fire scene and waited for him to set the fire, also pleaded guilty to the conspiracy charge, as well as a charge of aiding and abetting in the malicious damaging of a building by the use of fire. The second charge carries a five-year mandatory minimum term of imprisonment.

Sentencing of all three defendants will take place on a date to be set by the court. Treece is currently being held in the Faulkner County Jail for the arson. The sentences will be imposed under the United States Sentencing Guidelines according to the nature of the offenses and the criminal backgrounds, if any, of the defendants.

Credit Card Company Sued by Justice Department for Discriminating Against Hispanics

WASHINGTON, D.C.—A Delaware credit card company was sued today by the Justice Department for engaging in a pattern of discrimination against Hispanics.

The lawsuit, filed in U.S. District Court in Wilmington, Delaware, charges Associates National Bank, a consumer credit card bank headquartered in Wilmington, with violating the Equal Credit Opportunity Act by intentionally subjecting Spanish-language credit card applicants and cardholders to stricter underwriting standards and less favorable terms and conditions than those applied to non-Hispanic individuals.

"Credit card companies cannot treat applicants differently based on their national origin or ethnicity," said Bill Lann Lee, Acting Assistant Attorney General for Civil Rights. "Today's suit should put lenders on notice that they will be held to account under the law."

The Office of the Comptroller of the Currency (OCC), a federal financial regulatory agency, identified the problem during an April 1997 examination of the bank. After completing its examination, OCC referred the case to the Justice Department.

In its complaint, the Justice Department alleges that between January 1996 and April 1997, individuals who filled out the Spanish-language applications for an Associate National Bank/UNOCAL co-branded Master-Card were evaluated through a credit scoring system that had stricter standards than the scoring system used for English-language applicants. As a result, some Spanish-language applicants were denied credit on a discriminatory basis. The higher standards also caused some approved Spanish-language applicants to get lower credit limits than similarly-situated applicants who used English-language applications.

The complaint also alleges that the bank excluded Spanish-language cardholders from certain promotional credit services commonly offered to English-language applicants including skip-a-payment and balance consolidation offers.

The Justice Department estimates that approximately 1,800 Hispanic applicants were victims of the bank's discriminatory actions. Today's complaint seeks an order requiring the bank to stop discriminating against

Hispanics, pay compensatory and punitive damages to victims, and adopt a plan to remedy the bank's discriminatory practices.

"It is important that citizens of Delaware know that discrimination based on race or national origin will not be tolerated," said Carl Schnee, U.S. Attorney in Delaware. The lawsuit filed today is part of a continuing effort to assure that all citizens are treated equally."

Two Indiana Men Arrested for Cross Burning in Gary, Indiana

WASHINGTON, D.C.—Two Indiana men were arrested today for allegedly burning a cross on the property of a black family in Gary, Indiana, announced the Justice Department.

On October 20, 1999, Michael E. Riley, 36, from Gary, Indiana, and Ricky Lee Cumbow, 34, from Hammond, Indiana, were indicted by a federal grand jury in Hammond for conspiring to violate the civil rights of the victims. The indictment, unsealed today, alleges that in the early morning hours of May 3, 1998, Riley and Cumbow built a seven-foot-tall wooden cross and burned it in the backyard of a black couple, Ulysses Lacy and Carmen Estelle. The couple's seven-year-old son discovered the cross.

"We remain deeply committed to vigorously investigating and prosecuting arson attacks against individuals," said Bill Lann Lee, Acting Assistant Attorney General for Civil Rights. "We will not let up until all perpetrators of racial violence are brought to justice."

The offenses with which the defendants are charged carry a penalty in excess of 10 years. The case is expected to go to trial early next year. The investigation of the case is being conducted by the Federal Bureau of Investigation, Indianapolis Division, Merrillville Resident Agency. Prosecution of the case is being handled by Department of Justice attorneys Roy L. Austin, Jr. and Bharathi A. Venkatraman, both with the Criminal Section of the Civil Rights Division, along with assistance from the U.S. Attorney's Office. Today's arrests were made with the assistance of the Merrillville and Hammond, Indiana, Police Departments. The charges contained in the complaints are only allegations of guilt and are not proof of any crime.

Owner and Former Manager of Albuquerque, New Mexico, Apartment Complex Resolve Allegations of Housing Discrimination

WASHINGTON, D.C.—After a year of litigation, the owner and the former manager of an Albuquerque, New Mexico, apartment complex have agreed to pay $75,000 to resolve allegations that they refused to rent to African Americans and families with children, announced the Justice Department today.

The agreement, filed in U.S. District Court in Albuquerque, resolves a civil rights complaint filed by the Justice Department in July 1998, alleging that Anita Schikore, former manager of Monterey Manor Apartments in Albuquerque, violated the federal Fair Housing Act by falsely informing African

American apartment seekers that there were no apartments available and unlawfully discouraging people with children from living in the complex. Under the agreement, Schikore has admitted to engaging in discriminatory practices. The owner of Monterey Manor, Henry K. Vernon, and Schikore have agreed to compensate individuals whom the complex discriminated against and pay civil penalties to the U.S. Treasury. Vernon must also take steps to prevent future discrimination.

"No American should be turned away from a home they can afford because of their skin color or familial status," said Bill Lann Lee, Acting Assistant Attorney General for Civil Rights. "It has been more than 30 years since the Fair Housing Act became law and we are still fighting this kind of discrimination. We will continue to ensure, across the country, that the law is followed."

Under the agreement, which must be approved by the court, Vernon and Schikore are required to pay $10,000 to each of the two known victims of the complex's discriminatory policies. They must also establish a $20,000 settlement fund to compensate any as yet unidentified victims and provide $9,000 to the Albuquerque Legal Aid Society to promote area-wide compliance with fair housing laws. Under the terms of the agreement, Vernon will also pay a $25,000 civil

penalty and Schikore will pay a $1,000 penalty.

The agreement also requires Vernon to train all employees about their obligations under the Fair Housing Act and publicize new non-discrimination policies in newspaper advertisements. In addition, he must hire an independent third party to ensure that Monterey Manor is maintaining non-discrimination policies. "This important case demonstrates the United States' concern for unimpeded access to equitable housing," said John J. Kelly United States Attorney for the District of New Mexico. "Those who apply discriminatory practices in violation of the Fair Housing Act risk vigorous civil prosecution for their actions."

Some of the evidence against Monterey Manor was gathered through the Justice Department's fair housing testing program. During the tests, trained pairs of African American and white "testers" posed as prospective tenants to inquire about the availability of apartments. Their experiences were then compared to determine whether they were treated equally.

Individuals who believe they may have been the victims of housing discrimination at Monterey Manor should call the Housing Section of the Civil Rights Division of the Justice Department at 1-800-896-7743 or 202-514-4713.

Justice Department Sues Three Parsippany Apartment Complexes for Allegedly Discriminating Against African Americans

WASHINGTON, D.C.—The owners and managers of three Parsippany, New Jersey, apartment complexes were sued today by the Justice Department for allegedly refusing to rent to African Americans.

The lawsuit, filed in U.S. District Court in Newark, New Jersey, alleges that Garden Homes Management and the owners of Lakeview Garden Apartments (214 units), Westgate Garden Apartments (152 units), and Redstone Garden Apartments (92 units), told African Americans that apartments were not available while telling whites that apartments were available. Garden Homes Management, Corp., Westbound Homes, Inc., Redstone Garden Apartments, Inc, Joseph Wilf, and Cathy Rosenstein are named as defendants.

"We are committed to fighting housing discrimination which far too often goes uncovered," said Acting Assistant Attorney General for Civil Rights Bill Lann Lee. "Today's actions should warn all housing providers that housing discrimination is no longer immune to detection."

This is Justice Department's 56th case stemming from a nationwide fair housing testing program aimed at detecting illegal discrimination. Under the program, trained pairs of African American and white testers pose as prospective tenants and inquire about the availability of rental units. By comparing the experiences of the testers, investigators determine whether minorities were treated less favorably than whites. The

Northern New Jersey Fair Housing Council also participated in the tests for this case.

"This case demonstrates that we still must use the powers of the Justice Department to ensure equal housing opportunities," said Faith S. Hochberg, U.S. Attorney for New Jersey. "It is patently unfair and unjust for any person to be discriminated against simply for seeking to rent an apartment in New Jersey."

Today's lawsuit seeks an order preventing Garden Homes Management and the owners of the three complexes from engaging in further discriminatory practices, and requires the defendants to pay damages to any individuals identified as victims of the discrimination. Under the Fair Housing Act, a court may also require that each defendant pay a civil penalty up to $50,000 for the first violation and $100,000 for a subsequent violation.

Individuals who believe they may have been the victims of housing discrimination should call the Housing Section of the Civil Rights Division of the Justice Department at (800) 896-7743.

South Dakota Sanitary District Sued by Justice Department for Discriminating Against Native Americans

WASHINGTON, D.C.—A South Dakota sanitary district and county were sued today by the Justice Department for intentionally excluding Native Americans from their electoral process.

The complaint, filed in U.S. District Court in Sioux Falls, South Dakota, alleges that the Enemy Swim Sanitary District and Day County violated the Voting Rights Act of 1965 by excluding Native American citizens from the Enemy Swim Sanitary District. The sanitary district is comprised of several non-

contiguous pieces of land owned by white individuals, which represent only 13 percent of the land area around Enemy Swim Lake. The sanitary district was drawn to exclude the remaining 87 percent, owned by the Sisseton-Wahpeton Sioux Tribe and about 200 of its members. All of the registered voters in the sanitary district are white.

"Native American citizens were intentionally discriminated against in establishing the boundaries of the Enemy Swim Sanitary District," said Bill Lann Lee, Acting Assistant

Attorney General for Civil Rights. "We will not allow the sanitary district to continue denying this basic right to any individual on the basis of race".

Sanitary districts in South Dakota are governmental subdivisions incorporated for the purpose of addressing problems with waste water disposal. A sanitary district has the power to construct and operate storm sewers, sanitary sewers, waste disposal systems, and water systems. The district is governed by a board of trustees who are elected at-large and serve three-year staggered terms.

Enemy Swim Lake is located in Day County, a sparsely populated county in the northeast part of the state. The area is within the disestablished reservation of the Sisseton-Wahpeton Sioux Tribe, in what is known as a "checkerboard" area of non-Indian-owned parcels and adjacent Native American–owned parcels of land.

In a consent decree also filed today, Day County has agreed with the Justice Department that the Enemy Swim Sanitary District violates federal law and has agreed to approve incorporation of a sanitary district that is comprised of all voters, including the Native American citizens around and near Enemy Swim Lake. The Sanitary District defendants have refused to enter into this agreement.

Today's suit seeks an order dissolving the racially exclusionary sanitary district. The order further seeks to establish a sanitary district that includes all voters, including Native American citizens.

Three Florida Men Charged with Smuggling Individuals from Mexico and Forcing Them into Involuntary Servitude

WASHINGTON, D.C.—Three southwest Florida men have been arrested and charged with smuggling individuals from Mexico, holding them against their will, and forcing them to work in tomato fields in Immokolee, Florida, federal authorities with the National Worker Exploitation Task Force announced today.

A criminal complaint, filed and unsealed in U.S. District Court in Fort Myers, charged Abel Cuello, Jr., his brother Brasillo Cuello, Herman Covarrubias, and a fourth individual, with conspiracy to hold individuals in involuntary servitude, extortion, harboring aliens, and various violations of the Migrant and Seasonal Agricultural Worker Protection Act. The maximum penalty for all charges is thirty-six years in prison, a $250,000 fine, and three years supervised release. However, harboring illegal aliens can be punishable by up to ten years in prison per victim.

"The circumstances of this case are tragic," said Bill Lann Lee, Acting Assistant Attorney General for Civil Rights and co-chair of the Task Force. "But its discovery and the rapid response by law enforcement demonstrates that the work of the Task Force is paying off."

"This case reflects our commitment to bring to justice those employers who exploit and abuse their workers," said Henry Solano, Solicitor of the Department of Labor and co-chair of the Task Force.

This morning, agents of the U.S. Border Patrol, working with the Wage and Hour Division of the Department of Labor, and the Immigration and Naturalization Service (INS), arrested the three individuals and liberated twenty-seven victims. The fourth individual remains at large.

"This effectively dismantles an alien smuggling enterprise and brings its perpetrators forward to face these charges," added Charles Wilson, United States Attorney for the Middle District of Florida. "Today, we also send a clear and unmistakable message that this, or any, form of modern-day slavery has no place in America."

This case is the result of an interagency investigation by agents and prosecutors from the Border Patrol, INS, the Departments of Labor and Justice, and the U.S. Attorney's Office in Fort Myers, under the auspices of the National Worker Exploitation Task Force, which was founded last year to address the problem of modern-day slavery in the United States.

Indianness

Nicholas Peroff

◇◆◈◆◇

Study Questions
1. How does Peroff define indianness?
2. Peroff states that a "limited number of metaphors associated with several different communities within the larger American society supply most Americans with ideas about indianness." What are these metaphors?

Unlike Indianness, indianness is a product of the greater American society. It is a generic form of ethnic identity that is loosely based on a variety of metaphor associated with an almost infinite number of communities located within American society and, in fact, throughout the world. As with Indianness, indianness is a symbolic object, not a tangible object. It does not materially exist, but, again like Indianness, indianness tangibly affects the material world. Among other things, indianness influences the larger society's actions and behavior regarding American Indians.

Most people in American society know little or nothing about Indians or Indianness; however, they may be familiar with many expressions of indianness. Ideas or images that communicate indianness are a familiar feature in American movies, literature, and the media; in team logos, auto names, and in beer commercials. An especially prominent and relatively new variety of indianness can be found in the music, literature, and sweat lodge rituals of the New Age Movement (Parker, 1996).

Our knowledge of indianness and, indeed, most things is the product of the interactive, interpretive process of coming to know what we know in terms of what we

already know (Morgan, 1993). Most of what the general public knows about indianness is gradually acquired over time in the form of metaphor, images, or stereotypes of Indianness generated in a wide variety of communities within the dominant American society. As used here, the meaning of the word "community" is even more ambiguous than the definition of an interest group (Berry, 1996). The black community, gay community, and academic community are three examples of people recognized as a community by other people in American society because they are identified with an often indistinct, but powerful, connecting value or interest.

A limited number of metaphors associated with several different communities within the larger American society supply most Americans with their ideas about indianness. The environmental or "green" community contributes the metaphor "Indianness as harmony with nature" (e.g., Mander, 1991; Versluis, 1992).

Geographically defined communities such as the American Southwest or State of Oklahoma may contribute the metaphor "Indianness as tourist attraction." Many people within the health, education, social work, and other "helping communities" supply the metaphor

"Indian as victim" to explain the persistence of severe social and economic problems among American Indian minority populations.

One metaphor connected with virtually all of the relevant communities—from those already mentioned to others associated with the arts and entertainment industry, the media, politics, and especially with academia—has become the most powerful and pervasive portrait of indianness in America. The metaphor "Indian as historical artifact" advances the idea that:

All Indian tribes perceived their land as sacred territory from which they never moved for thousands of years, and which they worshipfully personified as Mother Earth, and upon which they lived in profound harmony; that to the Indian all creatures, all things, all thoughts, and all natural phenomena were pervasively infused with the sacred; and that, in defiance of the laws that govern cultural change everywhere else in the world, the beliefs of primeval Indians remain indelibly and irreversibly imprinted in the souls of their present-day descendants, having been passed down for endless generations unaltered by contact with the outside world, as if Native Americans alone among all the world's peoples existed utterly outside the flow of history (summary of Clifton, 1990, in Bordewich, 1996, pp. 210–211).

The irony that accompanies this lengthy and somewhat sarcastic quote is that James A. Clifton and many other academic writers in anthropology and elsewhere have been the very same people that have popularized and perpetuated this image of Indians as historical artifacts. American Indian author Vine Deloria, Jr. notes that:

It is they who have invented and continue to invent Indians. Not willing to admit it, they then blame us for perpetuating whatever images become popular among whites. These people are among the persistent crowd of people exploiting Indians while they pretend…to be advocating the real truth about Indians (Deloria, 1992, p. 410).

No metaphor or combination of metaphor will convey a true image of Indianness or capture the essence of an Indian identity. However, the widespread generation of Indian as artifact, Indian as victim, and other popular metaphors for Indianness by the numerous communities that make up the dominant society has led to the formation of indianness as an alternative representation of Indianness in American society.

References

Berry, J. (1996). *The Interest Group Society,* 4th edition. Glenview, IL: Scott, Foresman.

Bordewich, F. (1996). *Killing the White Man's Indian: Reinventing Native Americans at the End of the Twentieth Century.* New York: Doubleday.

Deloria, V. (1992). "Comfortable Fictions and the Struggle for Turf: An Essay Review. The Invented Indian: Cultural Fictions and Government Policies." *The American Indian Quarterly,* 16: 397–410.

Mander, J. (1991). *In the Absence of the Sacred.* San Francisco: Sierra Club Books.

Morgan, G. (1993). *Imaginization: The Art of Creative Management.* Beverly Hills, CA: Sage Publications.

Parker, S. (1996). "New Agers Stealing Cultural Traditions." *The Circle,* 17 (March): 19.

Versluis, A. (1992). *Sacred Earth: The Spiritual Landscape of Native America.* Rochester, VT: Inner Traditions International.

Brain's Use of Shortcuts Can Be a Route to Bias

K. C. COLE

◇◉◈◉◇

Study Questions
1. Define "cognitive weakpoints," "default assumptions," "availability-mediated influence," "believer perseverance," and "behavior confirmation biases."
2. How can each cognitive weakpoint lead to discrimination?

Affirmative action stirs up powerful emotions in both supporters and opponents. But while both sides battle for the hearts of voters, psychologists say the real issues have more to do with the mechanisms of the mind.

Human brains are finely tuned, decision-making machines designed to make quick judgments on a wide variety of confusing events. How far away is that car in the distance? Is that form in the shadows a garbage can or a man with a gun? Is that round red thing a cherry or a marble?

In general, the brain uses past experience to jump to the "most likely" conclusion. Yet these same assumptions can lead people grossly astray.

"This acceptance by the brain of the most probable answer," writes British perceptual psychologist Richard Gregory, makes it "difficult, perhaps somewhat impossible, to see very unusual objects."

When "unusual objects" are women and minorities, it may be impossible to see them as qualified for a variety of jobs, psychologists say.

"Even if you have absolutely no prejudice, you are influenced by your expectations," said Diane Halpern, professor of psychology at Cal State San Bernardino. "A small woman of color doesn't look like a corporate executive. If you look at heads of corporations, they are tall, slender, white males. They are not fat. They are not in a wheelchair. They are not too old. Anything that doesn't conform to the expectation is a misfit."

"Similarity is a strong predictor of attraction," said David Kravitz, psychologist at Florida International University. "So there is a natural human tendency to prefer and hire people like you."

A growing number of behavioral studies point to patterns of perception that influence how people view everything from the moon to minority job candidates. These patterns, experts say, confirm that perception is an active process in which people color the world with their expectations. They do not so much believe what they see as see what they believe.

The ideal of a society free of prejudice may not be possible, experts say, simply because of the makeup of the human mind. Stereotypes are not only inevitable, but essential for survival. If people couldn't make lightning-fast decisions on limited information, they would not be able to discriminate

429

between friend or foe, shadow or object, far or near. To a very real extent, people have to judge every book by its cover. And once a judgment is made, virtually no amount of contrary evidence can turn it around.

People aren't normally aware of the amount of guesswork that goes on in the brain because these perceptual tricks hit upon the right answer the vast majority of the time. Not only do perceptual processes work to ensure survival, they allow people to make music, play baseball, create art. In fact, one of the great puzzles of cognitive science is how a mind capable of dreaming up the music of Mozart and the equations of quantum mechanics can make so many egregious mistakes.

Social psychologists are finding that the occasional errors that the mind makes reveal the hidden rules it uses to make decisions. For example, the brain uses apparent size to judge distance: People don't mistake a car in the distance for a toy because the brain knows through past experience that distant objects appear smaller; therefore the brain compensates, automatically making it larger. But when the information is ambiguous, the brain often leaps to the wrong conclusion. For example, the moon appears to be much larger when it floats just above the horizon than when it shines overhead. The moon doesn't change size, but the brain's estimation of its distance does—in turn automatically changing its apparent size.

By studying how the mind can fool us, psychologists explore the nature of cognitive weak points. They have found that to a large extent, people see what they expect to see, and reject any information that would challenge their already established point of view. "It's the one thing that everyone agrees on," said psychologist Rachel Hare-Mustin, formerly of Harvard. "Unconscious prevailing ideologies are like sand at the picnic. They get into everything."

Errors about everyday objects tend to provide immediate feedback, which makes people unlikely to repeat them. Even a slight mistake in estimating the size of a step can lead to a serious fall.

But errors about other people can more easily slip by unnoticed. "If you're wrong about that car coming at you, it's going to run you down," said psychologist Jennifer Crocker of the State University of New York at Buffalo. "But if you're wrong about whether someone is stupid, you don't hire that person and you never find out how brilliant they are."

The subversive nature of unconscious thought is revealed by this riddle: A father and son are en route to a baseball game when their car stalls on the railroad tracks. The father can't restart the car. An oncoming train hits the car. The father dies. An ambulance rushes the boy to a nearby hospital. In the emergency room, the surgeon takes one look and says: "I can't operate on this child; he's my son."

As cognition researcher Douglas Hofstadter pointed out, even intelligent, broadminded people go out of their way to invent bizarre scenarios—sometimes involving extraterrestrials—to solve the riddle. What prevents most people from seeing that the surgeon is the boy's mother is the reliance of the brain on the "default assumption" that a surgeon is a man.

"A default assumption," Hofstadter explained, "is what holds true in what you might say is the 'simplest' or 'most likely' case. But the critical thing is that they are made automatically, not as a result of consideration and elimination."

Default assumptions are one of the strategies the brain uses to judge the most likely interpretation of an ambiguous situation. In effect, the brain calculates what psychologists call a "base rate"—the normal frequency of a certain event in a normal population.

Base rates have enormous survival value. A mail carrier who assumes that most pit bulls are dangerous is more likely to escape injury than a more open-minded colleague.

Other peculiarities of social perception have been uncovered in a wide variety of controlled experiments, mostly with college students. For example, subjects judge attractive colleagues as smarter, kinder and happier than their unattractive (but otherwise similar) counterparts.

They judge people perceived to be powerful as taller than less powerful people, even when they are actually the same height. They judge people living in poverty as less intelligent than people in affluent neighborhoods.

In one experiment, college students watched a short film of a girl taking a math test and getting a numerical grade. When the girl was portrayed in a suburban neighborhood, viewers remembered her score as higher than when she was shown in a ghetto—even though both the girl and the score were the same in both cases.

The brain also grabs for the most readily available image at hand. This automatic response—which psychologists refer to by the tongue-tangling term "availability-mediated influence"—can be easily manipulated.

In one frequently cited series of experiments, three groups of people were introduced to one of two bogus prison guards—one sweet-natured and humane, the other sadistic and brutish. All three groups were later asked to make inferences about "prison guards in general."

The first group was told that whatever guard they met was typical of all prison guards. The second group was told nothing. The third group was told that the guard they met was not at all typical; in fact, they were specifically warned that any inferences they made from this one case were likely to be wrong.

Nonetheless, all three groups described "prison guards in general" as either kind or brutish, depending on which guard they met.

The experiment, described in the classic book, "Human Inference" by Lee Ross of Stanford and Richard Nisbett of the University of Michigan, presents what the authors describe as "a humbling picture of human… frailty." When presented with a single vivid "available" example, the mind tends to bury all other evidence under the carpet of the unconscious.

This reliance on one vivid example sheds light on one of the most painful contradictions of the affirmative action debate. Many white males, studies show, are angry because they are convinced that less qualified women and minorities are taking their jobs.

Yet minorities and women still feel excluded—and apparently for good reason. The recently published report of the Glass Ceiling Commission, established by legislation introduced in 1990 by then-Senate minority leader Bob Dole, concluded that 95 percent of top positions are still occupied by white men, even though they constitute only 43 percent of the work force.

"So much of the public discourse on this is debate by anecdote," said William Bielby, chairman of the sociology department at UC Santa Barbara. "We hear from so many students that they have a white friend from high school who couldn't get into UC Santa Barbara, but a black kid got in with no problem. And we know how many black kids are on campus. If all those anecdotes were true, then 15 percent of our students, rather than 3 percent, would be black."

In the same way, Bielby said, it's easier to hang onto stereotypes in settings where only one or two women, for example, are in management positions. When only one woman occupies the executive suite, she becomes a target for all expectations about women in general. "But when the proportion of women is 40 percent or 50 percent," Bielby said, "[their colleagues] can see the extent to which the women differ among themselves and the men differ among themselves."

Psychologist Faye Crosby of Smith College conducted an experiment with a group of Yale undergraduate men that vividly showed how inequality becomes imperceptible on a case-by-case basis. Patterns of discrimination that are easy to see in a broad context become invisible when seen in individual instances. Crosby and her colleagues created bogus job descriptions of various men and women at a hypothetical company. The students were instructed to look for unfairness in the salaries. Unknown to them, the women's salaries were rigged to be 80 percent of the salaries of comparable men.

When the students compared one man with one woman at a time, they did not see any unfairness. But when they saw all the salaries of all the men and all the women at the same time, they could easily spot the pattern.

Crosby stresses that this inability to see unfairness on a case-by-case basis has nothing to do with sexism or bad attitudes. It has to do with how the mind works. "We're not saying people are stupid. It's just [a normal cognitive process] like optical illusions."

However one's perceptions are planted, they soon become almost impossible to root out.

In a process psychologists call "belief perseverance," people do almost anything to cling to cherished notions. "If we were constantly changing the way we view the world, things would be too confusing," Crocker said. So people tend to discount evidence that contradicts their "schema," or theory about the world. "If you believe lawyers are slimy and you meet some who aren't, you don't revise your schema; you say; oh, that's an exception."

People also routinely change their memories, Halpern said, to fit their beliefs. If you think that successful people have to be aggressive, and you work with a successful person who is not aggressive "you remember that person as more aggressive," Halpern said. "What we remember depends very much on our biases and beliefs."

These self-fulfilling prophecies, known to psychologists as "behavioral confirmation biases," were dramatically illustrated by a series of experiments in which similar black and white job applicants were questioned by a white interviewer while researchers watched behind a one-way mirror. When the job applicants were black, interviewers sat farther back in their chairs, avoided eye contact, stumbled over their speech and posed fewer questions.

The next part of the test was designed to look at the behavior of the job applicants. This time, the researchers became the interviewers. For consistency, all the applicants were white. With half of the applicants, the researchers intentionally mimicked the behaviors that the interviewers in the first part of the experiment used on blacks (sitting back, stumbling over words, and so on); with the other half, they behaved as the interviewers had with whites—that is, they sat forward in the chairs, maintained eye contact, spoke clearly and asked more questions.

Other researchers watching from behind one-way mirrors evaluated how the applicants seemed to perform during the interview. The result was that the white applicants, when treated as the black applicants had been, were rated less confident, less articulate, and less qualified for the job.

What makes these behaviors hard to correct is that they're completely unconscious; the brain jumps to conclusions in less than 100 milliseconds, "the time it takes to recognize your mother," Hofstadter noted.

In study after study, "the most important finding is that [biases] operate unconsciously,

The Lessons of Illusions

Psychologists use illusions to catch the brain in the act of jumping to conclusions. Most of the time, these perceptual shortcuts work quite well, so we don't notice them. But in unusual situations—such as considering women and minority applicants for jobs traditionally held by white males—the same tricks can lead to egregious mistakes. Many psychologists believe that the un-

Note: The moon on the right has been made smaller to simulate the illusion.

Source: The Exploratorium, San Francisco. Researched by K. C. Cole, *Los Angeles Times*

conscious mechanisms people employ to make judgments about other people are very similar to those behind visual illusions.

True Moon

- *The Illusion:* The moon appears larger when it's low on the horizon than when it's high overhead, even though the moon doesn't change size.

- *How It Works:* When the moon sits low in the sky, the horizon serves as a reference point, making the moon seem unnaturally bigger. (If you view the moon upside down and the horizon becomes the sky—thereby changing the apparent distance—the illusion disappears.)

- *What It Shows:* That the brain can jump to the wrong conclusions when information is ambiguous. Also, that knowing something is an illusion does not make the illusion go away.

Shape and Form

- *The Illusion:* A white triangle appears to float in front of three black circles, even though no triangle exists.

- *How It Works:* The brain constructs the triangle as the most likely solution to the figure of three pie-shaped wedges. People who don't immediately see the triangle usually find it after someone points it out to them.

- *What It Shows:* That people can see something that doesn't exist, especially if they go looking for it. Also, that it's much easier to see something familiar.

Paris, Paris

- *The Illusion:* A sign appears to read "Paris in the spring," but it actually has an extra "the."

- *How It Works:* Since people do not expect to see a double "the," most do not perceive it.

- *What It Shows:* That expectation influences what people see.

even in people who don't want them to," said Anthony G. Greenwald, psychologist at the University of Washington. One of the greatest misconceptions that people have, he said, "is that wanting to be fair is enough to enable you to be fair—not recognizing the unconscious forces that influence your judgments."

In the end, he says, the best approach to affirmative action may have nothing to do with putting people's hearts in the right place. Instead, it should come from understanding what goes on in the brain.

"If you understand that your car tends to drive to the left because your wheels are out of line, you can correct it," he said. Affirmative action, says Greenwald, is a way to compensate not only for past discrimination, but also for future discrimination "by persons who have no intent to discriminate."

Talking Past One Another

RICHARD T. SCHAEFER

<>◆◆◇◆◇

Study Questions
1. What are the two competing definitions of racism?
2. Do you think that differences in the meaning assigned to racism affect people's opinion on whether racism is a problem?

When it comes to talking about race, I contend that on college campuses as in the larger society Whites, Blacks, Asians, and Hispanics hold different views. It is not a variation in accent or vocabulary that is important, but how the dominant Whites and subordinated African Americans and other minority groups have come to view race.

Robert Blauner (1989; 1992) writes that Blacks and Whites basically talk past each other. Blauner reached these conclusions through his in-depth interviews with Blacks and Whites stretching back to 1968. While not intended as a random sample, Blauner's observations help to explain why national surveys continue to show such sharp differences between Whites and Blacks on questions about a broad range of issues from race to employment to welfare policies. By extension, his observations offer insight in the presence of racial prejudice and incidents on a college campus.

Blauner found that Black and White Americans differ on their interpretations of social change from the 1960s through the 1990s because their racial languages define central terms differently, especially "racism." Racism once meant a belief in the superiority of Whites based on the inherent inferiority of Blacks. But in the 1960s, academics and civil rights leaders broadened the meaning of racism. Blacks have tended to embrace the enlarged definition, while Whites have resisted it. Whites object when Blacks form their own groups because Whites equate color consciousness with racism. This is especially evident when we see (on predominantly White college campuses) White students puzzled and annoyed by Black fraternities, Black/Latino cultural houses, and Miss Black Homecoming Queen contests.

Racism was first widened to include "institutional racism," incorporating the social structures that lead to racial segregation. Clearly, in society and on college campuses, the term "racism" refers to an atmosphere that comforts people of one race while making people of other races uncomfortable and unwanted. Blacks may use the term to mean "racism as result," expressing the view that any underrepresentation of minorities shows that racism is at work. Again, few Whites accept this interpretation. This should not be surprising because accepting the view that racism is widespread challenges the legitimacy of whatever success White individuals have enjoyed (Bobo and Kluegel 1993).

Typical of this difference in Whites' and Blacks' attitudes was the aftermath of the 1992 acquittal of four White Los Angeles police officers charged in the beating of Rodney King. Large majorities of Whites and overwhelming majorities of African Americans told pollsters that the verdict was wrong and justice had not been served. Yet when asked if the verdict "shows that blacks cannot get justice in this country," the responses differed—78 percent of Blacks said yes, compared to only 25 percent of Whites (Duke 1992). Even broadly directed questions elicit vast differences in outlook. A 1994 national survey found that 60 percent of Whites "think blacks and other minorities have the same opportunities as whites in the U.S." Yet only 50 percent of Hispanics and 27 percent of Blacks held the same opinion (Fulwood 1994). These contrasting perspectives are what William A. Gamson and his colleagues have termed competing "issue cultures." People frame social issues in different ways, calling upon contrasting metaphors, phrases, and other symbols (Gamson and Lasch 1983; Gamson and Modigliani 1987; see also, Bobo and Kluegel 1993).

These expanded definitions of racism do not make sense to White college students, and Whites in general, who tend to view racism as a personal issue. By and large the content of college curricula does little to unravel these differences. Whites find it difficult to differentiate between the charge that a social structure or institution is racist and the accusation that they, as participants in that structure, are personally racist.

Judith Lichtenberg (1992, p. 3), a professor of philosophy, summarizes this dichotomy:

> In general, white people today use the word "racism" to refer to the explicit conscious belief in racial superiority (typically white over black, but also sometimes black over white). For the most part, black people mean something different by racism; they mean a set of practices and institu-

tions that result in the oppression of black people. Racism, in this view, is not a matter of what's in people's heads but of what happens in the world.

The expanded meaning of racism makes sense to many African Americans, Hispanics, Asian Americans, and Native Americans, "who live such experiences in their bones" (Blauner 1992). But these same expanded definitions of racism do not make sense to Whites, who find it difficult to differentiate between charges of a racist social structure and individual racists.

Whites' resistance to the view of racism as pervasive can be attributed to the dominant ideology in the United States that opportunity is plentiful, effort is economically rewarded and, hence, economic failure is largely deserved (Huber and Form 1973). Furthermore, Whites' own typical experience of relative economic success prevents their recognition of the continuing barriers to opportunity confronted by African Americans and other minorities (Kluegel and Smith 1986; Taylor and Pettigrew 1992).

African Americans talk and think of racism as an ongoing, pervasive condition of life, while Whites tend to talk and think of racism as individual actions, the bigoted exception. These differing perceptions help explain the frequent White response, "I am not racist," and Blacks' view that Whites are, at the very least, naive about the conditions in the nation they dominate.

The view emerging in post-1980 surveys indicates that Whites do not define racism as a serious problem. They object to measures seeking to reduce inequality on grounds they perceive as allegedly free of racial antipathy. Richard Lowry (1991) refers to this limited view of racial inequality and the mistaken perception that racial intolerance was a thing of the past as "yuppie racism."

Let's Spread the "Fun" Around: The Issue of Sports Team Names and Mascots

WARD CHURCHILL

◇•◆•◇

Study Questions
1. Before you read this article, did you have an opinion on the meaning of the "Tomahawk Chop"? What was that opinion?
2. Did your opinion change upon reading Ward's essay? Explain.
3. If your opinion changed to one against the "Chop," what elements of Ward's argument contributed to that change?
4. If your opinion remained in support or changed to one in support of the "Chop," why was Ward's essay unconvincing?

If people are genuinely interested in honoring Indians, try getting your government to live up to the more than 400 treaties it signed with our nations. Try respecting our religious freedom, which has been repeatedly denied in federal courts. Try stopping the ongoing theft of Indian water and other natural resources. Try reversing your colonial process that relegates us to the most impoverished, polluted, and desperate conditions in this country.... Try understanding that the mascot issue is only the tip of a very huge problem of continuing racism against American Indians. Then maybe your ["honors"] will mean something. Until then, it's just so much superficial, hypocritical puffery. People should remember that an honor isn't born when it parts the honorer's lips, it is born when it is accepted in the honoree's ear.

Glenn T. Morris
Colorado Aim

During the past couple of seasons, there has been an increasing wave of controversy regarding the names of professional sports teams like the Atlanta "Braves," Cleveland "Indians," Washington "Redskins," and Kansas City "Chiefs." The issue extends to the names of college teams like the Florida State University "Seminoles," University of Illinois "Fighting Illini," and so on, right on down to high school outfits like the Lamar (Colorado) "Savages." Also involved have been team adoption of "mascots," replete with feathers, buckskins, beads, spears, and "warpaint" (some fans have opted to adorn themselves in the same fashion), and nifty little "pep" gestures like the "Indian Chant" and "Tomahawk Chop."

A substantial number of American Indians have protested that use of native names, images, and symbols as sports team mascots, and the like, is, by definition, a virulently racist practice. Given the historical relationship between Indians and non-Indians during what has been called the "Conquest of America," American Indian Movement leader (and American Indian Anti-Defamation Council founder) Russell Means has compared the practice to contemporary Germans naming their soccer teams the "Jews," "Hebrews," and "Yids," while adorning their uniforms with grotesque caricatures of Jewish faces taken from the Nazis' antisemitic propaganda of the 1930s. Numerous demonstrations have occurred in conjunction with games—most notably during the November . 15, 1992, match-up between the Chiefs and Redskins in Kansas City—by angry Indians and their supporters.

In response, a number of players—especially African-Americans and other minority athletes—have been trotted out by professional team owners like Ted Turner, as well as university and public school officials, to announce that they mean not to insult, but instead to "honor," native people. They have been joined by the television networks and most major newspapers, all of which have editorialized that Indian discomfort with the situation is "no big deal," insisting that the whole thing is just "good, clean fun." The country needs more such fun, they've argued, and "a few disgruntled Native Americans" have no right to undermine the nation's enjoyment of its leisure time by complaining. This is especially the case, some have contended, "in hard times like these." It has even been contended that Indian outrage at being systematically degraded—rather than the degradation itself—creates "a serious barrier to the sort of intergroup communication so necessary in a multicultural society such as ours."

Okay, let's communicate. We may be frankly dubious that those advancing such positions really believe in their own rhetoric, but, just for the sake of argument, let's accept the premise that they are sincere. If what they are saying is true in any way at all, then isn't it time we spread such "inoffensiveness" and "good cheer" around among *all* groups so that *everybody* can participate *equally* in fostering the round of national laughs they call for? Sure it is—the country can't have too *much* fun or "inter-

group involvement"—so the more, the merrier. Simple consistency demands that anyone who thinks the Tomahawk Chop is a swell pastime must be just as hearty in their endorsement of the following ideas, which—by the "logic" used to defend the defamation of American Indians—should help us all *really* start yukking it up.

First, as a counterpart to the Redskins, we need an NFL team called "Niggers" to "honor" Afroamerica. Halftime festivities for fans might include a simulated stewing of the opposing coach in a large pot while players and cheerleaders dance around it, garbed in leopard skins and wearing fake bones in their noses. This concept obviously goes along with the kind of gaiety attending the Chop, but also with the actions of the Kansas City Chiefs, whose team members—prominently including black team members—lately appeared on a poster looking "fierce" and "savage" by way of wearing Indian regalia. Just a bit of harmless "morale boosting," says the Chiefs' front office. You bet.

So that the newly formed "Niggers" sports club won't end up too out of sync while expressing the "spirit" and "identity" of Afroamericans in the above fashion, a baseball franchise—let's call this one the "Sambos"—should be formed. How about a basketball team called the "Spearchuckers"? A hockey team called the "Jungle Bunnies"? Maybe the "essence" of these teams could be depicted by images of tiny black faces adorned with huge pairs of lips. The players could appear on TV every week or so gnawing on chicken legs and spitting watermelon seeds at one another. Catchy, eh? Well, there's "nothing to be upset about," according to those who love wearing "war bonnets" to the Super Bowl or having "Chief Illiniwik" dance around the sports arenas of Urbana, Illinois.

And why stop there? There are plenty of other groups to include. "Hispanics"? They can be "represented" by the Galveston "Greasers" and San Diego "Spics," at least until the Wisconsin "Wetbacks" and Baltimore "Beaners" get off the ground. Asian Americans? How about the "Slopes," "Dinks," "Gooks," and "Zipperheads"? Owners of the latter teams might get their logo ideas from editorial page cartoons printed in the nation's newspapers during World War II: slant-eyes, buck teeth, big glasses, but nothing racially insulting or derogatory, according to the editors and artists involved at the time. Indeed, this Second World War–vintage stuff can be seen as just another barrel of laughs, at least by what current editors say are their "local standards" concerning American Indians.

Let's see. Who's been left out? Teams like the Kansas City "Kikes," Hanover "Honkies," San Leandro "Shylocks," Daytona "Dagos," and Pittsburgh "Polacks" will fill a certain social void among white folk. Have a religious belief? Let's all go for the gusto and gear up the Milwaukee "Mackerel Snappers" and Hollywood "Holy Rollers." The Fighting Irish of Notre Dame can be rechristened the "Drunken Irish" or "Papist Pigs." Issues of gender and sexual preference can be addressed through creation of teams like the St. Louis "Sluts," Boston "Bimbos," Detroit "Dykes," and the Fresno "Faggots." How about the Gainesville "Gimps" and Richmond "Retards," so the physically and mentally impaired won't be excluded from our fun and games?

Now, don't go getting "overly sensitive" out there. *None* of this is demeaning or insulting, at least not when it's being done to Indians. Just ask the folks who are doing it, or their apologists like Andy Rooney in the national media. They'll tell you—as in fact they *have* been telling you—that there's been no harm done, regardless of what their victims think, feel, or say. The situation is exactly the same as when those with pre-

cisely the same mentality used to insist that Step'n'Fetchit was okay, or Rochester on the *Jack Benny Show,* or Amos and Andy, Charlie Chan, the Frito Bandito, or any of the other cutesey symbols making up the lexicon of American racism. Have we communicated yet?

Let's get just a little bit real here. The notion of "fun" embodied in rituals like the Tomahawk Chop must be understood for what it is. There's not a single non-Indian example deployed above which can be considered socially acceptable in even the most marginal sense. The reasons are obvious enough. So why is it different where American Indians are concerned? One can only conclude that, in contrast to the other groups at issue, Indians are (falsely) perceived as being too few, and therefore too weak, to defend themselves effectively against racist and otherwise offensive behavior. The sensibilities of those who take pleasure in things like the Chop are thus akin to those of schoolyard bullies and those twisted individuals who like to torture cats. At another level, their perspectives have much in common with those manifested more literally—and therefore more honestly—by groups like the Nazis, Aryan Nations, and Ku Klux Klan. Those who suggest this is "okay" should be treated accordingly by anyone who opposes nazism and comparable belief systems.

Fortunately, there are a few glimmers of hope that this may become the case. A few teams and their fans have gotten the message and have responded appropriately. One illustration is Stanford University, which opted to drop the name "Indians" with regard to its sports teams (and, contrary to the myth perpetuated by those who enjoy insulting Native Americans, Stanford has experienced *no* resulting drop-off in attendance at its games). Meanwhile, the local newspaper in Portland, Oregon, recently decided its long-standing editorial policy prohibiting use of racial epithets should include derogatory sports team names. The Redskins, for instance, are now simply referred to as being "the Washington team," and will continue to be described in this way until the franchise adopts an inoffensive moniker (newspaper sales in Portland have suffered no decline as a result).

Such examples are to be applauded and encouraged. They stand as figurative beacons in the night, proving beyond all doubt that it is quite possible to indulge in the pleasure of athletics without accepting blatant racism into the bargain. The extent to which they do not represent the norm of American attitudes and behavior is exactly the extent to which America remains afflicted with an ugly reality which is far different from the noble and enlightened "moral leadership" it professes to show the world. Clearly, the United States has a very long way to go before it measures up to such an image of itself.

The Rules of Passing

LAWRENCE OTIS GRAHAM

Study Questions
1. Why do you think people pass into the "white race?" List all the reasons identified in this article.
2. How do the rules of passing provide insights about shared histories?
3. Reevaluate the stories "Black Man with a Nose Job" and "Don't Want to Be Black Anymore" in light of the information presented in "The Rules of Passing."

During conversations with many light-complexioned blacks among the elite, one hears a wide range of family secrets and experiences. An Atlanta attorney who was born into a family where many relatives passed shared some conclusions after observing the way he saw black cousins and siblings pass into the white race. Although he used no such label, I have heard a number of "tips" repeated by other light-skinned blacks. For lack of a better term, I call this disturbing litany of tips "The Rules of Passing":

1. Passing will be easier if you attempt it while away at college—preferably on a campus that is predominantly white and is located in a small rural town.
2. Change your last name to one that is not associated with black family names. Avoid such surnames as Jones, Jackson, Johnson, Williams, Thomas, and Brown.
3. Recreate your family tree by describing yourself as an only child born of parents who died years ago, and who were also only children.
4. Relocate to a new community that insulates you from interacting with blacks and that is at least a few hundred miles from your family's home. Avoid cities like New Orleans and Charleston, South Car-

olina, where whites are adept at spotting light-skinned blacks who are passing.
5. Think of some manner in which to "kill yourself off" in the minds of black people who know you and your family. If your parents or siblings are willing participants in assisting you, they can say that you now live outside the country, that you have entered a cult or religious order, or even that you have died.
6. Realize that blacks—and not whites—are the ones who can threaten your security as a black person living a lie. Avoid any meaning interaction with black people. Affluent blacks who understand the "passing" phenomenon and may try to "out" you are particularly dangerous.
7. Develop associations with organizations and institutions that will buttress your new white résumé. Convert to the Presbyterian Church or the Republican Party. Contribute to charities like the Junior League or the Daughters of the American Revolution.
8. Recognize the physical features that can undermine your new identity. Avoid getting tanned at the beach. If your hair it not straight, keep it short, wear a hairpiece, or maintain weekly touchups.
9. Enhance those features that can support your new identity. Lightening your hair

color, narrowing your nose, thinning your lips, and adopting a more conservative style in clothing and speech are all simple steps that can aid your transition.

10. Realize that no one in your life (including a spouse) should be trusted with your secret, except for your adult-aged child, who, presumably, will maintain secrecy because of his or her own self-interest in living as a white person.

11. Avoid applying for high-profile positions or admission into selective clubs or lineage-obsessed institutions like secret societies or prestigious co-op boards, so that you will not be subjected to probing questions and searches.

12. Avoid the appearance of being secretive about your racial identity. If your physical appearance makes it possible, claim to be of white European background. If you have a darker complexion, claim to be a mixture that includes a white European background (e.g., Irish, Dutch, German, Polish) and a darker European or Middle Eastern background (e.g., Greek, Cuban, Lebanese, Portuguese). Never claim any ethnic group from continental Africa or Mexico or Central America.

13. Avoid sitting with or being photographed with black people because if you have any vaguely black features, those characteristics will be exaggerated and suddenly make you seem quite similar to "real blacks" standing near you. The similarities will quickly become obvious to all.

14. If the members of the black family you have "divorced" are willing to support your efforts to "pass," always meet them on neutral territory where neither you nor they live, work, or socialize. Never meet them at your home, and never meet them in settings that are predominantly white or that are places your white acquaintances might frequent.

15. If the black relatives you have "divorced" are unwilling to support your efforts, make a complete break from them, because they can too easily undo the facade you have created in your new community and new life.

16. To avoid the risk of giving birth to a "throwback child" with black features, consider adopting a white child.

17. If having your own child is a priority to you, you will be better able to explain your child's dark features if your spouse is a member of a dark-skinned ethnic group. Southern Italians, Greeks, Armenians, Brazilians, and Cubans are among the groups that fit this category.

"The Rules of Passing" have pretty much remained unchanged for families today, even though they were first established by northern and southern families who were avoiding the harsh discriminatory practices in existence during the slavery and early postslavery periods.

"Mother, I'm moving to Los Angeles and I will stay in touch, but I don't want you and Daddy to visit me there."

"Sheila, don't do this. Don't do this. It's a terrible life." Mrs. Harrison sat at her makeup table with the phone to her ear.

As her husband sat on a chair, he buried his head in his hands.

"Mother, I'm sorry, but I've made my mind up."

"But, Sheila, sweetheart, just come home and let's talk about this. We can figure it out; we can help you."

As she tells me the story of how she "lost" her child, Varnelle Harrison recalls how she attempted to talk her daughter out of passing. As she stares at the black-and-white photo of Sheila and her two other daughters standing in front of a summer beach cottage, she clenches a tissue in her left hand. Angry and somewhat embarrassed by her daughter's choice, she asks me not to use her or her daughter's real name (or identifying characteristics), even though she knows that her daughter has long since found a new identity.

"We had sort of expected that this call might come one day," says Harrison, a woman who, ironically, has strong ties to her black sorority, which she joined more than sixty years ago. "Some people don't understand why a black person who was born with a good background of educated and well-to-do parents would want to pass, but I think it's more likely that *we* would try to pass rather than a poor black person because we actually get to see what the most privileged white person has in life. We have the same education, the same money, and the same potential. In a way, we get so close that it becomes an awful temptation." For that reason, she wasn't terribly surprised that Sheila, a smart and ambitious child, would one day fall prey to that temptation.

Varnelle says it started becoming obvious when Sheila spent four years in college with only three visits to her parents' home. "She came home Christmas of freshman and sophomore year—and the summer in between," says Harrison as she recalls. "She told my husband and me that she was doubling up on coursework in order to graduate in three years, so she was working through vacations and doing research with professors during the summers."

It was all a lie, and Varnelle and her now-deceased husband, Roger, had an inkling of what was going on, particularly when Sheila had planned two visits with them and insisted that they stay at an inn that was forty-five minutes from campus.

When Sheila went away to college in the early 1950s, she picked a small women's college in the Northeast against the advice of her parents, who had both attended a black southern college.

"I told her she should be going to Howard, where she could meet some nice friends from good families," explains Varnelle, who is now almost ninety and has had limited contact with her daughter since that phone call. "But she came up with this college in New England that none of us had ever heard of. I remember asking her why she would ever want to go to a school in a place like that. And the minute I asked it, I knew the answer. It was devastating to my husband. And I think I just got angry."

Although she had been raised in a black neighborhood with an entire circle of well-to-do sophisticated black friends, Sheila had intentionally picked a white college in a rural community. Such an environment would allow her an easy transition out of a black culture. Her mother now concludes that it was Sheila's testing ground to see if she could live a life of passing.

"It was like she killed herself off as a black person, and then reemerged with an entirely new identity," says a childhood friend who knew Sheila as a black kid in their southern hometown.

"She almost never came home for summers during college—always telling her parents that she was doing extra papers and research with the hope of graduating early," says the childhood playmate. "Around her junior year, we started to hear rumors that she had suffered a breakdown and was institutionalized. Somebody else said she'd left the country and settled in India somewhere. And a couple of others—friends of Sheila's parents—told my parents that she'd killed herself. All these crazy stories to explain her disappearance. It was just a nontopic for Sheila's parents. They just never discussed her anymore."

According to a white classmate who claims to have known Sheila only as a white person, Sheila got married, unbeknownst to her parents, during the late part of her junior year to a local white high school graduate. "I think his last name was Masters," says the classmate. According to the former classmate, Masters was a quiet, rather simple, unsophisticated man who worked in a grocery store. Presumably, he was somebody that she knew would care little about her background and would be suitably impressed by the fact that she was a college student.

"I later got the sense," says Varnelle, who says it was years before she ever heard about a marriage—and to this day, she is not certain it took place—"that she told this boy that we were deceased and that she was an only child with no other family. I never met him or saw him, but he probably wasn't too concerned about her background. After all, unless you're in places like certain parts of South Carolina or Virginia, whites don't think about blacks passing that much. It's foreign to most white people."

Evidently, according to a former friend of Harrison's daugther, Masters was also somebody Sheila would not stay married to. Making the calculated decision that her husband's value was only in his name and white family heritage, she made no efforts to meet his friends or to build a life together. One black childhood friend learned that Sheila had taken off the next year from college and guessed that her intent was to gain a different graduation year—further altering her original school records. With a new last name, he concluded, her plan was to graduate and enter the real world with a new name and a new identity. When Mrs. Harrison hears this pieced together, she says, "Before my husband died, we pretty much figured out what she'd done, but I long ago stopped trying to understand the convoluted decisions our daughter made.

I'm not even sure she married this man. She may have just taken his name. It's like trying to figure one of those murder mystery novels."

At age twenty-two, only months before graduation, Sheila evidently parted from the white man who was believed to be her husband. Soon after graduating, she left town for Los Angeles with a completely new name and identity.

Today, Sheila has two different identities for two different communities. The black community in her hometown knew a Sheila Harrison, a black woman, who they believe, for the most part, is either dead, institutionalized, or living in some other country. The white community in her adoptive city and surounding environs know a Sheila Masters, a white socialite, whose Vermont doctor father and Greek mother died when Sheila was a child.

"I knew Sheila as a black person," says an elderly black physician who belonged to the same fraternity as her father. "And what's so amazing is that none of us have interacted with her since she re-created herself as a white woman. I have a pretty good idea of where she lives, what she does, and what she looks like. I had the opportunity to meet a white colleague who had actually been to Sheila's new home fifteen years ago. My colleague knows her only as a white person. From what I understand, when people ask her about her background, she says that her maiden name is Sheila Masters and that she is part Greek."

It seems that Sheila never mentions her former husband, but on the rare occasion when someone learns that she has previously been married, she will quite matter-of-factly offer the incredible story that "my name was originally Masters, but I ended up marrying a very distant cousin—also named Masters." With the dexterity of a double agent, Sheila has developed a clever way to guard her true identity and steer even the most curious genealogist directly into a white family tree. Of course, it was her former husband's family tree, but by claiming him as a distant cousin, she suddenly made it her family history too.

"I tried to rekindle my friendship with her," says a retired college professor who had grown up with Sheila and had been a friend of her father's. "I ran into her and confronted her in an airport several years ago, but the lies were so outrageous and so well rehearsed that I couldn't get through to her. It was so ridiculous to be keeping that story going now that she was successful and living a great life. It's not as if this was still the 1950s or 1960s anymore. She kept insisting that I was mistaking her for somebody else. Here she was with the same face, the same voice, and the same first name—and she's telling me that I'm confusing her with somebody else. It absolutely amazes me that white people can't see the black in her. She even has a southern black twang. But I guess the whites she socializes with have absolutely no ties to black people. If she's gone through that much trouble to live in the white race, all I can say is good riddance. They can have her."

A black secretary who worked for one of Sheila's white friends says, "When I first saw Mrs. Masters stop by to see my boss, I immediately assumed she might be black. Even with her white skin and the straight hair, in my eyes, there was nothing else she *could* be. But then I could tell the way she wouldn't meet my eyes when I greeted her that something was up. She was always direct with the white secretaries but not with me. She wasn't mean to me, but it was almost as if she was scared of me. And here she was, this rich, confident lady with all these rich white friends. I guess she was afraid they'd all dump her if they knew she was black." The secretary paused and shook her head in disgust.

"I hope you enjoy your new scarf," said the saleswoman as she slid the change across the counter and placed the large Goldsmith's shopping bag on the counter for Erma Clanton.

"I'm sure I will, thank you." As Clanton walked back past the silk scarves that she had been perusing, she stopped in front of one of the mirrors to adjust the lapel on her jacket. In the reflection, she caught a glimpse of someone in the background who looked familiar.

Erma turned around and made her way to the next department—ladies' hats. She looked around her and saw the glass countertops and small racks lined with the latest fashions from New York and abroad. What Erma had always liked about Goldsmith's was that it brought a big-city, northeastern flair to her hometown of Memphis. A large, sophisticated New York kind of store without the New York hustle and bustle.

"Sadie!" she called out, recognizing the profile that she had only glanced at earlier.

"Oh, my," responded a woman who was trying on a navy-blue hat with a spray of silk flowers in the back.

Erma had not seen Sadie (not her real name) since they had graduated from Booker T. Washington High School and gone off to college in the early 1950s. Almost a decade had passed, but she would have recognized her friend's bright-red hair and sharp olive features anywhere.

Sadie smiled faintly as the saleswoman removed the navy-blue hat and replaced it with a brown one. She spun around and rushed over to her friend, stopping Erma short.

"Girl, it is so good to see you." Erma put down her bag and leaned over to hug her old friend.

"No," the friend whispered briskly. "Erma, please don't hug me. Don't touch me."

Erma's outstretched arms froze strangely.

"I'm sorry, Erma. I'll grab your hands and shake them." The olive-complexioned hands very tenderly grabbed Erma's deep-brown wrists and brought them down to Erma's sides with a whisper, "It's very nice to see you, Erma, but not here."

As Erma glanced over Sadie's shoulder to the arched eyebrows of the white saleswoman, she was confused. Then she glanced up at the price tag that hung from the new hat on Sadie's head. She suddenly understood what was going on. Sadie was passing for white.

"Yes, Sadie, some other time."

"It had not occurred to me why Sadie wouldn't let me hug her until I saw the unpurchased hat on her head," explains Clanton, who is a retired professor from Memphis State University and who shares this memory with me during a recent visit to my aunt's home in Memphis. "At that time, blacks were not allowed to try hats on in department stores in Memphis. We had to either buy it or just look at it without touching it. So, when I realized she was trying a hat on with the assistance of the saleswoman, I realized she was passing. And if she'd hugged me, I would have blown her cover."

Erma shook her head—not with disgust over Sadie's actions, but more over the fact that she had not immediately recognized the situation.

One of the reasons many blacks have historically allowed their black brothers and sisters to pass without exposing them is either that it caught them off guard or that they were afraid of subjecting these individuals to consequences from the law or the general white public. Others neglected to expose these passing blacks because it sometimes gave them satisfaction to see one

of their own outsmart white people and the outrageous Jim Crow treatment of the black community. My father, who is the lightest-complexioned member of my immediate family but by no means light enough to pass, remembers a childhood acquaintance who used to pass whenever she went to the movie theater in Memphis.

"For Charlene, it was a big joke. A group of us would all walk over to the theater together, and about a block away, all the black-looking kids would drop behind and let her go ahead of us. When we got to the theater on Beale Street, we'd all see Charlene standing in line with the white people at the front door. She'd slyly wink at us, and then we'd go around to the side alley door where black patrons had to come in. Up in the balcony where blacks had to sit, we'd all be able to look down and see Charlene fooling the white kids that sat around her. When the show was over, we'd meet up about two blocks away and Charlene would be laughing about her prank."

The idea of "sticking it to white people" or beating them at their own game of racial segregation and favoritism has been an issue for many generations in the black community. While children might have done it as a prank, many parents and adults, like Sheila Harrison and Sadie, did it before—and continue it today—because of the economic advantages that are afforded to whites in the area of housing, employment, or treatment in public facilities. With the exception of Congressman Adam Clayton Powell, who had passed as white and dated white girls during his early college years at Colgate University in upstate New York, one rarely finds high-profile blacks attempting to lead double lives, so any advantages being gotten by black people who pass are usually individual and generally affect only the people who are being duped.

In her book *Ambiguous Lives,* George Washington University history professor Adele Logan Alexander looks at the generations of her family living as free blacks in the eighteenth and nineteenth centuries and points out that of her paternal grandmother's eight siblings—all of whom were light enough to pass—only one did. And among her father's siblings, she speculates that only one—a brother—passed, and that after he chose to do so, he created such selective rules about who could not meet his white wife that "the rest of my father's family simply got fed up with it."

"Just like my own relatives living during that time and later periods," says Alexander, "most educated or privileged blacks feel a sense of obligation to acknowledge their own black community and to give back to others who may not have the same advantages. Most are simply not willing to abandon an entire community."

Unfortunately, there is a high price to be paid by family members—particularly the children of blacks who pass. There are many stories of families who have been polarized on the issue of racial passing. I have at least a half-dozen cousins who are often mistaken for white and could pass if they chose. I feel grateful not to have lost them or other close relatives to the practice, but I can't help wondering what it must be like to be privy to remarks made by white people on the issue of race when they have no idea who is present.

There have been many blacks who have managed to divorce their parents or fool their friends and colleagues, but the passing blacks create an even more complex situation when they raise children. The passing black who marries a white will sometimes tell the spouse and sometimes not. If the white spouse objects, it's something that he

or she can avoid or dismiss through divorce. But what happens to the child of passing blacks? How are they affected by the lies and by the fact that their racial makeup is permanent and will always be called into question?

"Kids used to think I was adopted when I was in college. They'd see the photo of my parents in my dormitory room and say, 'Who's that?'" says Loretta Josephs, a fifty-two-year-old light-brown-complexioned woman who now wears her graying brown hair in small braids, as she tells the story of how she grew up as a dark-skinned child in a family that lived as white people. It took her twenty years to come to terms with the fact that her parents had developed all kinds of lies to avoid confronting the family's true racial makeup. And when she asks me to disguise her name (and certain identifying characteristics), it becomes obvious that she is still not ready to fully accept her family's situation in a public way. She admits that her parents went so far as hiring a black nanny who would pose as Loretta's mother in situations that might prove awkward for the other family members.

"My mother was white, and my father was black—but passing—so I was a real problem. My two older brothers came out real light, but I came out dark. I was a *throwback child.*"

As Josephs opens a large four-ring photo album, her point becomes immediately obvious. She sat peacefully in the dining room of her spacious colonial home while pointing out yellowed family photos taken in the 1940s. One photo showed a white couple on a picnic blanket with two white boys sitting in front of them. The boys, with clean-shaven heads, looked to be no more than four or five years old. They smiled broadly at the camera with complexions as milky-white as their parents'. The baby, dressed in a striped jumper, was also smiling—but she didn't seem to fit into the scene. She looked strangely out of place, even while being held in her mother's lap. The baby was black.

"That was me when I was ten months old. And as you can see, I was the darkest thing in that picture." The woman showed a succession of photos—all family gatherings—from birthday parties to outings at the park, Christmas tree poses, backyard cookouts. And in each one of them, Loretta was immediately identifiable. She was always the only black-looking child in the group. In a few of the photos, there was a black woman in a white uniform standing at the back.

"My parents hoped I would get lighter, because, as you can see from the pictures, we lived in a white world—went to a white church, lived in a white neighborhood. My mother used to scrub me twice a day—hoping that my skin would lighten up. She would make up a bath mixture in the tub using up a quart of milk, two squeezed lemons, and a teaspoon of liquid bleach. When she was done, she'd rub my knees and elbows with the halves of the lemon, all the while saying to me, 'Now, if you stay off your knees, they'll lighten up.'"

And there was something else Loretta remembers that was always kept near her bathroom tub.

"And she always kept a jar of Nadinola Bleaching Cream within reach. It was in the bedroom, in the kitchen cabinet, in the glove compartment of our car. Nadinola Cream— for clear complexions. That was a popular thing back then, but I remember you could only find it in the black neighborhoods, so my mother always had our maid get it for her. Of course I had no idea that all kids weren't scrubbed this way every morning and night. I thought it was normal."

Like many very young children of color-conscious parents, it was a long time before Loretta even noticed her own color difference. It was a long time before she noticed that she was considerably darker than her parents and brothers. Like other children, she saw size and gender as the primary differences between herself and her brothers and parents. The distinctions her parents drew and the rules they established seemed to be logical and fair when they were issued to her.

"When I was told by my parents not to play with the kids in the neighborhood, I thought it was because I was a girl and they were worried that I'd get hurt. When we went to the beach and they kept me fully clothed with a visored hat pulled tightly over my head and ears, I thought it was because it was unladylike to get tanned. As they held me under umbrellas, protecting me from what Mom called 'the sun's harsh rays,' they offered an innocent explanation for everything. They wouldn't allow me ever to pick up the telephone because they said little girls didn't do that. It wasn't until I was about five years old that I sensed real differences and started to realize there was more behind the special rules and special treatment. One example was when my mother used to hot-comb my hair with a blazing iron comb every morning. Once again, I thought all ladies got their hair hot-combed."

"One day, my brother Jimmy came in the room and asked, 'Why do you do that to Retty's hair?' My oldest brother, Sammy— who was eight or nine then said, 'Because she's got nigger hair when she wakes up every day.'"

"Even though Sammy didn't speak the words in a mean tone—and though I wasn't quite sure what 'nigger hair' was, I could immediately tell it got my mother mad. That night, my brothers and I heard my mother tell my father, 'You know, Sam, Retty's going to be a problem for us when she starts school in September.' All we could hear then was my father say, 'I'm sorry.' Then we heard mom start crying."

"About a month later, to our complete surprise," explained Josephs, "my mother announced that she and Dad had hired a maid."

"'Your father and I decided that with Retty starting school in two months,' my mother said gaily, 'I will need more help around the house. You boys are old enough to do your own things and get yourselves ready for school. But Retty will need extra help, since she's young. So the new maid will be helping Retty with her things.'"

"'So the maid will really be Retty's maid,' my father added—picking up almost exactly where mother had left off—as if with a script. 'She will walk Retty to school at St. Catherine's, take her to the playground on Saturdays, bring Retty to the doctor, and so forth.'"

"'St. Catherine's?' Jimmy asked. 'Isn't she going to *our* school?'"

"'No, Retty will not be going to the public school. As a girl, it's better for her in a nice Catholic school.'"

Loretta then remembers her father interrupting the discussion to explain how she and her brothers were to address the new maid. "'You are each to call her Mam when she gets here.'"

"'Mam?' my younger brother asked. 'What's her name?'"

"'Mam—that's her name and that's what you will call her.' My parents then got up from the dining-room table with their plates and went into the kitchen."

Loretta remembers her brother staring at her. A new school, a new maid, and new rules were all elicited by her coming of age. She admits she was confused. "All three of us were surprised. But my surprise soon turned into a feeling of superiority. My brothers glared at me and left the table."

The following month, when "Mam" joined her family and moved into a bedroom over the garage, Loretta was moved into a bedroom that allowed her to share Mam's bathroom. As her mother walked her brothers to school, Mam took Loretta by bus to an integrated Catholic school that was just on the other side of her town's border.

"By the time I was in the fifth or sixth grade, I realized a lot of things. I realized that neighbors were whispering things about me being a Negro, or that I was a half-breed, or that I was Mam's child. I realized also that my parents had kept me from answering the phone because people had been calling and saying racist things into the phone. But most devastating of all for me was when I realized that the reason why Mam was hired as 'my maid' was that she was, in a sense, acting as my 'mother' for the people who were watching from the outside world."

By the time Loretta was sent away to boarding school at age twelve while her brothers remained at home, she had stopped believing all of her parents' special rules about what young ladies were supposed to do. She realized that she was standing in the way of her family's ability to live as a white family in a white world. Today, living very obviously as a black woman, she says that her parents are deceased and that she has little contact with her brothers. Married to a black attorney who collects African art, she has no white friends and fully embraces her black identity. "I intentionally wear my hair in cornrows and get black in the sun," Josephs says with a slight chuckle that is belied by more than a few tears in her eyes. "I feel that I've got to make up for the years of blackness that my parents stole from me."

The phenomenon of passing is among the least-discussed issues within the community of the black elite. It is a source of great shame and annoyance, even among those people who recognize its necessity and its benefits from an economic perspective. Although I have known a few people who pass in order to gain short-term advantages such as better professional connections in business networking organizations or in order to purchase a co-op in a particular apartment building, most accomplish this by simply omitting information about themselves rather than actively lying about their family identity. The issue has less relevance in today's black community, because while most affluent blacks in America had historically also been light-skinned, today there are large numbers of blacks who are able to gain admission to top academic institutions, as well as to top employers, regardless of the shade of their Negroid complexion. As more and more opportunities open for blacks in housing and employment, the primary remaining reasons that certain blacks will choose to pass are those that determine their ability to maintain close intimate relationships with people who would otherwise not embrace them.

Childhood and Sexual Identity Under Slavery

ANTHONY S. PARENT, JR. AND SUSAN BROWN WALLACE

◇•◆•◇

Study Questions

1. How does the article help us to understand our shared history?
2. Relationships between "white" owners and "black" slaves were intimate, emotional, and complex. Explain what this means. How did these "interracial" relationships affect the status of multiracial offspring?
3. Does the information presented in this essay give further insight about "Black Man with a Nose Job," "Don't Want to Be Black Anymore," and "The Memoirs of Madison Hemings"? Explain.

In slavery, the message was that the woman's body was not her own; if she exercised a personal right she was not simply punished but publicly humiliated and dehumanized. The stripping of clothing meant that the violent act cut down to the primal essence of the victim and the slave community at large, revealing to the child her elemental vulnerability. A former woman slave remembered that "when they commenced selling the niggers they would have to strip naked" to be examined. "It was awful to see the condition of some of the women, especially. Some of them were pregnant." A former slave named Martha Harrison remembered that "the way they would whip you was like they done my oldest sister. They tied her, and they had a place just like they're gonna barbecue a hog; and they would strip you and tie you and lay you down." "When they would whip you they would tear your back all to pieces," remembered one ex-slave, who described himself as a fifteen-year-old boy when the war began. "Child, they didn't care for you. We had to stand in fear of them, we had no

protection. They would take your clothes off and whip you like you was no more than mules." Yet another recalled an incident when "they beat us till the blood run down our legs. When we left here we was naked; my sister was the weaver and she was weaving some clothes for us, and old mistress took that stuff off the loom and took it upstairs and hid it. We went away naked.... Yes, when we left there we had our dresses pulled round in front to hide our nakedness."

In developing a sense of sexual identity the prospect of sexually inspired physical violence was omnipresent. Children not only learned that white men commonly forced themselves upon black women but that the consequences of resisting could be fatal. Slave children learned that if women resisted they could be sold south, separated from their babies, and beaten. A slave woman remembered when she was a child on Dr. Gale's plantation that not all women had sexual relations with white men; of those who did, some went willingly but others were forced: "They had a horror of going to Mississippi and they would do anything to keep from it." At that time, Mississippi was seen as the worst place for a slave to be held. She recalled that her master allowed Aunt Mary Jane to marry a "yellow man" because he knew he could have her anytime he wanted. "He dressed her up in red—red dress, red band and rosette around her head, and a red sash with a big red bow." Her dark-skinned aunt "had two yellow girls to wait on her!" A dance followed the wedding, but the churched couple did not dance. The whites watched. A former slave from Hardeman County, Tennessee, recalled a slave named John, "a big double-jointed man," who confronted his owner for making advances to his wife. "John run old man Chapman, for some of the hands told him that Chapman had been after his wife, and John got after him about it. Old Chapman had a gun and John tried to take it away from him and Old Chapman shot him in the arm. . . . He taken his wife and went to Mississippi, and carried John's wife too. John kept on disputing with master and master tapped him over the head with his walking cane." Black men who resisted the rape of their wives and loved ones were choosing death. A slaveowner named Sam Watkins "would ship their husbands (slaves) out of bed and get in with their wives." One man killed Watkins, although "he knew it was death." According to Stephen M. Weissman, "The frequent disruptions of the black family unit were partially related to unconscious retaliatory envy. The white man's need to repress his childhood emotional tie to blacks often took the extreme form of seeing them as subhuman or nonhuman. Tenderness was replaced by cruelty in what could be described as a cultural reaction formation. The power and intensity of the white man's exaggerated sexual fear of the black man was probably related to the power and intensity of his own unconsciously determined inces-

tuous wishes toward black women and its accompanying retaliatory fears."[53] Boys and girls observed that the owners did not respect the sanctity of the marriage bed and that resistance had dire consequences.

In most cases, the children observed that slave women had little choice but to be involved in the liaisons that produced mixed-race children. In some cases, slave women might have sought the relationships, but the cost was great. These children were sometimes not trusted by the other slaves, because of their biological and social relationships with whites. The miscegenation added further confusion to a slave's sense of self-worth. Was it better to be half white, since being black was despised? Yet in many cases the offspring were treated just the same as blacks or were despised by the whites whom they resembled, and who feared them. Sometimes, slave children of owners and their mothers had special privilges. Most continued their status as slaves, although after slavery ended, some were deeded land and given some support by their white families.[54] One woman whose husband's father was the master remembered that "marsa had a brother to have a child by one of the slaves, 'Course he wouldn't own him, but everybody knowed it, he would give it things, but they treated him (the baby boy) like they did all the other slaves, no'm, didn't make no difference toward him. Well, some of them thought it was an honor to have the marsa, but I didn't want no white man foolin' with me." Another recalled, "I know plenty of slaves (women) who went with the old marster. They had to do it or get a killing. They couldn't help it. Some of them would raise large families by their owner. I know an old banker in Lebanon who gave one of his children a home after they come free." "Aunt Millie" who had master's son lived on a plantation but was free, paid for by a white person. They called her "widow woman" because she lived alone. A woman from Nashville remembered a man on the Pike. "I know when I went off he bought a woman, and this woman came from Arkansas, and this here man got with her and got this boy and she got him, and then she turned around and had a black one, and he turned around and sold it. He bought her from Miss Porter and she got jealous and she turned round and had a dark child and he sold [it]."

Issues of identity and sexuality were complicated further when the child was a blood relative of the slaveowner or his white employee. Some of the former slaves pointed out that the slaveowners tried not to show any favoritism. In some cases, they were sold by their relatives. What did it mean to be sold by your father? What did it mean to be seen as less than human by your relatives?[55] One ex-slave remembered that "some of them would treat these [mixed-blood] children better, and some of them wouldn't." Another ex-slave remembered that when he was twelve years old he was sold by his half-brother, "mighty near like Joseph." On the Gale plantation, a woman remembered, her "grandfather was an Irishman and he was a foreman, but he had to whip his children and grandchildren just like the others." Gale, himself, had his children work the same as other slaves and call him "marster," and the overseer whipped them like the others. "The only advantage they had was that Marster Gale wouldn't sell them." A witness, a fifteen-year-old boy when the war began, recalled that "they wouldn't make no difference in the half-white slaves. They would get whippings just like we would." Another remembered that the whites treated their children the same as other slaves. "They mighta liked them a little better, but they didn't want to show it." Still another recalled that the children were whipped the same as the others and sold from the block.

"They would take them to town and put them on the block, and he was the father of them." The commingling of race with sex and with the violent separations and whippings illustrate the sexual content of the violence about which Fanon wrote.

Often mistresses who felt threatened by the relationships that their husbands had with black women took out their frustration and anger on the resulting children. Dr. Gale's ex-slave remembered a practice that when whites married, the husband would be given a slave cook as a gift, by whom he then had children. They "sometimes favored him so much that the wife would be mean to them and make him sell them. If they had nice long hair she would cut it off and wouldn't let them wear it long like white children." Another informant recalled one family of half-white children of the master on the plantation. "The old lady would be meaner to them than she was to the black ones." She "would not have one of them for a house servant. She would get one right black and wouldn't have none of them in there looking as white as her." In another narrative, an ex-slave recounted the killing of a slave who was presumably half white. One can assume that because of the attention paid to her hair, it was not to her advantage that she bore some resemblance to a white woman. "A woman named Charlotte had real long hair and they cut one side of her hair off and left the other side long. They whipped her one evening for the longest, and told her to get over the barb wire fence, and she said she couldn't, and he jerked her through by the hair, and she never did come to. She was a corpse in ten minutes after they jerked her through."

In yet another case, a mistress was haunted by her slave grandson's similarity to her own son and, like Charlotte, his hair became the object of ridicule and torture.

This child lived in the house with the family but was accorded a special status. In this case the mistress would ask him what he had on his head. When he would answer "hair" she would tell him that it was wool. He told interviewers that she used to pull his hair out by the handfuls when he was a child. Again, the slave was subject to conflicting thoughts about his parentage, his bondage, and his physical appearance. In this case the slave grandson was given property at the war's end, but his memory of his grandmother's cruelty remained clear for many years. Yet his memory of his father turned vitriolic. "I was riding on a streetcar long after freedom and I passed the cemetery where my father was buried. I started cussing—'let me off this damn car and go see where my God damn father is buried, so I can spit on his grave, a God damn son-of-a-bitch.' I got no mercy on nobody who bring up their children like dogs. How could any father treat their child like that? Bring them up to be ignorant like they did us. If I had my way with them all I would like to have a chopping block and chop every one of their heads off." This man clearly had anger at his treatment by his master/father that had survived for decades.

Slave children, especially those of mixed race, might create in fantasy a family romance. The "family romance" is a psychoanalytic concept wherein the individual, in recalling events of his life, sometimes modifies and fantasizes a better scenario. An abused child, for instance, might fantasize that the abusing natural parent is really a step-parent, and when the powerful real parent realizes that he exists, he will be rescued. Weissman studied three biographies written by Douglass. He stresses that, in his opinion, Douglass develops a family romance, a set of fictional parents who create an idealized "good." This mental novel of early childhood is capable of being revised and rewritten at different stages of one's life. Like many mythological stories of birth, the hero is a secret, unacknowledged issue of parents of high station. The hero is raised by surrogate parents and in time comes to know the identity of his true parents.[56] Margaret Lavine's family romance contained a grandmother who was stolen from Spain and made a slave and a mother who had driven away the Indians. This former slave said that her mother, for whom she was named, was half Indian and half Spanish. Her father was white, "of course." Her mother was the overseer, hired the hands, and was "kind of the boss around there about things about the house....I remember mother crying and mistress got in bed with her. She slept right with mother. We had trundle beds then." Concerning Margaret and her siblings, the Yankees said to her mistress, "Goddamn, these must be your grandchildren the way you are carrying on about them." They very likely were.

In other instances, the children had fantasies about white women having close relationships with slaves who might have been biologically related to them. In some instances the relationships had a confusing mixture of love and degradation. In one case, the mistress was reported to have "saved" a pretty slave girl for her son. "A white woman would have a maid sometimes who was nice looking, and she would keep her and her son would have children by her." What was the message then? To be chosen as the pretty slave had advantages, but costs as well. Here, the man was not choosing the slave woman, but she was being chosen for him by another woman, who would be related to any progeny.

In some cases, slave children were treated as treasured pets of their white owners. Often the child was the pet of the mistress, given to her as a gift. In at least one instance, however, the child was also the valued pet of the master. An informant named Mrs. Moore, eleven years old when slavery ended, remembered that her mistress cried "'cause we were the same as her children" after her children were grown. She also remembered that "when I lived with the white folks, I stayed in the house most of the time," but unlike the white children "they fed me right there in the room, on the floor." One former slave noted that, from the time she was a baby, "I slept with ole mistiss till I was too big and used to kick her and they made me a pallet on the floor, and I never stayed in her bed anymore." Another former slave said that his mistress "mothered and raised" slave children. One woman remembered that when she was a child they sometimes paired children as companions when a slave and the mistress had children the same age. She recollected about her own situation: "I never called ole Miss nothing but 'mother' in my life." She slept in a trundle bed in the mistress's room as a child. This woman grew up to become a special maid to the mistress, and she traveled extensively with the mistress, unlike other slaves on the plantation. Like others, she spoke of the mistress's family as her "white family" when asked to describe the family of her childhood. Indeed, the relationship between slave children and the white owners was complex in such situations.

Like the woman who traveled with her mistress, another woman described her life as a special maid or nurse to her mistress. She described herself as being mulatto, having a Quaker father. This fact did not keep her from being given away as a gift to her mistress when she was five years old. She describes a case when she was put on dis-

play and revered by her owners. "My young master would have had a fit if I had married. I wasn't thinking about no marriage. I had my company to come to see me. They dressed me awfully nice. My mistress, she would say, 'Go wash,' meaning take a bath, and 'then I will come and dress you.' She would dress me in her clothes, from skin out. The boys just thought some of the girls were doll babies. That's what they thought about me, with my curls and dressed up so nice." She continued, "Yes, I went to parties and danced all night on Saturday night, dressed to death. I used to go to parties, and they all treated me nice. I never had a young man white or colored to say an ugly word to me, because my young master was very strict with me."

This passage indicates that in these situations the child, as her master's watch and ward, clearly had a status different from the other slaves, since her master would have been upset by either her mistreatment or sexual advances toward her. She was valued for her attractiveness to the "boys." One wonders, however, who the boys were, and what treatment the boys gave to her. In some ways, it sounds as if this attractive child might have been being prepared by her surrogate father to give sexual favors to the company, or for the master himself. She noted her curls. She also made reference to being dressed to death and dressed from the "skin out."

She was obviously aware of her similarity to and differences from whites and other slaves, as was an ex-slave named Lucy, who watched her mistress apply rouge to herself to "make her cheeks real nice and rosy; 'course me, smart, would go right behind her and rub my cheeks, too; and 'course I wasn't the right color. I would say, 'My cheeks don't git red as your'n,' and she would say, 'Lucy, you have to rub 'em harder,' he, he, he. I didn't know, I was so silly and young, but smart. Chile, I was sharp as a tack." For both slave girls described above, their developing sense of identity included incorporating aspects of both worlds, when indeed they did not fit comfortably into either. Similarly, another former slave vividly remembered that after being given to her new mistress at age six, the mistress washed her and made her new clothes—"a dress and some drawers and a drawer body." She said: "I was never dressed so fine in my life, and I just thought everybody was looking at me because I was dressed so fine.... The dress had some red in it and some big flowers in it, and I was looking at myself in the glass and I would pull up my dress and look at my pretty clean drawers and things, and when I went in the room where my mistress was I pulled it up again and started looking and saying to myself, 'Don't I look nice and clean under here,' and my mistress said, 'You mustn't do that, that's ugly,' and so then I went out in the woods where there was lots of cedars thick around, and I got down there and pulled up my dress and just looked and danced and danced."

Another woman was raised by her white mistress with her older brother when their mother died in childbirth. She noted that her mistress made an effort to "keep me from messing and mixing with everybody." The mistress was not happy if she played with slaves or poor white children. She went on to note that as a free adult, she continued to discriminate with regard to the persons with whom she interacted. Her father, who lived on another farm, continued to visit the children after the mother's death, every other week. After the war, her father came to retrieve her from the mistress, but she refused to leave with him. The mistress threatened to whip the girl if she showed any interest in leaving with her father. Finally, the father, after several trips, told the child how the mistress had mistreated her own mother. She then left with her father but returned many times to visit. This narrative accurately describes the ambivalence of the slaves, particularly those who felt favored by their owners. Despite the fact that they were mistreated, they often identified with whites. Likewise, another woman remembered that after the death of her mistress (whom she thought of as a mother), she told her master when asked if she would stay, "I'll go home" to Mississippi. Her master cried that it was her mistress's wish for her to stay with the white children. "I had a little boy [beau] down there I was crazy about, and I wanted to go back to him," yet she remained in Tennessee. The loss of parents (through absence or death) combined with living in the master's household was a confusing situation for a slave child. When racial origins were unknown, or racial identity was ambiguous, it often presented an even more confusing picture.

When slave children spoke of grooming, they often compared their physical features with those of white children. Invariably, the slave child did not benefit from the comparison. As noted earlier, the slave child was at both an advantage and a disadvantage if he had some characteristics in common with whites. Although skin color was often mentioned, hair was also a particular area of focus. White people resented slave children who had hair like that of whites, as shown in the cases above, where the former slaves remembered the mistress cutting off their hair and not letting them wear it like white children; the slave child's white grandmother pulling out his hair, referring to it as wool; the slave woman being jerked through the fence by her hair, resulting in her death. Children made references to the care of their hair during slavery. "Chillen was just as lousy as pigs. They had these combs that was just like cards you 'card' cotton with, and they would comb your head with them. They wouldn't get the lice out, but it would make it feel better. They had to use larkspur to get 'em out; that would always get lice out of your head." Another slave who was raised in Virginia noted, "In them days they made me comb my hair with an old kyard (card) what we used for spinning."

In a particular narrative, a slave noted that his hair was cared for by another species. "Me and my brother was in the trading yard before the Civil War. We stayed in there three or four weeks. They would fix us up and carry us in a great big old room and circle us all around every morning and every evening. They would have us up in a showroom to show us to the people. They would hit us in the breast to see if we was strong and sound. Monkeys would play with us and see if any boogies was in our heads. They would do pretty well if they found any, but if they didn't they would slap us. They had the monkeys there to keep our heads clean." This must have been a particularly confusing and humiliating experience for these two slave boys. Again, they were valued for their strength but humiliated by people and by monkeys.

In other cases, slave children were allowed to bathe nightly, and these children combed and wrapped their hair in cotton strings. Another slaved noted the difference in her grooming when staying with two different families. "I had never been clean like that before, and staying with them po' white folks I had had a time with those body lice. They would get so bad I would take my dress off and rub it in the suds and rinse it out in the branch; and sometimes I would be rinsing it and Mistress would call me, and I would be so scared I would put it on wet and run to her. I had a time, I tell you; they might nigh eat me up when I was staying there, and I was so glad to be clean." It was not important to many owners that slaves were groomed. Indeed, grooming was one of the indicators that a slave had a privileged status. For the slaves treated as pets, cleanliness was emphasized. Lucy remembered, "We had to [be] always nice and clean and everything." Elsewhere slave children were seen as stock animals, not in need of special grooming. Certainly, no one took time to help the slave child make his or her hair attractive, because parents had little time and owners understood this lack of grooming as one of the many ways slave children learned their slave role.

Notes

[53] Weissman, p. 750.

[54] Frederick Douglass was born of a slave mother and an unknown white man. He was separated from his mother at birth and raised by his maternal grandparents, who raised other grandchildren as well. Douglass was sent away for a time and then returned to live in his (presumably) master/father's home, where he received some affection. Douglass rejected the idea of slavery early in his life and met his hero William Lloyd Garrison, according to Weissman, at an abolitionist meeting in Nantucket. A strong bond of friendship ensued, and they traveled the abolitionist circuit, with Douglass emotionally recounting his life under slavery

and Garrison eloquently denouncing slavery in a manner that left the audience spellbound (ibid., pp. 729–50).

[55] Weissman emphasizes the inconsistent, disguised threads of positive feelings that Douglass had for his white family, saying "These relations were intimate with deep, unconscious, incestuous undercurrents. Douglass was raised as a second-class member of his master's family and received a great deal of special attention and consideration compared to the standard treatment of slave children." Weissman believes that this ambivalent form of black-white interaction was common during slavery and had some of its unconscious roots in early childhood experiences. Indeed for the slave with a white parent, the potential for the ambivalent feelings was great (Weissman, p. 749).

[56] Weissman, p. 729. For another example of a family romance, see the autobiography of Sella Martin written in 1867 (Blassingame, *Slave Testimony*, pp. 703–4).

Toward a New Vision: Race, Class, and Gender as Categories of Analysis and Connection

Patricia Hill Collins

Study Questions
1. Explain how race, class, and gender operate as interlocking categories that cultivate profound differences in our personal biographies.
2. Define the institutional, symbolic, and individual dimensions of oppression. Define the "oppressor within."
3. Give examples from Patricia Hill Collins' life that suggest she has come to recognize her own oppressor within. Describe the basic elements of the "new vision" Collins offers.

The true focus of revolutionary change is never merely the oppressive situations which we seek to escape, but that piece of the oppressor which is planted deep within each of us.

—Audre Lorde
Sister Outsider, 123

Audre Lorde's statement raises a troublesome issue for scholars and activists working for social change. While many of us have little difficulty assessing our own victimization within some major system of oppression, whether it be by race, social class, religion, sexual orientation, ethnicity, age, or gender, we typically fail to see how our thoughts and actions uphold someone else's subordination. Thus, White feminists routinely point with confidence to their oppression as women but resist seeing how much their white-skin privileges them. African-Americans who possess eloquent analyses of racism often persist in viewing poor White women as symbols of white power. The rad-ical left fares little better. "If only people of color and women could see their true class interests," they argue, "class solidarity would eliminate racism and sexism." In essence, each group identifies the type of oppression with which it feels most comfortable as being fundamental and classifies all other types as being of lesser importance.

Oppression is full of such contradictions. Errors in political judgment that we make concerning how we teach our courses, what we tell our children, and which organizations are worthy of our time, talents, and financial support flow smoothly from errors in theoretical analysis about the nature of oppression and activism. Once we realize that there are few pure victims or oppressors, and that each one of us derives varying amounts of penalty and privilege from the multiple systems of oppression that frame our lives, then we will be in a position to see the need for new ways of thought and action.

To get at that "piece of the oppressor which is planted deep within each of us," we need at least two things. First, we need new visions of what oppression is, new categories of analysis that are inclusive of race, class, and gender as distinctive yet interlocking structures of oppression. Adhering to a stance of comparing and ranking oppressions—the proverbial, "I'm more oppressed than you"— locks us all into a dangerous dance of competing for attention, resources, and theoretical supremacy. Instead, I suggest that we examine our different experiences within the more fundamental relationship of domination and subordination. To focus on the particular arrangements that race or class or gender take in our time and place without seeing these structures as sometimes parallel and sometimes interlocking dimensions of the more fundamental relationship of domination and subordination may temporarily ease our consciences. But while such thinking may lead to short-term social reforms, it is simply inadequate for the task of bringing about long-term social transformation.

While race, class, and gender as categories of analysis are essential in helping us understand the structural bases of domination and subordination, new ways of thinking that are not accompanied by new ways of acting offer incomplete prospects for change. To get at that "piece of the oppressor which is planted deep within each of us," we also need to change our daily behavior. Currently, we are all enmeshed in a complex web of problematic relationships that grant our mirror images full human subjectivity while stereotyping and objectifying those most different than ourselves. We often assume that the people we work with, teach, send our children to school with, and sit next to in conferences such as this, will act and feel in prescribed ways because they belong to given race, social class, or gender categories. These judgments by category must be replaced with fully human relationships that transcend the

legitimate differences created by race, class, and gender as categories of analysis. We require new categories of connection, new visions of what our relationships with one another can be.

Our task is immense. We must first recognize race, class, and gender as interlocking categories of analysis that together cultivate profound differences in our personal biographies. But then we must transcend those very differences by reconceptualizing race, class, and gender in order to create new categories of connection.

My presentation today addresses this need for new patterns of thought and action. I focus on two basic questions. First, how can we reconceptualize race, class, and gender as categories of analysis? Second, how can we transcend the barriers created by our experiences with race, class, and gender oppression in order to build the types of coalitions essential for social exchange? To address these questions I contend that we must acquire both new theories of how race, class, and gender have shaped the experiences not just of women of color, but of all groups. Moreover, we must see the connections between these categories of analysis and the personal issues in our everyday lives, particularly our scholarship, our teaching, and our relationships with our colleagues and students. As Audre Lorde points out, change starts with self, and relationships that we have with those around us must always be the primary site for social change.

How Can We Reconceptualize Race, Class, and Gender as Categories of *Analysis?*

To me, we must shift our discourse away from additive analyses of oppression (Spelman 1982; Collins 1989). Such approaches are typically based on two key premises. First, they depend on "either/or," dichotomous thinking. Persons, things and ideas are conceptualized in terms of their opposites. For example, Black/White, man/woman, thought/feeling, and fact/opinion are defined in oppositional terms. Thought and feeling are not seen as two different and interconnected ways of approaching truth that can co-exist in scholarship and teaching. Instead, feeling is defined as antithetical to reason, as it's opposite. In spite of the fact that we all have "both/and" identities (I am both a college professor and a mother—I don't stop being a mother when I drop my child off at school, or forget everything I learned while scrubbing the toilet), we persist in trying to classify each other in either/or categories. I live each day as an African-American woman—a race/gender specific experience. And I am not alone. Everyone in this room has a race/gender/class specific identity. Either/or, dichotomous thinking is especially troublesome when applied to theories of oppression because every individual must be classified as being either oppressed or not oppressed. The both/and position of simultaneously being oppressed and oppressor becomes conceptually impossible.

A second premise of additive analyses of oppression is that these dichotomous differences must be ranked. One side of the dichotomy is typically labeled dominant and the other subordinate. Thus, Whites rule Blacks, men are deemed superior to women, and reason is seen as being preferable to emotion. Applying this premise to discussions of oppression leads to the assumption that oppression can be quantified, and that some groups are oppressed more than others. I am frequently asked, "Which has been most oppressive to you, your status as a Black person or your status as a woman?" What I am really being asked to do is divide myself into little boxes and rank my various statuses. If I experience oppression as a both/and phenomenon, why should I analyze it any differently?

Additive analyses of oppression rest squarely on the twin pillars of either/or thinking and the necessity to quantify and rank all relationships in order to know where one stands. Such approaches typically see African-American women as being more oppressed than everyone else because the majority of Black women experience the negative effects of race, class, and gender oppression simultaneously. In essence, if you add together separate oppressions, you are left with a grand oppression greater than the sum of its parts.

I am not denying that specific groups experience oppression more harshly than others—lynching is certainly objectively worse than being held up as a sex object. But we must be careful not to confuse this issue of the saliency of one type of oppression in people's lives with a theoretical stance positing the interlocking nature of oppression. Race, class, and gender may all structure a situation but may not be equally visible and/or important in people's self-definitions. In certain contexts, such as the antebellum American South and contemporary South America, racial oppression is more visibly salient, while in other contexts, such as Haiti, El Salvador, and Nicaragua, social class oppression may be more apparent. For middle-class White women, gender may assume experiential primacy unavailable to poor Hispanic women struggling with the ongoing issues of low-paid jobs and the frustrations of the welfare bureaucracy. This recognition that one category may have salience over another for a given time and place does not minimize the theoretical importance of assuming that race, class, and gender as categories of analysis structure all relationships.

In order to move toward new visions of what oppression is, I think that we need to ask new questions. How are relationships of domination and subordination structured and maintained in the American political economy? How do race, class, and gender function as parallel and interlocking systems that shape this basic relationship of domination and subordination? Questions such as these promise to move us away from futile theoretical struggles concerned with ranking oppressions and toward analyses that assume race, class, and gender are all present in any given setting, even if one appears more visible and salient than the others. Our task becomes redefined as one of reconceptualizing oppression by uncovering the connections among race, class, and gender as categories of analysis.

Institutional Dimension of Oppression

Sandra Harding's contention that gender oppression is structured along three main dimensions—the institutional, the symbolic, and the individual—offers a useful model for a more comprehensive analysis encompassing race, class, and gender oppression (Harding 1989). Systemic relationships of domination and subordination structured through social institutions such as schools, businesses, hospitals, the work place, and government agencies represent the institutional dimension of oppression. Racism, sexism, and elitism all have concrete institutional locations. Even though the workings of the institutional dimension of oppression are often obscured with ideologies claiming equality of opportunity, in actuality, race, class, and gender place Asian-American women, Native American men, White men, African-American women, and other groups in distinct institutional niches with varying degrees of penalty and privilege.

Even though I realize that many in the current administration would not share this assumption, let us assume that the institutions of American society discriminate, whether by design or by accident. While many of us are familiar with how race, gender, and class operate separately to structure inequality, I want to focus on how these three systems interlock in structuring the institutional dimension of oppression. To get at the interlocking nature of race, class, and gender, I want you to think about the antebellum plantation as a guiding metaphor for a variety of American social institutions. Even though slavery is typically analyzed as a racist institution, and occasionally as a class institution, I suggest that slavery was a race, class, gender specific institution. Removing any one piece from our analysis diminishes our understanding of the true nature of relations of domination and subordination under slavery.

Slavery was a profoundly patriarchal institution. It rested on the dual tenets of White male authority and White male property, a joining of the political and the economic within the institution of the family. Heterosexism was assumed and all Whites were expected to marry. Control over affluent White women's sexuality remained key to slavery's survival because property was to be passed on to the legitimate heirs of the slave owner. Ensuring affluent White women's virginity and chastity was deeply intertwined with maintenance of property relations.

Under slavery, we see varying levels of institutional protection given to affluent White women, working-class, and poor White women, and enslaved African women. Poor White women enjoyed few of the protections held out to their upper-class sisters. Moreover, the devalued status of Black women was key in keeping all White women in their assigned places. Controlling Black women's fertility was also key to the continuation of slavery, for children born to slave mothers themselves were slaves.

African-American women shared the devalued status of chattel with their husbands, fathers, and sons. Racism stripped Blacks as a group of legal rights, education, and control over their own persons. African-Americans could be whipped, branded, sold, or killed, not because they were poor, or because they were women, but because they were Black. Racism ensured that Blacks would continue to serve Whites and suffer economic exploitation at the hands of all Whites.

So we have a very interesting chain of command on the plantation—the affluent White master as the reigning patriarch; his White wife helpmate to serve him, help him manage his property, and bring up his heirs; his faithful servants whose production and reproduction were tied to the requirements of the capitalist political economy; and largely propertyless, working-class White men and women watching from afar. In essence, the foundations for the contemporary roles of elite White women, poor Black women, working-class White men, and a series of other groups can be seen in stark relief in this fundamental American social institution. While Blacks experienced the most harsh treatment under slavery, and thus made slavery clearly visible as a racist institution, race, class, and gender interlocked in structuring slavery's systemic organization of domination and subordination.

Even today, the plantation remains a compelling metaphor for institutional oppression. Certainly the actual conditions of oppression are not as severe now as they were then. To argue, as some do, that things have not changed all that much denigrates the achievements of those who struggled for social change before us. But the basic relationships among Black men, Black women, elite White women, elite White men, working-class White men, and working-class White women as groups remain essentially intact.

A brief analysis of key American social institutions most controlled by elite White men should convince us of the interlocking nature of race, class, and gender in structuring the institutional dimension of oppression. For example, if you are from an American college or university, is your campus a modern plantation? Who controls your university's political economy? Are elite White men over represented among the upper administrators and trustees controlling your university's finances and policies? Are elite White men being joined by growing numbers of elite White women helpmates? What kinds of people are in your classrooms grooming the next generation who will occupy these and other decision-making positions? Who are the support staff that produce the mass mailings, order the supplies, fix the leaky pipes? Do African-Americans, Hispanics or other people of color form the majority of the invisible workers who feed you, wash your dishes, and clean up your offices and libraries after everyone else has gone home?

If your college is anything like mine, you know the answers to these questions. You may be affiliated with an institution that has Hispanic women as vice-presidents for finance, or substantial numbers of Black men among the faculty. If so, you are fortunate. Much more typical are colleges where a modified version of the plantation as a metaphor for the institutional dimension of oppression survives.

The Symbolic Dimension of Oppression

Widespread, societally sanctioned ideologies used to justify relations of domination and subordination comprise the symbolic dimension of oppression. Central to this process is the use of stereotypical or controlling images of diverse race, class, and gender groups. In order to assess the power of this dimension of oppression, I want you to make a list, either on paper or in your head, of "masculine" and "feminine" characteristics. If your list is anything like that compiled by most people, it reflects some variation of the following:

Masculine	Feminine
aggressive	passive
leader	follower
rational	emotional
strong	weak
intellectual	physical

Not only does this list reflect either/or dichotomous thinking and the need to rank both sides of the dichotomy, but ask yourself exactly which men and women you had in mind when compiling these characteristics. This list applies almost exclusively to middle-class White men and women. The allegedly "masculine" qualities that you probably listed are only acceptable when exhibited by elite White men, or when used by Black and Hispanic men against each other or against women of color. Aggressive Black and Hispanic men are seen as dangerous, not powerful, and are often penalized when they exhibit any of the allegedly "masculine" characteristics. Working-class and poor White men fare slightly better and are also denied the allegedly "masculine" symbols of leadership, intellectual competence, and human rationality. Women of color and working-class and poor White women are also not represented on this list, for they have never had the luxury of being "ladies." What appear to be universal categories representing all men and women instead are unmasked as being applicable to only a small group.

It is important to see how the symbolic images applied to different race, class, and gender groups interact in maintaining systems of domination and subordination. If I were to ask you to repeat the same assignment, only this time, by making separate lists for Black men, Black women, Hispanic women, and Hispanic men, I suspect that your gender symbolism would be quite different. In comparing all of the lists, you might begin to see the interdependence of symbols applied to all groups. For example, the elevated images of White womanhood need devalued images of Black womanhood in order to maintain credibility.

While the above exercise reveals the interlocking nature of race, class, and gender in structuring the symbolic dimension of oppression, part of its importance lies in demonstrating how race, class, and gender pervade a wide range of what appears to be universal language. Attending to diversity in our scholarship, in our teaching, and in our daily lives provides a new angle of vision on interpretations of reality thought to be natural, normal, and "true." Moreover, viewing images of masculinity and femininity as universal gender symbolism, rather than as symbolic images that are race, class, and gender specific, renders the experiences of people of color and of nonprivileged White women and men invisible. One way to dehumanize an individual or a group is to deny the reality of their experiences. So when we refuse to deal with race or class because they do not appear to be directly relevant to gender, we are actually becoming part of someone else's problem.

Assuming that everyone is affected differently by the same interlocking set of symbolic images allows us to move forward toward new analyses. Women of color and White women have different relationships to White male authority and this difference explains the distinct gender symbolism applied to both groups. Black women encounter controlling images such as the mammy, the matriarch, the mule, and the whore, that encourage others to reject us as fully human people. Ironically, the negative nature of these images simultaneously encourages us to reject them. In contrast, White women are offered seductive images, those that promise to reward them for supporting the status quo. And yet seductive images can be equally controlling. Consider, for example, the views of Nancy White, a 73-year-old Black woman, concerning images of rejection and seduction:

> My mother used to say that the black woman is the white man's mule and the white woman is his dog. Now, she said that to say this: we do the heavy work and get beat whether we do it well or not. But the white woman is closer to the master and he pats them on the head and lets them sleep in the house, but he ain't gon' treat neither one like he was dealing with a person. (Gwaltney, 148)

Both sets of images stimulate particular political stances. By broadening the analysis beyond the confines of race, we can see the varying levels of rejection and seduction available to each of us due to our race, class, and gender identity. Each of us lives with an allotted portion of institutional privilege and penalty, and with varying levels of rejection and seduction inherent in the symbolic images applied to us. This is the context in which we make our choices. Taken together, the institutional and symbolic dimensions of oppression create a structural backdrop against which all of us live our lives.

The Individual Dimension of Oppression

Whether we benefit or not, we all live within institutions that reproduce race, class, and gender oppression. Even if we never have any contact with members of other race, class, and gender groups, we all encounter images of these groups and are exposed to the symbolic meanings attached to those images. On this dimension of oppression, our individual biographies vary tremendously. As a result of our institutional and symbolic statuses, all of our choices become political acts.

Each of us must come to terms with the multiple ways in which race, class, and gender as categories of analysis frame our individual biographies. I have lived my entire life as an African-American woman from a working-class family and this basic fact has had a profound impact on my personal biography. Imagine how different your life might be if you had been born Black, or White, or poor, or of a different race/class/gender group than the one with which you are most familiar. The institutional treatment you would have received and the symbolic meanings attached to your very existence might differ dramatically from what you now consider to be natural, normal, and part of everyday life. You might be the same, but your personal biography might have been quite different.

I believe that each of us carries around the cumulative effect of our lives within multiple structures of oppression. If you want to see how much you have been affected by this whole thing, I ask you one simple question—who are your close friends? Who are the people with whom you can share your hopes, dreams, vulnerabilities, fears, and victories? Do they look like you? If they are all the same, circumstance may be the cause. For the first seven years of my life I saw only low-income Black people. My friends from those years reflected the composition of my community. But now that I am an adult, can the defense of circumstance explain the patterns of people that I trust as my friends and colleagues? When given other alternatives, if my friends and colleagues reflect the homogeneity of one race, class, and gender group, then these categories of analysis have indeed become barriers to connection.

I am not suggesting that people are doomed to follow the paths laid out for them by race, class, and gender as categories of analysis. While these three structures certainly frame my opportunity structure, I as an individual always have the choice of accepting things as they are, or trying to change them. As Nikki Giovanni points out, "we've got to live in the real world. If we don't like the world we're living in, change it. And if we can't change it, we change ourselves. We can do something" (Tate 1983, 68). While a piece of the oppressor may be planted deep within each of us, we each have the choice of accepting that piece or challenging it as part of the "true focus of revolutionary change."

How Can We Transcend the Barriers Created by Our Experiences with Race, Class, and Gender Oppression in Order to Build the Types of Coalitions Essential for Social Change?

Reconceptualizing oppression and seeing the barriers created by race, class, and gender as interlocking categories of analysis is a vital first step. But we must transcend these barriers by moving toward race, class, and gender as categories of connection, by building relationships and coalitions that will bring about social change. What are some of the issues involved in doing this?

Differences in Power and Privilege

First, we must recognize that our differing experiences with oppression create problems in the relationships among us. Each of us lives within a system that vests us with varying levels of power and privilege. These differences in power, whether structured along axes of race, class, gender, age, or sexual orientation, frame our relationships. African-American writer June Jordan describes her discomfort on a Caribbean vacation with Olive, the Black woman who cleaned her room:

> ...even though both "Olive" and "I" live inside a conflict neither one of us created, and even though both of us therefore hurt inside that conflict, I may be one of the monsters she needs to eliminate from her universe and, in a sense, she may be one of the monsters in mine. (1985, 47)

Differences in power constrain our ability to connect with one another even when we think we are engaged in dialogue across differences. Let me give you an example. One year, the students in my course "Sociology of the Black Community" got into a heated discussion about the reasons for the upsurge of racial incidents on college campuses. Black students complained vehemently about the apathy and resistance they felt most White students expressed about examining their own racism. Mark, a White male student, found their comments particularly unsettling. After claiming that all the Black people he had ever known had expressed no such beliefs to him, he questioned how representative the viewpoints of his fellow students actually were. When pushed further, Mark revealed that he had participated in conversations over the years with the Black domestic worker employed by his family. Since she had never expressed such strong feelings about White racism, Mark was genuinely shocked by class discussions. Ask yourselves whether that domestic worker was in a position to speak freely. Would it have been wise for her to do so in a situation where the power between the two parties was so unequal?

In extreme cases, members of privileged groups can erase the very presence of the less privileged. When I first moved to Cincinnati, my family and I went on a picnic at a local park. Picnicking next to us was a family of White Appalachians. When I went to push my daughter on the swings, several of the children came over. They had missing, yellowed, and broken teeth, they wore old clothing and their poverty was evident. I was shocked. Growing up in a large eastern city, I had never seen such awful poverty among Whites. The segregated neighborhoods in which I grew up made White poverty all but invisible. More importantly, the privileges attached to my newly acquired social class position allowed me to ignore and minimize the poverty among Whites that I did encounter. My reactions to those children made me realize how confining phrases such as "well, at least they're not Black" had become for me. In learning to grant human subjectivity to the Black victims of poverty, I had simultaneously learned to demean White victims of poverty. By applying categories of race to the objective conditions confronting me, I was quantifying and ranking oppressions and missing the very real suffering which, in fact, is the real issue.

One common pattern of relationships across differences in power is one that I label "voyeurism." From the perspective of the privileged, the lives of people of color, of the poor, and of women are interesting for their entertainment value. The privileged become voyeurs, passive onlookers who do not relate to the less powerful, but who are interested in seeing how the "different" live. Over the years, I have heard numerous African-American students complain about professors who never call on them except when a so-called Black issue is being dis-

cussed. The students' interest in discussing race or qualifications for doing so appear unimportant to the professor's efforts to use Black students' experiences as stories to make the material come alive for the White student audience. Asking Black students to perform on cue and provide a Black experience for their White classmates can be seen as voyeurism at its worst.

Members of subordinate groups do not willingly participate in such exchanges but often do so because members of dominant groups control the institutional and symbolic apparatuses of oppression. Racial/ethnic groups, women, and the poor have never had the luxury of being voyeurs of the lives of the privileged. Our ability to survive in hostile settings has hinged on our ability to learn intricate details about the behavior and world view of the powerful and adjust our behavior accordingly. I need only point to the difference in perception of those men and women in abusive relationships. Where men can view their girlfriends and wives as sex objects, helpmates, and a collection of stereotypical categories of voyeurism—women must be attuned to every nuance of their partners' behavior. Are women "naturally" better in relating to people with more power than themselves, or have circumstances mandated that men and women develop different skills? Another pattern in relationships among people of unequal power concerns a different form of exploitation. In scholarly enterprises, relationships among students and teachers, among researchers and their subjects, and even among us as colleagues in teaching and scholarship can contain elements of academic colonialism. Years ago, a Black co-worker of mine in the Roxbury section of Boston described the academic colonialism he saw among the teachers and scholars in that African-American community:

The people with notebooks from Harvard come around here and study us. They don't get to know us because they really don't want to and we don't want to let them. They see what they want to see, go back and write their books and get famous off of our problems.

Under academic colonialism, more powerful groups see their subordinates as people that they perceive as subordinate to them, not as entertainment as was the case in voyeurism, but as a resource to be benignly exploited for their own purposes.

The longstanding effort to "colorize" feminist theory by inserting the experiences of women of color, represents at best, genuine efforts to reduce bias in women's studies. But at its worst, colorization also contains elements of both voyeurism and academic colonialism. As a result of new technologies and perceived profitability, we can now watch black and white movie classics in color. While the tinted images we are offered may be more palatable to the modern viewer, we are still watching the same old movie that was offered to us before. Movie colorization adds little of substance—its contributions remain cosmetic. Similarly, women of color allegedly can teach White feminists nothing about feminism, but must confine ourselves to "colorizing" preexisting feminist theory. Rather than seeing women of color as fully human individuals, we are treated as the additive sum of our categories.

In the academy, patterns of relationships among those of unequal power such as voyeurism and academic colonialism foster reformist postures toward social change. While reformists may aim to make the movie more fun to watch by colorizing their scholarship and teaching via increased lip service to diversity, reformists typically insist on retaining their power to determine what is seen and by whom. In contrast, transformation involves rethinking these differences in power and privilege via dialogues among individuals from diverse groups.

Coming from a tradition where most relationships across difference are squarely rooted in relations of domination and subordination, we have much less experience relating to people as different but equal. The classroom is potentially one powerful and safe space where dialogues among individuals of unequal power relationships can occur. The relationship between Mark, the student in my class, and the domestic worker is typical of a whole series of relationships that people have when they relate across differences in power and privilege. The relationship among Mark and his classmates represents the power of the classroom to minimize those differences so that people of different levels of power can use race, class, and gender as categories of analysis in order to generate meaningful dialogues. In this case, the classroom equalized racial difference so that Black students who normally felt silenced spoke out. White students like Mark, generally unaware of how they had been privileged by their whiteness, lost that privilege in the classroom and thus became open to genuine dialogue.

Reconceptualizing course syllabi represents a comparable process of determining which groups are privileged by our current research and pedagogical techniques and which groups are penalized. Reforming these existing techniques can be a critical first step in moving toward a transformed curriculum reflecting race, class, and gender as interlocking categories of analysis. But while reform may be effective as a short-term strategy, it is unlikely to bring about fundamental transformation in the long term. To me, social transformations, whether of college curricula or of the communities in which we live and work, require moving outside our areas of specialization and groups of interest in order to build coalitions across differences.

Coalitions Around Common Causes

A second issue in building relationships and coalitions essential for social change concerns knowing the real reasons for coalition. Just what brings people together? One powerful catalyst fostering group solidarity is the presence of a common enemy. African-American, Hispanic, Asian-American, and women's studies all share the common intellectual heritage of challenging what passes for certified knowledge in the academy. But politically expedient relationships and coalitions like these are fragile because, as June Jordan points out:

> It occurs to me that much organizational grief could be avoided if people understood that partnership in misery does not necessarily provide for partnership for change: When we get the monsters off our backs all of us may want to run in very different directions. (1985, 47)

Sharing a common cause assists individuals and groups in maintaining relationships that transcend their differences. Building effective coalitions involves struggling to hear one another and developing empathy for each other's points of view. The coalitions that I have been involved in that lasted and that worked have been those where commitment to a specific issue mandated collaboration as the best strategy for addressing the issue at hand.

Several years ago, master's degree in hand, I chose to teach in an inner city, parochial school in danger of closing. The money was awful, the conditions were poor, but the need was great. In my job, I had to work with a range of individuals who, on the surface, had very little in common. We had White nuns, Black middle-class graduate students, Blacks from the "community," some of whom had been incarcerated and/or were affiliated with a range of federal anti-poverty programs. Parents formed another part of this community, Harvard faculty another, and a few well-meaning White liberals from Colorado were sprinkled in for good measure.

As you might imagine, tension was high. Initially, our differences seemed insurmountable. But as time passed, we found a common bond that we each brought to the school. In spite of profound differences in our personal biographies, differences that in other settings would have hampered our ability to relate to one another, we found that we were all deeply committed to the education of Black children. By learning to value each other's commitment and by recognizing that we each had different skills that were essential to actualizing that commitment, we built an effective coalition around a common cause. Our school was successful, and the children we taught benefited from the diversity we offered them.

I think that the process of curriculum transformation will require a process comparable to that of political organizing around common causes. None of us alone has a comprehensive vision of how race, class, and gender operate as categories of analysis or how they might be used as categories of connection. Our personal biographies offer us partial views. Few of us can manage to study race, class, and gender simultaneously. Instead, we each know more about some dimensions of this larger story and less about others. While we each may be committed to an inclusive, transformed curriculum, the task of building one is necessarily a collective effort. Just as the members of the school had special skills to offer to the task of building the school, we have areas of specialization and expertise, whether scholarly, theoretical, pedagogical, or within areas of race, class, or gender. We do not all have to do the same thing in the same way. Instead, we must support each other's efforts, realizing that they are all part of the larger enterprise of bringing about social change.

Building Empathy

A third issue involved in building the types of relationships and coalitions essential for social change concerns the issue of individual accountability. Race, class, and gender oppression form the structural backdrop against which we frame our relationship—these are the forces that encourage us to substitute voyeurism and academic colonialism for fully human relationships. But while we may not have created this situation, we are each responsible for making individual, personal choices concerning which elements of race, class, and gender oppression we will accept and which we will work to change.

One essential component of this accountability involves developing empathy for the experiences of individuals and groups different than ourselves. Empathy begins with taking an interest in the facts of other people lives, both as individuals and as groups. If you care about me, you should want to know not only the details of my personal biography but a sense of how race, class, and gender as categories of analysis created the institutional and symbolic backdrop for my personal biography. How can you hope to assess my character without knowing the details of the circumstances I face?

Moreover, by taking a theoretical stance that we have all been affected by race,

class, and gender as categories of analysis that have structured our treatment, we open up possibilities for using those same constructs as categories of connection in building empathy. For example, I have a good White woman friend with whom I share common interests and beliefs. But we know that our racial differences have provided us with different experiences. So we talk about them. We do not assume that because I am Black, race has only affected me and not her or that because I am a Black woman, race neutralizes the effect of gender in my life while accenting it in hers. We take those same categories of analysis that have created cleavages in our lives, in this case, categories of race and gender, and use them as categories of connection in building empathy for each other's experiences.

Finding common causes and building empathy is difficult, no matter which side of privilege we inhabit. Building empathy from the dominant side of privilege is difficult, simply because individuals from privileged backgrounds are not encouraged to do so. For example, in order for those of you who are White to develop empathy for the experiences of people of color, you must grapple with how your white skin has privileged you. This is difficult to do, because it not only entails the intellectual process of seeing how whiteness is elevated in institutions and symbols, but it also involves the often painful process of seeing how your whiteness has shaped your personal biography. Intellectual stances against the institutional and symbolic dimensions of racism are generally easier to maintain than sustained self-reflection about how racism has shaped all of our individual biographies. Were and are your fathers, uncles, and grandfathers really more capable than mine, or can their accomplishments be explained in part by the racism members of my family experienced?

Did your mothers stand silently by and watch all this happen? More importantly, how have they passed on the benefits of their whiteness to you?

These are difficult questions, and I have tremendous respect for my colleagues and students who are trying to answer them. Since there is no compelling reason to examine the source and meaning of one's own privilege, I know that those who do so have freely chosen this stance. They are making conscious efforts to root out the piece of the oppressor planted within them. To me, they are entitled to the support of people of color in their efforts. Men who declare themselves feminists, members of the middle class who ally themselves with anti-poverty struggles, heterosexuals who support gays and lesbians, are all trying to grow, and their efforts place them far ahead of the majority who never think of engaging in such important struggles.

Building empathy from the subordinate side of privilege is also difficult, but for different reasons. Members of subordinate groups are understandably reluctant to abandon a basic mistrust of members of powerful groups because this basic mistrust has traditionally been central to their survival. As a Black woman, it would be foolish for me to assume that White women, or Black men, or White men, or any other group with a history of exploiting African-American women have my best interests at heart. These groups enjoy varying amounts of privilege over me and therefore I must carefully watch them and be prepared for a relation of domination and subordination.

Like the privileged, members of subordinate groups must also work toward replacing judgments by category with new ways of thinking and acting. Refusing to do so stifles prospects for effective coalition and social change. Let me use another example from my own experiences. When I was an undergraduate, I had little time or patience for the theorizing of the privileged. My initial years at a private, elite institution were difficult, not because the coursework was challenging (it was, but that wasn't what distracted me) or because I had to work while my classmates lived on family allowances (I was used to work). The adjustment was difficult because I was surrounded by so many people who took their privilege for granted. Most of them felt entitled to their wealth. That astounded me.

I remember one incident of watching a White woman down the hall in my dormitory try to pick out which sweater to wear. The sweaters were piled up on her bed in all the colors of the rainbow, sweater after sweater. She asked my advice in a way that let me know that choosing a sweater was one of the most important decisions she had to make on a daily basis. Standing knee-deep in her sweaters, I realized how different our lives were. She did not have to worry about maintaining a solid academic average so that she could receive financial aid. Because she was in the majority, she was not treated as a representative of her race. She did not have to consider how her classroom comments or basic existence on campus contributed to the treatment her group would receive. Her allowance protected her from having to work, so she was free to spend her time studying, partying, or in her case, worrying about which sweater to wear. The degree of inequality in our lives and her unquestioned sense of entitlement concerning that inequality offended me. For a while, I categorized all affluent White women as being superficial, arrogant, overly concerned with material possessions, and part of my problem. But had I continued to classify people in this way, I would have missed out on making some very good friends whose discomfort with their inherited or acquired social class privileges pushed them to examine their position.

Since I opened with the words of Audre Lorde, it seems appropriate to close with another of her ideas. As we go forth to the remaining activities of this workshop, and beyond this workshop, we might do well to consider Lorde's perspective:

Each of us is called upon to take a stand. So in these days ahead, as we examine ourselves and each other, our works, our fears, our differences, our sisterhood and survivals, I urge you to tackle what is most difficult for us all, self-scrutiny of our complacencies, the idea that since each of us believes she is on the side of right, she need not examine her position. (1985)

I urge you to examine your position.

References

Butler, Johnnella. 1989. "Difficult Dialogues." *The Women's Review of Books 6,* no. 5.

Collins, Patricia Hill. 1989. "The Social Construction of Black Feminist Thought." *Signs.* Summer 1989.

Harding, Sandra. 1986. *The Science Question in Feminism.* Ithaca, NY: Cornell University Press.

Gwalatney, John Langston. 1980. *Drylongso: A Self-Portrait of Black America.* New York: Vintage.

Lorde, Audre. 1984. *Sister Outsider.* Trumansberg, NY: The Crossing Press.

———. 1985 "Sisterhood and Survival." Keynote address, conference on the Black Woman Writer and the Diaspora, Michigan State University.

Jordan, June. 1985. *On Call: Political Essays.* Boston: South End Press.

Spelman, Elizabeth. 1982. "Theories of Race and Gender: The Erasure of Black Women." *Quest* 5:32–36.

Tate, Claudia, ed. 1983. *Black Women Writers at Work.* New York: Continuum.

White-Blindness

Bruce N. Simon

◇◆◇◆◇

Study Questions

1. What are the two versions of color-blindness that Simon describes? What questions are associated with each version of color-blindness?
2. Which version does Simon recommend as the best approach for thinking about race? Why?

It's amazing how controversial such traditional legal doctrines as "innocent until proven guilty," "jury of one's peers," and "reasonable doubt" become when a black defendant stands accused of the murder of a white woman and man before a majority black jury, and is found not guilty. How easily presumption of innocence gets cast as racial loyalty. How quickly the people who decided that the state had not proved its case beyond a reasonable doubt are dismissed as unreasonable and perhaps incapable of reason. How smoothly the same fury that used to fuel lynch mobs claims the high moral ground by chastising the jury's failure of color-blindness.

I am referring to the O. J. Simpson spectacle—and particularly of white responses to it—but I am trying to raise larger questions about how we in the United States understand issues of race and racism, whiteness and color-blindness, democracy and justice. Were Johnnie Cochran's "playing the race card" and the jury's "choosing racial loyalty" over deliberation and evidence really the only times race impacted the Simpson case? Must our only response to the Simpson verdict and the Rodney King beating verdict be lamentations and jeremiads over the flagging commitment to color-

blindness in the post–Civil Rights era? Or is it instead that the many race-saturated public spectacles of the '90s call on us to question what is typically meant by color-blindness and rethink the problem it is supposed to solve?[1] It's striking that so many observers and commentators could deploy a rhetoric of color-blindness while at the same time repeating coded racialized narratives—and not only have the contradiction go unnoticed but have the latter legitimized by the former. In response, I think it's high time we distinguished between different versions of color-blindness and clarified what color-blindness for white people entails.[2]

To this end, let's consider the most controversial aspect of the Simpson case to many liberal and conservative commentators. Not the fact that he "got off." Not even the "racial divide" that opinion pollsters so suddenly discovered (after decades of ignoring or downplaying more telling evidence). No, what really irritated these commentators was the charge that their conviction of Simpson's guilt was not neutral or objective—that their whiteness interfered with their judgment, particularly in evaluating the plausibility and relevance of police racism and incompetence. I'm going to personalize this issue and imagine myself in a thought experiment as a potential juror faced with a similar charge. Adhering to one version of color-blindness would lead me to ask the following questions in response: (1) What does my being white have to do with considering the evidence and making a decision? (2) What does my racial identity, an accident of birth, have to do with issues of evaluation or judgment? (3) Hasn't the concept of race itself been shown to be incoherent, self-contradictory, fallacious, arbitrary, without basis in scientific fact or religious doctrine? So (4) what influence can an illusion have on me or my habits of thought? Given the currency of this version of color-blindness, I suspect that most people would say that the answers are simple: being white shouldn't affect how I consider the evidence; my white racial identity has nothing to do with how I evaluate or judge; yes, race has been shown to have no basis in science; and since race doesn't exist, it should have no influence on my thought. In other words, to proponents of this version of color-blindness, it would be racist for someone to insist that my being white could influence, much less interfere with, my judgment. Case closed.

But I don't think the answers to the above questions are at all simple—in fact, I think they are the wrong questions in the first place. Which is to say that I have my doubts about this version of color-blindness. I certainly understand and feel its appeal— particularly given the horrible history that race-thinking has been such a constitutive part of in modernity, from the slave trade and slavery to genocide to ethnic cleansing. And I certainly agree that the concept of race is without scientific basis. But I want to question the assumption that if we stop noticing race, if we stop talking about race, if we stop thinking of ourselves as belonging to any race, then the system of racial oppression that those who have identified

themselves as white have established will simply go away.[3] I want to question the assumption that to stop doing any of these things is at all simple or easy—or even desirable in all circumstances. I want to question the assumption that the best way to fight racism is to attack the notion of race by showing it to be a cognitive error.[4] For race is not only a concept, it is also a lived experience.[5]

Attention to race as social fact or lived experience does not conflict with the insight into the social construction of race, for we should not associate the idea of social construction with the notions of illusion or fallacy or cognitive error, but instead with such concepts as ideology and narrative.[6] Under this view, that is, I can fully agree that I am not "essentially" white, but at the same time I can't ignore, downplay, or dismiss the privilege being positioned as white tends to bestow, and not only in this country. Nor can I simply assume that how I've been positioned in and by U.S. race discourses and formations has nothing to do with how I experience or reflect upon the world. What this notion of race as social construction implies, then, is that some aspects of the version of color-blindness I've elaborated and criticized might be preserved as an end, but the model as currently understood has serious limitations as a means to justice in a multiracial democracy.

So let me pose an alternative set of questions that will bring out why I think my being white has a lot to do with how I might act as a juror: How does my self-perception and identification as "white" (both by myself and by others) affect my perceptions, experiences, thoughts, and judgments, not to mention my life chances? What does thinking of myself as "white" enable me to recognize or cause me to gloss over or elide? What relation does my "whiteness" have to other aspects of my identity—class, gender, sexuality, religion, political affiliations, order and area of birth, and on and on to even less obvious ones like the enjoyment I get out of watching "The Tick," "Daria," "The Simpsons," "Dr. Katz," "The Critic," and "Beavis and Butt-head"?

Here's why I think these questions are better than the four questions I asked while ventriloquizing the first version of color-blindness. For one thing, the earlier set of questions takes for granted as natural and eternal the existence of "the white race." I would counter that this concept is of relatively recent origin, and that thinking of whiteness or race as a simple biological fact is a mistake.[7] So when I say that it matters that I'm white in how I view the Simpson case, I don't mean inability to understand people of "other races" ("it's a white thing, I can't understand"). Rather, I mean that being treated as white throughout my entire life (along with a range of other socially significant conditions—male, middle class, short, Jewish, from upstate NY [no, not just north of New York City—the real thing!], and so on) has contributed toward shaping my habits of mind and emotions, including what I tend to take for granted and my gut reactions, my attitudes toward the police, crime, authority, and the law, where I've lived, whom I hang with and am close to, and so on. What I'm saying is that "being white" is a learned phenomenon, and until I started thinking about what kinds of lessons I was learning (usually after a friend took the time to call me out on something), I didn't even recognize that I was being taught, much less question its value or consider the possibility of change.

For another thing, the first four questions above assume that color-blindness is always in and of itself a good thing.[8] But think about that word. When you are color-blind, you only see in black and white, right? Isn't that counter-productive? Doesn't it actually reduce the question of race—the experience of living in a thoroughly racialized society—to a binary, instead of opening it up for interrogation? I can go on with this line of argument (the problems you run into when you reduce the complex history of racial discourse, racial projects, racial formations, and racial oppression to the realms of color, vision, and perception, particularly if you are committed to an anti-racist agenda that amounts to more than diversity management), but let's for the moment treat this kind of "I treat people as individuals" position charitably. I submit that if you are truly committed to color-blindness, then your task shouldn't be to go around lecturing to all those (usually people of color) who are still caught in the grips of race-consciousness, but instead to make the case to whites of the necessity of color-blindness, that is, the recognition and rejection of white racial privilege. Otherwise, a stated commitment to color-blindness will only function as an alibi for white blindness to history and to power. When "white-blindness" means that the most powerful institutions and actors stop furthering racial oppression by privileging whiteness, then, and only then, can a society legitimately call itself "color-blind." But by then using the limiting metaphor of vision and blindness to imagine racial justice will be unnecessary.

Historicizing the social construction of whiteness is an important part of recognizing the ways it operates today, so for those to whom these ideas are relatively new, I would like to recommend a few works that were crucial in advancing the analysis of "whiteness" and "the white race" and are indispensable still today:

- W. E. B. Du Bois, *The Souls of Black Folk* (especially the opening first few pages and the last chapter, but it runs throughout this 1903 book);
- W. E. B. Du Bois, "The Souls of White Folk," in his mid-'20s essay collection, *Darkwater;*
- W. E. B. Du Bois, *Black Reconstruction* (a thick tome from the early '30s that challenges the then-popular racist interpretations of the Reconstruction era [1865–1877], but still a classic, and the source of the "wages of whiteness" thesis);
- W. E. B. Du Bois, *Dusk of Dawn* (this 1940 autobiography/history of the pre-World War II era is still not often cited in discussions of Du Bois's career, but it is an absolutely crucial text for many reasons, including an imagined discussion with a white friend in the middle of the book);
- Ralph Ellison, *Shadow and Act* (largely ignored by whites in the academy in the 1950s, this is now the bible of the "race and American literature and culture" movement; see also "What America Would Be Like Without Blacks" in *Going to the Territory* for an update of his ideas, and of course read his novel *Invisible Man* if you haven't already);
- Malcolm X with Alex Haley, *The Autobiography of Malcolm X* (don't believe the hype that puts him as the black demon to Martin Luther King's black angel; read this for yourself—he's one of the best at exposing white supremacy, not only as it worked in the past, but how it is working in the present as well);
- Audre Lorde, *Sister Outsider* (a major collection of short and accessible essays that problematize the whiteness of the '70s women's movement and put racism squarely on the table in a challenging and constructive manner);
- James Baldwin, "On Being White . . . and Other Lies," in *Essence* (from 1984; good, short, accessible);

- bell hooks, "Representing Whiteness in the Black Imagination" (in the collection *Cultural Studies,* ed. Lawrence Grossberg, et al., and elsewhere);
- Toni Morrison, *Playing in the Dark* (recent but very influential book on the literary construction of blackness and whiteness, and of course don't forget to read all her novels and the less well-known essay collections she's edited—on the Anita Hill/Clarence Thomas and O. J. Simpson spectacles);
- Cheryl Harris, "Whiteness as Property," in *Critical Race Theory,* ed. Kimberlé Crenshaw, et al.;
- Patricia Williams, "The Ethnic Scarring of American Whiteness," in *The House That Race Built: Black Americans, U.S. Terrain,* ed. Wahneema Lubiano;
- Kimberlé Crenshaw, "Color Blindness, History, and the Law," in *The House That Race Built: Black Americans, U.S. Terrain,* ed. Wahneema Lubiano.

The reason I cite these classics along with the more recent African-Americanist work on whiteness is that any exploration of whiteness today is practically worthless if it doesn't engage, question, and respond to them. People of color have had to figure out white people and survive under white supremacy for centuries. These works represent the tip of the iceberg of black thinking on whiteness; I won't even try to survey the full range of thinking on whiteness by people of color. Nor is this the place to go into my response to the important work of a journal like *Race Traitor (http://www.postfun.com/racetraitor/)* or David Roediger's *Towards the Abolition of Whiteness* or Ian Haney López's *White by Law*. But I can at least recommend these and other recent works on the history and politics of whiteness: Richard Dyer, "White," *Screen* 29.1 (Winter 1988); Paul Kivel, *Uprooting Racism; Off White: Readings on Race, Power, and Society,* ed. Michelle Fine et al.; *Race*

Traitor, eds. Noel Ignatiev and John Harvey; Mab Segrest, *Memoir of a Race Traitor;* Vron Ware, *Beyond the Pale;* Ruth Frankenberg, *White Women, Race Matters;* Reginald Horsman, *Race and Manifest Destiny: The Origins of American Racial Anglo-Saxonism;* Alexander Saxton, *The Rise and Fall of the White Republic;* David Roediger, *The Wages of Whiteness;* Eric Lott, *Love and Theft;* Theodore Allen, *The Invention of the White Race;* Karen Sacks, "How Did Jews Become White Folks?" in *Race,* eds. Steven Gregory and Roger Sanjek; Noel Ignatiev, *How the Irish Became White,* and David Roediger, "White Workers, New Democrats, and Affirmative Action," Neil Gotanda, "Tales of Two Judges: Joyce Karlin in *People* v. *Soon Ja Du;* Lance Ito in *People* v. *O.J. Simpson,*" and Howard Winant, "Racial Dualism at Century's End," all in *The House That Race Built: Black Americans, U.S. Terrain,* ed. Wahneema Lubiano.

In closing, let's not forget that classic American literature has produced some profound analyses of the ideology of whiteness, most notably Herman Melville's *Moby-Dick* and "Benito Cereno"; Harriet Beecher Stowe's *Uncle Tom's Cabin;* Mark Twain's *Adventures of Huckleberry Finn* and "Pudd'nhead Wilson"; William Faulkner's *Absalom, Absalom, Light in August;* and *Go Down, Moses;* and Flannery O'Connor's "The Artificial Nigger" and "The Displaced Person."

Notes

[1] This, at least, is what such collections as *Race-ing Justice, En-gendering Power,* ed. Toni Morrison (NY: Pantheon, 1992); *Reading Rodney King/Reading Urban Uprising,* ed. Robert Gooding-Williams (NY: Routledge, 1993); and *Birth of a Nation'hood,* ed. Toni Morrison (NY: Pantheon, 1997) suggest.

[2] Given the relativist and pluralist rhetoric that contemporary white supremacists are now deploying, it is especially important to be clear when discussing color-blindness and race consciousness with respect to white people. On the new racism, see Pierre-Andre Taguieff, "From Race to Culture: The New Right's View of European Identity," trans. Deborah Cook, *Telos* 98–99 (Winter 1993–Fall 1994) 99–125; Etienne Balibar, "Is There a Neo-Racism?" trans. Chris Turner, in Etienne Balibar and Immanuel Wallerstein, *Race, Nation, Class: Ambiguous Identities* (NY: Verso, 1991) 17–28; Etienne Balibar, "Racism as Universalism," *Masses, Classes, Ideas: Studies on Politics and Philosophy before and after Marx* (NY: Routledge, 1994) 191–204; Slavoj Žižek, *Tarrying with the Negative: Kant, Hegel, and the Critique of Ideology* (Durham: Duke UP, 1993) 226; Judith Butler, "Endangered/Endangering: Schematic Racism and White Paranoia," in *Reading Rodney King/Reading Urban Uprising,* ed. Robert Gooding-Williams (NY: Routledge, 1993) 1–12; Avery Gordon and Christopher Newfield, "White Philosophy," *Critical Inquiry* 20 (Summer 1994) 737–757 (reprinted in *Identities,* ed. Kwame Anthony Appiah and Henry Louis Gates, Jr. [Chicago: U of Chicago P, 1995] 380–400); Kimberlé Crenshaw, "Color-Blind Dreams and Racial Nightmares: Refiguring Racism in the Post-Civil Rights Era," in *Birth of a Nation'hood,* ed. Toni Morrison (NY: Pantheon, 1997) 97–168.

[3] For an introduction to the idea of racial oppression, see Theodore Allen, *The Invention of the White Race—Volume One: Racial Oppression and Social Control* (NY: Verso, 1994) 1–51. Attending to racial oppression entails strict scrutiny toward biologically inflected notions of culture, as well, for "culture" is often invoked today to advance claims that in the past would

have been made in terms of race. In other words, anti-racism means more than making culture-based instead of nature-based claims (cf. note 2).

[4] For further questionings of this assumption, see Avery Gordon and Christopher Newfield, "White Philosophy," *Critical Inquiry* 20 (Summer 1994) 737–757 (reprinted in *Identities,* ed. Kwame Anthony Appiah and Henry Louis Gates, Jr. [Chicago: U of Chicago P, 1995] 380–400); and Gary Peller, "Race-Consciousness," in *Critical Race Theory,* ed. Kimberlé Crenshaw, et al. (NY: New P, 1995) 127–158.

[5] This apparently simple idea has far-reaching consequences; see Lucius Outlaw, "Toward a Critical Theory of 'Race,'" in *Anatomy of Racism,* ed. David Theo Goldberg (Minneapolis: U of Minnesota P, 1990) 58–82; Michael Omi and Howard Winant, *Racial Formation in the United States: From the 1960s to the 1990s,* 2nd ed. (NY: Routledge, 1994); Evelyn Brooks Higginbotham, "African-American Women's History and the Metalanguage of Race," in *"We Specialize in the Wholly Impossible": A Reader in Black Women's History,* ed. Darlene Clark Hine et al. (Brooklyn: Carlson, 1995) 3–24; Kenneth Mostern, "Three Theories of the Race of W. E. B. Du Bois," *Cultural Critique* 34 (Fall 1996) 27–63.

[6] For introductions to ideology, see James Kavanagh, "Ideology," in *Critical Terms for Literary Study,* eds. Frank Lentricchia and Thomas McLaughlin (Chicago: U of Chicago P, 1990) 306–320; and *Mapping Ideology,* ed. Slavoj Žižek (NY: Verso, 1994). For examples of reading race as ideology and as narrative, see Wahneema Lubiano, "Black Ladies, Welfare Queens, and State Minstrels: Ideological War by Narrative Means," in *Race-ing Justice, En-gendering Power,* ed. Toni Morrison (NY: Pantheon, 1992) 323–363; Wahneema Lubiano, "Like Being Mugged by a Metaphor: Multiculturalism and State Narratives," in *Mapping Multiculturalism,* eds. Avery Gordon and Christopher Newfield (Minneapolis: U of Minnesota P, 1996) 64–75.

[7] I discuss why this is so, at length, in my "race" page on the internet (*http://www.princeton.edu/~bnsimon/race.html*). For a small sample of the best scholarship challenging the notion that science has had, or should have, a monopoly on defining "race," see Reginald Horsman, *Race and Manifest Destiny: The Origins of American Racial Anglo-Saxonism* (Cambridge: Harvard UP, 1981); Audrey Smedley, *Race in North America: Origin and Evolution of a Worldview* (Boulder: Westview P, 1993); Theodore Allen, *The Invention of the White Race—Volume One: Racial Oppression and Social Control* (NY: Verso, 1994); Michael Omi and Howard Winant, *Racial Formation in the United States: From the 1960s to the 1990s,* 2nd ed. (NY: Routledge, 1994); Ian Haney López, *White by Law: The Legal Construction of Race* (NY: NYU P, 1996).

[8] For arguments challenging this assumption, see Neil Gotanda, "A Critique of 'Our Constitution Is Color-Blind,'" in *Critical Race Theory,* ed. Kimberlé Crenshaw, et al. (NY: New P, 1995) 257–275; and Kimberlé Crenshaw, "Color Blindness, History, and the Law," in *The House That Race Built: Black Americans, U.S. Terrain,* ed. Wahneema Lubiano (NY: Pantheon, 1997) 280–288.

The author thanks Wendy Chun, Joan Ferrante, and Wahneema Lubiano for their invaluable aid in translating this essay from web to print.

White Privilege Shapes the U.S.

ROBERT JENSEN

⋄⬦⬦⬦

Study Questions
1. What is white privilege?
2. How has Robert Jensen benefited from white privilege?
3. How does Jensen handle his white privilege?

Here's what white privilege sounds like: I am sitting in my University of Texas office, talking to a very bright and very conservative white student about affirmative action in college admissions, which he opposes and I support.

The student says he wants a level playing field with no unearned advantages for anyone. I ask him whether he thinks that in the United States being white has advantages. Have either of us, I ask, ever benefited from being white in a world run mostly by white people? Yes, he concedes, there is something real and tangible we could call white privilege.

So, if we live in a world of white privilege—unearned white privilege—how does that affect your notion of a level playing field? I ask. He paused for a moment and said, "That really doesn't matter."

That statement, I suggested to him, reveals the ultimate white privilege: the privilege to acknowledge you have unearned privilege but ignore what it means.

That exchange led me to rethink the way I talk about race and racism with students. It drove home to me the importance of confronting the dirty secret that we white people carry around with us everyday: In a world of white privilege, some of what we have is unearned. I think much of both the fear and anger that comes up around discussions of affirmative action has its roots in that secret. So these days, my goal is to talk openly and honestly about white supremacy and white privilege.

White privilege, like any social phenomenon, is complex. In a white supremacist culture, all white people have privilege, whether or not they are overtly racist themselves. There are general patterns, but such privilege plays out differently depending on context and other aspects of one's identity (in my case, being male gives me other kinds of privilege). Rather than try to tell others how white privilege has played out in their lives, I talk about how it has affected me.

I am as white as white gets in this country. I am of northern European heritage and I was raised in North Dakota, one of the whitest states in the country. I grew up in a virtually all-white world surrounded by racism, both personal and institutional. Because I didn't live near a reservation, I didn't even have exposure to the state's only numerically significant nonwhite population, American Indians.

I have struggled to resist that racist training and the ongoing racism of my culture. I like to think I have changed, even though I routinely trip over the lingering effects of that internalized racism and the institutional racism around me. But no matter how much I "fix" myself, one thing never changes—I walk through the world with white privilege.

What does that mean? Perhaps most importantly, when I seek admission to a university, apply for a job, or hunt for an apartment, I don't look threatening. Almost all of the people evaluating me for those things look like me—they are white. They see in me a reflection of themselves, and in a racist world that is an advantage. I smile. I am white. I am one of them. I am not dangerous. Even when I voice critical opinions, I am cut some slack. After all, I'm white.

My flaws also are more easily forgiven because I am white. Some complain that affirmative action has meant the university is saddled with mediocre minority professors. I have no doubt there are minority faculty who are mediocre, though I don't know very many. As Henry Louis Gates Jr. once pointed out, if affirmative action policies were in place for the next hundred years, it's possible that at the end of that time the university could have as many mediocre minority professors as it has mediocre white professors. That isn't meant as an insult to anyone, but is a simple observation that white privilege has meant that scores of second-rate white professors have slid through the system because their flaws were overlooked out of solidarity based on race, as well as on gender, class, and ideology.

Some people resist the assertions that the United States is still a bitterly racist society and that the racism has real effects on real people. But white folks have long cut other white folks a break. I know, because I am one of them.

I am not a genius—as I like to say, I'm not the sharpest knife in the drawer. I have been teaching full-time for six years, and I've published a reasonable amount of scholarship. Some of it is the unexceptional stuff one churns out to get tenure, and some of it, I would argue, actually is worth reading. I work hard, and I like to think that I'm a fairly decent teacher. Every once in awhile, I leave my office at the end of the day feeling like I really accomplished something. When I cash my paycheck, I don't feel guilty.

But, all that said, I know I did not get where I am by merit alone. I benefited from, among other things, white privilege. That doesn't mean that I don't deserve my job, or that if I weren't white I would never have gotten the job. It means simply that all through my life, I have soaked up benefits for being white. I grew up in fertile farm country taken by force from nonwhite indigenous people. I was educated in a well-funded, virtually all-white public school system in which I learned that white people like me made this country great. There I also was taught a variety of skills, including how to take standardized tests written by and for white people.

All my life I have been hired for jobs by white people. I was accepted for graduate school by white people. And I was hired for a teaching position at the predominantly white University of Texas, which had a white president, in a college headed by a white dean and in a department with a white chairman that at the time had one nonwhite tenured professor.

There certainly is individual variation in experience. Some white people have had it easier than me, probably because they came from wealthy families that gave them even more privilege. Some white people have had it tougher than me because they came from poorer families. White women face discrimination I will never know. But, in the end, white people all have drawn on white privilege somewhere in their lives.

Like anyone, I have overcome certain hardships in my life. I have worked hard to get where I am, and I work hard to stay there. But to feel good about myself and my work, I do not have to believe that "merit," as defined by white people in a white country, alone got me here. I can acknowledge that in addition to all that hard work, I got a significant boost from white privilege, which continues to protect me every day of my life from certain hardships.

At one time in my life, I would not have been able to say that, because I needed to believe that my success in life was due solely to my individual talent and effort. I saw myself as the heroic American, the rugged individualist. I was so deeply seduced by the culture's mythology that I couldn't see the fear that was binding me to those myths. Like all white Americans, I was living the fear that maybe I didn't really deserve my success, that maybe luck and privilege had more to do with it than brains and hard work. I was afraid I wasn't heroic or rugged, that I wasn't special.

I let go of some of that fear when I realized that, indeed, I wasn't special, but that I was still me. What I do well, I still can take in, even when I know that the rules under which I work in are stacked in my benefit. I believe that until we let go of the fiction that people have complete control over their fate—that we can will ourselves to be anything we choose—then we will live with that fear. Yes, we should all dream big and pursue our dreams and not let anyone or anything stop us. But we all are the product both of what we will ourselves to be and what the society in which we live lets us be.

White privilege is not something I get to decide whether or not I want to keep. Every time I walk into a store at the same time as a black man and the security guard follows him and leaves me alone to shop, I am benefiting from white privilege. There is not space here to list all the ways in which white privilege plays out in our daily lives, but it is clear that I will carry this privilege with me until the day white supremacy is erased from this society.

Frankly, I don't think I will live to see that day; I am realistic about the scope of the task. However, I continue to have hope, to believe in the creative power of human beings to engage the world honestly and act morally. A first step for white people, I think, is to not be afraid to admit that we have benefited from white privilege. It doesn't mean we are frauds who have no claim to our success. It means we face a choice about what we do with our success.

More Thoughts on Why the System of White Privilege is Wrong

Robert Jensen

Study Questions

1. How did "white" critics respond to Jensen's essay "White Privilege Shapes the U.S."?
2. Does Jensen believe white people should feel guilty about "white privilege"? Explain. How should white people view white privilege?

By writing about the politics of white privilege—and listening to the folks who responded to that writing—I have had to face one more way that privilege runs deep in my life, and it makes me uncomfortable. The discomfort tells me I might be on the right track.

Last year I published an article about white privilege in the Baltimore Sun that then went out over a wire service to other newspapers. Electronic copies proliferated and were picked up on Internet discussion lists, and the article took on a life of its own (the essay is available online at *http://uts.cc.utexas.edu/~rjen-sen/freelance/whiteprivilege.htm*)

As a result, every week over the past year I have received at least a dozen letters from people who want to talk about race. I learned not only more about my own privilege, but more about why many white folks can't come to terms with the truism I offered in that article: White people, whether overtly racist or not, benefit from living in a world mostly run by white people that has been built on the land and the backs of nonwhite people.

The reactions varied from racist rantings, to deeply felt expressions of pain and anger, to declarations of solidarity. But probably the most important response I got was from nonwhite folks, predominantly African-Americans, who said something like this: "Of course there is white privilege. I've been pointing it out to my white friends and co-workers for years. Isn't it funny that almost no one listens to me, but everyone takes notice when a white guy says it."

Those comments forced me again to ponder the privilege I live with. Who really does know more about white privilege, me or the people on the other side of that privilege? Me, or a black inner-city teenager who is automatically labeled a gang member and feared by many white folks? Me, or an American Indian on the streets of a U.S. city who is invisible to many white folks? Whose voices should we be paying attention to?

My voice gets heard in large part because I am a white man with a Ph.D. who holds a professional job with status. In most settings, I speak with the assumption that people not only will listen, but will take me seriously. I speak with the assumption that my motives will not be challenged; I can rely on the perception of me as a neutral authority, someone whose observations can be trusted. Every time I open my mouth, I draw on, and in some ways reinforce, my privilege, which is in large part tied to race.

Right now, I want to use that privilege to acknowledge the many nonwhite people who took the time to tell me about the enduring realities of racism in the United States. And, I want to talk to the white people who I think misread my essay and misunderstand what's at stake.

The responses of my white critics broke down into a few basic categories, around the following claims:

1. White privilege doesn't exist because affirmative action has made being white a disadvantage. The simple response: Extremely limited attempts to combat racism, such as affirmative action, do virtually nothing to erase the white privilege built over 500 years that pervades our society. As a friend of mine says, the only real disadvantage to being white is that it so often prevents people from understanding racial issues.

2. White privilege exists, but it can't be changed because it is natural for any group to favor its own, and besides, the worst manifestations of racism are over. Response: This approach makes human choices appear outside of human control, which is a dodge to avoid moral and political responsibility for the injustice we continue to live with.

3. White privilege exists, and that's generally been a good thing because white Europeans have civilized the world. Along the way some bad things may have happened, and we should take care to be nice to nonwhites to make up for that. Response: These folks often argued the curiously contradictory position that (1) nonwhites and their cultures are not inferior, but (2) white/European culture is superior. As for the civilizing effect of Europe, we might consider five centuries of inhuman, brutal colonialism and World Wars I and II, and then ask what "civilized" means.

4. White privilege exists because whites are inherently superior, and I am a weakling and a traitor for suggesting otherwise. Response: The Klan isn't dead.

There is much to say beyond those short responses, but for now I am more interested in one common assumption that all these correspondents made, that my comments on race and affirmative action were motivated by "white liberal guilt." The problem is, they got two out of the three terms wrong. I am white, but I'm not a liberal. In political terms, I'm a radical; I don't think liberalism offers real solutions because it doesn't attack the systems of power and structures of illegitimate authority that are the root cause of oppression, be it based on race, gender, sexuality, or class. These systems of oppression, which are enmeshed and interlocking, require radical solutions.

And I don't feel guilty. Guilt is appropriate when one has wronged another, when one has something to feel guilty about. In my life I have felt guilty for racist or sexist things I have said or done, even when they were done unconsciously. But that is guilt I felt because of specific acts, not for the color of my skin. Also, focusing on individual guilt feelings is counterproductive when it leads us to ponder the issue from a psychological point of view instead of a moral and political one.

So, I cannot, and indeed should not, feel either guilty or proud about being white, because it is a state of being I have no control over. However, as a member of a society—and especially as a privileged member of society—I have an obligation not simply to enjoy that privilege that comes with being white but to study and understand it, and work toward a more just world in which such unearned privilege is eliminated.

Some of my critics said that such a goal is ridiculous; after all, people have unearned privileges of all kinds. Several people pointed out that, for example, tall people have unearned privilege in basketball, and we don't ask tall people to stop playing basketball nor do we eliminate their advantage. The obvious difference is that racial categories are invented; they carry privilege or disadvantage only because people with power create and maintain the privilege for themselves at the expense of others. The privilege is rooted in violence and is maintained through that violence as well as more subtle means.

I can't change the world so that everyone is the same height, so that everyone has the same shot at being a pro basketball player. In fact, I wouldn't want to; it would be a drab and boring world if we could erase individual differences like that. But I can work with others to change the world to erase the effects of differences that have been created by one group to keep others down.

Not everyone who wrote to me understood this. In fact, the most creative piece of mail I received in response to the essay also was the most confused. In a padded envelope from Clement, Minn., came a brand-new can of Kiwi Shoe Polish, black. Because there was no note or letter, I have to guess at my correspondent's message, but I assume the person was suggesting that if I felt so bad about being white, I might want to make myself black.

But, of course, I don't feel bad about being white. The only motivation I might have to want to be black—to be something I am not—would be pathological guilt over my privilege. In these matters, guilt is a coward's way out, an attempt to avoid the moral and political questions. As I made clear in the original essay, there is no way to give up the privilege; the society we live in confers it upon us, no matter what we want.

So, I don't feel guilty about being white in a white supremacist society, but I feel an especially strong moral obligation to engage in collective political activity to try to change the society because I benefit from the injustice. I try to be reflective and accountable, though I am human and I make mistakes. I think a lot about how I may be expressing racism unconsciously, but I don't lay awake at night feeling guilty. Guilt is not a particularly productive emotion, and I don't wallow in it.

What matters is what we decide to do with the privilege. For me, that means speaking, knowing that I speak with a certain unearned privilege that gives me advantages I cannot justify. It also means learning to listen before I speak, and realizing that I am probably not as smart as I sometimes like to think I am.

It means listening when an elderly black man who sees the original article tacked up on the bulletin board outside my office while on a campus tour stops to chat. This man, who has lived with more kinds of racism than I can imagine through more decades than I have been alive, says to me, "White privilege, yes, good to keep an eye on that, son. Keep yourself honest. But don't forget to pay attention to the folks who live without the privilege."

It doesn't take black shoe polish to pay attention. It takes only a bit of empathy to listen, and a bit of courage to act.

APPENDIX A

◇◆◆◇

Race—U.S. Bureau of the Census (1996)

The concept of race as used [in 1990] by the Census Bureau reflects self-identification; it does not denote any clear-cut scientific definition of biological stock. The data for race represent self-classification by people according to the race with which they most closely identify. Furthermore, it is recognized that the categories of the race item include both racial and national origin or sociocultural groups.

During direct interviews conducted by enumerators, if a person could not provide a single response to the race question, he or she was asked to select, based on self-identification, the group which best described his or her racial identity. If a person could not provide a single race response, the race of the mother was used. If a single race response could not be provided for the person's mother, the first race reported by the person was used. In all cases where occupied housing units, households, or families are classified by race, the race of the householder was used.

The racial classification used by the Census Bureau generally adheres to the guidelines in Federal Statistical Directive No. 15, issued by the Office of Management and Budget, which provides standards on ethnic and racial categories for statistical reporting to be used by all federal agencies. The racial categories used in the 1990 census data products are provided below.

> *White*—Includes persons who indicated their race as "White" or reported entries such as Canadian, German, Italian, Lebanese, Near Easterner, Arab, or Polish.

> *Black*—Includes persons who indicated their race as "Black or Negro" or reported entries such as African American, Afro-American, Black Puerto Rican, Jamaican, Nigerian, West Indian, or Haitian.

> *American Indian, Eskimo, or Aleut*—Includes persons who classified themselves as such in one of the specific race categories identified below:

American Indian—Includes persons who indicated their race as "American Indian," entered the name of an Indian tribe, or reported such entries as Canadian Indian, French-American Indian, or Spanish-American Indian.

American Indian Tribe—Persons who identified themselves as American Indian were asked to report their enrolled or principal tribe. Therefore, tribal data in tabulations reflect the written tribal entries reported on the questionnaires. Some of the entries (for example, Iroquois, Sioux, Colorado River, and Flathead) represent nations or reservations.

The information on tribe is based on self-identification and therefore does not reflect any designation of a federal- or state-recognized tribe. Information on American Indian tribes is presented in summary tape files and special data products. The information is derived from the American Indian Detailed Tribal Classification List for the 1990 census. The classification list represents all tribes, bands, and clans that had a specified number of American Indians reported on the census questionnaire.

Eskimo—Includes persons who indicated their race as "Eskimo" or reported entries such as Arctic Slope, Inupiat, and Yupik.

Aleut—Includes persons who indicated their race as "Aleut" or reported entries such as Alutiiq, Egegik, and Pribilovian.

Asian or Pacific Islander—Includes persons who reported in one of the Asian or Pacific Islander groups listed on the questionnaire or who provided write-in responses such as Thai, Nepali, or Tongan. A more detailed listing of the groups comprising the Asian or Pacific Islander population is presented in Table 1 on p. 489. In some data products, information is presented separately for the Asian population and the Pacific Islander population.

Asian—Includes "Chinese," "Filipino," "Japanese," "Asian Indian," "Korean," "Vietnamese," and "Other Asian." In some tables, "Other Asian" may not be shown separately, but is included in the total Asian population.

Chinese—Includes persons who indicated their race as "Chinese" or who identified themselves as Cantonese, Tibetan, or Chinese American. In standard census reports, persons who reported as "Taiwanese" or "Formosan" are included here with Chinese. In special reports on the Asian or Pacific Islander population, information on persons who identified themselves as Taiwanese are shown separately.

Filipino—Includes persons who indicated their race as "Filipino" or reported entries such as Philipino, Philipine, or Filipino American.

Japanese—Includes persons who indicated their race as "Japanese" and persons who identified themselves as Nipponese or Japanese American.

Asian Indian—Includes persons who indicated their race as "Asian Indian" and persons who identified themselves as Bengalese, Bharat, Dravidian, East Indian, or Goanese.

Korean—Includes persons who indicated their race as "Korean" and persons who identified themselves as Korean American.

Vietnamese—Includes persons who indicated their race as "Vietnamese" and persons who identified themselves as Vietnamese American.

Cambodian—Includes persons who provided a write-in response such as Cambodian or Cambodia.

Hmong—Includes persons who provided a write-in response such as Hmong, Laohmong, or Mong.

Laotian—Includes persons who provided a write-in response such as Laotian, Laos, or Lao.

Thai—Includes persons who provided a write-in response such as Thai, Thailand, or Siamese.

Other Asian—Includes persons who provided a write-in response of Bangladeshi, Burmese, Indonesian, Pakistani, Sri Lankan, Amerasian, or Eurasian. See Table 1 for other groups comprising "Other Asian."

Pacific Islander—Includes persons who indicated their race as "Pacific Islander" by classifying themselves into one of the following groups or identifying themselves as one of the Pacific Islander cultural groups of Polynesian, Micronesian, or Melanesian.

  Hawaiian—Includes persons who indicated their race as "Hawaiian" as well as persons who identified themselves as Part Hawaiian or Native Hawaiian.

  Samoan—Includes persons who indicated their race as "Samoan" or persons who identified themselves as American Samoan or Western Samoan.

  Guamanian—Includes persons who indicated their race as "Guamanian" or persons who identified themselves as Chamorro or Guam.

Other Pacific Islander—Includes persons who provided a write-in response of a Pacific Islander group such as Tahitian, Northern Mariana Islander, Palauan, Fijian, or a cultural group such as Polynesian, Micronesian, or Melanesian. See Table 1 for other groups comprising "Other Pacific Islander."

Other Race—Includes all other persons not included in the "White," "Black," "American Indian, Eskimo, or Aleut," and the "Asian or Pacific Islander" race categories described above. Persons reporting in the "Other race" category and providing write-in entries such as multiracial, multiethnic, mixed, interracial, Wesort, or a Spanish/Hispanic origin group (such as Mexican, Cuban, or Puerto Rican) are included here.

Written entries to three categories on the race item—"Indian (Amer.),", "Other Asian or Pacific Islander (API)," and "Other race"—were reviewed, edited, and coded by subject matter specialists. (For more information on the coding operation, see the section below that discusses "Comparability.")

The written entries under "Indian (Amer.)" and "Other Asian or Pacific Islander (API)" were reviewed and coded during 100-percent processing of the 1990 census questionnaires. A substantial portion of the entries for the "Other race" category also were reviewed, edited, and coded during the 100-percent processing. The remaining entries under "Other race" underwent review and coding during sample processing. Most of the written entries reviewed and coded during sample processing were those indicating Hispanic origin such as Mexican, Cuban, or Puerto Rican.

If the race entry for a member of a household was missing on the questionnaire, race was assigned based upon the reported entries of race by other household members using specific rules of precedence of household relationship. For example, if race was missing for the daughter of the householder, then the race of her mother (as female householder or female spouse) would be assigned. If there was no female householder or spouse in the household, the daughter would be assigned her father's (male householder) race. If race was not reported for anyone in the household, the race of a householder in a previously processed household was assigned.

Limitation of the Data. In the 1980 census, a relatively high proportion (20 percent) of American Indians did not report any tribal entry in the race item. Evaluation of the precensus tests indicated that changes made for the 1990 race item should improve the reporting of tribes in the rural areas (especially on reservations) for the 1990 census. The results for urban areas were inconclusive. Also, the precensus tests indicated that there may be

Table 1   Asian or Pacific Islander Groups Reported in the 1990 Census

ASIAN	PACIFIC ISLANDER
Chinese	Hawaiian
Filipino	Samoan
Japanese	Guamanian
Asian Indian	Other Pacific Islander[1]
Korean	Carolinian
Vietnamese	Fijian
Cambodian	Kosraean
Hmong	Melanesian[3]
Laotian	Micronesian[3]
Thai	Northern Mariana Islander
Other Asian[1]	Palauan
Bangladeshi	Papua New Guinean
Bhutanese	Ponapean (Pohnpeian)
Borneo	Polynesian[3]
Burmese	Solomon Islander
Celebesian	Tahitian
Ceram	Tarawa Islander
Indochinese	Tokelauan
Indonesian	Tongan
Iwo-Jiman	Trukese (Chuukese)
Javanese	Yapese
Malayan	Pacific Islander, not specified
Maldivian	
Nepali	
Okinawan	
Pakistani	
Sikkim	
Singaporean	
Sri Lankan	
Sumatran	
Asian, not specified[2]	

[1]In some data products, specific groups listed under "Other Asian" or "Other Pacific Islander" are shown separately. Groups not shown are tabulated as "All other Asian" or "All other Pacific Islander," respectively.

[2]Includes entries such as Asian American, Asian, Asiatic, Amerasian, and Eurasian.

[3]Polynesian, Micronesian, and Melanesian are Pacific Islander cultural groups.

Source: U.S. Bureau of the Census (1990).

overreporting of the Cherokee tribe. An evaluation of 1980 census data showed overreporting of Cherokee in urban areas or areas where the number of American Indians was sparse.

In the 1990 census, respondents sometimes did not fill in a circle or filled the "Other race" circle and wrote in a response, such as Arab, Polish, or African American in the shared write-in box for "Other race" and "Other API" responses. During the automated coding process, these responses were edited and assigned to the appropriate racial designation. Also, some Hispanic origin persons did not fill in a circle, but provided entries such as Mexican or Puerto Rican. These persons were classified in the "Other race" category during the coding and editing process. There may be some minor differences between sample data and 100-percent data because sample processing included additional edits not included in the 100-percent processing.

Comparability. Differences between the 1990 census and earlier censuses affect the comparability of data for certain racial groups and American Indian tribes. The 1990 census was the first census to undertake, on a 100-percent basis, an automated review, edit, and coding operation for written responses to the race item. The automated coding system used in the 1990 census greatly reduced the potential for error associated with a clerical review. Specialists with a thorough knowledge of the race subject matter reviewed, edited, coded, and resolved inconsistent or incomplete responses. In the 1980 census, there was only a limited clerical review of the race responses on the 100-percent forms with a full clerical review conducted only on the sample questionnaires.

Another major difference between the 1990 and preceding censuses is the handling of the write-in responses for the Asian or Pacific Islander populations. In addition to the nine Asian or Pacific Islander categories shown on the questionnaire under the spanner "Asian or Pacific Islander (API)," the 1990 census race item provided a new residual category, "Other API," for Asian or Pacific Islander persons who did not report in one of the listed Asian or Pacific Islander groups. During the coding operation, write-in responses for "Other API" were reviewed, coded, and assigned to the appropriate classification. For example, in 1990, a write-in entry of Laotian, Thai, or Javanese is classified as "Other Asian," while a write-in entry of Tongan or Fijian is classified as "Other Pacific Islander." In the 1990 census, these persons were able to identify as "Other API" in both the 100-percent and sample operations.

In the 1980 census, the nine Asian or Pacific Islander groups were also listed separately. However, persons not belonging to these nine groups wrote in their specific racial group under the "Other" race category. Persons with a written entry such as Laotian, Thai, or Tongan, were tabulated and published as "Other race" in the 100-percent processing operation in 1980, but were reclassified as "Other Asian and Pacific Islander" in 1980 sample tabulations. In 1980 special reports on the Asian or Pacific Islander populations, data were shown separately for "Other Asian" and "Other Pacific Islander."

The 1970 questionnaire did not have separate race categories for Asian Indian, Vietnamese, Samoan, and Guamanian. These persons indicated their race in the "Other" category and later, through the editing process, were assigned to a specific group. For example, in 1970, Asian Indians were reclassified as "White," while Vietnamese, Guamanians, and Samoans were included in the "Other" category.

Another difference between 1990 and preceding censuses is the approach taken when persons of Spanish/Hispanic origin did not report in a specific race category but reported as "Other race" or "Other." These persons commonly provided a write-in entry such as Mexican, Venezuelan, or Latino. In the 1990 and 1980 censuses, these entries remained in the "Other race" or "Other" category, respectively. In the 1970 census, most of these persons were included in the "White" category.

Source: U.S. Bureau of the Census (1996).

Appendix B

◇◆◇◆◇

Federal and Program Uses
of the Data Derived from Race and Ethnicity
Questions — The U.S. Bureau
of the Census (1990)

Race and Ethnic Origin

U.S. CODE CITATION	USES OF THE DATA/PROGRAM/AGENCY
Subject: Race (Q4)	
5 U.S.C.	
7201	Establishment and evaluation of guidelines for Federal affirmative action plans under the Federal Equal Opportunity Recruitment Program (Equal Employment Opportunity Commission)
7 U.S.C.	
612c	Determine qualification for various programs such as the Food Stamp Program under the Food and Agriculture Act of 1977 (Department of Agriculture)
12 U.S.C.	
2809	Compilation of data on home mortgage lending patterns of depository institutions by race, geographic area, housing conditions, and income (Federal Financial Institutions Examination Council)
2901–2905	Determination of whether financial institutions are meeting credit needs of race/Hispanic origin groups in low- and moderate-income neighborhoods under the Community Reinvestment Act of 1977 (Federal Reserve Banks)
13 U.S.C.	
141	Review of State redistricting plans (Department of Justice)
15 U.S.C.	
631	Assistance to minority businesses in low-income areas under the Minority Business Development Program (Minority Business Development Agency—Department of Commerce)
1691 *et seq.*	Monitor compliance of nondiscrimination requirements of creditors under the Equal Credit Opportunity Act (Civil Rights Division—Department of Justice)
20 U.S.C.	
631	Planning school construction sites in school districts with increased enrollment due to Federal activities (Department of Education)

25 U.S.C.

13   Assessment of program needs for housing improvement under the Housing Improvement Program (Bureau of Indian Affairs—Department of the Interior and Indian Health Service—Department of Health and Human Services)

450, 450h   Funds allocation and planning and evaluation of tribal or Alaska Native village programs (Department of Health and Human Services and Bureau of Indian Affairs—Department of the Interior)

458   Planning needs of schools serving American Indian and Alaska Native children on or adjacent to reservations or Alaska Native villages under the Indian Education Assistance Act (Bureau of Indian Affairs—Department of the Interior)

1601 (P.L. 94-037)   Assessment of needs under the Indian Health Care Improvement Act (Indian Health Service—Department of Health and Human Services)

28 U.S.C.

1861–1871   Determination that jurors are randomly selected representing a cross-section of the community under the Jury Act (Department of Justice)

30 Federal
Register 12319

32 Federal
Register 14303   Monitor and enforce nondiscrimination by government contractors (Department of Labor—responsible for administering Executive Order 11246, as amended, and Department of Justice—authority to enforce E.O.)

31 U.S.C.

6708–6713   Revenue sharing funds allocation to tribal councils (Department of the Treasury) and enforcement of nondiscrimination of funds allocation (Department of Justice) under the State and Local Fiscal Assistance Act of 1972, as amended

42 U.S.C.

242k   Collection of vital, social, and health statistics (National Center for Health Statistics—Department of Health and Human Services)

628   Funds allocation to American Indian tribal organizations for child welfare services under the Adoption Assistance and Child Welfare Act of 1980 (Department of Health and Human Services)

1310   Research conducted on welfare dependency and income and employment characteristics to reduce dependency rates in Social Security Act programs (Social Security Administration—Department of Health and Human Services)

1786   Grants to American Indian tribes for supplemental food programs under the Child Nutrition Amendments of 1978 (Department of Agriculture)

1973aa–1a   Enforcement of bilingual election requirements of Voting Rights Act and Amendments of 1982 (Department of Justice)

1975c(4)   Commission on Civil Rights acts as clearinghouse for information on discrimination in housing, education, and employment under the Civil Rights Act of 1957, as amended

2000c–2	Technical assistance for school desegregation plans (Department of Education) and enforcement of desegregation plans (Department of Justice)
2000d	Monitor compliance with nondiscrimination requirements for variety of Federally assisted programs under the Civil Rights Act of 1964, as amended (various Federal agencies)
2000e	Evaluation of affirmative action programs and discrimination in employment in the private sector (Equal Employment Opportunity Commission) and enforcement of nondiscrimination in employment by State and local governments (Department of Justice) under the Civil Rights Act of 1964, as amended
2000f	Research on voting and voter registration (Commission on Civil Rights)
2001–2004	Planning new or renovation of existing sanitation facilities serving American Indian and Alaska Native houses, communities, and lands under the Indian Sanitation Facilities Act (Department of Health and Human Services)
2808	Grants to American Indian tribes and tribal organizations under the Community Services Block Grant Act (Department of Health and Human Services)
2992	Evaluation of program goals under the Native American Programs Act of 1974 as amended (Department of Health and Human Services)
42 U.S.C.—Con.	
3035a	Conduct demonstration projects addressing needs of low-income, minority, American Indian, older, and limited English-speaking persons under the Older Americans Act of 1965, as amended (Health Care Financing Administration—Department of Health and Human Services)
3057	Social and nutritional services for older American Indians under the Older Americans Act of 1965, as amended (Administration on Aging—Department of Health and Human Services)
3601 *et seq.*	Monitoring and enforcement of antidiscrimination provisions of Fair Housing Act of 1968, as amended (Department of Housing and Urban Development and Department of Justice)
3766c	Monitoring and enforcement of provisions of Omnibus Crime Control and Safe Streets Act of 1968, as amended, against discrimination by law enforcement agencies receiving Federal funds (Department of Justice)
8623–8629	Grants to American Indian tribes for home energy assistance to low-income households under the Low-Income Home Energy Assistance Act of 1981, as amended (Department of Health and Human Services)
9835	Grants to American Indian tribal organizations for preschool programs for low-income and handicapped children under the Head Start Program (Department of Health and Human Services)
P.L. 81-507	Collection of data on the need and availability for scientific and technical personnel (National Science Foundation)
P.L. 96-516	Provide data to Congress, Federal policymakers, and other data users on the status of women and minorities in science and engineering (National Science Foundation)

Public Health Act

Sec. 306
Collection of data on illness and disability (National Center for Health Statistics—Department of Health and Human Services)

Sec. 401
Research on the prevalence, causes, and prevention of cancer under the National Cancer Act (National Cancer Institute—Department of Health and Human Services)

Sec. 455e(2)
Research on the mental health problems of minorities (National Institute of Mental Health—Department of Health and Human Services)

Subject: Spanish/Hispanic Origin (Q7)

5 U.S.C.

7201
Establishment and evaluation of guidelines for Federal affirmative action plans under the Federal Equal Opportunity Recruitment Program (Equal Employment Opportunity Commission)

12 U.S.C.

2809
Compilation of data on home mortgage lending patterns of depository institutions by race, geographic area, housing conditions, and income (Federal Financial Institutions Examination Council)

12 U.S.C.—Con.

2901–2905
Determination of whether financial institutions are meeting credit needs of race/Hispanic origin groups in low- and moderate-income neighborhoods under the Community Reinvestment Act of 1977 (Federal Reserve Banks)

13 U.S.C.

141
Review of State redistricting plans (Department of Justice)

15 U.S.C.

631
Assistance to minority businesses in low-income areas under the Minority Business Development Program (Minority Business Development Agency—Department of Commerce)

1516a
Publication of social, health, and economic statistics of Spanish origin persons (Department of Agriculture, Department of Commerce, Department of Health and Human Services, and Department of Labor)

1691 *et seq.*
Monitor compliance of nondiscrimination requirements of creditors under the Equal Credit Opportunity Act (Civil Rights Division—Department of Justice)

29 U.S.C.

8
Development of methods for improving collection and analysis of unemployment data for Spanish origin persons (Department of Labor in cooperation with Department of Commerce)

30 Federal
Register 12319

32 Federal
Register 14303
Monitor and enforce nondiscrimination by government contractors (Department of Labor—responsible for administering Executive Order 11246, as amended, and Department of Justice—authority to enforce E.O.)

31 U.S.C.

6708–6713
Revenue sharing funds allocation to tribal councils (Department of the Treasury) and enforcement of nondiscrimination of funds allocation

	(Department of Justice) under the State and Local Fiscal Assistance Act of 1972, as amended
42 U.S.C.	
242k	Collection of vital, social, and health statistics (National Center for Health Statistics—Department of Health and Human Services)
1973aa–1a	Enforcement of bilingual election requirements of Voting Rights Act and Amendments of 1982 (Department of Justice)
1975c(4)	Commission on Civil Rights acts as clearinghouse for information on discrimination in housing, education, and employment under the Civil Rights Act of 1957, as amended
2000c–2	Technical assistance for school desegregation plans (Department of Education) and enforcement of desegregation plans (Department of Justice)
2000d	Monitor compliance with nondiscrimination requirements for variety of Federally assisted programs under the Civil Rights Act of 1964, as amended (various Federal agencies)
2000e	Evaluation of affirmative action programs and discrimination in employment in the private sector (Equal Employment Opportunity Commission) and enforcement of nondiscrimination in employment by State and local governments (Department of Justice) under the Civil Rights Act of 1964, as amended
2000f	Research on voting and voter registration (Commission on Civil Rights)
3035a	Conduct demonstration projects addressing needs of low-income, minority, American Indian, older, and limited English-speaking persons under the Older Americans Act of 1965, as amended (Health Care Financing Administration—Department of Health and Human Services)
3601 *et seq.*	Monitoring and enforcement of antidiscrimination provisions of Fair Housing Act of 1968, as amended (Department of Housing and Urban Development and Department of Justice)
3766c	Monitoring and enforcement of provisions of Omnibus Crime Control and Safe Streets Act of 1968, as amended, against discrimination by law enforcement agencies receiving Federal funds (Department of Justice)
P.L. 81–507	Collection of data on the need and availability for scientific and technical personnel (National Science Foundation)
P.L. 96–516	Provide data to Congress, Federal policymakers, and other data users on the status of women and minorities in science and engineering (National Science Foundation)

Subject: Ancestry (Q13)

5 U.S.C.	
7201	Establishment and evaluation of guidelines for Federal affirmative action plans under the Federal Equal Opportunity Recruitment Program (Equal Employment Opportunity Commission)
8 U.S.C.	
1521–1523	Employment assessment of refugee population and compilation of secondary migration data on refugees under the Refugee Education Assistance Act of 1980, as amended (Office of Refugee Resettlement—Department of Health and Human Services)

15 U.S.C.	
631	Assistance to minority businesses in low-income areas under the Minority Business Development Program (Minority Business Development Agency—Department of Commerce)
1691 *et seq.*	Monitor compliance of nondiscrimination requirements of creditors under the Equal Credit Opportunity Act (Civil Rights Division—Department of Justice)
30 Federal Register 12319	
32 Federal Register 14303	Monitor and enforce nondiscrimination by government contractors (Department of Labor—responsible for administering Executive Order 11246, as amended, and Department of Justice—authority to enforce E.O.)
42 U.S.C.	
242k	Collection of vital, social, and health statistics (National Center for Health Statistics—Department of Health and Human Services)
1310	Research conducted on welfare dependency and income and employment characteristics to reduce dependency rates in Social Security Act programs (Social Security Administration—Department of Health and Human Services)
1973aa–1a	Enforcement of bilingual election requirements of Voting Rights Act and Amendments of 1982 (Department of Justice)
1975c(4)	Commission on Civil Rights acts as clearinghouse for information on discrimination in housing, education, and employment under the Civil Rights Act of 1957, as amended
2000d	Monitor compliance with nondiscrimination requirements for variety of Federally-assisted programs under the Civil Rights Act of 1964, as amended (various Federal agencies)
2000e	Evaluation of affirmative action programs and discrimination in employment in the private sector (Equal Employment Opportunity Commission) and enforcement of nondiscrimination in employment by State and local governments (Department of Justice) under the Civil Rights Act of 1964, as amended
2000f	Research on voting and voter registration (Commission on Civil Rights)
3601 *et seq.*	Monitoring and enforcement of antidiscrimination provisions of Fair Housing Act of 1968, as amended (Department of Housing and Urban Development and Department of Justice)
3766c	Monitoring and enforcement of provisions of Omnibus Crime Control and Safe Streets Act of 1968, as amended, against discrimination by law enforcement agencies receiving Federal funds (Department of Justice)

APPENDIX C

◇•◆•◇

Answers to Table 5.2 Who Gets Caught?

Between January 1995 and September 1996 Maryland State Highway Patrol officers assigned to a stretch of highway known as I-95 stopped 823 drivers for traffic violations and then searched the cars for drugs. Use the information in Chart 1 to answer the questions below.

Looking only at the raw numbers in the "Yes" column, which group is more likely to have illegal substances in their cars? **Minority**

What percentage of all the cars stopped and searched is "minority?" **80.3%**

What percentage of all the cars stopped and searched is "white?'" **19.7%**

Maryland State Highway Patrol officers assigned to this section of I-95 were accused of *racial profiling*, the practice of using race as a basis for making some decision such as stopping drivers for traffic violations and/or searching cars for drugs. These numbers alone to not necessarily mean that the patrol officers[1] are guilty of this practice. Perhaps minority drivers make up 80.3 percent of all drivers on I-95 and are being pulled over in proportion

Chart 1 Illegal Substances Found in Cars of Those Motorists Stopped for Traffic Violations and Searched

| | DRUGS FOUND | | |
CLASSIFIED AS	YES	NO	TOTAL SEARCHED
Minority	188	473	661
White	47	115	162
Column Total	235	588	823

[1] We do not know the race of the highway patrol officers. But it is unlikely that they were all "white." The point is that we are *all* socialized to view some racial groups as more "deviant" than other racial groups.

to their actual numbers. Or perhaps minority drivers violate speeding laws more than "white" drivers do and thus deserve to be pulled over in greater numbers. Social Psychologist John Lamberth designed a study to determine if this was the case. Actual data was supplied and/or collected by the Maryland State Police and the ACLU. The researchers were asked to

✓ determine the percentage of cars driven by whites and nonwhite groups

✓ determine the percentage of cars speeding by race of driver

Chart 2   Percentage of Drivers Speeding by Racial Classification

	SPEEDING		
CLASSIFIED AS	**YES**	**NO**	**ROW TOTAL**
Black	938	35	973
White	4000	341	4341
Other	232	9	241
Unknown	184	2	186
Column Total	5354	387	5741

What percentage of drivers on the I-95 were classified as "black" **17.0%**, "white" **75.6%**, "other," **4.2%**, and "unknown" **3.2%**?

What percentage of all drivers speed? **93.3%**

What percentage of "black" drivers speed? **96.4%**

What percentage of "white" drivers speed? **92.1%**

What percentage of drivers' classified as "other" speed? **96.3%**

What percentage of drivers classified as "unknown" speed? **98.9%**

What percentage of all speeders are "black" **16.3%**, "white," **69.7%**, "other," **4.0%**, and "unknown" **3.2%**?

What conclusions can you draw about race classification and speeding?

Nearly all of the cars stopped were speeding, regardless of "race."

If racial profiling were not being used, what percentage of drivers stopped for traffic violation should have been minority (based on information in Chart 2)? **About 25%**

If racial profiling were not being used, what percentage of all the cars stopped and searched should have been "white?"' (based on information in Chart 2)? **About 75%**

In what percent of all minority cars searched were illegal substances found? **28.4%**

In what percent of all "white" cars searched were illegal substances found? **29.0%**

Do Maryland State Police stop and search black motorists at a rate disproportionate to their numbers on the highway? Explain.

Yes. 80% of the cars searched were driven by "minorities," yet only 25% of the cars on the freeway are driven by "minorities."

What conclusions can we draw about race and possession of illegal substances? (Can we say that minorities are more likely to use drugs than whites? Or is there some other explanation for the 188 minority people compared to the 47 white people in Chart 1?)

We cannot say that minorities are more likely to possess drugs than whites. Police stop more cars driven by minorities than whites for traffic violations and then search for illegal drugs. Seventy-five percent of the cars stopped and searched should have been driven by whites. If this were the case, the numbers shown in Chart 1 would be reversed.

Source: Lamberth, John. 1996. "Report of John Lamberth, Ph.D.," *http://www.aclu.org/court/ lamberth.html.*

REFERENCES

❖•❖•❖

Introduction

Fish, Jefferson M. 1995. "Mixed Blood." *Psychology Today*. (November/December): 55–61+.

FRONTLINE. 1985. "A Class Divided" (transcript #309). Boston: WGBH Educational Foundation.

Gates, Henry Louis, Jr. 1995. "The Political Scene: Powell and the Black Elite." *The New Yorker* (September 25):64–80.

Gerth, Hans and C. Wright Mills. 1954. *Character and Social Structure: The Psychology of Social Institutions*. London: Routledge & Kegan Paul.

Gross, Ariela J. 1998. "Litigating Whiteness: Trials of Racial Determination in the Nineteenth-Century South." *The Yale Law Journal* 105(1):109–188.

Kilker, Ernest Evans. 1993. "Black and White in America: The Culture and Politics of Racial Classification." *International Journal of Politics, Culture and Society* 7(2):229–258.

Lee, Sharon M. 1993. "Racial Classifications in the U.S. Census: 1890–1990." *Ethnic and Racial Studies* 16(1):75–94.

Page, Clarence. 1996. *Showing My Color: Impolite Essays on Race and Identity*. New York: HarperCollins.

del Pinal, Jorge and Susan J. Lapham. 1993. "Impact of Ethnic Data Needs in the United States." Pp. 448–449 in *Challenges of Measuring an Ethnic World: Science, Politics and Reality,* edited by Statistics Canada and U.S. Bureau of the Census. Washington, DC: U.S. Government Printing Office.

Rohrl, Vivian J. 1995. "The Anthropology of Race: A Study of Looking at Race." *Race, Gender, and Class* 2(2):85–97.

U.S. Bureau of the Census. 1993. *1990 Census of Population and Housing Content Reinterview Survey: Accuracy of Data for Selected Population and Housing Characteristics as Measured by Reinterview*. Washington DC: U.S. Government Printing Office.

———. 1996. 1990 *Census Lookup*. *http://venus.census.gov/cdrom/lookup/*.

———. 1994. *Current Population Survey Interview Manual*. Washington, DC: U.S. Government Printing Office.

———. 1999. *United States Census 2000*. Washington, DC: U.S. Government Printing Office.

Webster, Yehudi O. 1993. *The Racialization of America*. New York: St. Martin's Press.

Part 1

Adams, Yolanda. 1999. "Don't Want to Be Black Anymore." *Essence* 30(4):54.

Brodeur, Paul. 1978. "The Mashpees." *The New Yorker* (November 6):62–150.

Cambridge International Dictionary of English. 1995. New York: Cambridge University Press.

Castellini, Anna. Unpublished. Photos and research for "I Can't Imagine Being Any Race Other Than White." Northern Kentucky University student, Class of 2000.

Clifford, James. 1988. *The Predicament of Culture: Twentieth-Century Ethnography, Literature, and Art*. Cambridge, MA: Harvard University Press.

Dawkins, Paul Andrew. 1999. "Apologizing for Being a Black Male." *Essence* 30(6):64.

Egan, Timothy. 1996. "Expelled in 1877, Indian Tribe is Now Wanted as a Resource." *The New York Times* (July 22):A1+.

Elfers, Ray. Unpublished. Photos for "Can Family Members Really Belong to Different Races?" Northern Kentucky University student, Class of 1999.

Franklin, John Hope. 1990. Quoted in "That's History, Not Black History," by Mark Mcgurl. *The New York Times Book Review* (June 3):13.

Goffman, Erving. 1959. *The Presentation of Self in Everyday Life*. New York: Anchor.

———. 1963. *Stigma: Notes of the Management of Spoiled Identity*. Englewood Cliffs, NJ: Prentice-Hall.

Graham, Lawrence Otis. 1995. "Black Man with a Nose Job." Pp. 222–231 in *Member of the Club: Reflections on Life in a Racially Polarized World*. New York: HarperCollins.

Halter, Marilyn. 1993. "Identity Matters." Pp. 163–173 in *Between Race and Ethnicity: Cape Verdean American Immigrants, 1860–1965*. Champaign: University of Illinois Press.

Handler, Richard. 1986. "Authenticity." *Anthropology Today* 2(1):2–4.

Hongo, Garrett. 1994. "Asian-American Literature: Questions of Identity." *Amerasia Journal* 20(3):1–8.

———. 1995. "Introduction: Culture Wars in Asian America." Pp. 16–30 in *Under Western Eyes: Personal Essays from Asian America,* edited by G. Hongo. New York: Anchor.

Kim, Andrea. 1991. "Born and Raised in Hawaii, but Not Hawaiian." Pp. 24–31 in *Asian Americans: Oral Histories of First to Fourth Generation Americans from China, the Phillipines, Japan, India, the Pacific Islands, Vietnam, and Cambodia,* edited by Joann Faung Jean Lee. Jefferson, NC: McFarland & Company, Inc.

Kochiyama, Yuri. 1992. "Then Came the War." Pp. 10–18 in *Asian Americans,* edited by J. F. J. Lee. New York: The New Press.

Montagu, Ashley. 1964. "The Concept of Race in the Human Species in the Light of Genetics." Pp. 12–28 in *The Concept of Race,* edited by Ashley Montagu. New York: The Free Press.

Park, Robert. 1967. "Human Migration and the Marginal Man." Pp. 194–206 in *On Social Control and Collective Behavior: Selected Papers,* edited by Ralph H. Turner. Chicago: University of Chicago.

Riley, Patricia. 1992. "Adventures of an Indian Princess." Pp. 135–140 in *Earth Song, Sky Spirit,* edited by C. E. Trafzer. New York: Anchor.

Scales-Trent, Judy, 1995. "Choosing Up Sides." Pp. 61–65 in *Notes of a White Black Woman: Race, Color, Community*. University Park: The Pennsylvania State University Press.

Simmel, Georg. 1950. "The Stranger." Pp. 402–408 in *The Sociology of Georg Simmel,* translated, edited, and with an Introduction by K. H. Wolff. New York: The Free Press.

Tovares, Joseph. 1995. "Mojado Like Me." *http://www.hisp.com/mojado.html* (May).

Uehara-Carter, Mitzi. 1996. "On Being Blackanese." *http://www.webcom.com/~~intvoice/ mitzi.html* .

Ugwu-Oju, Dympna. 1995. "Convent Convenience" and "The Undoing of Mama's Handiwork." Pp. 272–282 in *What Will My Mother Say: A Tribal African Girl Comes of Age in America*. Chicago: Bonus.

Van't Hul, Sarah. "How It Was for Me." Pp. 210–214 in *Testimony,* edited by N. Tarpley. Boston: Beacon.

Part 2

Ancheta, Angelo N. 1998. "Race Relations in Black and White." Pp. 2–4 in *Race, Rights, and the Asian American Experience*. New Brunswick, NJ: Rutgers University Press.

Angelou, Maya. 1987. "Intra-Racism." Interview on the *Oprah Winfrey Show*. (Journal Graphics transcript #W172):2.

Black, L. Wade and Robert Thrower, Jr. 1996. *Getting Recognized*. (An Independent Film) wadeblack@mindspring.com.

Brown, Prince, Jr. 1998. "Biology and the Social Construction of the 'Race' Concept." Pp. 131–138 in *The Social Construction of Race and Ethnicity in the United States, 1/E* by Joan Ferrante and Prince Brown, Jr. New York: Addison Wesley.

Elfers, Ray. 2000. Photos for *Known Ancestries and Races*. Northern Kentucky University.

Finnegan, William. 1986. *Crossing the Line: A Year in the Land of Apartheid*. New York: Harper & Row.

Forbes, Jack D. 1990. "'Indian' and 'Black' as Radically Different Categories." Pp. 23–25 in "The Manipulation of Race, Caste and Identity: Classifying Afro Americans, Native Americans and Red-Black People." *The Journal of Ethnic Studies* 17(4).

Gimenez, Martha E. 1989. "Latino/'Hispanic'—Who Needs a Name?: The Case Against a Standardized Terminology." *International Journal of Health Services* 19(3):567–571.

Granberry, Michael. 1994. "A Tribes' Battle for It's Identity." *Los Angeles Times* (March 13):A1,A22+.

Green, V. 1978. "The Black Extended Family in the United States: Some Research Suggestions." Pp. 378–387 in *The Extended Family in Black Societies,* edited by D. B. Shimkin, E. M. Shimkin, and D. A. Frate. The Netherlands: Mouton DeGruyter.

Gross, Ariela J. 1998. "Litigating Whiteness: Trials of Racial Determination in the Nineteenth-Century South." *The Yale Law Journal* 105(1):109–188.

Haney López, Ian F. 1994. "The Social Construction of Race: Some Observations on Illusion, Fabrication, and Choice." *Harvard Civil Rights–Civil Liberties Law Review*. 29:39–53.

Knepper, Paul. 1995. "Historical Origins of the Prohibition of Multiracial Legal Identity in the States and the Nation." *State Constitutional Commentaries and Notes: A Quarterly Review* 5(2):14–20.

Lee, Sharon M. 1993. "Racial Classification in the U.S. Census: 1890–1990." *Ethnic and Racial Studies* 16(1):75–94.

Lock, Margaret. 1993. "The Concept of Race: An Ideological Construct." *Transcultural Psychiatric Research Review* 30:203–227.

Lovett, Laura L. 1998. "African and Cherokee by Choice." *American Indian Quarterly* 22(1 and 2):203–205.

Meier, August. 1949. "A Study of the Racial Ancestry of the Mississippi College Negro." *American Journal of Physical Anthropology* 7(1):227–240.

National Center for Health Statistics. 1993. "Advanced Report of Final Natality Statistics." *Monthly Vital Statistics Report* 41(9).

Pike County (Ohio) Republican, 1873. 1997. "Memoirs of Madison Hemings." Pp. 245–253 in *Thomas Jefferson and Sally Hemings: An American Controversy,* edited by Annette Gordon Reed. Charlottesville: University Press of Virginia.

Piper, Adrian. 1992. "Passing for White, Passing for Black." *Transition* 58:4–32.

Pollitzer, William S. 1972. "The Physical Anthropology and Genetics of Marginal People of the Southeastern United States." *American Anthropologist* 74(1–2):719–734.

Poston, Dudley L. Jr., Michael Xinxiang Mao, and Mei-Yu Yu. 1994. "The Global Distribution of the Overseas Chinese Around 1990." *Population and Development Review* 20(3): 631–645.

Scales-Trent, Judy. 1995. "Choosing Up Sides." Pp. 61–65 in *Notes of a White Black Woman: Race, Color, Community.* University Park: The Pennsylvania State University.

Strickland, Daryl. 1996. "Interracial Generation: 'We Are Who We Are.'" *The Seattle Times.* *http://webster3.seattletimes.com/topstories/browse/html/race_050596. html.*

TIME Magazine. 1941. "How to Tell Your Friends from the Japs." (December 22):33.

Trillin, Calvin. 1986. "American Chronicles: Black or White." *The New Yorker* (April 14): 62–78.

U.S. Bureau of the Census. 1989. *200 Years of U.S. Census Taking: Population and Housing Questions, 1790–1990.* Washington, DC: U.S. Government Printing Office.

———. 1994. *Current Population Survey Interviewing Manual.* Washington, DC: U.S. Government Printing Office.

———. 1996. "Race." In *Appendix B: Definition of Subject Characteristics. http://www .census.gov/td/stf3/append_b.html.*

U.S. Office of Management and Budget. 1997. *Revisions to Federal Statistical Directive No. 15.* Washington, DC:U.S. Government Printing Office.

Williams, David R., Risa Lavizzo-Mourey, and Rueben C. Warren. 1994. "The Concept of Race and Health Status in America." *Public Health Reports* 109(1):26–41.

Part 3

Bakalian, Anny. 1991. "From Being to Feeling Armenian: Assimilation and Identity Among Armenian Americans." Paper presented at the annual meeting of the American Sociological Association, Cincinnati, OH.

Cohen, David Steven. 1991. "Reflections on American Ethnicity." *New York History* 72(3): 321–336.

Espiritu, Yen Le. 1992. "Theories of Ethnicity." Pp. 3–5 in *Asian American Panethnicity: Bridging Institutions and Identities.* Philadelphia: Temple University Press.

Fair, Sara. Unpublished. "Juntos Como Hermanos: A Study of a Spanish-speaking Catholic Church." Northern Kentucky University student, Class of 2000.

Gimenez, Martha E. 1989. "Latino/'Hispanic'—Who Needs a Name?: The Case Against a Standardized Terminology." *International Journal of Health Services* 19(3):567–571.

Hirschman, Charles. 1993. "How to Measure Ethnicity: An Immodest Proposal." Pp. 547–560 in *Challenges of Measuring An Ethnic World: Science, Politics and Reality,* edited by Statistics Canada and U.S. Bureau of the Census. Washington, DC: U.S. Government Printing Office.

Infield, Henrik F. 1951. "The Concept of Jewish Culture and the State of Israel." *American Sociological Review* 16(4):506–513.

Leonard, Karen. 1993. "Historical Constructions of Ethnicity: Research on Punjabi Immigrants in California." *Journal of American Ethnic History* (Summer):3–26.

Mahmood, Cynthia K. and Sharon L. Armstrong. 1992. "Do Ethnic Groups Exist?: A Cognitive Perspective on the Concept of Cultures." *Ethnology* XXXI(1):1–14.

Nagel, Joane. 1995a. "Resource Competition Theories." *American Behavioral Scientist* 38(3):442–458, Thousand Oaks, CA: Sage.

———. 1995b. "American Indian Ethnic Renewal: Politics and the Resurgence of Identity." *American Sociological Review* 60(6):947–965.

———. 1994. "Constructing Ethnicity: Creating and Recreating Ethnic Identity and Culture." *Social Problems* 41(1):152–176.

Nathan, Andrew J. 1993. "Is Chinese Culture Distinctive?—A Review Article." *The Journal of Asian Studies* 52(4):923–936.

Novas, Himilice. 1994. "What's in a Name?" Pp.2–4 in *Everything You Need to Know about Latino History.*" New York: Dutton Signet.

Ortega, Rafael and Marcelle M. Willock. 1994. "To the Editor: When Is Ethnicity Relevant in a Case Report?" *Anesthesiology* 81(4):1082.

Rushdie, Salman. 1991. *Imaginary Homelands: Essays and Criticism 1981–1991.* New York: Viking Penguin.

Salins, Peter D. 1997. "Americans United by Myths." Pp. 101–121 in *Assimilation, American Style.* New York: Basic Books.

Sprott, Julie E. 1994. "'Symbolic Ethnicity' and Alaska Natives of Mixed Ancestry Living in Anchorage: Enduring Group or Sign of Impending Assimilation?" *Human Organization* 53(4):314–315.

Stavans, Ilan. 1995. *The Hispanic Condition: Reflections on Culture and Identity in America.* New York: HarperCollins.

Toro, Luis Angel. 1995. "A People Distinct From Others: Race and Identity in Federal Indian Law and the Hispanic Classification in OMB Directive No. 15." *Texas Tech Law Review* 26(1219):1259–1263.

U.S. Bureau of the Census. 1996a. *1990 Census Lookup. http://venus.census.gov/cdrom/lookup.*

———. 1996b. "Ancestry." In Appendix B: Definition of Subject Characteristics. *http://www.census.gov/td/stf3/append_b.html.*

———. 1994. *Current Population Survey Interviewing Manual.* Washington, DC: U.S. Government Printing Office.

U.S. Department of Interior. 1999. "Part 83—Procedures for Establishing That an American Indian Groups Exists as an Indian Tribe." *http://www.doi.gov/bie/acknowl.html.*

Vecoli, Rudolph J. 1997. "Are Italian Americans Just White Folks?" Pp. 307–318 in *Beyond the Godfather: Italian American Writers on the Real Italian American Experience,* edited by A. Kenneth Ciongoli and Jay Parini. Hanover, NH: University Press of New England.

Verkuyten, Matkel. 1991. "Self-Definition and Ingroup Formation Among Ethnic Minorities in the Netherlands." *Social Psychology Quarterly* 54(3):280–286.

Waters, Mary C. 1994. "Ethnic and Racial Identities of Second-Generation Black Immigrants in New York City." *International Migration Review* 28(4):795–820.

———. 1990. *Ethnic Options: Choosing Identities in America.* Berkeley: University of California Press.

White, Merry. 1988. *The Japanese Overseas: Can They Go Home Again?* New York: The Free Press.

Part 4

Altbach, Philip G. and Gail P. Kelly, eds. 1978. *Education and Colonialism.* New York: Longman.

Banks, James A. 1993. "The Canon Debate, Knowledge Construction, and Multicultural Education." *Education Researcher* 22(5):4–14.

Bell, Derrick. n.d. *Race, Racism and American Law.* Boston: Little, Brown.

Blauner, Robert. 1972. "Colonized and Immigrant Minorities," in *Nation of Nations,* edited by Peter I. Rose. New York: Random House.

———. 1969. "Internal Colonialism and Ghetto Revolt." *Social Problems* 16 (4):393–408.

Brown, Prince, Jr. 1995. "Why 'Race' Makes No Sense: The Case of Africans and Native Americans." Pp. 377–381 in *Sociology: A Global Perspective,* 2nd ed. by Joan Ferrante. Belmont, CA: Wadsworth.

Carnoy, Martin. 1974. *Education as Cultural Imperialism.* New York: David McKay.

Constitution of the State of California: Annotated California Codes. 1996. "Article XIX, Chinese." St. Paul: West.

Freeman, Bonnie C. 1978. "Female Education in Patriarchal Power System." Pp. 208–209 in *Education and Colonialism,* edited by Philip G. Altbach and Gail P. Kelley. New York: Longman.

Gallagher, Charles A. 1995. "White Reconstruction in the University." *Socialist Review 94* 24(1+2):165–187.

Genovese, Eugene. 1974. *Roll, Jordon Roll: The World the Slaves Made.* New York: Pantheon.

Gould, Stephen Jay. 1981a. *The Mismeasurement of Man.* New York: Norton.

———. 1981b. "The Politics of Census." *Natural History* 90(1):20–24.

———. 1983. *Hen's Teeth and Horse's Toes.* New York: Norton.

Grillo, Trina and Stephanie M. Wildman. 1991. "Obscuring the Importance of Race: The Implication of Making Comparisons Between Racism and Sexism (Or Other-Isms)." *Duke Law Journal* 1991(2):401–403.

Harris, Cheryl I. 1993. "Whiteness as Property." *Harvard Law Review* 106(8):1746–1750.

Hazel, Forest. 1985. "Black, White and Other." *Southern Exposure* 13(6):34–37.

Jordan, Withrop D. 1974. *The White Man's Burden: Historical Origins of Racism in the United States.* New York: Oxford University Press.

Marger, Martin N. 1991. *Race and Ethnic Relations: American and Global Perspectives.* Belmont, CA: Wadsworth.

Meneses, Eloise H. 1994.

Merton, Robert K. 1970. *Science, Technology and Society in Seventeenth Century England.* New York: Harper & Row.

———. 1976. *Sociological Ambivalence and Other Essays.* New York: The Free Press.

Morrison, Toni. 1989. "Unspeakable Things Unspoken: The Afro-American Presence in American Literature." *Michigan Quarterly Review* 28(1):1–34.

Nash, Manning. 1962. "Race and the Ideology of Race." *Current Anthropology* 3(3):285–293.

Park, Robert E. 1950. *Race and Culture.* New York: The Free Press.

Pope-Hennesy, James. 1967. *Sins of the Fathers: A Study of the Atlantic Slave Traders 1441–1807.* New York: Knopf.

Pulliam, John D. 1991. *History of Education in America.* Columbus: Merrill.

Rogers, J. A., 1972. *Sex and Race.* Vol. 3. St. Petersburg, FL: Helga M. Rogers.

Rose, Arnold. 1951. *The Roots of Prejudice.* Paris: UNESCO Courier.

Rothenberg, Paula S. 1988. *Racism and Sexism.* New York: St. Martin's Press.

Scales-Trent, Judy. 1995. "On Being Like a Mule." Pp. 99–183 in *Notes of a White Black Woman: Race, Color, Community.* University Park: The Pennsylvania State University.

Schaefer, Richard T. 1995. *Race and Ethnicity in the United States.* New York: HarperCollins.

UNESCO COURIER. 1981. "The Declaration of Athens." (May):28.

U.S. Reports. 1896. "Plessy v. Ferguson: Opinion of the U.S. Supreme Court." 163(537):535–564.

Zinn, Howard. 1995. *A People's History of the United States,* revised and updated. New York: HarperPerennial.

Part 5

Bateson, Mary Catherine. 1968. "Insight in a Bicultural Context." *Philippine Studies* 16: 605–621.

Barzun, Jacques. 1965. *Race: A Study in Superstition.* New York: TorchBook.

Behrangi, Samad. 1994. Quoted on p. 28 in "International Rural Education Teacher and Literary Critic: Samad Behrangi's Life and Thoughts." *Journal of Global Awareness* 2(1):27.

Berry, Michael. 1995. "Curse-Cultural Communication." *Word* 16(1):8.

Caldwell, Stephen H. and Rebecca Popenoe. 1995a. "Perceptions and Misperceptions of Skin Color." *Annals of Internal Medicine* 122(8):614–617.

———. 1995b. In Response to "Skin Color and Ethnicity." *Annals of Internal Medicine* 123(8):637.

Churchill, Ward. 1994. "Let's Spread the 'Fun' Around: The Issue of Sports Team Names and Mascots." Pp. 65–72 in *Indians Are Us?* Monroe, ME: CommonCourage.

Cole, K. C. 1995. "Brain's Use of Shortcuts Can Be a Route to Bias." *Los Angeles Times* (May 1):A8,A18–19.

Collins, Patricia Hill. 1993. "Toward a New Vision: Race, Class, and Gender as Categories of Analysis and Connection." *Race, Sex, and Class* 1(1):25–45.

Davis, F. James. 1978. *Minority-Dominant Relations: A Sociological Analysis.* Arlington Heights, IL: AHM.

Du Bois, W. E. B. 1899/1996 Reprint. *The Philadelphia Negro: A Social Study.* Philadelphia: The University of Pennsylvania Press.

Earnest, Les. 1989. "Can Computers Cope with Human Races?" *Communications of the ACM* 32(2):174–182.

Graham, Lawrence Otis. 1999. *Our Kind of People: Inside America's Black Upper Class.* New York: HarperCollins.

Jefferson, Thomas. 1815. "Virginia's Definition of a Mulatto." *The Jefferson Papers.* Washington, DC: Library of Congress.

Jensen, Robert. 1998. "White Privilege Shapes the U.S." *Baltimore Sun.* (July 19).

———. 1999. "More Thoughts on Why System of White Privilege is Wrong." *Baltimore Sun* (July 4).

Knepper, Paul. 1995. "Historical Origins of the Prohibition of Multiracial Legal Identity in the States and the Nation." *State Constitutional Commentaries and Notes: A Quarterly Review* 5(2):14–20.

Kuhn, Thomas. 1975. *The Structure of Scientific Revolutions.* Chicago: University of Chicago Press.

Lewis, David Levering. 1993. *W. E. B. Du Bois: Biography of a Race, 1868–1919.* New York: Holt.

Loewy, Erich H. 1998. "Making Good Again: Historical and Ethnical Questions." Pp. 185–195 in *Paying for the Past: The Struggle over Reparations for Surviving Victims of the Nazi Terror,* by Christian Pross. Baltimore, MD: The Johns Hopkins University Press.

Lorde, Audre. 1984. *Sister Outsider.* Trumansberg, NY: Crossing.

McBride, James. 1996. *The Color of Water: A Black Man's Tribute to His White Mother.* New York: Riverhead.

Mirza, M. N. and D. B. Dungworth. 1995. "The Potential Misuse of Genetic Analyses and the Social Construction of 'Race' and 'Ethnicity.'" *Oxford Journal of Archaeology* 14(3):345–354.

Parent, Anthony S., Jr. and Susan Brown Wallace. 1993. "Childhood and Sexual Identity Under Slavery." Pp. 19–57 in *American Sexual Politics: Sex, Gender, and Race Since the Civil War,* edited by John C. Fout and Maura Shaw Tantillo. Chicago: The University of Chicago Press.

Peroff, Nicholas C. 1997. "Indian Identity." *The Social Science Journal.* 34(4):485–495.

Reynoso, Cruz. 1992. "Ethnic Diversity: Its Historical and Constitutional Roots." *Villanova Law Review* 37(4):821–837.

Rohrl, Vivian J. 1995. "The Anthropology of Race: A Study of Ways of Looking at Race." *Race, Gender, and Class* 2(2):85–97.

Scales-Trent, Judy. 1995. *Notes of a White Black Woman: Race, Color, Community.* University Park: PA: The Pennsylvania State University.

Schaefer, Richard T. 1996. 1995 Presidential Address. "Education and Prejudice: Unraveling the Relationship." *The Sociological Quarterly* 37(1):1–16.

Simon, Bruce N. "White-Blindness." Unpublished. Princeton College.

U.S. Bureau of the Census. 1990. *Federal Legislative Uses of Decennial Census Data.* Washington, DC: U.S. Government Printing Office.

U.S. Department of Justice. 1999. "Selected Discrimination Cases Handled in 1999." Washington, DC: U.S. Government Printing Office.

Williams, Gregory Howard. 1995. *Life on the Color Line: The True Story of a White Boy Who Discovered He Was Black.* New York: Dutton.

Wright, Lawrence. 1994. "One Drop of Blood." *The New Yorker* (July 25):53–55.

TEXT CREDITS

◇◆◇

The numbers in parentheses after each entry are the page numbers on which the material appears.

Part 1

From "Adventures of an Indian Princess" by Patricia Riley in *Earth Song, Sky Spirit*, edited by C.E. Trafzer. Copyright © 1992 Patricia Riley. Reprinted by permission of the author. (29–32)

From "Black Man With a Nose Job" in *Member of the Club* by Lawrence Otis Graham, Copyright © 1995 Lawrence Otis Graham. Reprinted by permission of Harper-Collins Publishers, Inc. (33–38)

From "Culture Wars in Asian America" in *Under Western Eyes: Personal Essays from Asian America* by Garrett Hongo. Copyright © 1995 Garrett Hongo. Reprinted by permission of the author and the Liz Darhansoff Literary Agency, 179 Franklin Avenue, New York 10013–2857. (39–42)

From "Born and Raised in Hawaii, but Not Hawaiian" by Andrea Kim in *Asian American Experiences in the United States: Oral Histories of First to Fourth Generation Americans from China, the Philippines, Japan, India, the Pacific Islands, Vietnam and Cambodia*. Copyright © 1991 by Joann Faung Jean Lee. Reprinted by permission of McFarland & Company, Inc., Box 611, Jefferson, NC 28640. *www.mcfarlandpub.com*. (43–49)

From "Don't Want to Be Black Anymore" by Yolanda Adams. *Essence* magazine (August). Copyright © 1999 by Essence Communications, Inc. Reprinted by permission. (50–51)

From "On Being Blackanese" by Mitzi Uehara-Carter. http://www.webcom/~intvoice/mitzi.html (July 22). Copyright © 1996 Mitzi Uehara-Carter. Reprinted by permission of *Interracial Voice* and the author. (52–54)

From *What Will My Mother Say: A Tribal African Girl Comes of Age in America* by Dympna Ugwu-Oju. Copyright © 1995 Dympna Ugwu-Oju. Reprinted by permission of Bonus Books, Inc., 160 East Illinois Street, Chicago. (63–67)

From "Apologizing for Being a Black Male" by Paul Andrew Dawkins. *Essence* magazine (October). Copyright © 1999 by Essence Communications, Inc. Reprinted by permission. (68–69)

From "Choosing Up Sides" in *Notes of a White Black Woman: Race, Color, Community* by Judy Scales-Trent. Copyright © 1995 The Pennsylvania State University. Reproduced by permission of the publisher. (70–72)

From "Identity Matters: The Immigrant Children" in *Between Race and Ethnicity: Cape Verdean American Immigrants*, 1860–1965 by Marilyn Halter, Copyright © 1993 Board of Trustees University of Illinois. Reprinted by permission of the author and the University of Illinois Press. (73–80)

From "How It Was for Me" by Sarah Van't Hul in *Testimony: Young African-Americans on Self-Discovery and Black Identity* edited by Natasha Tarpley. Copyright © 1995 Natasha Tarpley. Reprinted by permission of Sarah Van't Hul. (81–84)

From "Mojado Like Me" by Joseph Tovares. http://www.hisp.com/mojado.html (May). Copyright © 1995 *Hispanic Magazine*. Reprinted by permission. (85–89)

From "Then Came the War" by Yuri Kochiyama. *Asian Americans,* edited by J.F.J. Lee. Copyright © 1992 Joann Faung Jean Lee. Reprinted by permission of The New Press, a division of W.W. Norton and Company, Inc. (90–97)

Part 2

From "Historical Origins of the Prohibition of Multiracial Legal Identity in the States and the Nation" by Paul Knepper. *State Constitutional Commentaries and Notes.* Copyright © 1995 Edwards McNall Burns Center for State Constitutional Studies, Rutgers–The State University of New Jersey. Reprinted by permission of *Albany Law Review,* Albany Law School, Albany, NY. (129–134)

From "Biology and the Social Construction of the 'Race' Concept" by Prince Brown Jr. Unpublished. Northern Kentucky University. Reprinted by permission of the author. (144–150)

From "The Social Construction of Race: Some Observations on Illusion, Fabrication, and Choice" by Ian F. Haney López. *Harvard Civil Rights-Civil Liberties Law Review.* Copyright © 1994 The President and Fellows of Harvard College. Reprinted by permission. (151–163)

From "The Manipulation of Race, Caste, and Identity: Classifying AfroAmericans, Native Americans, and Red-Black People" by Jack D. Forbes. Copyright © 1990 *The Journal of Ethnic Studies.* Reprinted by permission. (164–165)

Part 3

Part 4

The Center for Research on Women. 339 Clement Hall, Memphis, TN 38152. Reprinted by permission. (459–472)

From "White Blindness" by Bruce N. Simon. Unpublished. Princeton College. Reprinted by permission. (473–478)

From "White Privilege Shapes the U.S." by Robert Jensen. *The Baltimore Sun.* Copyright © 1998 by Robert William Jensen. Reprinted by permission. (479–481)

From "More Thoughts on Why System of White Privilege Is Wrong" by Robert Jensen. *The Baltimore Sun.* Copyright © 1999 by Robert William Jensen. Reprinted by permission. (482–484)

PHOTO CREDITS

⋄◆⬥◆⋄

INDEX